High Performance Fiber Reinforced Cement Composites (HPFRCC5)

High Performance Fiber Reinforced Cement Composites (HPFRCC5)
Mainz, Germany – July 10-13, 2007

Published by RILEM Publications S.A.R.L.
157 rue des Blains   F-92220 Bagneux - France
Tel : + 33 1 45 36 10 20   Fax : + 33 1 45 36 63 20
http://www.rilem.net   E-mail: dg@rilem.net
© 2007 RILEM – Tous droits réservés.   ISBN: 978-2-35158-046-2

RILEM, The International Union of Laboratories and Experts in Construction Materials, Systems and Structures, is a non profit-making, non-governmental technical association whose vocation is to contribute to progress in the construction sciences, techniques and industries, essentially by means of the communication it fosters between research and practice. RILEM's activity therefore aims at developing the knowledge of properties of materials and performance of structures, at defining the means for their assessment in laboratory and service conditions and at unifying measurement and testing methods used with this objective.

RILEM was founded in 1947, and has a membership of over 900 in some 70 countries. It forms an institutional framework for co-operation by experts to:
• optimise and harmonise test methods for measuring properties and performance of building and civil engineering materials and structures under laboratory and service environments,
• prepare technical recommendations for testing methods,
• prepare state-of-the-art reports to identify further research needs,
• collaborate with national or international associations in realising these objectives.

RILEM members include the leading building research and testing laboratories around the world, industrial research, manufacturing and contracting interests, as well as a significant number of individual members from industry and universities. RILEM's focus is on construction materials and their use in building and civil engineering structures, covering all phases of the building process from manufacture to use and recycling of materials.

RILEM meets these objectives through the work of its technical committees. Symposia, workshops and seminars are organised to facilitate the exchange of information and dissemination of knowledge. RILEM's primary output consists of technical recommendations. RILEM also publishes the journal *Materials and Structures* which provides a further avenue for reporting the work of its committees. Many other publications, in the form of reports, monographs, symposia and workshop proceedings are produced.

RILEM

Fifth International Workshop on

High Performance Fiber Reinforced Cement Composites (HPFRCC5)

Sponsored by RILEM, ACI, ACBM, IFS,
The University of Stuttgart and the University of Michigan

Mainz, Germany

July 10-13, 2007

EDITED BY

H.W. Reinhardt
Institut für Werkstoffe im Bauwesen
University of Stuttgart, Germany

AND

A.E. Naaman
Department of Civil and Environmental Engineering,
The University of Michigan, Ann Arbor, USA

RILEM Publications S.A.R.L.

RILEM Publications

RILEM Publications are presented in 6 collections, corresponding to the 5 clusters of active RILEM Technical Committees, sorted by fields of expertise, and a 6th multi-thematic collection dedicated to journals and compendiums:

A. Mechanical Performance and Fracture

B. Materials Characterization, Properties Evaluation and Processing

C. Design and Service Life

D. Performance and Deterioration Mechanisms

E. Special Construction Materials and Components

F. Journals and Compendiums

Each publication is assigned to one of the following series: reports (REP), proceedings (PRO), compendiums (COMP) and journals. The former CD-ROM series is now included in one of these series.

Each publication is available in at least one of the three following editions: print (PR), CD or DVD-ROM (CD), or online (OL).

Online editions are available through our web site, at http://www.rilem.org

The RILEM DVD-ROM, gathering several thousands of online articles, is also published and updated each year (internal publication, circulation restricted to RILEM Benefactor Members).

The following list is presenting our global offer, sorted by series.

PROCEEDINGS

PRO 1: Durability of High Performance Concrete (ISBN: 2-912143-03-9); *Edited by H. Sommer*

PRO 2: Chloride Penetration into Concrete (ISBN: 2-912143-00-04), *Edited by L.-O. Nilsson and J.-P. Ollivier*

PRO 3: Evaluation and Strengthening of Existing Masonry Structures (ISBN: 2-912143-02-0); *Edited by L. Binda and C. Modena*

PRO 4: Concrete: From Material to Structure (ISBN: 2-912143-04-7), *Edited by J.-P. Bournazel and Y. Malier*

PRO 5: The Role of Admixtures in High Performance Concrete (ISBN: 2-912143-05-5); *Edited by J. G. Cabrera and R. Rivera-Villarreal*

PRO 6: High Performance Fiber Reinforced Cement Composites (HPFRCC 3) (ISBN: 2-912143-06-3); *Edited by H. W. Reinhardt and A. E. Naaman*

PRO 7: 1st International RILEM Symposium on Self-Compacting Concrete (ISBN: 2-912143-09-8); *Edited by Å. Skarendahl and Ö. Petersson*

PRO 8: International RILEM Symposium on Timber Engineering (ISBN: 2-912143-10-1); *Edited by L. Boström*

PRO 9: 2nd International RILEM Symposium on Adhesion between Polymers and Concrete ISAP '99 (ISBN: 2-912143-11-X); *Edited by Y. Ohama and M. Puterman*

PRO 10: 3rd International RILEM Symposium on Durability of Building and Construction Sealants (ISBN: 2-912143-13-6); *Edited by A. T. Wolf*

PRO 11: 4th International RILEM Conference on Reflective Cracking in Pavements (ISBN: 2-912143-14-4); *Edited by A. O. Abd El Halim, D.A. Taylor and El H. H. Mohamed*

PRO 12: International RILEM Workshop on Historic Mortars: Characteristics and Tests (ISBN: 2-912143-15-2); *Edited by P. Bartos, C. Groot and J. J. Hughes*

PRO 13: 2nd International RILEM Symposium on Hydration and Setting (ISBN: 2-912143-16-0); *Edited by A. Nonat*

PRO 14: Integrated Life-Cycle Design of Materials and Structures (ILCDES 2000) (ISBN: 951-758-408-3), (ISSN: 0356-9403); *Edited by S. Sarja*

PRO 15: Fifth RILEM Symposium on Fibre-Reinforced Concretes (FRC) - BEFIB' 2000 (ISBN: 2-912143-18-7); *Edited by P. Rossi and G. Chanvillard*

PRO 16: Life Prediction and Management of Concrete Structures (ISBN: 2-912143-19-5); *Edited by D. Naus*

PRO 17: Shrinkage of Concrete - Shrinkage 2000 (ISBN: 2-912143-20-9) *Edited by V. Baroghel-Bouny and P.-C. Aïtcin*

PRO 18: Measurement and Interpretation of the On-Site Corrosion Rate (ISBN: 2-912143-21-7) *Edited by C. Andrade, C. Alonso, J. Fullea, J. Polimon and J. Rodriguez*

PRO 19: Testing and Modelling the Chloride Ingress into Concrete (ISBN: 2-912143-22-5); *Edited by C. Andrade and J. Kropp*

PRO 20: 1st International RILEM Workshop on Microbial Impacts on Building Materials (2000); *Edited by M. Ribas Silva (CD 02)*

PRO 21: International RILEM Symposium on Connections between Steel and Concrete (ISBN: 2-912143-25-X); *Edited by R. Eligehausen*

PRO 22: International RILEM Symposium on Joints in Timber Structures (ISBN: 2-912143-28-4); *Edited by S. Aicher and H.-W. Reinhardt*

PRO 23: International RILEM Conference on Early Age Cracking in Cementitious Systems (ISBN: 2-912143-29-2) *Edited by K. Kovler and A. Bentur*

PRO 24: 2nd International RILEM Workshop on Frost Resistance of Concrete (ISBN: 2-912143-30-6); *Edited by M. J. Setzer, R. Auberg and H.-J. Keck*

PRO 25: International RILEM Workshop on Frost Damage in Concrete (ISBN: 2-912143-31-4); *Edited by D. J. Janssen, M. J. Setzer and M. B. Snyder*

PRO 26: International RILEM Workshop on Historic Mortars: Characteristics and Tests (ISBN: 2-912143-34-9); *Edited by L. Binda and R. C. de Vekey*

PRO 27: International RILEM Symposium on Building Joint Sealants (1988) (CD03); *Edited by A.T. Wolf*

PRO 28: 6th International RILEM Symposium on Performance Testing and Evaluation of Bituminous Materials, PTEBM'03, Zurich, Switzerland (2003) (ISBN: 2-912143-35-7); *Edited by M.N. Partl, (CD06)*

PRO 29: 2nd International RILEM Workshop on Life Prediction and Ageing Management of Concrete Structures, Paris, France (2003) (ISBN: 2-912143-36-5); *Edited by D.J. Naus*

PRO 30: 4th International RILEM Workshop on High Performance Fiber Reinforced Cement Composites – HPFRCC 4, University of Michigan, Ann Arbor, USA (2003) (ISBN: 2-912143-37-3); *Edited by A.E. Naaman and H.W. Reinhardt*

PRO 31: International RILEM Workshop on Test and Design Methods for Steel Fibre Reinforced Concrete: Background and Experiences (2003) (ISBN: 2-912143-38-1) *Edited by B. Schnütgen and L. Vandewalle*

PRO 32: International Conference on Advances in Concrete and Structures (2003), 2 vol. (ISBN (set): 2-912143-41-1)

PRO 33: 3rd International Symposium on Self-Compacting Concrete (2003) (ISBN: 2-912143-42-X); *Edited by Ó. Wallevik and I. Níelsson*

PRO 34: International RILEM Conference on Microbial Impact on Building Materials (2003) (ISBN: 2-912143-43-8); *Edited by M. Ribas Silva*

PRO 35: International RILEM TC 186-ISA on Internal Sulfate Attack and Delayed Ettringite Formation (2002) (ISBN: 2-912143-44-6); *Edited by K. Scrivener and J. Skalny*

PRO 36: International RILEM Symposium on Concrete Science and Engineering – A Tribute to Arnon Bentur (2004) (ISBN: 2-912143-46-2) *Edited by K. Kovler, J. Marchand, S. Mindess and J. Weiss*

PRO 37: 5th International RILEM Conference on Cracking in Pavements – Mitigation, Risk Assessment and Prevention (2004), (ISBN: 2-912143-47-0) *Edited by C. Petit, I. Al-Qadi and A. Millien*

PRO 38: 3rd International RILEM Workshop on Testing and Modelling the Chloride Ingress into Concrete – (2002) (ISBN: 2-912143-48-9); *Edited by C. Andrade and J. Kropp*

PRO 39: 6th International RILEM Symposium on Fibre-Reinforced Concretes (BEFIB 2004), (ISBN: 2-912143-51-9); *Edited by M. Di Prisco, R. Felicetti and G. A. Plizzari*

PRO 40: International RILEM Conference on the Use of Recycled Materials in Buildings and Structures (2004) (ISBN: 2-912143-52-7); *Edited by E. Vázquez, Ch. F. Hendriks and G. M. T. Janssen*

PRO 41: RILEM International Symposium on Environment-Conscious Materials and Systems for Sustainable Development (2004) (ISBN: 2-912143-55-1); *Edited by N. Kashino and Y. Ohama*

PRO 42: SCC'2005 – China: 1st International Symposium on Design, Performance and Use of Self-Consolidating Concrete (2005) (ISBN: 2-912143-61-6); *Edited by Zhiwu Yu, Caijun Shi, Kamal Henri Khayat and Youjun Xie*

PRO 43: International RILEM Workshop on Bonded Concrete Overlays (2004) (e-ISBN: 2-912143-83-7); *Edited by J.L. Granju and J. Silfwerbrand*

PRO 44: 2nd International RILEM Workshop on Microbial Impacts on Building Materials (Brazil 2004) (CD11) e-ISBN: 2-912143-84-5; *Edited by M. Ribas Silva*

PRO 45: 2nd International Symposium on Nanotechnology in Construction, Bilbao, Spain - - ISBN: 2-912143-87-X - Soft cover; *Edited by Peter JM Bartos, Yolanda de Miguel and Antonio Porro*

PRO 46: ConcreteLife'06 - International RILEM-JCI Seminar on Concrete Durability and Service Life Planning: Curing, Crack Control, Performance in Harsh Environments (2006) - ISBN: 2-912143-89-6,; *Edited by K. Kovler*

PRO 47: , International RILEM Workshop on Performance Based Evaluation and Indicators for Concrete Durability (2006) - ISBN: 2-912143-95-0; *Edited by V. Baroghel-Bouny, C. Andrade, K. Scrivener and R. Torrent*

PRO 48: 1st International RILEM Symposium on Advances in Concrete through Science and Engineering (2004) *(e-ISBN: 2-912143-92-6)*

PRO 49: International RILEM Workshop on High Performance Fiber Reinforced Cementitious Composites in Structural Applications (2006) (ISBN: 2-912143-93-4); *Edited by G. Fischer and V.C. Li*

PRO 50: 1st International RILEM Symposium on Textile Reinforced Concrete (2006) (ISBN: 2-912143-97-7); *Edited by Josef Hegger, Wolfgang Brameshuber and Norbert Will*

PRO 51: 2nd International Symposium on Advances in Concrete through Science and Engineering (2006) (ISBN: 2-35158-003-6; e-ISBN: 2351580028); *Edited by J. Marchand, B. Bissonnette, R. Gagné, M. Jolin and F. Paradis*

PRO 52: Volume Changes of Hardening Concrete: Testing and Mitigation (2006) (ISBN: 2-35158-004-4; e-ISBN: 2351580052); *Edited by O. M. Jensen, P. Lura and K. Kovler*

PRO 53: High Performance Fiber Reinforced Cement Composites (HPFRCC5) (2007) (ISBN: 978-2-35158-046-2); *Edited by H.W. Reinhardt and A.E. Naaman*

PRO 54: 5th International RILEM Symposium on Self-Compacting Concrete (2007) (ISBN: 978-2-35158-047-9); *Edited by G. De Schutter and V. Boel*

REPORTS

Report 19: Considerations for Use in Managing the Aging of Nuclear Power Plant Concrete Structures (ISBN: 2-912143-07-1); *Edited* by D. J. Naus

Report 20: Engineering and Transport Properties of the Interfacial Transition Zone in Cementitious Composites (ISBN: 2-912143-08-X) *Edited by M. G. Alexander, G. Arliguie, G. Ballivy, A. Bentur and J. Marchand*

Report 21: Durability of Building Sealants (ISBN: 2-912143-12-8); *Edited by A. T. Wolf*

Report 22: Sustainable Raw Materials – Construction and Demolition Waste (ISBN: 2-912143-17-9); *Edited by C. F. Hendriks and H. S. Pietersen*

Report 23: Self-Compacting Concrete state-of-the-art report (ISBN: 2-912143-23-3); *Edited by Å. Skarendahl and Ö. Petersson*

Report 24: Workability and Rheology of Fresh Concrete: Compendium of Tests (ISBN: 2-912143-32-2); *Edited by P.J.M. Bartos, M. Sonebi and A.K. Tamimi*

Report 25: Early Age Cracking in Cementitious Systems (ISBN: 2-912143-33-0) *Edited by A. Bentur*

Report 26: Towards Sustainable Roofing (Joint Committee CIB/RILEM) (CD 07); *Edited* by Thomas W. Hutchinson and Keith Roberts

Report 27: Condition Assessment of Roofs (Joint Committee CIB/RILEM) (CD 08)

Report 28: Final report of RILEM TC 167-COM 'Characterisation of Old Mortars with Respect to their Repair' (e-ISBN: 2-912143-67-5); *Edited by C. Groot, G. Ashall and J. Hughes*

Report 29: Pavement Performance Prediction and Evaluation (PPPE): Interlaboratory Tests, (e-ISBN: 2-912143-68-3); *Edited by M. Partl and H. Piber, 2005, RILEM Publications S.A.R.L., Bagneux, France*

Report 30: Final Report of RILEM TC 198-URM 'Use of Recycled Materials', (ISBN: 2-912143-82-9; e-ISBN: 2-912143-69-1); *Edited by Ch. F. Hendriks, G.M.T. Janssen and E. Vázquez, 2005, RILEM Publications S.A.R.L., Bagneux, France*

Report 31: Final Report of RILEM TC 185-ATC 'Advanced testing of cement-based materials during setting and hardening', (ISBN: 2-912143-81-0; e-ISBN: 2-912143-70-5); *Edited by H.W. Reinhardt and C.U. Grosse*, 2005

Report 32: Probabilistic Assessment of Existing Structures. A JCSS publication (2001) - 176pp. ISBN 2-912143-24-1 - Hard back; *Edited* by D. Diamantidis

Report 35: Final Report of RILEM Technical Committee TC 188-CSC 'Casting of Self Compacting Concrete', (ISBN 2-35158-001-X; e-ISBN: 2-912143-98-5). - *Edited by Å. Skarendahl and P. Billberg*, 2006

Report 36: State-of-the-Art Report of RILEM Technical Committee TC 201-TRC 'Textile Reinforced Concrete', (ISBN 2-912143-99-3). - *Edited by W. Brameshuber*, 2006

Report 38: State-of-the-Art Report of RILEM Technical Committee TC 205-DSC 'Durability of Self-Compacting Concrete', (ISBN: 978-2-35158-048-6). - *Edited by G. De Schutter and K. Audenaert*, 2007

COMPENDIUMS

COMP 01: Trilingual Dictionary for Materials and Structures (English-French-German) (CD01) (1970)

COMP 02: 1947-1997: 50 years of evolution of Building Materials and Structures - e-ISBN: 2-912143-86-1; *Edited by F. Wittmann*

COMP 03: General Conference of RILEM TCs' Chairmen and RILEM Seminar 'Advancing the Knowledge in Materials and Structures' (CD10) (2000) e-ISBN: 2-912143-85-3

COMP 06: Concrete Science and Engineering Journal - Vol. 1, 2, 3, 4 (1999-2002) (CD05)

Contents

Preface

HPFRCC-5 will be the fifth workshop in a series dealing with High Performance Fiber Reinforced Cement Composites (HPFRCC). The four prior workshops have led to a definition of HPFRCC that mostly suggests a technical challenge. That is, composites that exhibit a strain hardening tensile stress-strain response accompanied by multiple cracking (and related relatively large energy absorption capacity). Researchers have tried to reduce the fiber content to a necessary minimum. By reducing fiber content, they are simplifying the production process, helping make standard mixing procedures acceptable, and opening the way to large scale practical applications.

The first international workshop on High Performance Fiber Reinforced Cement Composites was organized in Mainz, Germany, June 1991, under the auspices of RILEM and ACI. It was funded in part by US National Science Foundation (NSF) and by the Deutsche Forschungsgemeinschaft (the German NSF). Other co-sponsors included the center for Advanced Cement Based Materials (ACBM), the University of Michigan and the University of Stuttgart. The second workshop took place in Ann Arbor, Michigan, in June 1995, the third in Mainz Germany, in June 1999, and the fourth in Ann Arbor, Michigan, in June 2003 with same sponsors and co-sponsors. In each case hard-cover proceedings were published as a special RILEM publication. While the first workshop in 1991 included mostly US and German participants, subsequent workshops were opened to top researchers in the field from other countries. The last workshop in Ann Arbor 2003, assembled researchers from eighteen countries. The proceedings included 39 papers grouped in 7 different parts.

Since the first workshop, in 1991, continuous developments have occurred in new materials, processing, standardization, and in improved products for building and other structures. Also, enhanced theory and modeling of HPFRCC can now better describe their behavior and explain their reinforcing mechanisms. While in the first workshop, HPFRCC implied relatively high volume fractions of fibers (more than 4%), today HPFRCC can be engineered with as little as 1% fiber content. While the root definition of HPFRCC is simplest (that is to exhibit strain hardening and multiple cracking behavior in tension) to clearly differentiate them from other cement composites, this is not the only description of desirable performance. Durability, ductility, fire resistance, impact resistance, diffusion resistance, imperviousness, and constructability at reasonable cost, are other important attributes that need to be further clarified.

Typically in each workshop, a broad range of technical issues from microstructure characterization to design recommendations are covered; however, selected specific themes are emphasized. In this fifth workshop, the organizers recommended specific themes for which research information is needed. These are:

- tensile properties: characterization, testing and workability
- bending, shear and compression
- fresh state and hardening properties
- self-consolidating FRC mixtures
- permeability, durability and temperature effects
- retrofit and strengthening
- impact and blast loading
- seismic loading.

Papers addressing these themes are grouped in six separate parts of the proceedings.

The organizers hope that this new volume will help foster the continuous development and increasing utilization of HPFRCC in both stand-alone and structural applications.

H.W. Reinhardt

A.E. Naaman

HPFRCC5 - Workshop

Workshop Organization:

Co-Chairman: Hans W. Reinhardt, Institut für Werkstoffe im Bauwesen, University of Stuttgart, Germany

Co-Chairman: Antoine E. Naaman, Department of Civil and Environmental Engineering, University of Michigan, Ann Arbor, USA

Scientific Committee

Chair: J. Bolander, University of California, Davis, USA
Deputy Chair: A. Bentur, Technion - Israel Institute of Technology, Israel

Members:
- F. Ansari, University of Illinois at Chicago, USA
- G. Balazs, Budapest University of Technology, Hungary
- M. Behloul, Lafarge, France
- S. Billington, Stanford University, USA
- G. Campione, Universita di Palermo, Italy
- G. Chanvillard, Lafarge, France
- F. Dehn, University of Leipzig, Germany
- E. Denarié, EPFL, Lausanne, Switzerland
- A. Dubey, USG Corporation, USA
- H. Falkner, Technical University of Braunschweig, Germany
- L. Ferrara, Politecnico di Milano, Italy
- M.A. Glinicki, Polish Academy of Sciences, Poland
- C.U. Grosse, University of Stuttgart, Germany
- P. Hamelin, INSA-Lyon, France
- W. Hansen, University of Michigan, USA
- A. Katz, Technion, Haifa, Israel
- K. Kosa, Kyushu Institute of Technology, Japan
- N. Krstulovic-Opara, Arup, USA
- A. Lambrechts, Bekaert, Belgium
- D. Lange, University of Illinois at Urbana-Champaign, USA
- V.C. Li, University of Michigan, USA
- I. Markovic, Delft University of Technology, The Netherlands
- V. Mechtcherine, Technical University of Dresden, Germany
- H. Mihashi, Tohoku University, Japan
- B. Mobasher, Arizona State University, Tempe, USA
- H.S. Müller, University of Karlsruhe, Germany
- G.J. Parra-Montesinos, University of Michigan, USA
- A. Peled, Ben Gurion University, Israel
- M. di Prisco, Politecnico di Milano, Italy

- G. Plizzari, Universita de Bergamo, Italy
- P. Rossi, LCPC, France
- M. Schmidt, University of Kassel, Germany
- C. Sujivorakul, King Mongkut's University of Technology Thonburi, Thailand
- L. Vandewalle, Katholieke Universiteit Leuven, Belgium
- F.H. Wittmann, Aedificat Institute, Freiburg, Germany

International Committee

Chair: N. Banthia, University of British Columbia, Canada
Deputy Chair: S.P. Shah, Northwestern University, USA

Members:
- W. Brameshuber, RWTH Aachen, Germany
- A.M. Brandt, Polish Academy of Sciences, Poland
- K.P. Chong, National Science Foundation, USA
- M. Curbach, Technical University of Dresden, Germany
- G. Fischer, Technical University of Denmark, Lyngby, Denmark
- H. Fukuyama, Building Research Institute, Tsukuba, Japan
- P. Gambarova, Politecnico di Milano, Italy
- M. Harajli, American University of Beirut, Lebanon
- S. Karihaloo, University of Cardiff, UK
- M. Maalej, University of Sharjah, UAE
- C. Meyer, Columbia University, USA
- J.G.M. van Mier, ETH Zürich, Switzerland
- S. Mindess, University of British Columbia, Canada
- B.H. Oh, Seoul National University, Korea
- G. Ong, National University of Singapore
- P. Paramasivam, National University of Singapore
- J. Pera, INSA de Lyon, France
- K. Rokugo, Gifu University, Japan
- H. Stang, Technical University of Denmark, Denmark
- Sun Wei, Southeast University, Nanjing, P.R. China
- L. Taerwe, University of Gent, Belgium
- K.H. Tan, National University of Singapore
- R.D. Toledo Filho, COPPE/UFRJ, Brasil
- T.C. Triantafillou, University of Patras, Greece
- J.C. Walraven, Delft University of Technology, The Netherlands
- J. Wastiels, Vrije Universiteit Brussel (VUB), Brussels, Belgium
- G. van Zijl, University of Stellenbosch, South Africa

Sponsorship

RILEM
American Concrete Institute
University of Michigan
University of Stuttgart
NSF Center for Advanced Cement Based Materials
International Ferrocement Society (IFS)

Funding

Deutsche Forschungsgemeinschaft, Germany
The US National Science Foundation

Local Organization
- Prof. Dr. H.W. Reinhardt
- Dr. C.U. Grosse
- Dr. M. Krüger
- Ms. S. Stumpp

Production Assistant
- S. Stumpp, University of Stuttgart

Acknowledgments

This workshop was sponsored by RILEM (International Union of Laboratories and Experts in Construction Materials, Systems and Structures), and co-sponsored by the American Concrete Institute (ACI), the center for Advanced Cement Based Materials (ACBM), and the International Ferrocement Society (IFS). It was made possible by grants from the German Deutsche Forschungsgemeinschaft (DFG); the US National Science Foundation (NSF), Division of Civil and Mechanical Systems, with P. Balaguru as cognizant program director; the University of Stuttgart; and the University of Michigan. The support of the above organizations is gratefully acknowledged.

The organizers would like to thank all members of the Scientific and International Committees for enthusiastically supporting the organization of this fifth workshop, and all the authors who have contributed the valuable papers that make these proceedings. Special thanks are due to Ms. Simone Stumpp for preparing with great care and efficiency the camera ready material for printing. Once more, H.W. Reinhardt and A.E. Naaman would like to express their deep gratitude to the Alexander von Humboldt Foundation for giving them the opportunity to initiate, in 1990, a long-term continually productive cooperation.

H.W. Reinhardt
A.E. Naaman

PART ONE

TENSILE PROPERTIES: CHARACTERIZATION, TESTING AND MODELING

MEASUREMENT OF TENSILE PROPERTIES OF FIBER REINFORCED CONCRETE: DRAFT SUBMITTED TO ACI COMMITTEE 544

Antoine E. Naaman (1), Gregor Fischer (2), and Neven Krstulovic-Opara (3)

(1) Civil and Environmental Engineering, University of Michigan, USA

(2) Civil Engineering, Technical University of Denmark, Denmark

(3) Arup Energy, Houston, Texas, USA

Abstract

The constitutive properties of structural materials are essential for modeling structural response for analysis, evaluation, and design. This is particularly true for the tensile properties of fiber reinforced concrete should its contribution be considered in the design of structural concrete members. This short paper summarizes a chapter of a draft document currently under preparation by ACI Committee 544, Fiber Reinforced Concrete, on the Measurements of Properties of Fiber Reinforced Concrete; in particular, Chapter 3, Tensile Properties, is addressed. Following a simple classification of the behavior of FRC composites as either tension strain-hardening or strain-softening, the types of tensile stress-strain or stress-elongation response that can be experimentally obtained as well as the key elements of each response are explained. Several types of specimens, their preferred size, and the loading conditions are described. Some recommendation is provided for the measurements of strains and crack opening.

1. INTRODUCTION

The constitutive properties of structural materials are essential for modeling structural response for analysis, evaluation, and design. This is particularly true for the tensile properties of fiber reinforced concrete should its contribution be considered in the design of structural concrete members.

2. TENSILE STRESS-STRAIN RESPONSE

The importance of the tensile properties of fiber reinforced cement composites is stressed in every book and publication dealing with them. Many experimental tensile tests (direct or indirect) have been tried and results published; yet no comprehensive agreed upon tensile test standard has been established to date.

3

Several technical organizations (ASTM, JCI, RILEM) have developed bending tests meant to simulate the characteristics of FRC composites in tension; this is because bending tests are simpler to carry out than tensile tests. However, such tests are insufficient to characterize tensile response, particularly when strain-hardening behavior and multiple cracking in tension are present and crack width is a criterion. Similarly, the indirect tensile test carried out by a split cylinder test is not meaningful since it does not simulate the true state of stress in a composite subjected to tension (see also section below).

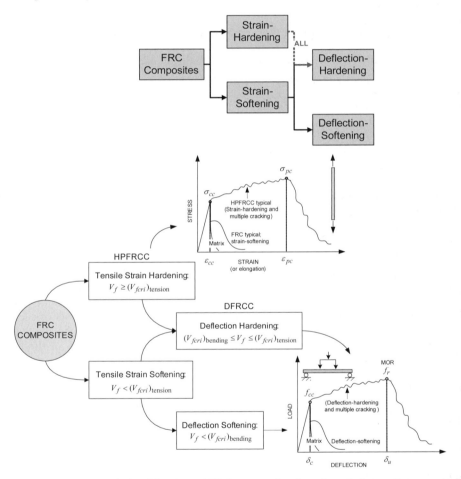

Figure 1: Suggested classification of FRC composites based on their tensile response [1, 2, 3]

Recognizing this gap, Naaman and Reinhardt [1] described several needs in order to promote increased structural applications of fiber reinforced concrete, among which the urgent need to develop a rational tensile test for fiber reinforced cement composites, the need to specify different performance levels for their key properties, and the need to show how a particular fiber and fiber concrete mixture can lead to a prescribed level of performance.

The discussion following the 2003 fourth international workshop on High Performance Fiber Reinforced Cement Composites (HPFRCC-4) led to suggesting a general classification of FRC composites such as shown in Fig. 1 [2, 3]. One key distinguishing material characteristic is whether the response of the composite is strain-hardening or strain-softening in tension, and within this last category, whether it is deflection-hardening or deflection-softening. Practically all fiber reinforced cement composites currently available are covered by the simple classification of Fig. 1. While the upper part of Fig. 1 is simplest for illustration, the lower part provides additional information about shape of the response curve and likely conditions to achieve such response in term of the critical volume fraction of fibers.

The classification of the tensile response (that is, strain-hardening or strain-softening) relates to a fundamental property, but the correlation with bending response relates to structural behavior. It is observed that a strain-hardening composite is considered mechanically more performant than a strain-softening one, while a tension strain-softening composite can be deflection-hardening or deflection-softening. Deflection-hardening composites are useful in structural applications where bending prevails [4], while deflection-softening composites cover a wide range of practical applications starting at the lower end by the control of plastic shrinkage cracking of concrete, to the higher end where they are used in concrete pavements and slabs on grade. Finally note that a strain-hardening composite generates multiple cracking during the hardening process leading to significantly increased toughness and energy absorption capacity, while a strain-softening composite undergoes immediate crack localization at first cracking and thus will generate only one structural or percolation crack.

Fig. 2 (adapted from [5]) illustrates the characteristics stress versus elongation curve of a strain-hardening versus a strain-softening FRC composite. In this figure, σ_{cc} represents the stress at first structural cracking (percolation crack) and σ_{pc} represents the maximum post-cracking stress attained. A strain-hardening composite can be most simply characterized by the condition: $\sigma_{pc} > \sigma_{cc}$ (assuming an elastic-plastic response or better), while for a strain softening composite: $\sigma_{pc} \leq \sigma_{cc}$. Fig. 2a is a true stress-strain response; the softening branch after maximum stress is not shown. Fig. 2b is a strain versus crack-opening response, since following first cracking the composite cannot develop sufficient strength to induce more than one crack (localized cracking). In either figure the x axis also represents the elongation of the specimen under load. In each figure two curves are given, one full and one dotted, to illustrate typical ranges observed. For a strain hardening material (Fig. 2a), everything else being equal, steel fibers (high elastic modulus) lead to a stiffer post-cracking branch (dotted curve) while polymeric fibers (lower elastic modulus) lead to a softer response. In Fig. 2b, a softer fiber leads to a crack width at maximum post-cracking stress larger than a stiffer one.

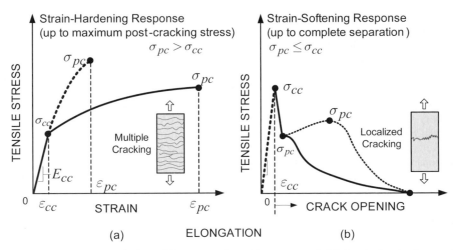

Figure 2: Key characteristics of the stress-elongation curve of: (a) Strain-hardening, and (b) Strain softening FRC composites subjected to direct tension [5]

While no standard test has been so far developed by ACI to determine the direct tensile properties of FRC composites, it is essential to keep in mind Figs. 2a and 2b in order to make sure that a standard test allows the measurement of the key properties shown in these figures, such as $\sigma_{cc}, \sigma_{pc}, \varepsilon_{cc}, \varepsilon_{pc}$ and the elastic modulus of the composite. Moreover, it is recommended to record crack distribution, spacing, and width at maximum post-cracking stress or ultimate.

For a more comprehensive test, it is also recommended to monitor and quantify the crack formation at various stages of the deformation process. For this purpose, digital image analysis can be applied. In this process images of the FRC specimen are taken at various stages of the stress-elongation test, then analyzed for crack formation, width and spacing. Data are processed to yield statistical distribution of variables such as maximum, minimum, and average crack width at various stages of loading [6, 7]. Such information can be important for evaluating structural performance for service loads and at ultimate.

3. TYPE OF TENSILE TESTS OF FRC COMPOSITES

Fig. 3 illustrates examples of specimens for tensile testing. The specimen shown in Fig. 3a is appropriate for thin sheets and plates. In such a specimen, the ends are taken in sandwich by thin aluminum plates bonded to their surface; the plates serve to minimize damage due to the jaws of the tensile grips used to transfer the load. Fig. 3b shows a dog-bone shaped specimen which is characterized by a cross section that decreases significantly from the loading end to the body of the specimen; such a reduction helps insure that failure occurs within the body of the specimen allowing strains $(\Delta L / L)$ to be measured within the gauge length, L. In Fig. 3c, the specimen can be a prism or a cylinder with its ends bonded to stiff steel loading platens. Fig. 3d shows a notched tensile prism (or cylinder) used to evaluate the stress versus crack-opening or displacement $(\sigma - \delta)$ under tensile loading.

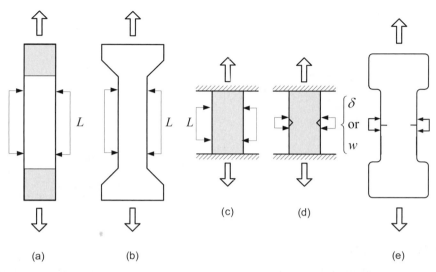

Figure 3: Examples of tensile tests of FRC composites: (a) Thin sheets; (b) Dog-bone shaped, hinged ends; (c) Bonded ends fixed against rotation; (d) Bonded ends notched and fixed against rotation; (e) Hinged ends notched

Loading conditions at the end of the tensile specimens can vary from pin-pin, to fixed-pin, or to fixed-fixed. Typically the specimens of Figs. 3a and 3b are pin-pin loaded while the specimens of Figs. 3c and 3d are preferably fixed-fixed loaded. Fixed-fixed implies no end rotation but displacement in the loading direction, while fixed-pin would allow both rotation and displacement at one end.

The tests described in Figs. 3a, 3b, and 3c are suitable for strain-hardening FRC composites. The stress is calculated from the load and the strain is calculated from the displacement as shown in Fig. 4. The notched prism tests of Figs. 3d and 3e are particularly suitable to determine the stress versus displacement (or crack opening) response which is considered a constitutive property of the composite (Fig. 2b). They are also suitable for a "strain-softening" FRC composite where localized failure is expected. Such tests can also be used, to supplement information from tests in Figs. 3a, 3b, and 3c, to evaluate the stress versus crack-opening of a strain-hardening FRC composite (after peak stress or crack localization). Furthermore, Yang and Fischer [6] have shown that information from a sufficient number of such tests (Fig. 3d) and their variability can be used to predict the entire tensile stress-strain response of a strain hardening FRC composite.

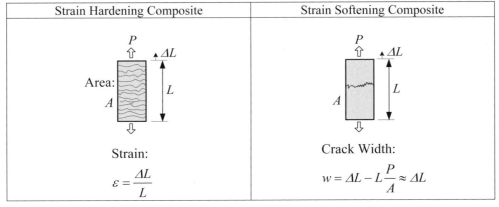

Strain Hardening Composite	Strain Softening Composite
Area: A, P, ΔL, L	A, P, ΔL, L
Strain: $$\varepsilon = \frac{\Delta L}{L}$$	Crack Width: $$w = \Delta L - L\frac{P}{A} \approx \Delta L$$

Figure 4: Computation of strain or approximate crack opening

4. SPECIMEN SIZE

Since no standard test has been developed for FRC composites, available research investigations on the subject show a wide variety of sizes. Since size effects are significant, correlation between different investigations cannot be properly carried out. Until a standard test is developed, the following recommendation made by Naaman and Reinhardt [2005, Ref. 5] could be used as a guide for specimen size:

- Use prisms of square or circular cross-section, with a side or diameter equal at least to 50 mm, 3 times the fiber length, and/or 6 times the size of maximum aggregate, whichever is larger.
- Gauge length for measuring strain should be at least 2 to 3 times the minimum size (side or diameter) of the tensile prism.
- For tests involving thin sheets, the specimen section could be rectangular with the longer side satisfying at least the above criteria and the smaller side equal to the thickness of the sheet.
- Tensile prisms with dog-bone shaped ends or especially confined ends are often used for direct tensile tests and, when carried out properly, should lead to most realistic results.

5. SPLIT CYLINDER TENSILE TEST

This section is reproduced, as is, from the 1999 report of ACI Committee 544 [8].
"Results from the split cylinder tensile strength test (ASTM C 496) for FRC specimens are difficult to interpret after the first matrix cracking and should not be used beyond the first crack because of unknown stress distributions after the first crack. The precise identification of the first crack in the split cylinder test can be difficult without strain gages or other sophisticated means of crack detection, such as acoustic emission or laser holography. The relationship between splitting tensile strength and direct tensile strength or modulus of rupture has not been determined.

The split cylinder tensile test has been used in production applications as a quality control test, after relationships have been developed with other properties when using a constant mixture."

ACKNOWLEDGMENTS

The research described here was sponsored in part by the National Science Foundation under Grant No. CMS 0408623 to the first author, and by the University of Michigan. Their support is gratefully acknowledged. The opinions expressed in this paper are those of the authors and do not necessarily reflect the views of the sponsor.

REFERENCES

[1] Naaman, A.E., and Reinhardt, H.W., "Fiber Reinforced Concrete: Current Needs for Structural Implementation," Proceedings of US-European Workshop on Advanced Fiber Reinforced Concrete, G.A. Plizzari and M. di Prisco, Editors, Bergamo, Italy, September 2004.

[2] Naaman, A.E., and Reinhardt, H.W., "High Performance Fiber Reinforced Cement Composites, HPFRCC 4: International RILEM Workshop, Summary Report, Materials and Structures 36 (2003), pp 710-712.

[3] Naaman, A.E., and Reinhardt, H.W., "Setting the Stage: toward Performance Based Classification of FRC Composites," in High Performance Fiber Reinforced Cement Composites (HPFRCC-4), A.E. Naaman and H.W. Reinhardt, Editors, RILEM Publications, Pro. 30, June 2003, pp. 1-4.

[4] Naaman, A.E., "Strain Hardening and Deflection Hardening Fiber Reinforced Cement Composites," in High Performance Fiber Reinforced Cement Composites (HPFRCC-4), A.E. Naaman and H.W. Reinhardt, Editors, RILEM Publications, Pro. 30, June 2003, pp. 95-113.

[5] Naaman, A.E., and Reinhardt, H.W., "Proposed Classification of HPFRC Composites Based on their Tensile Response," in Proceedings of a Symposium honoring S. Mindess, edited by A. Bentur, S.P. Shah, and N. Banthia, University of British Columbia, August 2005.

[6] Yang, J., and Fischer, G., "Implications of the Fiber Bridging Stress – Crack Opening Relationship on Properties of Fiber Reinforced Cementitious Composites in Uniaxial Tension", paper presented at the International Workshop on Applications High Performance Fiber Reinforced Cementitious Composites in Structural Applications, Honolulu, USA, May 2005. RILEM Proceedings PRO 49, ed. by G. Fischer and V.C. Li, Bagneux, France, pp 93-105

[7] Peled A. and Mobasher, B., "Pultruded Fabric-Cement Composites," ACI Materials Journal, Vol. 102, No. 1, Jan.-Feb. 2005, pp. 15-23.

[8] ACI Committee 544, "Measurements of Properties of Fiber Reinforced Concrete," ACI 544.2R-89 (Reapproved 1999), in Manual of Concrete Practice, American Concrete Institute, Farmington Hills, MI, 2002.

APPENDIX A – EXAMPLES OF TENSILE TEST METHODS AND SET-UP

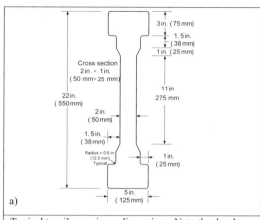

Typical tensile specimen dimensions. Note the dog-bone shaped ends have a double transition in width reduction to minimize failure near the grips. The end parts are additionally reinforced by two layers of steel wire mesh extending about 25 mm into the narrowest part of the specimen.	Typical specimen under test. The free length allows measurements of elongation, thus strain, over a gauge length of up to 200 mm.

Figure A1: Typical tensile tests with hinged ends conditions used by Naaman and Co-workers at the University of Michigan

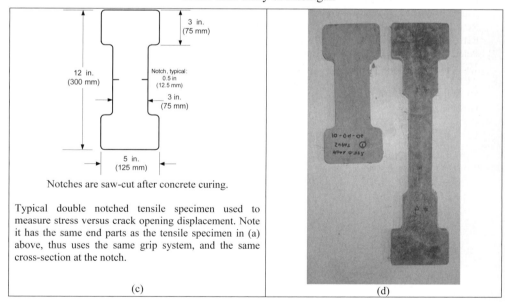

Notches are saw-cut after concrete curing.

Typical double notched tensile specimen used to measure stress versus crack opening displacement. Note it has the same end parts as the tensile specimen in (a) above, thus uses the same grip system, and the same cross-section at the notch.

(c)

(d)

Figure A1: continued: Typical tensile tests with hinged ends conditions used by Naaman and Co-workers at the University of Michigan

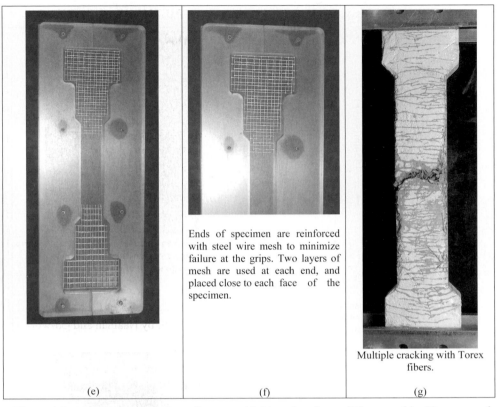

Ends of specimen are reinforced with steel wire mesh to minimize failure at the grips. Two layers of mesh are used at each end, and placed close to each face of the specimen.

Multiple cracking with Torex fibers.

(e)   (f)   (g)

Figure A1: continued: Typical tensile tests with hinged ends conditions used by Naaman and Co-workers at the University of Michigan

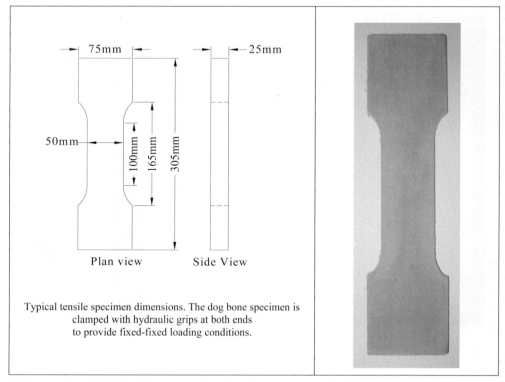

Figure A2: Typical tensile test specimens with fixed end conditions used by Fischer and co-workers at the Technical University of Denmark

TESTING BEHAVIOUR OF STRAIN HARDENING CEMENT-BASED COMPOSITES IN TENSION – SUMMARY OF RECENT RESEARCH

Viktor Mechtcherine

Institute for Building Materials, TU Dresden, Germany

Abstract

This paper summarizes the findings of recent research with regard to the testing of Strain Hardening Cement-based Composites (SHCC) in tension. It presents advantages and shortcomings of various test set-ups, as well as effects of various testing parameters, on the mechanical performance measured for such materials. A recommendation for a suitable test methodology is then mapped out based on these discussions.

1.   INTRODUCTION

The most important and decisive characteristic of SHCC subjected to uni-axial tension is the strain hardening accompanied by multiple crack formation and, therefore, considerable non-elastic deformations. Testing, to determine whether or not a cementitious fibre-reinforced composite can be classified as SHCC, as well as quantifying material characteristics, presents challenging tasks. These tasks require suitable testing methods that deliver an unaltered picture of the characteristic behaviour of such newly developed composite materials.

Uni-axial tension tests are generally accepted as the most direct and sound procedure to determine the stress-deformation behaviour under tension of strain hardening cement-based composites. This type of test – although simple in concept – is quite sensitive to the particularities of the test set-up used (e.g. the degree of hindrance of specimen rotation), specimen geometry (size effect, effect of notches), etc. This paper will first provide an overview of different test set-ups used by the author and other researchers in the last few years. And, second, summarize the results obtained from studies which have addressed the effects of various testing parameters on the mechanical performance of SHCC. Finally, based upon these observations and considerations, a recommendation will be mapped out for a suitable test methodology capable of being adopted as standard testing.

2.   EFFECT OF TEST SET-UP

2.1   Shape and dimensions of the specimens

The most commonly used geometry for specimens of testing of SHCC behaviour under tension are so-called dog-bone shaped prisms. This shape enables the avoidance of failure in the area of load introduction in the specimen which, otherwise, occurs due to an unfavourable multi-axial stress state and/or an abrupt change of stiffness in the transition region from loading plates to the specimen. A smooth transition from a wider part of the specimen to the narrow, middle portion, as used in the experiments [1, 2] appears to be, at least theoretically, the most appropriate geometric shape needed to avoid local stress concentrations, cf. Fig. 1 (a, b, d). However, a sharper transition, when the narrower portion of the specimen builds a defined angle with the wider portion of the specimen, was adopted for the tests by [2, 3], (see e.g. Fig. 1 (c)). This situation does not seem to negatively influence the results. Fig. 1 provides geometrical data for the specimen mentioned.

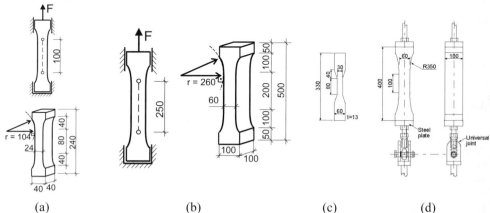

(a)   (b)   (c)   (d)

Figure 1: Geometries of dog-bone shaped prisms: a) and b) according to Mechtcherine and Schulze [1], c) and d) acc. to Kanabuko et al. [2]

Coupon (plate type) specimens were used in a series of tests by Li [4] and Wang and Li [5]. Each specimen measured 304.8 mm by 76.2 mm by 12.7 mm. In general, a characteristic strain-hardening behaviour could be successfully documented. However, as indicated by Li [4], the final crack formation typically occurred in the region near the loading grips. Similar results were observed in experiments by Wittek [6] on prisms measuring 160 mm by 40 mm by 40 mm despite the fact that the specimens were glued into the machine using a special adapter, which should have provided for a smoother change of stiffness within the transition region of the "loading plates/specimen".

In [2, 7] un-notched cylinder specimens, which were without cross-sectional changes, were used. These can be easily produced using "conventional" moulds. Another advantage of such geometry is that it corresponds to the shape of cores which may be taken from structural elements to test in-situ properties of SHCC. However, in addition to the problems described for the un-notched prisms and plates without cross-sectional change, an unfavourable orientation of fibres with regard to the direction of tensile loading in the case of cast cylinder specimens should be considered, (see also Section 2.2).

In order to avoid the phenomena of failure in the region of load introduction, dog-bone cylinders were used by Kanabuko et al. [2]. Alternatively, sheets of glass fibre or similar material can be glued to the specimen flanks in the transition region from the loading plates to the specimens, as described in [2].

Notched prisms and notched cylinders are commonly used for the testing of post-peak behaviour of stress-softening cementitious materials subjected to tension. Notches are necessary for such quasi-brittle materials, in order to enable stable crack development in these deformation-controlled tests using small gauge lengths and correspondingly achieving an adequate steering of the testing machine. Stress concentrations and a multi-axial stress state at the notches is the benefit for anticipating the failure region.

A few series of tests on notched prisms were carried out by various research groups [8, 9, 10] based upon the notion of localising the final crack prior to testing. Fig. 2 displays typical stress-deformation relationships obtained from the uni-axial tension tests which were performed on un-notched and notched prisms, respectively. Not only was there an absence of reduction in the tensile strength f_t, but, rather a slight increase was observed in the direct tension tests on notched specimens compared to the tests on un-notched prisms. This is a typical result for ductile materials (e.g., steel) when considering the SHCC investigated. The reason for this phenomenon is most likely the existence of a multi-axial state of stresses in the notched region.

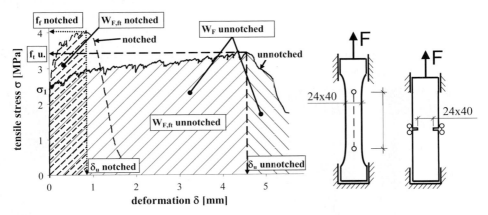

Figure 2: Uni-axial tension tests: stress-deformation relationships obtained from notched and un-notched prisms according to Mechtcherine and Schulze [9]

As a result of the concentration of cracks around the notched cross-section of notched specimens, much smaller total deformations δ_u could be measured at the maximum load. It is worthy to note that the ultimate strain ε_u (equal to the ultimate deformation δ_u divided by the gauge length) was higher for notched specimens indicating denser cracking – a phenomenon, which could be clearly confirmed by the observation of surface crack patterns of specimens.

2.2   Specimen production method, casting direction
The distribution and orientation of fibres in a structural member or in a specimen made of SHCC are very essential to mechanical performance. Both of these properties, but, in particular, the fibre orientation, depend on the direction of SHCC casting, as well as in some cases, the particular geometry of the member or the method of specimen production.

The bend tests performed by van Zijl [3] on specimens produced by a variety of methods (extrusion and spinning, respectively) clearly show the corresponding effects on the mechanical performance of SHCC.

The most extensive study on the effect of the casting direction was performed in Japan as a Round Robin test [2]. According to the results obtained, the mechanical performance of the specimens loaded in the direction of casting was considerably higher with regard to the ultimate strain capacity. Remarkably, the dog-bone cylinder, which was cast vertically, did not show any strain hardening. The statistics given in [2] illustrate that the scatter of the results was more pronounced during testing of the vertically cast specimens.

2.3   Attachment of the specimen to the testing machine, boundary conditions

The type and preciseness of attachment of the specimens to the testing machine may have a pronounced effect on test results. Generally, two main types of boundary loading conditions are associated with the tensile tests both with and without hindering the specimen rotation, respectively.

In order to prevent specimen rotation, the specimens can be wedged by being glued between the load cell and the base plate of the machine. In this case, the accuracy of the specimen positioning is of major significance in order to assure the centricity of loading. Due to the heterogeneity of composite materials, some secondary flexure is inevitably introduced at the onset of local cracking which then disappears once cracking has spanned the entire cross-section. The secondary flexure can be completely avoided using a test set-up with adjusting gears as described in [10]. However, this type of testing is very elaborate and for this reason, not recommended for common use.

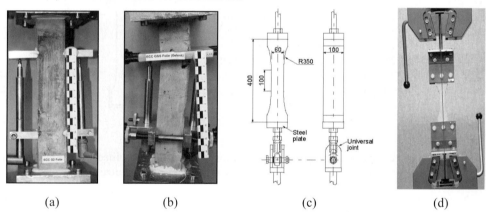

| (a) | (b) | (c) | (d) |

Figure 3: Variants of the attachment of the specimen to the testing machine: (a) non-rotational boundaries [9], (b) rotational boundaries [9], (c) pin-fixed boundaries [2], (d) fixed boundaries with reduced rotational stiffness [3]

Calottes are normally installed between the load carrying portion of the machine and the metal adapters fixed to the ends of the specimens for tension tests without hindrance to the specimen rotation.

Mechtcherine and Schulze [9] performed tests on SHCC both with non-rotational and rotational loading plates, cf. Fig. 3 (a) and (b). During the tests with rotational loading boundaries, deformations increased more significantly on the side of the prism where the initial crack appeared. A multiple-crack formation appears on both sides of the specimen during the tests where the deformation discrepancy measured continuously increased. This implies that the crack formation proceeds faster on one side; therefore, the specimen loading becomes increasingly eccentric. However, the crack formation irregularity in this case does not occur during testing in which the rotation of the specimen is hindered. But, rather, both sides of the specimen display almost identical curves until ultimate strain occurs.

When considering the average curves of both sides of the specimen, which are normally considered when characterising the material behaviour, it is determined that the measured σ-ε relationships obtained from the test with rotational loading plates, are lower than the σ-ε curves obtained from the test in which rotational hindrance played a factor [9]. Smaller values of the initial crack stress σ_1, the tensile strength f_t and the ultimate strain ε_u at failure are determined accordingly.

A set-up with a non-rotational loading plate on one specimen end and a calotte on the other end, a so-called pin-fixed arrangement as used by Kanabuko et al. [2], can be regarded as a compromise solution. However, such a set-up not only incorporates the advantages of both basic set-ups, but it incorporates their shortcomings, as well.

Gluing is one method often implemented to attach the specimen to the adapters. For the corresponding tests on ordinary concrete, a "slice" of cement rich material is sawn from the ends of specimens before gluing in order to obtain a good introduction of forces into the specimen via coarse aggregate grains and, consequently, to avoid joint failure. For SHCC, with its very fine fillers and, conversely, lack of coarse aggregates, the sawing does not render much improvement even if high strength epoxy is used as glue. A more effective measure is to glue the specimens to the adapters which "embrace" the flanks at the specimen ends as has been practiced by Mechtcherine and Schulze [9, 11].

However, the procedure of gluing specimens between loading plates is time-consuming. For this reason, different types of grips have been developed in order to facilitate the mounting of specimens into testing machines, cf. e.g. Fig. 3 (d) according to van Zijl [3]. A disadvantageous side-effect of using such adapters is that the testing system becomes softer and the secondary flexure associated with a partial rotation of the specimen at the onset of cracking becomes more pronounced. Furthermore, some bending moments may occur after gripping the specimen.

3.   EFFECTS OF OTHER TESTING PARAMETERS

3.1   Age of the specimens

Wang and Li [5] investigated the development of tensile strain capacity relative to age and found the strain capacity 24 hours after casting to be about 2.3%. The ultimate strain in "early-age" increases with time and rises above 4% after 7 days; later a decrease occurs only to be followed by a plateau of slightly more than 3% after a time period of approximately 30 days. This change in strain capacity reflects the evolution of matrix toughness and interfacial bond properties. The tensile strength of SHCC tested increased from 3.0 MPa to 5.4 MPa within a time period of 1 to 90 days after casting [5]. There was no observed age effect based upon the tensile strength of SHCC on notched specimens at the material ages of 14, 28 and 90 days, respectively according to the results of experimental work performed by Yang and Fischer [8], However, the deformation at peak load decreased considerably with an increase in age.

3.2   Curing conditions

According to the current regulations, ordinary concrete or mortar specimens are to be stored in water until testing in order to determine the material behaviour in tension. The formation of residual stresses due to moisture gradients (and consequently, a decrease in tensile strength) should therefore be avoided. The results obtained by Mechtcherine and Schulze [11] illustrate that curing conditions of SHCC also have a considerable effect on tension test results.

Slightly higher values for the stress at first cracking were obtained from the tests on drying specimens compared to results from tests on sealed specimens; see [11]. The values of the tensile strength f_t and the ultimate strain ε_u were slightly lower overall for both un-notched and notched prisms in the case of unsealed specimens, cf. Fig. 4.

Water storage of the specimens resulted in a significant reduction of tensile strength in comparison to sealed or drying specimens. At the same time, the stress-deformation curves for the specimens cured in water clearly showed a less steep descending branch in comparison to the other types of curing in the experiments on notched prisms (Fig. 5, right). This phenomenon unquestionably resulted from the specific properties of the matrix and, in particular, the interface between the matrix and fibres which was a result of various curing conditions. However, particular mechanisms must still yet be clarified.

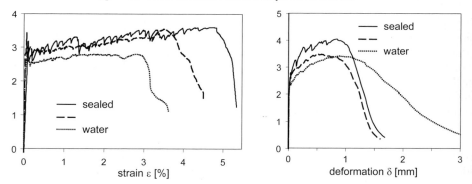

Figure 4: Effect of curing on the results of tension tests performed on small un-notched (left) and notched (right) prisms, according to Mechtcherine and Schulze [11]

3.3   Size effects

The specimen size can affect the measured mechanical behaviour of SHCC in various ways. On the one hand, the orientation of the fibres depends on the size and shape of moulds: the fibres are aligned in the direction of the walls at both the mould walls and eventually at the specimens' surfaces (so-called wall-effect). The orientation of fibres becomes more irregular with increasing distance from the specimen surfaces. As a result, the average performance values measured for SHCC on small specimens with a narrow cross-section were higher in comparison to the corresponding values obtained from tests on larger specimens. This holds true for the case when the loading direction is congruent with the primary direction of the fibre orientation (see e.g. the results presented in [1, 2, 11]).

On the other hand, the presence of some local material imperfections, such as larger voids due to incomplete de-airing, influence the mechanical performance of smaller specimens more significantly than the performance of large specimens in which the ratio of the defect size to specimen size is much smaller. The fact that a more pronounced scattering of these results is obtained from small specimens compared to larger specimens as observed in [2] may be regarded as characteristic.

These considerations take into account the size of the cross-section; however, the specimen length most certainly influences the test results. No reports could be found in literature which could illustrate this effect. Preliminary tests by the author showed that specimens with a constant cross-section provide higher values, as expected, with regard to the deformation measured for the entire specimen length, while the tensile strength and the strain capacity decrease. This result appears to be meaningful since, the probability of a "weaker link" existing over the length measured increases, as well, with increased specimen length. More tests are still needed in order to quantify this effect.

3.4   Loading rate

The tests performed by Yang and Li [12] showed a pronounced increase in values for the stress at first crack σ_1 and tensile strength f_t, as well as a considerable decrease in strain capacity for SHCC with an increasing loading rate. Similar results were obtained by Douglas and Billington [7] for a less ductile SHCC. They observed multiple cracking only for the quasi-static strain rate. This multiple cracking was essentially not present for the two fastest strain rates. In contrast to the findings published in [7, 12], Boshoff [15] observed no considerable effect of the loading rate on the tensile strength and strain capacity of SHCC, while increase in the stress at first crack was very pronounced.

According to Yang and Li [12], the sensitivity of the material behaviour relative to the loading rate (i.e. the loss of ductility with increasing strain rate) primarily depends on the kind of interface chemical bond between fibres and matrix. They showed that a weakening of the chemical bond interface had a positive effect on decreasing the rate dependence. This approach is suitable for SHCC with PVA fibres in which the interface chemical bond is rather strong. On the contrary, PE (polyethylene) fibres show no chemical bond in cement-based composites due to the hydrophobic nature of PE. Hence, a lower rate dependency in PE-ECC can be expected when compared with that of PVA-ECC. This assumption is supported by observations in the test results of Maalej et al [13].

3.5   Type of test control

All experiments referred to in this document were carried out using either displacement control (displacement of the cross-head of the testing machine) or deformation control (deformation measured directly at the specimen). Due to the ductility of the material and, as a rule, large gauge length the particular choice of either of these two control techniques has no significant effect on test results. In principle, it is possible to test SHCC using load control, as well, as demonstrated by Mechtcherine and Schulze [11]. These load tests are not recommended for the derivation of the characteristic material behaviour under tensile loading, but they may be used for quality control of SHCC if no displacement controlled testing machine is available.

4.   EVALUATION / UTILISATION OF THE TEST RESULTS

As a rule, a quite straightforward procedure is used to evaluate the results of tensile tests. The modulus of elasticity E_0, the stress at first cracking σ_1, the tensile strength f_t, as well as the strain capacity ε_u, are all derived for each specimen from the average stress-strain curve obtained from measurements by two (primarily), three or four LVDTs fixed to specimen flanks. These material parameters can be utilized directly as input values for a corresponding material law describing behaviour of SHCC in tension, see e.g. [11, 14].

Additionally, the area under the curve can be calculated, as it has been commonly done in fracture mechanics investigations. In such cases, the term "specific work of fracture W_F," which is commonly used in fracture mechanics, should be used instead of the term "fracture energy G_F" in order to avoid misconceptions. By definition, the fracture energy is the energy needed for the complete opening of a <u>single</u> major crack of a unit area. However, in the case of hardening materials, the area under the stress-deformation curve gives the energy consumed for the formation and propagation not of a single crack but of numerous parallel cracks. The expression chosen, "<u>specific</u> work of fracture", indicates that in the case of multiple cracking, the energy consumed is divided by the cross-sectional area, as well. This enables a better comparison of the results from various tests (different test set-ups: e.g., tensile tests/bend tests; various geometries, etc.) with regard to energy consumption due to cracking.

The shape of the curve, itself, provides some information about the cracking process and, in general, can be correlated to the crack number and crack width. Abrupt leaps of the curve indicate the formation of new cracks and the amplitude of these leaps appears to correlate to the corresponding crack opening widths.

A comparison of the stress-deformation curves obtained from the individual LVDTs attached to the specimen flanks provided information as to if and to what extent the rotation of the specimen cross-section occurred. The significance was, however, reduced when only two LVDTs were used. With three or four LVDTs, every inequality of the strain distribution within the specimen cross-section could be detected.

The scatter of the test results with regard to the tensile strength f_t with a variation coefficient of approx. 10% according to [11] or 3.7% to 14.5 according to [2] corresponds to the usual scatters for laboratory testing of tensile strength of ordinary cement-based materials such as concrete or mortar. The values of the stress at first cracking show a larger scatter with a variation coefficient of approximately 20% according to [11] or 9.6% to 32.4% according to [2]. The highest variation coefficient can be stated for the strain capacity as such: in the investigation by Kanabuko et al. [2], it was 22.5% to 73.9%, while Mechtcherine and Schulze [11] reported an average value of approximately 25%. In [2], particularly higher scatters were observed in both the tests on small specimens and the tests on specimens without a narrower portion.

The quasi-ductility of SHCC is a result of a gradual formation of a large number of fine cracks, more or less uniformly distributed over the length of the specimen. An observation of the crack formation and opening is an important part of the mechanical testing of SHCC with regard to more profound interpretation of the measured curves and, in some respect, to an estimation of SHCC durability. Until now, little systematic work has been done with regard to the crack detection and evaluation procedures.

5.   CONCLUSIONS

The following main conclusions with regard to the testing of SHCC in tension can be drawn from the test results presented in the previous sections:

5.1   Specimen shape

Only tests on un-notched specimen reproduce the characteristic material behaviour of SHCC subjected to tensile stress. The stress-strain relationships obtained from these tests can be considered as material-specific. Dog-bone shaped specimens should therefore be used in order to avoid a premature material failure in the regions of load introduction at the specimen ends.

The complex stress conditions in the notched specimens which depend on the notch geometry and irregular cracking in the area limited by the gauges render the interpretation of the results obtained from the tests on such specimens extremely difficult and not suitable for the derivation of the characteristic material behaviour. However, the tests on notched specimens may be used to some extent for quality control of products made of SHCC.

5.2 Casting direction and specimen size

The casting direction, as well as the specimen size and geometry, influence the fibre orientation in the specimen. Depending on the direction of the eventual loading, this orientation may or may not be favourable with regard to the mechanical performance (ductility) of SHCC. While an increase in specimen size leads to a moderate decrease of average mechanical performance, an unfavourable fibre orientation causes a dramatic reduction of the ductility of the material measured.

For the standard testing, the use of horizontally cast dog-bone shaped prisms seems to be the most appropriate. For some particular applications, in which an unfavourable orientation of fibres in the structure is likely, additional tests on specimens having a relevant fibre orientation should be performed. For this, one option might be to cast the portion of the structural element under consideration and eventually cut the specimen from the regions in question. A reasonable specimen size should only be chosen after considering the size of the concrete section which is to be constructed.

5.3 Curing of specimens and specimen age

The type of curing or storage influences the performance of SHCC. Choosing the type of curing relative to a specimen needs to be oriented to the prospective concrete manufacturing conditions, as well as building use. Otherwise, the most neutral curing method best suited for a standard test is sealing (no water absorption, no water loss).

The specimen age affects the performance of SHCC, as well. An age of 28 days is proposed for the standard testing which is commonly used for the testing of hardened concrete and mortar. Testing at a different age(s) may be needed for special applications.

5.4 Type of loading boundaries

The use of non-rotational loading plates has been proven to be beneficial for the implementation of tensile tests. To a large extent, a uniform strain distribution is attained throughout the cross-section when implementing such a test set-up in contrast to tests using rotational loading plates.

5.5 Type of test control

Indication of a specific velocity of the crosshead is sufficient for stable test implementation in order to control tests. A closed-loop test control, using deformation measurements by means of LVTDs attached to the specimen, are certainly applicable, as well. If load controlled testing equipment is the only type of testing equipment available, then this kind of test may be used for quality control of SHCC.

REFERENCES

[1] Mechtcherine, V., Schulze, J.: Testing the behaviour of strain hardening cementitious composites in tension. Int. RILEM Workshop on HPFRCC in Structural Applications, Honolulu, May 2005, G. Fischer & V. C. Li (eds.), RILEM Publications S.A.R.L., PRO 49, pp. 37-46.

[2] Kanakubo, T., Shimizu, K., Katagiri, M., Kanda, T., Fukuyama, H., Rokugo, K.: Tensile Characteristics Evaluation of DFRCC – Round Robin Test Results by JCI-TC – Testing Method and Modelling of HPFRCC. Int. RILEM Workshop on HPFRCC in Structural Applications, Honolulu, May 2005, G. Fischer & V. C. Li (eds.), RILEM Publications S.A.R.L., PRO 49, pp. 27-36.

[3] van Zijl, G.: Optimisation of the composition and fabrication methods; Applications for precast concrete members. In: Ultra-ductile concrete with short fibres – Development, Testing, Applications, V. Mechtcherine (ed.), ibidem Verlag, Stuttgart, 2005, 37-54.

[4] Li, V.C.: Engineered cementitious composites (ECC) – Tailored composites through micromechanical modelling. In: Fiber Reinforced Comcrete: Present and the Future, N. Banthia, A. Bentur, and A. Mufti, Canadian Society of Civil Engineers, 1997.

[5] Wang, S., Li, V.C.: Cementitious Composites: Material Design and Performances. Int. RILEM Workshop on HPFRCC in Structural Applications, Honolulu, May 2005, G. Fischer & V. C. Li (eds.), RILEM Publications S.A.R.L., PRO 49, pp. 65-74.

[6] Wittek, Th.: Ultra-ductile concretes – Material design, production and optimization of properties. Diploma thesis, TU Kaiserslautern, Institute for Building Materials, Germany, 2004 (in German).

[7] Douglas, K. S., Billington, S. L.: Rate dependence in high-performance fiber reinforced cement-based composites for seismic applications. Int. RILEM Workshop on HPFRCC in Structural Applications, Honolulu, May 2005, G. Fischer & V. C. Li (eds.), RILEM Publications S.A.R.L., PRO 49, pp. 17-26.

[8] Yang, J., Fischer, G.: Investigation of the Fiber Bridging Stress–Crack Opening Relationship of Fiber Reinforced Cementitious Composites. Int. RILEM Workshop on HPFRCC in Structural Applications, Honolulu, May 2005, G. Fischer & V. C. Li (eds.), RILEM Publications S.A.R.L., PRO 49, pp. 93-105.

[9] Mechtcherine, V., Schulze, J.: Ultra-ductile concrete – material design concept and testing. CPI Concrete Plant International, No. 5, pp. 88-98, 2005.

[10] Mihashi, H., Kikuchi, T., Akita, H., Fantilli, A.: Polyvinyl Alcohol Fiber Reinforced Engineered. Int. RILEM Workshop on HPFRCC in Structural Applications, Honolulu, May 2005, G. Fischer & V. C. Li (eds.), RILEM Publications S.A.R.L., PRO 49, pp. 7-16.

[11] Mechtcherine, V., Schulze, J.: Ultra-ductile concrete – Material Design and Testing. In: Ultra-ductile concrete with short fibres – Development, Testing, Applications, V. Mechtcherine (ed.), ibidem Verlag, Stuttgart, 2005.

[12] Yang, E., Li, V.C.: Rate dependence in Engineered Cementitious Composites. Int. RILEM Workshop on HPFRCC in Structural Applications, Honolulu, May 2005, G. Fischer & V. C. Li (eds.), RILEM Publications S.A.R.L., PRO 49, pp. 83-92.

[13] Maalej, M., Zhang, J., Quek, S.T., and Lee, S.C., "High-Velocity Impact Resistance of Hybrid-fiber Engineered Cementitious Composites," Proc. of the Fifth Int. Conf. on Fracture Mechanics of Concrete and Concrete Structures (FraMCoS-5), Vail, Colorado, USA, pp.1051-1058, 2004.

[14] Rokugo, K.: Applications of Strain Hardening Cementitious Composites with Multiple Cracks in Japan. In: Ultra-ductile concrete with short fibres – Development, Testing, Applications, V. Mechtcherine, V. (Ed.), ibidem Verlag, Stuttgart, 2005.

[15] Boshoff, W.P: Time-dependant behaviour of ECC. PhD thesis, University of Stellenbosch, 2007.

IMPROVING THE MECHANICAL PROPERTIES OF HFC BY ADJUSTING THE FILLING METHOD

Patrick Stähli, Martin Sutter and Jan G.M. van Mier

Institute of Building Materials, ETH Zurich, Switzerland

Abstract

In this paper we investigated the relation between rheological properties, casting procedure and tensile strength of HFC. Tensile properties were determined in a newly developed test set-up in which the specimen supports have no restrained freedom of movements. This goal has been achieved by means of an arrangement based on 'pendulum-bars'. Rheological tests were carried out on HFC using the same amount of super-plasticizer but cast by means of different mixing procedures. Four different casting methods and two different fibre mixtures have been investigated. It is shown that the performance of super-plasticizer can be improved, and with equal amounts of super-plasticizer but different mixing procedures the flow properties can be increased as well. The experiments showed that the casting method and the flow properties have a significant influence on the fibre alignment and the mechanical properties of HFC.

1 INTRODUCTION

In a material like hybrid fibre concrete (HFC) the important properties to be improved are tensile strength and ductility. These properties can be improved by adding different types of fibres [1-4] or by aligning the fibres in the stress direction. A uniaxial tension test is privileged and recommended to test such an improved material. A uniaxial tension test allows determining the "real" tensile strength and ductility because the stress state is well defined and rather uniformly distributed over the whole cross-section up till peak stress. To be able to test the ductility the supports of the test set-up should have no restrained freedom of movements during the whole test. This has been achieved by means of an arrangement based on 'pendulum-bars' [5] (see Fig. 1). The diameter of the smallest cross-section of the dog-bone shaped tensile test specimens should be at least three times the length of the largest fibre to reduce the influence of the wall effect.

Preliminary tests showed that the fibres can align in the direction of the flow of the material [6]. Therefore, each element/structure has its own characteristic and a standard test can not be performed for HFC or for (probably most) ordinary fibre reinforced concrete (FRC). That means that such materials should preferably be used in a prefabrication plant, where the material flow during the casting process can be well controlled, and with that the fibre alignment. Similar elements can be produced with one mould and the same material flow i.e. the same fibre alignment and therefore the same mechanical properties for all elements can be guaranteed.

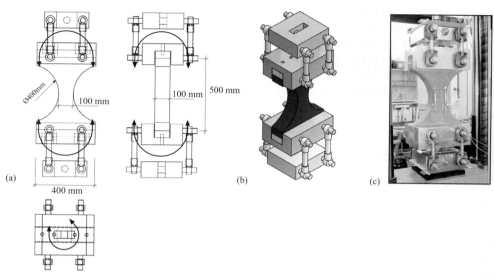

Figure 1: 2D (a), 3D (b) sketch and an image (c) of the 'pendulum-bar' tensile test set-up (see [5])

This paper presents the results of experiments of HFC and FRC cast with four different filling methods using the above mentioned tensile test set-up. The rheological properties were determined for each mixture using the SegBox (see [1]) and small and large slump flow tests (see [5]). These tests show that the influence of the mixing procedure, viz. how the super-plasticizer is added to the mix, has a significant influence.

2   MIXING PROCEDURE AND MATERIAL

In order to optimize the rheological properties and to minimize the amount of water and super-plasticizer a test series was carried out where the mixing sequence varied. For each mixture two mixing procedures were performed. In a first procedure the whole amount of super-plasticizer and water were added together and mixed for 5 minutes. Afterwards the fibres were added and the whole batch was mixed for another 5 minutes. Small slump flow tests were carried out and the diameter of the slump flow was measured. In a second procedure only a part of the super-plasticizer was added together with the water and mixed for 5 minutes. The remaining super-plasticizer was added together with the fibres and mixed for the remaining 5 minutes. Fig. 2 shows the mixing procedure for the second version. Table 1 gives an overview of the used fibre mixes and Fig. 3 shows images of the respective small slump flow results. This figure shows that in some cases the material mixed with the second procedure flew twice as far (the diameter of the small slump flow cone is 10 cm) as the one mixed with the first/common procedure. These results show that the performance of the super-plasticizer can be increased by adding it in two steps. The majority of the superplasticizer should be added with the water; the remainder with the fibres. This increase in the "flow-ability" can be caused by the fact that the aggregates and the cement were already saturated with the initial water and super-plasticizer mix, i.e. part of the firstly added super-plasticizer was absorbed by the aggregates and its performance could not develop. The remaining super-plasticizer was not absorbed anymore and therefore the performance is much enhanced. For the common mixing procedure part of the whole super-plasticizer can be absorbed by the aggregates and less 'free' super-plasticizer can have an effect of the flow ability.

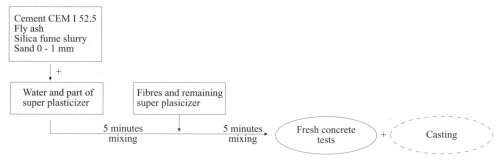

Figure 2: Alternative mixing procedure to increase the influence of super-plasticizer

2.1 Material

For all investigated mixtures the same matrix was used. The matrix was composed as follows: 1000 kg/m^3 CEM I 52.5R, 200 kg/m^3 fly-ash, 100 kg/m^3 Microsilica and 800 kg/m^3 sand with a maximum diameter of 1 mm. The water to binder ratio was kept constant at 0.18.

Table 1: Overview of the concrete mixtures used for the rheological tests

Mixture Code[1]	3 0 0	*3 0 0*	0 3 0	*0 3 0*	0 0 3	*0 0 3*	1 1 1	*1 1 1*	3 1 1	*3 1 1*
Small fibre Ø0.15/6 mm	3%	3%	-	-	-	-	1%	1%	3%	3%
Middle fibre Ø0.20/12 mm	-	-	3%	3%	-	-	1%	1%	1%	1%
Large fibre Ø0.6/30 mm	-	-	-	-	3%	3%	1%	1%	1%	1%
Super-plasticizer (BASF Glenium ACE 30)	2.3%	2.15%	2.6%	2.3%	2.5%	2.0%	2.45 %	2.3%	2.6%	2.3%
Remaining super-plasticizer	-	0.15%	-	0.3%	-	0.5%	-	0.15 %	-	0.3%

* The mixtures where the super-plasticizer was added in two parts (second version) are shown in *italics*
1) The mixture code shows the percentage of short, middle and large fibres respectively

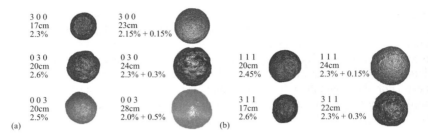

Figure 3: Images of the slump flows for (a) FRC mixtures and for (b) HFC mixtures, showing the mixture code the diameter of the slump flow test and the amount of super-plasticizer

Another test for describing the fresh concrete properties is the so-called SegBox experiment (see [1]). Such tests were performed on most of the preliminary tests (a total of 14 different mixtures with different amounts of super-plasticizer and fibres were carried out) which led to the mixtures in Table 1. The results of SegBox and the small slump flow tests are shown in the slump flow vs. self-levelling degree diagram in Fig. 4.

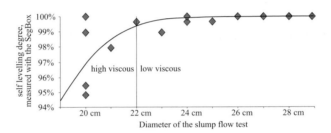

Figure 4: Diameter of the small slump flow vs. self levelling degree diagram

In Fig. 4 a line at a slump flow diameter of 22cm is draw. This line divides the diagram in a high- and a low-viscous part. This diagram shows that with an increasing slump flow the degree of self-levelling increases. At a diameter of 22 cm the material is self-levelling. Knowing this limit was very important for performing further experiments with low and high viscous materials that are presented on paragraph 4.

3 FILLING METHODS

Investigations on new filling methods are needed due to the fact that the fibres align with the flow of the fresh material [6]. Four different filling methods were investigated. First, the conventional method (Fig. 5, conventional method) where the concrete was filled from the top and the material could not flow in the mould itself. The second and third methods where the so called 'U-mould' (Fig. 5, fill and climb method) was used the material was filled in the first mould and then the concrete flew through a connection part and could finally climb into the second mould. The difference between the fill and climb method is the flowing distance of the material. The last method was the 90° filling method where the mould lied on the ground while filling the material (Fig. 5, 90° method). On both sides of the mould additional mould parts were attached so that the material could really flow through the whole mould. For each filling method two different mixtures were produced, a low and a high viscous mixture. 3% of the large Ø0.6 mm x 30 mm straight fibres were added to be able to look at the fibre alignment and distribution in the hardened state.

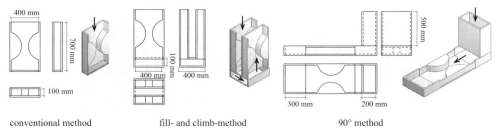

conventional method   fill- and climb-method   90° method

Figure 5: Sketches of the different considered filling methods

4   RESULTS

4.1   Fibre alignment and distribution

As mentioned, two different mixtures with different viscosities were produced for each filling method. One day after casting the specimens were demoulded and cut in such a way that the fibres in the middle of the specimen were visible. These sections were photographed, the individual images were stitched together and filtered. The final images are shown in Figs. 6 to 8. The pixel size is 0.1 mm for all the images. Fig. 6 clearly shows the different fibre distributions for the different viscous mixtures using the conventional filling method. It can be seen that the low viscous mix tended to segregate and that the distribution is not uniform over the whole cross section. Some aligned fibres can be seen in the upper left part of the detail image of the cross section of the low viscous specimen. These fibres probably aligned while sinking down. On the other hand, the highly viscous mixture shows uniformly distributed fibres and no visibly aligned fibres.

0°, conventional low-viscous   0°, conventional high-viscous

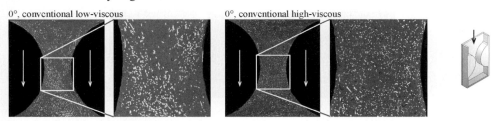

Figure 6: Cross-sections of two specimens filled with the conventional method

Fig. 7 shows images of the cross section four specimens filled using the 'U-mould'. For each 'U-mould' two filling method were investigated, the fill and the climb method. For both viscosities the filling specimens shows some fibre alignment in the centre part but the alignment in the climbing specimens is much stronger. The climbing specimen with the low viscous mixture shows the strongest fibre alignment but the total visible number of the fibres is not as large as the one from the mixture with the high viscosity. It seems that the material could not transport the fibres all the way up into the climb specimen. The reason why the fill specimens also show some fibre alignment is that even there the material flew during the casting process. When the material started to level out all the material flowed and the fibres could align in both specimens.

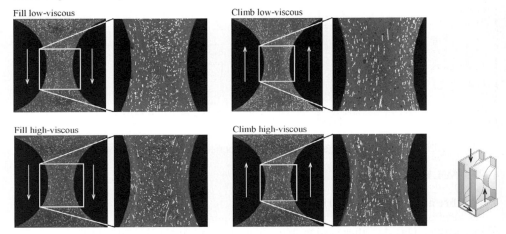

Figure 7: Cross-section of the specimens filled with the fill- and climb-method

The results from the 90° method are shown in Fig. 8. For both mixtures fibre alignment can be observed but the low viscous mixture shows some segregation, therefore less fibres than for the high viscous mixture are present. In summary it can be said that these methods are really different methods with different fibre distributions and alignments. Further more, it can be said that the filling method together with the viscosity has an additional influence on the aligning and distribution of the fibres. At present the results are quantified through fibre counting and orientation analysis.

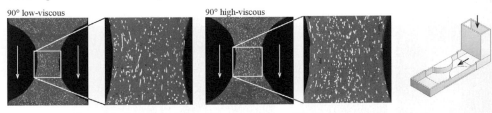

Figure 8: Cross sections of two specimens filled with the 90° method

4.2 Mechanical properties

To confirm the influence of the filling method on the mechanical properties uniaxial tensile tests using the 'pendulum-bar' test set-up (Fig. 1) were performed. Two different hybrid fibre concrete (HFC) mixtures with different amounts of fibres (see Table 2) were used. The first mixture contained 3% of the small Ø0.15 mm x 6 mm fibres and 1% for the middle Ø0.2 mm x 12 mm and the large Ø0.6 mm x 30 mm fibres. The second mixture only differed in the amount of the small fibre; only 2% were added to the mixture. The conventional method was performed for both mixtures. The 'U-mould' was only cast using the first, the

3 1 1 mixture, and the 90° was used for the second, the 2 1 1 mixture only. The mechanical and theological properties of both mixtures were more or less identical except of the bending strength: the elastic bending strength of the 2 1 1 was only 70% of the one from the 3 1 1 mixture. This is because the 3 1 1 mixture has 1% more of the small Ø0.15 mm x 6 mm fibres. The values of the uniaxial tensile strength results were adjusted according to their bending strength to allow for comparison of the results (Table 3). Because the fibre distribution and alignment in 'dog-bone' shaped specimens is dependent on the viscosity the bending strength derived from four-point bending test using 70 mm x 70 mm x 280 mm prisms was taken to adjust the results.

Table 2: Overview of the concrete mixtures used for the mechanical tests

	3 1 1	2 1 1
Fibre Ø0.15/6 mm	3%	3%
Fibre Ø0.20/12 mm	1%	1%
Fibre Ø0.6/30 mm	1%	1%
Super-plasticizer	2.3%	2.3%
Residual super-plasticizer	0.3%	0.3%
Slump small	27 cm	26 cm
Slump large	84 cm	-
Air content	2.8%	2.8%
Young's Modulus [GPa]	38.4	39.5
Compression Strength [MPa]	133.7	126.4
Elastic Bending Strength f_b [MPa]	31.0	21.1

Table 3: Overview of the mechanical properties of the two mixtures

	Tensile strength f_t [MPa]	$\eta = f_t/f_b$	$\kappa = \eta/\eta_{min}$ [%]
3 1 1 0°	9.31	0.3	130%
3 1 1 fill	12.61	0.41	178%
3 1 1 climb	13.67	0.44	191%
2 1 1 0°	4.74	0.23	100%
2 1 1 90°	11.49	0.54	235%

*the tensile strength was adjusted to the four point bending strength

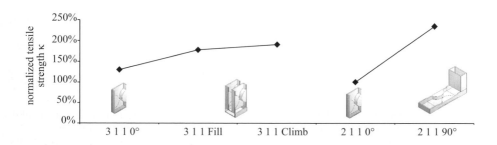

Figure 9: Normalized results derived from the 'pendulum-bar' tensile test

Fig. 9 shows that the influences of the filling methods are significant. It can be seen that the 90° method has the largest increase in tensile strength. In the authors opinion there is a reason why the increase of the tensile strength between the 2 1 1 0° and 2 1 1 90° was that much higher than for the 3 1 1 mixtures; the large fibres segregated and for the 90° specimens they lied at the bottom of the mould, but for the 0° and the climb specimens the fibres settled. Therefore the performance of the fibres in the 90° specimens was over-estimated and under-estimated for the 0° and climb specimens. Thus the increase of the normalized tensile strength between the 2 1 1 0° and the 2 1 1 90° specimens is over-estimated (see Fig. 9).

5   CONCLUSIONS

The performance of the super-plasticizer can be increased by adding it in two steps. The majority should be added with the water and the residual together with the fibres. (see paragraph 2). Using such a two-step procedure the performance of the super-plasticizer can increase the small slump flow of by more than 50%.

The fibre alignment is dependent on the flow behaviours of the fresh concrete, the filling method and the flow distance of the material. The longer and 'faster' the material can flow, the better the fibres are aligned. (see paragraph 4.1)

The tensile strength is also dependent on the filling method. There is a direct relation between filling method, fibre alignment and tensile strength. Using a suitable filling method, the fibres align and the tensile strength increases. This can be used to advance the pre-cast concrete industry.

ACKNOWLEDGEMENTS

The authors are indebted to the colleagues at the Institute of Building Materials, Messrs Claudio Derungs, Leonardo Bressan and Antoni Amerana. Support by Holcim, BASF and Walter Trindler from Empa for sieving the sand is gratefully acknowledged.

REFERENCES

[1] Stähli, P., Van Mier, J.G.M. (2007), Manufacturing, Fibre Anisotropy and Fracture of Hybrid Fibre Concrete, Eng.Frac.Mech. 74, 223-242.
[2] Rossi, P. and Renwez, S. High performance multi-modal fibre reinforced cement composites (HPMFRCC). In: Proceedings 4th International Symposium on High Strength/High Performance Concrete. Paris: RILEM Publications; 1996, p. 687-694.
[3] Markovic, I. (2006), High-Performance Hybrid-Fibre Concrete, PhD thesis, Delft University of Technology.
[4] Markovic, I., Walraven, J.C., Van Mier, J.G.M. (2003), Development of high performance hybrid fibre concrete, In Proceedings of the fourth international RILEM Workshop in High Performance Fibre Reinforced Composites, June 15-18, 2003, Ann Arbor, USA, ed. A.E. Naaman and H.W. Reinhardt
[5] Stähli, P., Van Mier, J.G.M. (2007), Effect of manufacturing methods on tensile properties of fibre concrete, In Proceedings 6th International Conference on 'Fracture Mechanics of Concrete and Concrete Structures' (FraMCoS-VI), June 18-22, 2007, Catania, Italy, ed. V. C. Li et al
[6] Stähli, P., Custer, R., Van Mier, J.G.M., (2007), On flow properties, fibre distribution, fibre orientation and flexural behaviour of FRC, Materials and Structures, RILEM, Online First article,
[7] Stähli, P., Van Mier, J.G.M. (2004), Three-Fibre-Type Hybrid Fibre Concrete, In Proceedings 5th International Conference on 'Fracture Mechanics of Concrete and Concrete Structures' (FraMCoS-V), April 12-16, 2004, Vail, Colorado, ed. V. C. Li et al, pp. 1105-1112.

CHALLENGES FOR STRAIN HARDENING CEMENTITIOUS COMPOSITES – DEFORMABILITY VERSUS MATRIX DENSITY

Minoru Kunieda [1], Emmanuel Denarié [2], Eugen Brühwiler [2] and Hikaru Nakamura [1]

(1) Dept. of Civil Engineering, Nagoya University, Japan

(2) MCS, Ecole Polytechnique Fédérale de Lausanne (EPFL), Switzerland

Abstract

Recently, fiber reinforced cementitious materials with novel properties have been developed. Here, novel properties mean "high tensile strain capacity with strain hardening and multiple fine cracks" and "high durability due to dense matrix with extremely low water to binder ratio". Although each property mentioned above is individually important, Ultra High Performance Strain Hardening Cementitious Composites (UHP-SHCC) with outstanding mechanical and protective performance are required for sustainable structures. This paper summarizes some issues on the recent fiber reinforced materials concerning each material design concept. This paper also presents the author's trials in order to develop UHP-SHCC by means of an optimization procedure based on uniaxial tensile, air permeability and capillary absorption tests.

1.   INTRODUCTION

In the last ten years, the material developments on fiber reinforced cementitious materials had two typical directions as follows (see Fig. 1):
- high tensile strain capacity with strain hardening and multiple fine cracks. Typical materials are Strain Hardening Cementitious Composites (SHCC) such as Engineered Cementitious Composites (ECC) [1], which exhibit tensile strain capacity more than 1 or 2%. In addition to these novel mechanical properties, the limited crack width gives the advantage of durability in cracked SHCC compared to ordinary concrete. However, the durability in terms of capillary absorption of the matrix itself is similar to an ordinary cement mortar, because higher water to binder ratio of the matrix has been adopted to obtain the ductility. There are existing applications on the surface repair of deteriorated concrete structures, the energy absorption damper for seismic loading and so forth [2].
- high durability (i.e. very low permeability) due to dense matrix with extremely low water to binder ratio. Typical material is Ultra High Performance Fiber Reinforced Concrete (UHPFRC) such as Reactive Powder Concrete (RPC) [3]. These materials exhibit a high tensile strength and a very high specific work of fracture. But most often their tensile strain hardening is limited. In addition, some of these materials require special curing techniques

to fully benefit from their excellent properties. The pre-cast members made of the UHPFRC have been applied to the new structures [4], and UHPFRC has been also cast at construction site for a rehabilitation application [5].

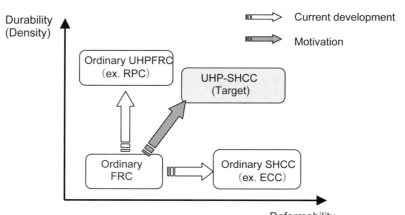

Figure 1: Material developments in FRC (schematic image)

This paper summarizes some issues on recent fiber reinforced materials such as SHCC and UHPFRC, from the viewpoint of their material design concepts. This paper also presents the results of material development focusing on uniaxial tensile tests and protective properties, comparing with ordinary fiber reinforced materials such as SHCC and existing UHPFRC

2.   MATERIAL DESIGN CONCEPTS

2.1   Ordinary SHCC

The material design concepts on ordinary SHCC are to optimize the properties of matrix, fiber and their interface, to achieve several percent strain hardening with multiple cracking under tension. Engineered Cementitious Composites (ECC), which are developed by Li [1], are one type of SHCC, and their novel mechanical properties can be designed by the micromechanics approach. This concept achieves the steady state cracking in composites with lower fiber content (i.e. less than about 2% in volume). The concept is based on energetic criteria using complementary energy and fiber bridging behaviour. In order to obtain the optimized volume fraction of fibers V_f, low matrix toughness J_{tip}, high interfacial bond strength τ and snubbing friction g, high aspect ratio L_f/d_f, in addition to wider crack opening δ_0 that is related to stiffness and shape of fibers are required.

Naaman [6] also proposed the material design concept for cement composites with strain hardening response, using average bond strength τ, tensile strength of matrix σ_{mu}, aspect ratio of fiber L_f/d_f and several factors on fiber distribution [6]. The proposed criterion is based on the verification in stress level (i.e. comparison between cracking stress and post-cracking one).

2.2   UHPFRC

There are some specific composites such as Densified Small Particle (DSP) Concrete [7], Reactive Powder Concrete (RPC) [3] and Multi-Scale Cement Composite (MSCC) [8, 9]. The material design concept is completely different from the previous SHCC. The matrix has ultra high strength (150-250MPa in compression and 45-65GPa in elastic modulus), and it involves the optimization of mixture by packing of fine particles [3, 10], extremely lower water to binder ratio and special heat curing in some cases. These materials also exhibit a very high specific work of fracture but most often their tensile strain hardening in tension is limited.

2.3   Further material developments (motivations)

Although each material property obtained from the above design concepts is individually important, Ultra High Performance-Strain Hardening Cementitious Composites (UHP-SHCC) with outstanding protective (extremely low permeability) and mechanical (high strength and significant tensile strain hardening) properties are required for sustainable structures. In addition, further material developments involve indices, test methods and procedures for the optimization. In this research, the following indices were proposed:
- Mechanical performance: uniaxial tensile test
- Protective performance: air permeability test and capillary absorption test

3.   PROTECTIVE PERFORMANCE RELATED TO MATRIX DENSITY

3.1   Air permeability test

The protective performance can be assessed through the tests that measure the penetration of substances. Here, gas and liquid transport are closely correlated as demonstrated by Bamforth [11] and Torrent et al. [12, 13]. Torrent et al. [12, 13] proposed the Torrent Permeability Tester. The main advantages are its fully non-destructive character and its ease of operation. The air permeability index kT is calculated according to the model from Torrent et al. [12], on the basis of the air flow measurement (pressure values) in the inner chamber.

3.2   Capillary absorption test

Transportation of substance is strongly affected by the pore structure within a cement based material. The capillary absorption is one of the effective indices to represent the protective performance related to the matrix density. The test method has been specified in DIN 52617. The capillary absorption was calculated by following equation:

$$m(t) = \alpha \cdot S \cdot \sqrt{t} \tag{1}$$

Here, m(t) is the amount of absorbed water (g/m^2). α is the coefficient of capillary absorption ($g/m^2\sqrt{h}$). S is the surface area contacted with water (m^2), and t is the duration (h).

4.   MATERIAL DEVELOPMENTS FOCUSING ON DEFORMABILITY AND MATRIX DENSITY

4.1   Developed UHP-SHCC

Mix proportions of developed UHP-SHCC are shown in Table 1. Water to binder ratio (W/B) was 0.22. Portland cement (CEM I 52.5) was used, and 20% of the cement was replaced by silica fume. The quartz sand (less than 0.5mm in diameter) was used as the fine aggregate. High strength PE fibers were chosen for this material. For the geometry of the fibers (diameter of the fiber was 0.012mm), two kinds of fiber lengths were adopted: one was 3mm, and the other was 6mm. Volume fractions of those fibers were 0.5% and 2.0%, respectively. The measured slump flow and air content were 40×35cm and 10.0%, respectively.

Table 1: Mix proportions of developed UHP-SHCC

	W/B	S/B[1]	Air (%)	Unit content (kg/m^3)					
				Water	Cement	Fine agg.	Silica fume	Superplasticizer	Fiber
UHP-SHCC	0.22	0.050	10.0	330	1198	75	300	44.9	24.3

[1] Sand to binder ratio

Table 2: Specimens

	Test type			
	Uniaxial tension	Compression	Air permeability	Capillary absorption
Size of specimens	Dumbbell shaped specimen 200 × 700 × 50mm	Cylindrical specimen Ø 110 × 220mm	Plate specimen 200 × 500 × 30mm (200×500×100mm[1])	Cylindrical specimen Ø 49 × 30mm[2]
Number of specimens	5	3	1	3

[1] UHP-SHCC:30mm, N-SHCC:100mm
[2] Cored from plate specimen after the air permeability test

Tensile and compressive strength tests were carried out at 26-28 days. The size and number of the specimens are tabulated in Table 2. For the tensile test, the dumb-bell shaped specimens having tested length of 300mm were used as shown in Fig. 2 [14, 15]. The displacement with measurement length of 350mm was measured by LVDTs, as shown in Fig. 2. For the compressive test, the cylindrical specimens with 110mm in diameter and 220mm in length were fabricated.

A plate specimen with the size of 30×200×500mm for both air permeability and capillary absorption tests was cured, and kept in wet condition up to the day before the test. And then, the specimen was exposed to dry condition for 1day. At the age of 28 days, the air permeability coefficient was measured three times at different place within the plate specimen. After the air permeability measurements, the three cylindrical specimens with the diameter and height of 49mm and 30mm respectively were cored from the plate specimen to conduct the capillary absorption tests.

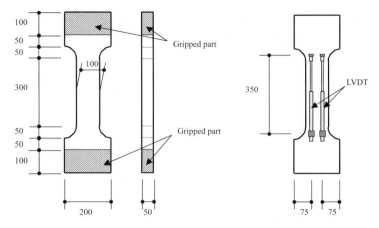

Figure 2: Geometry of dumb-bell shaped specimens for tensile test

4.2   Comparative materials

Two kinds of materials were used for a comparison.

N-SHCC: Water to binder ratio (W/B) was 0.45 with fly ash. PVA fibers having length of 12mm and diameter of 0.036mm were used. Volume fraction of the fiber was 2.0%.

UHPFRC: UHPFRC of Recipe CM23 [5] developed at EPFL was chosen. This material was a type of CEMTEC$_{multiscale}$® [16]. Water to binder ratio (W/B) was 0.125. Both longer steel fiber (10mm in length and 0.2mm in diameter) and steel wool were used to be 705kg in the total dosage.

4.3   Mechanical performance (deformability)

Compressive and tensile strengths obtained from each test are tabulated in Table 3, with the elastic modulus of UHP-SHCC and UHPFRC. The compressive and tensile strengths of UHP-SHCC were more than two times higher than those of N-SHCC. UHPFRC had quite higher compressive and tensile strengths because of extremely low water to binder ratio.

Table 3: Strengths of each material

Series	Compressive (MPa)	Elastic modulus (GPa)	Tensile (MPa)
UHP-SHCC	83	25.3	4.35
N-SHCC	20.2	-	1.91
UHPFRC [5]	182	46.8	13.5

Fig. 3 shows the relationship between tensile stress and strain of UHP-SHCC, N-SHCC and UHPFRC. The stress of plateau (strain hardening) in the curve of UHP-SHCC (4-5MPa) was about two times higher than that of N-SHCC (about 2 MPa). The ultimate strain, which is the strain just before the onset of the descending branch, was more than about 1.0% for UHP-SHCC and N-SHCC (Fig. 3). Note that the strength and strain obtained from this test for UHP-SHCC were similar to the ordinary test results with higher water to binder ratio and PVA fiber. Kanakubo [17] revealed that the test results in tensile tests were strongly affected by the specimen size and boundary conditions, and the large test specimens with fixed ends showed lower strength and strain. It seems that the test setup conducted in this research gives a lower boundary of the material response close to a pure uniaxial tensile stress state. UHPFRC had tensile strength higher than 12MPa with strain hardening of 0.15% (Fig.3).

Obtained crack patterns in UHP-SHCC are shown in Fig. 4. The well-distributed fine cracks can be observed in UHP-SHCC specimen. The averaged crack spacing was less than 5mm through the visual observation. The crack width of each crack in UHP-SHCC was smaller than that in N-SHCC. The reasons are: (1) the stiffness of PE fiber (about 88GPa) was higher than that of PVA fiber (about 40GPa), (2) the low water to binder ratio and silica fume improved the bond property, and (3) the volume fraction in UHP-SHCC (2.5%) was slightly higher than that of N-SHCC (2.0%).

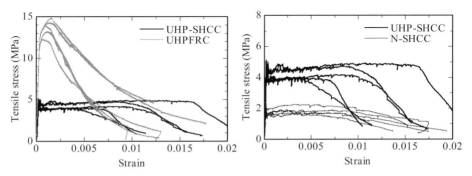

Figure 3: Stress strain relations in uniaxial tensile tests (left: UHP-SHCC and N-SHCC), right: UHP-SHCC and UHPFRC)

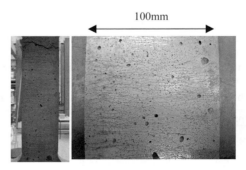

Figure 4: Crack patterns of UHP-SHCC

4.4 Protective performance (matrix density)

Fig. 5 shows the results on the air permeability and capillary absorption tests for UHP-SHCC (28 days), N-SHCC and UHPFRC (58 days). For the capillary absorption, the amount of absorbed water during 24hours was used for the calculation.

Regarding N-SHCC, the tests were carried out at 28 days and 91 days, to consider the hydration with fly ash. The permeability coefficient of the developed UHP-SHCC was 0.007×10^{-16} m^2, and that of N-SHCC at 28 days was 1.210×10^{-16} m^2. In addition, the permeability coefficient of N-SHCC at 91 days was 0.452×10^{-16} m^2, and was improved by long term hydration process. However, the resistance against air permeability of UHP-SHCC was about 60 times lower than that of N-SHCC. The permeability coefficient of UHPFRC was 0.004×10^{-16} m^2 indicating excellent protective performance.

The coefficient of capillary absorption in N-SHCC at 91 days was 449 ($g/m^2\sqrt{h}$). Hence, the coefficients of capillary absorption in UHP-SHCC and UHPFRC were 104 ($g/m^2\sqrt{h}$) and 45 ($g/m^2\sqrt{h}$), respectively. Martinola et al. [18] also carried out the similar capillary absorption tests for ordinary SHCC with water to cement ratio measuring 0.21-0.63, and they revealed that capillary absorption was significantly affected by water to cement ratio of composites (SHCC).

As shown in Fig. 5, significant correlation between capillary absorption and air permeability was observed in this test. It was confirmed that the permeability coefficient kT was one of the effective indices for the material design focusing on the durability of SHCC.

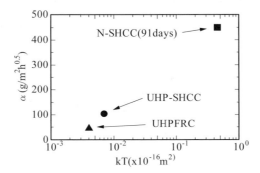

Figure 5: Results of capillary absorption and air permeability tests

5.   CONCLUDING REMARKS

In this paper, the material development focusing on both mechanical and protective performances was carried out, and following conclusions were obtained.
(1) New strain hardening composite (UHP-SHCC) with a dense matrix was developed and tested.
(2) This material combines an excellent protective performance comparable to UHPFRC with a significantly higher tensile strain hardening (up to 2 %).
(3) Air permeability and capillary absorption tests are complementary methods useful for the validation of the protective properties of SHCC / UHPFRC / UHP-SHCC.
(4) Uniaxial tensile tests with a fixed boundary set-up are a prerequisite to determine in a reliable way the tensile response of strain hardening materials.

ACKNOWLEDGEMENTS

The first author visited EPFL as visiting scholar of the exchange program between the Japan Society for the Promotion of Science (JSPS) and the Swiss National Science Foundation (SNSF). This research was one of the activities during the stay. PE and PVA fibers were provided by Toyobo Co., Ltd and Kuraray Co., Ltd, respectively. Chemical admixture was provided by NMB. The authors would like to acknowledge those supports.

REFERENCES

[1]   Li, V.C. 'From Micromechanics to Structural Engineering –The Design of Cementitious Composites for Civil Engineering Applications', *Structural Engineering/ Earthquake Engineering*, JSCE, 10(2) (1993) 37s-48s.
[2]   Kunieda, M. and Rokugo, K. 'Recent Progress of HPFRCC in Japan - Required Performance and Applications -', *Journal of Advanced Concrete Technology*, 4(1) (2006) 19-33.
[3]   Richard, P. and Cheyrezy, M. 'Composition of reactive powder concretes', *Cement and Concrete Research*, 25(7) (1995) 1501-1511.
[4]   Tanaka, Y., Ootake, A., Uzawa, T., Tsuka, T., Kano, K. and Shimoyama, Y. 'Structural Performance of a 50m Span Footbridge Applying Fiber Reinforced Reactive Powder Concrete', Proc. of the JCI International Workshop on Ductile Fiber Reinforced Cementitious Composites (DFRCC 2002), Takayama, 2002, 209-218.
[5]   Denarié, E. and Brühwiler, E. 'Structural Rehabilitations with Ultra-High Performance Fibre Reinforced Concrete (UHPFRC) ', *Restoration of Buildings and Monuments*, 12(5/6) (2006) 453-468.
[6]   Naaman, A.E. 'Strain Hardening and Deflection Hardening Fiber Reinforced Cement Composites', High Performance Fiber Reinforced Cement Composites (HPFRCC4), Proceedings of the fourth international RILEM workshop, Ann Arbor, 2003, 95-113.
[7]   Bache, H.H. 'Introduction to compact reinforced composite', Nord. Concr. Res., 6 (1987) 19-33.
[8]   Rossi, P., Acker, P. and Malier, Y. 'Effect of Steel Fibers at Two Different Stages: the material and Structures', *Material and Structures*, 20(120) (1987) 436-439.
[9]   Rossi, P. 'Ultra-high Performance Fiber Reinforced Concrete (UHPFRC): an Overview', Proc. of the Fifth International RILEM Symposium on Fiber-Reinforced Concrete (BEFIB'2000), 2000, 87-100.
[10] Larrard, F. and Sedran, T. 'Optimization of Ultra-High-Performance Concrete by the Use of a Packing Model', *Cement and Concrete Research*, 24(6) (1994) 997-1009.
[11] Bamforth, P.B. 'The Relationship between Permeability Coefficients for Concrete Obtained using Liquid and Gas', *Magazine of Concrete Research*, 39(138) (1987) 3-11.
[12] Torrent, R.: 'A Two-chamber Vacuum Cell for Measuring the Coefficient of Permeability to Air of the Concrete Cover on Site', *Materials and Structures*, 25 (1992) 358-365.
[13] Torrent, R. 'The Gas-permeability of High-Performance Concretes: Site and Laboratory Tests', High Performance Concrete, Performance and Quality of Concrete Structures, ACI Special Publication 186, (1999) 291-308.
[14] Denarié, E., Rossi, P., Woodward, R. and Brühwiler, E. 'Guidelines for the Use of UHPFRC for Rehabilitation of Concrete Highway Structures', deliverable SAMARIS D25b, European project 5th FWP / SAMARIS Sustainable and Advanced MAterials for Road Infrastructures, http://samaris.zag.si/, 2006.
[15] Denarié, E. and Brühwiler, E. 'Tailored Composite UHPFRC-concrete Structures', MMMCP Symposium, 16th European Conference of Fracture, ECF 16, Greece, 2006.
[16] Rossi, P. 'Development of New Cement Composite Material for Construction', Proc. of the International Conference on Innovations and Developments, 2002, 17-29.
[17] Kanakubo, T. 'Tensile Characteristics Evaluation Method for Ductile Fiber-Reinforced Cementitious Composite', *Journal of Advanced Concrete Technology*, 4(1) (2006) 3-17.
[18] Martinola, G., Bäuml, M.F. and Wittmann, F.H. 'Modified ECC Applied as an Effective Chloride Barrier', Proc. of the JCI International Workshop on Ductile Fiber Reinforced Cementitious Composites (DFRCC 2002), Takayama, 2002, 171-180.

EXPERIMENTAL OBSERVATIONS ON THE TENSILE RESPONSE OF FIBER REINFORCED CEMENT COMPOSITES WITH DIFFERENT FIBERS

Supat Suwannakarn, Sherif El-Tawil and Antoine E Naaman

Dept. of Civil and Environmental Engineering, University of Michigan, USA

Abstract

The application of high performance fiber reinforced cement composites (HPFRCC) in structural systems depends primarily on the material's tensile response, which is a direct function of fiber and matrix characteristics, the bond between them, and the fiber content or volume fraction. In general, improved material response is observed with an increase in the fiber volume fraction, as long as the fiber content does not impede mixing.

This paper discusses the results of an extensive experimental program that was undertaken to investigate the direct tensile response of HPFRCC. Care is taken to ensure that strains are accurately measured and that reasonably-sized specimens are uniformly used throughout the testing program. The main variables considered include the type (Torex, High strength Hooked, PVA, and Spectra) and volume ratio (ranging from 0.75% to 2.0%) of the fibers. Experimental observations pertaining to the initial linear-elastic response, multiple cracking, localization behavior, and statistical variability in the results are presented.

1.   INTRODUCTION

Fiber reinforced cement composites (FRCC) are comprised of a cementitious matrix in which short discontinuous fibers are embedded. The material response of a FRCC depends on many factors, such as fiber properties (geometry, length, strength, and elastic modulus), fiber orientation, volume fraction of the fibers, matrix properties (strength, composition), and the characteristics of the bond between fibers and matrix [1, 2]. The main function of the discontinuous fibers within the brittle cementitious matrix is realized only after the matrix cracks. The fibers prevent a sudden loss in load-carrying capacity of the cracked composite by providing a load transfer mechanism across the crack.

According to Naaman and Reinhardt [1, 3, 4, 5], high performance fiber reinforced cementitious composites (HPFRCC) are defined as FRCC that exhibit post-cracking strain hardening response accompanied by multiple cracking. In contrast, ordinary FRCC soften once the matrix cracks. In general, the tensile stress-elongation response of HPFRCC is comprised of three parts; the elastic stage, wherein the matrix is not cracked, the strain-hardening and multiple cracking stage, and the damage localization or crack opening stage.

The composite exhibits linear behavior up to first cracking in the elastic stage. Strain hardening dominates the multiple cracking stage, at the end of which the stress increases to a maximum. In the third stage, which is characterized by softening behavior, damage localization occurs via crack width growth in the most critical crack.

2.   OBJECTIVE

The objective of this study is to investigate the tensile response of selected HPFRCC as a function of two variables, namely type and quantity of fibers. The test parameters for the direct tensile test include four types of fibers, two of which are polymeric (i.e., Spectra and PVA) and two of which are steel fibers (i.e., Torex and High strength Hooked fiber). Four volume fractions of fibers are considered (i.e., 0.75%, 1.0%, 1.5%, and 2.0%). The paper discusses and compares the observed experimental responses including initial linear-elastic behavior, multiple cracking, localization behavior, and the statistical variability in the results.

3.   EXPERIMENTAL PROGRAM

The experimental program consisted of about 200 direct tensile tests of dogbone- shaped HPFRCC specimens. The cross-sectional area of a typical specimen is 2 square inches and the geometric details are shown in Fig. 1. Fig. 2 shows the test setup. The mix used in this study is regular mortar with an unconfined compressive strength of 55.16 MPa (8 ksi). The mixture ratios, based on weight of cement, sand, fly ash, and water, are 1, 1, 0.15, and 0.35, respectively. Fiber properties are summarized in Table 1. All four fibers used in this study are shown in Fig. 3.

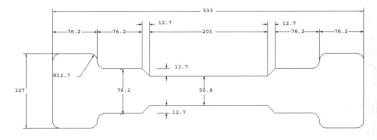
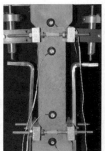

Figure 1: Dimensions of dogbone shaped specimen (mm)   Figure 2: Test setup

Table 1: Fiber properties

Fiber type	Diameter (mm)	Length (mm)	Density (g/cc)	Tensile Strength (MPa)	Elastic modulus (MPa)
PVA	0.19	12	1.31	900	29000
Spectra	0.038	38	0.97	2585	117000
Torex	0.3	30	7.9	2760	200000
High strength Hooked	0.4	30	7.9	2100	200000

(a) PVA

(b) Spectra

(c) High strength Hooked

(d) Torex

Figure 3: Fibers types

Specimen Preparation

Care was taken during the mixing process to prevent clumping of the fibers. The dry components of the mortar mix were first combined with approximately 25% of the total water required. The fibers along with the remaining 75% of the water were intermittently added as the mixing process progressed. Particular care was paid while casting the Spectra specimens because it was observed that Spectra fibers could potentially trap large amounts of air in comparison with the other fibers used in this study. After mixing, the specimens were kept under preventive cover while still in the molds for 24 hours. After that, the specimens were removed from the molds and placed to cure in a water tank for at least 14 days. Next, they were left to air dry for a period of at least 48 hours prior to testing. After drying, thin poly-urethane spray was applied to the surface of the specimens to aid in crack detection during and after testing. It should be noted that HPFRCC reinforced PVA specimens are not equivalent to ECC specification [6].

4.   MEASUREMENTS

As each specimen was being tested, its elongation was obtained from a high-accuracy optical measurement system (Optotrak) as well as from two LVDTs, which were placed on the two opposite sides of the specimen. Four Optotrak markers were placed on the specimens' surface as shown in Fig. 2. The gauge length for both types of measurement system was 177.8 mm (7 inches). All tests were carried out using an MTS hydraulic testing machine, which strained the specimen in displacement control at a rate of 0.762 mm per minute (0.03 inch per minute). A data acquisition system was used to record the force readings from the load cell of the testing machine as well as displacement information from the LVDTs and the optical system. An image-processing unit comprised of a camera equipped with a special high-magnification lens was used for crack detection and observation of crack propagation behavior during the test. Pictures were taken at regular time increments.

5.   ANALYSIS OF RESULTS

5.1   Direct Tensile Response

As previously discussed and as shown in Fig. 4, the tensile behavior of a typical HPFRCC specimen is comprised of three phases: elastic phase, multiple cracking phase, and localization phase. While no cracks occur in the first phase, the second phase is characterized by the creation of many cracks primarily oriented perpendicular to the axis of the specimen. Virtually no matrix spalling occurs at the surface of the specimen in this stage. Better fiber quality and an increase in fiber content both lead to a denser crack pattern, high peak stress, and greater energy absorption.

Pictures taken during the tests revealed that cracks typically commence from either side of a specimen and propagate towards the other side. It could sometimes be observed that some cracks stopped growing and that the largest or widest crack observed at the multiple cracking stage was not necessarily the crack that eventually localized. As shown in Fig. 5, the stress drops wherever a crack grows significantly, then picks up again as the composite system redistributes the unbalanced loads released as a result of the cracking process. Localization failure eventually takes place as a result of the opening of the dominant crack leading to softening response (Fig. 6). When this happens, no new cracks initiate in the specimen and existing cracks gradually close as the applied load reduces due to softening. At this stage, loading eccentricities created by an uneven distribution of fibers at the cross-section of the localizing crack force the specimen to no longer remain straight.

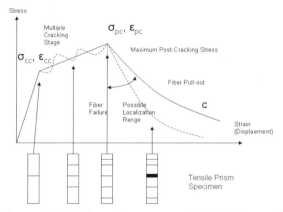

Figure 4: Typical tensile response of HPFRCC in tension

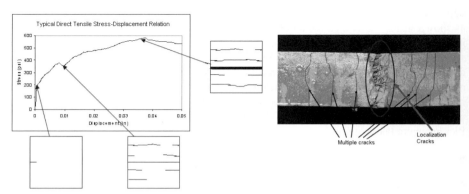

Figure 5: Typical direct tensile stress-displacement

Figure 6: Illustration of multiple cracks and localization crack

5.2 Comparison of direct tensile response of HPFRCC with different types and volume fractions of fibers

Fig. 7 shows the effect of fiber content on the response of PVA specimens. Each curve in the figure is an average of at least 3 test results. It is clear from Fig. 7 that the highest fiber content (V_f = 2.0%) leads to the highest tensile strength and that the strength drops as the fiber content drops. The average maximum stresses for PVA specimens with volume fractions of 2.0%, 1.5%, and 1.0% are 1.447, 1.296, 1.013 MPa (210, 188, and 147 psi), respectively. The trend is more subdued in Spectra specimens, where, as shown in Fig.. 8, average maximum stresses for specimens with volume fractions of 2.0%, 1.5%, and 1.0% are respectively 2.71, 2.70 and 2.54 MPa (394, 393, and 369 psi). Although the volume fraction does not appear to influence the strength greatly, it does affect the post-cracking ductility and energy absorption capacity. For example, as shown in Fig. 8, Spectra specimens with V_f = 2.0% show substantially higher ductility and energy absorption capacity after cracking compared to specimens with a lower V_f.

The results of specimens reinforced with High strength Hooked steel fibers at different volume fractions are shown in Fig. 9. As with the polymeric fibers, Fig. 9 shows that the strength and energy absorption capacity are directly influenced by V_f. However, the effectiveness of V_f appears to diminish as V_f increases. For example, increasing V_f from 0.75% to 1% caused a 63% increase in peak stress, whereas increasing V_f from 1% to 1.5% caused only a 6% increase in peak strength. This can be attributed in part to statistical variability and group effect, which appears to be more pronounced in High strength Hooked fibers than in the polymeric fibers. The group effect is the phenomenon whereby the behavior of a single fiber is adversely affected by its proximity to other fibers, i.e. the fiber's efficiency drops when it is in group compared to when it is acting alone.

The results of specimens reinforced with Torex steel fibers at different volume fractions are shown in Fig. 10. The same trends seen for specimens with High strength Hooked fibers are evident in Torex specimens, including sensitivity to the group effect.

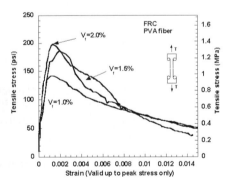

Figure 7: Tensile response of HPFRCCs - PVA

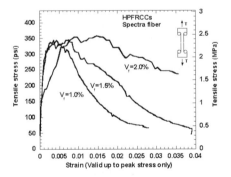

Figure 8: Tensile response of HPFRCCs - Spectra

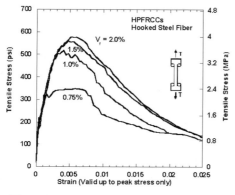

Figure 9: Tensile response of HPFRCCs - High strength Hooked

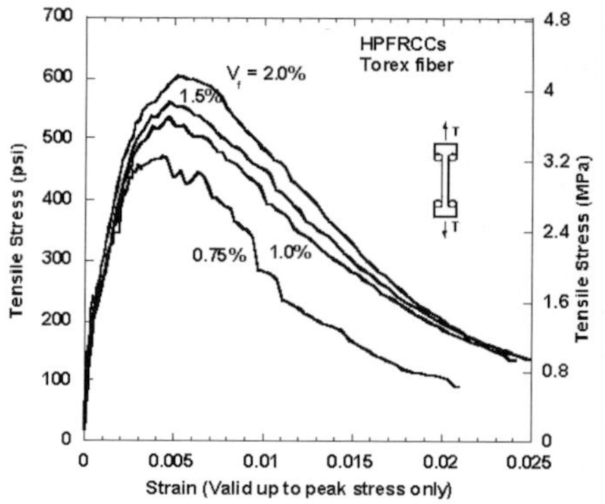

Figure 10: Tensile response of HPFRCCs - Torex

Figs. 11, 12, and 13 compare the response of specimens with different types of fibers for the same V_f. It is evident from the figures that specimens reinforced with PVA have the lowest strength. High strength Hooked and Torex specimens have approximately the same ultimate strength, whereas Spectra specimens are in between the PVA and steel reinforced specimens.

At the highest V_f (2%), Spectra specimens exhibit the highest ductility amongst the 4 types of fibers. These specimens are able to maintain hardening response up to about 2% strain. In contrast, High strength Hooked and Torex fibers start to soften at about 0.5 - 0.6% strain Fig. 13.

The coefficient of variation of strength for different V_f is plotted in Fig. 14. Each point in the figure represents results from at least 6 specimens, i.e. series with less than 6 specimens are excluded from the plot. It is clear from the figure that there does not appear to be a well-defined relationship between V_f and the coefficient of variation that holds for all fiber types. For example, the coefficient of variation drops rapidly as V_f increases for the PVA fibers, but an opposite trend occurs for Spectra fibers. The coefficient of variation appears to be almost constant for Torex fibers (about 0.2) while no conclusions can be drawn regarding High strength Hooked fibers because an insufficient number of points were available.

Another important conclusion from Fig. 14 is that the coefficient of variation is relatively high for all series, with the highest value (0.36) occurring for 1% PVA specimens. The high variability in strength is also evident in Fig. 15 and Fig. 16, both of which show the ranges and averages of the collected data. The upper boundary of each shaded part represents the maximum recorded strengths, while the lower boundary represents the lowest recorded strengths. The solid line running through the middle of each shaded region is the average line. The circles at each V_f represent individual test results at that V_f and the distribution of points again gives an idea of the large statistical spread in the data.

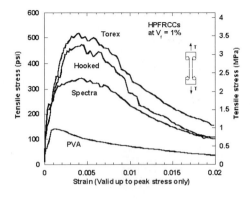

Figure 11: Tensile response of HPFRCCs at
$V_f = 1.0\%$

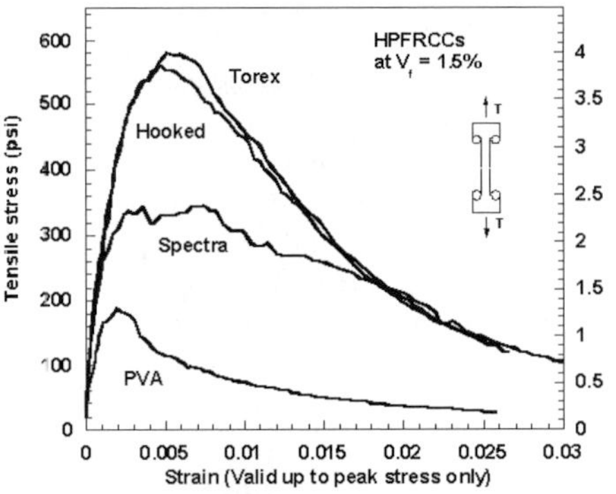

Figure 12: Tensile response of HPFRCCs
at $V_f = 1.5\%$

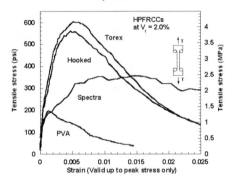

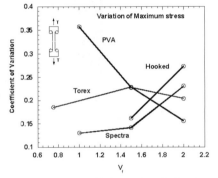

Figure 13: Tensile response of HPFRCCs at
$V_f = 2.0\%$

Figure 14: Coefficient of variation in
maximum tensile stress

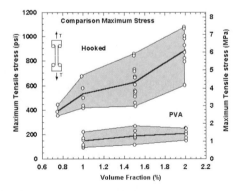

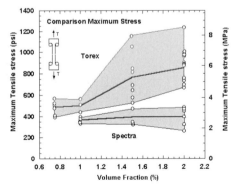

Figure 15: Strength range and average
(High strength Hooked and PVA)

Figure 16: Strength range and average
(Torex and Spectra)

6.   ONGOING RESEARCH

The direct tensile test measures the aggregate displacement contributions of all the cracks in the dogbone specimen in addition to the fiber and matrix contributions in between the cracks. In order to better understand the cracking behavior of HPFRCC, an ongoing effort is being undertaken to study the response of notched specimens whose response is dominated by a single crack (as shown in Fig. 17). Fig. 18 shows some preliminary data, which will eventually be correlated to the direct tension test data with the objective of developing both deterministic and stochastic tensile models for HPFRCC.

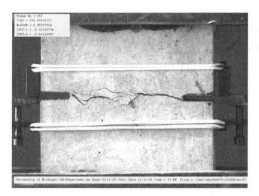

Figure 17: Crack in a notched specimen

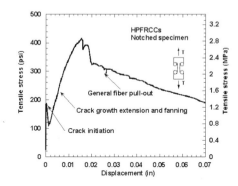

Figure 18: Tensile response of notched specimen

7.   SUMMARY AND CONCLUSIONS

The results of an extensive experimental program that was undertaken to investigate the direct tensile response of HPFRCC were presented and discussed. The main variables considered include the type (Torex, High strength Hooked, PVA, and Spectra) and volume ratio (ranging from 0.75% to 2.0%) of the fibers. The following conclusions can be drawn from the data presented:

1. The specimens tested were able to achieve 'high performance' behavior, i.e their tensile response exhibited strain-hardening and multiple cracking behavior after first cracking. This was true for all types of fibers and fiber contents studied.
2. For the same volume fraction of fibers, specimens with Torex, High strength Hooked, and Spectra fibers showed better overall behavior than specimens with PVA fibers. Moreover, their post-cracking strength was 1.5 to 3 times their strength at first cracking, while for specimens with PVA fibers, the post-cracking strength was only 10% to 50% higher than the cracking strength.
3. For the same type of fiber, increasing the volume fraction leads to a marked improvement in the post-cracking strength, ductility, and energy absorption capacity of the composites.
4. Torex reinforced specimens provided the best tensile strength (4.2 MPa (610 psi) for V_f=2.0%), while Spectra reinforced specimens provided the best ductility, e.g. they were able to maintain hardening response up to about 2% strain.
5. High strength Hooked and Torex fibers provide comparable responses for the range of V_f studied.
6. There is a large statistical spread in the data.

REFERENCES

[1] Naaman, A.E, "Ferrocement & Laminated Cementitious Composites," Techno Press 3000, Ann Arbor, 2000, 372 Pages.
[2] Visalvanich, K and A.E. Naaman, "Fracture Model for Fiber Reinforced Concrete", ACI Journal, March-April 1983
[3] Chandrangsu, K and A.E. Naaman, Comparison of Tensile and Bending response of three high performance fiber reinforced cement composites, HPFRCC4 Workshop, Ann Arbor, USA, 2003
[4] Naaman, A.E.; Moavenzadeh, F and McGarry, F., "Probabilistic Analysis of Fiber Reinforced Concrete, "Journal of Engineering Mechanics Division, ASCE, V. 100, No. EM2, Apr. 1974, pp.397-413
[5] Naaman, A.E. and Reinhardt, H.W., "Characterization of High Performance Fiber Reinforced Cement Composites," Proceedings of 2nd International Workshop on HPFRCC, Chapter 41, in High Performance Fiber Reinforced Cement Composites: HPFRCC 2, RILEM, No 31, 1996, pp. 1-24.
[6] Li, V.C.; Wang, S and Wu, C, "Tensile Strain-Hardening Behavior of Polyvinyl Alcohol Engineered Cementitious Composite (PVA-ECC), ACI Material Journal, November-December 2001, pp 483-492

BACK ANALYSIS OF TENSILE STRESS-STRAIN RELATIONSHIP OF HPFRCC

Yuichi Uchida, Masanori Kawai and Keitetsu Rokugo

Gifu University, Japan

Abstract

A method of inversely estimating the tensile stress-strain relationship of a HPFRCC from its moment-curvature relationship obtained from bending tests was investigated. It was confirmed that the tensile stress-strain relationship can be determined by carrying out sequential analysis from the starting point of a moment-curvature relationship. The results of such back analysis of bending test data nearly agreed with the results of uniaxial tension test, but the ultimate strain widely varied in both test and analysis.

1.   INTRODUCTION

"High performance fiber reinforced cement composite (HPFRCC)" is a material in which fine cracks occur one after another as the tensile stress increases, macroscopically showing perfect plasticity or strain hardening [1]. Though uniaxial tension testing is desirable for evaluating its performance in tension, it is not necessarily easy on a practical level. For this reason, the authors investigated a method of inversely estimating its tensile stress-strain relationship by back analysis from the results of bending testing, which is easier to carry out.

2.   OUTLINE OF BACK ANALYSIS

This analysis method is based on fiber analysis. In contrast to normal analysis to determine the moment-curvature (M-ϕ) relationship of a material by giving its stress-strain curve, back analysis inversely estimates the stress-strain relationship from the M-ϕ relationship.

Fig. 1 shows the analysis flow. Using the strain on the tension edge as the increment parameter, tensile stresses are assumed for the strain on the tension edge at each step, and the one with which the calculated M-ϕ comes in line with the experimental M-ϕ curve is determined as the tensile stress. In the following step, the stress for only the increment of the tensile strain is identified without changing the tensile stress-strain curve determined up to the previous step.

3.   CHECKING THE ACCURACY OF BACK ANALYSIS

3.1   Basic accuracy of analysis

In order to check the accuracy of this analysis method, a tensile stress-strain relationship as shown in Fig. 2 and compressive stress-strain relationship as shown in Fig. 3 were assumed as the input values for a cross-sectional size of 100 by 100 mm. Normal analysis was conducted to obtain the M-ϕ curve shown in Fig. 4. This was then back-analyzed to inversely estimate the tensile stress-strain relationship. As a result, the analyzed values were found to nearly agree with the input values as shown in Fig. 2.

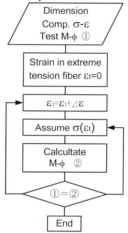

Figure 1: Analysis flow

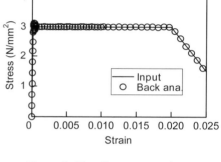

Figure 2: Tensile stress-strain curve

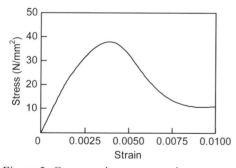

Figure 3: Compressive stress-strain curve

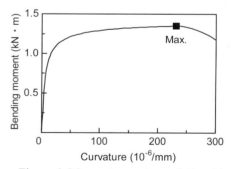

Figure 4: Moment-curvature relationship

3.2   Comparison with JCI's evaluation method

The Japan Concrete Institute (JCI) has proposed a method of calculating the tensile strength and ultimate tensile strain from the results of bending testing [2] (hereafter referred to as the JCI method). This is a method whereby a perfect plasticity-type stress-strain relationship is assumed using the bending moment and curvature at the peak load in bending testing to evaluate the tensile strength and ultimate tensile strain. In this study, the results obtained from the JCI method and the present analysis method were compared.

The analysis results of the JCI method and the present back analysis method were compared by assuming that a bending moment-curvature relationship shown in Fig. 5 was obtained from bending tests. Note that the three curves in Fig. 5 were calculated by assuming typical tensile stress-strain curves for three possible post-cracking patterns of HPFRCC: (A) softening, (B) perfect plasticity, and (C) hardening. Strictly speaking, fiber analysis should not be applied to softening, because it is associated with localization of failure. In this case, however, back analysis was carried out by assuming that failure was uniformly distributed.

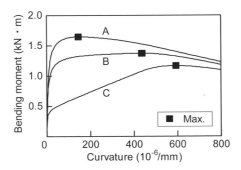

Figure 5: Assumed moment-curvature relationship

The results of estimation by back analysis and the JCI method are shown in Fig. 6. Whereas the results by both methods completely agreed in the case of perfect plasticity (B), they widely differed in the cases of softening and hardening, particularly in regard to the ultimate strain. This is because the JCI method only uses the bending moment and curvature at the peak load for its calculation, without evaluating the behavior before the peak.

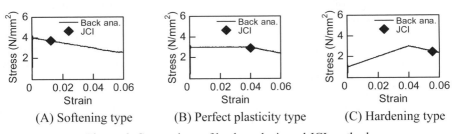

Figure 6: Comparison of back analysis and JCI method

4. EFFECT OF COMPRESSIVE STRESS-STRAIN RELATIONSHIP ON THE ANALYSIS RESULTS

4.1 Overview
In this analysis, the compressive stress-strain relationship of the subject material should be established beforehand. Though the compressive stress-strain relationship can be readily

obtained by conducting compression testing, it is also necessary to investigate its effect on the analysis results.

A back analysis simulation was therefore carried out using a compressive stress-strain relationship as a parameter. Fig. 7 shows the relationship used for the analysis. A model consisting of a quadratic parabola up to the compressive strength point, a plastic zone, and a linear softening zone was assumed here, in which three strains were selected as the turning points toward softening (E, F, and G). A model shown in Fig. 8 was used for the tensile stress-strain relationship. Note that a larger ultimate tensile strain than the value given in the model shown in Fig. 2 was adopted to clarify the effect of the compressive stress-strain relationship.

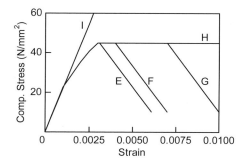 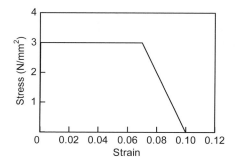

Figure 7: Assumed comp. stress-strain curve   Figure 8: Assumed tensile stress-strain curve

4.2   Effect on M-ϕ relationship and JCI method

Fig. 9 shows the M-ϕ relationship calculated by assuming a cross-sectional size of 100 by 100 mm. This figure also shows the point of maximum capacity (max), point at which the strain on the compression edge reaches the turning point toward compression softening on the stress-strain curve (C-sof), and point at which the strain on the tension edge reaches the turning point toward tension softening (T-sof), as well as their curvature values.

The overall shape of the M-ϕ relationship is scarcely affected by the changes in the compressive stress-strain relationship. When closely examined, however, the curvature at the maximum capacity is found to change corresponding to the strain at the turning point toward softening on the compressive stress-strain relationship. Also, in the cases of E and F, compression softening begins before reaching the maximum capacity, thus preceding tension softening. Therefore, the maximum capacity is attained by compression softening in the cases of E and F, whereas it is attained by tension softening in the case of G.

In regard to the application of the JCI method to the M-ϕ relationship shown in Fig. 9, the point of maximum capacity varies in the analysis depending on the compressive stress-strain relationship, leading to the evaluation of different ultimate tensile strains, even if the tensile stress-strain relationship is the same. However, the overall shape of the M-ϕ relationship is scarcely affected by the difference in the compressive stress-strain relationship. It is also considered impossible to experimentally read the changes in the point of maximum capacity as shown in Fig. 9 by being disturbed by data scatters and measurement errors. The JCI method is therefore deemed practically insensitive to compressive stress-strain relationships.

4.3   Effect on back analysis

In order to investigate the effect of a compressive stress-strain relationship on back analysis, back analysis was carried out using E, F, G, and H (perfect plasticity) and I (linear elasticity) shown in Fig. 7 as the compressive stress-strain relationship, assuming that the M-φ relationship shown in Fig. 9 was experimentally measured.

The results of back analysis are shown in Fig. 10. The results with G naturally agree with the input values. On the other hand, when adopting E and F, in which the point where softening begins is lower than the true value as represented by G, the stress turns up in the middle of the plastic zone of the tensile stress-strain curve toward the point where softening begins. This phenomenon is explained as follows: When E or F is adopted, the strain on the compression edge enters the softening zone while the strain on the tension edge is still in the plastic zone. This should reduce the moment, but the input M-φ relationship has no reduction in the moment. The tensile stress is therefore increased to compensate for the loss in the moment due to compression softening.

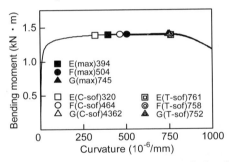

Figure 9: Calculated moment-curvature relationship

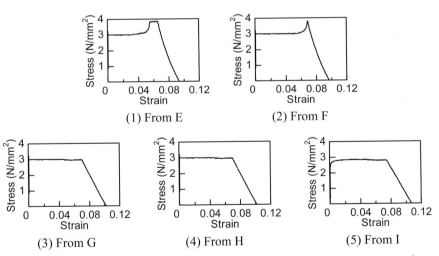

Figure 10: Estimated tensile stress-strain curve from different compressive stress-strain curve

When H having no compressive softening is adopted as the compressive stress-strain curve, the analysis results nearly agree with the input values. This is because the strain on the compression edge does not enter the softening zone in this case even after the M-ϕ relationship enters the softening zone, leaving the tension softening predominant over the softening of the M-ϕ relationship.

When the compressive stress-strain relationship is assumed to be linearly elastic, the tensile stress is evaluated to be slightly lower because of the compressive stress greater than the true value, but the overall shape of the curve nearly agrees with the input value.

Accordingly, the compressive stress-strain relationship can affect the results of back analysis, but the effect can be practically avoided by adopting a stress-strain relationship of a perfect plasticity type.

5. EXAMPLES OF APPLYING BACK ANALYSIS TO TEST VALUES

5.1 Overview

Back analysis was conducted using test values with the aim of confirming its effectiveness. In the experiment, HPFRCC containing 2.0% mixed fiber (polyvinyl alcohol fibe (length: 12mm) and polyethylene fiber (9mm)) of the same batch was fabricated into both uniaxial tension specimens and flexure specimens, which were subjected to testing to measure the tensile stress-strain relationship and M-ϕ relationship, respectively. Back analysis was then applied to the measured M-ϕ relationship to determine the tensile stress-strain relationship, and this was compared with the measured tensile stress-strain relationship.

Beam specimens measuring 15*30*330 mm were subjected to bending testing under third point loading with a span length of 240 mm as shown in Fig.11. The deflection at three points on the tension edge, i.e., two points directly below the loading points and the center of the span, were measured during testing to determine the mean curvature within the constant moment span. The bending tests were carried out in lengthwise (height: 30 mm, width: 15 mm, marked with 'V') and crosswise (height: 15mm, width: 30mm, marked with 'H') because the section of beam specimen is rectangle.

Dumb-bell specimens as shown in Fig. 12 were used for direct tension testing. The mean tensile strain of each specimen, with the cross-sectional size of its test zone being 15*30 mm, was measured with respect to a gage length of 80 mm. Both tensile and beam specimens have the same section to eliminate the size effect. The loading was applied with a constant displacement rate via pin supports at both ends of each specimen.

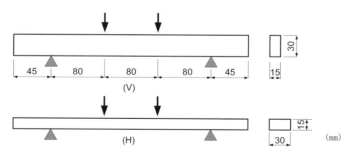

Figure 11: Beam specimen

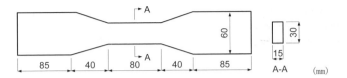

Figure 12: Uniaxial tension specimen

5.2   Test and analysis results

Figs. 13 and 14 show the tensile stress-strain relationship and M-ϕ relationship measured in the tests. The scatter of strength was marginal, but that of ultimate strain or curvature was relatively large in all cases.

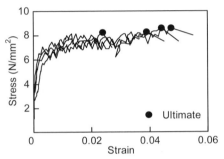

Figure 13: Results of tension test

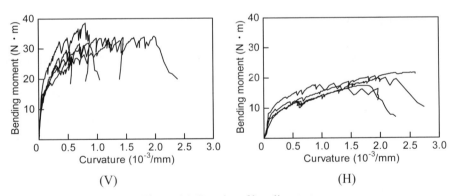

Figure 14: Results of bending test

When carrying out back analysis, the compression test values were used for the area up to the strength point of the compressive stress-strain relationship, and the subsequent area was assumed to be of the perfect plasticity type. In regard to the M-ϕ relationship, smoothed curves were used, because if measured values are used as they are, their small oscillation can oscillate the back analysis results, eventually preventing the solution from converging.

Fig. 15 shows the tensile stress-strain relationships obtained from back analysis. As compared the estimated curves for lengthwise bending (V) with crosswise bending (H), the strength of lengthwise bending was lower than that of crosswise bending, but the ultimate strain of the lengthwise bending was larger than that of crosswise bending. These results may be caused by the size effect on the bending behaviour of HPFRCC.

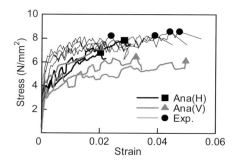

Figure 15: Estimated tensile stress-strain curves

The cracking strength (equivalent to yielding strength of the elasto-plasticity stress strain curve) estimated by the back analysis was lower than the measured value in tension test. The ultimate strength of back analysis of the crosswise bending (H) nearly agreed with the measured value of tension test. On the other hand, the ultimate strain of tension test was close to that of back analysis of longwise bending (V), but both estimated and measured values widely varied from 2% to 5%. These results therefore cannot be determined as characteristic of back analysis.

6.   CONCLUSIONS

Major results obtained from the present study are as follows:
-   It was confirmed that the tensile stress-strain relationship can be estimated from the moment-curvature relationship.
-   The back analysis method is more effective than the JCI method, particularly in estimating the ultimate strain.
-   Though the compressive stress-strain relationship affects the results of back analysis, such an effect can be practically avoided by using a stress-strain relationship of the perfect plasticity type.
-   When back analysis was applied to bending test results, the estimated strength tended to be lower than the measured value in tension test. The ultimate strain widely varied in both test and analysis.

REFERENCES

[1] Naaman, A.E. and Reinhardt, H.W., 'Characterization of High Performance Fiber Reinforced Cement Composites,' in 'High Performance Fiber Reinforced Cement Composites: HPFRCC2,' RILEM, No.31, E.&FN Spon, London, 1996, 1-24.
[2] Japan Concrete Institute: Method of test for bending moment-curvature curve of fiber-reinforced cementitious composites JCI-S-003-2005 (http://www.jci-web.jp/jci_standard/)

EXPERIMENTAL INVESTIGATION FOR CHARACTERIZING OPENING DISPLACEMENT OF MULTIPLE TENSILE CRACKS ON ECC

Tetsushi Kanda [1], **Yoshinori Hiraishi** [2], **Ichiro Fukuda** [2] **and Kumiko Suda** [3]

(1) Building Construction Group, Kajima Technical Research Institute, Tokyo, Japan

(2) Civil Engineering Group, Kajima Technical Research Institute, Tokyo, Japan

(3) Civil Engineering Design Head Office, Kajima Corporation, Tokyo, Japan

Abstract

A testing method of crack opening displacement (COD) measurement for highly ductile cementitious composites, ECC, was proposed on the basis of uniaxial tensile test and verified experimentally. A simplified method of counting the number of cracks, as well as the method directly observing COD, was found to be useful giving averaged COD in a satisfactory accuracy. The maximum COD of ECC taking into account possible variation at a tensile strain between 0.2 and 1.0 percent resulted in a constant value regardless of tensile strains.

1. INTRODUCTION

Engineered cementitious composites, ECC, is a highly ductile composite material with a tensile strain capability comparable to that of steel (see demonstrative flexural deformation in Fig. 1). The excellent tensile strain capability of ECC is originated from the bridging effects of short fibers capable of transferring tensile stress after cracking resulting in formation of multiple cracks. This leads to a characteristic of ECC that each crack opening displacement (COD, hereafter) is controlled to be sufficiently small. Cracks in the normal concrete resulted from excessive loading or drying shrinkage often poses substantial degradation to the structural members, while ECC members may be ensured a higher durability thanks to a range of CODs controlled to have negligible effects on its durability [1].

Practical application of the high durability design requires quantitative knowledge of the COD generated in ECC, while simple and reliable method capable of determining the COD has never been established.

This study proposed a method that can determine the COD of ECC on the basis of uniaxial tensile test and showed its verification through experiments. Experimental results of COD were statistically reevaluated and a simplified method of COD measurement was also verified. Possible maximum COD of ECC in practice and effects of tensile strain in ECC on the COD were evaluated as a basic data for design.

Figure 1: Demonstrative flexural behavior of ECC   Figure 2: Method of tensile test

2. EXPERIMENT

2.1 Objectives

Normal concrete is a tensile softening material that undergoes abrupt increase in COD and decrease in sustained load when sufficiently large tensile or bending loads are applied to cause cracks. In reinforced concrete structure, COD of concrete is a structural property and largely depends on loads and structural section design such as reinforcement ratio and diameter. On the other hand, ECC is a tensile hardening material capable of maintaining its load bearing capacity and unvaried COD after cracking. The COD is affected by properties of the fiber, bonding performance between fiber and matrix and loads and hence the COD can be regarded as a material property. The experiment was performed to determine CODs in ECC under tensile loads and to evaluate average COD, maximum COD and relationship between COD and tensile strain.

2.2 Experimental Program

(1) Uniaxial tensile test

Experiments were performed using uniaxial direct tensile test method [2] as shown in Figs. 2 and 3. Dimensions of the specimen are shown also in Fig. 2. The specimen was a dumbbell shaped plate placed in a steel mold horizontally and the upper surface was trowelled subsequently. Detailed dimensions of specimen and the permissible range of dimensional error are shown in Table 1.

Table 1: Detailed dimensions of specimen and permissible errors (unit: mm)

	Width of parallel	Gauge length	Length of parallel	Thickness
Dimensional size	30	80	80	13
Permissible error	±1	±1	±1	±1

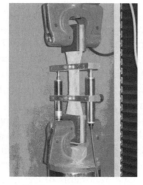

Figure 3: Execution of tensile test

Figure 4: Chucking mechanism and boundary conditions of tensile test

A pneumatic chuck (Fig. 4) was used to assure the axial tensile load to the specimen as shown in Fig. 2. The boundary conditions of specimen at loading were a fixed end at one end and a pin joint at the other end as shown in Fig. 4. A deflection-controlled loading was applied at a head speed of 0.5 mm per minute.

(2) Crack opening displacement

COD measurement under loading is not an established practice. In this experiment, a digital microscope with a CCD camera was adopted and CODs were directly observed. Measurement procedure was as follows. First, a deflection was maintained when strain reached a specified value ε_m. Next, displacement gauges were removed and all the cracks were captured as a digital image with a contact type microscope at a magnification of 175 times. Finally, COD was determined by image processing. Both sides of a specimen, trowelled surface and the formed surface, were processed and, for a future reference, residual cracks were also observed and recorded.

(3) Parameters and specimen preparation

Specified strain ε_m at the entire test length was 0.2, 0.3 and 1.0 percent. A polyvinylalcohol (PVA) fiber with a length of 12 mm and diameter of 0.04 mm was introduced at two percent by volume. More details are given in the literature [3]. Eight specimens per ε_m were prepared. ECC of the same batch was used for the specimens of the conventional tensile test where loading continued until fracture. Tests were performed at the age of eight weeks when the underwater curing at a temperature of 20 °C was expired.

3. RESULTS

3.1. Tensile performance of ECC

An example of stress-strain curve to the fracture is shown in Fig. 5. The ECC specimens show a pseudo strain-hardening characteristic withstanding the load at a strain level greater than one percent and show saw-shaped stress peaks with an increase in tensile strain. The stress peaks indicate the formation of multiple cracks.

3.2. COD measurement

Measured stress-strain curves of three specimens with a respective ε_m of 0.2, 0.5 and 1.0 percent are shown in Fig. 6. For any ε_m, saw-shaped stress peaks were observed implying multiple crack formation. An image data for a COD determination is shown in Fig. 7 where a crack is clearly shown at the center of the photo. A COD distribution of three specimens in Fig. 6 is shown in Fig. 8. It is shown that the COD at ε_m =0.2 distributes over a comparatively narrow range from 0.04 mm to 0.12 mm while those at ε_m =0.5 and ε_m =1.0 distribute over a wide range from 0.04 mm or less to approximately 0.2 mm.

COD distributions over the entire data by the strain level ε_m are shown in Fig. 9 where (a) and (b) show those of the formed surface and the trowelled surface respectively. It is shown in these figures that COD distribute over a wide range from 0.04 mm or less to approximately 0.2 mm, as in the case shown in Fig. 8, while the major distribution is found in a range from 0.04 to 0.12 mm and no significant difference is found between surface treatments of the specimen.

Residual COD distributions after unloading are shown in Fig. 10 where (a) and (b) show those of the formed surface and the trowelled surface respectively. It is seen in the figures that there is no significant difference in COD distribution between surface treatments of the specimen, and the overall COD is smaller than that during loading showing apparent decrease by unloading. This alerts a risk in underestimating CODs in the existing structures when measured as a residual COD.

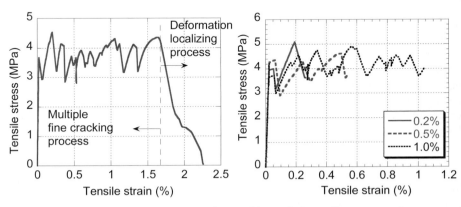

Figure 5: An example of tensile stress-strain curve

Figure 6: A tensile stress-strain curve until the COD is measured

Figure 7: An example of crack image data

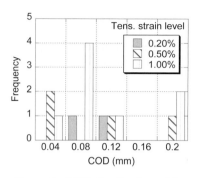

Figure 8: COD distribution of three specimens

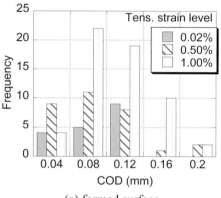

(a) formed surface

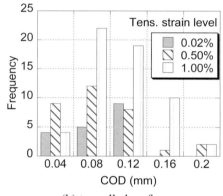

(b) trowelled surface

Figure 9: Distribution of COD (all specimens)

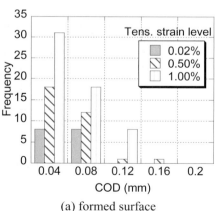

(a) formed surface

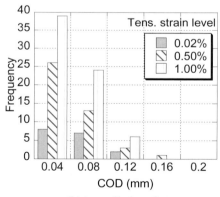

(b) trowelled surface

Figure 10: Distribution of residual COD (all specimens)

4. STOCHASTIC ESTIMATION OF COD

4.1. Investigation Method

Because a large variation of COD was found as shown in Fig. 9, estimation of COD needs a stochastic approach. Statistical properties of COD are given as follows. First, the average COD μ_w that is the expected value of COD can be given by the equation (1),

$$\mu_w = \frac{1}{N_{sp}} \sum_{i=1}^{N_{sp}} \mu_w^i \tag{1}$$

where $\mu_w^i = \frac{1}{N_{cr}^i} \sum_{j=1}^{N_{cr}^i} w_j^i$, w_j^i is measured COD of specimen i at a strain level of ε_m and N_{sp}, N_{cr} are the number of specimen and number of sampled COD of specimen i at a strain level of ε_m respectively.

Coefficient of variation δ_w is given by the equation (2),

$$\delta_w = \frac{\sigma_w}{\mu_w} \tag{2}$$

where $\sigma_w = \sqrt{\frac{1}{(N-1)} \sum_{i=1}^{N_{sp}} \sum_{j=1}^{N_i} \left(w_j^i - \mu_w\right)^2}$.

4.2 Calculation of statistical values

Statistical properties of the COD data are shown in Table 2 where average COD refer to a simple average of the CODs at formed surface or trowelled surface. Also in this table, the average number of crack refers to a number of crack per specimen averaged over eight specimens. The average number of crack shows an increase with an increase in strain level ε_m while μ_w shows constant value of approx. 0.08 mm regardless of strain level ε_m. The coefficient of variation for the COD δ_w is quite large at the maximum of 0.6.

Table 2: Statistical values of COD and the maximum COD

	Formed surface			Trowelled surface			Mean		
Tensile strain e_m (%)	0,2	0,5	1,0	0,2	0,5	1,0	0,2	0,5	1,0
Average COD m_w (mm)	0,0727	0,0739	0,0882	0,087	0,057	0,0725	0,080	0,065	0,080
Average number of crack	2,3	4,4	7,1	2,1	5,5	8,9	2,2	5,0	8,0
Coeff. of variation of COD d_w	0,40	0,63	0,42	0,49	0,69	0,63	-	-	-
Max. COD w_{lim} (mm)	0,12	0,15	0,15	0,16	0,12	0,15	0,14	0,14	0,15
Estimated average COD $_cm_w$ (mm)	0,069	0,091	0,11	0,080	0,074	0,092	0,075	0,083	0,10

5. PROPOSAL OF SIMPLIFIED ESTIMATION METHOD FOR AVERAGE COD

5.1. Simplified estimation method for average COD

The digital microscope method described in 2.2 (2) is a direct and precise method for COD measurement but the equipment is not easily available and may not be a widely applicable one.

Counting the number of crack is a simple method to estimate the average COD and discussed hereafter.

Strain of ECC under tensile stress can be given with average COD as follows.

$$\varepsilon_m = \frac{\mu_w^i \cdot N_{cr}^i}{L_m} + \frac{\sigma_m}{E_c} \qquad (3)$$

where σ_m is stress corresponding to ε_m, L_m is the distance between measuring points and E_c is elastic modulus. The first term of the right-hand side of equation (3) is the crack contribution to strain and the second term is the elastic strain. When the number of crack N_{cr}^i is given by tensile test and ε_m, σ_m and L_m are known, estimated average COD $_c\mu_w$ can be given by equation (4). Thus it is possible for the following equation to estimate the average COD simply by counting the number of crack only.

$$_c\mu_w = \frac{1}{N_{sp}}\sum_{i=1}^{N_{sp}} {}_c\mu_w^i \qquad (4)$$

where $_c\mu_w^i = \dfrac{L_m\left(\varepsilon_m - \dfrac{\sigma_m}{E_c}\right)}{N_{cr}^i}$.

5.2. Verification of the simplified estimation method

Estimated $_c\mu_w$ and comparison with μ_w are shown in Table 2 and Fig. 11 respectively. In this estimation, E_c of 16 kN/mm^2 based on experience and L_m of 80 mm after Fig. 1 were used. Results described in Table 2 and Fig. 11 show that $_c\mu_w$ can represent μ_w in a sufficient accuracy, hence the average COD can be estimated precisely and easily by counting the number of crack.

6. DISCUSSION ON THE MAXIMUM COD

Based on the statistical values in Table 2, the upper limit of the confidence interval at a risk of 5 percent was calculated. The maximum COD w_{lim}, which is an upper limit that can be anticipated in engineering, is given by equation (5),

$$w_{lim} = \frac{1}{N_{sp}}\sum_{i=1}^{N_{sp}} w_{lim}^i \qquad (5)$$

where $w_{lim}^i = \mu_w^i(1 + 1.645\delta_w)$.

Result of calculation for w_{lim} is shown in Fig. 12. For comparison, an example of stress-strain curve obtained by tensile test and average COD μ_w are also shown. It is seen that, at a strain greater than 0.2 percent, w_{lim} and μ_w are almost constant regardless of strain. In this strain range, w_{lim} is approx. 0.15 mm. These suggest that average COD that may occur in ECC tested in this experiment is 0.08 mm and at the maximum 0.15 mm when strain level is less than 1.0 percent.

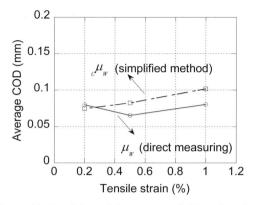

Figure 11: Precision of the average COD estimation

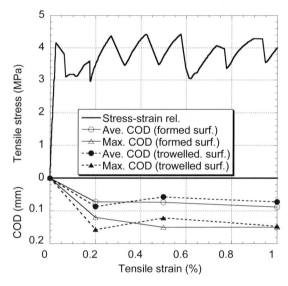

Figure 12: Effects of tensile strain level on the COD

7. CONCLUSIONS

COD generated in ECC was focused in this study and a method capable of measuring the COD directly has been proposed. Results of experiment for verification of the method can be summarized as follows.

(1) Variation of COD was significantly large with a coefficient of variation of 0.6 at the maximum and needed a stochastic approach.

(2) COD during loading was larger than the residual COD measured after unloading.

(3) Average COD can be determined not only by the direct method but estimated by a simpler method counting the number of cracks in a satisfactory precision.

(4) The maximum COD with the upper limit of the confidence interval at a risk of 5 percent was found to be almost constant regardless of the strain level and the proposed method showed that it was approximately 0.15 mm within a tensile strain of ECC less than 1 percent.

ACKNOWLEDGEMENT

Authors express their gratitude for valuable advice of the members of the High Performance Fiber Reinforced Cementitious Composite Committee of Japanese Society of Civil Engineers that given during the execution of this study.

REFERENCES

[1] Japan Concrete Institute, 'Technology of Highly Ductile Cementitious Composite – Present and Future', (2002) (in Japanese).
[2] Kanda, T. and Li, V. C., 'A new micromechanics design theory for pseudo strain hardening cementitious composite', *J. of Engineering Mechanics*, ASCE, 125 (4) (1999) 373-381.
[3] Kanda et al., 'Full Scale Processing Investigation for ECC Pre-cast Structural Element', *Journal of Asian Architecture and Building Engineering*, 5 (2), 333-340 (2006)

CORRELATION BETWEEN SINGLE FIBER PULLOUT AND TENSILE RESPONSE OF FRC COMPOSITES WITH HIGH STRENGTH STEEL FIBERS

Dong Joo Kim, Sherif El-Tawil, and Antoine E. Naaman

Civil and Environmental Engineering, University of Michigan, USA

Abstract

This paper describes the results of experimental tests designed to correlate the pull-out response of two types of high strength steel fibers [Hooked and Torex fibers] with the tensile response of fiber reinforced cement composites using such fibers. The focus is mostly on HPFRCC or strain-hardening composites in tension and the parameter studied include fiber type. Experimental results reveal that a strong correlation exists between pull-out behavior and tensile response, especially in terms of the extent of slip before bond decays and the strain-capacity of the composite prior to localization. While the bond strength is important, the extent of slip prior to bond softening is also most critical. It is concluded that extensive slip hardening in the fiber pullout behavior leads to high strain capacity composites with multiple micro-cracks.

1.   INTRODUCTION

The tensile behavior of fiber reinforced cement composites (FRCCs) depends on numerous parameters including the matrix and fiber properties and the bond at the fiber-matrix interface. Compared with conventional FRC composites, high performance FRC composites (HPFRCC) are characterized by a strain-hardening behavior in tension accompanied by multiple cracking. Such characteristic leads to high ductility, durability, and energy absorption capacity.

The condition to develop strain-hardening and multiple cracking behavior is simple to set, namely; the post cracking strength of composites should be higher that their first cracking strength [1, 2]. Moreover, the slip-hardening in single fiber pullout behavior, should it exist, is believed to be a key for the strain-hardening behavior of the composite [3]. Both Torex (twisted fibers of polygonal cross-section) and Hooked ends steel fibers show slip-hardening behavior under pull-out, primarily because of the plastic energy capacity of steel [4, 5]. However, the extent of slip before bond decay is very different for both types of fibers [6].

The main objective of this study is to evaluate the correlation that exists between the extent of slip before bond decay in a single fiber pull-out, and the tensile response of a composite made with such fiber. Experimental test results are provided and analyzed using equivalent bond strength derived from the fiber pullout energy.

2. PULLOUT MECHANISM AND PULLOUT ENERGY

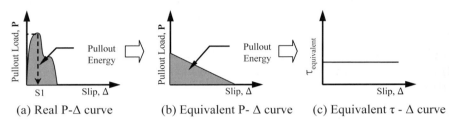

(a) Real P-Δ curve   (b) Equivalent P- Δ curve   (c) Equivalent τ - Δ curve

Figure 1: Hooked fiber pull-out behavior

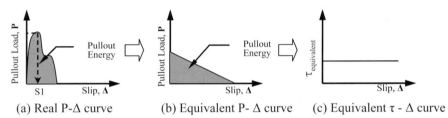

(a) Real P-Δ curve   (b) Equivalent P- Δ curve   (c) Equivalent τ - Δ curve

Figure 2: Torex fiber pull-out behavior

Fiber pullout resistance is based on the bond mechanisms at the interface between fiber and matrix. Bond characteristics between fiber and matrix generally comprise adhesion, friction and mechanical components. The pullout resistance of deformed steel fibers is primarily controlled by the mechanical component, whereas that of smooth steel fiber is mainly dependent upon the frictional component. The Hooked steel fiber is one of the most widely used steel fibers which utilize the plastic energy of deformation of steel [7]; however, it uses only a small portion of fiber length to enhance pullout resistance as induced by the formation of two plastic hinges at the end hook. Plastic hinge formation results in slip-hardening response up to a certain slip (S1 in Fig. 1a). The pull-out mechanism of Torex fiber is based on the untwisting torsional moment resistance of the fiber which is distributed throughout the fiber embedment length [8]; therefore, everything else being equal, the extent of slip of a Torex fiber before bond decays (S2 in Fig. 2a) is much higher than that of a Hooked fiber (S1 in Fig. 1a), i.e. S2 >> S1. This big difference in slip capacity leads to a substantial increase in pullout energy during single fiber pullout and in improved energy absorption capacity of the composite.

3. PULLOUT ENERGY AND EQUIVALENT BOND STRENGTH

To achieve strain-hardening behavior, the maximum post-cracking strength, σ_{pc}, should be higher than the first cracking strength, σ_{cc} [1, 2]. The post-cracking strength is directly dependent on the average bond strength at the fiber matrix interface, which is assumed to be a constant over a relatively small level of slip. Assuming that the bond strength remains a constant over the entire embedment length, the authors suggest that an equivalent bond strength can be calculated from the pullout energy obtained from a single fiber pullout test

If the equivalent bond strength is assumed constant, the shape of the pullout load versus slip curve will be triangular such as shown in the middle part of Figs. 1, 2. Using the pull-out energy (area under each curve) leads to the equivalent bond strength for a typical Hooked and Torex steel fiber as illustrated in Fig. 1c, 2c. It is observed that, even if the maximum pull-out load is the same for two fibers, their equivalent bond strength can be significantly different depending on their pull-out energy. Mathematically, the equivalent bond strength can be estimated from the following equations.

$$E_{pullout} = P\Delta/2 = \left(\pi d_f \tau_{eq} \times \left(L_f/2\right)\right) \times \left(L_f/2\right)/2 = \tau_{eq} \times \pi d_f L_f^{2}/8 \;\rightarrow\; \tau_{eq} = 8E_{pullout}/\pi d_f L_f^{2} \tag{1}$$

4. EQUIVALENT BOND STRENGTH AND TENSILE BEHAVIOR

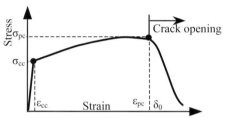

Figure 3: Typical stress-elongation curve of HPFRCC

The equivalent bond strength concept makes it possible and simple to utilize the equations for first-cracking strength and post-cracking strength based on the mechanics of composite materials suggested by Naaman [9, 1] because these equations assume a constant bond strength.

Typical stress-elongation curve of a strain-hardening FRC composite is shown in Fig. 3. Multiple cracking occurs along the strain hardening portion of the curve. The strain capacity at maximum stress is based on both the number of multiple cracks and the width of cracks. These can also be estimated, assuming the equivalent bond strength is known as described next. The equations suggested by Naaman [9, 1] for first cracking strength and the post cracking strength are used here:

First cracking strength : $\sigma_{cc} = \sigma_{mu}\left(1 - V_f\right) + \alpha\tau_{eq}V_f\left(L_f/d_f\right)$ (2)

Post cracking strength: $\sigma_{pc} = \lambda\tau_{eq}V_f\left(L_f/d_f\right)$ (3)

The average crack spacing and crack width derived for the case of continuous reinforcement [10, 11] are assumed to apply here provided an equivalent bond strength is used. Note that the equation can also be put in terms of the specific surface of fiber reinforcement. Thus, assuming a tensile prism model leads to:

Average crack spacing: $\Delta L_{av} = \eta \dfrac{A_m \sigma_m}{p\tau_{eq}} = \eta \dfrac{A_m \sigma_m}{\left(N_F \cdot \pi d_f\right)\tau_{eq}}$ (4)

Crack opening due to fiber stretch:

$$W_{st} = \Delta L_{ax} \left[\left(\varepsilon_f \right)_{ax} - \left(\varepsilon_m \right)_{ax} \right] = \Delta L_{av} \left[\frac{N}{A_f E_f} - \frac{p\tau}{4 A_f E_f} \Delta L_{av} \right] - \Delta L_{av} \left[\frac{p\tau \times \Delta L_{av}}{4 A_m E_m} - \varepsilon_{SH} \right] \cong \Delta L_{av} \frac{N}{A_f E_f} \quad (5)$$

Where, V_f = fiber volume fraction, L_f = fiber length, d_f = fiber diameter, L_f/d_f = fiber aspect ratio, σ_{mu} = tensile strength of matrix, τ_{eq} = equivalent bond strength, $\left(\varepsilon_f \right)_{av}$ = Average strain in fiber, $\left(\varepsilon_m \right)_{av}$ = Average strain in matrix, $\left(\sigma_f \right)_{av}$ = Average strain in fiber, $\left(\sigma_m \right)_{av}$ = Average strain in matrix, p = total fiber perimeter (i.e., sum of perimeters of all fibers per unit volume), N_f = Number of fibers crossing a unit area of matrix, A_m = area of matrix in tensile prism model, W_{st} = Crack opening due to fiber stretch, A_f = average area of fibers crossing a unit area of composites, E_m = Matrix modulus of elasticity, E_f = Fiber modulus of elasticity, N = Applied Load, α = factor equal to the product of several coefficient for considering average stress, random distribution, fiber orientation, λ = factor equal to the product of several coefficients for considering average pullout length, group reduction, orientation effect, η = factor for the range between minimum and maximum crack spacing ($1 \le \eta \le 2$).

5. EXPERIMENTS

Experimental tests were carried out to investigate the correlation between single fiber pullout behavior and the tensile behavior of strain-hardening FRC composites (HPFRCC). Hooked and Torex steel fibers were investigated since they both show slip-hardening behavior under pull-out but with significantly different slip capacity before bond decay.

5.1 Materials
The matrix mix properties are shown in Table 1 and the key properties of the fibers are shown in Table 2.

Table 1: Composition of matrix mixtures by weight ratio and compressive strength

Matrix	Cement (Type III)	Fly ash	Sand (Flint)	Silica Fume	Super - Plasticizer	VMA	Water	f_c', ksi (MPa)
Mortar	1.00	0.15	1.00	-	0.009	0.006	0.35	7 (49)

Table 2: Properties of Fibers used in this study

Fiber Type	Diameter in (mm)	Length in(mm)	Density g/cc	Tensile strength ksi (MPa)	Elastic Modulus ksi (GPa)
Hooked	0.016 (0.4)	1.18 (30)	7.9	304 (2100)	29000 (200)
Torex	0.012 (0.3)*	1.18 (30)	7.9	400 (2760)**	29000 (200)

* Equivalent diameter   ** Tensile strength of the fiber after twisting

Note that the reason for which VMA (viscosity modifying agent) was used is because this project was in support of another project involving the use of self-consolidating HPFRCC for application in seismic resistant structures. VMA is added to the matrix to increase viscosity, reduce fiber segregation and ensure uniform fiber distribution during mixing.

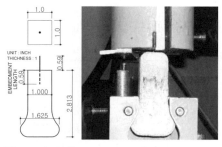
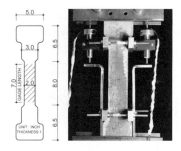

Figure 4: Pull out test specimen and setup   Figure 5: Tensile test specimen and setup

5.2   Single Fiber Pullout Test

The geometry of pullout test specimen and test set up are shown in Fig. 4. This test simulates the case of fibers bridging the crack surface of a tensile prism and undergoing the different pullout mechanisms influencing slip capacity and fiber pullout energy. In performing single fiber pullout test, extreme care should be taken in gripping the fiber as close as possible to the free surface of the prism to minimize the effect of deformation from fiber elongation.

5.3   Tensile Test

The tensile behavior of HPFRCC is highly dependent on the fiber reinforcing parameters and the equivalent bond stress. Tests on tensile prisms were carried out to correlate with results on pull-out load and energy obtained from tests using single fiber pull-out. Tensile test specimen (double-dogbone shaped) and test set-up are shown in Fig. 5. Cross section dimensions of specimen are 2 x 1 in. (50 mm x 25 mm) and the elongation (thus strain) was measured over a gage length of 7 in (= 178 mm) using the average reading of 2 LVDTs.

The fiber volume fraction was 2% in both Hooked and Torex fiber reinforced specimen and the same matrix composition (compressive strength 7ksi (48.3 MPa)) was used to eliminate the influence of any other parameters. The direct tensile test as shown in Fig. 5 allows identification of the following characteristics: first cracking strength, post cracking strength, strain capacity, cracking behavior, and strain energy to peak stress.

6.   RESULTS

6.1   Single Fiber Pullout behavior

Single fiber pullout test were performed and the results are shown in Fig. 6. The embedded length was taken as 0.59 in (15 mm). The pullout response of Torex fibers shows considerable slip before bond decays (more than 0.4 inch (10 mm)). In contrast, high strength Hooked fibers slipped less than 0.05 inch (1.27 mm) before the resistance started to decay. The typical shapes of both Torex and Hooked fibers before and after the pullout test are shown Fig. 6g, h.

Both Hooked and TOREX fibers have comparable mechanical bond resistance when computed from the peak pull-out load (Fig. 6a, b). If the fiber tensile stress under pull-out is plotted versus slip (Fig. 6c, d), then the pull-out stress until a slip of 0.03 in. (0.76 mm) is about the same in the two fibers, that is, about 190 ksi (1311 MPa). The slip at the peak stress for the Hooked fiber is 0.03 in. (0.76 mm) and is followed by a rapid decay; however, after that slip, the Torex fibers show dramatic enhancement in both stress and slip up to a slip of about 0.45 in (11.4 mm), which represents 76% of embedded fiber length (Fig. 6e, f).

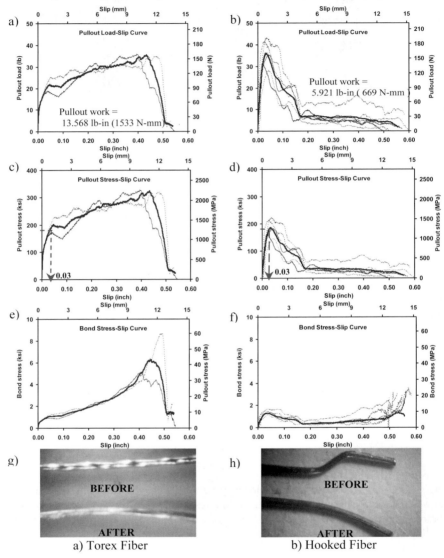

Figure 6: Single fiber pull-out test results

This big difference in slip capacity leads to a considerable difference in pullout energy. Pullout energy was calculated from the average pullout load versus slip curves of Hooked and Torex fibers. The pullout work obtained for Torex fiber was = 13.568 lb-in (1533 N-mm) is more than twice that obtained for Hooked fibers (5.921 lb-in = 669 N-mm).

Even though there is a big difference in pullout energy between Hooked and Torex fibers, it should be noted that the slip capacity at peak stress of Hooked fiber before bond decays (0.03 inch = 0.76 mm) is still sufficient to induce significant multiple cracking in a tensile composite. Since fiber embedment length varies from 0 to $L_f/2$ at any crack section, an average bond stress along the fiber embedment length is used in estimating the composite tensile behavior.

The equivalent bond stress was calculated from the experimentally measured pullout work using Eq. (1). The equivalent bond stress is thus a constant that is assumed to be slip-independent.

$$\underline{\text{Hooked Fiber}} : \tau_{eq} = \frac{8 \times PulloutWork}{\pi d_f L_f^2} = \frac{8 \times 5.921}{\pi (0.4/25.4)1.18^2} = 686\,psi = 4.73\,MPa \qquad (6)$$

$$\underline{\text{Torex Fiber}} : \tau_{eq} = \frac{8 \times PulloutWork}{\pi d_f L_f^2} = \frac{8 \times 13.568}{\pi (0.3/25.4)1.18^2} = 2100\,psi = 14.49\,MPa \qquad (7)$$

These values will be used later on to explain some aspects of the tensile response and crack distribution in composites subjected to tension.

6.2 Tensile behavior

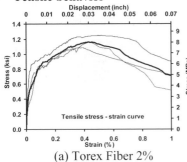

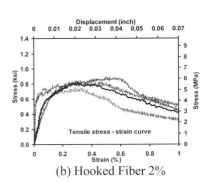

(a) Torex Fiber 2%   (b) Hooked Fiber 2%

Figure 7: Tensile stress – strain curve

Table 3: Tensile test results

	TOREX FIBER 2%	HOOKED FIBER 2%
First Cracking strength, σ_{cc}	0.826ksi = 5.70MPa	0.575ksi = 3.97MPa
Post Cracking strength, σ_{pc}	1.157ksi = 7.98MPa	0.783 ksi = 5.40MPa
Strain capacity at peak stress, ε_{pc}	0.47%	0.33%
Number of cracks	60	15
Average crack spacing	0.116inch = 2.96mm	0.467inch =11.85mm
Crack opening at Post Cracking (Based on strain capacity and Number of Cracks)	13.92μm	39.12μm
Permanent average crack width	9.06μm	22.12μm
Crack opening due to fiber stretch	13.92–9.06=4.86μm	39.12–22.12 = 17μm

Tensile test results are shown in Fig. 7 and Table 3. Both Hooked and Torex fiber reinforced specimens with 2% fiber volume ratio show strain hardening behavior. Three specimens were tested for each series, and the averages are discussed next. For the hooked fiber reinforced tensile prisms, the first cracking strength was 0.575 ksi (3.97 MPa), the post-cracking strength was 0.783 ksi (5.40 MPa) and the corresponding strain was 0.33%. Torex fiber reinforced specimens showed a higher load carrying capacity: first cracking strength = 0.826 ksi (5.70 MPa), post-cracking strength = 1.157 ksi (7.98 MPa), and a strain of 0.47% at peak stress. It is clear in this comparison between Hooked and Torex steel fibers that, everything else being equal, the Torex fiber leads to a significantly better performance in terms of both strength and strain capacity prior to decay.

Note also that the cracking behavior of the tensile specimen with Torex fibers is quite different from that with Hooked fibers as shown in Fig. 8. For the Torex fiber reinforced specimen, the average number of observed cracks is 60 and the average crack spacing is 2.96 mm (= 177.8/60); the average crack opening at post cracking strength 1.157 ksi (= 7.98 MPa) is 13.92 μm (Table 7, Fig. 8). For the Hooked fiber reinforced specimen, the average number of observed cracks was 15, and their average spacing was 11.85 mm; the average crack width was 39.12 μm (Table 7, Fig. 8).

Crack spacing and pattern

Crack width

(a) Torex Fiber   (b) Hooked Fiber

Figure 8: Cracking pattern and crack width

7. COMPARISON BETWEEN EXPERIMENTALLY OBSERVED AND ANALYTICALLY PREDICTED CRACK SPACING AND WIDTH

Predicted theoretical values of crack spacing and crack width for Torex and Hooked fiber reinforced tensile specimens are calculated using Equations (4), (5) in which the equivalent bond strength is obtained from Eqs. (6), (7). In estimating theoretical crack widths due to the average tensile strain in the fiber, the post-cracking strength was used to calculate the applied tensile force N, for both Torex and Hooked fibers. The corresponding values of crack widths are given in Table 4 and compared to the experimental observations. On the other hand, Fig. 8 illustrates examples of residual crack width observed.

7.1 Torex Fiber

Average number of fibers at bridging a typical cross section of the tensile prism:

$$N_f = \alpha_2 \frac{4V_F}{\pi d_f^2} A_c = 0.5 \times \frac{4 \times 0.02}{3.14 \times 0.011811023^2} \times 2 = 182 \, \text{ea}$$

Average crack spacing [4]: $\Delta L_{average} = 1.5 \times \dfrac{(2-0.04)\times 0.504}{(182 \times \pi \times (0.3/25.4))\times 2.1} = 0.1045 inch = 2.66mm$

Predicted number of cracks: $Gagelength/Crackspacing = 7/0.1045 = 67$ ea

Crack opening due to fiber stretch [5]: $W_{st} = \Delta L_{av}\dfrac{N}{A_r E_r} = \mu\dfrac{A_m \sigma_{mu}}{(N_f \cdot \pi d_f)\tau_{eq}} \times \dfrac{\sigma_{pc} A_c}{A_r E_r}$

$= 1.5 \times \dfrac{(2-0.04)\times 0.504}{(182 \times \pi \times (0.3/25.4))\times 2.1} \times \dfrac{1.157 \times 2}{0.04 \times 29000} = 0.000208 inch = 0.0053mm = 5.3 \mu m$

7.2 Hooked Fiber

Average number of fibers bridging a typical cross section of the tensile prism:

$N_f = \alpha_2 \dfrac{4V_F}{\pi d_f^2} A_c = 0.5 \times \dfrac{4 \times 0.02}{3.14 \times 0.015748^2} \times 2 = 103$ ea

Average crack spacing [4] : $\Delta L_{average} = 1.5 \times \dfrac{(2-0.04)\times 0.504}{(103 \times \pi \times (0.4/25.4))\times 0.686} = 0.424 inch = 10.77mm$

Predicted number of cracks: $Gagelength/Crackspacing = 7/0.424 = 16$ ea

Crack opening due to fiber stretch: $W_{st} = \Delta L_{av}\dfrac{N}{A_r E_r} = \mu\dfrac{A_m \sigma_{mu}}{(N_f \cdot \pi d_f)\tau_{eq}} \times \dfrac{\sigma_{pc} A_c}{A_r E_r}$

$= 1.5 \times \dfrac{(2-0.04)\times 0.504}{(103 \times \pi \times (0.4/25.4))\times 0.686} \times \dfrac{0.783 \times 2}{0.04 \times 29000} = 0.00057 inch = 0.0145mm = 14.53 \mu m$

Table 4: Comparison of cracking behavior between predicted and actual test results

	Torex Fiber 2%		Hooked Fiber 2%	
	Predicted	Actual	Predicted	Actual
Crack spacing	2.66mm	2.96mm	10.77mm	11.85mm
Number of cracks	67 ea	60 ea	16 ea	15 ea
Crack opening due to fiber stretch	5.3 μm	4.86 μm	14.53 μm	17.00 μm

The above analytical calculations for the crack spacing are very close to the results observed in the experimental tensile tests (Tables 3, 4) suggesting that the analytical procedure used here can be very useful. The results confirm that the better tensile response of specimens reinforced with Torex fibers is due to the high equivalent bond strength that develops along the entire fiber embedment length. This high equivalent bond strength is due to the large slip capacity before bond softening in the fiber pull-out versus slip behavior of Torex fiber.

8. CONCLUSIONS

This study investigated the correlation between single fiber pullout and tensile response of FRC composites with high strength steel Torex and Hooked fibers. Even though both Torex and Hooked fibers show slip-hardening behavior due to their mechanical bond, the extent of slip prior to bond softening (or decay) is very different for each fiber. Differences in the slip capacity are theorized to be partly responsible for the observed differences in strain capacity and multiple cracking development in the FRC composites. The following specific conclusions may be drawn from the limited study described herein:

- The combined effects of high slip-hardening capacity and high slip before bond decay in fiber pull-out behavior helps achieve strain-hardening FRC composites with higher strain capacity in tension and better multiple cracking development.
- Torex fiber shows slip-hardening behavior up to 76 % of the fiber embedment length. This large slip capacity significantly increases the energy required to pull out the fiber.
- The high pull-out energy of Torex fibers leads to a high equivalent bond strength, which can be used to predict crack spacing at crack saturation in strain-hardening FRC composites.
- The very fine crack widths at saturated micro-cracking associated with Torex fibers implies that Torex reinforced composites are likely to have excellent durability.

ACKNOWLEDGMENTS

The research described here was sponsored in part by the National Science Foundation under Grants No. CMS 0408623 and 0530383, and by the University of Michigan. Their support is gratefully acknowledged. The opinions expressed in this paper are those of the authors and do not necessarily reflect the views of the sponsor.

REFERENCES

[1]   Naaman, A.E., "High Performance Fiber Reinforced Cement Composites," Concrete Structures for the future, IABSE Symposium, Paris, France, September 1987, pp. 371-376

[2]   Naaman, A.E., and Reinhardt, H.W., "Characterization of High Performance Fiber Reinforced Cement Composites," Proceedings of 2nd International Workshop on HPFRCC, Chapter 41, in High Performance Fiber Reinforced Cement Composites: HPFRCC 2, A.E. Naaman and H.W. Reinhardt, Editors, RILEM, No. 31, E. & FN Spon, London, 1996, pp. 1-24.

[3]   Sujivorakul, C, and Naaman, A.E., "Tensile Response of HPFRC Composites using Twisted Polygonal Steel Fibers", accepted for publication in proceedings of Fiber Reinforced Concrete: Innovation for Value, ACI Convention, Toronto, ACI Special Publication, in print, 2003.

[4]   Sujivorakul, C., Waas, A.M., and Naaman, A.E., "Pullout Response of a Smooth Fiber with End Anchorage," Journal of Engineering Mechanics, American Society of Civil Engineers, Vol. 126, No. 9, September 2000, pp.986-993.

[5]   Naaman, A.E., "Fibers with Slip-Hardening Bond," in High Performance Fiber Reinforced Cement Composites – HPFRCC 3,' H.W. Reinhardt and A.E. Naaman, Editors, RILEM Pro 6, RILEM Publications S.A.R.L., Cachan, France, May 1999, pp. 371-385.

[6]   Sujivorakul, C., "Development of High Performance Fiber Reinforced Cement Composites using Twisted Polygonal Steel Fibers," Ph.D. Thesis, 2002, University of Michigan, Ann Arbor.

[7]   Naaman, A.E., and Najm, H., "Bond-Slip Mechanics of steel Fibers in Concrete," ACI Materials Journal, Vol. 88, No.2, April 1991, pp. 135-145.

[8]   Naaman, A.E., and Sujivorakul, C., "Pull-out Mechanism of Twisted Steel Fibers Embedded in Concrete "Proceedings of International Conference on Applications of Shotcrete, Tasmania, Australia, April 2001.

[9]   Naaman, A.E, "A Statistical Theory of Strength for Fiber Reinforced Concrete," Ph.D. Thesis, Massachusetts Institute of Technology, 1972, 196 pages.

[10] Naaman, A.E., "Reinforcing Mechanisms in Ferrocement," M.S. Thesis, Massachusetts Institute of Technology, Civil Engineering Department, 1970, 152 pages.

[11] Naaman, A.E., "Ferrocement & Laminated Cementitious Composites", Techno Press 3000, Ann Arbor, Michigan, 2000

LARGE SCALE TENSILE TESTS OF HIGH PERFORMANCE FIBER REINFORCED CEMENT COMPOSITES

Shih-Ho Chao [1], **Wen-Cheng Liao** [1], **Thanasak Wongtanakitcharoen** [2], **and Antoine E. Naaman** [1]

(1) University of Michigan, Ann Arbor, USA

(2) Department of Highways, Thailand

Abstract

The macro-scale properties of high performance fiber reinforced cement composites (HPFRCC) depend on their stress-strain characterization under tension; hence direct tensile tests are essential for determining the fundamental tensile behavior of HPFRC composites. Most tensile tests for obtaining the tensile response of FRC composites are carried out on relatively small-size specimens which do not account for more realistic fiber distribution and content variability in full scale structural applications. Moreover, they do not incorporate the tension stiffening effect due to the presence of continuous reinforcement in real structural concrete elements. In this study, long prismatic specimens of dimensions $64 \times 76 \times 3050$ mm reinforced with one unstressed prestressing steel tendon along their longitudinal axis were tested in tension under monotonic load. The tensile load was applied to the prestressing tendon and strains in the tendon (inside and outside the matrix) as well as in the FRC material along the specimen were recorded. The advantage of using a prestressing steel tendon is that a strain as high as 0.9% can be applied while the tendon remains linear elastic, thus allowing a stable environment for loading-unloading and for measurements of crack width and spacing. In this study, the stress-strain curves of HPFRC composites (here a self-consolidating concrete mixture is used) obtained from long-prism tests were compared to curves obtained from small scale direct tensile tests of dog-bone shaped specimens without continuous reinforcement. It was observed that the onset of damage localization following peak stress is significantly delayed in the presence of continuous reinforcement. The strain capacity of an HPFRC composite was also considerably enhanced due to the presence of the reinforcing steel strand.

1. INTRODUCTION

HPFRCCs are characterized by their strain-hardening response under tension accompanied by multiple cracking; generally, a direct tensile test is the best way to determine the fundamental tensile behavior of HPFRC composites, which is essential in design and modelling. Currently, however, most tensile tests for obtaining the tensile response of FRC composites are carried out on relatively small-size specimens that do not account for more realistic variability in fiber distribution in full scale structural elements, and possible scale effects. Moreover, they do not incorporate the tension stiffening effect due to the presence of continuous reinforcement in a real structural concrete element. In this study, large scale HPFRCC tensile prisms reinforced with an unstressed prestressing steel strand along their longitudinal axis were tested in tension under monotonic load and their response was compared to that of typical tensile dog-bone shaped specimens.

2. EXPERIMENTAL PROGRAM

2.1 Materials

The HPFRCC used in this study is one of a series of self-consolidating high performance fiber reinforced concrete (SCHPFRC) developed at the University of Michigan [1] for seismic applications, as part of a NSF-NEES project. This mixture has a maximum coarse aggregate size of 12.7 mm and 1.5% volume fraction of high strength steel hooked fibers. Average 28-day compressive strength based on 100 mm × 200 mm cylinders is approximately 50 MPa. Details of matrix composition and fiber properties are given in Tables 1 and 2, respectively. Figure 1 shows the steel fiber type used in this study. Note that in order to obtain a self-consolidating mixture, a strict mixing procedure (involving mixing steps and mixing time) must be followed.

The reinforcement used is an unstressed prestressing steel tendon (seven-wire strand), having a nominal diameter of 12.7 mm and ultimate tensile strength of 1860 MPa.

Table 1: Relative composition of concrete mixture by weight and compressive strength

Cement (Type III)	Fly Ash*	Sand**	Coarse Aggregate †	Super-plasticizer	Water	VMA ††	Steel Fiber	f_c' (MPa)
1.0	0.5	1.7	1	0.003	0.6	0.0095	0.244	50

*Type C ; **Flint Sand ASTM 50-70; † Maximum Size of 12.7 mm ; †† Viscosity Modifying Agent

Table 2: Properties of fiber used in this study

Fiber Type	Diameter, (mm)	Length, (mm)	Density, (g/cc)	Tensile Strength, (MPa)	Elastic Modulus, (GPa)
Hooked	0.38	30	7.9	2300	200

Figure 1: Steel hooked fiber used in this study

2.2 Specimen Geometry and Test Setup for Large Scale Tensile Test

Details of the specimen geometry, test setup, and instrumentation are shown in Figure 2. The long prismatic specimen has a cross-sectional dimension of 64 mm x 76 mm.

It has been established that the presence of continuous reinforcement helps concrete to carry tension between cracks through transfer of bond forces. This in turn results in better control on member stiffness, deformation, and crack widths in RC members as compared to plain concrete members [2]. In this study, an unstressed prestressing steel strand was placed at the centroid of the specimen to simulate the presence of reinforcing steel in HPFRCCs. The advantage of using a prestressing steel tendon is that a strain as high as 0.9% can be applied while the tendon remains linear elastic ([3], Chapter 12), thus allowing a stable environment for loading-unloading and for measurements of crack width and spacing at every loading step. Moreover, tests conducted by [4] have shown that HPFRC composites lead to a much higher bond strength between a seven-wire strand and surrounding matrix than plain concrete (as high as three times), thus ensuring the tension stiffening effect in the test specimens.

The specimen was placed in a prestressing bed and supported by a few steel strips which allowed the specimen to move easily on its bed support during tension. The strand going through the specimen was attached at each end by a prestressing chuck. The tensile load was applied monotonically to the strand through a hydraulic jack and recorded by a pair of load cells at both ends of the prestressing bed (Figure 2a). Five zones in the middle of the specimen were selected to record the strains in the concrete through the use of linear variable differential transformers (LVDTs), as shown in Figure 2b (Zones 1 thru 5). The gauge length of each zone was 250 mm. Elongation of the entire specimen was also monitored by two LVDTs attached to the ends of the specimen. Strains in the strand (inside the matrix) were measured by strain gauges attached at pre-designated locations corresponding to the middle points of the five zones (Zones 1 thru 5) mentioned above. Strain gauges were also mounted on the strand outside the matrix (Figure 2b) in order to obtain the stress-strain curve of the bare strand.

The experimental procedure of the large scale tensile test is shown in Figure 3.

2.3 Specimen Geometry and Test Setup for Small Scale Tensile Test

For comparison purposes, a small scale tensile test was also carried out by using dog-bone shaped specimens as illustrated in Figure 4. These specimens have a cross-sectional dimension of $25\,mm \times 50\,mm$, therefore leading to a somewhat two-dimensional distribution of fibers (Note the fiber length is 30 mm). Same matrix (Table 1) was used for the small tensile specimens but without continuous reinforcement. The applied load was monitored by the load cell of the testing machine and elongation was recorded by a pair of LVDTs attached to the specimen, with a gauge length about 175 mm. It is noted that this type of direct tensile test has been extensively used previously to obtain tensile stress-strain responses in FRCCs with great success [5, 6].

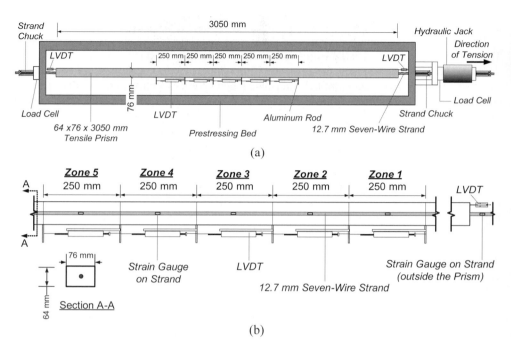

(a)

(b)

Figure 2: (a) Geometry of large scale tensile specimen and test setup; (b) Instrumentation

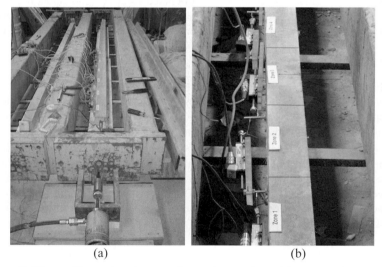

(a)   (b)

Figure 3: Photos illustrating the experimental procedure: (a) Prestressing bed and
application of tensile load; (b) Typical zones for measurements

(c)

Figure 3 (continued): (c) Tracing of cracks and measurement of crack width

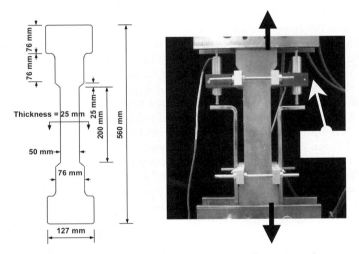

Figure 4: Geometry of small scale specimen and test setup layout

3. EXPERIMENTAL RESULTS

3.1 Calculation of Stress in HPFRCC

The stress in the fiber concrete for the large scale tensile test was calculated by:

$$\sigma_c = \left(F - E_s \varepsilon_s\right)/\left(A_t - A_s\right) \tag{1}$$

where σ_c is the tensile stress in fiber concrete (MPa); F is the total force measured by load cell (kN); E_s is the elastic modulus of strand (MPa) ; ε_s is the strain in strand measured by strain gauge (mm/mm); A_t is the gross cross-sectional area of the specimen (= 4860 mm^2) ;

A_s is the nominal cross-sectional area of a 12.7 mm seven-wire strand (= 100 mm^2). It was mentioned previously that a prestressing steel strand remains linear elastic when the strain reaches as high as 0.9%. This was indeed the case in the strand used in this study, as indicated by the stress-strain relation obtained based on strain gauges mounted outside the matrix; the curve was linear with an elastic modulus of 206 GPa. Since the specimen was able to move freely during testing with minor frictional force, the force measured by the load cell (F) can be taken as constant along the specimen and used for Zones 1 thru 5. The force sustained by the fiber concrete was calculated by the difference between F and force in the strand, $E_s\varepsilon_s$. The average tensile stress was then obtained by dividing the force difference using the net concrete area, $A_t - A_s$. The tensile strains in the fiber concrete were obtained by dividing the elongation (measured through LVDTs) by the gauge length of each zone (= 250 mm).

3.2 Stress-Strain Response Obtained from Large Scale Specimen

Typical tensile load-elongation responses of the composite and bare strand in Zone 3 are shown in Figure 5a. Stress-strain response of the HPFRCC material were obtained based on Equation 1 and plotted in Figure 5b, along with an envelope curve. The unloading loops were the result of softening of the hydraulic jack during crack measurement and photographing. Figure 5 shows that the HPFRCC used in this study exhibited tensile strain-hardening behavior up to 0.7% composite strain, along with extensive multiple cracking as shown in Figure 8b. The stress-strain curve is generally very stable without any sudden degradation in strength. This can be attributed to the presence of the longitudinal reinforcement, which was able to redistribute tensile stress through bond when cracks occurred.

Figure 6 shows the relation between average concrete tensile strain versus average crack number (within the range of 250 mm) and average crack width based on the measurements from Zones 1 thru 5. It was observed that generally there were one or two primary cracks in each zone, which have wider width than the remainder cracks. The width of a primary crack was measured by an 8X magnifier with a minimum reticle scale of 0.05 mm. Although the width of primary cracks increased with the concrete strains, no localization occurred. Additional secondary cracks can still develop and their average crack width was less than 50 μm, even when maximum loading condition (matrix tensile strain of 0.7%) was reached. The residual width of the primary cracks after unloading was generally from 0.05 mm to 0.2 mm. It is noted that the yield strain and strain at onset of strain-hardening of a typical Grade 420 M deformed reinforcing bar are approximately 0.2% and 0.6%, respectively. This signifies that the HPFRCC used in this study can still sustain load with no degradation even when a deformed reinforcing bar has yielded and strain-hardened [7]. This is essential for RC elements, especially when subjected to large inelastic deformation, to prevent earlier degradation due to concrete softening.

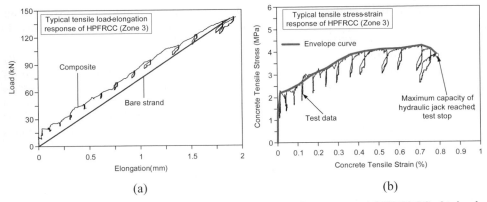

(a)   (b)

Figure 5: Typical tensile load-elongation and stress-strain responses of HPFRCC obtained from large scale tensile test

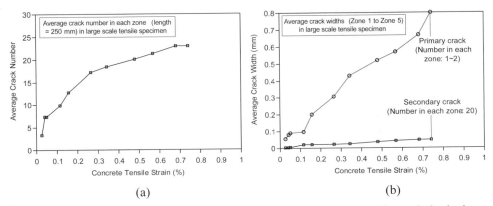

(a)   (b)

Figure 6: Average crack number and width versus average concrete tensile strain in the large scale tensile specimen

3.3 Comparison between Results from Large and Small Scale Specimens

Figure 7 compares the tensile stress-strain responses of small and large scale specimens using the same HPFRC composite. Two observations can be made:

1) The tensile strength (or peak stress) of the small scale specimen is higher than that of the large scale specimen. This can be attributed to scale effects and to the possible two-dimensional versus three-dimensional fiber orientations in each specimen, respectively. Everything else being equal, the tensile capacity of a fiber reinforced cement composite is affected by the fiber orientation. This can be accounted for by a "bridging efficiency" factor, which defines the amount of fibers bridging across a crack with respect to fiber orientation effect. Generally, the 3-D random distribution leads to the lowest bridging efficiency due to loss of fiber bridging when oriented at high angles with respect to the tensile stress direction. Krenchel [8] derived analytically efficiency ratios for 1-D: 2-D: 3-

D fiber distribution leading to numerical values of 1, 0.636, and 0.5, respectively. This translates into a composite tensile capacity ratio of 2-D/3-D = 1.27, which generally agrees with the observation shown in Figure 7.

2) The onset of damage localization as a result of fiber pullout at peak stress is significantly delayed in the presence of continuous reinforcement. Indeed, the tensile strain up to the peak strength in the large scale specimen is more than two times that of the small scale specimen. The smaller strain in the small specimen possibly resulted from the fact that smaller specimens are more sensitive to defects such as non-uniformly distributed fibers and coarse aggregates. In addition, without continuous reinforcement, crack extension is more likely to become unstable during stressing.

It is seen from this study that a small scale tensile specimen with no continuous reinforcement can slightly overestimate the tensile strength and overly underestimate the strain capacity in a conventionally reinforced full scale structural element.

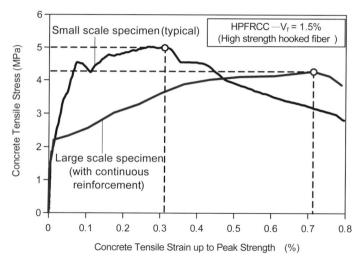

Figure 7: Comparison of stress-strain responses between small and large scale specimens using SCHPFRC mixture [1]

3.4 Crack Distribution

Figure 8 shows the crack distributions in the small and large scale specimens. As can be seen, the specimen with no continuous reinforcement developed a smaller number of cracks before damage localization started; the gauge length was 175 mm. On the other hand, the large scale specimen with continuous reinforcement developed extensive multiple cracks and no significant damage localization was observed up to about 0.8% strain which was the limit of the test set-up. The average visible crack spacing at crack saturation was approximately 10 mm.

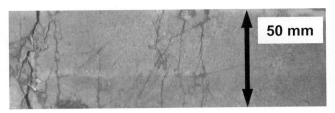

(a) Small scale tensile specimen (dog-bone shaped; gauge length = 175 mm)

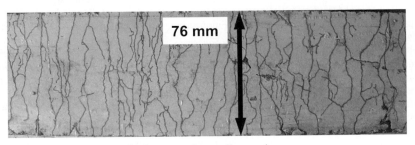

(b) Large scale tensile specimen

Figure 8: Crack distributions in smaller and large scale tensile specimens at the end of tests

4. CONCLUSIONS

1. Direct tensile stress-strain curves of strain-hardening FRC composites are needed for material characterization in structural modelling and applications. However, such curves are very sensitive to scale effects and may be significantly influenced by the presence of conventional reinforcement (such as reinforcing bars or prestressing strands).
2. The use of a large scale tensile specimen allowing three-dimensional fiber distribution and incorporating the presence of continuous reinforcement lead to a stress-strain response more realistic for use in structural elements than a pure tensile test.
3. The procedure described here whereas a long tensile prism is strained through a single concentric prestressing strand is recommended as a reliable method of testing. The advantage of using a prestressing steel tendon as continuous reinforcement is that a strain as high as 0.9% can be applied incrementally while the tendon remains linear elastic, thus allowing a stable environment for loading-unloading and for measurements of crack width and spacing. For higher strain capacity, a carbon bar or a glass bar could also be used, although their bond properties may be different from those of steel bars or strands.
4. The peak tensile strength obtained from small scale specimens was generally higher than that of larger scale specimen.
5. The tensile strain at the onset of damage localization in the large scale specimens where reinforcing strand was used was about twice that observed in the small scale specimens where no reinforcement was used. This leads to a significantly better crack development as well as a significant increase in energy absorption capacity.

ACKNOWLEDGEMENTS

The research described herein was sponsored by the National Science Foundation under Grant No. CMS 0408623 and by the University of Michigan. Their support is gratefully acknowledged. The opinions expressed in this paper are those of the authors and do not necessarily reflect the views of the sponsor.

REFERENCES

[1] Liao, W.-C., Chao, S.-H., Park, S.-Y. and Naaman, A. E., 'Self-Consolidating High Performance Fiber Reinforced Concrete (SCHPFRC)—Preliminary Investigation', Report No. UMCEE 06-02, Department of Civil and Environmental Engineering, University of Michigan, Ann Arbor, MI, 2006.

[2] Fields, K. and Bischoff, P. H., 'Tension Stiffening and Cracking of High-Strength Reinforced Concrete Tension Members', ACI Structural Journal, **101** (4), July-August, (2004) 447-456.

[3] Naaman, A. E., 'Prestressed Concrete Analysis and Design—Fundamentals', 2nd Edn (Techno Press 3000, 2004), Ann Arbor, Michigan, 1072 pp.

[4] Chao, S.-H., Naaman, A. E. and Parra-Montesinos, G. J., 'Bond Behavior of Strands Embedded in Fiber Reinforced Cementitious Composites', PCI Journal, **51** (6), November-December. (2006), Precast/Prestressed Concrete Institute, 56-71.

[5] Sujivorakul, C., and Naaman, A.E., 'Tensile Response of HPFRC Composites Using Twisted Polygonal Steel Fibers', in Innovations in Fiber-Reinforced Concrete for Value, N. Banthia, M. Criswell, P. Tatnall, and K. Folliard, Editors, ACI Special Publication, SP216, American Concrete Institute, 2003, pp. 161-179.

[6] Chandrangsu, K., and Naaman, A.E., 'Comparison of Tensile and Bending Response of Three High Performance Fiber Reinforced Cement Composites', in High Performance Fiber Reinforced Cement Composites (HPFRCC-4), A.E. Naaman and H.W. Reinhardt, Editors, RILEM Publications, Pro. 30, June 2003, pp. 259-274.

[7] Naaman, A.E., and Reinhardt, H.W., 'Proposed Classification of FRC Composites Based on their Tensile Response', Materials and Structures, **39**, page 547-555, 2006. Also, Proceedings of symposium honoring S. Mindess, N. Banthia, Editor, University of British Columbia, Canada, August 2005. Electronic proceedings, 13 pages.

[8] Krenchel, H., 'Fiber Reinforcement', Akademisk Forlag, Copenhagen, Denmark, Engl. Translation (1964).

TENSILE CREEP OF SHCC

William P. Boshoff and Gideon P.A.G. van Zijl

Stellenbosch University, South Africa

Abstract

The possibilities for the use of SHCC as a construction material have attracted the attention of the construction industries world wide due to the superior properties of this material. It shows high ductility in tension which has the ability to absorb orders more energy compared to ordinary concrete. Due to the multiple cracking phenomenon it can improve the durability of the material and so reduce the life cycle cost of a structure.

The micro-mechanical modelling and the structural benefits of SHCC have been the focus of many research groups, but certain important aspects of the material have received little attention, for example the time-dependant properties. The effect of tensile creep and creep fracture have to date not been investigated.

This paper reports on recent research done on the tensile creep and shrinkage of SHCC. Tensile creep tests were done on the macro-level as well as on the single fibre level. The effect of cracking on the creep strain was also investigated. Single fibre pull-out tests were performed to study this important mechanism of time dependence. The results of these tests are presented and the implications for time-dependent behaviour of SHCC discussed.

1.   INTRODUCTION

SHCC (Strain Hardening Cement-based Composites) have become an appealing possibility as a building material in advanced structural systems. SHCC are a special class of HPFRCC (High Performance Fibre Reinforced Cement-based Composites). SHCC have not only received attention from the structural engineering industry, but are also the research focus of many international research groups who are doing fundamental research of the material behaviour and its application.

SHCC is distinguishable from ordinary FRC (Fibre Reinforce Concrete) as it shows steel like pseudo strain-hardening in tension over a significant tensile strain. This phenomenon is achieved by multiple cracking which can result in a strain extension of up to 5 % without softening. This behaviour is achieved by engineering the composite, which consists of cement, cement extenders, aggregates and fibres [1], [2]. An example of the importance of the micro-mechanical tailoring is the adjustment of the surface of PVA fibres when it was introduced to SHCC to ensure this ductile behaviour [3]. Even though FRC has been researched for many decades [4], SHCC development only began recently in the early 1990's [5], [6], [7].

The time-dependant behaviour of any building material, which includes shrinkage, creep and a rate-effect, is an important property that should be understood and quantified. The time-dependant behaviour should be taken into account in the design guidelines for SHCC. Only recently has the rate-effect been investigated [8], [9], [10], [11] but research in the creep and mechanisms causing creep of SHCC is still lacking.

Creep and creep fracture are important phenomena of any cement-based material. Creep fracture can occur after a period of time if a load is applied to the material which is lower than the static ultimate load. Another important uncertainty is the possible loss of ductility when a sustained load is applied. Before these phenomena can be quantified, insight is required in the mechanisms causing this behaviour.

In this paper, results of tensile creep tests as well as shrinkage tests are reported. The aim of these tests was to understand the mechanisms rather than to quantify the phenomena, which is a next step in this research project. Tensile creep tests were done on cracked and uncracked specimens. To further explore the cause of the tensile creep, creep tests were done on fibres and single fibres embedded in the matrix.

2. EXPERIMENTAL PROGRAM

The experimental program to investigate the tensile creep behaviour of SHCC consisted out of four parts. Firstly, tensile creep and shrinkage tests were done to investigate the tensile creep behaviour of uncracked SHCC. Secondly, tensile creep tests were done on specimens that were pre-cracked to gain insight in the creep behaviour of cracked SHCC. A test was also done to investigate the tensile creep of a single fibre. Lastly, single fibre pull-out creep tests were done to determine the influence of the time-dependant fibre pull-out on the tensile creep behaviour of SHCC.

All tests were done using the same mix proportions, namely a water/binder ratio of 0.4 and an aggregate/binder ratio of 0.5. The binder consisted of CEM I 42.5 cement, a fly ash filler marketed as PozzFill by Ash Resources, South Africa, and Corex Slag of origin of the Saldanha Steel Refinery in the Western Cape Province, South Africa used in the ratio of 45:50:5 by mass respectively. A fine sand was used as the aggregate. PVA (Polyvinyl Alcohol) fibres with a length of 12 mm and a 40 μm diameter were added at 2 % by volume. Note that the rheology refinement was achieved by the addition of a superplasticizer and a viscosity modification agent. The cross sectional dimensions of the gauge area of the tensile specimens are 16 mm x 30 mm. All specimens were water cured for 14 days before testing commenced. The complete mixing and casting procedure and the specimen geometry are described in detail in [11].

2.1 Tensile creep and shrinkage

To investigate the tensile creep behaviour of SHCC, tensile creep tests as well as shrinkage tests were done. All the specimens were tested unsealed, so the shrinkage values are required to distinguish which part of the time-dependant strain response of the loaded specimens is creep. It is acknowledged that the true basic creep cannot be calculated using this method of testing unsealed specimens [12], [13] and that the creep values presented in this paper will be specimen size-dependant due to the inclusion of drying creep. The results will however give meaningful insight into the tensile creep behaviour of an uncracked SHCC specimen.

The creep test setup was designed and built to apply the creep load with free hanging weights acting on the specimens with a lever arm. The load is applied to two specimens in series. The setup can be seen in Fig. 1a. Two LVDT's were fixed to an aluminium frame that was clamped over the gauge length of 88 mm to measure the strain, shown in Fig. 2b. The climate room where the tests were performed was controlled to be at a constant temperature of 23±1 °C and a relative humidity of 65±5 %. The shrinkage tests were done by placing the specimens on frictionless rollers.

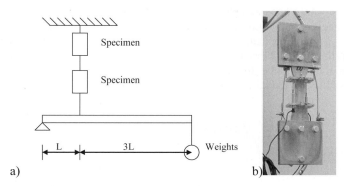

a)   b)

Figure 1: a) The tensile creep test setup. b) The creep specimen in the creep frame with the strain measuring instrument attached.

Two specimens were used for each of the shrinkage and creep tests. The specimens were kept moist using a small brush to ensure that shrinkage did not start before the onset of the test. Al specimens were tested at an age of 14 days. The creep load was chosen at 50 % of the static ultimate load. This ultimate stress was found to be 2.79 MPa for this specific mix and type of specimens tested under the same conditions [11].

2.2   Tensile creep of cracked specimens

The true benefit of SHCC is only utilised after the material has cracked. The creep of a cracked SHCC is thus important as it would be the condition of SHCC in its intended use. For this reason tensile creep tests were done on SHCC specimens that were cracked under controlled conditions before the tensile creep load was applied.

The test setup and procedure is the same as for the tests in Section 2.1, save for the exception that the specimens were loaded to 1 % tensile strain and released before the creep load was applied. The tensile strain was applied using a Zwick Materials Testing Machine using displacement control. Eight specimens were tested in total using four different load levels. The test program is shown in Table 1.

Table 1: Test program for the tensile creep tests on cracked specimens.

Loading as % of ultimate strength	30 %	50 %	70 %	80 %
Actual applied stress [MPa]	0.81	1.32	1.87	2.11
Number of specimens	2	2	2	2

Photographs were taken of the specimens over time to monitor crack growth and the time-dependant widening of the cracks.

2.3 Fibre pull-out creep

To study a possible source of the tensile creep behaviour, creep tests were done on the single fibre level. Single fibres were embedded in the matrix at a specific embedment length. A sustained load was applied to the embedded fibres individually to simulate a creep load.

A schematic representation of the test setup is shown in Fig. 2 and is described in detail in [11]. A series of rate-dependant pull-out tests were done in [11] using the same procedures and mix proportions as for these tests. [11] found that the average interfacial shear resistance, τ_0, which is the pull-out force divided by the interfacial shear area, of the fibres was 2.4 MPa. A creep load of 50 % of the ultimate resistance was chosen.

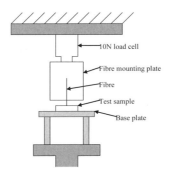

Figure 2: Schematic representation of the single fibre pull-out test setup.

Two sets of creep tests were done. For the one set the creep load was applied to the fibres and sustained. For the other set the fibres were debonded from the matrix before the creep load was applied. The debonding was achieved by pulling the fibre with a constant pull-out rate from the matrix using the actuator until a slight load drop or change of gradient occurs in the force-displacement response. This indicates that the fibre has debonded completely. The test program and the actual embedment lengths for each specimen are shown in Table 2.

Table 2. Test program for the time-dependant fibre pull-out creep tests.

	Debonded tests			Fully bonded tests		
Number of specimens	3			3		
Actual embedment lengths [mm]	1.3	1.3	1.4	1.4	1.5	1.35
Loading, τ_0 [MPa]	1.2 MPa			1.2 MPa		

2.4 Fibre Creep

To investigate the possibility that fibre creep could attribute to the tensile creep of a cracked section, a test was done on a single fibre using a sustained creep load.

The fibre was tested in the setup shown in Fig. 2 with a minor adjustment to include a second fibre mounting plate fixed to the base plate. Due to the possible time-dependant slippage of the fibre-glue interface, the creep extension was measured using a microscope rather than the displacement of the actuator. The fibre diameter of 40 μm was used as a scale for the measurement. A load of 800 MPa was applied to the fibre, i.e. half the fibre capacity.

3.   EXPERIMENTAL RESULTS

3.1   Tensile creep and shrinkage

The measured strain responses of the shrinkage and creep specimens are shown in Fig. 3a. Note that the initial strain that occurred during the load application has been subtracted from the response of the loaded specimens. It is clear that the shrinkage dominated the response. The time-dependant strain response of one of the loaded creep specimens showed a sudden increase after about 4 hours after the commencement of the load. The effect of this sudden increase can be seen in Fig. 3a. The reason for this sudden increase was the formation of a crack. It should also be noted that the creep rate is higher of the specimen that cracked compared to the uncracked specimen.

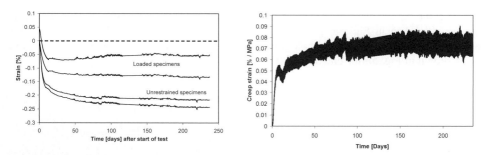

Figure 3: a) Individual creep and shrinkage responses of the uncracked specimens. b) The tensile creep envelope excluding the initial strain.

The shrinkage response is typical for a cement-based material and the shrinkage apparently converges to a value of about 0.23 % after 8 months of monitoring. To find the creep strain, the shrinkage strain needs to be deducted from the strain of the loaded specimens of which the initial strain has already been subtracted. The resulting creep envelope is shown in Fig. 3b. Note that the response of the creep specimen that cracked was discarded for the calculation of the envelope.

3.2   Tensile creep of cracked specimens

The average strain response at each load level of the cracked creep test specimens is shown in Fig. 4a. Note that only for the 30 % load level the shrinkage was dominant. The creep compliance, C_c, also known as the specific creep, can be calculated with:

$$C_c = \frac{\varepsilon_c}{\sigma} \tag{1}$$

with ε_c the creep strain at a given time and σ the applied stress. After the shrinkage values were deducted from the results, the average creep compliance at 8 months was calculated for each load level. These values are shown together with the creep compliance of the uncracked specimens in Fig. 4b.

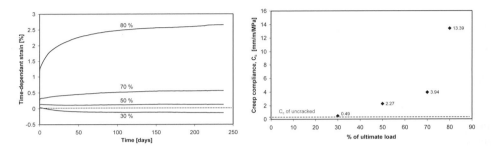

Figure 4: a) The average responses of the cracked creep specimens at different load levels. b) The calculated creep compliance's of the cracked creep specimens.

During the first few hours of the load application, sudden jumps occurred in the strain response as shown in Fig. 5a. It is believed that these jumps indicate the initiation of new cracks. It is however clear from photographs taken that the crack widths increased over time. This is shown in Fig. 5b for one of the 80 % creep specimens.

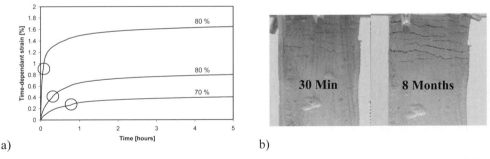

a)   b)

Figure 5: a) Sudden jumps in the response indicating crack formation. b) Photographs showing the increase of crack width over time.

3.3   Fibre pull-out creep

All six the fibres that were under a sustained creep load of 50 % of the static ultimate resistance pulled out completely within 80 hours. The time to failure for each test and the averages for the sets are shown in Fig. 6a.

3.4   Fibre creep

The distance between two points on a fibre was monitored using a microscope over a period of 60 hours. For the creep of the fibre to have any significant influence on the tensile creep of SHCC, there should be at least an increase of 0.5 % of the length during this duration as calculated by [11]. The postulated increase is also shown in Fig. 6b and it is clear that no significant creep of the fibre was found.

4.   DISCUSSION OF RESULTS

A relative large shrinkage value of 0.23 % was found after 8 months. Even though this shrinkage magnitude is alarming, it should not pose a problem in most application of SHCC as the tensile capacity of SHCC is in the order of 5 %, thus the shrinkage strain should be easily absorbed.

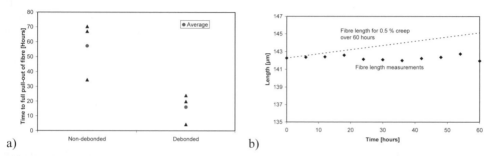

Figure 6: a) Time to complete pull-out of the single fibre pull-out creep tests. b) The length measurements of the fibre creep test with a line to indicate what the response would be if a linear creep of 0.5 % over 60 hours would realise.

In Fig. 3a it is shown that the shrinkage phenomenon clearly dominates the creep behaviour if the material is uncracked and loaded at 50 %. However, if the material is cracked to 1 % tensile strain, the shrinkage only dominates at a load of 30 % as shown in Fig. 4a.

It is important to note that at a creep load of 50 %, the creep strain is about 4 times more if the specimens were pre-cracked to 1 % tensile strain compared to the uncracked specimens. This clearly shows that the creep strain increases with an increase of cracks in a section. This was also confirmed by the uncracked creep tests where a significant increase of creep strain and rate was found after the one creep specimen cracked.

The creep strain of the cracked specimens showed an exponential increase of the creep strain with an increase of the creep level. This clearly shows that the creep of a cracked section is not linearly proportional to the load level, but increases rapidly with an increase of load.

To find the source of the tensile creep strains in a cracked section, creep tests were done on a single fibre level. The fibre itself was shown not to have any significant contribution to the SHCC tensile creep. However, fibres embedded in the matrix did show significant creep when a sustained pull-out force was applied. All the tested specimens pulled out completely in less than 80 hours with a force of half the static pull-out resistance. Fibres that were debonded in the matrix before the start of the creep load showed a higher creep rate. This showed that the source of the increased creep when a specimen is cracked is due to the time-dependant pull-out of the fibres.

A final source of the tensile creep strain is the formation of (further) multiple cracking over time. This phenomenon increases the phenomological tensile creep strain, even though cracking is not commonly considered as a source of creep. This source of time dependence was confirmed with the increase of creep when one of the uncracked creep specimens cracked and is also indicated by the sudden jumps shown in Fig. 5a, the response of the cracked creep tests.

5.   CONCLUSIONS

The mechanisms behind the tensile creep of SHCC was investigated and identified. The following significant conclusions can be drawn:

- Tensile creep of SHCC was found to consist out of three parts, namely the matrix creep, time-dependant fibre pull-out and the formation of (further) multiple cracking over time.
- The creep strain of a cracked SHCC specimen increases exponentially with an increase of the tensile creep load.
- The magnitude of the tensile creep was found to not only be dependant on the load level, but also the number of cracks in the SHCC section.
- The increase of the creep strain of a cracked section compared to an uncracked section can be attributed to the time-dependant fibre pull-out and not to the creep of the fibres.

REFERENCES

[1] Li, V.C., 1998, "Engineered Cementitious Composites - Tailored Composites Through Micromechanical Modeling," in Fiber Reinforced Concrete: Present and the Future edited by N. Banthia, A. Bentur, A. and A. Mufti, Canadian Society for Civil Engineering, Montreal, pp. 64-97.

[2] Li, V. C., Wang, S., Wu, C., 2001, "Tensile Strain-hardening Behavior of PVA-ECC," ACI Materials Journal, Vol. 98, No. 6, pp 483-492.

[3] Li, V. C., Wu, C., Wang, S., Ogawa,. A., Saito, T., 2002, "Interface Tailoring for Strain-hardening PVA-ECC," ACI Materials Journal, Vol. 99, No. 5, pp 463-472.

[4] Hannant, D.J., 1978, "Fibre Cements and Fibre Concretes," John Wiley & Sons, Ltd., New York, United States of America.

[5] Li, V.C., and Wang, Y., and Backer, S., 1990, "Effect of Inclining Angle, Bundling, and Surface Treatment on Synthetic Fiber Pull-Out from a Cement Matrix," J. Composites, Vol. 21, No. 2, pp 132-140.

[6] Li, V.C., 1992, "Post-Crack Scaling Relations for Fiber-Reinforced Cementitious Composties," ASCE J. of Materials in Civil Engineering, Vol. 4, No. 1, pp 41-57.

[7] Li, V. C., 1993, "From Micromechanics to Structural Engineering□ The Design of Cementitious Composites for Civil Engineering Applications," J. Struct. Mech. Earthquake Eng., JSCE, Vol. 10, No. 2, 37-48.

[8] Maalej, M., Quek, S.T., Zhang, J., 2005, "Behaviour of Hybrid-Fibre Engineered Cemetitious Composites Subjected to Dynamic Tensile Loading a Projectile Impact," Journal of Materials in Civil Engineering, ASCE, pp 143-152.

[9] Yang, E., Li, V.C., 2005, "Rate dependence in Engineered Cementitious Composites," Proceedings of HPFRCC Conference, Rilem PRO 49, Hawaii, pp 83-92.

[10] Douglas, K.S., Billington, S.L., 2005, "Rate dependencies in high-performance fibre-reinforced cement-based composites for seismic application," Proceedings of HPFRCC Conference, Rilem PRO 49, Hawaii, pp 17-25.

[11] Boshoff, W.P., 2007, "Time-dependant behaviour of Engineered Cement-based Composites", Dissertation, University of Stellenbosch, South Africa.

[12] Pickett, G., 1942, "The effect of change in moisture content on the creep of concrete under a sustained load," Journal of the ACI, Vol. 38, pp 333-355.
[13] Wittmann, F.G. and Roelfstra, P.E., 1980, "Total deformation of loaded drying concrete," Cement and Concrete Research, Vol. 10, pp 601-610.

BEHAVIOUR OF STRAIN-HARDENING CEMENT-BASED COMPOSITES (SHCC) UNDER REPEATED TENSILE LOADING

Petr Jun and Viktor Mechtcherine

Institute for Building Materials, TU Dresden, Germany

Abstract

This paper presents selected results of an experimental investigation regarding the behaviour of a Strain Hardening Cement-based Composite (SHCC) subjected to cyclic tensile loading. A series of uni-axial tensile tests was performed on unnotched, dog-bone shaped prisms containing 2.25% by volume of polymeric fibre by using various loading regimes, i.e., deformation-controlled monotonic and cyclic loading, as well as a load-controlled cyclic regime. The results obtained from the tests revealed no pronounced effect of the cyclic loading on the material performance. The material stiffness decreased considerably with an increasing number of loading cycles. The crack pattern and crack widths as observed on the specimen's surfaces did not differ significantly for the various loading regimes used.

1.   INTRODUCTION

This paper addresses the group of fibre, reinforced cement-based composites which exhibits strain hardening, quasi-ductile behaviour due to bridging of fine multiple cracks by short, well-distributed fibres. The characteristic behaviour of such Strain-Hardening Cement-based Composites (SHCC) was studied in tension under monotonic, quasi-static loading during the last few years quite intensively; see e.g. [1, 2]. However, in practice, the majority of concrete structures is exposed to more or less severe cyclic loadings such as traffic loads, temperature changes, wind gusts and, in some cases, sea waves, vibrations due to the operation of machinery or, in extreme circumstances, earthquake. Therefore, a profound knowledge of the fatigue behaviour of SHCC is indispensable for a safe and economical design of structural members, as well as building elements for which such materials may be used.

As of yet, only a few investigations on SHCC behaviour under cyclic loading have been performed. Fukuyama et al. [3] investigated the cyclic tension-compression behaviour of two SHCC materials that possessed a strain capacity of 0.5% and 1.0%, respectively; only about five cycles were needed until the strain capacity expired while the cyclic tension response accurately reflected the corresponding curve obtained from a monotonic tension test. In contrast to this result, Douglas and Billington [4] found that the envelop stress-strain curve from the cyclic tests was less than the relationship as measured in the monotonic regime (i.e., cyclic test curve was located below the monotonic curve). This difference was particularly pronounced in experiments with high strain rates. The SHCC investigated showed a strain capacity of approximately 0.5% when subjected to monotonic, quasi-static loading.

Mechtcherine and Jun [5, 6] investigated an SHCC with a strain capacity that was clearly above 2% in all tests. In this investigation, a higher number of loading cycles was used compared to earlier studies. Furthermore, two different types of loading regimes were applied: deformation-controlled (monotonic and cyclic) and load-controlled (cyclic and creep) tests. The effect of additional parameters (i.e., specimen size, curing conditions) was investigated, as well.

This paper presents selected results from the experimental investigation performed to date with the goal to provide a more detailed discussion of the behaviour of material subjected to cyclic tensile loading. As it was shown in the previous publication [5], the curing conditions, as well as varying specimen size, in general, does not significantly alter the effect of the loading type. Therefore, these testing parameters are not considered in this paper.

2. MATERIAL COMPOSITION

SHCC, unlike common fibre reinforced concrete, is a micro-mechanically designed material. The approach for such material design was developed by Li [7] for a composite which he called ECC (Engineered Cementitious Composite). However, a more specific term, SHCC, is used in this paper in conjunction with international research activities conducted in this field.

The SHCC composition used for these experiments is delineated as follows. It was developed in previous investigations by the authors; see e.g. [1]. A mix containing a combination of 42.5 R Portland cement (30% by mass) and fly ash (70% by mass) was utilized as a binder. The fine aggregate consisted of a uniformly, graded silica sand with particle size of 0.06 mm to 0.20 mm. Furthermore, PVA fibres, 2.25% by volume with a length of 12 mm, were applied. A super plasticizer (SP) and a viscosity agent (VA) were added to the mix in order to adjust its rheological properties. Further details are given in Table 1.

Table 1: SHCC composition used for experiments

Cement [kg/m^3]	Fly ash [kg/m^3]	Silica sand [kg/m^3]	Water [kg/m^3]	SP [kg/m^3]	VA [kg/m^3]	PVA fibres [kg/m^3]
321.0	749.1	535.0	334.5	16.6	3.2	29.3

3. TEST SET-UP, TESTING PROCEDURE AND EXPERIMENTAL PROGRAM

3.1 Specimens geometry, casting, curing, set-up

Based on the findings of previous investigations [1, 2], unnotched, dog-bone shaped prisms were chosen as specimens for this study. The prisms possessed a cross-sectional area of 24 mm x 40 mm. The gauge length was 100 mm. Fig. 1 gives further geometric data for the specimens.

All specimens were cast horizontally in metal forms. The moulds were stored 2 days in a climate box (T = 25°C, RH = 65%). The specimens were wrapped in a plastic foil and stored until testing at room temperature after de-moulding. All specimens were tested at a concrete age of 28 to 32 days.

The uni-axial tension tests were performed with non-rotatable boundaries. The deformations were measured by means of two LVDTs fixed to the specimen as displayed in Fig. 1 (one LVDT attached to the front side of the prism and another attached to the rear side). The specimen surfaces were then covered with a thin, brittle white paint in order to facilitate the monitoring of crack development.

a) side view   b) geometry of the specimen

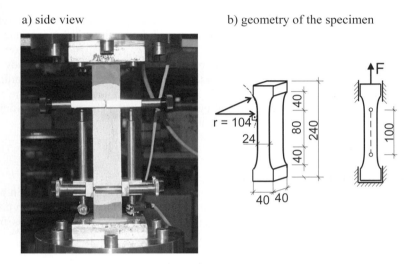

Figure 1: Test set-up used: a) side view and b) geometry of the specimen used for the tensile tests; geometrical data is given in mm

The uni-axial tension test series was followed by a set of compression tests. The compressive strength was derived from 12 displacement controlled tests on cubes with a side length of 100 mm. The average compressive strength of the SHCC was 33.7 MPa. The findings obtained concerning the stress-strain curves and the crack pattern observed will be published elsewhere.

3.2 Testing procedure

Three types of experiments were performed with regard to the loading procedure: 1) monotonic deformation-controlled tests; 2) cyclic deformation-controlled tests; and 3) cyclic load-controlled tests.

The deformation rate was held constant at 0.01 mm/s in the deformation-controlled tests which corresponds to a strain rate of 10^{-4} 1/s for a gauge length of 100 mm. For the deformation-controlled cyclic tests, the increase of the total deformation within the measuring length was given by the deformation increment $\Delta\delta$ which was chosen to equal 0.1 mm; this corresponds to a constant (i.e., from cycle to cycle) strain increment of 0.1%. When the preset value $\Delta\delta$ in the following cycle was reached, the specimen was unloaded until the lower reversal point δ_{min} was attained. The lower reversal point δ_{min} was defined as a function of the lower load level F_{min} = const = 0 N.

In the load controlled cyclic tests, the specimen was first loaded monotonically until the strain value 0.5% was reached. The specimen was then unloaded and subsequently cyclically reloaded in a load control regime with predefined lower and upper load limits. The preloading in the monotonic regime was needed due to an observed presence of a pronounced scatter of the stress at first cracking σ_l. The knowledge of the behaviour of a particular specimen at the onset of cracking allowed for a more purposeful choice of the upper stress limit σ_{up} for cyclic loading. The lower limit was held constant at $F_{min} = 0$ N while the upper limit σ_{up} was chosen under careful consideration of the material behaviour measured during the initial monotonic loading regime.

Since the stress-strain curves under monotonic loading were rather unsteady in this investigation, the choice of the upper limit value σ_{up} was not very straightforward; details pertaining to this can be found in [5].

The load frequency in the load-controlled cyclic tests was 0.5 Hz, i.e., each loading cycle took 2 seconds.

4. EXPERIMENTAL RESULTS

4.1 Behaviour under monotonic loading

The behaviour of SHCC under monotonic tensile loading was studied in detail in previous investigations, e.g., [2]. Therefore, the results from the monotonic tests obtained in this study will be presented and discussed solely as a reference to the corresponding results from the cyclic tests.

4.2 Results of deformation controlled cyclic tests

Fig. 2 shows representative results from deformation-controlled cyclic tests in comparison to the curves obtained using the monotonic loading regime. Both diagrams (Fig. 2, left-hand and right-hand) were obtained under the same testing conditions and are presented here in order to illustrate the observed variability in the curve shape as recorded for individual specimens.

Nearly no relative effect can be observed on the shape of the stress-strain diagram when only considering the envelop curves given the relatively moderate number of loading cycles. The lack of a pronounced distinction in the course of the envelope curve naturally results in only minor differences to the average values of stress at initial cracking σ_l, tensile strength f_t, as well as the strain capacity ε_{tu}, for the various loading regimes; see Table 2.

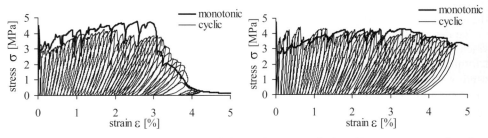

Figure 2: Results representative of the deformation-controlled cyclic tests compared to the curves obtained using monotonic loading

Table 2: Statistical evaluation of the mechanical performance of the SHCC investigated under various loading regimes.

Type of loading	Number of cycles N [-]	Stress at first cracking σ_1 [MPa]	Tensile strength f_t [MPa]	Upper stress (l. con.) σ_{up} [MPa]	Strain capacity ε_{tu} [%]
		Average value (standard deviation)			
		5 specimens per loading type			
Monotonic, deformation-controlled	1	3.6 (0.7)	4.7 (0.3)	-	2.5 (0.8)
Cyclic, deformation-controlled	24 (6)*	3.9 (0.7)	4.3 (0.1)	-	2.4 (0.6)
Cyclic, load-controlled	1840 (1200)	3.4 (0.4)	3.9 (0.2)**	3.4 (0.3)	2.4 (0.3)

* Number of cycles before the material strain capacity is reached
** Values belong to the monotonic curves prior to changing to the load-controlled regime.

The curves obtained from the cyclic tests show characteristic hystereses. From this, it can be clearly recognised that the high strains are, to a great extent, a result of non-elastic deformations (see strains at zero stress). Furthermore, the stiffness of the composite gradually decreases as the inclinations of the hysteresis curves decline with regard to the strain axis.

Table 3 provides values of the secant modulus of elasticity for several chosen strain levels. As the strain level is gradually increased from 0.5% to 3.0%, tests indicate a very pronounced decrease of the secant modulus of elasticity by approximately a factor of four.

Table 3: Change of SHCC stiffness with increasing induced strain levels as observed in deformation-controlled cyclic tests

Strain under load [%]	Secant modulus E [GPa] average value (standard deviation)
0.5	20.4 (3.1)
1.0	14.3 (2.7)
1.5	10.8 (2.2)
2.0	8.0 (1.5)
3.0	5.1 (1.4)

4.3 Results of load-controlled cyclic tests

Fig. 3 presents two of the stress-strain curves obtained from load-controlled cyclic tests. After switching to the load-controlled regime at the strain of 0.5%, the individual hysteresis curves lie in close proximity to one another and are not easily recognizable given the scale used. The shape of individual hystereses for a chosen strain level is presented and discussed in Section 4.4. On average, 1840 load cycles were needed to bring the specimen to failure.

The strain capacity was practically the same in this series as in both the monotonic and the deformation-controlled cyclic tests (see also Table 2).

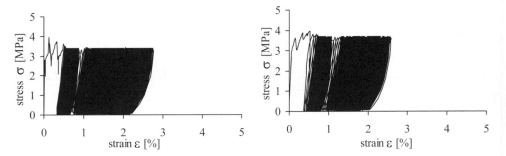

Figure 3: Representative stress-strain curves from the load-controlled cyclic tests

Table 4 gives values of the secant modulus of elasticity for several chosen strain levels. A pronounced decrease of the material stiffness can be seen in all tests. The degree of the stiffness reduction is, however, smaller than that obtained in the deformation-controlled cyclic tests (cf. Table 3).

Table 4: Statistical evaluation of the load-controlled tests - the secant modulus of elasticity

Strain under load [%]	Secant modulus E [GPa] average value (standard deviation)
0.5	17.1 (5.7)
1.0	13.6 (1.3)
1.5	9.9 (1.0)
2.0	7.5 (0.8)

4.4 Shape of the hystereses in the cyclic tests

In previous sections, the secant modulus of elasticity was presented and discussed as an appropriate measure for the change of SHCC stiffness those results from repeated loading. The shape of the individual hystereses of the stress-strain curves is another feature characterising the material response. This feature will be considered here for both cyclic loading regimes.

Fig. 4 shows representative shapes of the chosen individual cycles obtained from deformation-controlled and load-controlled tests of the prisms used. These cycles are numbered according to their succession. In both types of tests, material stiffness gradually decreases while the hysteresis loops become wider and rounder. The change of the loop shape is more pronounced for deformation-controlled tests due to the fact that these curves contain a considerable portion of in-elastic deformation that increases as the number of loading cycles increases. In contrast to this, only a very small portion of in-elastic deformation was recorded for individual hysteresis loops in the load-controlled cyclic tests. Therefore, the SHCC behaviour in the individual load cycles can be described as nearly non-linear elastic.

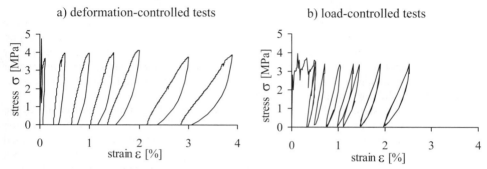

Figure 4: Representative shapes of the individual cycles chosen as obtained from
a) deformation-controlled and b) load-controlled tests

4.5   Comparison of the crack system

Development of the cracks on the specimen's surfaces was monitored during the tests; a number of high resolution digital photographs was taken at given strain levels and visually evaluated afterwards. Only cracks that propagated throughout the specimen were taken into account; no crack branches or one-sided cracks were taken into consideration. Statistical evaluation of the crack numbers observed in the different types of tests at the respective strain levels of 0.5%, 1.0% and 2.0% is presented in Table 5.

Table 5: Crack number comparison

Type of loading	Strain ε [%]	Number of cracks n [-] average values (stand. deviation)
monotonic	0.5	no record
	1.0	8 (2)
	2.0	12 (3)
cyclic, deformation controlled	0.5	4 (0)
	1.0	6 (1)
	2.0	9 (1)
cyclic, load controlled	0.5	5 (1)
	1.0	8 (2)
	2.0	12 (2)

Basically, the number of cracks increases with increasing strain level while the average and maximum crack widths become slightly larger. Generally, the values do not differ much with regard to the loading regime. On average, the deformation-controlled cyclic tests provided fewer cracks with slightly larger crack openings in comparison to the other two types of tests conducted. More testing is needed in order to prove if this difference is statistically significant.

5. CONCLUSIONS

The following conclusions can be drawn about the effect of the loading regime on the performance of SHCC from the test results obtained.

In the deformation-controlled regime, the repeated loading caused a decrease in the tensile strength of SHCC compared with the results from the monotonic tests. However, there was no pronounced effect on the strain capacity of the material for the relatively small number of loading cycles applied. Further experiments are needed in order to study the influence of a larger number of loading cycles on the material behaviour. The repeated loading in the load-controlled regime did not affect the strain capacity of SHCC.

The analysis of hystereses of the stress-strain curves showed a pronounced decrease of the material stiffness with an increasing number of loading cycles; the hysteresis loops became wider, as well. The hystereses obtained from the deformation-controlled cyclic tests revealed a considerable inelastic deformation portion in every loop. The load-controlled cyclic tests provided loop shapes which contained only minimal inelastic portions; however, due to a large number of load cycles in these tests, the accumulated inelastic deformations were comparable to those obtained from the deformation-controlled tests for the same strain levels.

The number of cracks, as well as the crack widths, as observed on the specimen's surfaces did not vary much given the different loading conditions.

REFERENCES

[1] Mechtcherine, V. and Schulze, J., 'Ultra-ductile concrete – Material design concept and testing', Ultra-ductile concrete with short fibres – Development, Testing, Applications, V. Mechtcherine (ed.), (ibidem-Verlag, Stuttgart: 11-36, 2005).

[2] Mechtcherine, V. and Schulze, J., 'Testing the behaviour of strain hardening cementitious composites in tension', Int. RILEM Workshop on HPFRCC in Structural Applications, Honolulu, May 2005, G. Fischer & V. C. Li (eds.), (RILEM Publications S.A.R.L., PRO 49: 37-46, 2006).

[3] Fukuyama, H. and Haruhiko, S. and Yang, I., 'HPFRCC Damper for Structural Control', Proceedings of the JCI International Workshop on Ductile Fiber Reinforced Cementitious Composites (DFRCC), Japan Concrete Institute: 219-228, (Takayama, Japan, 2002).

[4] Douglas, K.S. and Billington, S.L., 'Rate-dependence in high-performance fiber-reinforced cement-based composites for seismic applications', Int. RILEM Workshop on HPFRCC in Structural Applications, Honolulu, May 2005, G. Fischer & V. C. Li (eds.), (RILEM Publications S.A.R.L., PRO 49: 17-26, 2006).

[5] Mechtcherine, V. and Jun, P., 'Stress-strain behaviour of strain-hardening cement-based composites (SHCC) under repeated tensile loading', 6. Int. Conference on Fracture Mechanics of Concrete Structures, FRAMCOS-6, (Catania, Italy, 2007), accepted for publication.

[6] Jun, P. and Mechtcherine, V., 'Behaviour of strain-hardening cement-based composites (SHCC) under cyclic tensile loading', 5. Int. Conference on Concrete under Severe Conditions CONSEC'07, (Tours, France, 2007), accepted for publication.

[7] Li, V. C., 'From micromechanics to structural engineering – The design of cementitious composites for civil engineering applications', JSCE J. of Struc. Mechanics and Earthquake Engineering. 10 (2): 37-48, (1993).

INFLUENCE OF SHORT FIBRES ON STRENGTH, DUCTILITY AND CRACK DEVELOPMENT OF TEXTILE REINFORCED CONCRETE

Marcus Hinzen and Wolfgang Brameshuber

Institute of Buildings Materials Research (ibac), RWTH Aachen University, Germany

Abstract

Nowadays thin-walled load bearing structures can be realised using textile reinforced concrete. The required tensile strength is achieved by embedding several layers of textile. By means of the laminating technique the number of textile layers that can be included into the concrete could be increased. To further increase serviceability and load bearing capacity and to optimise the crack development, fine grained concrete mixes with short fibres can be used. Within the scope of this study, the influence of short fibres made of steel, glass, carbon and synthetics on the stress-strain curve of tensile specimens was investigated. Therefore examinations of concrete specimens with solely textile layers and with solely short fibres as well as with combinations of both were carried out. The paper presents the results of these examinations and describes the effect of short fibres on strength, crack development and ductility of textile reinforced concrete.

1.   INTRODUCTION

The positive properties of steel, glass or polypropylene fibres at the application in concrete have often been emphasised in literature [1, 2, 3]. The more special types of short fibres as carbon, aramid and polyvinyl alcohol (PVA) have so far been considered to a lesser extend. Above all, however, due to their special properties, the fine grained concrete mixes developed within the scope of the Collaborative Research Centre 532 necessitate a re-examination of all fibres mentioned. Here, the main focus is directed on the positive properties of the short fibres at a simultaneous use of glass fabrics. After the first crack of the matrix, customary textile reinforced tensile specimens feature a crack formation phase with small increases in load and high strains. After the load has been completely transferred to the textile, the load is increased until the textile fails (Fig. 2). It is the aim to improve this brittle material behaviour of textile reinforced concrete precisely in the area of the crack formation by means of a more ductile fibre reinforced fine grained concrete mix. In preceding examinations on the influence of short fibres on the fine grained concrete properties [4], the strength-improving effect as well as an improvement of the post-cracking behaviour could be demonstrated in bending tests. The findings obtained, however, can be transferred to a uniaxial tensile test only in a limited way. As such examinations are rather time consuming, in the present paper only fibres are examined which yielded good results in preliminary tests [4]. To describe the influence of the single fibres on the properties of the textile reinforced concrete, first, the stress-strain relations of tensile specimens are presented which contain either only textiles or only short fibres or a combination of both. In doing so, the influence of the short fibres on a higher strength, an improved crack formation and a better ductility shall be considered.

2. EXPERIMENTAL PROGRAMME

2.1. Materials, mixes and specimens

The fine grained concrete mix used in the tensile specimen tests is based on a standard mix developed in the Collaborative Research Centre 532 [5]. Basically, the mixes feature a very flowable consistency which is yielded by the application of a maximum grain size of 0.6 mm, a high binder content as well as different pozzolanic additives and superplasticisers. In the basic mix applied here, the binder content was further increased to yield a better workability and the content of silica fume was increased to improve the contact area between fibre and matrix. The mix proportions of the basic mix without fibres as well as the compressive and the flexural strength are shown in Table 1.

Table 1: Basic mix proportions and mechanical properties

Mix components	Unit	Amount
Cement CEM I 52.5 N		700
Fly ash		150
Silica fume	kg/m^3	150
Water		400
Quartz powder		218
Sand		384
Superplasticiser	% by mass of binder content	0.37[*] / 0.75[*]
Binder content	kg/m^3	1000
w/b ratio	-	0.4
Compressive strength f_c (7d)	N/mm^2	53
Flexural strength $f_{ct,fl}$ (7d)		8.2

* depending on the type of short fibres

In comparison to the previous examinations [4], the number of short fibres to be examined could be reduced considerably. It became obvious that carbon fibres with a length of 3 mm can very effectively be applied to increase the first crack load in a bending test. Furthermore, the water dispersible glass fibres and the PVA fibres displayed the best crack forming properties. In the range of macro-fibres the choice could be reduced to steel and aramid fibres, respectively, which both led to a good post-cracking behaviour in bending tests. A survey of the fibres applied here is given in Table 2. As textile reinforcement, a bi-directional alkali resistant (AR) glass fabric with a cross sectional area of 71.65 mm^2/m in the longitudinal direction was applied (Figure 1(a)). The investigations were conducted on dog bone shaped tensile specimens with a cross sectional area of 10 x 60 mm^2 and a length of 500 mm (Figure 1(b)). Five short fibre mixes which are compiled in Table 3 resulted from the combination of the basic mix and the respective short fibre type. With the exception of the carbon fibres, a fibre content of 2 % by volume was added. For reasons of workability, the carbon fibre content had to be reduced. A content of 0.6 % by volume was determined in preliminary tests and yielded good results at a workability comparable to the 2 % mixes. Of all short fibre concretes tensile specimens with and without textiles were produced. In addition, reference samples with textile and the basic mix without short fibres were produced.

Table 2: Fibre types and properties

Fibre	Type	Dimensions			E	Tensile Strength	Density
		L	D	Geometry			
		mm	μm		N/mm^2	N/mm^2	g/cm^3
S	Steel	12.7	175	Straight	210000	2200	7.85
A	Aramid	20	12	Straight, strands	73000	3400	1.39
G	Glass	6	20	Straight, water dispersible	72000	1700	2.68
C	Carbon	3	7	Straight, water dispersible	238000	3950	1.79
P	PVA[*]	8	40	Straight	42000	1600	1.3

* Polyvinyl alcohol

Table 3: Short fibre mixes

Name	FC-2S	FC-2A	FC-2G	FC-2P	FC-0.6C
Fine grained concrete	Basic mix (Table 1)				
Fibre material	Steel (S)	Aramid (A)	Glass (G)	PVA (P)	Carbon (C)
Content in % by vol.	2	2	2	2	0.6

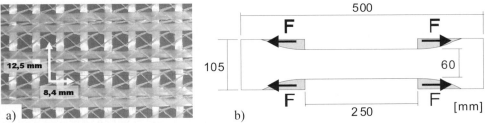

Figure 1: (a) Applied AR glass fabric of the Institut für Textiltechnik, RWTH Aachen University, Germany; (b) test specimen with dimensions and load introduction

2.2. Production and execution of the test

All mixes were mixed in a mortar mixer for 5 minutes. At the mixes containing short fibres, the short fibres were stirred in during a mixing break. All specimens were produced horizontally. At the specimens produced without textiles, the mixes containing short fibres were cast into the formwork and properly screeded. Specimens containing textiles were produced with the so-called laminating technique. Here, layers of fine grained concrete and textile are alternately rolled into the framework until the requested amount of layers is reached. Two layers of textile were used at the specimens examined here which corresponds to a reinforcement content of 10.8 mm^2 in the cross section. All test specimens were cured at a temperature of 20°C and a relative humidity of 95 % for 24 hours. Afterwards, they were sealed and stored for 26 days at 20°C. One day before testing, the specimens were prepared and stored at 20°C and 65 % RH. The tests were carried out on a universal testing machine controlled by cross-head displacement at a rate of 1 mm/min. The axial load was applied in the waist shaped area of the test specimens. The force was measured by a load cell and the elongation by one inductive gauge on each side.

3.   RESULTS AND DISCUSSION

In the following the stress-strain curves of all five short fibre concretes are demonstrated in Fig. 2. They each comprise the stress-strain curve of the reference specimen containing only two layers of AR glass, the stress-strain curves of the short fibre concretes without textile as well as the stress-strain curves of the specimens with the short fibre mixes and textile. Additionally, the calculated cumulative curve of the specimens containing solely textile and solely short fibres are drawn to demonstrate possible synergy effects at the experimental stress-strain curves of specimens containing textile and short fibres. As a matter of course a comparison of both curves is only valid after the first crack of the concrete.

3.1. Influence on strength

In Fig. 2 it becomes obvious that the maximum strengths of the specimens with a simultaneous application of textile and short fibres in the case of steel, aramid and PVA fibres range above the sum of the single strengths of textile reinforced concrete and fibre reinforced concrete. Thus, in these cases synergy effects become apparent. This was not the case at the glass and carbon fibres. As the maximum strength is generally determined by the amount of textile layers at a textile reinforced concrete, strength increasing effects induced by short fibres play a rather inferior role at the final strength. At the increase of the first crack load of the concrete, however, they gain importance as with textiles, at least with a small amount of layers, an increase in the first crack load is not to be expected [6]. At the modified fine grained concrete mix applied here, initially a reduced first crack load in the uniaxial tensile test occurred in the examinations compared to the basic mix presented by Brockmann [5]. Presumably, this has to be ascribed to a higher notch sensitivity due to the higher binder content and to micro cracks induced by shrinkage. In most cases, however, this disadvantage could be balanced by the addition of short fibres. Nevertheless, the mix applied will be further optimised in the future.

Apart from the aramid and the PVA fibres, the first crack load could be improved with all short fibre types and be raised to the expected level of about 4 N/mm^2 ($\hat{=}$ 2.4 kN). In general, the first crack load of the concrete is mainly increased by high-modulus micro-fibres as e. g. glass or carbon. At high fibre contents, however, it can also be increased by macro-fibres with a very high Young's Modulus as e. g. steel. In the case of the aramid fibres, both properties are less distinct and PVA has a relatively low Young's Modulus. In comparison, despite the reduced fibre content, the carbon fibres were highly efficient because they met both criteria. Surprisingly good results were shown by the glass fibres at the increase of the first crack load in the uniaxial tensile test. In preceding bending tests [4] glass fibres had yielded worse results compared to carbon fibres. At the combination of short fibres and textile, the first crack load could further be increased compared to the first crack load of the mere short fibre concrete. Assuming that two layers of textile do not increase the first crack load of the concrete [6], synergy effects between textile and short fibres thus become apparent at these fibre types concerning the first crack load.

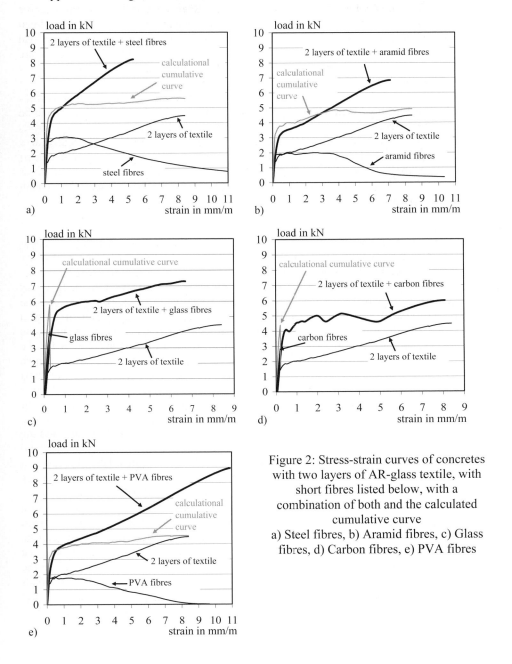

Figure 2: Stress-strain curves of concretes with two layers of AR-glass textile, with short fibres listed below, with a combination of both and the calculated cumulative curve
a) Steel fibres, b) Aramid fibres, c) Glass fibres, d) Carbon fibres, e) PVA fibres

3.2. Influence on ductility

The positive influence of the short fibre reinforced fine grained concrete mixes becomes particularly obvious at the post-cracking behaviour of the specimens. All stress-strain curves of the short fibre and simultaneously textile reinforced specimens exceed the calculational cumulative curve of both single curves in large areas. Thus, not only an increase in the load level and the ductility is possible due to the addition of short fibres and textile, but there are also synergy effects beyond that when comparing overall strains. This behaviour is particularly distinct at the carbon and glass fibres. Although both types of fibres failed in a brittle way during the test at relatively small strains, their effect in combination with textiles seems to last considerably longer (Fig. 2). In the case of the steel and aramid fibres, it can be assumed that these fibres take part in the load transfer also at high strains. At the PVA fibres, despite their own very low load level, the strength can be increased significantly at a combination with the textile. In the area of the crack formation, it becomes obvious that, apart from the carbon fibres, the gradient of the curves becomes smoother with all types of fibres which is also reflected in a finer crack formation (Chapter 3.3). As expected, an improvement could not be yielded with carbon fibres in this place due to the brittleness of the fibres.

3.3. Influence on crack development

At the application of glass fibre textiles or short fibres very small crack widths may occur in the concrete which are invisible to the naked eye. A visualisation of the cracks by humidifying the specimen with water did not show satisfactory results in all cases due to the different surface conditions of the specimens. Therefore, a dye penetration method was applied which also furnished good results at Jesse [6]. According to this, before testing, the specimens were coated with a thin, brittle layer of lacquer which was wiped off with a pigmented ink after the test. After the cleaning of the smooth surface, pigments remain in the cracks showing the crack pattern. The results are demonstrated in Fig. 3 and Fig. 4 for the reference specimen with two layers of AR glass as well as for the specimens which additionally contain short fibres. The crack pattern of the reference specimen without short fibres showed crack distances of 8 – 15 mm. This crack behaviour could not be further improved by the additional application carbon fibres. This was to be expected, as, due to their brittle fracture behaviour, the carbon fibres fail as a rule with the first crack of the concrete. With a Young's modulus of 42000 N/mm^2, the PVA fibres feature the lowest stiffness and the first cracks are formed by the stiffer textile. However, PVA fibres have a high chemical bond to the matrix and can participate in the load introduction at higher strains. For this reason, a very good crack pattern could be achieved with crack distances of 1 – 2 mm. With a Young's modulus of 73000 N/mm^2, the aramid fibres have the same stiffness as the textile and thus can take part in the load introduction. The thereby shortened load introduction length led to a decrease in the crack distance to 3 – 6 mm. The application of steel fibres led to similar crack distances. Due to the significantly higher Young's modulus, smaller crack widths can be expected at the steel fibres than at the aramid fibres. More detailed examinations of the crack width are presently not available. Similar to the aramid fibres, the glass fibres feature the same stiffness as the textile. Owing to their small diameter and the large bond area the loads can be introduced into the concrete in an even shorter way. Thus, along with the water dispersible glass fibres, crack distances of less than 1 mm could be reached.

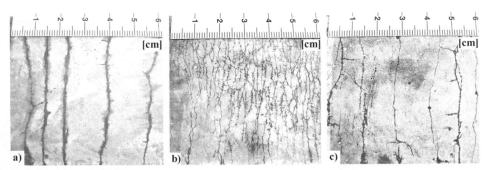

Figure 3: (a) Crack pattern of a specimen with two layers of textile; (b) with additionally 2 % by vol. of PVA fibres; (c) with additionally 0.6 % by vol. of carbon fibres

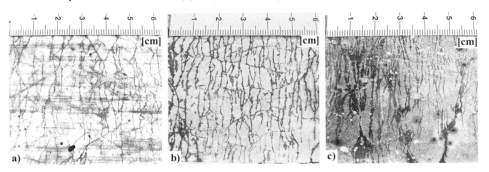

Figure 4: (a) crack pattern of a specimen with two layers of textile and additionally 2 % by vol. of aramid fibres; (b) with additionally 2 % by vol. of steel fibres; (c) with additionally 2 % by vol. of glass fibres

4.   CONCLUSIONS

The present paper shows the positive influence of short fibres on the serviceability and the load bearing capacity of textile reinforced concrete. With the exception of the carbon fibres, all short fibres could improve the ductility in the area of the load transfer from the concrete to the textile. Additionally, the crack pattern could be improved significantly with glass, aramid, PVA and steel fibres. When comparing overall strains, all fibre types seem to entail synergy effects at the ductility in the post-cracking area. Except for the aramid and PVA fibres, all fibres could contribute towards an increase in the first crack load. In principle, the maximum strength could be increased by the addition of short fibres. Beyond that, there were synergy effects at the maximum strength in the case of steel, aramid and PVA fibres.

REFERENCES

[1]   Banthia, N.; Soleimani, S.M.: Flexural Response of Hybrid Fiber-Reinforced Cementitious Composites. In: ACI Materials Journal 102 (2005), Nr. 6, pp 382-389
[2]   Butler, M.; Hempel, R.; Schiekel, M.: The Influence of Short Glass Fibres on the Working Capacity of Textile Reinforced Concrete. Bagneux: RILEM, 2006. - In: Textile Reinforced

Concrete. Proceedings of the 1st International RILEM Symposium, Aachen, 6./7. September 2006, (Hegger, J. ; Brameshuber, W. ; Will, N. (Eds.)), pp 45-54

[3]   Markovic, I.; Walraven, J.C.; Mier van, J.G.M.: Development of High Performance Hybrid Fibre Concrete. Bagneux: RILEM, 2003. - In: Fourth International Workshop on High Performance Fiber Reinforced Cement Composites (HPFRCC4), Ann Arbor, USA, June, 15-18, 2003, (Naaman, A.E. ; Reinhardt, H.W. (Eds.)), pp 277-300

[4]   Hinzen, M.; Brameshuber, W.: Hybrid Short Fibres in Fine Grained Concrete. Bagneux: RILEM, 2006. - In: Textile Reinforced Concrete. Proceedings of the 1st International RILEM Symposium, Aachen, 6./7. September 2006, (Hegger, J. ; Brameshuber, W. ; Will, N. (Eds.)), pp 23-32

[5]   Brameshuber, W.; Brockmann, T.: Development and Optimization of Cementitious Matrices for Textile Reinforced Elements. London: Concrete Society, 2001. - In: Proceedings of the 12th International Congress of the International Glassfibre Reinforced Concrete Association, Dublin, 14-16 May 2001, pp 237-249

[6]   Jesse, F.: Tragverhalten von Filamentgarnen in zementgebundener Matrix. Dresden, Technische Universität, Fakultät Baunigenieurwesen, Dissertation, 2004

HYBRID-FIBER REINFORCED CEMENT COMPOSITES: MODELING ISSUES

John E. Bolander, Sri Ramya Duddukuri and Zhen Li

Dept. Civil and Environmental Engineering, University of California, Davis, USA

Abstract

The potential benefits of hybrid-fiber reinforced cement composites (hybrid-FRCC) are evident in previous experimental work. The benefits include improved strength and toughness of the material, which can lead to thinner and lighter structural members, and improved durability performance. In materials composed of both macro- and microfibers, the different fiber types play fundamentally different roles. It is thought that microfibers improve tensile strength by restraining microcrack growth and coalescence; macrofibers improve material toughness by maintaining stress transfer mechanisms over larger crack openings. Conventional experimental techniques provide only a partial understanding of the individual and combined actions of each fiber type. Model-based simulation can be used to complement knowledge gained through experimentation.

This paper discusses some basic issues related to modeling hybrid-FRCC. Approaches that explicitly represent the individual fibers in the composite are favored. Key benefits of such an approach are the abilities to directly account for fiber distribution effects and discriminate between the actions of each fiber type during fracture development

1.   INTRODUCTION

Hybrid-FRCC materials are potentially stronger, tougher and/or more economical relative to designs based on monofiber reinforcement. The combined use of multiple fiber types in concrete was introduced two decades ago [1] and is a current topic in the cement composites literature [2-5]. The performance optimization of hybrid fiber composites is more difficult, due to the additional design parameters associated with multiple fiber types. Numerical modeling can be used to supplement experimental results for the optimization of material properties.

Of the many potential fiber combinations, micro/macro-fiber combinations are of special interest. The categorization of fibers as either micro- or macrofibers is generally based on fiber diameter. Microfibers have diameters on the scale of the cement grains, whereas macrofibers have significantly larger diameters. This paper discusses some of the objectives and modeling issues for micro/macro hybrid-FRCC. Modeling the tensile behavior is of primary importance, as many other properties directly follow or can be inferred from material response to tensile loading.

2.   MICRO/MACRO-FIBER COMPOSITES

A large number of microfibers are needed to achieve ordinary volume fractions due to their small diameter and relatively small length. When properly dispersed throughout the material domain, and strongly bonded to the cement-based matrix, microfibers are effective in restricting microcrack growth, which is the precursor to macrocrack formation and strength loss. Experimental work has shown significant improvements in strength through the introduction of microfibers. However, the extent of load transfer across developing cracks is limited by the fiber length and thus microfiber composites generally provide less toughness, in comparison with materials reinforced with macrofibers. Whereas microfibers are often straight, the geometry of macrofibers is often modified to improve mechanical bonding.

From that perspective, micro- and macrofibers have been used within the same mix to improve both strength and toughness. Van Mier [5] describes four stages in the tensile response of fiber reinforced cement composites, including hybrid-FRCC:

- elastic behavior prior to microcrack growth or formation;

- stable microcracking;

- distributed macrocrack formation and growth; and

- fracture localization resisted by fiber bridging and pullout.

During the latter stages of the response curve, microfibers provide both direct and indirect contributions to fracture resistance [4]. Direct contributions include bridging actions across cracks that are loading. Indirect contributions include improving the pullout performance of macrofibers. For example, microfibers improve the confinement provided by the matrix, thus fostering full plastic deformation of hooked ends of steel fibers during pullout.

3.   SEVERAL MODELING ISSUES

Many of the basic mechanisms of fracture in hybrid-FRCC have been identified and are understood in a qualitative sense. To support material design and optimization for target applications, however, better quantitative understanding is needed at, and between, the various scales of interest. Progress can be made through numerical modeling, as a complement to physical experimentation. Models of fiber reinforced composite materials can be roughly categorized into: 1) macromodels that represent the effects of fiber additions in an average sense; and 2) micromechanical models in which the fibers and their interactions with the cement-based matrix are explicitly represented. Recognizing that each approach has advantages and disadvantages, the following discussions favor the second of these two modeling approaches.

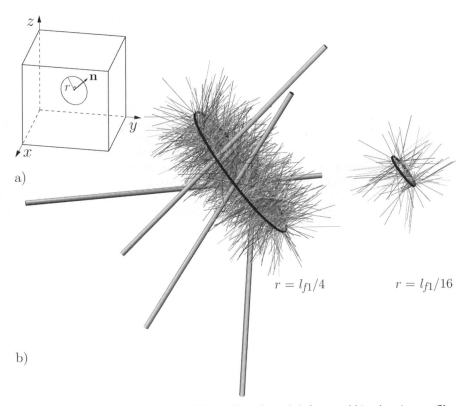

Figure 1: a) Material volume containing a disc-shaped defect; and b) micro/macrofiber combinations that bridge defects of differing size

3.1 Explicit modeling of fibers

The primary advantages of modeling each fiber as a discrete entity include: 1) quantitative linkage between properties defined at the fiber scale and composite performance measures, such as strength, toughness, and permeability; and 2) for hybrid-FRCC, the ability to discriminate between the actions of each fiber type.

Figure 1a shows a material volume with a disc-shaped defect, defined by its center coordinates, radius r, and surface-normal direction $\mathbf{n}$. Consider one of the hybrid-FRCC materials tested by Lawler et al. [3], which contains steel macrofibers (length $l_{f1} = 30$ mm; diameter $d_1 = 0.5$ mm; volume fraction $V_{f1} = 0.5\%$) and steel microfibers ($l_{f2} = 6$ mm; $d_2 = 22$ μm; $V_{f2} = 0.5\%$). Both fiber types are distributed throughout the material volume using pseudo-random numbers to define the fiber centroid coordinates and axis orientation. Fiber placement respects the domain boundaries, and fiber-fiber intersection is avoided, but the other potential effects of segregation and fiber interaction (e.g. clumping) are not included. For the larger defect size of $r = l_{f1}/4$, both micro- and macrofibers bridge the flaw surfaces (Fig. 1b). For the smaller defect size of $r = l_{f1}/16$, the defect surfaces are bridged only by microfibers. These figures are useful in illustrating, for the same volume fraction of each fiber type, the dramatic differences in the number of fibers and their dispersion within the material volume. The explicit representation of fibers [6, 7] enables a more direct accounting for these types of differences and their associated effects on fracture.

The nature of fiber-matrix bond is central to the performance of FRCC and thus the effects of fiber geometry are another important issue. Straight, smooth fibers are easiest to model in that their pullout from the matrix can be described in terms of the constitutive properties of the interface [8], embedded length, fiber angle to the crack surface, and so forth. However, steel macrofibers generally have hooked ends, or some other form of geometric variation, and much of the energy consumption during pullout is associated with plastic deformation of those features. As noted above, the inclusion of microfibers improves fracture resistance both directly, through the pinning of microcracks and the bridging of opening macrocracks, and indirectly by improving the confining actions of the matrix about such macrofibers. Whereas models that explicitly represent fibers seem particularly well suited for simulating these phenomena, the effects of variations in fiber geometry are difficult to model.

3.2   Material component distribution effects

Prior to in-service loading, various defects are present due to the methods of processing, early age cracking due to hygral and/or thermal gradients, and other factors inherent to cement-based materials. In addition, processing methods affect the spatial and orientation distributions of the various inclusions, including fibers. It is possible to obtain three-dimensional descriptions of material structure using, for example, computed x-ray tomography. Numerical models can utilize such information, including initial defect distributions and their evolution under loading, in two ways: 1) forward analyses by which composite performance is simulated using a relevant set of microstructural properties; and 2) inverse analyses by which microstructural properties are determined from other appropriate measurements. Computational inverse techniques are of current interest, since many important microstructural properties are difficult to measure in situ.

The distributions of fibers in cement composites are generally non-uniform due to boundary effects, segregation, fiber-fiber interactions, and various effects of the production process. Simulations and experiments have shown that regions with fewer and/or unfavorably aligned fibers act as defects within the loaded composite [6, 9]. If defects are regarded as initial (or developing) cracks that are not pinned by fibers, then the smallest maximum defect size is achieved with uniformly distributed fibers. With hybrid-FRCC, the degree of non-uniformity of the component distributions can be different, depending on the fiber. The macroscopic notions of volume fraction and average spacing factor, etc., do not provide a complete picture of fiber efficiency. Rather, the modeling of fibers as individual entities enables the direct study of such distribution effects on post-cracking strength and toughness.

3.3   Interaction effects between material components

Material design seeks positive interactions amongst the material components (e.g. cement-based matrix, fibers, and aggregate inclusions) both prior to and during fracture. Experimental programs have provided insight into various forms of component interaction, yet quantitative interpretations at the material scale are few. Numerical modeling is a means for supplementing the scarce, limited data in this area.

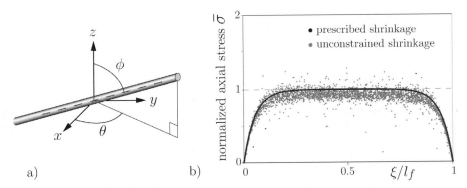

Figure 2: a) Fiber orientation (θ, ϕ) with respect to coordinate axes; and b) fiber axial stress values (adapted from Li et al. [10])

Li et al. [10] have used discrete fiber models for the simulation of FRCC under drying shrinkage. Figure 2 shows axial stresses measured before cracking at various locations along the length of each fiber, where ξ is the distance from the fiber end and stress has been normalized by the product of the fiber elastic modulus and the prescribed shrinkage strain. For the case where uniform shrinkage strains are imposed on the model, the collection of stress values appears as a solid line that agrees with elastic shear lag theory. For the more realistic case where matrix shrinkage is not artificially constrained, the stress values exhibit scatter and, for the most part, are reduced due to the effects of fiber restraint. The scatter in stress values is mainly due to interaction of the stress fields associated with each randomly positioned fiber, which is a form of group effect.

Likewise, nonuniformity of the fiber distribution affects stresses carried by the cement-based matrix prior to fracture. Regions with fewer fibers tend to be more highly stressed, which promotes crack formation at these less favorable locations [6]. The explicit, micromechanical modeling of various interactions between the fibers and matrix (e.g. spalling of the matrix local to the fiber entry point) is possible with sufficient model resolution, but such simulations are necessarily three-dimensional and computational expense becomes an issue even for moderately sized domains. Cracks propagating through FRCC tend to be distributed and discontinuous (at least in the early stages of fracture), leading to matrix-fiber interactions that can be quite different from those obtained during fiber pullout from the surface of an intact specimen. Furthermore, it is not clear how our knowledge of fracture of unreinforced cement composites can be used in the modeling of FRCC, since the presence of fibers greatly modifies fracture of the matrix. Accurate estimations of crack widths and crack connectivity are important for simulating the durability mechanics of cement-based composites. The extent of the elastic stage is more limited in concrete materials with coarse aggregates, since the matrix-aggregate interface is generally weaker and therefore more susceptible to microcracking. An explicit modeling of such aggregates is necessary for cases where the aggregate inclusions are not small relative to the fiber lengths.

4.   CONCLUSION

The potential benefits of hybrid-FRCC are evident in previous experimental work. The benefits include improved strength and toughness of the material, which can lead to thinner and lighter structural members, and improved durability performance. Relative to monofiber composites, the design of hybrid-FRCC materials presents additional challenges, due to the larger parameter space and potential for additional interactions between the material components. Computer modeling is a means for supplementing limited test/field data and enabling investigations outside of the parameter range covered by physical testing. It can provide a precisely controlled environment for studying the interrelation between material and structural behavior, which facilitates movement from an empirically based understanding of structural performance to one based on materials science and engineering. Although this sounds attractive, there are significant barriers and gaps in our abilities to model fiber reinforced cement composites. A few such issues have been discussed in this paper, with attention to the explicit, three-dimensional modeling of fibers within micro/macro hybrid-FRCC. The transition from microcrack growth and coalescence to macrocrack propagation spans the material and structural scales, since realistic structural boundary conditions are needed to simulate macrocrack growth. The number of microfibers and/or defects becomes tremendously large even when considering small structural components, so that multiscale approaches appear to be necessary.

REFERENCES

[1] Rossi, P., Acker, P. and Malier, Y., 'Effect of steel fibres at two stages: the material and the structure', *Materials and Structures* **20** (1987) 436-439.

[2] Mobasher, B. and Li, C.Y., 'Mechanical properties of hybrid cement-based composites', *ACI Materials Journal* **93** (3) (1996) 284–92.

[3] Lawler, J.S., Wilhelm, T., Zampini, D. and Shah, S.P., 'Fracture processes of hybrid fiber-reinforced mortar', *Materials and Structures*, **36**(3) (2003) 197-208.

[4] Markovic, I., Walraven, J.C., van Mier, J.G.M., 'Development of high performance hybrid fibre concrete', in Proceedings of 4th International Workshop on 'High Performance Fiber Reinforced Cement Composites', Ann Arbor, Michigan, June 2003 (RILEM 2003) 277-300.

[5] van Mier, J.G.M., 'Cementitious composites with high tensile strength and ductility through hybrid fibres', in '6th RILEM Symposium on Fibre-Reinforced Concretes (BEFIB 2004)', Varenna, 2004, 219-238.

[6] Bolander, J.E. and Saito, S., 'Discrete modelling of short-fiber reinforcement in cementitious composites', *Advanced Cement Based Materials* **6** (1997) 76-86.

[7] Bolander, J.E. and Sukumar, N., 'Irregular lattice model for quasistatic crack propagation', *Physical Review B* **71**, 094106, 2005 (12 pages).

[8] Naaman, A.E., Namur, G., Alwan, J., Najm, H., 'Fiber pullout and bond slip. I: Analytical study', *J. Structural Engineering* **117**(9) (1991) 2769-2790.

[9] Akkaya, Y., Shah, S.P. and Ankenman, B., 'Effect of Fiber Dispersion on Multiple Cracking of Cement composites', *J. Engineering Mechanics* **127**(4) (2001) 311-316.

[10] Li, Z., Perez Lara, M. and Bolander, J.E., 'Restraining effects of fibers during non-uniform drying of cement composites', *Cement and Concrete Research* **36**(9) (2006) 1643-1652.

EFFECT OF REINFORCING FIBER TYPES ON THE FRACTURE PROCESS AND ACOUSTIC EMISSION ACTIVITY CHARACTERISTICS IN HIGH PERFORMANCE FIBER-REINFORCED CEMENTITIOUS COMPOSITES

Sun-Woo Kim, Hyun-Do Yun, Esther Jeon and Su-Man Jeon

Dept. of Architectural Engineering, Chungnam National University, Republic of Korea

Abstract

Fiber is an important ingredient in high performance fiber-reinforced cementitious composite (HPFRCC), which can control fracture of cementitious composite by bridging action. The properties of reinforcing fiber, such as tensile strength, aspect ratio and elastic modulus, have great effect on the fracture behavior of HPFRCC. Acoustic emission (AE) method was used to evaluate the characteristics of fracture process and the micro-failure mechanism of HPFRCC. This investigation of distress attempts to relate external behavior to internal signals of distress through acoustic emission. This helps to identify critical internal distress vis-a-vis external level of stress. For these purposes, three kinds of fibers were used: PP (Polypropylene), PE (Polyethylene), SC (Steel cord). In this study, the AE characteristics of HPFRCC reinforced with different fiber types (PE.15, PP2.0, SC0.75+PE0.75) distributions under four-point-bending were studied. The result shows that the AE technique is a valuable tool to study the failure mechanism of HPFRCC.

1.   INTRODUCTION

Recently, there have been many studies to improve material property (brittle failure mechanism) of concrete by reinforcing fiber in cement composites. HPFRCC represents various tensile performances (2 ~ 4 % of deformation capacity) according to tensile strength, elastic modulus, volume fraction and type of fiber used. Also, there has been renewed vigor in the field of fiber-reinforced cement-based composites, because of the development of hybrid fiber systems, where two or more types of fiber are combined to produce a composite that derives benefits from each of the individual fibers and exhibits a synergistic response [1, 2]. Therefore, it is needed to study fracture characteristics and damage process of cement composites by reinforcing fiber.

AE signals are low-level sonic or ultrasonic signals that are generated as a result of material deformation, degradation, or damage [3]. When a microcrack forms in a composite, stored elastic strain energy is released. This generates a stress wave that travels through the material. AE sensors can detect this stress wave. Monitoring of the AE behavior of specimens allows the degree of damage to the specimen to be identified, including microscopic events that accumulate prior to crack formation, and macroscopic events associated with crack extension. In cement composites, the AE activity is primarily associated with the cracking of the cement matrix. It can be assumed that microcracks form at the time that the AE sensors detect the first stress wave.

The objective of this study is to investigate the flexural fracture of cement composites reinforced with single and hybrid fibers to examine their flexural behavior, fracture behavior, and the progress of damage in HPFRCCs using the AE technique, and to establish the correlation between the acoustic activity and the process of fracture.

2. EXPERIMENTAL PROGRAMS

2.1 Specimen and Material

The specimen used in this study is a rectangular cement composite beam as shown in Figure 1. All beams have cross-sectional areas of 100 x 100 mm^2, and net span of 400 mm as listed in Table 1. The main variable in this study used was reinforcing fiber type. The fibers used were PP, PE, and SC as shown in Figure 2 and Table 2. The proportion of the cement composites mixtures is shown in Table 3. High-early strength cement and silica powder with a maximum size of $G_{max} = 0.1$ mm were used in the specimens employed in the bending tests. The water-to-cement ratio of the HPFRCCs was 0.45, and the specified compressive strength of the cylindrical specimens was 50 MPa. The top of the specimens was capped by a vinyl cap after a period of 24 hours after casting to prevent shrinkage strain of the top surface. The specimens were remolded after a period of 1 day, and were cured in water at 40±5 ℃ for a period of 7 days before the tests were carried out.

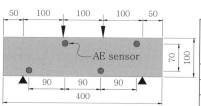

Figure 1: Detail of specimen [mm]

Table 1: Example of construction of a table

Specimen	Section [mm^2]	Length [mm]	Net span [mm]	Specific comp. strength [MPa]
Concrete				
PP2.0	100x100	400	300	50
PE1.5				
SCPE				

(a) PP   (b) PE   (c) SC

Figure 2: Shape of fibers

Table 2: Mechanical properties of fiber

Fibers	Density [g/cm^3]	Length [mm]	Dia. [μm]	Aspect ratio	Tensile strength [MPa]	Elastic modulus [GPa]
PP	900	15	40	375	600	5
PE	970	15	12	1250	2500	75
Steelcord	7850	32	405	79	2300	206

Table 3: Mixture proportions of cement composites

Specimen	W/C	Fiber volume fraction, V_f[Vol. %]			Unit weight [kg/m³]		
		PE	SC	PP	Cement	Sand	Water
Concrete	0.37	-	-	-	459.0	759.0	170.0
PP		-	-	2.00	1036.0	414.4	466.2
PE	0.45	1.50	-	-	1041.5	416.6	468.7
SCPE		0.75	0.75	-	1041.5	416.6	468.7

2.2   Test Setup and Instrumentation

All beams were tested under four-point loading to investigate the microscopic fracture behavior and the degree of damage in the cement composites using the AE technique. The tests were carried out using a displacement control (1.0 mm/min) with a universal testing machine (UTM) as shown in Figure 3. As the load increased, the AE signals were generated by crack initiation and propagation within the specimen. The AE signals were detected by the AE sensors attached to the side of the specimen. A preamplifier was used to amplify the AE signal waveform. The threshold level was fixed at 40dB to eliminate any electric or mechanical noise.

Figure 3: Test setup and AE measurement system

3.   RESULTS AND DISCUSSIONS

3.1   AE Parameter and Fracture Mechanism of HPFRCCs

The four-point bending test was performed to evaluate the degree of damage and microscopic fracture mechanism of cement composite by considering the corresponding AE signal characteristics. Figure 4 shows load vs. deflection relationship of all specimens. Figure 4 shows that concrete specimen has 225~467 % higher initial stiffness compared with HPFRCC specimens, respectively. It may be the reason that HPFRCCs were mixed with silica powder instead of the coarse aggregate to improve bond strength between reinforcing fiber and cement composites. HPFRCC specimens represented much more deflection, above 2.5 mm, whereas concrete specimen showed 0.046 mm of deflection at peak strength. Especially, SCPE specimen showed 68.01 kN of peak strength and 26.39 kN/mm of peak stiffness because macro-cracks were bridged by SC.

The relationship between the load and AE events of specimen is shown in Figure 5. As shown in Figure 5, a few AE events by the local stress were generated at the first stage of the load. As the load increased gradually, the number of AE events rarely increased until 80% of peak stress in concrete specimen. At 80% of peak stress, the number of AE events increased rapidly and specimen represent brittle failure mode. In HPFRCCs specimens, after 40% of peak stress, the number of AE events increased gradually up to failure. It was estimated that reinforcing fibers in cement composites prevent brittle failure of HPFRCCs because the flexural tensile stress in cement composites was redistributed by fibers' bridging action. Based on the analysis of the data from individual event signals stored in the AE measurement system, the increase in the number of AE events generally corresponded to events having larger ring-down counts and longer duration times.

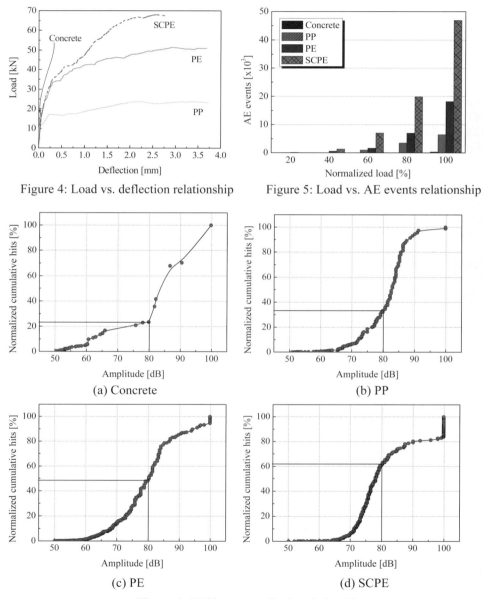

Figure 4: Load vs. deflection relationship   Figure 5: Load vs. AE events relationship

(a) Concrete   (b) PP

(c) PE   (d) SCPE

Figure 6: AE hits vs. amplitude relationship

Therefore, it is thought that the SC macro-fibers may lead to AE signals being generated with longer durations when HPFRCCs is subjected to flexural tensile stress.

The relationship between the cumulative hits and amplitude is shown in Figure 6. As shown in Figure 6, it is observed that distribution of amplitude is different between concrete and HPFRCCs at flexural/tension cracking. At tension cracking, wide distribution area was observed in concrete specimen as shown in Figure 6(a) because fracture of concrete is tension fracture result in loss of bond stress between aggregate and cement paste. But narrow distribution area of AE amplitude was observed in HPFRCCs specimen as shown in Figure 6(b) to 6(d) based on bridging action between cement matrix and micro/macro-fibers. Normalized cumulative AE hits number is 22 % at 80 dB of amplitude, whereas PP, PE, SCPE specimen represent 33 %, 48 %, 62%, respectively.

3.2   Two-dimensional AE Source Location and Crack Propagation of HPFRCCs

Figure 8 shows the result of the two-dimensional AE source location. AE source were generated along the produced cracks on the four types of specimens as shown in Figure 7. It was found at the beginning of loading on the all specimens that a few AE sources were generated at the center of the lower surface of the specimen where the maximum bending moment applies. These AE signals were due to the local stress concentration of voids in the cement composites and micro-cracks initiation.

However, at the moment the crack was initiated on the specimens, a lot of AE sources were generated along the main crack. Figure 8(a) is the result of AE source location on the concrete

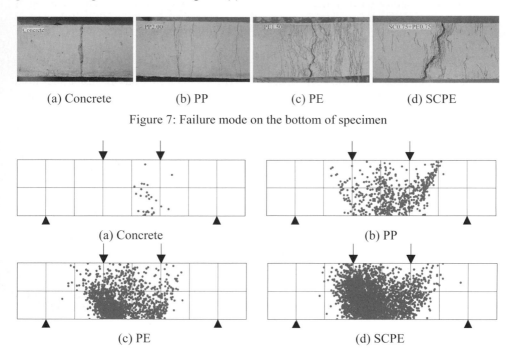

| (a) Concrete | (b) PP | (c) PE | (d) SCPE |

Figure 7: Failure mode on the bottom of specimen

| (a) Concrete | (b) PP |

| (c) PE | (d) SCPE |

Figure 8: The result of AE source location on the side of specimens by AE method

specimen. At the beginning of the load, the crack was not observed on the surface of the specimen. A few number of AE sources have been generated at the middle of specimen, and the specimen represented brittle failure mode as shown in Figure 7(a). In the case of HPFRCC specimen, however, multiple micro-cracks were observed as the load increased gradually and many AE sources were measured along the crack line as soon as the micro crack was initiated at the centre of the lower surface of the specimen. Especially, a great number of AE sources were observed along wide area of specimen in PE and SCPE specimen due to micro/macro reinforcing fibers have controlled micro/macro crack propagation in cement composite. This result concurs with the relationship between the crack propagation and AE source location show that two-dimensional AE source location was the best technique to understand the degree of damage and crack propagation in the HPFRCCs.

4. CONCLUSIONS

– It was observed that the number of AE events increased gradually until failure stage because of micro-crack initiation originating from the micro-bond fractures occurring between the fiber and cement matrix by bridging action while the number of AE events in concrete specimen increased rapidly at failure stage.
– As the result on distribution of AE amplitude, it was confirmed that fracture mechanism between concrete and HPFRCC is different. Also, the fracture mechanism of HPFRCCs was characterized by a reinforcing fiber type.
– Based on AE source location data by triangular method, it is possible to detect damage of cement composite reinforced with various fibers. Therefore, it was confirmed that stress distribution in the HPFRCCs can be estimated by AE method.

ACKNOWLEDGEMENTS

This research was supported by grants (04-core technology-C02-02) from the Infra Structure Assessment Research Center constituted by the funds of Ministry of Construction & Transportation in Korea.

REFERENCES

[1] Yun. et al., 'Response of High Performance Hybrid Fiber-Reinforced Cement Composites to Cyclic Tension', Proceeding of Architectural Institute of Korea. 24(2) October, 2004 119-122.
[2] Yun. et al., 'Hysteretic Characteristics of Seismic Devices using High Performance Fiber Reinforced Cement Composites', Journal of Architectural Institute of Korea. 21(1) (2005) 51-58.
[3] A.K. Maji, S.P. Shah, 'Process Zone and Acoustic Emission Measurement in Concrete', Experimental Mechanics (1988)
[4] Han. et al., 'Crack Source location Technique for Plain Concrete Beam using Acoustic Emission', Journal of Korea Concrete Institute, 13(2) (2001) 107-113.
[5] Uomoto. T., 'Application of Acoustic Emission to the Field of Concrete Engineering', J. Acoustic Emission. 6(3) (1987) 137-144.
[6] Keru Wu, Bing Chen, Wu Yao, 'Study on the AE characteristics of fracture process of mortar, concrete and steel-fiber-reinforced concrete beams', Cement and Concrete Research, 30 (2000) 1495-1500.

MULTI-CRACK FORMATION IN STRAIN HARDENING CEMENT-BASED COMPOSITES

Folker H. Wittmann [1], **Tina Wilhelm** [2], **Françoise Beltzung** [3] **and Peter Grübl** [2]

(1) Aedificat Institute Freiburg, Germany

(2) Institute for Concrete Structures, University of Technology (TU), Darmstadt, Germany

(3) University of Applied Sciences of North-west Switzerland, Basel, Switzerland

Abstract

It has been shown by numerous authors that strain hardening cement-based materials can be produced by adding high performance polymer fibres such as PVA and PE fibres to fresh fine mortar. The complex interaction between the high performance fibres and the cement-based matrix leads to multi-crack formation. The surface of strain hardening cement-based materials (SHCC) has been observed by means of a high resolution digital camera while a steadily growing deformation has been imposed. From the observed data the displacements and deformations of elements of the stochastic pattern on the surface can be obtained by numerical evaluation. This method is based on principles of pattern recognition. As we had expected it can be observed that PVA fibres stabilize fictitious cracks in the strained matrix. With increasing strain a process of complex redistribution of stresses and strains can be observed. The width of most cracks widens while at a given strain some cracks are closed again. If pseudo-ductility is to be simulated in a realistic way, these processes, which to the knowledge of the authors, are described for the first time in this contribution have to be taken into consideration.

1. INTRODUCTION

Cement-based materials such as concrete and mortar are most frequently applied materials in industrialized countries. Advanced technologies allow us to produce special types of concrete for many applications. High strength concrete with compressive strength well beyond 120 N/mm^2 has become a usual building material in practice. Service-life of many reinforced concrete structures, however, is not long enough in many cases. One major reason for this is crack formation in the concrete cover. Concrete is a rather brittle material and the combination of hygral, thermal, and mechanical strains imposed under usual conditions cannot be absorbed without crack formation.

With the advent of high performance polymer fibers it became possible to produce cement-based materials with pronounced pseudo strain hardening. In an optimized system ultimate strains of 5 % can be achieved. Kanda & Li [1, 2] developed a design theory for pseudo strain hardening cement-based materials based on earlier work by Marshall & Cox [3]. Other authors optimize the composition of cement-based materials using neural networks to evaluate experimental results [4] or just by trial and error.

In any case pseudo strain hardening can be assumed to be due to crack bridging by fibers. Hardened cement paste has a wide pore size distribution. The largest flaw in the porous structure essentially controls strength [5]. It has been shown that very high strength hardened cement paste can be produced by eliminating large flaws [6]. This material was called MDF: Macro Defect Free cement-based material [7]. MDF, however, is a very brittle material.

In the case of materials with pseudo strain hardening micro cracks in the porous structure are not eliminated but bridged by fibers. High ductility is reached when the number of fibers, their size and mechanical properties can avoid unstable crack propagation. This crack arresting mechanism must be activated in pre-existing cracks and in cracks, which occur under applied load [2]. Then and only then multi crack formation leads to pseudo ductility. In order to understand these complex mechanisms in concrete better it would be helpful if we could observe crack formation under imposed deformation.

Pseudo ductile deformation is accompanied by continuous crack formation. That means the cement-based material undergoes progressive damage as the deformation increases. With respect to durability of the damaged material it is important to know the width of the produced cracks. As long as the crack width remains below a critical value it may be assumed that durability is not affected [8, 9]. If we could observe the process of crack formation and the widening of cracks under imposed deformation we would be able to discern optimized fiber reinforced cement-based materials from less suitable materials and we could define ultimate strain capacity of strain hardening cement-based materials with respect to durability.

It is not easy to check the validity of models to describe the complex load transfer from cracking material to fibers in fiber reinforced cement-based materials under progressive imposed deformation. One possibility is to observe crack formation on a surface by means of optical methods. Hack et al. [10] has applied electronic speckle pattern interferometry to observe crack formation in concrete. Rastogi and Denarié [11] have used the holographic moiré method. Sunderland et al. [12] observed crack growth in concrete by means of the confocal microscope. Jaquot and Rastogi [13] have described the optical basis of interferometry in some detail.

We have applied the method of digital image correlation to study strains and crack formation on the surface of cement-based materials. This method is based on pattern recognition. The stochastic pattern on the surface of a sample is deformed by an applied load and from this deformation local strains and crack formation can be deduced by means of suitable software. The method is described in detail by Winter [14]. Choi and Shah [15] studied the fracture mechanism under compressive load with a similar method. The application of this powerful method to study strain fields and crack formation in composite cement-based materials (2D model concrete) is described in the PhD Thesis of T. Wilhelm [16].

2 EXPERIMENTAL

Specimens with the following dimensions have been prepared: 80 x 80 x 35 mm. A dry mix provided by Technochem, Italy, together with 2 % PVA fibers have been used to prepare a strain hardening cement-based composite (SHCC). The fresh fine mortar has been cast in

PVC moulds and cured under sealed conditions for 7 days. The specimens were tested at an age of 3 months.

The specimen has been glued into a testing machine by high strength epoxy. After hardening of the glue an area of 60 x 60 mm2 has been photographed by means of a high-resolution digital camera. As a deformation has been imposed by tensile stress digital prints have been taken in regular intervals. At the end of the test more than 200 exposures have been taken and stored in a computer.

The software program ARAMIS was used to evaluate selected exposures. In this way it is possible to determine principal strains, vertical or horizontal displacements.

3   RESULTS AND DISCUSSION

3.1   Principal strains on the surface

The testing machine allowed to determine the stress-strain diagram of the SHCC. A typical result is shown in Fig. 1. First a nearly linear relation between stress and strain is observed. After a maxium stress is reached the stress first decreases with further increasing strain until an intermediate minimum stress is reached. Further imposed deformation leads to strain hardening. Fig. 1 indicates that the material under investigation is not optimized. The drop after the maximum stress is reached is too big.

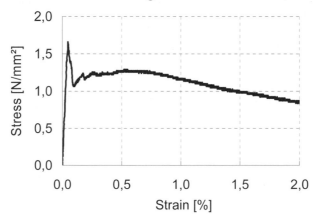

Figure 1: Stress-strain relation of the SHCC under investigation

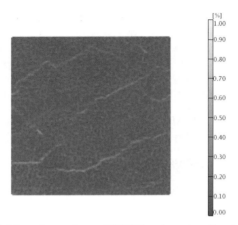

Figure 2: Principal strain field on the surface of SHCC under a tensile stress corresponding to approximately 55 % of the ultimate load. The strain of a unit with length 0.78 mm is shown in % as grey tones

The results obtained with the digital camera can be further evaluated in different ways. In Fig. 2 the principal strains within the observed area are shown as measured at a tensile stress corresponding to 55 % of the ultimate tensile load bearing capacity. The direction of the tensile stress is parallel to the left and right borders of the figure. A characteristic crack pattern is visible. At stresses below this load level, no cracks can be observed with the chosen scale. The width of cracks in Fig. 2 can be estimated. The grey tone corresponds approximately to a strain of $\varepsilon = 0.3$ %. This strain is measured along the edge of one unit, which in this case is $\Delta l = 0.78$ mm. Hence the length change in the damaged zone is

$$\Delta l = \varepsilon \, l_0 = 0.3 \cdot 10^{-2} \cdot 0.78 = 0.0023 \text{ mm} \tag{1}$$

(In a colour visualisation the crack width can be estimated more precisely.)

In Fig. 3 the crack pattern as observed at the maximum of the stress-strain diagram is shown. When we compare results shown in Figs. 2 and 3 we observe that the crack width has increased and few new cracks have been formed. Near the left lower corner of Fig. 3 a crack normal to the applied tensile stress reaches a width of 0.0055 mm.

All cracks shown in Figs 2 and 3 have a crack width below 10 μm. These fine cracks must be considered to be fictitious cracks in terms of non-linear fracture mechanics. That means that the cement-based matrix contributes to load transfer in cracks shown in Figs. 2 and 3 and that fictitious cracks are stabilized in the presence of PVA fibers. Under tensile load there is obviously intense interaction between the cement-based matrix and the fibers. We must abandon simple models, in which real cracks are assumed to be formed and then bridged by fibers. This may be a suitable model to represent the behavior of brittle ceramic matrices reinforced with fibers. In the case of cement-based matrices the contribution of the load transfer within the fictitious crack without fibers has to be taken into consideration as well.

The patterns shown in Figs 4 and 5 have been observed at macroscopic strains of 0.5 % and 1 % respectively. It can be observed that the width of some cracks does not increase, while some cracks situated in the center of the observed area widen considerably. Some cracks have reached a width of 0.0078 mm, and the width of the totally white crack is even wider but cannot be determined any more in this way of data processing. We can also observe that the diagonal crack shown in the upper left corner of Fig. 3 practically vanishes at an imposed strain of 0.5 %; but it reopens at an imposed strain of about 1 %. Quite obviously there is a complex redistribution of stresses and strains in the material before localization of one fatal crack takes place. It is also of interest to note that in going from a macroscopic strain of 0.5 % to 1 % new and wide cracks are being formed in parallel to the existing cracks.

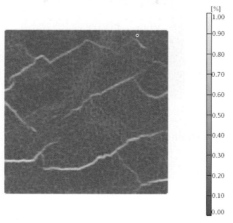

Figure 3: Principal strain field on the surface of SHCC under tensile stress corresponding to approximately to the ultimate load capacity

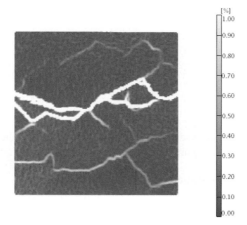

Figure 4: Principal strain field on the surface of SHCC as observed at an imposed macroscopic strain of 0.5 %

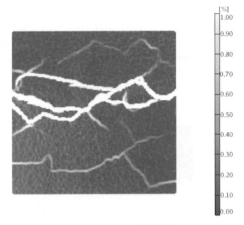

Figure 5: Principal strain field on the surface of SHCC as observed at an imposed macroscopic strain of 1 %

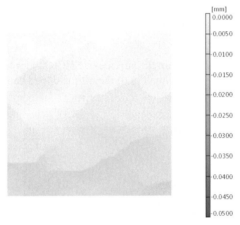

Figure 6: Displacements in y-direction in the observed area on the surface of SHCC at the maximum stress. This figure corresponds to the principal strains as shown in Fig. 3

3.2 Displacements in y-direction

In Figs. 2 to 5 principal strains are shown. In addition displacements in y-direction have been determined from the original data. Tensile stress has been applied in y-direction. In Figs. 6 and 7 y-coordinates are measured from the upper edge to the lower edge.

The displacement in y-direction close to the maximum load is shown in Fig. 6. This figure corresponds to the results shown in Fig. 3. If we determine the difference of the displacements in the lower part of the figure from the grey tones of the lowest field and the adjacent field above, we can estimate the crack width to be 0.005 mm. This value agrees very well with the crack width as determined from the principal strains shown in Fig. 3.

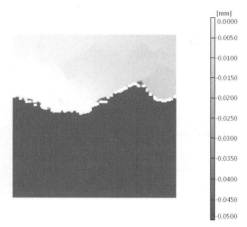

Figure 7: Displacements in the y-direction in the observed area on the surface of SHCC at an imposed strain of approximately 0.5 %. This figure corresponds to the principal strains as shown in Fig. 4

In Fig. 4 the principal strains at an imposed macroscopic strain of approximately 0.5 % are shown. When we determine the displacements in y-direction from the same data, we obtain the pattern shown in Fig. 7. The lower half of Fig. 7 is homogeneously dark. The displacement is equal or bigger than the maximum measurable value of 0.05 mm. We can still conclude that the big crack running from left to right has an opening bigger than 0.05 mm at the left edge and an opening bigger than 0.025 at the right edge. The left part has been obviously unloaded by the opening of the wide crack. Crack formation imposes a certain rotation of the separated parts. This is certainly the reason why cracks as shown in the upper left corner have closed again at an imposed strain of 0.5 %.

3.3   Crack opening

In order to get quantitative values of the development of the width of different cracks the crack width has been determined at two selected points of the surface. Results are shown in Fig. 8. The two selected points are lying on two different micro-cracks and are shown in the insert of Fig. 8. It can be seen that the crack width starts to grow at both points at an imposed global strain of 0.1 %. At a global strain of about 0.12 % both cracks reach a width of about 0.002 mm. As the imposed strain increases the crack width called P1-P1 further increases while the crack with P1-P2 decreases. After having reached a crack width of about 0.004 at a strain of about 0.125 % the crack width of crack P1-P1 also decreases with increasing imposed strain. But at a strain of 0.15 % the crack width of crack P1-P2 starts to grow rapidly. The crack width of crack P1-P1 remains at the same time nearly closed.

Micro-cracks in SHCC may open under imposed strain roughly normal to the applied load. At a later stage due to formation and growth of other cracks initial cracks may close again. This complex process of local unloading is an essential part of the apparent ductility of SHCC. A chain model built up with coupled parallel chains and with a stochastic distribution of the strength of the chain elements will most probably describe the apparent ductility and failure of SHCC in a realistic way.

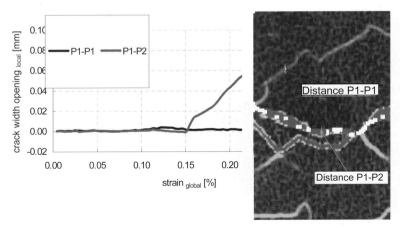

Figure 8: Development of the crack width at two selected points on two different cracks. The selected points are shown in the insert

3.4   Visual observation

The dominating crack, which has been developed at a macroscopic strain of approximately 0.5 % and which is clearly visible in Fig. 7 finally became the separating crack of this sample. In Fig. 9 a photograph of the separating crack as observed after failure is shown. It can be seen that failure mechanism essentially is fiber pullout.

Figure 9: Final macroscopic separating crack in SHCC after failure

Fig. 9 can be compared with Fig. 5 in which the crack pattern at an imposed strain of 1 % is shown. Most of the fine cracks are closed again after failure and they cannot be observed in

Fig. 9. But some of the wider cracks visible in Fig. 5 can still be recognized in Fig 9 as thin lines.

4. CONCLUSIONS

An advanced optical method has been applied to study principal strain fields and crack formation on the surface of SHCC. Records have been taken by means of a high-resolution digital camera and have been numerically processed.

Multi-crack formation can be followed with this method as function of imposed macroscopic strain. It turns out that PVA fibers stabilize fictitious cracks in SHCC. In the fictitious crack load is transferred by fibers but in addition by the remaining load bearing capacity of the damaged cement-based matrix. This combination of load transfer must be considered to be the major mechanism for obtaining large deformations, strain hardening, and pseudo ductility of SHCC.

Complex redistribution of strains and fictitious cracks can be observed. Results presented in this contribution shall serve as a basis for further optimizing SHCC for practical applications. The influence of the observed damage on durability has to be further investigated.

ACKNOWLEDGEMENT

The authors gratefully acknowledge supply of the dry mix of SHCC by TECNOCHEM Italiana.

REFERENCES

[1] Kanda, T. & Li, V. C. 1999. New micro-mechanics design theory for pseudo strain hardening cementitious composites. Journal of Engineering Mechnics, ASCE, 124 (4): 373-381.
[2] Kanda, T. & Li, V. C. 2006. Practical criteria for saturated pseudo strain hardening behavior in ECC. Journal of Advanced Concrete Technology 4: 59-72
[3] Marshall, T. B. & Cox, B. N. (1988). A J-Integral method for calculating steady-state matrix cracking stresses in composites. Mechanics of Materials 7:127-133.
[4] Wittmann F. H. & Martinola G. 1993. Optimization of concrete properties by neural networks. In Dhir R. K. & Jones M. C. (eds.) Concrete 2000, Economic and Durable Construction through Excellence, E & FN Spon, London, Vol. II: 1889-1893.
[5] Wittmann F. H. 1983. Structure of concrete with respect to crack formation. In Fracture Mechanics of Concrete. Wittmann F. H. (ed.). Elsevier Science Publishers, Amsterdam, pp.43-74
[6] Higgins D. D. & Bailey J. E. 1976. Fracture measurements on cement paste. Journal of Materials Science 11: 1955-2003
[7] Lewis J. A., Boyer M. & Bentz, D. P. 1994. Binder distribution in Macro-Defect-Free cements: relation between percolation properties and moisture absorption kinetics. Journal of the American Ceramic Society 77(3): 711-719
[8] Wittmann F. H. 2006. Specific aspects of durability of strain hardening cement-based composites. Int. Journ. Restoration of Buildings and Monuments 12 (2): 109-118.
[9] Lepech M. D. & Li, V. C. 2006. Long term durability performance of engineered cementitious composites. Int. Journ. Restoration of Buildings and Monuments 12 (2): 119-132
[10] Hack, E., Steiger, T., & Sadouki H. 1995. Application of electronic speckle pattern interferometry (ESPI) to observe the fracture process zone. In Fracture Mechanics of Concrete Structures, Proceedings FRAMCOS-2, Wittmann F. H. (ed.). Aedificatio Publishers, Freiburg: 229-238

[11] Rastogi, P. K. & Denarié E. 1994. Measurement of the length of fracture process zone in fiber-reinforced concrete using holographic moiré. Exp. Techn. 18 (4): 11-17

[12] Sunderland H., Tolou A., Denarié E., L. Job & Huet C. 1995. Use of the confocal microscope to study pre-existing microcracks and crack growth in concrete. In Fracture Mechanics of Concrete Strucutres, Proceedings FRAMCOS-2. Wittmann F. H. (ed.). Aedificatio Publishers: 239-248

[13] Jaquot, P. & Rastogi P. K. (1983). Speckle metrology and holographic interferometry applied to the study of cracks in concrete. In Wittmann F. H. (ed.) Fracture Mechanics of Concrete. Elsevier Scientific Publishers, Amsterdam: 113-155

[14] Winter D. 1993. Optische Verschiebungsmessungen nach dem Objektrasterprinzip mit Hilfe eines Flächen orientierten Ansatzes. Internal Report, Institut für Technische Mechanik, Abteilung Experimentelle Mechanik. TU Braunschweig.

[15] Choi, S. & Shah, S. P. 1998. Fracture mechanism in cement-based materials subjected to compression. J. Eng. Mechanics, 124 (1): 94-102

[16] Wilhelm T. 2006. Ein experimentell begründetes mikromechanisches Modell zur Bescheibung von Bruchvorgängen in Beton bei äusserer Krafteinwirkung. Dissertation TU Darmstadt, Germany

PART TWO

BENDING, SHEAR

AND COMPRESSION

EXPERIMENTAL AND NUMERICAL INVESTIGATION OF SHEAR BEHAVIOR OF PVA-ECC IN STRUCTURAL ELEMENTS

Petr Kabele [1] **and Toshiyuki Kanakubo** [2]

(1) Faculty of Civil Engineering, Czech Technical University in Prague, Czech Republic

(2) Institute of Engineering Mechanics and Systems, University of Tsukuba, Japan

Abstract

Combined experimental and analytical approach is used to investigate shear behavior of reinforced ECC structural elements. The experimental part consists of a self-contained program, which includes material tests under uniaxial tension and compression, reinforcement bond tests, and bending shear tests on beams. Experiments on selected beams are reproduced numerically. By comparing the experimental and numerical results we identify the importance of accounting for various mechanisms on the material scale (e.g., bond between ECC and reinforcement or crack sliding resistance) and verify if the uniaxial material tests truly represent the material behavior in a structural member.

1. INTRODUCTION

Due to their high tensile strain capacity and damage tolerance, Engineered Cementitious Composites (ECC) appear as an attractive alternative for replacing concrete in shear-critical structural elements and details. A large number of experimental studies have shown that using ECC in conjunction with conventional reinforcement (R/ECC) in such elements indeed leads to a significant qualitative improvement of their structural behavior, namely in terms of load and displacement capacity. Recent move from prescriptive to performance-based structural design opens new possibilities for utilizing ECC materials in engineering practice. To this end, however, it is desirable to gain a deeper understanding of the fundamental mechanisms responsible for the cited structural performance improvements. It is also necessary to quantify the performance gains and relate them to elementary material properties, such as compressive strength, tensile strength, and tensile strain capacity. The present paper addresses these issues by means of combining experimental investigation and subsequent numerical simulation of the experiments.

2. EXPERIMENTAL PROGRAM

The experimental part consisted of material tests in uniaxial tension and compression, pull-out tests of bond between ECC and reinforcement, and bending shear tests on beam specimens. The samples for the material tests and the beam specimens were cast from the same mix batch. Although the whole experimental program involved several cementitious materials [1], in the present paper we will focus only on the most commonly used ECC with 2% volume fraction of PVA fibers (PVA-ECC).

2.1 Mechanical properties of PVA-ECC

Mix proportions of the ECC used for the experiments and the main parameters of the PVA fiber, as provided by the manufacturer, are summarized in Table 1.

Table 1: Mix and fiber properties of PVA-ECC

Mix properties				Fiber properties				
Water to binder ratio	Sand to binder ratio	Air content (%)	Fiber volume fraction (%)	Type	Length (mm)	Diameter (mm)	Tensile strength (MPa)	Elastic modulus (GPa)
0.42	0.77	10	2	PVA	12	0.04	1600	40

Compressive behavior of the ECC material was tested on cylinder specimens with diameter of 100 mm and height of 200 mm under displacement control. Load-contraction curves including ascending and descending parts were recorded (Fig. 1). Uniaxial tension tests were conducted to obtain tensile behavior of PVA-ECC. The adopted test setup, which has been developed by the authors of ref. [1], is shown in Fig. 2. This tensile specimen is used to minimize the influence of fiber orientation and is expected to capture more precisely tensile performance of ECC in large-size members. Cross-sectional dimensions in the tested region are 100 mm × 60 mm, which is at least 5 times larger than the fiber length. Support conditions are one of the important factors for conducting uniaxial tension test on cementitious materials. In actual loading, it is impossible to perform "pure tension" because of the non-uniformity of the material itself and variations in specimen shapes and setup conditions. The "pin-fix" ends condition is selected as a suitable way to decrease the effect of the moment due to eccentricity of tensile load and of the secondary moment after cracking [2]. Comparisons with uniaxial tension test results performed by other test methods using the same PVA-ECC can be found in ref. [2].

Tensile stress – tensile strain curves are shown in Fig. 3. The first crack strength was around 3 MPa and the tensile strength was in the range of 3.5 – 4 MPa. Pseudo strain hardening behavior was recognized.

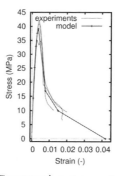

Figure 1: Compressive stress –strain curves

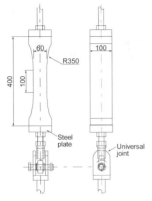

Figure 2: Uniaxial tension test   Figure 3: Tensile stress –strain curve

2.2   ECC-reinforcement bond properties

To investigate the local bond behavior between PVA-ECC and steel reinforcement, pull out bond tests were conducted. In the case of ordinary RC members, bond splitting failure often takes place with disintegration of surrounding concrete. In the case of R/ECC members, however, it is expected that ECC provides confinement against the splitting force caused by deformed bars, which results in higher bond strength.

(1) Specimen and loading method

As shown in Fig. 4, specimens with a bond length of four times of the reinforcement diameter (d_b) were tested. Deformed steel reinforcement bar D16 (16 mm in diameter) was arranged in the center position of the specimen. Slits on four sides of the specimen were designed in order to stimulate bond splitting failure [3]. The distance between bar surface and the slit corresponded to the thickness of cover concrete (C). The thickness of cover concrete was varied by changing the length of the slit. The test parameter was the normalized thickness of cover concrete C/d_b, which was varied between 1.5 and 3.5. Monotonic pull-out load was applied until failure occurred. The pull-out load and the slip of the free end of the reinforcement were monitored and recorded.

(2) Test results

Typically, the reinforcement was pulled out from the specimen and some radial cracks on the loaded surface were observed. But, as opposed to ordinary concrete, the ECC specimen did not disintegrate along these cracks due to the bridging action of fibers. Consequently the composite provided a better confinement to the reinforcing bar.

The measured bond stress – slip curves are shown in Fig. 5. Bond stress was calculated as the average shear stress on the reinforcement surface. Obviously, bond strength increases with increasing thickness of cover material. With a reference to publications [3] and [4] it can be noted that the bond strength of R/ECC specimens is typically 1.5 – 2 times higher than that of RC specimens due to the confinement effect. Bond stress – slip curves of R/ECC specimens have almost the same tendency as those of RC specimens subjected to direct lateral confinement force.

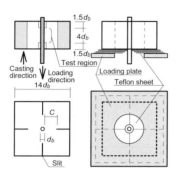

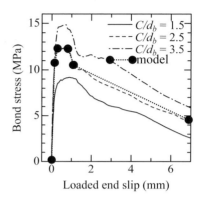

Bond stress (MPa)

Loaded end slip (mm)

$C/d_b = 1.5$
$C/d_b = 2.5$
$C/d_b = 3.5$
model

Figure 4: Specimen for bond test

Figure 5: Bond stress – slip curves

2.3 Bending shear tests on beams

(1) Specimen and loading method

Shear behavior of R/ECC elements was tested on beam specimens monotonically loaded by anti-symmetrical moment (so-called Ohno method). Fig. 6 shows the boundary conditions as well as specimen dimensions and typical reinforcement arrangement. All tested specimens had the same shear span ratio of 1.5. The variable parameters of the series were the stirrup reinforcement ratio and the main bar strength – see Table 2. Beam specimens named by F were designed to undergo flexural yielding before shear failure. Other specimens were designed to fail in shear before flexural yielding.

Table 2: List of beam specimens and tests results

Specimen	Main bar		Stirrup			Maximum load (kN)	Failure mode
	Arrange	σ_y (MPa)	Arrange	p_w (%)	σ_y (MPa)		
PVA20-00	8-D13 p_t=2.43%	720	-	0.00	-	182.7	Shear
PVA20-15			2-D4@93	0.15	295	205.8	Shear
PVA20-30			2-D4@47	0.30		208.6	Shear
PVA20-60		711	2-D6@59	0.60		310.2	Shear
PVA20-89			2-D6@40	0.89	334	341.2	Shear
PVA20-89F		438	2-D6@40	0.89		272.4	F. Yield

(2) Test results

Overall behavior of the beams is shown in Fig. 7 in terms of shear load (one third of total load P) vs. translational angle (rotation of the side stubs about support pins). Specimens after loading are depicted in Fig. 8. First bending and shear cracks were observed at about 0.0025 rad. Consequently, diagonal multiple cracking was taking place. In beam specimens of shear failure type, attaining a peak load was associated with opening of one of the inclined cracks while the width of other cracks was decreasing. In PVA20-89F specimen, opening of a localized flexural crack was accompanied with overall hardening behavior due to yielding of the main reinforcement. Observed maximum shear forces are indicated in Table 2. The shear load carrying capacity increases as stirrup ratio also increases.

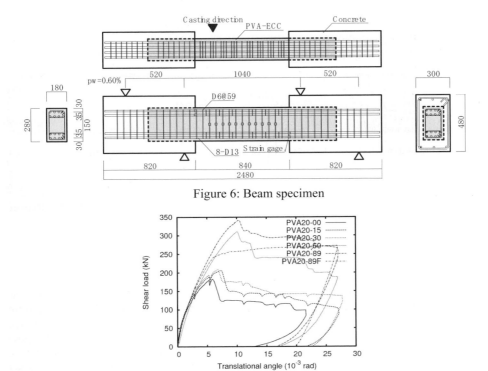

Figure 6: Beam specimen

Figure 7: Results of the beam tests

3. NUMERICAL STUDY

3.1 Computational model

We used finite element program Atena [5] to perform numerical simulations of selected experiments on Ohno beams. Plane stress idealization of the problem was adopted. A finite element mesh typically consisted of about 3200 elements. Highly refined mesh, with element size around 1 cm, was used for the sheared central part of the beams.

ECC material was represented with constitutive model proposed for pseudo strain-hardening fiber reinforced cementitious composites by Kabele [6]. The constitutive law is obtained as a relation between overall stress and overall strain of a representative volume element, which contains up to two mutually perpendicular sets of parallel distributed cracks. A crack set, perpendicular to the principal stress direction, forms once the maximum principal stress attains the first crack strength. Consequently, the overall response in the crack-normal direction is governed by a linear hardening relationship, which is determined from a uniaxial tension test. If the principal stress direction changes, cracks' direction remains fixed, but they may slide. It is assumed that sliding is resisted by bridging fibers acting as elastic beams. The corresponding tangential traction is obtained by homogenizing the effect of individual fibers over a crack area. Localized softening cracks are treated by the crack band approach. The fracture model is combined with a concrete plasticity model for compressive behavior [5].

Behavior of conventional reinforcement was modeled as elastic - perfectly plastic. Reinforcing bars were represented by truss elements. Their interaction with surrounding cementitious material was modeled by perfect bond or bond - slip relationship.

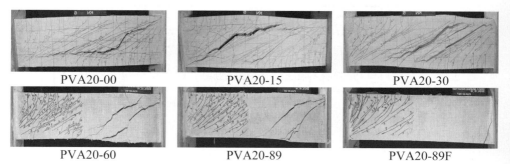

Figure 8: Beam specimens after loading

3.2   Reproduction - beam without stirrups

With the aim of investigating the effect of various fracture mechanisms on the shear behavior of R/ECC members, we attempted to reproduce the behavior of beam PVA20-00 (i.e., the beam lacking shear reinforcement) using our computational model. The compressive plasticity model of ECC was calibrated to fit the uniaxial test data as shown in Fig. 3. Shear modulus of fibers G_{fib}, which is a major parameter controlling the behavior of cracked ECC in shear, was set to 110 MPa, based on previous studies [6]. Tensile stress – strain (or crack width, for softening) relationship was approximated by a tri-linear fit to the uniaxial test data as shown in Fig. 3 (line "tens 1"): the first crack strength, ultimate strength, and strain capacity (strain at maximum load) were determined as average values of the experimental results. Perfect bond of the conventional reinforcement was assumed. Fig. 9 compares the calculated shear load vs. translational angle curve (line "bond 1") with experimental one. Despite showing stiffer behavior in the early loading stage, the analysis overestimated both the peak load and displacement.

In order to verify whether the assumption of perfect bond could be responsible for the higher stiffness, analyses with bond - slip relationship applied to the interface between the main reinforcement and ECC were carried out. To this end, the experimentally determined bond - slip relation was approximated by a piecewise linear curve as shown in Fig. 5. Two cases were considered: 1) the curve was fitted including the initial elastic part ("bond 2"), and 2) the initial elastic deformation was subtracted, i.e., bond was represented by rigid – hardening - softening relation ("bond 3"). Results are compared in Fig. 9 and indicate that the effect is very small. However, closer inspection of the numerical results revealed that, regardless of the bond model used, intense cracking of ECC occurred along a portion of the main bars (see Fig. 12), which could be also interpreted as a sort of debonding. For the analyses discussed hereafter, model "bond 3" was used.

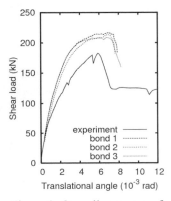

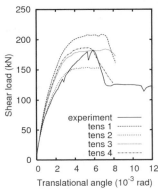

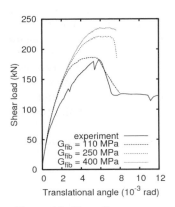

Figure 9: Overall response of beam PVA20-00 – influence of bond

Figure 10: Overall response of beam PVA20-00 – influence of tensile properties

Figure 11: Overall response of beam PVA20-00 – influence of fiber stiffness

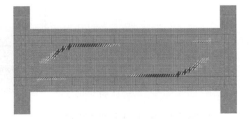

Figure 12: Calculated cracking of beam PVA20-00 – immediately after peak

Figure 13: Calculated cracking of beam PVA20-00 – final state

In a next step, considering that the tensile behavior of ECC has a dominant effect on the beams' response [1], the input uniaxial stress-strain relation "tens1" was modified as follows (see also Fig. 3): 1) both first-crack and ultimate strengths were reduced by factor ½ ("tens 2"), 2) both first-crack and ultimate strengths were reduced by factor ¾ ("tens 3"), 3) the hardening curve was a linear lower bound fit to the experimental curves and the strain capacity was reduced to 0.01 ("tens 4"). It is evident from Fig. 10 that the load and deformational capacity of the beam was best matched when approximation "tens 4" was adopted.

The last parameter whose effect we investigated was the fiber shear modulus G_{fib}. Synthetic fibers usually exhibit high anisotropy, which results in shear modulus two orders of magnitude lower than the axial Young modulus [7]. However, the exact value of G_{fib} for the used type of PVA fiber is not known. Fig. 11 shows that G_{fib} had a strong effect on the calculated load carrying capacity. The best result was obtained with G_{fib} equal to 110 MPa, which corresponded to a very high anisotropy ratio E_{fib}/G_{fib} of 363.

Figs. 12 and 13 show the cracking state of beam PVA20-00 calculated with the best choice of parameters ("tens 4", "bond 3", $G_{fib} = 110$ MPa). It is seen that extensive multiple cracking eventually localized into inclined cracks in a similar manner as in the experiment (Fig. 8).

3.3 Prediction - beam with stirrups

In order to validate the above results a prediction of the response of beam PVA20-30 was carried out. To this end, we used identical assumptions, material models, and parameters as those with witch the best results were obtained for specimen PVA20-00 ("tens 4", "bond 3", $G_{fib} = 110$ MPa). Fig. 14 shows that, again, a reasonably good agreement in the load carrying and deformation capacity was obtained.

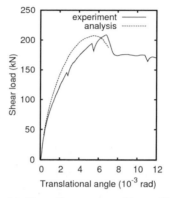

Figure 14: Overall response of beam PVA20-30

4. CONCLUDING REMARKS

Based on the comparison of experiments and numerical analyses, we can draw the following conclusions related to the shear behavior of R/ECC beams with no or light conventional shear reinforcement:

− The overall load and deformational capacity of the beams is determined by localization of fracture into inclined cracks, which is preceded by multiple cracking of ECC and partial debonding of the main bars.
− The fact that multiple cracks undergo not only opening but also sliding has a strong effect on the load carrying capacity of the beams. It is possible that bridging fibers are damaged by the relative slip of crack surfaces. Consequently, only a fraction of the ECC's tensile strength and strain capacity, which has been measured in a uniaxial test, is actually utilized in the R/ECC member. Also, this mechanism may explain why it was necessary to use apparently a very low shear modulus of fibers to match the experimental results.
− The bond failure revealed by numerical simulation of the beam test had a different nature from that of the bond test discussed in section 2.2. While in the bond test failure occurred due to radial cracks, which facilitated the bar pullout, in the beam, cohesion was lost due to extensive multiple cracking and crack sliding of ECC along the reinforcement layer.

ACKNOWLEDGEMENTS

Part of the presented research (carried out by PK) has been supported by the Czech Science Foundation grant GACR 103/05/0896 and the Ministry of Education, Youth and Sports of the Czech Republic contract MSM6840770003. The experimental programs were performed in cooperation with Dr. T. Kanda and Mr. S. Nagai in Kajima Corporation.

REFERENCES

[1] Shimizu, K., Kanakubo, T., Kanda T. and Nagai, S. 'Shear Behavior of Steel Reinforced PVA-ECC Beams', Conference Proceedings DVD, 13th World Conference on Earthquake Engineering, Vancouver, B.C., Canada, August 1-6, (2004), Paper No. 704

[2] Kanakubo, T, 'Tensile Characteristics Evaluation Method for Ductile Fiber-Reinforced Cementitious Composites', *Journal of Advanced Concrete Technology*, **4** (1) (2006) 3-17.

[3] Sakai, T., Kanakubo, T., Yonemaru, K. and Fukuyama, H., 'Bond Splitting Behavior of Continuous Fiber Reinforced Concrete Members', on 'Fiber Reinforced Polymer for Reinforced Concrete Structures', (ACI SP-188, 1999) 1131-1144.

[4] Yasojima, A. and Kanakubo, T. 'Effect of Lateral Confinement in Bond Splitting Behavior of RC Members', Conference Proceedings DVD, 13th World Conference on Earthquake Engineering, Vancouver, B.C., Canada, August 1-6, (2004), Paper No. 644.

[5] ATENA Program Documentation, www.cervenka.cz, (Cervenka Consulting, Prague, Czech Republic, 2005).

[6] Kabele, P. 'Equivalent Continuum Model of Multiple Cracking', *Engineering Mechanics* (Association for Engineering Mechanics, Czech Republic) **9** (1/2) (2002) 75-90.

[7] Vigo, T., Kinzig, B. 'Composite applications: the role of matrix, fiber, and interface' (VHC Publishers, 1992).

THE ROLE OF HPFRCC IN COMPRESSION ON THE POST-PEAK RESPONSE OF STRUCTURAL MEMBERS

Alessandro P. Fantilli [(1)], **Hirozo Mihashi** [(2)] **and Paolo Vallini** [(1)]

(1) Department of Structural and Geotechnical Engineering, Politecnico di Torino, Italy

(2) Department of Architecture and Building Science, Tohoku University, Japan

Abstract

To model the post-peak response in compression, stress- inelastic displacement relationships are defined in the present paper. A unique function, able to characterize different cement-based materials, is introduced. Structural analyses are developed in members reinforced with steel bars and made, respectively, of ordinary concrete (RC) and High-Performance Fiber Reinforced Cementitious Concrete (R/HPFRCC). Referring to load-midspan deflection curves of simply supported beams, only if the proposed function is taken into account, a good agreement between numerical results and experimental data can be obtained. Moreover, the higher ductility of R/HPFRCC beams in bending is clearly evident.

1.   INTRODUCTION

The stress-strain relationships of cement-based materials in compression (Fig. 1a) can be divided into two parts (Fig. 1b). In the first part, when stresses are lower than the strength f'_c (and $\varepsilon_c < \varepsilon_{c1}$), the specimen can be considered undamaged. In the case of plain concrete, the ascending branch of σ_c-ε_c can be defined by the Sargin's relationship proposed by CEB-FIP Model Code [1]. As soon as the peak stress is reached, localized damage develops and strain softening begins. In this stage, the progressive sliding of two blocks of cement-based material is evident. In Fig. 1a, the angle between the horizontal axe of the specimen and the sliding surfaces is assumed to be $\alpha = 18°$, according to some experimental observations [2]. In the case of compressed concrete, a similar value of α is obtained through the Mohr-Coulomb failure criterion, if the tensile strength is assumed to be 1/10 of that in compression ($f_{ct} = 0.1$ f'_c). For this reason, the value of α only depends on the strength of materials, and therefore it can change only in the presence of an efficient confinement (that is, the presence of stirrups).

The inelastic displacement w of the specimen, and the consequent sliding s of the blocks along the sliding surface, rule the average post-peak compressive strain ε_c of the specimen. Referring to the specimen depicted in Fig. 1a, post peak strains can be defined by the following equation [3] (Fig. 1b):

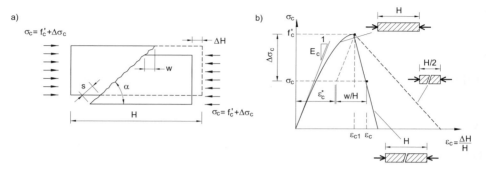

Figure 1: Cement-based materials in compression: a) crushing failure in a compressed specimen; b) possible stress-strain relationships σ_c-ε_c.

$$\varepsilon_c = \varepsilon_c^* + \frac{w}{H} = \varepsilon_{c1} - \frac{\Delta\sigma_c}{E_c} + \frac{w}{H} \tag{1}$$

where, ε_{c1} = strain at compressive strength f'_c ; $\Delta\sigma_c$ = stress decrement after the peak; and H = height of the specimen.

According to test measurements [3-4], the post-peak slope of σ_c-ε_c increases in longer specimens (Fig. 1b), due to the ratio w/H involved in the evaluation of ε_c (Eq. 1)

The stress decrement $\Delta\sigma_c$ can be defined as:

$$\Delta\sigma_c = f'_c - \sigma_c = f'_c \cdot [1 - F(w)] \tag{2}$$

where, $F(w)$ = non-dimensional function which connects the inelastic displacement w and the relative stress σ_c / f'_c during softening (Fig. 2a); f'_c = compressive strength (assumed to be positive).

Substituting Eq. (2) into Eq. (1), it is possible to obtain a new equation for ε_c:

$$\varepsilon_c = \varepsilon_{c1} - \frac{f'_c \cdot [1 - F(w)]}{E_c} + \frac{w}{H} \qquad \text{for } \varepsilon_c > \varepsilon_{c1} \tag{3}$$

2. UNIAXIAL COMPRESSION TESTS ON CYLINDRICAL SPECIMENS

Eq. (3), adopted for the post-peak stage of a generic cement-based material in compression, is based on the definition of $F(w)$, which has to be considered as a material property. In all the cement-based composites, this function should be evaluated experimentally on cylindrical specimens, as performed by Jansen and Shah [4] for plain concrete (Fig. 2a). In the case of fiber-reinforced composites, test campaigns for defining $F(w)$ cannot be found in the literature. Only the influence of the fibers on σ_c-ε_c relationships has been measured in the existing experimental data [5]. In particular, test results clearly show the dependence of the adsorbed energy on the type of fiber, on the aspect ratio l/D (l= length of the fiber, D = diameter of the fiber), and on the fiber volume content V_f .

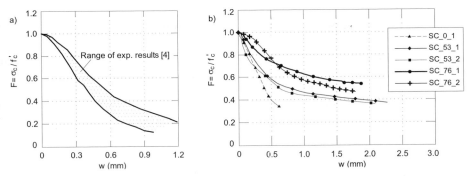

Figure 2: $F(w)$ curves obtained from tests on cylindrical specimens: a) plain concrete specimens [4]; b) HPFRCC specimens made of steel cords [6].

For these reasons, starting from uniaxial compression tests on cylindrical specimens, $F(w)$ relationships are here defined in different cement-based materials. In particular for plain concrete, the post peak response in compression can be obtained from the results of Jansen and Shah [4], which are reported in Fig. 2a in terms of $F = \sigma_c / f'_c$ versus w. In addition, five tests on cylindrical specimens (H=100÷200 mm) are here used to define the post peak behaviour of the HPFRCC tailored by Mihashi and co-workers [6-8]. It is a normal strength composite ($f'_c = 40÷50$ MPa), made of steel cords ($V_f = 0÷1\%$), having an aspect ratio of $l/D = 76.2$, added to a cement-based matrix already reinforced with polyethylene fibers (1% in volume). If the reinforcing index (RI= $l/D \cdot V_f$) is only referred to steel cords, in the considered specimens RI varies form 0 to 76.2%. An acronym has been assigned to each specimen reported in Fig. 2b. It is composed by two capital letters (SC= HPFRCC made of steel cord), followed by two numbers (that is, the value of RI, and the number of the specimen having that reinforcing index).

3.   AN EMPIRICAL FORMULATION OF $F(W)$

For the specimens reported in Fig. 2, a general definition of $F(w)$ seems not possible for all the inelastic displacements, because tests are generally concluded when $F(w) \cong 0.2$. At the corresponding inelastic displacement, compressive stresses σ_c stabilize to a non-zero residual value, which increases with the increase of RI (Fig. 2b). To model the post-peak response of concrete structures, it is necessary to define $F(w)$ also for higher values of w. Since no experimental data are available for modelling the tail of $F(w)$, it can be theoretically defined by considering that the curve should vanish with the increase of w, and should have an order of continuity with the previous part. For the sake of simplicity, $F(w)$ is assumed to be composed, both in the first and the second part, by bivariate polynomial functions (Fig. 3a):

$$F(w) = \frac{\sigma}{f'_c} = 1 + a \cdot w^2 + b \cdot w \qquad \text{if} \quad 0 \le w \le -\frac{b}{2 \cdot a} \qquad (4a)$$

$$F(w) = \frac{\sigma}{f'_c} = -\left(1 - \frac{b^2}{4 \cdot a}\right) \cdot \left(\frac{4 \cdot a^2}{b^2} w^2 + \frac{4 \cdot a}{b} w\right) \qquad \text{if} \quad -\frac{b}{2 \cdot a} < w \le -\frac{b}{a} \qquad (4b)$$

$$F(w) = \frac{\sigma}{f'_c} = 0 \qquad\qquad\qquad \text{if} \quad w > -\frac{b}{a} \qquad\qquad (4c)$$

As can be easily observed in Fig. 3a, the parabolas (Eqs. 3a-b) are defined by the same coefficients a, b and have the same extreme point at $w = -0.5\ b/a$. While $w = -\ b/a$ (i.e. twice the value at extreme point) is considered the maximum value of the inelastic displacement for which $F(w)$ is assumed to be higher than zero. However, both the coefficients can be defined only through the first parabola (Eq. 4a), because of the reduced range of experimental observations.

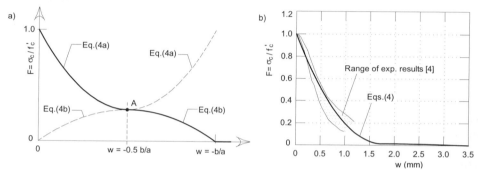

Figure 3: The function $F(w)$ for cement-based materials: a) schematic representation of Eqs. (4); b) comparison between the proposed $F(w)$ for plain concrete and the range experimentally measured by Jansen and Shah [4].

3.1 a, b for plain concrete

For plain concrete specimens (Fig. 2a), the values a = 0.320 mm^{-2} and b = -1.12 mm^{-1} are obtained by means of the least square approximation of the experimental data [4]. However, as shown in Fig. 3b, the measured range only covers the first part of the theoretical $F(w)$ curve.

3.2 a, b for HPFRCC made of steel cords

The coefficients a, b are computed separately in specimens having the same reinforcing index RI. By means of least square approximation algorithm, three values can be obtained for the coefficients a (Fig. 4a) and b (Fig. 4b), respectively. As Figs. 4a-b show, in this case a, b can be written as linear functions of RI:

$$a = (-0.00761 \cdot RI + 0.704) \cdot mm^{-2} \qquad\qquad (5a)$$

$$b = (0.00130 \cdot RI - 1.53) \cdot mm^{-1} \qquad\qquad (5b)$$

The values of a, b obtained by means of Eqs. (5) clearly show the different post peak responses obtained by changing the mixture of cement-based composites. In other words, the evaluation of a, b cannot be of general validity, but should be experimentally evaluated for each kind of reinforcing fiber and matrix.

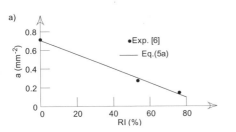 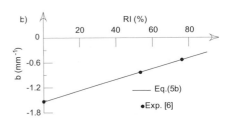

Figure 4: Coefficients a, b for HPFRCC specimens containing steel cords [6]; a) linear approximation of the coefficient a; b) linear approximation of the coefficient b.

4. STRUCTURAL ANALYSIS OF SIMPLY SUPPORTED BEAMS

Only if strain localization phenomena are taken into account, can the post peak stage of beams in bending be correctly predicted by structural analysis. Although structures can be affected by shear and tensile cracks, only beams in bending which fail via crushing of compressed concrete are here considered. In particular, beams in four-point bending, and in three-point bending, with a span/height ratio higher than 10, are analyzed. According to Hillerborg [9], due to this crushing, moment-curvature relationships (M-μ) cannot be evaluated from stress-strain response of materials. On the contrary, stress-inelastic displacement relationships have to be taken into consideration in a more effective approach, like that proposed by Fantilli et al. [10].

If the complete constitutive relationships of a cement-based material are known, the mechanical response of a simply supported beam can be adequately predicted. Thus, in beams which fail via the crushing in compression, the accuracy of the proposed $F(w)$ can be estimated from the comparison between predicted results and experimental data. To this aim, load-midspan deflection curves of simply supported beams are analyzed in the next paragraphs. Both the three-point bending beams and the constant moment zone of the four-point bending beams do not have steel stirrups, therefore their post-peak response is only affected by the presence of fibers.

4.1 Four-point bending tests of Mansur et al. [11]

To study the behaviour of over reinforced four-point bending beams (Fig. 5a), a wide test campaign was conducted by Mansur et al. [11]. In particular, the behaviour of a beam, named B4-0.0C and made of plain high-strength concrete is here taken into consideration. The geometrical dimensions of the beam are shown in Fig. 5a. As it is over-reinforced, crushing failures in compression have been observed prior to the yielding of the steel bars in tension.

To predict the structural response of this beam, the mechanical model proposed by Fantilli et al. [10] can be used, after defining the constitutive relationships of materials. The pre-peak response can be reproduced by the Sargin's relationship proposed by CEB-FIP Model Code [1] (based on the parameters f'_c, E_c, and ε_{c1} experimentally measured). The post-peak stage in compression is described by the function $F(w)$ (Eqs. 4), and the coefficients $a = 0.320$ mm^{-2} and $b = -1.12$ mm^{-1} previously obtained.

For the sake of simplicity, tensile stresses of concrete are neglected, because they give an irrelevant structural contribution during the failure stage of over-reinforced beams.

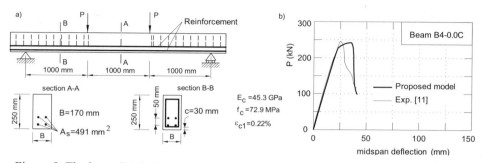

Figure 5: The beam B4-0.0C tested by Mansur et al. [11]; a) geometrical and mechanical properties; b) load-midspan deflection curves.

In fact, at this stage, due to the presence of high curvatures and, consequently, of high tensile stresses in the steel bars, cracks are completely developed and tension stiffening does not affect the ductility of concrete beams [12].

The load-midspan deflection diagrams theoretically computed and experimentally measured are reported in Fig. 5b. Since a good agreement can be seen between the two curves, the effectiveness of the adopted functions $F(w)$ to describe the crushing of plain concrete is definitely proven.

4.2   Three-point bending tests of Mihashi et al. [6]

To complete the investigation on the $F(w)$ relationships, the behaviour of three beams (Fig. 6a), named HSC_1, HSC_2 and HSC_3, is here analyzed. The beams have been tested in three-point bending by Mihashi et al. [6], to investigate the mechanical response of structures made of high-performance concrete and traditional steel reinforcing bars (R/HPFRCC). The HPFRCC is obtained by a mixture of 1% in volume of steel cord in a cement-based mortar, already reinforced by polyethylene fibers (1% in volume). Although the considered beams are normally reinforced, crushing in the compressed zone is systematically observed after yielding of steel bars.

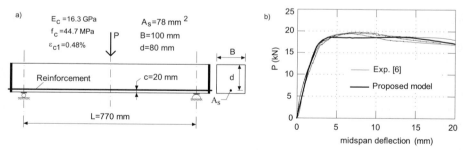

Figure 6: The beams tested by Mihashi et al. [6]; a) geometrical and mechanical properties; b) load-midspan deflection curves.

As widely discussed by the Authors of this paper [13], it is reasonable to expect such behaviour from R/HPFRCC members in bending. The capability of cement-based composites to sustain tensile stresses also at high strains, can correspond to an increase of the steel reinforcement area in tension [13]. Thus, such tests can be used here in order to verify the effectiveness of the proposed model to predict the crushing of R/HPFRCC beams in bending.

Unlike the beams tested by Mansur et al. [11], the contribution of tension stiffening cannot be neglected in the evaluation of the whole structural response of these beams. It can be taken into account by means of a suitable stress-strain relationship for HPFRCC in tension, which has been experimentally evaluated from tensile tests [6], together with the stress-strain relationship of steel reinforcing bar. Similarly to ordinary concrete, the pre-peak response of compressed HPFRCC can be reproduced by the Sargin's relationship proposed by CEB-FIP Model Code [1] (defined by the parameters f_c, E_c, and ε_{c1} experimentally measured). For the three beams, the post-peak stage in compression is described by the function $F(w)$ of Eqs. (4), in which the coefficients a, b are computed by means of Eqs. (5) (RI=76.2%).

A good agreement between numerical and experimental results is evidenced in Fig. 6b. Therefore, the functions $F(w)$ are also effective in describing the crushing failure of R/HPFRCC beams in bending.

4.3   Some numerical results

To compare the different responses of beams made of ordinary concrete and HRFRCC, which fail via concrete crushing in compression, numerical analyses are here developed for the beam depicted in Fig. 7a. In particular, load-midspan deflection diagrams of such a beam are computed in two different cases (Fig. 7b). In Case_1, the beam is made of ordinary concrete, whose mechanical properties (f_c, E_c, ε_{c1}) are those measured by Mihashi et al. [6]. Its post-peak stage in compression is described by the function $F(w)$ of Eqs. (4) and the coefficients $a = 0.320$ mm^{-2} and $b = -1.12$ mm^{-1}. Case_2 regards a beam made of the HPFRCC tailored by Mihashi et al. [6], and already described in the previous paragraph.

In both the cases, reinforcement areas A_s are chosen in order to have the same maximum load P (that is, $A_s = 205$ mm^2 in Case_1, and $A_s = 156$ mm^2 in Case_2). Although the beams show the same bearing capacity (Fig. 7b), the load-midspan deflection diagram of Case_2 (R/HPFRCC beam) appears more ductile.

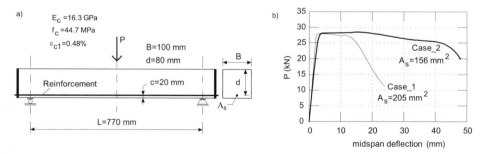

Figure 7: The beams of Case_1 and Case_2; a) geometrical and mechanical properties; b) load-midspan deflection curves.

5. CONCLUSIONS

With the goal of modelling the failure stage of RC and R/HPFRCC beams, a characterization of two cement-based materials has been presented. In particular, a unique function $F(w)$ has been introduced to define the post-peak behaviour of plain concrete and HPFRCC in compression. In this way, the ultimate stages of simply supported beams in bending can be analyzed. Based on the results of this investigation, it is possible to conclude that the ductility of R/HPFRCC beams is higher than that of RC beams, because of the highly ductile post-peak response of HPFRCC in compression.

ACKNOWLEDGEMENTS

The authors wish to express their gratitude to the Italian Ministry of University and Research for financing this research work (PRIN 2004-2005).

REFERENCES

[1] CEB (Comite Euro-International du Beton), "CEB-FIP Model Code 1990". *Bulletin d'information n°203-205*. (Thomas Telford, London, 1993).

[2] Fujita, Y., Ishimaru, R., Hanai, S., and Suenaga, Y., "Study on internal friction angle and tensile strength of plain concrete". Proceedings of the third international conference on Fracture Mechanics of Concrete Structures (FRAMCOS 3), Gifu, Japan, 1998, (Aedificatio Publishers, 1998) 325-334.

[3] van Mier, J. G. M., "Strain softening of Concrete under Multiaxial Loading Conditions". Doctoral thesis. (Delft University of Technology, The Netherlands, 1984).

[4] Jansen, D. C., and Shah, S. P., "Effect of length on compressive strain softening of concrete", *ASCE Journal of Engineering Mechanics* **123**(1) (1997) 25-35.

[5] Fanella, D. A., and Naaman, A. E., "Stress-strain Properties of Fiber Reinforced Mortar in Compression", *ACI Journal* **82**(4) (1985) 475-483.

[6] Mihashi, H., Kikuchi, T., Akita, H., and Fantilli, A. P., "Testing Method and Modeling of HPFRCC", In International RILEM Workshop on High Performance Fiber Reinforced Cementitious Composites (HPFRCC) in Structural Applications, Honolulu, Hawaii, 2005. (RILEM Publications SARL, 2006) 7-16.

[7] Kawamata, A, Mihashi, H., and Fukuyama, H., "Properties of Hybrid Fiber Reinforced Cement-based Composites", *Journal of Advanced Concrete Technology* **1**(3) (2003) 283-290.

[8] Otsuka, K., Mihashi, H., Kiyota, M., Mori, S., and Kawamata, A., "Observation of Multiple Cracking in Hybrid FRCC at Micro and Meso Levels", *Journal of Advanced Concrete Technology* **1**(3) (2003) 291-298.

[9] Hillerborg, A., "Fracture mechanics concepts applied to moment capacity and rotational capacity of reinforced concrete beams", *Engineering Fracture Mechanics* **35**(1/2/3) (1990) 233-240.

[10] Fantilli, A.P., Ferretti, D., Iori, I., and Vallini, P., "Mechanical Model for the Failure of Compressed Concrete in Reinforced Concrete Beams", *ASCE Journal of Structural Engineering* **128**(5) (2002) 637-645.

[11] Mansur, M.A., Chin, M.S., and Wee, T.H., "Flexural Behavior of High-Strength Concrete beams", *ACI Structural Journal* **94**(6) (1997) 663-674.

[12] Fantilli, A. P., Iori I., and Vallini, P., "Mechanical Model for the Confined Compressed Concrete of RC Beams". Concrete Structures in the 21st century: Proceedings of the 1st fib Congress, Osaka, Japan, 2002, 43-52.

[13] Fantilli, A.P., Mihashi, H. and Vallini, P., "Strain compatibility between HPFRCC and steel reinforcement", *Materials and Structures* **38**(5) (2005) 495-503.

FLEXURAL MODELLING OF STRAIN SOFTENING AND STRAIN HARDENING FIBER REINFORCED CONCRETE

Chote Soranakom and Barzin Mobasher

Department of Civil & Environmental Engineering, Arizona State University, USA

Abstract
Parameterized material models for modeling strain softening and strain hardening fiber reinforced concrete are presented. The models are expressed as closed-form solutions of moment-curvature response, which can be used with crack localization rules to predict flexural response of a beam under four point bending test. A parametric study of post crack tensile strength in the strain softening model is conducted to demonstrate two sub-class behaviors: deflection softening and deflection hardening. Uniaxial and flexural test results of steel and glass fiber reinforced are selected to demonstrate the applicability of the algorithm to predict load deflection responses. The simulations reveal that the direct use of tensile response from uniaxial test under-predicted the flexural response of four point bending test, implying the discrepancy between the two test methods. A uniformly increase in tension capacity is found necessary to enable the predictions to match the experimental results.

1. Introduction

With an increased use of fiber reinforced concrete in structural applications, proper characterization techniques and development of design guides are needed [1, 2]. High Performance Fiber Reinforced Concrete (HPFRC) with significant ductility are characterized by multiple cracking mechanisms which lead to a relatively high elastic limit, and stress carrying capacity in the post cracking region extending over a large strain range [3, 4]. Naaman and Reinhardt [5] defined the formulation and testing conditions for strain hardening and strain-softening in tension test. Within the last category, additional two terms for bending test are defined; deflection-hardening is used to describe the material that has post crack flexural strength higher than the cracking strength and deflection-softening for materials with a descending stress beyond the first crack flexural strength. In order to utilize varieties of fiber reinforced concrete products, two simple parameterized material models applicable for modeling strain softening and hardening material are presented in this paper.

2. STRAIN SOFTENING FIBER REINFORCED CONCRETE

Strain softening fiber reinforced concrete [6] can be adequately described by uniaxial tension and compression models as shown in Fig. 1(a) and (b), respectively. The tension response is assumed to behave linearly elastic up to the cracking tensile strength σ_{cr} and drop to the post crack tensile strength σ_p thereafter. The compression response is assumed to be elastic perfectly plastic with the yield compressive stress σ_{cy} starting at the yield compressive strain ε_{cy}. The ultimate tensile and compressive strains (ε_{tu} and ε_{cu}) in the model limit the strength of material. As shown in the figures, all strain quantities are expressed as combination of normalized parameters (β_{tu}, ω, λ, and λ_{cu}) and the first cracking tensile strain ε_{cr}. Similarly, the stresses are expressed as normalized parameters (μ and ω) and the cracking tensile strength σ_{cr} or $\varepsilon_{cr}E$.

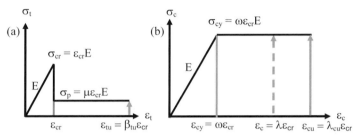

Figure 1: Parameterized strain softening fiber reinforced concrete model; (a) Tension model; (b) Compression model

The closed form solutions for moment curvature diagram was derived explicitly in [6] by first drawing stress strain diagram according to the applied normalized top compressive strain λ in 3 stages: elastic tension and compression ($0<\lambda\leq1$), post-peak tension, elastic compression ($1<\lambda\leq\omega$) and post-peak tension, plastic compression ($\omega<\lambda\leq\lambda_{cu}$). The neutral axis depth ratio k is found by solving equilibrium of forces. The moment capacity is then calculated using tension and compression forces and the neutral axis location; the corresponding curvature is obtained by dividing the top compressive strain with the neutral axis depth. Finally, the moment M and curvature ϕ are normalized with their cracking moment M_{cr} and cracking curvature ϕ_{cr} to obtained the normalized moment M' and curvature ϕ', respectively [6]. Expressions for calculating neutral axis depth ratio, moment and curvature are given in Eqs (1) and (2) and Table 1:

$$M = M_{cr}\, M'; \qquad M_{cr} = \frac{1}{6}bd^2 E\varepsilon_{cr} \tag{1}$$

$$\phi = \phi_{cr}\, \phi'; \qquad \phi_{cr} = \frac{2\varepsilon_{cr}}{d} \tag{2}$$

For a given set of material parameters and dimensions of a beam cross section, the moment curvature diagram can be generated by substituting an incremental normalized top compressive strain λ from zero up to the ultimate compressive strain λ_{cu} using the expressions given in Table 1. One can show that after cracking, the post crack moment curvature response depends mainly on the normalized post crack tensile strength parameter μ. The moment-curvature response becomes elastic perfectly plastic when μ reaches the critical value of μ_{crit}, given by

$$\mu_{crit} = \frac{\omega}{3\omega-1} \qquad (3)$$

This critical parameter represents the transition from a deflection softening to a deflection hardening material. For typical steel fiber reinforced concrete SFRC with ω between 6 and 12, μ_{crit} varies in a narrow range 0.353 - 0.343. This indicates that the post crack tensile strength in a SFRC must be at least 35% of its tensile strength before it can exhibit deflection hardening. This value is in agreement with the values reported by other researchers as well. [7, 8].

Table 1: Neutral axis depth ratio and normalized moment curvature expression for three stages of applied normalized top compressive strain

	Stage	k	M'	ϕ'
Linear tension & comp.	$0 \leq \lambda \leq 1$	$\frac{1}{2}$	$\frac{\lambda}{2k}$	
Softening tension & linear comp.	$1 < \lambda \leq \omega$	$\frac{2\mu\lambda}{\lambda^2 + 2\mu(\lambda+1)-1}$	$\frac{(2\lambda^3 + 3\mu\lambda^2 - 3\mu+2)k^2}{\lambda^2} - 3\mu(2k-1)$	$\frac{\lambda}{2k}$
Softening tension & plastic comp.	$\omega < \lambda \leq \lambda_{cu}$	$\frac{2\mu\lambda}{-\omega^2 + 2\lambda(\omega+\mu)+2\mu-1}$	$\frac{(3\omega\lambda^2 - \omega^3 + 3\mu\lambda^2 - 3\mu+2)k^2}{\lambda^2} - 3\mu(2k-1)$	

3. STRAIN SOFTENING/HARDENGING FIBER REINFORCED CONCRETE

The parameterized material model for strain softening fiber reinforced concrete can be extended to strain hardening material, with three additional non-dimensional variables: γ, η and α to describe material characteristics. Fig. 2 shows a parameterized strain softening/hardening fiber reinforced concrete model [9]. The second model can simulate both strain softening and hardening materials, the simplicity of the first model is more convenient and suitable to be used as a design guide line for typical low content steel fiber reinforced concrete. Compared to the softening model in Fig 1, the strain softening/hardening model in Fig. 2 is different in three aspects. First, the compressive modulus E_c can be different from the tensile modulus E. Second, a transition zone is added between the first cracking tensile strain, ε_{cr}, and the ultimate strain ε_{trn} in tension model to account for strain hardening after cracking. Strain softening or hardening can be defined by negative or positive cracking modulus E_{cr}. Finally, the post crack tensile strength parameter μ may vary by a range of values $1 < \mu < \eta(1-\alpha)$ to simulate the post peak stress, which may not necessary be defined as a continuous function from the end of the second segment. Similar to the strain softening model, all strain quantities are expressed as combination of normalized parameters (α, β_{tu}, ω, λ, and λ_{cu}) and the first cracking tensile strain ε_{cr}; stresses are expressed as normalized parameters (μ and ω) and the cracking tensile strength σ_{cr} or $\varepsilon_{cr}E$; modulus are expressed as normalized parameters (η and γ) and the tensile modulus E.

The closed form solution for moment curvature diagram can be obtained by the same procedure as the strain softening material. The expressions will be released in an upcoming publication [9].

4. CRACK LOCALIZATION RULES

As a flexural specimen is loaded beyond the peak strength, the load decreases and two distinct zones develop as the deformation localizes in the cracking region while the remainder of the specimen undergoes general unloading. The deflection response depends on the relative sizes of these two zones. If cracks concentrate in a narrow localized region, the deflection shows a brittle response, even exhibiting snap-back unloading. On the contrary, if cracks are distributed over a larger area, dissipation of energy results in a more ductile response and gradual unloading. Crack localization rules are introduced in the moment curvature diagram to predict deformation with both localized and non-localized regions.

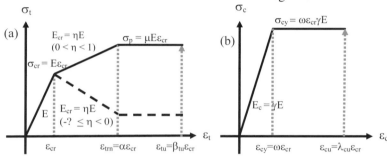

Figure 2: Parameterized strain softening/hardening fiber reinforced concrete model; (a) Tension model; (b) Compression model

Fig. 3(a) and (b) present the schematic moment-curvature diagram and a half model of a beam between the support and mid span under four point bending test. Smeared crack is assumed to localize in the mid-zone; while the zones outside the cracking region undergo unloading during softening. The length of the localized zone is defined as parameter c, representing a fraction of spacing $S=L/3$, where L is the clear span. For a reinforced cement composite with a uniform distribution of cracks in the mid span, a default value of $c=0.5$ is used.

The moment-curvature diagram is used to determine the bending curvature distribution along the length of a beam corresponding to the internal moment distribution at any given load step. In general case as shown in the solid curve of Fig. 3(a), the diagram is divided into two portions: an ascending curve from 0 to M_{max} and a descending curve from M_{max} to M_{fail}. For some low-fiber volume fractions where the post-peak response sharply drops after cracking and slowly increase afterwards, the moment curvature response is expressed in three portions: an ascending curve from 0 to $M_{max1}(=Mcr)$, a descending curve from M_{max1} to M_{low} and ascending curve again from M_{low} to M_{max2}. In this case, there are two local maxima and either one could be the global maximum, depending on the absolute magnitude.

To predict load-deflection response of four-point bending test, the load steps P_i are obtained from discrete data points along the generated moment curvature diagram.

$$P_i = \frac{6M_i}{L}, \qquad i=1,2,3,..N \qquad (4)$$

where, M_i is a discrete moment along the moment curvature diagram, L is the clear span and N is number of data points along the moment curvature diagram, equal to number of load steps. The corresponding curvature is obtained from this moment-curvature relationship. When the specimen is loaded from 0 to M_{max} (or M_{max1}), the ascending portion of the diagram is used. Beyond the maximum load, as the specimen undergoes unloading, the curvature along the beam depends on the localized or non-localized zones and its prior strain history (uncracked or cracked). For a section in the non-localized zone, the curvature of an uncracked section that the moment remains below the cracking moment M_{cr} is reduced linearly and elastically during unloading. If the section has been loaded beyond M_{cr} but less than M_{max}, the unloading curvature of cracked sections follows a quasi-linear recovery path expressed as:

$$\phi_j = \phi_{j-1} - \xi \frac{(M_{j-1} - M_j)}{EI}$$

(5)

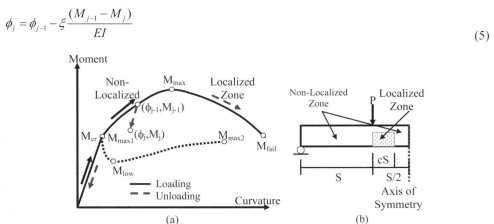

Figure 3: Crack localization rules; (a) moment curvature diagram; (b) half model of four point bending test

where ϕ_{j-1} and M_{j-1} represent moment and curvature at the previous load step and ϕ_j, and M_j are the current step. E and I represent the elastic modulus and the moment of inertia of uncracked section. The unloading factor ξ is between 0 and 1; $\xi = 0$ indicates no curvature recovery while $\xi = 1$ is unloading with initial stiffness EI. The default $\xi = 0$ was used in the present study. Unloading curvature in the localized zone is determined from the descending portion of the curve (M_{max} to M_{fail}) or (M_{max1} to M_{low}). For a special case of low fiber content that the moment curvature diagram is divided into 3 portions, the curvature corresponding to the load step beyond the M_{low} is determined by the third portion, (M_{low} to M_{max2}).

5. ALGORITHM TO PREDICT LOAD DEFLECTION RESPONSE OF FOUR POINT BENDING TEST

The load deflection response of a beam can be obtained by using the moment-curvature response, crack localization rules, and moment-area method:
1. For a given cross section and material parameters, moment curvature diagram can be generated for N discrete data points using the closed form solutions.
2. Using the value of moment, a load vector P containing N steps is calculated by Eq. (4).
3. Beam length L is discretized into finite sections between the support and mid span (half model). The static moment distribution is calculated corresponding to load vector P.

4. Curvature corresponding to the moment at a discrete section is obtained from the moment curvature diagram and crack localization rules.
5. Deflection at mid-span is calculated by taking the first moment of the curvature distribution between the support and mid-span.
6. Steps 3-5 are repeated for N load steps to obtain a complete load deflection response.

6. PARAMETRIC STUDY OF THE EFFECT OF POST CRACK TENSILE STRENTH

In a strain softening material model as shown in Fig. 1, the post crack tensile strength parameter μ plays an important role in the flexural behavior. A typical steel fiber reinforce concrete with a compressive to tensile strength ratio ω of 10, ultimate compressive strain ε_{cu} of 0.004 and ultimate tensile strain ε_{tu} of 0.015 is used to demonstrate the effect of this parameter. Neutral axis dept ratio k and normalized moment-curvature M'-ϕ', are independent of the size of the beam and two intrinsic material parameters, Young modulus E, and first cracking strain ε_{cr}.

Fig. 4(a) shows the effect of parameter μ to the neutral axis depth ratio k at various stages of normalized top compressive strain λ. It can be seen that the k value of brittle material with $\mu = 0.01$ drops very rapidly from 0.5 to 0 at very low value of normalized top compressive strain. As the parameter μ increases, the drop rate of k value decreases and the beam section can develop larger normalized top compressive strain. Fig. 4(b) clearly shows that μ_{crit} of 0.35 causes normalized moment curvature response to behave elastic perfectly plastic; the material with
$\mu < 0.35$ shows deflection softening while the material with $\mu > 0.35$ shows deflection hardening response.

7. ANALYSIS OF FOUR POINT BENDING

The closed form solutions for moment curvature diagram were used to predict load deformation response in a four point bending test for steel and glass fiber reinforced concrete. The material parameters for tension model were found by fitting the model to the uniaxial tension result. The material parameters for compression model are less sensitive to the prediction of the load deflection; thus, they were estimated from the uniaxial compressive strength.

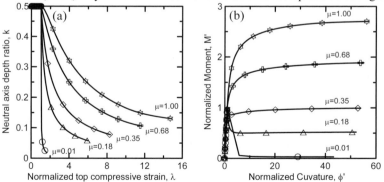

Figure 4: Parametric study the effect of post cracking tensile stress parameter μ

6.1 Simulation of strain softening fiber reinforced concrete

Two sets of steel fiber reinforced concrete specimens H1 and H21 by Lim et. al. [10, 11] that show deflection softening and hardening responses under four point bending test were used to demonstrate the model's simulation of load deflection response using the strain softening material model. Two mixes designated H1 and H21 contain hook fibers at V_f= 0.5% and 1.0%, respectively. The details of the samples and parameters for simulation are listed in Table 2.

Table 2: Details of the mixes and Parameter estimations in simulations of load deflection responses of fiber reinforced concrete

Set	class	b x d x L mm	E GPa	ε_{cr} x10^{-6}	μ	ω	γ	η	α	β_{tu}	λ_{cu}	Modifying factors
SFRC (H1)	SS-DS	100x100 x750	25.4	110.6	0.24	10.3	-	-	-	135.6	36.2	1.61ε_{cr}
SFRC (H21)	SS-DH	100x100 x750	25.4	116.2	0.83	9.8	-	-	-	129.1	34.4	1.02ε_{cr}
GFRC	SH	50x10 x175	7.5	1000	0.65	2.53	2.02	0.04	24	60	8	1.30ε_{cr}

Note that Acronym SS-DS, SS-DH and SH refer to strain softening-deflection softening, strain softening-deflection hardening and strain hardening materials, respectively.

Fig. 5 shows the input tensile uniaxial tests used in prediction of flexural response. Fig. 5(a) shows the uniaxial tension test result of deflection softening mix H1 (V_f=0.5%) with circular symbols and the fitted tension model in solid curve. The parameters of compression model are presented in Table 2. Fig. 5(b) revealed that the direct use of the uniaxial tension test under-predict the flexural response. By examining the load deflection response, the concrete cracks at load P_{cr}=6.0 kN. With a clear span L=750 mm, beam width b=100 mm and beam depth d=100 mm, the nominal flexural stress for four-point bending is 4.50 MPa, which is 1.61 times the experimental uniaxial tensile strength of 2.80 MPa. This discrepancy is attributed to the differences in the stress profiles of the tension and flexural experiments. In the uniaxial tension test, the entire volume of the specimen is a potential zone for crack initiation. On the other hand, in the flexural test, only a small tension region at the centerline extreme tension fiber of the beam is subjected to an equivalent tensile stress. The experimental tensile strength obtained from the flexural test is likely to be higher than uniaxial test results. For brittle materials with high compressive to tensile strength ratios, the flexural behavior is dominated by the tensile strength of material. In order to compensate the under predicted response, the tension model could be uniformly increased by as much as the degree of under-prediction. This increase can be done by modifying the first cracking tensile strain ε_{cr} with a factor of 1.61 as other associated strains and stress will be increased by the same factor as shown in the dash line in Fig. 5(a). The modified model leads to a good match of the experimental result as shown in the dash line in Fig. 5(b).

Another set of deflection hardening specimen H21 (V_f=1.0%) is presented in Fig.5 (c) and (d). The uniaxial tension test result and its fitted tension model are shown in Fig. 5(c) and the predicted flexural response is shown in Fig. 5(d). The predicted response is slightly lower than the experimental result. By increasing the first cracking tensile strain by a factor of 1.02

as shown by the dash line in Fig 5(c), the prediction matches the experimental results as indicated by the dash line in Fig. 5(d).

6.2 Simulation of strain hardening fiber reinforced concrete

One set of unaged glass fiber reinforced concrete (GFRC) specimen was used from published literature [12] to demonstrate the use of strain hardening/softening model to predict the flexural behavior of strain hardening material under four point bending. The uniaxial tension specimens were notched while the flexural specimens were unnotched. The proportion of the mix (cement : sand : metakaolin : water : polymer) was 100 : 100 : 25 : 44 : 12. AR-glass fiber content of 5% by weight of composite was used.

The uniaxial tension test result was used to fit the tension model to obtain the material parameters as shown by the solid line in Fig. 6(a). Since there was no compression test data available, the ultimate compressive strength f_c' was assumed to be 45 MPa, the compressive yield stress f_{cy} of $0.85fc'$, the compressive modulus E_c was estimated from the initial slope of the load deflection response and the normalized compressive yield strain was obtained by $\omega=f_{cy}/(E_c\varepsilon_{cr})$. The ultimate compressive strain ε_{cu} was assumed to 0.008. Table 2 provides material parameters for tension and compression models used in simulation of a flexural sample. Fig. 6(a) shows the tension test results of GFRC along with the fitted tension model and the modified tension model. Fig. 6(b) shows that the fitted model under-predicted the peak experimental load by the ratio of 1.30 (experiment 1.0 kN vs. predicted 0.77 kN). As discussed before, this discrepancy is caused by the differences in the stress profiles of the tension and flexural experiments. Also the notched tension specimen generally yield lower tensile stress strain response than those of unnotched specimens. The modification to the first cracking strain by a factor of 1.30 ε_{cr} was necessary for a good prediction of load deflection response.

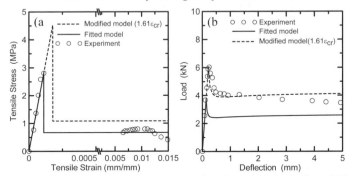

Figure 5: Tension models and the predicted load deflection responses of steel fiber reinforced concrete under four point bending: (a) and (b) Tension model and load deflection response for H1;

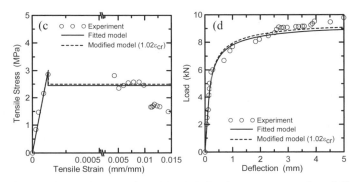

Figure 5: Tension models and the predicted load deflection responses of steel fiber reinforced concrete under four point bending: (c) and (d) Tension model and load deflection response for H21

8. CONCLUSIONS

Flexural response of fiber reinforced concrete products with different levels of pre- and post peak tensile response can be adequately predicted using two simple parameterized material models: strain softening and strain soft/hardening models. Closed form solutions for generating moment curvature diagrams based on these two models were also derived for estimation of flexural capacity and load deformation of flexural members. The algorithm to predict load deflection of a beam under the four point bending test using a moment-curvature response with crack localization rules was also presented. According to the strain softening model, for a typical compressive to tensile strength ratio of between 6-12, the critical post crack tensile strength $\mu_{crit} = 0.35$ characterizes two subclasses of materials: deflection softening ($\mu < 0.35$) and deflection hardening ($\mu > 0.35$). The simulation of steel and glass fiber reinforced concrete revealed that the direct use of the tensile response under-predicted the flexural response. This discrepancy was in part due to a difference in stress distribution between the uniaxial tension and bending tests. Since the flexural strength of concrete member is generally governed by the tensile strength of material, the under-predicted load deformation response can be corrected by increasing the tension capacity. This can be achieved by multiplying a scaling parameter to the first cracking strain; other associated tensile strains and stress will be subsequently increased by the same scale. With proper scaling parameters, the predicted responses agree well with experimental observations.

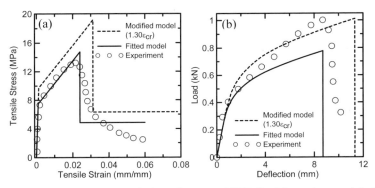

Figure 6: Simulation of glass fiber reinforced cement (GFRC): (a) tension model; (b) flexural response

ACKNOWLEDGEMENT

The authors gratefully acknowledge the support of National Science Foundation, Award # 0324669-03, Program manager: Dr. P. Balaguru for the support of this research.

REFERENCES

[1] Priestley, M.J.N., Verma, R., and Xiao, Y., 'Seismic Shear Strength of Reinforced Concrete Columns', *ASCE Journal of Structural Engineering*, 120(8), (1994) 2310-2328.

[2] Parra-Montesinos, G.J., 'High-Performance Fiber Reinforced Cement Composites: A New Alternative for Seismic Design of Structures', *ACI Structural J.*, 102(5) (2005) 668-675.

[3] Mobasher, B. and Shah, S.P., 'Test Parameters for Evaluating Toughness of Glass-Fiber Reinforced Concrete Panels', *ACI Materials Journal,* 86(5) (1989) 448-458.

[4] Mobasher, B. and Li, C.Y., 'Mechanical Properties of Hybrid Cement-Based Composites', *ACI Materials Journal*, 93(3) (1996) 284-293.

[5] Naaman, A. E. and Reinhardt H. W., 'Proposed Classification of HPFRC Composites Based on Their Tensile Response', *Materials and Structures*, 39 (2006) 547–555.

[6] Soranakom, C., and Mobasher, B., "Closed Form Solutions for Flexural Response of Fiber Reinforced Concrete Beams," ASCE *Journal of Engineering Mechanics*, 2007. *(Accepted for Publication)*.

[7] Nemegeer-Harelbeke, D., Design Guidelines for Dramix Steel Fibre Reinforced Concrete, Bekaert, 1998.

[8] Barros, J. A. O., Cunha, V. M. C. F., Ribero, A. F., and Antunes, J. A. B., (2004) "Post-cracking Behaviour of Steel Fibre Reinforced Concrete," Materials and Structures, Vol. 37.

[9] Soranakom, C., and Mobasher, B., "Modeling the Flexural Response of Strain Softening and Strain Hardening Cement Composites," *Cement and Concrete Composites,* 2007. *(in preparation)*

[10] Lim, T.Y., Paramasivam, P. and Lee, S.L., 'Analytical Model for Tensile Behavior of Steel-Fiber Concrete', *ACI Material Journal*, 84(4) (1987) 286-551.

[11] Lim, T.Y., Paramasivam, P. and Lee, S.L., 'Bending Behavior of Steel-Fiber Concrete Beams', *ACI Structural Journal*, 84(6) (1987) 524-536.

[12] Marikunte, S., and Aldea, C., and Shah, S.P., "Durability of Glass Fiber Reinforced Cement Composites: Effect of Silica Fume and Metakaolin," *Adv Cement Based Materials*, V.5, No.3-4, Apr.-May. 1997, pp. 100-108.

MECHANICAL CHARACTERISTICS OF EXTRUDED SHCC

Christo R. Visser and Gideon P.A.G. van Zijl

Department of Civil Engineering, University of Stellenbosch, South Africa

Abstract

Strain Hardening Cement-based Composites (SHCC), is a class of High Performance Fibre Reinforced Cement Composites (HPFRCC), which has significant pseudo strain-hardening in tension. Extrusion may present a suitable manufacturing process for SHCC if the mix rheology is optimised and matrix-fibre properties are balanced through appropriate micromechanical considerations. This paper reports the results of mechanical testing of extruded SHCC containing polymeric fibres. Attention is given to fibre orientation and tensile mechanical properties such as E-modulus, first cracking strength and ductility. The properties are compared with those of cast SHCC of equivalent mix proportioning.

1. INTRODUCTION

SHCC is a relatively new class of HPFRCC construction material and the interest in the structural use thereof is rapidly growing. SHCC exhibits significant pseudo strain-hardening behaviour in direct tension and in bending. This is maintained over a large tensile strain, giving SHCC a high ductility and energy absorbing capacity.

The work presented in this paper focuses on developing an extrusion process for SHCC with the idea to produce prefabricated elements for the construction industry. Extrusion not only has all the benefits of pre-casting, such as quality-control, more accurate geometrical tolerances and higher construction speed, but also an increased production rate compared to ordinary pre-casting methods. However, special attention is required to ensure that the ductile, pseudo strain-hardening character of SHCC is achieved despite the formation of elements under high pressure and shear in the plastic moulding process of extrusion. Firstly a mix with the correct rheology has to be designed to enable the extrusion of cement-based composites containing soft polymeric fibres, while maintaining appropriate dispersal, stretch and orientation of the fibres in the matrix. Polymeric fibres which have been found to be optimal for SHCC, having appropriate aspect ratios, mechanical properties of strength and stiffness, as well as suitable bonding properties for suitable interfacing with cement-based matrices to ensure pseudo strain-hardening. In particular, Polyvinyl Alcohol (PVA) fibres of 12 mm length have been used widely in cast mixes and are used in this paper for both cast and extrusion processing of specimens. Extrusion of PVA fibres of lengths up to 6 mm has been shown the be challenging, leading to reduced alignment of the fibres by the extrusion process and fibre breakage during mechanical testing in tension and bending due to strong bonding with the extrusion-densified matrix [1].

Furthermore the mechanical properties of extruded SHCC have to be determined to enable structural design for its use a construction material. Several structural applications demand high stiffness. A relatively low E-modulus has been a persisting problem with SHCC It may be required that high stiffness prevails in the uncracked service conditions to ensure structural serviceability, while the high energy dissipation quality in the pseudo strain-hardening, multiple cracking phase is released during calamities. Furthermore, application of SHCC in composite sections, for example reinforced concrete with SHCC over- or underlays, may lead to stress peaks and damage in the RC if a significant difference in the E-moduli exists. In this paper special attention is given to the E-modulus of extruded SHCC. Direct tensile mechanical behaviour of extruded PVA SHCC is compared with that of equivalent SHCC specimens prepared by casting.

2. EXPERIMENTAL PROGRAM

2.1 Mix design

The experimental program can be divided into three parts: 1) to successfully extrude PVA SHCC containing 12 mm PVA fibres, 2) to study the fibre orientation in an extruded composite and 3) to determine the tensile mechanical characteristics of extruded PVA SHCC. SHCC uses the same materials as FRC, namely water, cement, sand, fibres and chemical additives. However, particles sizes are limited and an optimal combination of the ingredients, based on micro-mechanical principles, is sought to achieve the strain hardening, ductile response of SHCC. Furthermore, it has proved difficult to successfully extrude SHCC with polymeric fibres of relatively large length. Extrusion of cement composites with PVA fibres of length 2 mm, 4 mm and 6 mm respectively has been reported [1], finding reduced mechanical performance in terms of a lower tensile ductility with increased fibre lengths. Table 1 shows a mix that was designed in the current project for the extrusion of SHCC using PVA fibres of length 12 mm, diameter 40 μm and $E_f = 40$ GPa. A mix designed for comparison purposes of cast specimens, using the same fibres is also shown in Table 1.

Two significant differences can be seen in the mixes. Firstly, in the casting mix a portion of the cement is replaced with Ground Granulated Corex Slag (GGCS) and secondly, the casting mix has a higher water:binder (w/b) ratio. This difference in the w/b ratio is to establish a more workable, wet mix for casting while the extrusion mix is dough-like and dry.

2.2 Specimen preparation and testing

2.2.1 Extrusion

SHCC pastes are difficult to characterize with normal concrete rheology models. A more appropriate technique has to be adopted to characterize extrusion mix designs. According to Srinivasan et al. (1999) [2], extrudable SHCC can be effectively developed with the aid of an extrusion rheometer. However, for this study an indirect method was adopted in testing the behaviour of the hardened extrusion products. Thereby, an indirect measure of fibre dispersion is followed, by concluding that the degree of multiple cracking and ductility indicates the degree of fibre dispersion and, therefore, successful extrusion. Highly ductile, strain hardening tensile/ flexural response indicates good fibre dispersal, while brittle failure at low tensile strain indicates poor fibre dispersal. The mix was prepared in a 50L pan mixer and then extruded with a plate piston extruder. The mix was visually inspected for fibre distribution, i.e. no fibre balls, extrude-ability, i.e. no segregation, and form retention. Plates with nominal cross-section of 70 mm x 15 mm were extruded and cut to lengths of 500 mm.

Table 1: Mix design for the extrusion of PVA-SHCC

	Constituent	Ratio		kg/m^3	Vol. portion
Extrusion mix:	water	water:binder	0.250	312.90	$V_p = 0.750$
	binder: Cement - OPC	cement:binder	0.500	625.80	
	Fly Ash (FA)	FA:binder	0.500	625.80	
	super-plasticizer (SP)	SP:binder	0.012	15.00	
	aggregate - dune sand	aggregate:binder	0.500	625.80	$V_a = 0.230$
	PVA fibres (12mm)	fibres:mix volume	0.020	26.00	$V_f = 0.020$
Cast mix:	water	water:binder	0.400	419.64	$V_p = 0.0786$
	binder:Cement - OPC	cement:binder	0.450	472.10	
	Fly Ash (FA)	FA:binder	0.500	524.55	
	Slag (GGCS)	GGCS:binder	0.050	52.46	
	Super-plasticizer (SP)	SP:binder	0.012	12.59	
	Aggregate - dune sand	aggregate:binder	0.500	524.55	$V_a = 0.194$
	PVA fibres (12mm)	fibres:mix volume	0.020	26.00	$V_f = 0.020$

The plates were then placed in a climate room to cure at 100% relative humidity and a temperature of 23°C.Tests were conducted after 14 days of curing, when the specimens were removed from the climate room and towel dried just before testing. For this research the method for determining the tensile mechanical properties and performance of extruded SHCC is bending tests for determining flexural strength or indirect tension strength. Three-point bending tests were conducted over a span of 400 mm with the use of a Zwick Z250 testing machine. The tests were conducted by displacement control at a rate of 3 mm/minute. The load was applied at mid-span, with the built-in load Zwick cell measuring the applied load and the Zwick crosshead LVDT measuring the deflection at mid-span. The data was then converted to an output file and displayed on a computer in the form of an applied load vs. mid-span deflection curve.

2.2.2 Orthotropy

The determination of the orientation of PVA fibres in SHCC is difficult since a method does not yet exist to accurately quantify or determine such non-metallic fibres. The primary reason for this is the low colour contrast between the fibres and the cement material. Research done by Torigoe (2003) [3], led to claims that PVA fibres can be seen as green to yellow spots in a cross-section of the composite with the use of a fluorescence technique. This was deemed impractical for this research, since it would require the use of complicated equipment which might give an indication of fibre dispersal, but not of the fibre orientation.

An easier and more effective way had to be found to determine or quantify the orientation of fibres within a composite. By using three-point bending, a comparison can be made between the fibre orientation in the longitudinal and orthogonal direction of a composite by comparing the mechanical responses of the composite for bending in each direction. It is acknowledged that this is an indirect method, and does not reflect the influence of fibre orientation alone.

The same procedure described above was used to produce extruded plates. From these plates, samples were cut with nominal dimensions 70 mm x 30 mm x 15 mm for the orthogonal and the longitudinal direction to be tested in both these directions at spans of 60 mm. The length to depth ratio of these specimens approaches the aspect ratio of deep beams, but they were only used to compare the mechanical responses in the two directions. These specimens were cut from the cured extrudate one day before testing and then placed back in the climate room to be tested the next day. The three-point bending tests were conducted with the use of a Zwick Z250 testing machine at 14 days after curing and the specimens were towel dried just before testing. The tests were conducted by displacement control at a rate of 0.5mm/minute.

2.2.3 Mechanical characteristics of SHCC in direct tension

Extruded plates were again produced for this part of the research. From these plates dogbone specimens, as shown in Fig. 1 were cut. The specimens were tested in direct tension at 14 days after curing, in a Zwick Z250 testing machine at a speed of 0.5 mm/min. The applied load was measured with a 500 kg HBM load cell and the elongation was measured with the use of two HBM 10mm, spring-type, LVDT's. The average reading of the two LVDT's was used to calculate the deformation over a gauge length of 80 mm. The results from these tests were compared with the results of direct tension tests for cast composites that were conducted by W.P. Boshoff (2007) [4] at the University in previous studies.

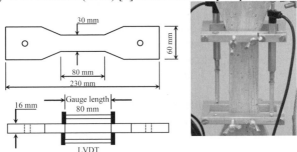

Figure 1: Test set up for direct tensile tests on SHCC.

3.   EXPERIMENTAL RESULTS

3.1   Extrusion

The flexural and direct tensile behaviour of the extruded and cast SHCC specimens are shown in Fig. 2. From the strain-hardening, ductile responses observed in Fig. 2 it may be concluded that successful extrusion was performed on a suitable mix of appropriate rheology, which achieved reasonable fibre dispersion. It produced a composite with mechanical properties of high tensile and flexural strength (average MOR = 11.8 MPa at relatively young age of 14 days) and significant ductility and toughness, although less than that of cast specimens. The choice of the mix was confirmed with reasonably repeatable matrix characteristics, reflected by first crack strength, ultimate load and ductility.

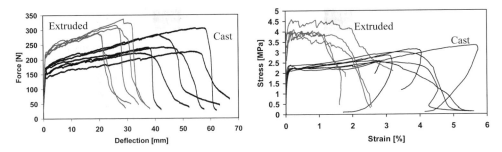

Figure 2: SHCC (a) three-point bending and (b) direct tensile responses.

3.2 Orthotropy

Ten specimens each for the longitudinal and orthogonal direction were tested in three-point flexural bending. During the testing it was evident that all the specimens tested for the longitudinal direction formed multiple micro-cracks, while the specimens tested for the orthogonal direction formed one localized crack. This is reflected in the load vs. deflection curves for the two directions shown in Fig. 3, (a) and (b).

All the specimens tested for the longitudinal direction reached a high strength and then displayed a strain hardening response. The specimens tested for the orthogonal direction on the other hand reached a lower strength at the first crack and then had a brittle response. Some of the composites displayed an increase in strength after the first crack occurred for bending in the orthogonal plain. From the results it can be concluded that the fibres are predominantly orientated in the longitudinal direction. Nevertheless some of the specimens tested for the orthogonal direction exhibited an increase in strength after the first crack, indicating that some fibres are orientated in that direction. This marks a significant modification of the mechanical behaviour of SHCC if it is produced by extrusion, as opposed to casting.

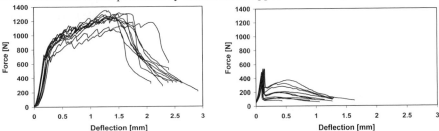

Figure 3: Three-point flexural bending in the (a) longitudinal and (b) orthogonal direction.

4. TENSILE MECHANICAL BEHAVIOUR

4.1 E-modulus of cast SHCC specimens

A secant method was applied to compute E-moduli (Fig. 4) from the direct tensile responses at stress levels one third of the first cracking stress and a low pre-stress ($\sigma_0 = 0,1$ N/mm^2) and the corresponding strains as follows:

$$E_c = \frac{\frac{1}{3}\sigma_t - \sigma_0}{\varepsilon_{(\frac{1}{3}\sigma_t)} - \varepsilon_0} \tag{1}$$

4.1.1 E-modulus of cast SHCC specimens

Considering the volume portions of the main phases in SHCC to be that of matrix (V_m) and fibre (V_f) with respective elastic moduli E_m and E_f, the composite elastic modulus can be expressed as follows:

$$E_c = V_m E_m + \eta V_f E_f \tag{2}$$

based on homogenisation of the stress and strain fields in the two phases. A fibre efficiency coefficient (η) provides for the fact that the fibres are discontinuous and not all aligned in the main stress direction. To study the influence of the heterogeneities in the matrix, it is further subdivided into aggregate (V_a) and paste (V_p), with respective elastic moduli E_a and E_p. Considering only the matrix, the elastic modulus of the matrix (E_m) can be expressed as follows [5]:

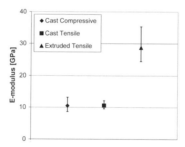

Figure 4: E-moduli of cast SHCC in compression and tension, extruded SHCC in tension.

$$E_m = \frac{(1+V_a)E_a + V_p E_p}{V_p E_a + (1+V_a)E_p} E_p \tag{3}$$

An alternative formulation is based on a representative matrix volume with a central concentration of solid aggregate surrounded by hardened cement paste:

$$\frac{1}{E_m} = \frac{\left(1-\sqrt{V_a}\right)}{E_p} + \frac{\sqrt{V_a}}{E_a\sqrt{V_a} + E_p\left(1-\sqrt{V_a}\right)} \tag{4}$$

Eq. (2) shows an insignificant contribution of low volume PVA fibres to the composite E-modulus, considering an upper bound of $\eta = 1$. This is confirmed by results of direct tensile tests of SHCC specimens of the same mix as reported in this paper, but with fibres volumes of 2% and 2.5% [6]. However, the inclusion of aggregate in proportions such as in this test program ($V_a^{cast} = 0.194$ and $V_a^{extrude} = 0.23$) significantly contributes to E_m, cf. (3) or (4), and thus to the E_c, cf. (2). This is confirmed by experimentally determined E_c [7] of cast SHCC of the same type as in Table 1, but with varying aggregate, Fig. 5. In this figure the E-moduli computed from eqs. (3) or (4) and eq. (2) for various a/b ratio's are also shown. Due to uncertainty of E_a for the aggregate used, two values (E_a = 72 GPa and E_a = 100 GPa) are used, along with E_p = 5.3 GPa, which produces E_c = 6 GPa as suggested by the E-modulus measured for the case a/b = 0. A significant dependence of E_c on aggregate content is apparent. The computed values underestimate the measured increase in E_c in the higher a/b range. Note that the E-moduli of Fig. 5 are for specimens cured in water for 14 days, and subsequently tested at the age of 14 days. Similar tests on a SHCC at 28 days showed a similar influence of aggregate content on E_c, but with roughly doubled value at the higher age [8]. Fig. 5(b) shows the evolution of E_c for the SHCC reported in the current paper (a/b = 0.5), confirming that the 28 day E-modulus is significantly higher than the 14 day value.

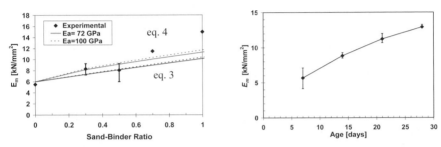

Figure 5: Influence of (a) aggregate content and (b) aging (a/b=0.5) on SHCC E-modulus [7].

4.1.2   E-modulus of extruded SHCC specimens

The extruded SHCC has a lower w/b = 0.25 ratio than the cast mix (w/b = 0.4) to ensure the correct extrusion rheology. Thereby, the aggregate content in the extrusion mix is effectively increased ($V_a^{extrude}$ = 0.23). This aggregate volume portion can be achieved in a cast mix with w/b = 0.4 and a/b = 0.6. For such a mix Fig. 2a suggests E_c to be in the region of 8-10GPa. However, an average of $E_a^{extrude}$ = 28.7GPa was measured. To explain this significant difference, another mechanism is considered, namely paste porosity. It is known that a reduced w/b is linked to reduced porosity (p) and increased E-modulus of hardened cement paste. The governing mechanism of reduced porosity here is the extrusion pressure, whereby air is forced from the paste. Experimental evidence indicates a cubic relation between the paste E-modulus and porosity [9]:

$$E_p = E_p^* \left(1-p\right)^3 \tag{5}$$

where E_p^* is the paste modulus for zero porosity (p = 0). By substituting the E_p = 5.3 GPa into (5), a porosity of 37.9% and 30.8% respectively is computed from (3) and (4) for E_c = 8.7 GPa. These levels of porosity are not uncommon in cement pastes. Furthermore, keeping in mind that this is the porosity of the paste, which comprises 75% of the composite ($V_p^{extrude}$ = 0.75), an overall void content of 28% (3) and 23% (4) respectively is suggested. Air content values of about 15% have been measured by the authors for fresh SHCC mixes with V_f = 2%. It is postulated that the extrusion process forces the entrained air from the composite, and is thereby the main mechanism of increased stiffness of the hardened SHCC produced by extrusion. The quantification of the porosities and air contents of cast versus extruded SHCC remains to be performed in further experimentation. An indication of reduced porosity through extrusion is given by increased density of the extrudate [10].

4.2 Matrix tensile strength

Another indication of densification of the composite by extrusion is given by the increased tensile strength. It is commonly agreed that reduced porosity not only leads to increased E-modulus as argued in the previous section, but also increased strength. However, as for stiffness, increased a/b ratio causes a second mechanism of increased strength. It is believed that the increased tortuosity of cracks leads to higher tensile strength. This was confirmed in an experimental program [7] for the same SHCC as reported in this paper, but for various a/b ratios, Fig. 6. A typical stress-strain result is shown in the figure (left) and the trend of increased first cracking stress with increased a/b ratio is shown on the right. However, it is clear that the matrix strength increase by extrusion is beyond that expected from these two mechanisms. As in the previous section, it is argued that the significant reduction in porosity caused by high pressure extrusion leads to the observed strong increase in first cracking stress.

4.3 Ductility of extruded SHCC specimens

From Fig. 3 it is apparent that increased matrix strength, be it through increased a/b ratio or by reduced porosity (extrusion) causes reduced tensile ductility. This is in agreement with micro-mechanical considerations whereby increased crack tip toughness relative to fibre pull-out complementary energy requires a larger critical fibre volume, i.e. a larger fibre content to ensure tensile strain hardening. A balance between required mechanical properties (E-modulus, tensile strength, tensile ductility) must be found to ensure that optimal behaviour of structural elements fabricated of SHCC is obtained.

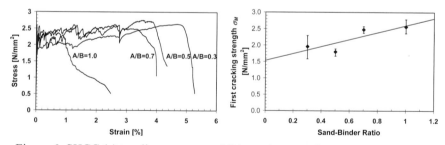

Figure 6: SHCC (a) tensile response and (b) matrix strength versus aggregate content [7].

5. CONCLUSION

At the onset of this research the aim was to: 1) to successfully extrude PVA SHCC containing 12 mm PVA fibres, 2) to study the fibre orientation within an extruded composite and 3) to determine the mechanical characteristics of extruded PVA SHCC in direct tension. Tests and experiments were conducted and based on their results the following conclusions can be made:

- A mix was designed for the extrusion of PVA SHCC containing 12 mm fibres. Mechanical testing in bending and tension confirmed that the mix is appropriate for extrusion, indicated by strain hardening, ductile responses.

- The reasonably repeatable responses in terms of first cracking and ultimate strength indicate that extrusion produced consistent matrix properties and fibre dispersal.
- Bending tests in orthogonal directions showed that extrusion predominantly orientates the fibres in the longitudinal direction. There is nevertheless an indication that some fibres are orientated in the orthogonal direction.
- The elastic modulus of SHCC elements is increased when produced with extrusion. This is due to the higher aggregate content and a lower porosity of extruded products.

REFERENCES

[1] Peled, A. and Shah, S.P. 'Processing effects in cementitious composites: extrusion and casting', *ASCE J Materials in Civil Eng.* **15** (2) (2003) 192-199.
[2] Srinivasan, R., DeFord, D. and Shah, S.P. 'The use of extrusion rheometry in the development of extruded fiber-reinforced cement composites.', *Concrete Science and Engineering* **1** 26-36.
[3] Torigoe, S., Horikoshi, T., Ogawa, A., Saito, A., and Hamada, T., Study on Evaluation Method for PVA Fibre Distribution in Engineered Cementitious Composite, Journal of Advanced Concrete Technology, V.1, No.3, November 2003, 265-268.
[4] Boshoff, W.P., "Time-dependant behaviour of Engineered Cement-based Composites," Dissertation, University of Stellenbosch, South Africa, 2007.
[5] Hashin, Z. 'The elastic moduli of heterogeneous materials',*J Appl. Mech.* **29** (1962) 143-150.
[6] Shang, Q. and van Zijl, G.P.A.G. 'Characterising the shear behaviour of SHCC', *Journal of the South African Institution of Civil Engineers,* accepted for publication.
[7] Van Zijl, G.P.A.G. 'The role of aggregate in HPFRCC', *Concrete / Beton* **110** (2005) 7-13.
[8] Li, V.C., Mishra, D.K. and Wu, H.-C. 'Matrix design for pseudo-strain-hardening fibre reinforced composites', *Materials and Structures* **28** (1995) 586-595.
[9] Helmuth, R.A. and Turk, D.M. Symposium on Structure of Portland Cement Paste, Special Report 90, National Acadamy of Sciences, Washington (1966).
[10] De Koker, D., 'Manufacturing Processes for Engineered Cement-Based Composite Material Products', *M.Sc.Eng. thesis report*, Stellenbosch, South Africa, December 2004.

EFFECT OF REINFORCEMENT RATIO ON THE MECHANICAL RESPONSE OF COMPRESSION MOLDED SISAL FIBER TEXTILE REINFORCED CONCRETE

Flávio A. Silva, Romildo D. Toledo Filho, João A. Melo Filho and Eduardo M.R. Fairbairn

Department of Civil Engineering, COPPE/UFRJ, Brazil

Abstract
   This work presents results of an experimental program on the mechanical properties of a new class of textile composite developed using vegetable sisal fiber as reinforcement. A multi-layer composite was manufactured by a hand lay out of the fibers in 5 layers and posterior compression. The single filament fibers were stitched together, side by side, forming a unidirectional fabric. The influence of reinforcement ratio, ranging from 2 to 10 %, was investigated by means of direct tension and four point bending tests. Results have indicated that 10% is the fiber volume fraction that maximizes the mechanical properties of the composites. Maximum strength values under four point bending, direct tension and bending toughness of, respectively, 18.53 MPa, 8.03 MPa and 20.30 kJ/m^2 were obtained, indicating the potentiality of the new material for structural applications in the sustainable construction industry.

1. INTRODUCTION

   For the past 30 years several researches on the use of sisal fibers as reinforcement in thin section cement composite materials has been performed [1-11]. The majority of this research concerns the use of sisal as a pulp or short fiber as a randomly dispersed reinforcement. The composites reinforced by short fibers presents a reinforcement ratio (V_f) normally ranging from 2 to 3% with the fiber length ranging from 20-50 mm while the ones reinforced by sisal pulp presents a maximum V_f of 14% with fiber length less than 2 mm. The use of larger quantities of fiber or higher fiber lengths resulted in fiber balling or agglomeration, which decreases the performance of the composites. These composites present, in general, a strain softening behavior under direct tension loads. Although the impact behavior, toughness and bending strength can be improved over the non-reinforced matrix, these composites does not present adequate properties for structural applications and their use are mainly devoted to fabricate non-structural elements such as partitioning boards and roofing elements for low cost housing. Finding a substitute for asbestos cement is certainly another concern of the researchers working with sisal fiber as reinforcement of cement composites [9]. Recently, the use of synthetic textile fabrics showed to be adequate for reinforcement of even and curved components in different loading directions resulting in high tensile strength and high energy absorption capacity materials [12-16]. The ease and reproducible positioning of the yarns in the shape of textile fabrics are another advantage of this material. With the objective of developing sisal fiber-composites with high tensile strength and toughness for semi-structural and structural applications, a sisal textile fabric, developed by stitching the single filament fibers side by side in one direction, was used as reinforcement in a multi layer compression molded composite. An investigation on the effect of the reinforcement ratio, which ranged from 2 to 10%, on the mechanical properties of the composites was performed. For that, direct tension and four point bending tests were performed.

2. EXPERIMENTAL PROGRAM

2.1 Materials and Processing

The sisal fibers were produced in Valente-Bahia, Brazil. They presented an average density, elastic modulus and tensile strength of 0.90 g/cm^3, 19 GPa and 577 MPa, respectively [9]. The fibers (Agave sisalana) were extracted from the sisal plant (see Fig. 1a) leaves in the form of long fiber bundles. A sisal plant produces from 200 to 250 leaves before flowering [17], each of which contains approximately 700-1400 fiber bundles with a length of 0.5-1.0 m [18]. The sisal leaf is a sandwich structure composed of 4% fiber, 0.75 % cuticle, 8% dry matter and 87.25% water [17], which is reinforced by three types of fibers: structural, arch and xylem fibers (see Fig. 1 c). These three different types of fibers were also reported by Bisanda and Ansell [19] and by Nutman [20]. The structural fibers gives to the sisal leaf its stiffness and they are found in the periphery of the leaf.

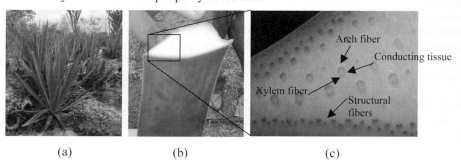

(a)   (b)   (c)

Figure 1: The sisal plant (a), leaf (b) and leaf cross section showing the different types of fibers (c).

The structural sisal fibers present a small, rarely circular and usually horse shoe shape (see Fig. 2 a). The arch fibers occur in association with the conducting tissues (see Fig. 2 b) and they are usually developed in the median line of the leaf. The xylem occurs opposite to the arch fibers. According to Nutman [20], they are composed of thin walled cells, and are invariably broken up and lost during the process of fiber extraction. Every fiber contains numerous elongated individual fibers, which are about 1-8 mm in length and 6 to 30 µm in diameter [17].

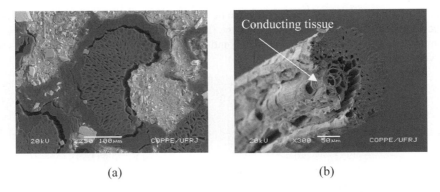

(a)   (b)

Figure 2: Sisal fibers: (a) horse shoe shaped structural fiber and (b) arch fiber with conducting tissue.

Chemically the sisal fibers comprise cellulose (~ 70%), hemicellulose (~ 12%), lignin (~10%) and a small amount of pectin, waxes and fat (~ 2%). Cellulose $(C_6H_{10}O_5)_n$ is a polymer derived from glucose that is just one of a number of monosaccharides having the same chemical composition, $C_6H_{12}O_6$ [21]. Hemicellulose are amorphous short-chained isotropic polysaccharides and polyuronides, often of very similar sugars, e.g. galactose and mannose and rarely if ever crystalline [21]. The polysaccharide hemicellulose are chemically linked or partly intermingled and oriented with cellulose molecules. Lignin is a short chain isotropic and non-crystalline made up of units from phenylpropane. It is found in the middle lamella of the fiber and in the walls of the fibrillae. About 25% of the total lignin is to be found in the middle lamella. Since the middle lamella is very thin, the concentration of lignin is correspondingly high (~ 70%).

The mix design of the matrix used in the present study was 1:1:0.3 (cement:sand:water in mass). The Portland cement used was of CPII F-32 defined by the Brazilian standard [22] as composed with filler (in mass: 85% < clinker < 91%; 3% < gypsum < 5%; 6% < filler < 10%) with 32 MPa of compressive strength at 28 days. River sand with a maximum diameter of 1.18 mm and a density of 2.67 g/cm³ were used in all composites. A naphthalene superplasticizer (SP) Fosroc Reax Conplast SP 430 with a content of solids of 44 % was used for increasing the fluidity of the matrix. The consistency of the matrix was determined by the flow table spread test (FTS). A FTS of 38 cm was obtained for the used dosage (0.7%) of superplasticizer (SP dry extract/cement mass in %).

The matrix was produced using a bench-mounted mechanical mixer with a capacity of 20 liters. The cement and sand were dry mixed for 30 seconds (for homogenization) with the subsequent addition of the superplasticizer diluted in the water. The whole mixture was then mixed for 3 minutes.

For manufacturing the composite with the sisal fabrics, the mortar mix was placed in a steel mould by a manual lay-out technique, one layer at a time, followed by one layer of fibers (see Fig. 3 (a) and (b)). Flat laminates were produced with the dimensions of 400 mm x 250 mm x 12 mm. Composites with five layers were produced using the technique described and then compressed at a pressure of 3 MPa (see Fig. 3 c). The pressure of 3 MPa was chosen after an optimization process in which pressures ranging from 0 to 4 MPa were tested. Details of this study can be found elsewhere [23]. The composites were fog cured for 28 days in a cure chamber with 100% relative humidity (RH) and 23 ± 1°C. The composites were denominated as M1F2, M1F4, M1F6, M1F8 and M1F10. The last numbers corresponds to the fiber volume fraction of the composite.

(a)   (b)   (c)

Figure 3: Molding procedure: (a) pouring the matrix material, (b) placing the sisal fabric and (c) applying pressure.

2.2 Mechanical characterization

To determine the mechanical properties of the studied composites at 28 days of age, a Shimadzu UH-F 1000 kN was used. Direct tension and four point bending tests were performed. The direct tension and bending tests were carried out at a crosshead rate of 0.1 mm/min and 0.5 mm/min, respectively. Three specimens with the dimensions of 400 mm x 100 mm x 12 mm (length x width x thickness), diamond sawed from the flat laminate produced as explained before, were tested under a four-point bending (300 mm span). Deflections at mid-span were measured using an electrical transducer (LVDT) and the loads and corresponding deflections were continuously recorded using a 32-bit data acquisition system taking four readings per second.

Direct tension tests were carried out on specimens of 400 mm x 50 mm x 12 mm (200 mm height between grips). Steel plates were epoxy glued at the extremities (last 100 mm) of the specimens to allow fixing the samples in the hydraulic grips. The displacement measurements were realized using two LVDTs mounted apart in the central part of the specimen on a base of 100 mm. The displacements were recorded using the same data acquisition system used for the bending tests.

3. RESULTS AND DISCUSSION

Typical equivalent bending stress-deflection curves and tension stress-displacement curves of the sisal fiber textile composites are presented, respectively, in Fig. 4 and 5. Bending first-cracking (FCS) and post cracking strength (PCS), (determined, respectively, from the first crack load and maximum load carried out by the composite after the first crack event using the bending formula $\sigma_u = 6M/bd^2$, where b is the width and d the thickness) bending toughness (calculated from the area under the load-deflection curves obtained under bending up to a post-peak deflection corresponding to 40% of the peak load [24]) and direct tension first and post-cracking strength are presented in Table 1.

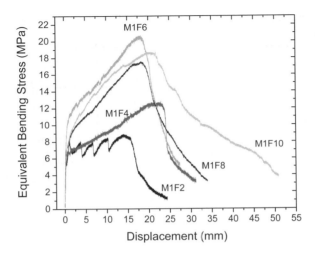

Figure 4: Effect of reinforcement ratio on the behavior under bending loads of the sisal fiber textile reinforced composite.

The results indicate that the average values of first-crack strength, under bending, of the studied composites ranged from about 6.5 MPa to 7.5 MPa. Considering that most of the standard deviation ranged from about 0.7 to 1.6 MPa, it can be concluded that this parameter is not significantly influenced by the fiber volume fraction. Regarding to the post cracking bending strength, an expressive increase in this property can be observed with the increment of the reinforcement ratio. The increase, however, is more expressive for volume fractions up to 6%. For example, the increment in PCS of composites M1F4 and M1F6, in comparison with M1F2, are 60% and 130%, respectively. The composites M1F8 and M1F10 presented nearly the same PCS as M1F6. It is also important to observe that all composites with volume fraction equal or above 4% presented a deflection hardening with multiple cracking behavior. The composite M1F2 also presented a multiple cracking fracture with a pseudo-hardening behavior under bending loads. The bending toughness of the composites was also significantly increased with the increase in reinforcement. For example, the toughness of composite M1F2 is increased by about 3.2 and 5.1 times when increasing the reinforcement ratio to 6% and 10%, respectively. It is important to observe that most of the textile composites presented post cracking strength higher than the first cracking strength for displacements at mid-span ranging from 25 to 45 mm (see composites M1F4-M1F10). This behavior indicates the remarkable ductile behavior of the developed textile composite due to the nature of the flexible vegetable reinforcement used.

Table 1: Summary of the results of four point bending and direct tension tests (average values ± standard deviation).

Composites	Four Point Bending			Direct Tension	
	First crack strength (MPa)	Post Cracking strength (MPa)	Toughness (kJ/m²)	First crack strength (MPa)	Post Cracking Strength (MPa)
M1F2	7.01 ± 1.01	8.00 ± 1.24	3.99 ± 0.92	5.06 ± 2.08	5.62 ± 1.31
M1F4	7.27 ± 0.70	12.80 ± 3.14	9.59 ± 2.80	5.49 ± 0.50	6.65 ± 0.53
M1F6	7.60 ± 0.89	18.31 ± 3.76	12.79 ± 4.92	5.85 ± 0.48	7.21 ± 0.65
M1F8	6.48 ± 0.18	18.53 ± 1.49	13.93 ± 1.78	3.98 ± 0.67	7.05 ± 0.82
M1F10	6.49 ± 1.57	17.99 ± 3.07	20.30 ± 2.70	4.34 ± 0.31	8.03 ± 1.02

A multiple cracking behavior with strain hardening under tension load was observed for the composites with V_f of 4% and higher (see Fig. 5). The reinforcement ratio of 2% was not high enough to increase significantly (see Table 1) the tensile strength of the composite. The softening in the stress – displacement curve occurred for a displacement of about 0.75mm. A maximum of two macroscopic visible cracks were observed in the tested specimens (see Fig. 6 a). When the V_f was increased to 4%, a higher number of cracks was observed (see Fig. 6 b) and the stress-displacement curve presented a pseudo-hardening behavior up to a displacement of about 1.5mm. The post-cracking strength presented an average value 20% higher than its FCS. The composites with a reinforcement ratio of 6, 8 and 10% presented higher number of cracks with a closer spacing, especially the composite M1F10 (see Fig. 6 c, d and e).

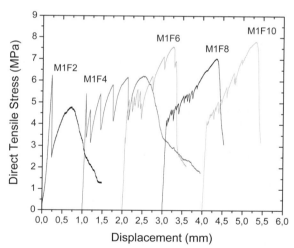

Figure 5: Effect of reinforcement ratio on the behavior under direct tension loads of the sisal fiber textile reinforced composite

The post cracking strength of the composites M1F8 and M1F10 were significantly improved almost doubling their FCS. From the obtained results it can be concluded that the composite M1F10 is the one with maximum PCS under direct tension and maximum bending toughness what indicates that the V_f of 10% was the reinforcement ratio that maximized the mechanical properties of the developed textile composite.

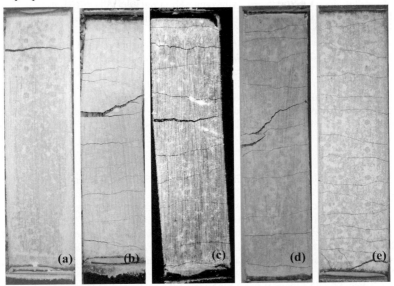

Figure 6: Cracking patterns under direct tension: (a) M1F2, (b) M1F4, (c) M1F6, (d) M1F8 and (e) M1F10.

4. CONCLUSIONS

The results of the present investigation indicate that sisal fiber textile cement composites reinforced with a reinforcement ratio of 4% and above present a deflection hardening behavior. Under direct tension only for fiber volume fractions of 6% and higher a tension hardening behavior is observed. When increasing the fiber volume fraction from 2 to 10% an increase of about 5 times in bending toughness was obtained while the bending PCS is increased by 2.3 times. For the same amounts of fibers, the direct tension post cracking strength was increased by about 45%. Maximum strength values under four point bending, direct tension and bending toughness of, respectively, 18.53 MPa, 8.03 MPa and 20.30 kJ/m^2 were obtained, indicating the enormous potentiality of the newly developed material for use in structural applications in the sustainable construction industry.

REFERENCES

[1] Swift, D.F., Smith, R.B.L., 'The flexural Strength of Cement-Based Composites Using Low Modulus (sisal) Fibers', *Composites* (1979) 145-148.
[2] Coutts, R.S.P., Warden, P.G., 'Sisal Pulp Reinforced Cement Mortar', *Cement & Concrete Composites.* **14** (1992) 17-21.
[3] Savastano Jr., H., Warden, P.G. and Coutts, R.S.P., 'Mechanically pulped sisal as reinforcement in cementitious matrices', *Cement and Concrete Composites* **25** (2003) 311-319.
[4] Toledo Filho, R.D., Ghavami, K., England, G.L., Scrivener, K., 'Development of vegetable fiber-mortar composites of improved durability', *Cement & Concrete Composites* **25** (2003) 185-196.

[5]   Toledo Filho, R.D., Ghavami, K., England, G.L., Scrivener, K., 'Development of vegetable fiber-mortar composites of improved durability', *Cement & Concrete Composites* **25** (2003) 185-196.

[6]   Toledo Filho, R. D., Joseph, K., Ghavami, K., England, G.L., 'The use of sisal fiber as reinforcement in cement based composites', *Brazilian Journal of Agricultural and Environmental Engineering* **3** (1999) 245-256.

[7]   Silva, F. A., Ghavami, K., d'Almeida, J.R.M., 'Toughness of Cementitious Composites Reinforced by Randomly Sisal Pulps', in Eleventh International Conference on Composites Engineering - ICCE-11, 2004, Hilton Head Island - SC. Proceedings of the Eleventh International Conference on Composites Engineering. Hilton Head Island - SC: ICCE - 11, 2004.

[8]   Silva, F.A., Ghavami, K., d'Almeida, J.R.M., 'Interfacial transition zone in fiber reinforced cement-based composites', in Conferência Brasileira de Materiais e Tecnologias Não-Convencionais: Habitações e Infra-Estrutura de Interesse Social - Brasil Nocmat 2004, 2004, Pirassununga. Anais do Brasil NOCMAT 2004. Rio de Janeiro: ABMTENC, 2004.

[9]   Toledo Filho, R. D., 'Natural fiber reinforced mortar composites: experimental characterization', Ph.D. Thesis, DEC-PUC-Rio, Brazil, 1997, 472 p.

[10] Gram, H.E., 'Durability of natural fibers in concrete', Swedish Cement and Concrete Research Institute, Research Fo. 1983, 225 pp.

[11] Guimarães, S.S., 'Some experiments in vegetable fiber-cement composites in Symposium on Building Materials for Low Income Housing', Bangkok, (1987), 167-175.

[12] Peled, A. and Bentur, A., 'Geometrical chacracteristics and efficiency of textile fabrics for reinforcing cement composites', *Cement and Concrete Research* **30** (2000) 781-790.

[13] Peled, A. and Mobasher, B., 'Pultruded Fabric-Cement Composites', *ACI Materials Journal* **1** (2005) 15-23.

[14] Brameshuber, W. (Ed.) State of the Art Report of Rilem Technical Committee 201-TRC: Textile Reinforced Concrete (2006) 187-210.

[15] Mobasher, B. and Pivacek, A., 'A Filament Winding Technique for Manufacturing Cement Based Cross Ply Laminates', *Cement and Concrete Composites* **20** (1998) 405-415.

[16] Peled, A. and Mobasher, B., 'The Pultrusion Technology for the Production of Fabric-Cement Composites', in Proceedings of the 7th International Symposium on Brittle Matrix Composites (BMC7), Warsaw, Poland, (2003) 505-514.

[17] Murherjee, P.S., Satyanarayana, K.G., 'Structure properties of some vegetable fibers, part 1. Sisal fibre', *Journal of Materials Science* **19** (1984) 3925-34.

[18] Oksman, K., Wallstrom, L. and Toledo Filho, R.D., 'Morphology and mechanical properties of unidirectional sisal-epoxy composites' *Journal of Applied Polymer Science* **84** (2002) 2358-2365.

[19] Bisanda, E.T.N. and Ansell, M.P., 'Properties of sisal-CNSL composites', *Journal of Materials Science* **27** (1992) 1690-1700.

[20] Nutman, F.J. 'Agave fibres Pt. I. Morphology, histology, length and fineness; frading problems', *Empire Journal of Experimental Agriculture* **5** (1936) 75-95

[21] Walker, J.C.F., 'Primary Wood Processing: Principles and Practice', Chapman and Hall, 1993.

[22] NBR 11578, Cimento Portland Composto. Associação Brasileira de Normas Técnicas (ABNT), Julho, 1991 (In Portuguese).

[23] Melo Filho, J.A., 'Development and experimental characterization of cement based laminates reinforced with long sisal fibers', M.Sc. thesis, COPPE/UFRJ, Rio de Janeiro, Brazil, 2005. (In Portuguese).

[24] Rilem Technical Committee 49 TFR, 'Testing methods for fiber reinforced cement based composites', *Materiaux et Constructions* **17** (1984) 441-456.

LOAD-BEARING BEHAVIOUR OF POLYMER-IMPREGNATED TEXTILES IN CONCRETE

Ulrich Dilthey [1], **Markus Schleser** [1], **Josef Hegger** [2] and **Stefan Voss** [2]

(1) Welding and Joining Institute, RWTH Aachen University, Germany

(2) Institute of Structural Concrete, RWTH Aachen University, Germany

Abstract

It is possible to substantially improve the load-bearing behaviour of textile-reinforced concrete by using liquid polymers for impregnation of the textiles. For the work referred to in this paper, the influence of epoxy impregnation on the load-bearing behaviour of alkali-resistant glass-fibre textiles has been tested by means of tensile and bending tests. The main influential factors on the observed load bearing and failure behaviour have, moreover, been identified and evaluated by means of mechanical tests on filament and bond tests on the roving.

1.   INTRODUCTION

The use of alkali-resistant textile structures made of high-performance filament yarns as reinforcement for concrete elements allows, through the omission of minimum concrete covers for corrosion protection, the serial production of particularly thin and high-strength prefabricated concrete elements. The alkali-resistant (AR)-glass fibre is an efficient reinforcement material with high strengths and good availability. The practical application of elements which are reinforced with AR-glass fibres meet special demands regarding the load-bearing behaviour, the durability and the serviceability of the material. One of the main problems is the insufficient utilisation of the reinforcement in the composite compared to the strength of the basic material. This mainly originates from the incomplete penetration of the concrete matrix into the rovings and the resulting insufficient activation of the inner filaments.

So different strategies for improving the bond behaviour have been suggested. Those strategies include, among other things, the increased penetration of the rovings with concrete, the development of hybrid yarn structures and the application of polymers. The designated aim of impregnating the textiles with polymers is to improve the bond between the filaments and, at the same time, ensure a good load transmission into the concrete.

The influence which impregnation with epoxy exerts on the load-bearing behaviour of AR-glass fibre textile in concrete is examined and evaluated within the scope of this work by means of tensile and bending tests on textile reinforced concrete elements.

2.   IMPREGNATION OF THE TEXTILES

The textile impregnation has been carried out in the Welding and Joining Institute (ISF) of the RWTH Aachen University, Germany. A biaxial AR-glass fibre fabric which consisted of 2400 tex rovings (arranged vertical to each other) with a grid spacing of 8 mm each has been used for textile reinforcement (Figure 1). For the tests on filaments and rovings, those were taken from the fabric. For impregnation, epoxy resin on the basis of bisphenol-A-epichlorhydrin, together with amine hardener has been used. Within the scope of comparative tensile tests using different polymer systems, the application of high-module epoxy led to the highest ultimate load increase [1]. The mechanical properties of the used epoxy have been characterised by means of film tensile testing in accordance with DIN EN ISO 527. After curing at room temperature a medium tensile strength of 47 MPa and a Young's modulus of 3.700 MPa was measured.

Fiber material : AR-glass
Rovingtiter :   2400 tex
Grid spacing :   8mm x 8 mm

Figure 1: AR-glass fabric used for the investigations

Impregnation has been carried out on the unit which has been developed in the ISF, Figure 2. In a first step, the fabrics ends are fixed inflexibly. Subsequently, the fabrics are manually pulled between two pressure rolls through a polymer bath. This ensures the complete impregnation of the entire reinforcement cross-section. Further pressure rolls serve the purpose of squeezing out and stripping off the dispensable polymer, Figure 3.

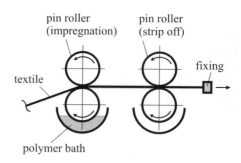

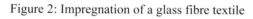

Figure 2: Impregnation of a glass fibre textile

Figure 3: Schematic diagram

3. INVESTIGATION OF MATERIAL CHARACTERISTICS

For testing the tensile strength of coated rovings, they were, from both sides, sealed into epoxy blocks with a length of 80 mm. The epoxy blocks serve for the mounting of the specimens into the clamp jaws of the tension testing machine. Through the comparatively homogeneous load introduction, the blocks reduce the risk of breaking the clamped fibre materials which are notch-stress sensitive. Tensile test specimens with free lengths of 125 mm and 500 mm have been tested. The traverse speed was, in both cases, 10 mm/min. Further information about the test appears in [2, 3].

The results of the tensile tests carried out on impregnated rovings are shown in Figure 4. The average values of the test series, each consisting of five single tests, resulted for the specimens with a free length of 125 mm in a tensile strength of 1885 MPa and a Young's modulus of 63200 MPa. In comparison with this, the specimens with a free length of 500 mm had a tensile strength of 1668 MPa and a Young's modulus of 72630 MPa. The differences result from the following, decisive effects:

- The quantity of critical damage along the individual filaments increases with the increasing length of the roving. The result is a reduced load-bearing cross-section and thus a reduction of strength.
- The resin blocks between the clamping jaws are deforming under load and lead thus to additional specimen deformation which is a result of clamping. The contribution towards the entire length alteration of the specimen decreases with increasing specimen length which results in less strain and in a higher modulus of elasticity.

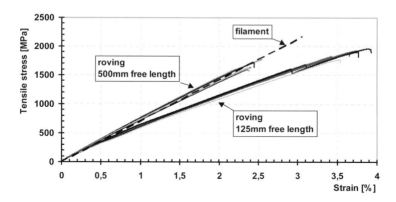

Figure 4: Results from tensile tests carried out on coated rovings

To compare the stress-strain behaviour of the rovings and the basic material, tensile tests on the single filament were carried out. Therefore, a filament with a length of 5 mm which has been detached off the 2400 tex roving is glued onto a paper frame and torn - after having been clamped into the testing machine and after the cutting of the supporting frame. A more detailed description of the test method appears in [4]. In this particular case, a test series with 10 filaments resulted in an average tensile strength of 2138 MPa and a modulus of elasticity of 71850 MPa.

A transfer of the load characteristics of single filaments to the load characteristics of the rovings is hardly possible. The main reason is that the rovings show, partially, considerable deviations from the ideal structure and also have a complex load transmission behaviour between the filaments. Subsequently, the filaments show locally different states of strain. The polymer impregnation and the connected good load transmission between the filaments allowed, to a large extent, the homogenisation of the individual filaments' strain. A composite cross-section is produced where torn filaments contribute towards the load transfer at another point. The comparison of the roving tensile-test specimen and the filament tensile-test specimen allows to derive the following conclusions:

- The strain of the filament tensile-test specimens is determined via CCD cameras directly on the filament. Deformations which result from clamping are not detected. For this reason the modulus of elasticity which has been determined for the filaments is correlating rather with the longer roving tensile-test specimens than with the short ones.
- With a decreasing filament length the number of critical imperfections is decreasing and the strength increases. The determined filament strength is thus correlating rather with the short roving tensile-test specimens than with the long ones.

A look at corresponding parameter studies shows that the test results are, besides the above-mentioned effects of differences in free length, type of clamping and deformation measurement, also significantly influenced by other factors, as, for example, the elongation rate. It is, therefore, hardly possible to compare the results with other test methods, for example in [5].

4.   EXPERIMENTAL INVESTIGATIONS

For testing the bond behaviour and the load-bearing behaviour of the textile reinforcement under centrical tensile stress, different tension member tests have been carried out. For the production of the specimens a fine grained concrete matrix based on Portland cement was used. The matrix is characterised by high strength, good flowability and aggregates which are adapted to the textile structures. A detailed description of the matrix composition and the characteristics of the hardened concrete are given in [6].

4.1   Tensile tests on the component

The effect of different impregnation materials on the ultimate load capacity of TRC was investigated at the ISF within the scope of tension member tests. For this purpose textile reinforced concrete strips with the dimensions of L/W/H = 500/100/10 [mm] were produced in a vertical formwork and stored for 28 days in standard climate (95% rel. atmospheric humidity, 20°C). The load transmission into the specimens was accomplished via gimbal-mounted steel clamping jaws (length 100 mm) which had been pressed on the specimens by six screws, Figure 5. Through the cardanic suspension of the tension member in the testing machine, the unintended initiation of bending moments was avoided. The tests were carried out displacement-controlled with a speed of 1 mm/min. The deformation of the specimens was measured between the steel clamps by means of potentiometric displacement transducers (experimental set-up, see Figure 5).

For the comparative investigation of the tensile load-bearing behaviour of textile-reinforced members tests were accomplished at the Institute of Structural Concrete (IMB), RWTH Aachen University. The specimens had a length of 1.0 m, a cross section thickness of

10 mm and a width of 100 mm in the measuring range, Figure 6. The load was applied by gimbal-mounted steel jaws adapted to the waisted specimen geometry. During the tests the load and the elongation of the measuring range were detected. The tests were carried out displacement-controlled with a deformation speed of 1 mm/min.

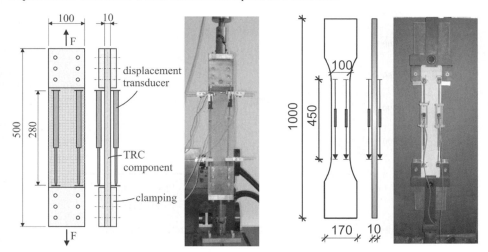

Figure 5: Tensile test ISF   Figure 6: Tensile test IMB

The comparison of both test set-ups enables the determination of the influence of the load-introduction method on the test results.

4.2   Bending tests

In addition to the tensile tests the load-bearing behaviour of specimens reinforced with the epoxy-impregnated AR-glass fabric was tested by a four-point bending test, Figure 7. The specimens had a length of 700 mm, a width of 150 mm and a thickness of 25 mm, see Figure 8. They were reinforced with one layer of the epoxy-impregnated AR-glass fabric. The reinforcement was placed 5 mm from the bottom edge in the tensile zone of the plate. The test was carried out displacement-controlled with a speed of 1 mm/min.

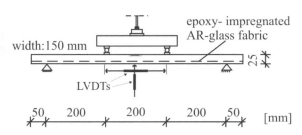

Figure 7: Bending-test   Figure 8: Set-up of bending test

4.3   Test results

The textile stress-strain curves of representative tensile tests, bending test and filament test are shown in Figure 9.

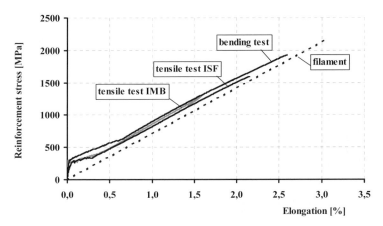

Figure 9: Stress-strain curves of the tests on the component

Until the formation of the first cracks, the load increases linearly with the applied deformation. After the concrete tensile strength has been reached, the crack formation phase starts where the load slightly increases due to the scattering concrete tensile strength. The crack distance in the completed crack pattern amounts about 10 mm. The stress-strain curve then proceeds along with the Young's modulus of the reinforcement until the breaking of the reinforcement. Unlike steel reinforced concrete, there is no yielding plateau due to the linear-elastic material behaviour of the textile reinforcement. A close look at the textile stress-strain curves, Figure 9, shows that the described load-bearing behaviour is setting exactly for the tensile member test of the ISF and the bending test. The Young's modulus in the tensile member test amounted approx. 70300 MPa, whereas the Young's modulus that was determined in the filament-tension test is approx. 71850 MPa. The differences originate from the differing free lengths of the filaments, the resulting different elongation rates and the difficult determination of the exact cross-section area of roving and filament. The textile fails in the ISF tension member test at a maximum textile tensile tension of approx. 1600 MPa and in the bending test a tensile strength of 1920 MPa was calculated. The failure of the reinforcement goes along with partially flaking off of the reinforcement. Methods for calculation of the load-bearing behaviour of textile reinforced concrete elements are given in [7].

The flaking off of the concrete coverage was observed in the IMB tensile test, too (Figure 10). In this case this mechanism caused the anchorage failure of the AR-glass fabric and as a result the tensile strength of the reinforcement material was not completely utilised. The load introduction as well as additional curvature of the reinforced concrete element due to bending thus seem to have a significant influence on the load-bearing behaviour. In the tensile test of the ISF (Figure 5) the lateral pressure caused by the clamping leads to a complete anchorage of the reinforcement. In the same way the curvature of the plate in the bending test causes lateral pressure on the reinforcement and enhances the bond performance even if the concrete coverage is partially flaked off. For the modelling of the load-bearing behaviour of elements reinforced by epoxy-impregnated AR-glass fabrics thus the loading, the load-introduction mechanism as well as the bending of the element have to be taken into consideration.

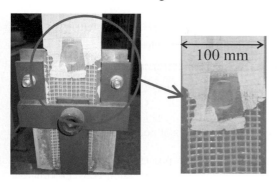
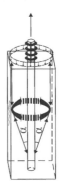

Figure 10: Concrete flaking   Figure 11: Hoop tension [8]

The formation of longitudinal cracks and the chipping of the concrete cover have already been observed in tests with different impregnated reinforcements and have been subject of several publications, i.a. [8]. In the case of steel reinforced concrete, Tepfers [9] specifies the high bonding forces to be the reason for longitudinal crack formation. They occur under an unfavourable, i.e. steep angle α and lead to high coil tensions in the concrete, Figure 11. The concentrated transmission of bonding forces under an unfavourable angle is together with an insufficient adhesion between concrete and reinforcement responsible for the appearance of longitudinal cracks and concrete flaking. In the following, the force transmission between impregnated reinforcement and concrete is, therefore, examined in more detail.

5.   BOND CHARACTERIZATION

For the evaluation of the load transmission from the concrete into the impregnated reinforcement and concrete, double-sided pull-out tests were carried out with using the non-impregnated base material and the epoxy-impregnated roving. A description of the experimental set-up is given in [1]. The test results show that the impregnation allows the transmission of high bond forces. The pull-out force of the impregnated roving is more than tripled compared to the non-impregnated roving, Figure 12.

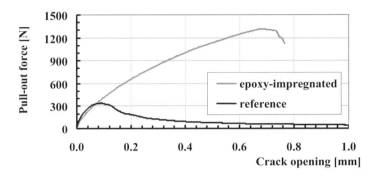

Figure 12: Crack opening/textile-stress-strain-curves of double-sided pull-out tests

Since the epoxy-impregnated glass textiles do not possess a systematic pattern, the following mechanisms are responsible for the good force transmission between concrete and impregnated reinforcement:
- Positive fit through the transverse reinforcement with a distance of 8 mm
- Chemical/physical (adhesive) bonding between concrete and polymer
- Positive fit caused by alterations of the cross-section and micro profiling of the impregnated roving

Since tension member tests of textiles with a transverse reinforcement distance of 8 mm and 16 mm resulted in almost congruent test diagrams, it is possible to exclude a significant influence of the transverse reinforcement, Figure 13.

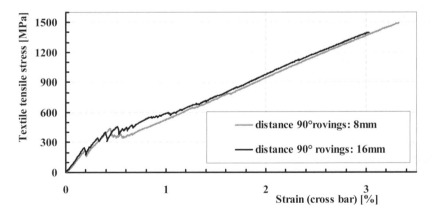

Figure 13: Tension member tests ISF for different transverse reinforcements

The adhesion between concrete and polymer has been evaluated by means of pull-off tests. The low determined pull-off tensions with values smaller than 0.5 N/mm² prove that there is no significant adhesion between concrete and polymer. This fact is confirmed by the complete debonding at the interface in the case of textile fracture.

The results from the different bond tests thus identify the positive fit caused by alterations of the cross-section and the micro-profiling of the impregnated roving to be the main reasons for the good force transmission between concrete and reinforcement. The alterations of the cross-section are produced by the knitting thread which is enwinding the roving in the textile, the non-ideal orientation of the individual filaments and deviations in the impregnation regularity. Another contribution results from the slight waviness of the textile, since it is impossible to implement the reinforcement in a completely stretched state, even if under tension.

6.   CONCLUSIONS

The activation of the total cross-sectional area of alkali-resistant glass rovings can be significantly improved by the impregnation with epoxy-resin. In tensile and bending tests on textile reinforced concrete components the calculated strength of the reinforcement amounted about 1600 to 1900 MPa, which is equivalent to 75 to 90% of the filament tensile strength. The tests revealed that the load-introduction method as well as curvature of the element caused by bending loading have an influence on the anchorage and the load-bearing behaviour of the reinforcement. Clamping of the component by steel plates and the curvature of plates in bending tests lead to additional lateral pressure on the reinforcement improving the anchorage strength. Without these the bond characteristics of epoxy-impregnated AR-glass rovings tend to cause the flaking off of the concrete coverage. Additional investigations are required to determine the main effects in more detail and to improve the bond performance to that effect that the concrete flaking can be prevented.

ACKNOWLEDGEMENTS

The authors thank the Deutsche Forschungsgemeinschaft (DFG) in context of the Collaborative Research Center 532 "Textile Reinforced Concrete - Development of a new technology" for their financial support.

REFERENCES

[1] Dilthey, U. and Schleser, M., 'Composite Improvement of Textile Reinforced Concrete by Polymeric Impregnation of the Textiles', in 'Proceedings: ISPIC International Symposium Polymers in Concrete 2006', 2th-4th April 2006, University of Minho Guimaraes, Portugal, 2006

[2] Hanisch, V., Roye, A. and Gries, T. 'Characterization of textile structures for use in concrete', in 'Part 1: Strength of 2D structures and initial stages of simulation of deformation', Technical Textiles 47, August 2004, E104-E105.

[3] Dilthey, U., Schleser, M., Hanisch, V. and Gries, T. 'Yarn tensile test of polymer-impregnated textiles for the reinforcement of concrete', Technical Textiles 49, 2006, 41 – 43.

[4] Banholzer, B., 'Textile Reinforced Concrete (TRC): Bond Behaviour of a multi-filament yarn embedded in a cementitious matrix', PhD-Thesis, RWTH Aachen University, 2004.

[5] RILEM Publications S. A. R. L.: Report 36, 'Textile Reinforced Concrete', State-of-the-Art Report of RILEM Technical Committee 201-TRC, (Brameshuber, W.), 2006.

[6] Brockmann, T., 'Mechanical and fracture mechanical properties of fine grained concrete for textile reinforced composites', PhD-Thesis, RWTH Aachen University, 2006.

[7] Voss, S., Hegger, J., 'Dimensioning of Textile Reinforced Concrete Structures', Proceedings of 1st International RILEM Conference on Textile reinforced Concrete, 06.- 07.09.2006, Aachen, 151-160.

[8] Hegger, J. and Niewels, J., 'Textile Carbon Reinforcement for Base Slabs of Self-Consolidating Concrete', in 'Proceedings of the 7th International Symposium on the Utilization of High-Strength/High Performance Concrete', Washington D.C., USA, ACI SP-228, Vol. 1, 317- -332.

[9] Tepfers, R., 'A theory of bond applied to overlapped tensile reinforcement splices for deformed bars', Göteborg, Chalmers University of Technology, Division of Concrete Structures, PhD-thesis, 1973.

EFFECT OF CONFINEMENT ON SFRHPC SUBJECTED TO UNIAXIAL COMPRESSION

Namasivayam Ganesan, Pookattu Vattrambath Indira and Ruby Abraham

Department of Civil Engg, National Institute of Technology, Calicut, India

Abstract

An experimental investigation was carried out to study the effect of confinement on the strength and behaviour of Steel Fibre reinforced High Performance Concrete (SFRHPC). The investigation consists of casting and testing of 80 SFRHPC cylindrical specimens of 150mm x 300 mm in size. The specimens were subjected to both monotonically increasing load and cyclic loading. The fibres considered in this study include corrugated steel fibres having aspect ratio 66. Four values of volume fraction of fibres viz. 0.25,0.50,0.75 and 1.0 were used. The confinement was provided in the form of spirals having different values of pitch viz. 25 mm, 50 mm and 75 mm. Out of the 80 specimens 40 were subjected to monotonically increasing loading and the remaining were subjected to cyclic loading. Tests reveal that increase in the volumetric ratio of transverse reinforcement increases the ultimate strength of High Performance Concrete (HPC) and SFRHPC. However the percentage of increase is higher for SFRHPC specimens than for HPC. Strain at peak load was found to be significantly improved as the confinement increased. Combined effect of confinement and fibre improved several engineering properties such as strain at peak load, ultimate strength, energy absorption capacity etc. These results indicate that SFRHPC with proper confinement could be used in structures subjected to extreme load conditions such as seismic loading, blast and impact loading.

1. INTRODUCTION

High Performance Concrete (HPC) is a novel construction material with improved properties like higher strength, durability, and constructionability than conventional concrete. Addition of fibres to HPC increases many of the engineering properties such as strength, ductility and fatigue strength [1-4]. The main function of fibres in members subjected to compression are to resist the opening of cracks due to micro cracking, increase the ability of the composite to withstand loads and to allow larger strains in the neighbourhood of fibres. Behaviour of confined normal concrete has been extensively studied during the last several decades [5-11]. It has been understood from the studies that strength and ductility could be improved significantly by providing proper confinement. Inelastic deformability of reinforced concrete column is essential for the overall strength and stability of structures subjected to seismic forces. Specifications for confinement in the existing codes are limited to normal concrete. Confinement increases the capacity of concrete to sustain large deformation without a substantial strength loss. It also increases the compressive strength, which offset the strength loss from spalling of cover concrete. Effectiveness of confinement depends on volumetric ratio of confinement, compressive strength of concrete, type of aggregate used etc. Although adequate information on the effect of confinement in conventional concrete is available in literature; effect of confinement in HPC and SFRHPC is not fully investigated. A complete knowledge of stress strain behaviour of SFRHPC is essential for predicting the behaviour of structural elements using this material. Considering this an attempt has been made to evaluate the behaviour of HPC and SFRHPC with different values of volumetric ratio of confinement in the case of specimen subjected to monotonic and cyclic loading. Cyclic loading tests are of practical relevance for understanding the behaviour of compression members subjected to repeatedly applied loading.

2. EXPERIMENTAL PROGRAMME

Tests were conducted on a total of 80 cylindrical specimens of size 150mm x 300mm. Eight numbers of specimens were cast using HPC and remaining using SFRHPC with different volume fractions of steel fibres viz. 0.25, 0.50, 0.75 and 1.0%. Plain mild steel bars of 6 mm diameter having yield strength of 250 MPa were used for making spiral reinforcement cages of 110 mm diameter as shown in Fig.1. The pitch of the spiral used was 75, 50 and 25 mm corresponding to volumetric ratios of 1.36, 2.05 and 4.10 percentage. Two specimens were used for each combination of variables considered. In order to study the effect of confinement under monotonic and cyclic loading, half the specimens were subjected to monotonic loading and the remaining were subjected to cyclic loading.

2.1 Mix Proportions

HPC mix proportion for M60 grade concrete was obtained based on the guidelines given in modified ACI 211 method suggested by Aitcin [12]. Part of cement was replaced by micro-fillers such as silica fume and fly ash. In this study 10% replacement of cement by silica fume and 20% replacement by fly ash was considered. Workability of the mix was kept constant at 0.9 compaction factor. Same mix proportion was maintained for SFRHPC mix. In order to maintain uniform workability, dosage of super plasticizer was adjusted in SFRHPC mixes. Details of materials obtained based on the mix design are given in Table 1.

2.2 Preparation of Test specimens

For casting the specimens, cast iron moulds of 150mm diameter and 300mm height were fabricated. Special provision was made to insert the plates for fixing the LVDT so that the core strain can be measured accurately. Before casting, spiral reinforcement cage having diameter of 110 mm was placed inside the mould. A drum type mixer with 1.5 cft (0.062 m³) capacity was used for mixing. Required quantities of steel fibres were added slowly at a constant rate during mixing. Superplasticizer was also added in the mix along with 50% of mixing water. The concrete mix was poured in to the mould in layers and the mould was vibrated on a vibrating table for through compaction. The top surface was levelled using a smooth trowel after compaction. Immediately after casting, moulds were covered with wet gunny bags to avoid moisture loss. After 24 hours, the specimens were demoulded and cured for 28 days. Details of specimens are given in Table 2. A total number of 20 combinations of variables have been considered in the study. For each combination of variables, 2 specimens have been tested and the average value is reported for both monotonic and cyclic loading. Thus a total number of 80 specimens have been tested.

Table 1: Mix Proportions of High performance concrete (kg/m^3)

Cement	Fly ash	Silica fume	Sand	Coarse aggregate	Water	Superplasticizer
353	98	39	658	1048	162	10.78

2.3 Testing of Specimens

In the case of monotonic loading, specimens were subjected to monotonic axial compression until failure using Universal testing machine of 300t (2942.1kN) capacity. In the case of cyclic loading, the specimens were loaded up to a designated loading of 15 t (147.15kN), then unloaded and reloaded to the next increment. Both loading and unloading were carried out at a constant rate of loading (140kg/cm^2/min). The deformations over a gauge length of 100mm were recorded during testing using LVDT. From the core deformations, core strains were computed. Fig. 2 shows the test set up.

Table 2: Details of specimens

Serial no.	Specimen Designation	No. of specimens tested	Volume fraction of fibres (V_f) (%)	Pitch of Spiral (mm)	Volumetric ratio of spiral reinforcement (ρ_s) %
1	HP0	4	0.00	-	-
2	HP7	4	0.00	75	1.36
3	HP5	4	0.00	50	2.05
4	HP2	4	0.00	25	4.10
5	F1 HP0	4	0.25	-	-
6	F1HP7	4	0.25	75	1.36
7	F1HP5	4	0.25	50	2.05
8	F1HP2	4	0.25	25	4.10
9	F2 HP0	4	0.50	-	-
10	F2HP7	4	0.50	75	1.36
11	F2HP5	4	0.50	50	2.05
12	F2HP2	4	0.50	25	4.10
13	F3 HP0	4	0.75	-	-
14	F3HP7	4	0.75	75	1.36
15	F3HP5	4	0.75	50	2.05
16	F3HP2	4	0.75	25	4.10
17	F4 HP0	4	1.00	-	-
18	F4HP7	4	1.00	75	1.36
19	F4HP5	4	1.00	50	2.05
20	F4HP2	4	1.00	25	4.10

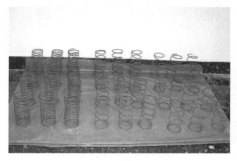

Figure 1: Spiral reinforcements used   Figure 2: Test set up

3. BEHAVIOUR OF SPECIMENS

a) Monotonic loading

In the case of HPC specimens without confinement and fibres, as the loading was increased, cracks formed suddenly and brittle failure occurred. However, in the case of HPC specimens with confinement, spalling of cover concrete took place at a strain of approximately 0.0015. The core concrete was found to be intact in the case of specimens with higher volumetric ratio of confinement. However in the case of specimens with lower volumetric ratio of confinement, some portion of core concrete was found to have spallen after the spalling of cover concrete. Fig. 3 shows the tested confined HPC specimens.

In the case of SFRHPC specimens without confinement, as the loading is increased, cracks were observed at the initial stages. Further increase of loading caused development of additional cracks. Finally failure occurred due to bulging of the specimens exposing visible fibres stitching the adjacent concrete pieces and spalling of some portion of concrete.

For confined SFRHPC specimens, initial cracks developed as in the case of unconfined specimens. As the loading is further increased, several finer cracks developed and the cover concrete was found to be intact and connected to the core concrete. Even after the final stage, the dimensional stability of the specimen was not disturbed. Fig. 4 shows tested confined SFRHPC specimens.

b) Cyclic loading

The behaviour of specimens was found to be similar to that under monotonic loading. However the load carrying capacity and the strain at peak load were found to have improved significantly in the case of confined HPC and SFRHPC specimens. The reason for this is explained in subsequent sections.

Figure 3: Tested HPC specimens Figure 4: Tested SFRHPC specimens

4. ANALYSIS OF TEST RESULTS

4.1 Effect of volumetric ratio of confinement (ρ_s) and volume fraction (V_f) of fibres

An attempt has been made to analyse the test results and evaluate the strength enhancement and deformability. Strength enhancement was expressed as ratio of confined to unconfined strength. Deformability of confined concrete was evaluated in terms of strain ductility ratio. It is defined as ratio of axial strain of confined concrete at 85% peak stress on the descending branch to that of strain of unconfined concrete corresponding to peak stress [13]. Table 3 shows the strength enhancement, strain at ultimate load and strain ductility ratio for various volumetric ratio of confinement and various volumetric ratios of fibres. When volumetric ratio of confinement increased from 1.36 percent to 4.10 percent the strain ductility ratio increased considerably. This increase is more significant in cases where volume fraction of fibres is 1%. This indicates that combined effect of fibres and confinement can be effectively utilized for enhancement of ductility.

In the case of cyclic loading also, same procedure was adopted for determining strength enhancement ratio and strain ductility ratio and the results are given in Table 4. Similar to previous case, strength enhancement is not prominent under compression. But strain ductility ratio was found to increase consistently and is significantly higher for specimens with $V_f = 1\%$ and $\rho_s = 4.10\%$.

Table 3: Effect of ρ_s and V_f on strength enhancement and strain ductility ratio (Monotonic Loading)

Specimen No.	V_f (%)	s/h	ρ_s (%)	$\varepsilon_u * 10^3$	Strength Enhancement	Strain Ductility ratio
HP0	0.00	0.00	0.00	2.05	1.00	1.33
HP7	0.00	0.25	1.36	3.44	1.91	2.31
HP5	0.00	0.16	2.05	3.52	2.17	2.19
HP2	0.00	0.08	4.10	5.04	2.14	3.87
F1HP0	0.25	0.00	0.00	2.00	1.00	1.33
F1HP7	0.25	0.25	1.36	2.30	1.92	1.82
F1HP5	0.25	0.16	2.05	3.00	2.02	2.50
F1HP2	0.25	0.08	4.10	3.78	2.14	3.42
F2HP0	0.50	0.00	0.00	2.51	1.00	1.79
F2HP7	0.50	0.25	1.36	3.42	2.01	2.29

F2HP5	0.50	0.16	2.05	3.48	2.10	3.06
F2HP2	0.50	0.08	4.10	4.20	2.17	3.84
F3HP0	0.75	0.00	0.00	2.55	1.00	1.76
F3HP7	0.75	0.25	1.36	3.06	2.01	2.58
F3HP5	0.75	0.16	2.05	2.90	2.00	3.13
F3HP2	0.75	0.08	4.10	4.60	2.10	4.35
F4HP0	1.00	0.00	0.00	3.21	1.00	2.16
F4HP7	1.00	0.25	1.36	3.90	1.97	3.14
F4HP5	1.00	0.16	2.05	5.54	2.05	4.20
F4HP2	1.00	0.08	4.10	6.61	2.09	6.32

Table 4: Effect of ρ_s and V_f on strength enhancement and strain ductility ratio (Cyclic Loading)

Specimen No.	V_f (%)	s/h	ρ_s (%)	$\varepsilon_u * 10^3$	Strength Enhancement	Strain Ductility ratio
HP0	0.00	0.00	0.00	2.21	1.00	1.18
HP7	0.00	0.25	1.36	3.48	1.90	1.86
HP5	0.00	0.16	2.05	3.00	1.99	2.05
HP2	0.00	0.08	4.10	4.08	2.19	2.85
F1HP0	0.25	0.00	0.00	2.25	1.00	1.62
F1HP7	0.25	0.25	1.36	2.28	2.03	1.75
F1HP5	0.25	0.16	2.05	2.30	2.02	2.34
F1HP2	0.25	0.08	4.10	4.51	2.21	3.49
F2HP0	0.50	0.00	0.00	2.10	1.00	1.80
F2HP7	0.50	0.25	1.36	3.21	2.00	2.19
F2HP5	0.50	0.16	2.05	3.33	2.07	3.33
F2HP2	0.50	0.08	4.10	4.83	2.09	4.38
F3HP0	0.75	0.00	0.00	2.00	1.00	1.87
F3HP7	0.75	0.25	1.36	2.73	2.05	2.70
F3HP5	0.75	0.16	2.05	2.43	2.03	3.15
F3HP2	0.75	0.08	4.10	3.15	1.99	4.25
F4HP0	1.00	0.00	0.00	3.20	1.00	1.95
F4HP7	1.00	0.25	1.36	3.25	1.88	3.00
F4HP5	1.00	0.16	2.05	6.00	1.90	3.66
F4HP2	1.00	0.08	4.10	6.00	2.09	6.25

4.2 Stress strain behaviour

a) Monotonic loading

The stress- strain values of the tested specimens were computed and plots have been prepared for all the specimens. Fig. 5 shows the typical stress strain plots for confined SFRHPC specimens with different values of volumetric ratio of confinement. It may be noted from the figure that all the specimens displayed linear behaviour at the initial stages of loading. Beyond about one third of ultimate stress, the curves started deviating from linearity.

In the case of specimens with higher value of volumetric ratio of confinement, the curves became flat. This indicates the post peak softening behaviour of SFRHPC specimens with high volumetric ratio of confinement. In fact this is the one which impart high ductility to the structure.

Fig. 6 shows a typical plot of stress strain curves of specimens having same volumetric ratio of confinement but different percent volume fraction of fibres. It may be noted from the figure that linear behaviour of stress strain curves have been observed at initial stages for all the specimens as in the case of specimens with different confinement as discussed earlier. In this plot also, specimens with higher quantity of fibres exhibited flat post peak descending branches of the curve. Curves became more and more flat as the fibre content increases. This indicates that specimens with higher volume fraction of fibres show higher ductility. However during casting it was noted that mix was found to be not workable at values of volume fraction above 1%due to balling effect.

The reason for the development of high strength and ductility are due to the following. At the initial stages of loading, micro cracks develop inside the concrete. These cracks are intercepted by fibres, which are oriented at random. The fibres, which cross the cracks generally, will delay the propagation of cracks and hence the cracks have to take a meandering path. During this course the material demand higher energy for the propagation of cracks, which results in higher, load carrying capacity and ductility.

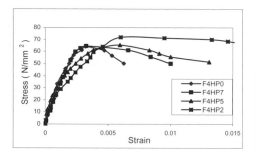

Figure 5: Stress Strain plots for SFRHPC (V_f=1%) with different values of ρ_s

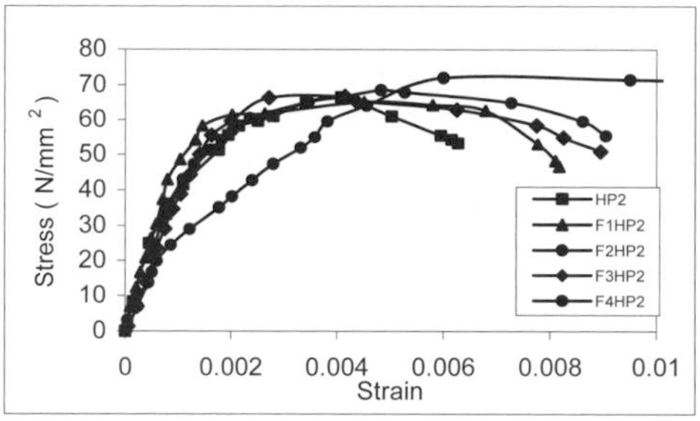

Figure 6: Comparison of stress strain curves of specimens (ρ_s= 4.10%)

b) Cyclic loading

The recorded values of load and deformations have been used to obtain the cyclic stress-strain curves for the specimens. Fig. 7 shows a typical plot of stress versus strain for the cyclically loaded specimens. An envelope curve can be drawn by joining the peak points of all cycles. Fig. 8 shows the envelope curve obtained for specimens with different values of volumetric ratio of confinement. From the figure it can be seen that as the volumetric ratio of confinement increases, performance in terms of energy absorption capacity (area under the stress strain curve) and ductility increases. This indicates the importance of high amount of volumetric ratio of confinement.

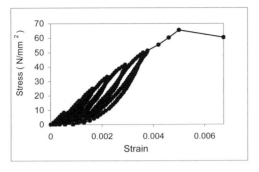

Figure 7: Typical stress strain curve under cyclic loading

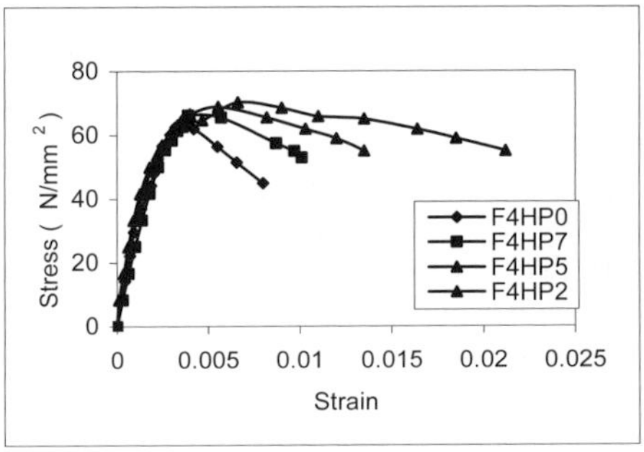

Figure 8: Comparison of envelope plots for different confinement (V_f=1%)

4.3 Comparison between monotonic loading and cyclic loading

It has been shown from the earlier research that in the case of plain concrete, the envelope curve obtained for the positive cyclic loading matches with that of stress strain curve due to monotonically increasing load. An attempt has been made to compare the envelope curves for HPC and SFRHPC obtained for cyclic loading tests with the curves of monotonically increasing load. Typical comparison of stress strain plots is shown in Fig. 9. Results show that the load carrying capacity and strain at peak load for cyclically loaded specimens are slightly higher than that of monotonic loading. This can be attributed to the following reason. When the specimen is loaded at a particular stress level, micro cracks develop in the specimen and during unloading these cracks close partially or completely and the tip of the cracks become blunt. On reloading, crack reopens and deviates from original path, which may demand higher energy for further propagation [14]. This causes a difference in the stress strain curves of cyclic loading and monotonically increasing loading.

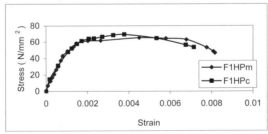

Figure 9: Comparison of stress-strain plots (Monotonic and Cyclic loading)

5. CONCLUSIONS

1. Increase in the volumetric ratio of transverse reinforcement increases the ultimate strength of HPC and SFRHPC. However the percentage of increase is higher for SFRHPC specimens than for HPC
2. Peak strain was found to be higher as the confinement increases. Addition of steel fibres improved this peak strain further.
3. The addition of fibres improves the dimensional stability of the structure to a great extent.

4. For cyclically loaded specimens, it may be noted that at initial stages of loading residual strain is small. However after the formation of cracks, residual strain increases rapidly showing the predominance of inelastic deformation after cracking.

Notations

h   - Height of specimen ε_u -   Strain at ultimate stress
s   - Pitch of spiral ρ_s -   Volumetric ratio of spiral reinforcement
V_f - Volume fraction of fibres

ACKNOWLEDGEMENTS

This experimental investigation is part of the research project on 'High Performance steel Fibre Reinforced Concrete' funded by MHRD, Government of India and project on "Strength and Ductility of High performance Concrete Flexural Members Subjected to Seismic Forces" funded by Kerala State Council for Science Technology and Environment, Government of Kerala. Financial support rendered by them is greatly acknowledged.

REFERENCES

[1]   Singh, B., Kumar, P. and Kaushik, S. K., 'High Performance Composites for the New Millennium,' Journal of Structural Engineering, 28 (1) (2001) 17-26.
[2]   Aitcin, P.C., 'Developments in the Application of High-Performance Concretes,' Construction and Building Materials, 9 (1) (1995) 13-17.
[3]   Mesbah, H. A., Lachemi, M. and Aitcin, P. C., 2002, 'Determination of Elastic Properties of High-Performance Concrete at Early Ages,' ACI Materials Journals, 99 (1) (2002) 37-41.
[4]   Malhotra, V. M., Zhang, M H., Read, P. H. and Ryell, J., 'Long-Term Mechanical Properties And Durability Characteristics of High-Strength/ High-Performance Concrete Incorporating Supplementary Cementing Materials under Outdoor exposure Conditions,'ACI Materials Journal, 97 (5) (2000) 518-525.
[5]   Ahmad, S.H., and Shah, S.P., 'Stress-Strain Curves of Concrete Confined by Spiral Reinforcement,' ACI Journal, 79 (6) (1982) 484-490.
[6]   Bahn, Byong Youl, and Hsu, C.T., 'Stress-Strain Behaviour of Concrete under Cyclic Loading,' ACI Materials Journal, 95 (2) (1998) 178-193.
[7]   Burdette, Edwin G., and Hilsdorf, H.K., 'Behaviour of Laterally Reinforced Concrete Columns,' Journal of Structural Division, ASCE, 97 (2) (1971) 587-602.
[8]   Desayi, P., Iyenkar, K.T.S., and Reddy, T.S, 'Stress-Strain Characteristics of Concrete Confined in Steel Spirals Under Repeated Loading,' Materials and Construction, 12, (71) (1979) 375-383.
[9]   Ganesan, N., and Murthy, R.J.V., 'Strength and Behaviour of Confined Steel fibre Reinforced Concrete Columns', ACI Materials Journal, (1990) 221-227.
[10] Charles, K.D., and Robert, P., 'Flexural Members with Confined Concrete, Journal of Structural Division,' ASCE, 97 (7) (1971) 1969-1990.
[11] Li. B, Park. R,' Confining Reinforcement for High strength Concrete columns', ACI Structural Journal, (2004) 314-320.Aitcin, P.C., High Performance Concrete (E&FN Spon, London, 1994)
[13] Razvi, S., and Saatcioglu, M., 'Strength and Deformability of Confined High-Strength Concrete Columns,' ACI Structural Journal, 91 (6) (1994) 678-688.
[14] Ganesan, N. and Indira, P.V., 'Cyclic Loading of Confined Latex Modified Steel Fibre Concrete,' Proceedings of the National Seminar on 'Recent trends in Concrete and Steel Structures', India, April, 1997.

OUTLINE OF JSCE RECOMMENDATION FOR DESIGN AND CONSTRUCTION OF MULTIPLE FINE CRACKING TYPE FIBER REINFORCED CEMENTITIOUS COMPOSITE (HPFRCC)

Keitetsu Rokugo [(1)], **Tetsushi Kanda** [(2)], **Hiroshi Yokota** [(3)] **and Noboru Sakata** [(2)]

(1) Department of Civil Engineering, Gifu University, Gifu, Japan

(2) Kajima Technical Research Institute, Tokyo, Japan

(3) Structural Mechanics Division, Port and Airport Research Institute, Yokosuka, Japan

Abstract

Multiple fine cracking type fiber reinforced cementitious composite (hereafter referred to HPFRCC) is a cement-based material on which worldwide active research has been conducted and particular attention has been focused in recent years. The Japan Society of Civil Engineers (JSCE) has published the world's first design recommendation for HPFRCC. Characteristics of HPFRCC include a strain hardening tensile stress-strain behavior like steel and crack width controlling capability keeping crack width in a permissible range. Appropriate use of the tensile performance can work out a structural component excellent in both durability and mechanical performance. This paper introduces the JSCE design recommendation of HPFRCC.

1. INTRODUCTION

Multiple fine cracking type fiber reinforced cementitious composite (hereafter referred to HPFRCC- high performance fiber reinforced cement composite) is a cement-based composite material on which worldwide active research has been conducted and particular attention has been focused in recent years. HPFRCC marks a strain hardening tensile stress-strain behavior like steel and exhibits excellent crack width controlling capability allowing multiple fine cracks at tensile loading [1]. A number of HPFRCC structures have been realized in Japan [2], for which a technical committee in Japan Concrete Institute, Performance Evaluation of Highly Ductile Cementitous Composite (Chairman Prof. Rokugo, from 2001 to 2004), played an important role [3].

Inheritance of the JCI technical committee was to organize a new committee of drafting the recommendation for multiple fine cracking type fiber reinforced cementitious composite (Chairman Prof. Rokugo, from 2005 to 2007) in Japan Society of Civil Engineers which led to the publication of world's first recommendation (draft) for design and construction of HPFRCC [4]. Outline of the recommendation is dealt with in this paper.

2. OUTLINE OF THE RECOMMENDATION

The JSCE committee was organized with commission of consulting companies, construction companies and construction materials manufacturers who are interested in application of HPFRCC. During the 2-year term, active discussions on material, design and construction were made and reflected in the recommendation.

Contents of the recommendation are shown in Fig. 1. The recommendation specifies that structural performance, serviceability and resistance to the environmental actions have to be verified on the basis of performance verification concept. Test methods for measuring tensile strength, tensile strain capacity, and crack width are also specified because tensile performance is one of the most important material property in the design of HPFRCC. The test methods enable us to define material properties regarding tensile yield strength, ultimate tensile strain capacity, and maximum crack width for given HPFRCCs, which are subjected to the design verification. This recommendation allows cracks not only in ultimate limit state but also in service condition of a member. The serviceability limit state design is required to verify the resistance to the environmental actions (durability) throughout the design life on the basis of the calculated tensile strain or crack width nucleated in members subjected to service conditions.

The recommendation is provided for synthetic short fiber reinforced cementitious composite materials that exhibit a pseudo strain-hardening behavior and form multiple fine cracks under uniaxial tensile loading. More specifically, the targeted materials are those which exhibit mean ultimate tensile strain capacity of more than 0.5 percent and mean crack width of less than 0.2 mm as determined with test methods specified in the recommendation. Applicable range of the recommendation also includes steel reinforced HPFRCC members (R/HPFRCC, hereafter) and existing R/C structures covered with HPFRCC layer (HPFRCC-covered R/C, hereafter), but excludes monolithic use of HPFRCC in members.

3. CHARACTERISTICS OF HPFRCC

HPFRCC covered in the recommendation is a composite material with a synthetic short fiber such as polyvinyl alcohol (PVA) or polyethylene (PE) at a fiber-volume fraction of less than around 0.02. The features of HPFRCC in relation with other fiber reinforced cementitious materials are illustrated in Fig. 2. Characteristics of HPFRCC are best manifested when compared with ultra high-strength fiber reinforced concrete (UFC) [5] in Fig. 2. UFC can use design strengths of more than 150 N/mm^2 for compressive strength and 5 N/mm^2 for tensile strength, which are characteristics of UFC far greater than those of HPFRCC. However, UFC shows multiple fine crack formation like in HPFRCC only under bending and not under uniaxial tension leading to a limitation in reflecting the multiple fine crack performance into structural design as a material property. Unlike HPFRCC, UFC does not show the strain-hardening or plastic type tensile stress-strain behavior but shows so-called quasi-brittle behavior where early-stage damage concentration takes place at the initial cracks. The difference in materials property leads to a different principle of designing structural members between HPFRCC and UFC. UFC is designed to control the number of cracks as small as possible while HPFRCC design allows cracks in service to draw the best characteristics. Construction of HPFRCC is divided into two types, sprayed type and casting type. The former is applied to repair/retrofitting while the latter is for new constructions.

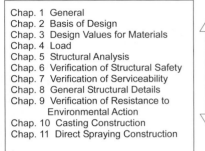

Chap. 1 General
Chap. 2 Basis of Design
Chap. 3 Design Values for Materials
Chap. 4 Load
Chap. 5 Structural Analysis
Chap. 6 Verification of Structural Safety
Chap. 7 Verification of Serviceability
Chap. 8 General Structural Details
Chap. 9 Verification of Resistance to
          Environmental Action
Chap. 10 Casting Construction
Chap. 11 Direct Spraying Construction

Figure 1: Contents of the
Recommendation

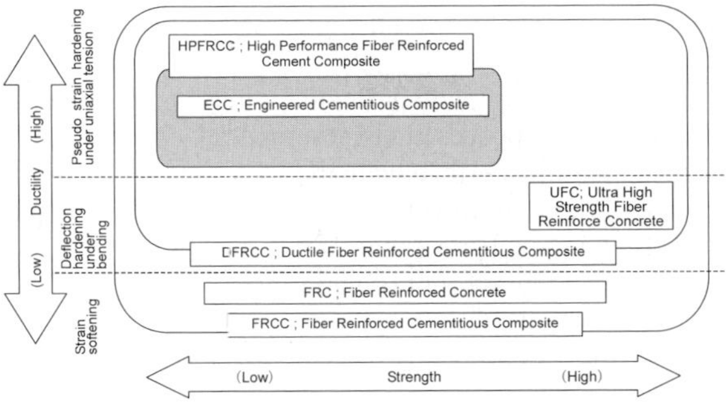

Figure 2: Classification of materials

4. ADVANTAGES IN APPLYING HPFRCC

Tensile and shear load bearing capacities of R/HPFRCC members are deducible by superimposing those of the reinforcing steel and HPFRCC. This contribution of HPFRCC is originated from the fact that the tensile performance of HPFRCC can be maintained at a region exceeding the yield strain of the steel. This contribution results in improvement of cost effectiveness and performance of the structural members, which appears more significant if serviceability limit state governs structural section design.

Unlike other structural systems, HPFRCC members also show a unique feature in protecting steel reinforcements. When crack forms in R/C members, the crack allows corrosive mass transport resulting in the corrosion-induced performance degradation. In R/HPFRCC or HPFRCC-covered R/C members, on the other hand, crack width in HPFRCC becomes smaller and hence the carbonation rate and chloride migration rate are suppressed obviously exhibiting higher corrosion protection capability than that of R/C components. Thus these HPFRCC members can be expected to have a longer design life owing to their protective capability against corrosion-induced degradation and other environmental actions. Results of application of the characteristic are compiled as an appendix of the recommendation.

5. MATERIAL PROPERTIES AND DESIGN VALUES

A unique feature of HPFRCC lies in tensile performance including pseudo strain-hardening tensile stress-strain behavior and crack width controlling capability, while compressive performance is not very different from that of the normal concrete. To reflect the tensile performance in structural design, three major material properties, tensile yield strength, ultimate tensile strain capacity and maximum crack width, are defined. The first two characteristics can be determined by a proposed uniaxial direct tensile test [6] as shown in Fig. 3. When the tensile stress-strain relation is determined with the proposed method, sample data of the tensile yield strength and the ultimate tensile strain capacity can be obtained as shown in Fig. 4, and the characteristic values of tensile yield strength f_{tyk} and ultimate tensile strain capacity ε_{tuk} are to be determined taking account of their variations. Examples of variation in the tensile yield strength and the ultimate tensile strain capacity are shown in Figs. 5 and 6. A schematic representation of the characteristic values and the measured sample data is shown in Fig. 7.

The characteristic value of crack width is defined as the maximum crack width for which a test method is proposed. In this test method, crack widths as shown in Fig. 8 are measured under the tensile loading performed in the same way as in Fig. 3. The crack width measurement can be executed either with direct microscope observation or indirect estimation based on the number of cracks and the tensile strain. When the crack width is obtained, the maximum crack width is determined taking account of variations as shown in Fig. 9.

6. VERIFICATION FOR STRUCTURAL PERFORMANCE

6.1 Verification of structural safety

(1) Bending moments

Regarding the structural safety verification of members in bending, design capacity of cross-section can be determined reflecting the contribution of the design tensile yield strength of HPFRCC to the steel reinforcement within the range of design ultimate tensile strain of HPFRCC. These design values for material performance are determined below material characteristic values considering safety factors. Assumption in stress and strain distribution in R/HPFRCC member section is shown in Fig. 10, where tensile stress of HPFRCC is added as a component of tensile stress resultant unlike R/C members. Since the design ultimate tensile strain capacity of HPFRCC normally exceeds the yield strain of steel, it is possible in the calculation of design flexural moment capacity of members to superimpose the tensile yield strength of HPFRCC on the tensile yield strength of steel. Estimating design capacity of member cross-section normally adopts so-called fiber model to calculate the moment-curvature relation, where the elasto-plastic model, as shown in Fig. 7, is used to represent the tensile stress-strain relation of HPFRCC. Result of the design capacity estimation and the experiment for the flexural behavior of a beam are compared in Fig. 11, where ECC is a sort of HPFRCC. In this estimation, the tensile yield strength and the ultimate tensile strain capacity of HPFRCC are not the design value but greater mean values obtained in experiments.

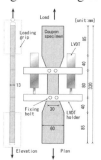 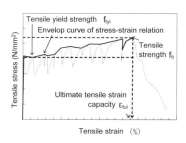

Figure 3: Direct uniaxial tensile test   Figure 4: Method of tensile characteristics evaluation

Also in Fig. 11, analysis and the experimental result show good agreement demonstrating the appropriateness of the assumption made in flexural moment capacity design, though the moment-curvature relation is modified as load-displacement relation.

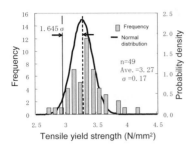

Figure 5: Distribution of measured tensile yield strengths

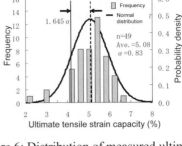

Figure 6: Distribution of measured ultimate strains

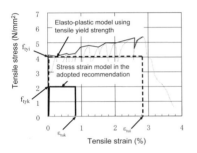

Figure 7: Measured tensile stress and characteristic values

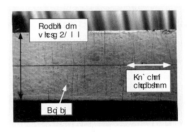

Figure 8: Multiple fine cracks in ECC

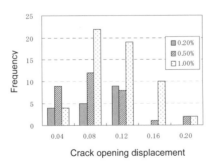

Figure 9: Distribution of measured crack widths at different tensile strain level

(2) Shear forces

Structural safety verification for shear forces can be performed by calculating the design shear capacity with the following equation,

$$V_{yd} = V_{cd} + V_{sd} + V_{fd} + V_{ped} \qquad (1)$$

where V_{cd} : design shear capacity of linear member without shear reinforcing steel, excluding the share of reinforcing fiber in HPFRCC, V_{sd} : design shear capacity of shear reinforcing steel,

V_{fd} : design shear capacity of reinforcing fiber in HPFRCC, V_{ped} : effective tensile force of axial tendon in parallel to shear force. The resulting design shear capacity has a fiber contribution term V_{fd} in addition to V_{cd}, V_{sd} and V_{ped} that comprises the shear capacity of R/C member. In equation (1), values of V_{sd} and V_{ped} are based on those of R/C member while a reduction of 70 percent to R/C member is applied to V_{cd} because cracks are allowed in service condition.

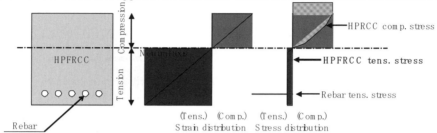

Figure 10: Schematic diagram of bending strain and stress distributions

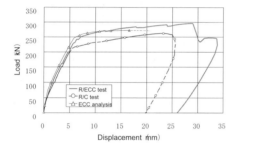

Figure 11: Example of proportioning and load-displacement curve

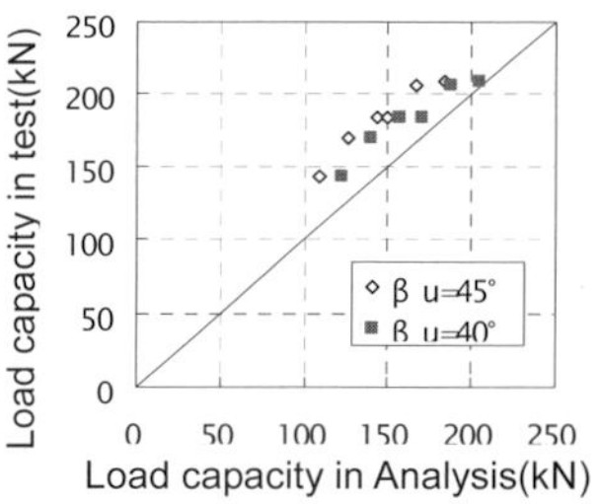

Figure 12: Comparison with sear test result and calculation

Although V_{fd} is a function of β_u, an angle made by the crack plane with the axis, it is fixed to $\beta_u =45°$ to keep the safe side.

Result of calculation with equation (1) and the shear experimental results are compared in Fig. 12, where the design tensile yield strength of HPFRCC is replaced with the mean value of measured tensile yield strength that exhibits a greater value. This figure shows that estimation with equation (1) results in a safe estimation of the experimental results.

6.2 Verification of serviceability

Serviceability verification in the recommendation is featured by (i) cracks are allowed in service condition and the crack width is treated as a material property not as structural performance, (ii) limitation in stress or strain in service condition is set not only for steel stress but also for tensile strain in HPFRCC. As stated in (i), crack width in HPFRCC is not greatly affected by structural design parameters such as tension reinforcement ratio and cover thickness but by the material property before reaching ultimate tensile strain capacity, while that in normal R/C member is controlled by the structural design parameters. This concept is manifested in Fig. 13. This figure shows a relationship between tensile strain and crack width, where the mean crack width refers to the averaged width of multiple cracks that occur at a tensile strain and the maximum crack width refers to a characteristic value of crack obtained stochastically taking account of variations as stated above. As seen in this figure, variation of crack width in HPFRCC is small even though the tensile strain develops and may be regarded nearly constant until the tensile strain reaches the ultimate state except for small strain ranges, i.e. HPFRCC can control crack width without help of steel reinforcement.

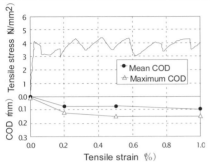

Figure 13: Effects of tensile strain on crack width

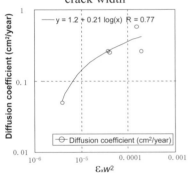

Figure 15: Example of measured chloride ion diffusivity

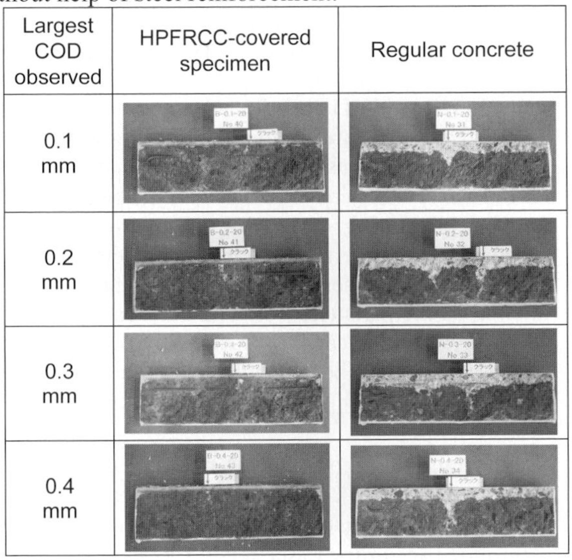

Largest COD observed	HPFRCC-covered specimen	Regular concrete
0.1 mm		
0.2 mm		
0.3 mm		
0.4 mm		

Figure 14: Effects of cracks on carbonation depth

To guarantee this design, serviceability verification requires the tensile strain of HPFRCC in service condition to be less than the ultimate tensile strain capacity to control the crack width at service loads less than the maximum crack width that is a material property of HPFRCC.

7. VERIFICATION FOR RESISTANCE TO ENVIRONMENTAL ACTIONS

7.1   Verification for reinforcement corrosion induced by carbonation

Verification for resistance to environmental actions also pays a special attention to cracks. Carbonation generally develops faster at a cracked region as in R/C structures where reinforcement corrosion occurs around the carbonated/cracked regions. However, crack width of HPFRCC can be controlled to be smaller than that of R/C members and it is experimentally verified that the development of carbonation at the cracked region is not significant compared to a region without cracks (Fig. 14). Hence the corrosion of steel reinforcement can be verified in the same way as the case without cracks by a permissible crack width below which the crack width of a member in service is controlled.

For carbonation related verification, confirmation is needed whether a calculated depth comprising designed carbonation depth plus remaining depth corrected with a structure factor exceeds the cover depth or not, as performed in R/C members [7]. The characteristic value of carbonation rate factor for HPFRCC has to be set properly on the basis of testing but, as confirmed, the value may be equal to that of concrete when water-cement ratio is the same. Crack width should be examined by confirming that the maximum crack width, as explained in the serviceability verification, is less than the permissible crack width.

7.2 Verification for reinforcement corrosion induced by chloride ion ingress

Verification regarding the chloride ingress is performed with the workflow as shown in Table 1 where it has to be confirmed that the designed chloride ion concentration at steel reinforcement location is lower than the permissible value for steel corrosion at the specified cover depth during design life. The design value of chloride ion diffusivity in HPFRCC employed in this verification has to be determined taking into account possible tensile strain and crack width in service condition. Verification of R/C members takes crack width and crack interval as the parameters [7] and verification in HPFRCC members in principal follows this concept. A formula capable of estimating chloride ion diffusivity taking into account the above factors is newly proposed on the basis of experimental results as shown in Fig. 15.

$$D_d = D_k + D_0 \log\left(\varepsilon \cdot w^2\right) \tag{2}$$

where D_d: design value of chloride diffusivity (cm^2/year), D_k: constant depending on materials (cm^2/year), D_0: constant representing contribution of cracks and tensile strain on the chloride diffusivity of HPFRCC, ε: tensile strain which is resulted by service load and determined according to section 7.2 "Computation of stress and strain" of the recommendation, w: characteristic value of the maximum crack width (mm).

Table 1: Verification procedure for chloride ion induced steel corrosion in HPFRCC

Stage	Estimation	Input	Output
0	Strain computation referring to Chap.7 of Serviceability verification of structure.	Ellipsis	Tensile strain at extreme tension fiber resulted by service load.
1	Estimation of maximum crack width.	Design value of tensile strain.	Characteristic value of maximum crack width.
2	Estimation of chloride ion diffusivity.	Maximum crack width and tensile strain.	Design value of chloride ion diffusivity in HPFRCC with cracks.
3	Estimation of chloride ion concentration at steel reinforcement.	Design value of chloride ion diffusivity in HPFRCC with cracks, design life and design value of cover thickness.	Resulted chloride ion concentration at steel reinforcement during design life.
4	Verification of steel corrosion.	Resulted chloride ion concentration at steel reinforcement during design life, Permissible chloride ion concentration for steel reinforcement corrosion.	Permissible chloride ion concentration for steel reinforcement corrosion ≥ Resulted chloride ion concentration at steel reinforcement during design life → End of verification

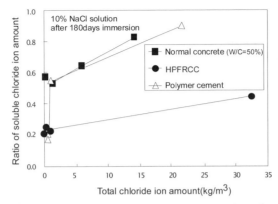

Figure 16: Example of permissible chloride ion concentrations for steel corrosion

The permissible chloride ion concentration for steel corrosion is 1.2 kg/m^3 same as in normal concrete while the value can be set higher according to experimental data as shown in Fig. 16. This appears due to HPFRCC's higher chloride ion binding capability originated from its high unit cement content and variety of admixtures. The advantage of HPFRCC is demonstrated in Fig.16. It is shown in this figure that the fraction of free chloride ion in HPFRCC after immersion test in 10-percent NaCl solution ranges from 0.2 to 0.4 while that in normal concrete with a water-cement ratio of 0.5 ranges from 0.6 to 0.8 proving the higher chloride ion binding capability of HPFRCC.

8. SELECTION OF MATERIALS, MANUFACTURING AND CONSTRUCTION

The constituent of HPFRCC has to be sufficiently stable and durable during the design life of structures. Specifically, selection of the synthetic fibers that has never been present in the normal concrete has to be confirmed by testing its stability over the design life. The confirmation test methods including high temperature accelerated test under alkali environment are compiled in the appendix of the recommendation.

Manufacture and construction of HPFRCC members are described in chapters 11 and 12 of the recommendation. Basics of mix design and mixing are presented and the confirmation of performance of HPFRCC by inspection is emphasized. Examples of inspection items are shown in Table 2 where the principal inspection items are tensile performance and crack width.

Conventional construction method of concrete can be applied to HPFRCC. Because the tensile performance of HPFRCC is important in the design consideration, notations are given on the layered placement and placing joints that greatly affect the performance of the completed structures. Methods of performance confirmation for placing joints are compiled in the supplemental section of the recommendation.

9. CONCLUSIONS

Application of HPFRCC is still in incunabula and associated with problems to be solved, while it poses a unique feature that has never been presented by the existing cement-based materials. A worldwide active research and development of HPFRCC imply a possibility to realize concrete structures with excellent safety, serviceability and durability performance. It is our anticipation that the publication of the recommendation could contribute to the realization of the excellent concrete structure.

Table 2: Items for HPFRCC inspection

Item	Test method	Timing and iteration	Criteria
Mix proportion	Weighing of each material	All batches	Within a permissible range of error.
Fresh state	Visual observation by experts	At construction	Good workability, stable and uniform quality.
Fluidity	Flow value. JIS A 1150	At the start of construction.	Adoptable to conditions required by the construction methods.
Segregation resistance	V-funnel test		
Unit mass	JIS A 1116	At sampling.	
Mixing temperature	Temperature measurement	When there are any changes in quality.	
Compressive strength	JIS A 1108	Once a day or every 20 to 150 m³ depending on the importance of structure and on construction scale.	Probability of lowering the design value has to be less than 5 percent, as estimated with appropriate consumer's and producer's risk.
Tensile yield strength	Uniaxial direct tensile strength test (Test methods 2 of the recommendation)		
Ultimate tensile strength			
Maximum crack width	Crack width testing (Test methods 3 and 4 of the recommendation)		

ACKNOWLEDGEMENTS

Authors thank to all the members of the JSCE committee of drafting the recommendation for multiple fine cracking type fiber reinforced cementitious composite for their generous cooperation.

REFERENCES

[1] Naaman, A. E. and Reinhardt, H. W. eds., 'High performance fiber reinforced cement composites 2 (HPFRCC2)', RILEM Proceedings 31, (E&FN Spon, London, 1995).

[2] 'Performance Evaluation and Structural Use of Highly Ductile Cementitious Composite II', Technical Committee Report, (Japan Concrete Institute, 2004).

[3] Kanda, T., Sakata, N., Kunieda, M. and Rokugo, K., 'State-of-the-art of High Performance Fiber Reinforced Cement Composite Research', Concrete Journal, 44(3) (2006), 3-10.

[4] 'Recommendations for Design and Construction of High Performance Fiber Reinforced Cement Composite with Multiple Fine Cracks (Draft)', Concrete Library 127, (Japan Society of Civil Engineers, 2007).

[5] 'Recommendations for Design and Construction of Ultra High-Strength Fiber Reinforced Concrete Structures (Draft)', Concrete Library 113, (Japan Society of Civil Engineers, 2004).

[6] Inakuma, T., Kanda, T., Lim, S. and Uchida, Y., 'Evaluation of Tensile Properties in High Performance Fiber Reinforced Cement Composites', Concrete Journal, 44(7) (2006), 3-10.

[7] 'Standard Specifications for Concrete Structures – 2002 "*Materials and Construction*", JSCE Guidelines for Concrete No. 6 (Japan Society of Civil Engineers, 2002).

HPFRCC FIELD OF APPLICATIONS: DUCTAL® RECENT EXPERIENCE

Mouloud Behloul

Lafarge, France

Abstract

Ductal®, a new material technology developed over the last decade, is a combination of superior technical characteristics of strength, ductility and durability, whilst providing high quality surface aspect on moldable products.

This technology offers flexural resistance exceeding 40 MPa with ductility and compression strength beyond 200 MPa. As a result of its tensile strength and ductility it is possible to avoid reinforcement bars in structural elements.

Ductal® covers a range of formulations that can be adapted to meet specific demands of different customer segments, enhancing the usage value and contributing to the overall construction performance, reducing labour requirement, enhancing durability, lowering maintenance need and increasing total life cycle.

Ductal®'s unique combination of superior properties enables designers to create thinner sections, longer spans and higher structures that are lighter, innovative in geometry and form, while providing superior durability and impermeability against corrosion, abrasion and impact.

A number of reference prototypes in Ductal® already exist in different countries both in structural and architectural segments. A number of selected references as the recent footbridges, retrofitting elements and architectural realisations will be illustrated in this article. Currently there are many other innovative applications of this material in projects at different stages of development.

1. INTRODUCTION

Ductal®, the outcome of the research over the last 10 years in the area of concrete, is a new construction material technology belonging to UHPFRC family, with very high durability, compressive strength, flexural resistance with ductility and aesthetics [1]. Through the development period, several prototypes have been produced, prior to make an extensive use in civil works, structural and architectural various applications [2].

In France, new recommendations for the use of ultrahigh strength concretes reinforced with fibres have been issued in May 2002 [3]. These recommendations were established by a BFUP working group (Béton Fibré Ultra Performant) coordinated by SETRA (Road and traffic govern-mental agency) and with representatives of construction industries (contractors, control agencies, suppliers, certification authorities).

2. DUCTAL® TECHNOLOGY

Ductal® is based on the principle that a material with a minimum of defects such as micro-cracks and pore spaces will achieve a greater percentage of the potential ultimate load carrying capacity defined by its component materials, and it will also have greater durability. By applying this principle as a guideline, a concrete has been proportioned to provide a very dense mixture that will minimise voids and a very high compressive strength, but with not enough ductility compared to a conventional mortar. The inclusion of adequate fibres improves drastically tensile strength and provides a substantial level of ductility.

The various Ductal® formulations are all based on an optimized composition combining homogeneity and adequate granular compactness. To enhance and to stabilize the performances, especially mechanical ones, the option of heat treatment can be chosen. For each application according to technical and economical challenges, adequate adjustments are made within Ductal® technology in order to achieve the most adapted product to the customer requirements.

As described above, Ductal® is an Ultra-High Performance Concrete reinforced with fibres. These fibres can be made of steel (Ductal®-FM), made of organic material (Ductal®-FO) or combination of both steel and organic material (Ductal® AF). The fresh mix of all these ranges of material have very useful properties in term of fluidity and self placing. Most of the standard industrial batching facilities are able to mix Ductal® requiring only minor adjustments.

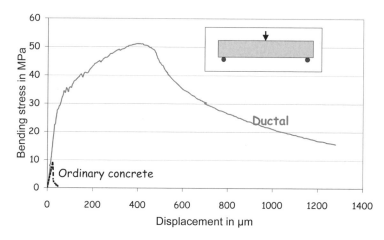

Figure 1: Ductal®-FM behaviour in bending

Ductal®-FM, used for structural applications, includes small steel fibres at a dosage of 2% per volume, and of 0.20 mm in diameter and 12 mm in length. In a typical load deflection graph of a sample under three-point loading, the material exhibits linear behaviour up to its first crack stress, a post-first-crack strain hardening phase up to its ultimate flexural load, and a post-ultimate-load strain softening phase. It has an ultimate bending stress that is over twice its first crack stress and more than ten times the ultimate stress of conventional concrete (Fig. 1).

Table 1: Main properties of the material with steel fibres or organic fibres

		Ductal®-FM or Ductal®-AF With Thermal Treatment	Ductal®-FO Without Thermal Treatment
Density		2500 kg /m^3	2350 kg/m^3
Compressive Strength	Mean value	180 – 200 MPa	130 – 160 MPa
	Characteristical value	150 – 180 MPa	100 – 140 MPa
Flexural Strength (4*4*16 cm)	Mean value	40 – 45 MPa	18 – 25 MPa
	Characteristical value	30-40 MPa	15-20 MPa
Tensile Strength	Mean value	11 MPa	8 MPa
	Characteristical value	8 MPa	5 MPa
Residual tensile strength (0.3 mm)	Mean value	10 MPa	4 MPa
	Characteristical value	8 MPa	3 MPa
Young Modulus (E)		50 GPa	45 GPa
Poisson Ratio		0.2	0.2
Shrinkage		< 10 µm/m	550 µm/m
Creep factor		0.3	0.8
Thermal expansion coefficient		11.8 µm/m/°C	11.8 µm/m/°C

The Ductal® microstructure is completely closed, making it resistant to abrasion, corrosion or chemical attacks. Such superior characteristics give the material ultra-high performance durability properties. Table 2 hereafter shows some durability properties of heat treated Ductal®-FM and a comparison with ordinary concrete and high performance concrete properties.

Table 2: Ductal® main durability properties

Durability indicator	Ordinary concrete	HPC	Ductal®-FM
Water porosity (%)	12-16	9-12	2-6
Oxygen permeability(m²)	$10^{-15} – 10^{-16}$	10^{-17}	$<10^{-19}$
Carbonation depth (mm) after one month of accelerated tests	10	2	< 0.1
Abrasion test I=V/V$_{glass}$	4	2.8	1.3-1.7

3. DUCTAL® RECENT REFERENCES

The ultra high performance of Ductal® opens applications in following different domains:
- Bridges and footbridges
- Durability oriented applications
- Architectural applications

3.1 Bridges and footbridges

A material with such high ultimate compressive and flexural-tensile strength offers interesting opportunities in the field of prestressed concrete. As might be expected, the high flexural tension capacity also gives rise to extremely high shear capacity. This allows Ductal® to carry the shear load in the structure, without providing auxiliary shear reinforcement.

The elimination of passive reinforcement makes it possible to use thinner sections and a wider variety of innovative and acceptable cross-sectional shapes. The current structural precast shapes used for prestressed beams in bridges and buildings have been shaped for concretes with much lower strength properties. Their dimensions and design would not allow to take advantage of very high performances of Ductal®. In order to make the best use of the higher mechanical properties, there are several opportunities to introduce new shapes in prestressed beam design. Through such re-design approach of the elements the beam dead load can be reduced by a factor of three.

Among these kind of applications we can list 3 traffic bridges: the Shepherds Bridge erected in Australia [4], the Wapello bridge in Iowa-US and the Kuyshu expressway bridge erected in Japan [5]; 5 footbridges: Sherbrooke footbridge in Canada – Seonyu footbridge in Korea [6] – Sermaises footbridge in France- Sakata Mirai and Akakura footbridges in Japan. Also an important work is performed in the US by the FHWA (Federal High-Way Administration) in order to design short span bridges made of Ductal® [7]. Hereafter, the saint-Pierre-La-Cour bridge and the Glenmore footbridge, recently erected, are presented.

Saint-Pierre-la-Cour bridge

The "Conseil Général" of the Mayenne ordered a bypass from the town of Saint-Pierre-la-Cour. It was in this context that the first bridge in France made of Ductal® was built to cross a railway line. This bridge, with a span of 19 m and 12.6 m wide, supports a continuous reinforced concrete road of 7.6 m, a pavement and a cycle track (Fig. 2)

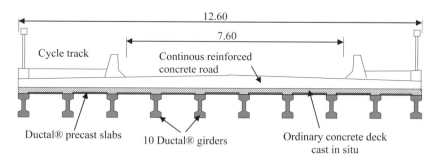

Figure 2: Transversal section of the bridge

The ten 20-meters length prestressed girders without re-bars and 83 precast slabs they support are all made of Ductal® (Fig. 3 and 4). Although not exceeding 25 mm thick, the precast slabs support a conventional 20-cm concrete apron. All the girders and precast slabs were laid in two days, thanks to the speed this technique affords.

A comparison with a traditional solution indicates a reduction of the weight of the bridge deck by a factor 2.2. The characteristics of the structure are enhanced by the fact that the underside of the concrete deck and its reinforcements are protected against any damage thanks to Ductal ultra high durability performances. Durability that limits maintenance budgets and provides a more globally economic solution.

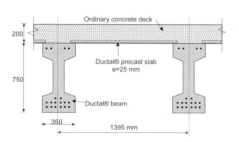

Description of the composite solution   Erection of the bridge

Figure 3: Saint-Pierre-La-Cour bridge description and construction

Figure 4: View of the Saint-Pierre-La-Cour bridge after completion

Glenmore/Legsby Road Pedestrian Overpass

The Glenmore/Legsby Pedestrian Overpass is a single span, 53-metre bridge that stretches across 8 lanes of traffic in the city of Calgary, Alberta, Canada. It is just the second pedestrian bridge in North America to be built with Ductal®. It consists of two cantilevered, high performance concrete abutments and a drop-in, "T-section" Ductal® girder with an arch. The architectural and structural designs are part of an innovative design program for the City of

Calgary - which encourages and allows the use of new materials in the construction of various infrastructure projects.

The Ductal® girder is 33.6m long, 1.1m deep at mid-span, has a 3.6m wide deck, and weighs approximately 100 tons (Fig. 5). It is constructed with Ductal®-FM and post-tensioned with 42 – 15 mm strands. Glass fibre-reinforced plastic (GFRP) bars were utilized by the designers as a redundant passive reinforcing system.

The girder production at the Lafarge precast facility in Calgary involved the largest single monolithic pour of Ductal® in the world (to date), requiring 40 m^3 of material. After pouring, the girder was thermally heat treated for over 48 hours at 90°C. Full and partial service load tests were performed on the girder with uniformly distributed live loads. The deflections of the girder were significantly less than predicted and demonstrated the reserve capacity of the structural system.

Transportation of the girder   Erection of the footbridge

Figure 5: Glenmore footbridge

Some advantages of using Ductal® for the drop-in girder are as follows:
- An aesthetically pleasing solution.
- Greater structural strength with reduced weight.
- A single-span bridge was quickly installed (with minimal disruption to traffic) to stretch across an 8-lane highway.
- High resistance against chloride ingress (due to salting of the roads) during winter months.
- Smooth surface finish (to satisfy the required architectural look).
- Superior durability.
- Low maintenance.

With completion of this unique, innovative bridge expected in spring, 2007, the fast-growing City of Calgary leads the way as an innovative, leading edge city for the 21st century.

3.2   Durability Oriented Applications

The durability of Ductal® is as important as the mechanical strength. Combining strength and durability, Ductal® can be an ideal solution for structures in severe environment [8]. Also the durability of the material lowers the maintenance costs and makes the solution very competitive.

Ductal® was used in several durability /fire resistance oriented applications like the beams and girders (more than 2000) used for the Cattenom power plant cooling tower-France, the retained earth anchorages (more than 6000) used in Reunion Island –France- and the Ductal®-AF used for the construction of composite columns in the Reina Sofia Museum in Madrid (Spain). Recently Ductal® was used for the fabrication of the troughs of Gold Bar waste water treatment.

The Gold Bar wastewater treatment plant in Edmonton, AB, Canada, is the sole facility serving the city of Edmonton and its surrounding suburbs. The plant's collection tanks are located directly over the sheet-steel plate-settlers; structural strength, durability and lightness were therefore key requirements. Traditional cement would have called for extra support and stainless steel might have seemed the logical choice for this project, but the cost was prohibitive. The Stantec design consultants were familiar with Ductal's unique properties and decided that Ductal® troughs offered a viable, new solution. 200 pieces of Ductal®-FM U-shaped forms, 5 m long, 800 mm high, 600 mm wide, 17 mm thick were made and installed (Fig. 6).

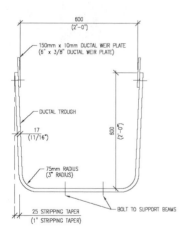

Transversal section   Troughs after installation

Figure 6: Gold Bar troughs

As a result, the physical property requirements were met and the solution offered the following advantages:

- Greater structural strengths to simplify the design and reduce the weight,
- High resistance to the corrosive wastewater environment,

- Lighter structure, installation was easier,
- Dense, smooth surface finish to prevent water infiltration and contamination,
- Easy-to-clean.

3.3   Architectural Applications

The use of a concrete-like material but with almost unlimited possibilities of appearance, texture and colour has excited the architects by giving them access to unexpected new world of shapes and volumes. Ductal® was used in several architecturally oriented applications like the bus shelters in Tucson (USA), sun shades in France, façade panels in Monaco, Kyoto clock tower in Japan and the canopies of LRT station of Shawnessy in Canada (Fig. 7). Recently, Ductal® was used for the construction of the façade of building located at Thiais in France; this project is presented hereafter.

Figure 7: Ductal®-FO canopies - LRT Train Station, Shawnessy

The RATP administrative centre in Thiais is responsible for the traffic management of 300 buses and provision of 24-hour facilities for 800 drivers. Located in an industrial zone on the outskirts of Paris, this project was designed by Dominique Marrec and Emmanuel Combarel.

Mirroring the variety of coatings within the bus depot, a double skin first follows and then lifts the pavement. The result is a non-directive setting in which users are free to determine what they want to conceal and what they want to leave open to view (Fig. 8).

The architects wanted to focus on the mineral nature of the site and propose a building that acts as a continuation of the ground surface and emerges like a deformation of that surface.

Figure 8: Thiais bus station – By D.Marrec and E.Combarel

It was this approach that gave the idea of a skin that would blur distinctions between traffic flows and building while giving the site a strong visual identity.

Two implementation techniques come together here: heavy prefabrication and siding, as the 3cm thick skin provides a pavement that is partly open to traffic and rises up, sweeping away any thickness, to lose itself in the sky.

The Lego-like framework offers anti-slip properties, gives colour-stippling effects that break up the play of lights and mirrors from the tinted external exterior bonded glass bays (Fig. 9). This skin uses Ductal® not only for its structural properties but also for its visual aspect, its depth of colour and quality of finish.

Figure 9: Thiais project- Details of the façade

4. CONCLUSION

Ductal® is a new technology of ultra high strength concretes that constitutes a breakthrough in concrete mix design. This family of products is characterised by a very dense microstructure and very high compressive strength achieving and possibly exceeding 200 MPa. Steel and organic fibres or combination of both are one of the major components of the material enhancing the bending strength, the ductility and fire resistance.

The three main categories of applications are:

- Bridges and footbridges: The very high mechanical properties combined with prestressing technology offer to engineers and architects lot of opportunities to design elegant structures by avoiding heavy steel reinforcement. Ductal® technology gives access to very thin slender and elegant structures like footbridges.
- Durability oriented applications: the very dense microstructure of the Ductal® matrix offers a material which resists to very aggressive media and opens therefore a very wide range of applications.
- Architectural applications: a very wide range of textures and colours effects are accessible to Ductal®. Such properties provide architects with very high potential of innovative design in all elements that build up new architecture.

REFERENCES

[1] Orange, G.; Dugat, J.; Acker, P.; "A new generation of UHP concrete : Ductal®. Damage resistance and micromechanical analysis"; Proc. of the 3rd Internat. RILEM Workshop, HPFRCC3-1999, 101-111.

[2] Behloul, M.; Durukal, A.; Batoz, J.-F.; Chanvillard, G.; "Ductal® : Ultra High-Performance Concrete Technology with Ductility"; International Rilem Symposium on Fibre Reinforced Concretes BEFIB'2004, September 22-24 – Varenna, 2004.

[3] BFUP-AFGC; "Ultra High Performance Fibre-Reinforced Concretes, Interim Recommendations"; AFGC publication, France, 2002. Comparison on 30m-span bridge

[4] Cavill, B. and Chirgwin, G; "The worlds first Ductal road bridge Sherpherds gully creek bridge, NSW"; 21st Biennial Conference of the Concrete Institute of Australia, Brisbane, 2003.

[5] Okuma, H et al; "The first highway bridge applying ultra high strength fibre reinforced concrete in Japan"; 7th International Conference on short and medium span bridges. Montreal, Canada, 2006.

[6] Behloul, M.; Lee, KC.; "Ductal® Seonyu footbridge" ; Structural Concrete. 4 (4), 2003, 195-201.

[7] Graybeal, B.; Hartamann, J.; Perry, V.; "Ultra-high performance concrete for highway bridge"; FIB Symposium, Avignon - 26-28 April 2004.

[8] Behloul, M.; Arsenault, J "Ductal® : a durable material for durable structures"; CONSEC'07, concrete under severe conditions ; Tours, France, 4-6 June 2007.

SIMPLIFIED ANALYTICAL MODEL FOR BEARING CAPACITY OF FRC CORBELS

Guiseppe Campione, Lidia La Mendola, Maria L. Mangiavillano and Maurizio Papia

Dipartimento di Ingegneria Strutturale e Geotecnica, Università di Palermo, Italy

Abstract

A simplified analytical model is proposed able to calculate the shear strength of fibrous reinforced concrete (FRC) corbels. The model is based on the truss analogy and it is able to consider the influence of the type of concrete grade (normal and high strength concretes), of the fiber percentage and of the arrangement and percentage of the steel bars. Finally, the experimental results recently generated by the authors and those available in the literature are compared with the results obtained through the proposed model and with existing analytical expressions present in the literature showing good agreement.

1. INTRODUCTION

Corbels and deep members are structural members very commonly used in reinforced concrete structures and particularly in precast structures where their principal function is the transfer of vertical and horizontal forces to principal members. Corbels and deep beams are structural members characterized by a shear span-depth ratio generally very low (lower than unity for corbels and lower than two for deep beams) and subjected to concentrate forces as in the support zones. For these reasons they are host zones of static and geometric discontinuities and the hypothesis assumed for members in flexure that sections remain plane after deformation, is not valid in this case. There are zones therefore, well known in the literature as D-regions, in which three-dimensional states of stress occur and classical bending theory cannot be applied. Many studies in the literature are addressed to determining experimentally and analytically the strength of such elements when subjected to vertical and horizontal forces and to highlighting the role of the parameters which influence the performance of corbels including shape and dimension of corbels, type of longitudinal and transverse steel reinforcements, and strength of concrete. It has been widely shown that to increase the strength and improve the ductility of corbels it is necessary to increase the percentages of transverse steel (generally constituted by horizontal stirrups or inclined bars) or to integrate or partially substitute the secondary shear steel reinforcements by using fiber reinforced concrete (FRC). These studies (see e.g. [1, 2, 3] also stress the use of fibers in producing significant increases in the bearing capacity and ductility of corbels. The aim of the present study is to investigate the bearing capacity of corbels cast with ordinary reinforced concrete or fibrous concrete and to propose a simple analytical procedure based on the individuation of strut and tie mechanisms.

2. CODE PRESCRIPTIONS AND EXISTING ANALYTICAL MODELS

European and International code prescriptions [4, 5] consider corbels and give clear indications on evaluation of the shear strength of these elements also introducing limitations on the percentage of reinforcing bars and on the geometry of corbels respecting the aim of assigning strength to the brittle mechanisms. In the following section code prescriptions on the arrangement of concrete corbels are given with reference to the case of Fig. 1, by using the symbols contained in the same figure.

a)   b)

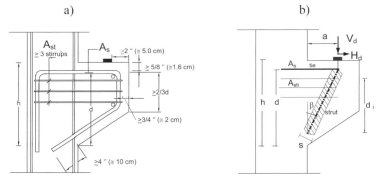

Figure 1: Steel arrangements in ordinary concrete corbels and simplified strength model

Some of the existing analytical expressions given in the literature for the calculation of the ultimate strength of corbels with reference to the use of steel bars (main and secondary) and plain concrete or steel bars and fibrous concrete, will also be presented and discussed.

When considering the corbels and depending on shear span-depth ratio (a/h) the Eurocode 2 advises carrying out the calculation for $0.4 \cdot h \leq a \leq h$ by a simple model strut-and-tie, if $a > h$ the calculus is in accordance with the beam theory. Finally adequate models for $a < 0.4 \cdot h$ are advised. If horizontal force H_d acts simultaneously to vertical force V_d its value has to be limited in relation to the value of vertical force to avoid drastic reduction in the bearing capacity of corbel and proposed limiting H_d to $H_{dmax} = 0.2 V_d$.

Moreover, Eurocode 2 to corbels with $h \geq 300\,mm$, prescribed that the area of horizontal main bars A_s must satisfy the relation:

$$A_s \geq 0.4 \cdot A_c \cdot \frac{f_{cd}}{f_{yd}} \qquad \text{in S.I. units} \qquad (1)$$

in which $A_c = b \cdot h$ is the area of the fixed section of the corbel, b is the width, f_{cd} and f_{yd} are the design strength values of concrete and steel respectively. In addition to reducing the cracking spacing and producing confinement effects in the compressed strut, horizontal stirrups (or inclined bars) having area $A_{st,}$ higher than $0.4A_s$, have to be utilised and distributed through depth d.

Similar prescriptions are given in ACI 318-02 which refer specifically to chamfered corbels where inclined reinforcements are placed. In particular the above mentioned code prescribes: - minimum value of mechanical percentage of steel bars expressed by means of $\omega = (A_s \cdot f_{yd})/(b \cdot d \cdot f_{cd})$ has to be between 0.04 and 0.15; - steel bars distributed in the height of the corbel (secondary reinforcements) and situated in a perpendicular direction to the shear force V_d and placed from the top of the corbel in the height 2/3 d, must consist of least three stirrups, and the gross-area has to be not less than 0.5% $b \cdot d$; - stirrups have to be bent in a U shape in such way as to wrap the vertical bars situated on the internal side, or if welded to these, anchored appropriately to support to corbels. As already mentioned, almost all codes give practical design rules to avoid brittle failure ensuring the development of a well defined strength mechanism which generally occurs in the formation of a strut and tie resistant mechanism. From theoretical point of view the European and International codes also give analytical expressions for the shear strength prediction of corbels. ACI 318-02 give analytical expressions for the calculation of the shear strength of chamfered corbels with main bars valid for both normal and high strength concrete. This procedure refers to four typical modes of failure: the first is the failure mode due to shear constraint occurring at the interface between column and corbel, and which can occurs with very small shear span ratio and reduced percentages of reinforcement; the second is due to yielding of the main bars; the third occurs when the failure mechanism is tied to the crushing of compressed regions; and finally the fourth consists of premature failure in the loaded section.

There is particular interest in the recent model proposed in [6] which allows the calculation of the shear strength of corbels in the presence of horizontal stirrups also. In particular the model is valid for a/d ≤1 and analyses only the failure mode due to the crushing of concrete strut. In this case prediction of the shear strength is based on a simplified strut-and-tie mechanism which takes into account the bi-axial state of stresses in compressed strut and considers the effective contribution due to the stirrups. Moreover, it covers a wide range of experimental data present in the literature.

Several models are also available for fibrous concrete corbels. Some of these are of empirical nature [2], some others are derived by a mechanical model such as that proposed by [7] in which it was demonstrated that it is possible to calculate the shear strength of corbels in FRC by using two different methods: the first referring to an equivalent truss structure and the second referring to a beam model. The truss model is identified by a single truss consisting of a diagonal member formed by a region of compressed concrete and by a horizontal member subject to tension and simulating the presence of main and secondary steel bars. The model also takes the presence of fibers into account by means of the contribution expressed through the indirect tensile splitting strength of concrete. The beam model relates the external load to the ultimate flexural moment carried out by the fixed section and it also takes the presence of bars and fibers into account.

3. PROPOSED MODEL AND COMPARISON WITH EXPERIMENTAL DATA

The model presented here (developed in detail in [8, 9]) is able to determine the bearing capacity of corbels reinforced by main and transverse steel bars and in the presence of fibrous concrete. In the present paper we refers only to corbels in plain or fibrous concrete with main steel. Therefore we refer to the single truss model in Fig. 2. The truss structure consists of a compressed member inclined by an angle α with respect to the horizontal direction and main steel A_s placed at distance z from the centre of the compressed zone.

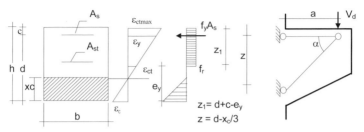

Figure 2: Equivalent truss model

The angle α is related to the arm of the internal forces z and to the shear span by a simple geometrical relation.

In the case of fibrous concrete the presence of fibers is considered in both the trusses including that of the vertical resistant forces exercised by fibers through the fracture plan (inclined α). This force is expressed by means of the residual tensile strength of the composite f_r (defined below) and by means of the depth of the tensile zone in which the resultant of the residual stress is projected to direction α. Both in the cases of plain and fibrous concrete corbels the strength reduction of compressed strut due to biaxial state of stresses (softening of concrete) is considered as well as the reduction coefficient proposed by [6] in the form:

$$\chi = 0.74 \cdot \left(\frac{f_c'}{105}\right)^3 - 1.28 \cdot \left(\frac{f_c'}{105}\right)^2 + 0.22 \cdot \left(\frac{f_c'}{105}\right) + 0.87 \qquad \text{for } 10 < f_c' < 105 \text{ MPa} \qquad (2)$$

It should also be noted that the addition of steel fibers to the concrete elements improves the bi-axial strength with respect to ordinary concrete, but, because little experimental information is available, in the present paper it assumes the softening coefficient given by Eq. (2) for fibrous concrete also.

To define the position of the neutral axis and to define z (see Fig. 2), we refer, as suggested in the literature [6], to the neutral axis position derived from elastic analysis of the fixed section. To obtain the neutral axis position stresses distribution of Fig. 2 is assumed.

From the translational equilibrium we obtain the following equation:

$$\frac{1}{2} \cdot \frac{E_c \cdot f_y}{E_s} \cdot \frac{x_c}{d - x_c} \cdot b \cdot x_c - f_y \cdot A_s - f_r \cdot b \cdot (d + c - e_y) = 0 \qquad (3)$$

in which x_c is the position of neutral axis and e_y is the distance between the more compressed fiber of the transverse cross-section, the fiber at which the maximum tensile strength in concrete is reached and E_c is the modulus of elasticity of concrete in compression. Its value can be obtained by considering the plane section hypothesis resulting:

$$e_y = \frac{\dfrac{f_t}{E_{ct}} \cdot (d - x_c) + \varepsilon_y \cdot x_c}{\varepsilon_y} \qquad (4)$$

E_{ct} being the elasticity modulus of concrete in tension.

The values of x_c and e_y are obtained by introducing Eq. (4) in Eq. (3); in this way the following second degree equation for position of the neutral axis is obtained:

$$\left[\frac{1}{2} \cdot \frac{E_c \cdot f_y}{E_s} \cdot b + f_r \cdot b \cdot \left(\frac{\varepsilon_{ct} - \varepsilon_y}{\varepsilon_y} \right) \right] \cdot x_c^2 + \left(f_r \cdot b \cdot c + f_y \cdot A_s \right) \cdot x_c +$$

$$+ \left(f_r \cdot b \cdot d^2 \cdot \frac{\varepsilon_{ct}}{\varepsilon_y} - f_r \cdot b \cdot h \cdot d - f_y \cdot d \cdot A_s \right) = 0 \qquad (5)$$

c being the distance between the centre of the main steel and the most stressed fiber in tension.

The tensile strength f_{ctf} of the fibrous concrete can be assumed for moderate content of fibers giving strain softening behaviour of material approximately equal to that of the plain concrete f_t, (the latter assumed as $f_t = 0.7 \cdot \sqrt{f_c'}$, f_c' in MPa, as suggested in [5]).

Referring to the residual tensile strength f_r of FRC steel fibers an investigation by [10] recently showed that it can be assumed as:

$$f_r = 0.2 \cdot \sqrt{f_c'} \cdot F \qquad\qquad f_c' \text{ in MPa} \qquad (6)$$

F being the fiber factor expressed as $F = v_f \cdot L_f \cdot \lambda / D$, with $\lambda = 1$ for hooked fibers and 0.5 for straight fibers. The values assumed for λ are the same as suggested by the author and also are in agreement with the results obtained in [11] from which it emerges that the pull-out resistance of straight fibers is less than for hooked or crimped steel fibers (having a similar aspect ratio). It should be noted that the value for the residual tensile strength f_r expressed only in terms of fiber volume and aspect ratio and compressive strength (Eq. 6) is specific for steel fibers.

In the case of corbels with main steel bars the area of the strut is assumed to be equal to $A_c = h_{eff} b$, being h_{eff} the effective depth of the strut and assumed to be equal to $x_c \cdot \cos\alpha$, as shown in Fig. 3.

It is possible to obtain the ultimate load by imposing the condition of failure of the main steel reinforcement or of the compressed concrete; by using the equilibrium equation it can be obtained:

$$V_{n1} = f_y \cdot A_s \cdot \tan\alpha \qquad (7)$$

in the case of yielding of steel where $\tan\alpha = z/a$ and:

$$V_{n2} = \chi \cdot f_c' \cdot b \cdot x_c \cdot \cos\alpha \cdot \sin\alpha \qquad (8)$$

in the case of failure of the compressed zone.

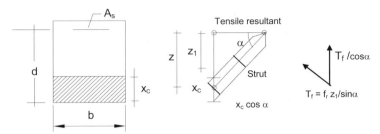

Figure 3: Definition of depth of the strut and shear contribution due to fibers

It must be noted that some authors, including [6], assume that the width of the strut is equal to x_c, instead of $x_c \cos\alpha$. In the present study, the assumption that the width of the strut is equal to $x_c \cos\alpha$, is related to the fact that the truss model adopted is in strict correlation with the beam model and for this reason it appears appropriate to consider the projection of x_c along the direction of the strut. With reference to fibrous concrete, considering the vertical projection of the bridging action exerted by the fibers across diagonal cracks (see Fig. 3), we have:

$$V_f = \frac{f_r \cdot z_1 \cdot b}{\sin\alpha \cdot \cos\alpha} \tag{9}$$

The last term is to be added to those obtained using Eq. (7) and Eq. (8).

Specifically Eq. (9) was derived considering f_r to be perpendicular to the direction of the strut and acting for a length $z_1/\sin\alpha$ corresponding to the tensile zone z_1 of the fixed cross-section. Excluding failures mode due to shear constrained or due to bond failure of the main bars and utilizing the previous Eqs. (7), (8) by means of Eq. (9) it is possible to obtain the shear strength V_n, by means of V_{n1} e V_{n2}, expressed as:

$$V_{n1} = f_y \cdot A_s \cdot \frac{d - \dfrac{x_c}{3}}{a} + \frac{b}{\sin\alpha \cdot \cos\alpha} \cdot 0.2 \cdot \sqrt{f_c'} \cdot F \cdot \left[(d - x_c) \cdot \left(1 - \frac{f_{ctf}}{f_y} \cdot \frac{E_s}{E_{ct}} \right) + c \right] \tag{10}$$

$$V_{n2} = \chi \cdot f_c' \cdot (b \cdot x_c \cdot \cos\alpha) \cdot \sin\alpha + \frac{b}{\sin\alpha \cdot \cos\alpha} \cdot 0.2 \cdot \sqrt{f_c'} \cdot F \cdot \left[(d - x_c) \cdot \left(1 - \frac{f_{ctf}}{f_y} \cdot \frac{E_s}{E_{ct}} \right) + c \right] \tag{11}$$

Dividing both expressions for bd and introducing k ($k=x_c/d$ with x_c given by Eq. (5) and introducing the geometrical ratio of main steel ($\rho = A_s/(b \cdot d)$) it results:

$$v_{n1} = \rho \cdot f_y \cdot \frac{d}{a} \cdot \left(1 - \frac{k}{3} \right) + \frac{0.2 \cdot \sqrt{f_c'} \cdot F}{\sin\alpha \cdot \cos\alpha} \cdot \left[(1 - k) \cdot \left(1 - \frac{f_{ctf}}{f_y} \cdot \frac{E_s}{E_{ct}} \right) + \frac{c}{d} \right] \tag{12}$$

$$v_{n2} = \chi \cdot f_c' \cdot k \cdot \sin\alpha \cdot \cos\alpha + \frac{0.2 \cdot \sqrt{f_c'} \cdot F}{\sin\alpha \cdot \cos\alpha} \cdot \left[(1 - k) \cdot \left(1 - \frac{f_{ctf}}{f_y} \cdot \frac{E_s}{E_{ct}} \right) + \frac{c}{d} \right] \tag{13}$$

As suggested in international codes (e.g. [5]) the strength of corbel can be assumed as the minimum value among v_{n1} and v_{n2}.

It has to be observed that in all the expressions proposed the contribution due to the fibers can be estimated in approximate way and if the angle is settled 45° in the single truss as:

$$v_f \cong 0.4 \cdot \sqrt{f_c'} \cdot F \cdot \left[(1-k) + \frac{c}{d} \right] \qquad (14)$$

To validate the mentioned model a comparison with the experimental results given in the literature in terms of bearing capacity of corbels is given. Analytical prediction is made by using the current model and the model of [12] and the one of [7]. In particular 79 experimental data for the corbels in fibrous concrete are collected. These data refer to: 12 data from [1], 64 data from [2], 3 data from [8]. In the graph in the ordinate there is the predicted value and in the abscissa the experimental ones. The comparison between analytical and experimental results shows good agreement.

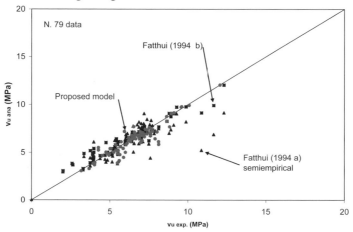

Figure 4: Comparison between analytical and experimental results for fibrous concrete corbels with main steel bars

4. CONCLUSIONS

In the present paper an analytical model based on an equivalent truss structure which also considers the presence of fibers is proposed and verified against experimental data existing in the literature. The model highlights the role of the single contributions (bars, concrete, fibers) in the resistant mechanisms of corbels and takes into account the failure mode of compressed strut or yielding of main steel reinforcement including the presence of fibers by means of the residual post-cracking strength for which the author proposed a simple expression calibrated for hooked steel fibers. Moreover, the model proposed can be useful in addition to the others available in the literature for design purpose of fibrous reinforced concrete corbels for which little information is available in the codes.

ACKNOWLEDGEMENTS

Support of this research by the Ministero dell'Istruzione, dell'Università e della Ricerca is gratefully acknowledged.

REFERENCES

[1] Fattuhi, N.I. and Hughes, B.P., 'Ductility of reinforced concrete corbels containing either steel fibers or stirrups', *ACI Structural Journal* **86** (6) (1989) 644-651.

[2] Fattuhi, N.I., 'Strength of SFRC corbels subjected to vertical load', *ACI Structural Journal* **116** (3) (1990) 701-718.

[3] Foster, S.J., Powell, R.E. and Selim, H.S., 'Performance of high-strength concrete corbels', *ACI Structural Journal* **93** (5) (1996) 555-563.

[4] Eurocodice 2, 'Progettazione delle strutture di calcestruzzo (UNI ENV 1992-1-1)', *Commissione " Ingegneria Strutturale"*, Milano.

[5] ACI Committee 318. (2002), 'Building code requirements for reinforced concrete (ACI 318-95), and Commentary ACI 318RM-02', *American Concrete Institute*, Detroit, Michigan.

[6] Russo, G., Venir, R., Pauletta, M. and Somma, G., 'Reinforced concrete corbels shear strength model and design formula', *ACI Structural Journal* **103** (1) (2006) 3-7.

[7] Fattuhi, N.I., 'Reinforced corbels made with plain and fibrous concretes', *ACI Structural Journal* **91** (5) (1994) 530-536.

[8] Campione, G., La Mendola, L. and Papia, M., 'Flexural behaviour of concrete corbels containing steel fibers or wrapped with FRP sheets', *Materials and Structures* **38** (280) (2005) 617-625.

[9] Campione, G., La Mendola, L. and Mangiavillano, M.L., 'Steel fibers reinforced concrete corbels: experimental behavior and shear strength prediction' accepted on *ACI Structural Journal* (2007).

[10] Campione, G., La Mendola, L. and Papia, M., 'Shear strength of steel fiber reinforced concrete beams with stirrups', *Structural Engineering and Mechanics* **24** (1) (2006) 107-136.

[11] Banthia, N. and Trottier, J.F., 'Concrete reinforced with deformed steel fibers, part I: bond-slip mechanism', *ACI Structural Journal* **91** (5) (1994) 435-446.

[12] Fattuhi, N.I., 'Strength of FRC corbels in flexure', *Journal of Structural Engineering ASCE* **120** (2) (1994) 360-377.

THREE DIMENSIONAL PLASTICITY MODEL FOR HIGH PERFORMANCE FIBER REINFORCED CEMENT COMPOSITES

Kittinun Sirijaroonchai and Sherif El-Tawil

Department of Civil and Environmental Engineering, University of Michigan, USA

Abstract

Many researchers have proposed in the past micro-mechanical models to describe the behavior of high performance fiber reinforced cementitious composites (HPFRCC). The goal of the majority of these models is to reproduce macro-scale constitutive properties, such as stress versus strain relationships, as a function of the properties of the fiber, matrix and the interaction between fibers and matrix. Although such models can accurately represent behavior under a variety of conditions, they are computationally expensive and cannot be conveniently used to simulate the overall response of structures constructed with HPFRCC. A 3-D model that can directly represent HPFRCC behavior at the macro-scale level is proposed in this paper. The model is rooted in fundamental plasticity theory and, since it requires modest computational resources, can be used in large-scale computational structural simulations. Although the proposed model is versatile enough to represent HPFRCC with any type of fiber, it is calibrated for two types of commercially available fibers, namely hooked and Spectra fibers, with volume fractions ranging from 1% to 2%. The model produces results that match experimental results well. The model formulation and validation exercises are presented.

1. INTRODUCTION

Inelastic analysis models for HPFRCCs can be broadly categorized by their resolution in modeling nonlinear behavior as micro-scale models, macro-scale models, and structural-scale models. Micro-scale models describe the interaction among the three phases of the material, i.e. fiber, matrix, and interfacial zones. The basic concepts behind such models can be found, for example, in [1, 2, 3]. Macro-scale models, on the other hand, focus on phenomenological behavior at the point level. They are capable of explicitly accounting for key phenomena such as hardening and softening in compression, crushing behavior, and post-cracking and post-peak response in tension. Structural-scale models implicitly capture the essence of structural behavior at the domain level, for example, cross-sectional moment versus curvature behavior and panel shear force versus distortion relationships. They are generally favored by practitioners because they are computationally expedient and because they produce data that is intuitive and that deals directly with design variables such as moments, rotations, etc. Examples of models operating at this scale level are found in [4, 5].

Since micro-scale models focus on the behavior of the constituents of HPFRCC, they have high computational demands which severely limit their use in analysis applications involving large structures. Macro-scale models, on the other hand, are significantly more computationally efficient than micro-scale models because they capture only the overall stress-strain response. They can therefore be practically used in continuum finite element simulations of structural members and systems. The focus of the presented work is to develop a plasticity macro-scale model for HPFRCC. The proposed model is based upon fundamental plasticity theory and is calibrated using basic experimental data.

2. BASIC EXPERIMENTS

Basic experiments were conducted to develop the data necessary to calibrate the proposed plasticity model. The experiments focused on only two types of commercially available fibers, namely hooked and Spectra fibers, with volume fractions ranging from 1.0% to 2%. The mortar used in the HPFRCC has a compressive strength of 55.16 MPa (8 ksi) and the mix proportion by weight is 1-cement: 1-sand: 0.15-fly ash: 0.4-water (mixed with super-plasticizer to enhance flowability). Three different types of compression tests and direct tension tests are performed to characterize the failure surface and determine key parameters. The results are summarized in Fig. 1, where each curve shown is an average of at least 3 test results.

Unconfined compression tests, which are performed on 75 x 150-mm cylinders, clearly demonstrate the beneficial effects of the fibers on HPFRCC compressive behavior. As shown in Fig. 2, the fibers provide a confining effect similar to that of a confining steel tube, which improves strength and post-peak ductility. These effects can be observed in Fig. 1a, which shows the uniaxial compressive response of the various HPFRCC mixes tested in this program. Compared to pure mortar, which loses strength abruptly after reaching the peak, all the HPFRCC mixes considered behaved in a ductile manner, sustaining stress levels higher than 10% of the peak capacity at strains up to 5%.

The biaxial compression tests involved testing 140 x 140 x 38 mm^3 panels under equal biaxial loads. The panels behaved in a much less ductile manner than the unconfined cylinders and generally failed abruptly by in-plane splitting (Fig. 1b). The relative thinness of the panels may have promoted some in-plane alignment of the fibers, which could have resulted in the observed unexpected brittleness in behavior. In other words, the out-of-plane response, which precipitated failure, may not have fully benefited from the presence of the fibers. Nevertheless, the biaxial tests provided useful information about biaxial strength, which is helpful in calibrating the plasticity model.

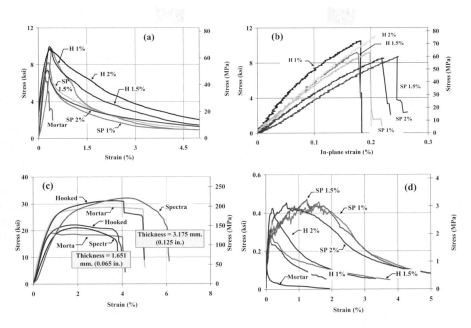

Figure 1: Experimental results: (a) unconfined uniaxial; (b) equal biaxial compression-
compression; (c) triaxial compression; (d) direct tension

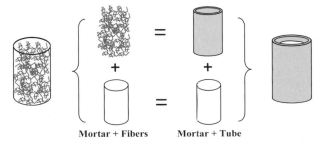

Mortar + Fibers   Mortar + Tube

Figure 2: Fibers provide effective confinement in the uniaxial compression test

The triaxial tests were passive tests in the sense that the confining pressure came about
from confining steel tubes. Two different thicknesses for the steel tubes are used (1.65 mm
and 3.175 mm). The key observation from these tests is that the confining effect of the fibers
is small compared to that afforded by the tubes, which causes the confined compressive
responses for all mixes to be quite similar (Fig. 1c). This implies it is reasonable to assume
that the shape of the plasticity surfaces depends mostly on the strength of the matrix and not
on fiber content.

The tensile stress-strain behavior is obtained from tension testing of coupons. Fig. 1d
shows the tensile responses obtained in this research.

3. PLASTICITY MODEL

The compressive behavior of HPFRCC differs from its tensile response in several aspects, e.g. strength and its corresponding strain, ductility, etc. Therefore, the plasticity model is split into two distinct parts, namely, compression and tension models.

3.1 Compression response

HPFRCC response in compression is linear elastic up to about one-third of the compressive strength, after which the response become nonlinear. The shape of the HPFRCC stress-strain curve under unconfined compression is almost identical to that for regular concrete up to the peak response. Beyond the peak, however, HPFRCC behavior differs substantially from regular concrete because of the confining effect of the fibers (Fig. 2).

The plasticity model proposed for HPFRCC is a modified version of the four-parameter HTC concrete model previously published by [6] and modified by [7]. This model is particularly useful because it captures two unique features of the experimentally observed responses of HPFRCC: 1) the nonlinear compressive and tensile curves in the meridian plane; and 2) the somewhat triangular shape in the π-plane (Fig. 3). Imran and Pantazopoulou [7] extended the basic HTC model to account for the triaxial behavior of concrete by introducing a softening parameter (I_1^{trans}) to permit smooth transition from the relatively brittle behavior under low confinement to more ductile behavior under higher confinement. Imran and Pantazopoulou [7] also introduced a non-associative flow rule to allow the model to capture volumetric contraction and expansion. Under compressive loading, concrete first suffers volumetric contraction followed by expansion after the peak stress is exceeded.

The yield surface for the model is described by Eqs. 1 and 2 (a list of notations can be found in Appendix I).

$$F(\sigma,k,r,s) = F_1(\sigma,k) + F_2(\sigma,r) + F_3(\sigma,s) \tag{1}$$

$$F_1(\sigma,k) = \frac{AJ_2}{kf_c} + B\sqrt{J_2} + Ck\sigma_1 + DkI_1 + E_{htc}\frac{(1-k)}{kf_c}I_1^2 - kf_c \tag{2a}$$

$$F_2(\sigma,r) = -(1-r)\frac{I_1}{I_1^{trans}}f_c + (1-r)f_c \tag{2b}$$

$$F_3(\sigma,s) = -Imp(1-s)\frac{I_1}{I_1^{trans}}f_c \tag{2c}$$

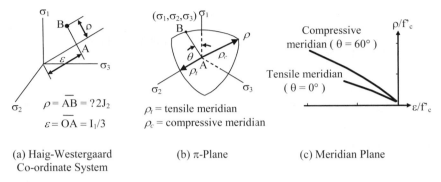

(a) Haig-Westergaard   (b) π-Plane   (c) Meridian Plane
Co-ordinate System

Figure 3: Failure surface of original the HTC model [6]

Where:

$$k = \frac{2\sqrt{\varepsilon_p \varepsilon_{p,max}} - \varepsilon_p}{\varepsilon_{p,max}}(1-k_0) + k_0 \qquad \text{: Hardening parameter} \qquad (3a)$$

$$r = \frac{1}{2} + \frac{1}{2}\cos\left[\frac{\pi(\varepsilon_p - \varepsilon_{p,max})}{(\varepsilon_{p,ult} - \varepsilon_{p,max})}\right] \qquad \text{: Softening parameter (Cosine)} \qquad (3b)$$

$$s = \exp^{-1}\left[\frac{A(\varepsilon_p - \varepsilon_{p,int})}{\varepsilon_{p,ult} - \varepsilon_{p,int}}\right] \qquad \text{: Softening parameter (Exponential)} \qquad (3c)$$

The Drucker-Prager yield function is used as the plastic potential function:

$$g(\sigma,k) = a\frac{I_1}{3} + \sqrt{2J_2} - c \qquad \text{: Drucker-Prager plastic potential function} \qquad (4)$$

where

$$a = \frac{a_u}{(1-\eta)}\left(\frac{\varepsilon_p}{\varepsilon_{p,max}} - \eta\right) \qquad \text{: Drucker-Prager constant} \qquad (5)$$

Based on experimental observations for HPFRCC, the post-peak region of the compressive response is assumed to begin with a cosine shape that eventually transitions into an exponential function. This is shown in Fig. 4a.

3.2 Tension response

In contrast to regular concrete where localization and subsequent softening occurs once the first crack is reached, HPFRCC exhibits hardening behavior until crack saturation occurs. In other words, the ability of HPFRCC to strain harden then soften gradually make it a good candidate for a plasticity model. In the proposed model, the Tresca yield surface is modified by adding a pressure dependent term (I_1) to accurately capture the tensile response of HPFRCC. The assumed Tresca yield surface has sharp corners and therefore violates

Drucker's postulate. The power term '*n*' is added in Eq. 6 to smooth the corner of the yield surface. These modifications are illustrated in Fig. 5 along with the original Tresca and von Mises surfaces for comparison. As a result of these two modifications, the tensile strength under a state of equal biaxial tension is lower than the uniaxial case.

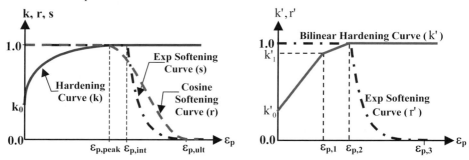

Figure 4: Plot of hardening and softening parameters as a function of equivalent plastic strain (ε_p) from Eq. (3) and Eq. (7)

$$F(\sigma,k,r,f_t)=2\sqrt{J_2}\left[\sin\left(\theta+\frac{\pi}{2}\right)\right]^n+aI_1^m-2kf_t+(1-r)f_t=0 \tag{6}$$

Where

$$k'=\frac{(k'_1-k'_0)}{\varepsilon_{p,1}}\varepsilon_p+k'_0 \qquad : \quad 0<\varepsilon_p\le\varepsilon_{p,1} \tag{7a}$$

$$k'=\frac{(1-k'_1)}{\varepsilon_{p,2}-\varepsilon_{p,1}}(\varepsilon_p-\varepsilon_{p,1})+k'_1 \qquad : \quad \varepsilon_{p,1}<\varepsilon_p\le\varepsilon_{p,2} \tag{7b}$$

$$r'=\exp\left[s\frac{(\varepsilon_p-\varepsilon_{p,2})}{(\varepsilon_{p,3}-\varepsilon_{p,2})}\right] \qquad : \quad \varepsilon_{p,2}<\varepsilon_p\le\varepsilon_{p,3} \tag{7c}$$

4. MODEL CALIBRATION, IMPLEMENTATION AND VALIDATION

The proposed plasticity model is implemented as a user-defined model in LS-DYNA [8]. Two different numerical approaches, i.e. explicit and implicit schemes, are used to integrate the model. The incremental form of the yield surface is used to derive the consistency parameter in the explicit scheme, whereas in the implicit scheme, the current yield surface is used to obtain the consistency parameter [9].

The calibration parameters obtained from the experiments are listed in Appendix I. Since the model captures softening, a simple regularization scheme whereby the softening parameters are made a function of element size is used to ensure mesh size independence.

4.1 Simulation of unconfined uniaxial compression test

A standard unconfined compression test on a 75 x 150 mm cylinder with 1.5% hooked fibers is simulated using the plasticity model. A comparison between the simulation and test results is shown in Fig. 6a. It is clear from Fig. 6a that the model is able to reasonably capture all pertinent aspects of the stress-strain response.

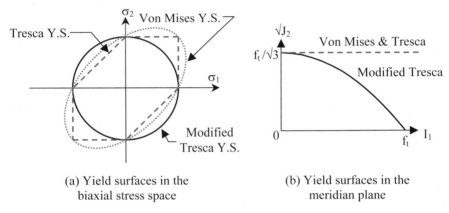

(a) Yield surfaces in the
biaxial stress space

(b) Yield surfaces in the
meridian plane

Figure 5: Yield surface of tension response in the biaxial stress space and in the meridian plane

4.2 Uniaxial tension (dog-bone test)

A direct tension test on a dog-bone specimen with 1.5% hooked fibers is simulated using the developed model. A comparison between the simulation and test results is shown in Fig. 6b. It is clear once again from Fig. 6b that the model is able to reasonably capture all pertinent aspects of the stress-strain response.

4.3 Two-span continuous beam

Since the model was calibrated to test results of which the test data in Fig. 6 is part of, the two previous simulation exercises are not really a validation of the model. They merely show that the model is able to capture all important aspects of behavior. To gain confidence in the model, its results are compared to independently produced test data. A two-span continuous beam tested in [10] is chosen for this purpose. The beam is constructed with 1.5% Spectra and one layer of No.3 deformed bar placing at 4.5 in. from the top. The loading position and dimensions of the beam are given in Fig. 7a, while the deformed shape is shown in Fig. 8. Additional information about test setup and material properties can be found in [10]. It is clear from Fig. 7b that the simulated overall response matches well with the measured experimental data. The final mode of failure was also simulated correctly.

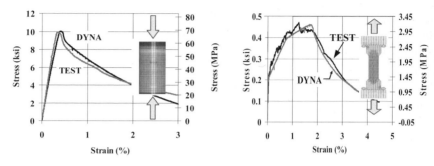

(a) Response of unconfined uniaxial
compression (Hooked 1.5%)

(b) Response of uniaxial tension
(Spectra 1.5%)

Figure 6: Comparison between test results and simulations

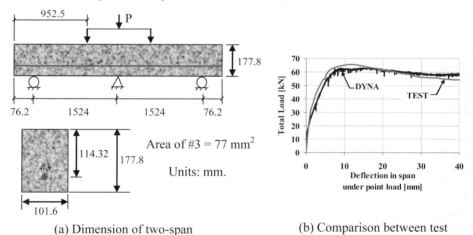

(a) Dimension of two-span
continuous beam

(b) Comparison between test
result and simulation (DYNA)

Figure 7: Response of two-span continuous beam constructing with Spectra 1.5%

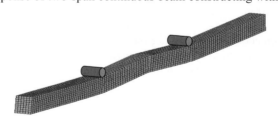

Figure 8: Deformed shape of two-span continuous beam

5. CONCLUSION

This paper presented a macro-scale plasticity model for HPFRCC. The 3-D model can capture the essential aspects of both compression and tension responses of HPFRCC. A limited validation study shows that the developed model is reasonably accurate that it represents a promising way to efficiently model the response of large structures or systems constructed with HPFRCC materials. The authors are currently working to further validate the model and to incorporate cyclic and rate of loading effects into the model.

ACKNOWLEDGEMENTS

The research described here was sponsored in part by the National Science Foundation under Grant No. CMS 0530383, and by the University of Michigan. Their support is gratefully acknowledged. The opinions expressed in this paper are those of the authors and do not necessarily reflect the views of the sponsor.

REFERENCES

[1] Naaman, A.E., 'A statistical theory of strength for fiber reinforced concrete', Ph.D. Dissertation, Massachusetts Institute of Technology (1986) 196 pp.

[2] Li, V.C., 'Post-crack scaling relations for fiber-reinforced cementitious composites', *ASCE J. of Materials in Civil Engineering*, **4(1)** (1992) 41-57.

[3] Hansen, W. and Tjiptobroto, P., 'Energy based model for predicting the elastic tensile strain capacity of high performance fiber reinforced composites (FRC)', *Nordic concrete research* **10** (1991) 48 pp.

[4] Stang, H. and Olesen, J.F. 'On the interpretation of bending tests on FRC-materials' Fracture Mechanics of Concrete Structures **1** (1998) 511-520.

[5] Olesen, J.F., 'Fictitious crack propagation in fiber-reinforced concrete beams', J. Engrg. Mech. **127(3)** (March 2001) 272-280.

[6] Hsieh, S. S., Ting, E. C., and Chen, W.F., 'Application of a plastic-fracture model to concrete structures' *Comp. and Struct.* **28(3)** (1988) 373-393.

[7] Imran, I. and Pantazopoulou, S. J., 'Plasticity model for concrete under triaxial compression', *J. Engrg. Mech.* **127** (3) (March, 2001) 281-290.

[8] Hallquist, J.O. 'LS-DYNA keyword user's manual version 971', (September, 2006), 2209 pages.

[9] Ortiz, M. and Simo, J.C., 'An analysis of a new class of integration algorithms for elastoplastic constitutive relations', Int. J. for Numer. Methods Eng. 23 (1986) 353-366.

[10] Chandrangsu, K., 'Innovative bridge deck with reduced reinforcement and strain-hardening fiber reinforced cementitious composites' Ph.D. Dissertation, University of Michigan, Ann Arbor (2003) 265 pp.

APPENDIX I. NOTATIONS AND MATERIAL PARAMETERS

The following model parameters are obtained from the experiments described in Section 2. Since the softening parameters of both compression and tension are affected by the size of the element, the parameters given below are for elements that measure 13 mm. diagonally. The parameters need to be recalibrated when different element sizes are used. Note that the volume fraction unit is in percentage.

Material Parameter	Notation	Spectra	Hooked	Mortar
COMPRESSION PARAMETERS				
Material parameters in compression yield surface	A	3.55		
	B	0.902		
	C	0.604		
	D	0.655		
	E_{htc}	3.190		
	$I_{1,trans}$	280.931		
Initial hardening	k_0	0.37		
Compressive strength [MPa]	f'_c	54.042	68.074	45.78
Young's modulus [MPa]	E_c	18028.45	21568.024	30338.29
Unconfined Drucker-Prager constant	a_u	0.63	0.63	0.63
Transition point volumetric strain from contraction to expansion	η	0.34	0.34	0.34
Equivalent plastic strain at peak, at the beginning of exponential softening curve, and at the end of softening, respectively.	$\varepsilon_{p,max}$	1.00E-5	1.00E-03	0.8E-03
	$\varepsilon_{p,int}$	$0.0058V_f - 0.0055$	$0.0136V_f - 0.0192$	1.00E-03
	$\varepsilon_{p,ult}$	$0.009V_f - 0.0068$	$0.015V_f - 0.0165$	1.50E-03
Slope of exp. soft. function	A	0.028	0.028	0.00
Weight factor between cosine and exponential function	IMP	3.20	1.00	0.00
TENSION PARAMETERS				
Material parameters in tension yield surface	n	0.25	0.25	0.25
	a	0.5	0.5	0.5
	m	2.0	2.0	2.0
Tensile strength [MPa]	f_t	3.178	$1.1V_f + 0.467$	0.818
Initial and intermediate hardening	k'_0	0.37	0.37	0.37
	k'_1	0.80	0.9	0.9
Equivalent plastic strain at intermediate, peak point and the end of softening respectively.	$\varepsilon_{p,1}$	$0.001V_f + 0.0032$	5.0E-04	5.0E-05
	$\varepsilon_{p,2}$	$-0.007V_f + 0.0298$	$0.0006V_f + 0.0005$	7.0E-05
	$\varepsilon_{p,3}$	0.2	$0.02V_f + 0.2217$	1.0E-02
Slope of exp. soft. function	s	-0.731	-20.731	-9.731

PART THREE

FRESH STATE AND
HARDENING PROPERTIES

INFLUENCE OF DIFFERENT MIXING PARAMETERS ON FRESH PROPERTIES OF ULTRA HIGH STRENGTH HYBRID FIBRE CONCRETE (HFC)

Frank Dehn, Marko Orgass and Andreas König

MFPA Leipzig GmbH, Germany

Abstract

In order to optimise the performance of ultra high strength hybrid fibre concrete (HFC) the mix design has to be co-ordinated with the production process. On this account, the influence of varying mixing parameters on the fresh properties of a certain type of HFC with a self-compacting ultra-high strength matrix and a representative steel fibre content was studied within an extensive research program. For the experiments the use of a high performance mixer was essential. Basically, the investigated HFC contained short straight (2 % by vol.) and long hooked (1 % by vol.) steel fibres. The aim was to produce a flowable hybrid fibre concrete by changing only the mixing parameters. Exemplary, the results for the following mixing parameters are summarized in this paper: mixing order and mixing speed. The composition of the mixture was not changed. From the experimental study a direct interrelationship between the mixing parameters and the fresh concrete properties can be derived by recording all relevant mixer data and testing the fresh concrete properties simultaneously. The paper will emphasize the necessity of implementing rheological tests when projecting such high performance cementitious materials.

1 INTRODUCTION

Like with all materials, there is a direct relationship between the micro-structure and the performance capacity of a material. The micro-structure is influenced above all by the mix design, but also by the nature of the manufacturing and curing process. Due to the large number of different starting materials with regard to ultra high strength fibre concrete, the mixing process or the applicable mixing technology plays a decisive role.

The ultra high strength HPC with a self-compacting consistency contained a content of altogether 3 % by vol. of different steel fibres. The compression strength amounted 145 N/mm² and the flexural tensile strength 25 N/mm² after 28 days (according to RILEM TC 162-TDF) [1]. For the experiments a high performance mixer has been applied. This high performance mixer allowed a continuous recording of various data - such as concrete temperature, energy requirement/consumption, etc. In order to investigate the influence of the used mixing technology parameters like varying mixing tools, the implementation of mixing breaks, and the mixing order and speed have been changed. The results for the last-mentioned parameters are summarized exemplarily below.

2   MIXING TECHNOLOGY - GENERAL SPECIFICATIONS

Basically, the term „mixing" is deemed to mean the introduction of particles of one material among particles of a different material by stirring, rolling, kneading or emulsifying, whereby the primary goal of all mixing procedures is to produce a uniform distribution or a homogeneous product. In view of the fact that a large number of different constituents are mixed in the production of ultra high strength hybrid fibre concrete, it is necessary to enlarge the term of mixing. In general, mixing is considered to be a change in location which can be divided into two different processes. During the first process (the distributive mixing) a low shearing speed leads to a simple positional change. In the second phase (the dispersive mixing) agglomerates are broken down under high shearing speeds. Provided that suitable mixing technologies are used, this produces a homogeneous mass, but also a comminution effect, the triggering of chemical reaction products between various materials (cement hydration), the dissolution of materials in fluids and the deglomeration effect in fibre agglomerations.

3   EXPERIMENTAL PROGRAM

3.1   Materials

For the experiments a self-compacting ultra high strength concrete mixture was developed. A steel fibre mix made of 2 % by vol. of 6 mm short, straight fibres and 1 % by vol. of 35 mm long fibres fitted with final hooks was used for the mixture. Despite the high steel fibre content, it was possible to guarantee a sufficient workability with adherence to a uniform distribution of fibres. No fibre agglomeration was identified, despite the high viscosity of the concrete. Table 1 shows the recipe that was developed.

Table 1 : Concrete composition

Ingredients		HFC
Air content	% by vol.	1.5
CEM I 42.5 R-HS	kg/m³	665
Quartz sand	kg/m³	993
Quartz powder	kg/m³	285
Silica fume	kg/m³	200
Superplasticizer	% by mass of cement	7
Water	kg/m³	198.2
Steel fibres 6 mm	% by vol.	2.0
Steel fibres 35 mm	% by vol.	1.0
w/c ratio	-	0.298

3.2 Mixing System

The selection of a suitable mixing system with which extremely varied mixing parameters can be set variably is of decisive importance [2]. This is why a high performance mixer was used. It enables the variation of a large number of parameters and the evaluation of their effects by recording various performance indicators. The mixer consists of two parts, the slanted mixing container with its drive and the computer-assisted control unit (Fig. 1). The rotating mixing container is arranged inclined towards the rotating axis. The mixing tool is located on the inside, arranged eccentrically towards the mixing container axis, while the upper area houses a stationary, installed, combined tool, the deflector or stripper. A so-called pin agitator is used as a mixing tool (Fig. 2).

Figure 1: High performance mixer   Figure 2: Mixing tool

3.3 Testing program

In the implementation of the test, only the parameter to be analysed was changed, while the mixing recipe and the remaining mixing parameters remained unchanged. In order to indicate the effects of the individual mixing parameters, a series of fresh concrete tests were conducted in a defined order after the completion of the mixing procedure in addition to recording the power consumption data of the mixer. The power consumption curves recorded by the mixer describe what energy requirement is necessary in order to achieve a predefined rotational speed. This means that it is possible, similar to the effects of a rheometer, to measure the required energy and the resistance produced in the material to be mixed. The recorded energy requirement permits to derive statements concerning the degree of workability. If the energy requirement rises while the rotational speed remains the same during the mixing process, the flow behaviour of the fresh concrete deteriorates accordingly.

4 EXPERIMENTAL RESULTS

4.1 Mixing order

Essentially, the different addition times of the superplasticizer were analysed under this aspect. Three different mixing phases can be recognised on the basis of the power consumptions (Fig. 3).

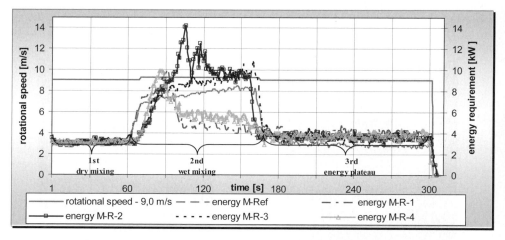

Figure 3: Energy requirement - recording during the mixing process

The first phase includes the dry mixing with a low and constant power consumption. After 60 seconds, in phase 2, 100 % water and superplasticizer are added in different quantitative ratios at different times (wet mixing). The addition of water, which takes place at the same time in all tests, leads to a wetting of the surfaces of the different materials, which causes an increase in bonding forces on the wet surfaces. This becomes manifest in a strong rise in power consumption. Depending on the dosage quantity of the superplasticizer, the power consumption of the mixing tool drops differently following the strong rise in power. The reduction in power consumption is based on the mechanical work introduced by the mixer. The applied shearing forces cancel the prevalent bonding forces of the materials wetted with water. It is not until now that, in addition to the free water molecules and sulphate ions, PCE molecules can react optimally, which is clearly visible in the decrease of the power curves. The third phase starts after a mixing period of 150 seconds. The third phase is characterised by the stabilisation of all power consumptions on a constant energy plateau. A uniform change in the slump flow and V-funnel flow time was observed in the fresh concrete tests and this suggests an influence exerted by the superplasticizer addition time on the flow properties of the concrete. With the improvement in the flowability, specified by the slump flow, the viscosity falls. This is characterised by a reduction in the V-funnel flow time. The temporally separate addition of water and superplasticizer leads to a high degree of workability in the form of a high slump flow and a low V-funnel flow time. Conversely, the workability reduces with simultaneous addition of water and superplasticizer (Fig. 4).

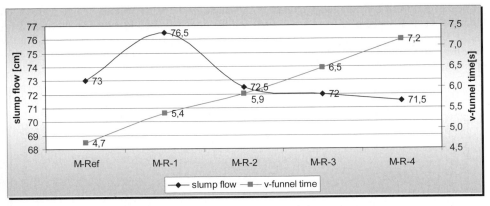

Figure 4: Flow properties - mixing order

4.2   Mixing speed

Numerous tests in the past have shown that the acceleration of differently sized particles in the mixing container leads to a strong separation effect in the different constituents, depending on the mixing speed. For example, heavy particles are thrown out into the outside regions of the mixing container due to a larger impulse. Conversely, light particles are located on the inside, close to the mixing tool. The tests show that after setting of an optimum mixing speed, the degree of homogeneity, depicted in the so-called variation curve, rises sharply with an increase in speed. This behaviour is presented in Fig. 5 on the basis of our own test.

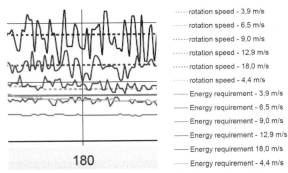

Figure 5: Energy requirement detail after 180s mixing time

In order to reach a comprehensive conclusion on the flow properties with the mixing speed as the selected test parameter, we can only draw on the fresh concrete test. Graphic depiction of the various slump flows and the V-funnel flow times in Fig. 6 shows that the workability improves up to a specific point by increasing the mixing speed. After reaching a mixing speed of 9.0 m/s which is the specific optimum for this mixture, any increase in speed leads to a deterioration in the flow properties (Fig. 6). The temperature of the fresh concrete rose sharply with an increase in the mixing speed. Accordingly, at the end of the mixing process, there was a temperature difference of no more than 14 °C between the fastest (33 °C) and the slowest (19 °C) rotational speed. Our own tests on self-compacting concretes have shown that there is a direct relationship between flow properties and fresh concrete temperatures. For example, if the fresh concrete temperature is too high, the reaction speed of C3A is accelerated and the effectiveness of the PCE molecules is reduced, which leads to significantly lower flow properties. Therefore it can be supposed that the flow properties which deteriorate above a mixing speed of 9.0 m/s will be influenced by the suboptimum position of the starting materials and the rising temperature of the fresh concrete.

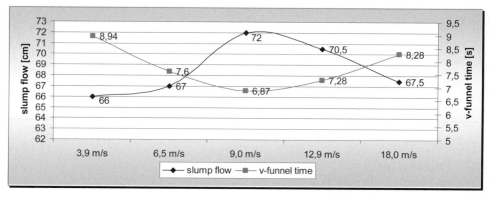

Figure 6: Flow properties - mixing speed

5   CONCLUSIONS

Current knowledge concerning mixing technology deals primarily with the influence of conventional mixing systems on the uniformity of the mixing material in systems consisting of 3 materials. However, in view of the fact that the complexity of the chemical and physical processes increases during and shortly after the mixing phase with the number of different materials taking effect, this knowledge is only restrictedly applicable. Today instead, it is necessary to align the traditional process procedures with the production of systems consisting of 5 materials. Within this framework, the mixing technology that must be used represents one of the most important process stages. For this reason, the self-compacting, ultra high strength hybrid fibre concrete was produced by using a high performance (intensive) mixing system which enabled to change the individual mixing parameters and to evaluate their influence by recording the power data.

The results of the mixing power data and the fresh concrete tests show that there is a direct relationship between the selection of mixing parameters and the fresh concrete properties. For example, following a delayed and separate addition of water and highly effective superplasticizer on a PCE basis, significantly better flow behaviour is manifest. This became evident by the rise in slump flow, the reduction in V-funnel flow time and a lower mixing power. Changes in the mixing tool speed caused a strong influence on the fresh concrete properties. In these tests, an optimum intensity was achieved at the rotational speed of 9.0 m/s. The fresh concrete properties deteriorated with an increase or a decrease in this speed.

REFERENCES

[1]   RILEM TC 162 "Test and design methods for steel fibre reinforced concrete"
[2]   Beitzel, H.: Herstellung und Verarbeitung von Beton. Betonkalender 2003, Bd. 2, S. 71-125

ON THE CONNECTIONS BETWEEN FRESH STATE BEHAVIOR, FIBER DISPERSION AND TOUGHNESS PROPERTIES OF STEEL FIBER REINFORCED CONCRETE

Liberato Ferrara, Daniele Dozio and Marco di Prisco

Department of Structural Engineering, Politecnico di Milano, Italy

Abstract

The connections between fresh and hardened state properties of fiber reinforced concrete and issues related to fiber dispersion have been a research challenge in the very last years. The topic is addressed in this work with reference to "self compacting" concrete with three different types of steel fiber reinforcement.

Fresh state properties were measured through the slump flow, V funnel and L-box tests. Plate specimens 1000 x 500 x 70 mm have been cast in such a way that the concrete flow was parallel to their long side. Beams 150 mm wide and 600 mm long and disks with a 150 mm diameter were sawn from the plates and tested respectively in 4 point bending and splitting. Beams were cut with their axis either parallel or normal to the flow direction of the fresh concrete in the plate; the same procedure was followed for the diameter axis of preferential fracture in split disks.

The results show a strong correlation between the fresh state properties, the dispersion and orientation of fibers, as influenced by the casting process, and the mechanical properties of the composite. An omni-comprehensive approach to the problem is currently under development aiming at a "design" of the material and of the casting process tailored to the dedicated application and to the anticipated structural performance.

1. INTRODUCTION

The addition of fibers into self compacting concrete may take advantage of its high performance in the fresh state to achieve a more uniform dispersion of fibers, which is critical for a wider and reliable structural use of fiber reinforced cement composites. The compactness of the SCC matrix, due to the higher amount of fine and extra-fine particles, may improve interface zone properties, and consequently also the fiber-matrix bond, leading to enhanced post-cracking toughness and energy absorption capacity. The synergy between self compacting and fiber reinforced technologies, thanks to the elimination of vibration and the reduction or even the complete substitution of conventional reinforcement with fibers, is likely to improve the economic efficiency of the construction process, through increased speed of construction, reduction or suitably focused rearrangement of labor resources, costs and energy consumption, better working environment, with reduced noise and health hazards, also contributing to a more reliable quality control.

The robustness of a fiber reinforced self consolidating concrete (SCSFRC) relies first of all on a rational mix design methodology, which has to encompass the influence of fibers on the grading of solid skeleton [1, 2] and the target fresh state performance, either in terms of fundamental rheological and field test measurements [3]. The fresh state behavior and the mix design proportions have been shown to significantly influence the fiber dispersion and orientation, furthermore affected by the casting process and structure geometry. Fiber dispersion related issues have hence to be carefully considered when measuring the mechanical properties of the composite in the sight of anticipating the structure performance [4]. Non destructive monitoring techniques of fiber dispersion in structural elements are currently under development [5, 6].

In this work the connections between fresh and hardened state properties and fiber dispersion have been investigated with reference to self compacting concretes with three different types of steel fiber reinforcement. The reliability of the mix design was assessed by means of a method recently proposed by the first author [7]. Plate specimens 1000 x 500 x 70 mm were cast in such a way that the concrete flow was parallel to their long side. Beams 150 mm wide and 600 mm long and 150 mm diameter disks were sawn from the plates and tested respectively in 4 point bending and splitting. After testing fibers of the fracture surface was counted. Beams were cut with their axis either parallel or normal to the flow direction of the fresh concrete in the plate and the same happened for the diameter axis of preferential fracture in split disks. The results show a strong correlation between the fresh state properties, the dispersion and orientation of fibers, as influenced by the casting process, and the mechanical properties of the composite. These have been shown to be significantly correlated to the same parameters assumed to characterize the fresh state behavior.

2. SELF CONSOLIDATING STEEL FIBER REINFORCED CONCRETE: MIX DESIGN AND FRESH STATE CHARACTERIZATION

The mix design of the self consolidating fiber reinforced concrete (SCSFRC), as summarized in Table 1, has been optimized for the incorporation of 50 kg of steel fibers per cubic meter of bulk concrete. Three different types of hooked-end fiber reinforcement have been considered: high carbon fibers 30 mm long and with an aspect ratio equal to 80; low carbon fibers 30 mm long and with an aspect ratio equal to 45 and finally a blend of low carbon fibers either 60 mm long with a diameter equal to 0.8 mm and 30 mm long with a diameter equal to 0.6 mm, added in equal quantities to the concrete. All mixes also contained 3 kg per cubic meter of bulk concrete of polypropylene fibers 12 mm long.

The grading of fine and coarse aggregates was calibrated through some trial and error adjustments to account for the presence of the predetermined amount of fibers; it was targeted for the optimum packing density to the well known Bolomey, with a workability index A equal to 30.

The grading of solid skeleton, as above detailed and incorporating the different types of fibers, was back-analyzed in the framework of a mix-design method for SCSFRC recently proposed [7], in which fibers are handled as an equivalent aggregate, the diameter of which is calculated on the basis of the specific surface area:

$$d_{eq,fiber} = \frac{3\,L_f}{1+2\dfrac{L_f}{d_f}}\;\frac{\gamma_{fiber}}{\gamma_{aggregate}} \tag{1}$$

Table 1: Mix design for self consolidating steel fiber reinforced concrete

Constituent	Quantity [kg/m^3]	Density (kg/dm^3)
Gravel (max d_a 20 mm)	510.9	2.67
Mixed sand (max d_a 10 mm)	789.1	2.70
Sieved sand (max d_a 4 mm)	375.1	2.69
Calcareous filler	98.2	2.70
Cement type 52.5R	400	3.10
Superplasticizer	3.5	1.05
Water	198	1.00
Steel fibers	50	7.85
Polypropylene fibers	3	1.00

In Table 2 data are shown for the three different types of fiber reinforcement, together with the average diameter and the void ratio V_{void} for the solid skeleton, graded as in Table 1 (the void ratio was measured according to ASTM C29/29). It has to be observed that the solid skeletons are almost equivalent in terms of average aggregate diameter of the particles, with some differences detected in the case of the fibers with the highest aspect ratio, for which also the highest void ratio was measured: the larger number of thinner fibers has a stronger perturbation effect on the packing density.

Table 2: Model parameters for mix design of self consolidating fiber reinforced concretes

Fiber type	$d_{eq,fiber}$ (mm)	d_{av} (mm)	V_{void}	d_{ss} (mm)
Fibers 30/0.375	1.63	5.511	30%	0.466
Fibers 30/0.62	2.68	5.542	27.8%	0.504
fibers 60/08+ Fibers 30/06	3.47 2.60	5.552	28.2%	0.500

The mix design of concrete was optimized for a paste volume ratio V_{paste} equal to 0.367. In the framework of the mix-design method previously recalled the average aggregate spacing, correlated to the thickness of the excess paste enveloping the solid particles, d_{ss}, regarded as spherical for the sake of simplicity, can be calculated as:

$$d_{ss} = d_{av}\left[\sqrt[3]{1+\frac{V_{paste}-V_{void}}{V_{concrete}-V_{paste}}}-1\right] \tag{2}$$

were d_{av} is the average diameter of the solid particles, computed simply on the basis of the actual grading curve. d_{ss} stands hence as an indicator of the degree of suspension into the cement paste of the solid particles, which are featured by the above detailed grading and by the consequently related void ratio (experimentally measured). For the given solid skeleton the fresh state properties of concrete are hence likely to be jointly governed by the rheology of the cement paste and by the parameter d_{ss}, with its physical meaning as above.

In this framework an investigation has been first of all performed on the rheological behavior of the cement paste, as formulated from the SCC mix design: the paste composition is characterized by a solid volume fraction equal to 0.455 (w/b $\cong$ 0.4) and by a filler to binder volume ratio equal to 0.22; the dosage of the superplasticizer (SP) is equal to 0.7% of the solid fraction mass. The rheological behavior of the fluid cement paste has been investigated through mini-cone slump and Marsh cone tests. For the former the flow spread diameter has been measured, which is believed to be an indicator of the material yield stress [8]. The Marsh cone test has been performed by using two different nozzle radii (4 and 5.5 mm) both with a filling height H = 0.265 m (1.7 liters), and the time for a prescribed amount of material (1 lt) to flow was in both cases measured. This twofold test configuration may give information on both the yield stress and the viscosity of the material [9]. For three nominally identical paste batches an average flow spread diameter equal to 470 mm was measured, which would correspond to a value of the yield stress τ_0 equal to 0.063 Pa. [8]. As far the Marsh cone test, the following flow times for 1 lt of paste, over 1.7 lt poured into the cone, have been measured (average of three values):
- nozzle radius 4 mm   T = 25 sec
- nozzle radius 5.5 mm   T = 10 sec
which correspond, for τ_0 = 0.063 Pa, to a "Bingham viscosity" equal to 0.2 Pas [9].

Table 3: Fresh state characterization of (self-consolidating) fiber reinforced concrete

Mix	Fiber type	d_{ss} (mm)	Slump flow diameter (mm)	T_{50} (sec)	V funnel time (sec)	L_{box}		
						T_{200} (sec)	T_{400} (sec)	h_{min}/h_{max}
A	Fibers 60/0.8+ Fibers 30/0.6	0.500	700	6	6	1	2.5	difficult measure
B	Fibers 30/0.375	0.466	650	5	blockage	blockage		
C	Fibers 30/0.62	0.504	740	3	8	1	2	0.857 (90/105)

The characterization in the fresh state was hence performed through the following tests:
- slump flow, in which both the flow diameter and the time employed to reach a 500 mm spread (T_{50}) were measured;
- V funnel, measuring the efflux time;
- L-box, where the time to reach a 200 mm and a 400 mm distance from the movable shutter and the ratio between the minimum and maximum height in the horizontal leg of the L-box was measured. It has to be remarked that the spacing of the bars in the L-box device was suitably modified and related to the fiber length (96 mm in all three cases).
The results of the tests, summarized in Table 3, can be interestingly correlated to the average aggregate spacing of the solid skeleton particles, which differ for the three different types of fiber reinforcement incorporated, once the rheological properties of the paste were measured as above. The model requires the knowledge of the apparent viscosity (shear stress vs. shear strain rate ratio) at a prescribed shear strain rate (100 s^{-1}) to define an optimum flow diameter vs. apparent viscosity ratio, which has to satisfy minimum and maximum requirements, also defined as a function of the average diameter of the solid skeleton particles, in order to guarantee proper deformability and segregation resistance respectively.

From previous experience performed [7, 10] a ratio between the above said apparent viscosity and the equivalent Bingham viscosity equal to 2.25 can be reliably assumed. This yields to an average flow-apparent viscosity ratio equal to 1044 mm/Pas for the case at issue.

Experimental data points are plot in the framework of the mix-design model lines; these have been drawn form [11] (Fig. 9), for an average aggregate diameter equal to 5.675 mm, very close to the values characterizing the three mixes herein dealt with (Table 2). Fig. 1 is self explaining: for the given average aggregate diameter and a given set of rheological properties of the cement paste, a lower d_{ss} results in a more tight suspension of the solid particles in the enveloping fluid paste and hence in a less workable concrete. Alternatively, to achieve the target values of the deformability and fluidity parameters of the fresh concrete, once the solid skeleton has been suitably graded, for a lower d_{ss} a cement paste is needed featured by a higher value of the flow-viscosity ratio while lower values of this ratio are sufficient for more dilute suspensions (higher d_{ss}).

The efficacy of the model predictions even when applied to back analyze a set of data other than the one employed for its formulation stands as a proof of its reliability.

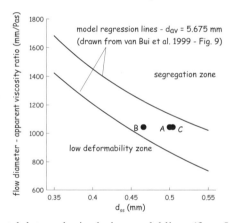

Figure 1: Experimental data and mix-design model lines (from Van Bui et al., 1999)

3. FIBER DISPERSION AND TOUGHNESS

In order to evaluate the effect of fiber dispersion and orientation as governed by the casting process, through the fresh state properties of concrete, for each of the three mixes described one slab 1000 x 500 x 70 mm was been cast, allowing the concrete to flow parallel to the long side. From each plate four beam specimens were and for 150 mm diameter disks were drilled, according to the scheme shown in Fig. 2, to be tested respectively in 4 point bending and tension splitting, as described in section 1.

3.1 4-point bending tests on beams

The tests have been performed under crack opening control according to the scheme shown in Fig. 3. The Crack Opening Displacement (COD) ratio has been kept equal to 8.33 x 10^{-4} mm/sec up to 0.65 mm and then uniformly ramped up by 2.5 x 10^{-3} mm/sec increments every 120 seconds up to 8.33 x 10^{-3} mm/sec. The tests have been stopped once an imposed displacement equal to 40 mm was reached.

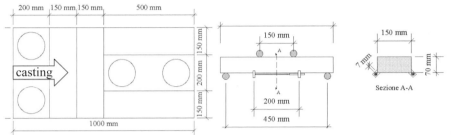

Figure 2: Scheme for cutting beams and drilling disks from the plate

Figure 3: Scheme and measuring instruments for 4pb tests

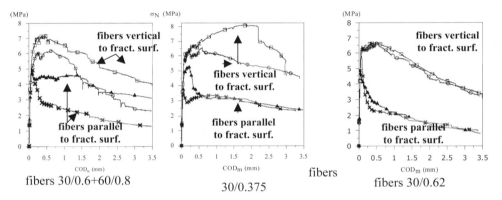

fibers 30/0.6+60/0.8

fibers 30/0.375

fibers 30/0.62

Figure 4: 4pb tests: stress-crack opening for fibers parallel and vertical to fracture surface

From nominal stress vs. crack opening curves (Fig. 4) the influence of the casting process on the fiber orientation on the mechanical properties of the material clearly appears: in all cases a higher energy absorption capacity was measured for beams tested with their axis parallel to the flow direction than when at a right angle. It also clearly appears that when fibers are oriented vertically to the fracture surface a significant post-cracking hardening is measured, while, for fibers mostly parallel to it, a softening behavior characterizes the post-cracking response of the composite. A more significant "disturbance effect" on the first cracking strength can be also observed for fibers vertical to the fracture surface (Table 4).

Results of 4pb tests have been processed and analyzed as prescribed in the recently issued Italian guidelines for SFRC structures [12], computing, besides the first cracking strength f_{ctf}:
- the equivalent stress $\sigma_{eq,I}$ in the COD range $3w_I$-$5w_I$, with w_I crack opening at first cracking, defined as the maximum load in the COD range 0-0.1 mm;
- the residual stress $\sigma_{eq,II}$, in the COD range $0.8w_u$-$1.2w_u$, where w_u is equal to 3 mm.
Their values, and their ratios (Table 4) confirm what above said with reference to Fig. 4.

The number of fibers on the fracture surface has been hence counted: the surface has been divided into three equally thick layers. Results in Table 4 (the average values between two measurements have been reported for each case, with the related scattering) refer to the intrados, central and extrados layers respectively. It is worth remarking that beams were tested upside down with respect to the casting direction and hence the intrados of the beam in the testing configuration corresponds to the free surface of the plate when cast. A reasonable resistance to downward settlement of fibers appears, as well as an acceptable dispersion within the plates, the experimental scattering between the number of fibers, with reference to the investigated positions, being always lower than 20%, with very few exceptions.

From the specific number of fibers N_f, the fiber cross section area A_f and volume fraction V_f (0.64%).the orientation factor α has been calculated [13]:

$$\alpha = N_f \frac{A_f}{V_f} \qquad (3)$$

Table 4: 4pb tests: compressive, first cracking, post-cracking strengths, toughness indicators, specific number of fibers on the fracture surface layers and orientation factor

Mix	Casting direction	f_c (N/mm²)	f_{ctf} (N/mm²)	$\sigma_{eq,I}$ (N/mm²)	$\sigma_{eq,II}$ (N/mm²)	$\frac{\sigma_{eq,I}}{f_{ctf}}$	$\frac{\sigma_{eq,II}}{\sigma_{eq,I}}$	specific n° fibers / cm²	α
A	normal to fract. surface	54.4	5.02 (± 0.5%)	6.47 (± 4.7%)	3.47 (±13.4%)	1.29	0.54	bottom: 0.39 (±8%) center: 0.62 (±41%) top: 0.75 (±23%)	0.42
A	parallel to fract. surface	54.4	5.68 (± 8.1%)	3.73 (± 9.5%)	2.34 (±19.4%)	0.66	0.63	bottom: 0.40 (±8%) center: 0.58 (±20%) top: 0.26 (±10%)	0.25
B	normal to fract. surface	57.1	4.36 (± 15%)	6.32 (± 2.3%)	5.63 (± 6.0%)	1.45	0.89	bottom: 2.51 (±5%) center: 2.41 (±4%) top: 3.0 (±17%)	0.46
B	parallel to fract. surface	57.1	5.44 (± 6.7%)	3.39 (± 5.3%)	2.52 (± 1.0%)	0.62	0.74	bottom: 1.2 (±17%) center: 1.75 (±15%) top: 1.33 (±39%)	0.25
C	normal to fract. surface	61.1	5.32 (± 9.2%)	6.47 (± 0.9%)	3.67 (± 1.2%)	1.22	0.57	bottom: 0.8 (±8%) center: 1.25 (±17%) top: 1.49 (±5%)	0.54
C	Parallel to fract. surface	61.1	6.38 (± 1.4%)	3.21 (± 9.3%)	1.09 (± 3.7%)	0.50	0.34	bottom: 0.69 (±3%) center: 0.52 (±27%) top: 0.70 (±4%)	0.30

3.2 Splitting tension tests

The splitting tension tests have been performed on the 150 mm diameter cores drilled from the plates. The test was displacement controlled and the crack opening over a gauge length equal to 40 mm on both sides of the disk at center height was measured.

In Table 5 the first cracking and the maximum load are listed and correlated to the number of fibers on the diameter fracture plane (average value between two nominally identical tests with related scattering). The effect of fiber orientation can be appreciated from the ratio between the maximum and first cracking loads: fibers with a preferred orientation at a right angle to the diameter fracture plane justify a significant increase of post-cracking load bearing capacity. The specific number of fibers on the fracture surface and the values of the orientation factors, computed as above, stand as a further confirmation, when compared to the results obtained from beams, of the effectiveness of the self consolidating mixtures in guaranteeing a uniform dispersion of fibers.

Table 5: Tension splitting tests: compressive strength, first cracking and maximum load; specific number of fibers on the fracture plane and fiber orientation factor α

Mix	Casting direction	f_c (N/mm^2)	P_{crack} (kN)	P_{max} (kN)	P_{max}/P_{crack}	specific n° fibers /cm^2	α
A	Normal to Fracture surface	54.4	51.7 (± 13.6%)	65.0 (± 17.7%)	1.26	0.618 (± 12%)	0.39
	Parallel to fracture surface		54.7 (± 6.3%)	57.9 (± 3.3%)	1.06	0.348 (± 11%)	0.21
B	Normal to Fracture surface	57.1	64.0 (± 2.8%)	79.0 (± 3.5%)	1.23	2.55 (± 10%)	0.44
	Parallel to fracture surface		55.2 (± 4.9%)	59.1 (± 11.0%)	1.07	1.55 (± 9%)	0.27
C	Normal to Fracture surface	61.1	58.3 (± 16.3%)	68.7 (± 1.0%)	1.18	1.05 (± 10%)	0.50
	Parallel to fracture surface		59.4 (± 2.5%)	61.8 (± 1.1%)	1.04	0.547 (± 10%)	0.26

3.3   Performance analysis of the hardened fiber reinforced concrete

As a final goal of the work the results from 4pb tests have been processed in order to seek a common correlation for all the investigated types of fiber, between the performance of the fiber reinforced composite in the hardened state and a parameter, suitable to include in its definition the different characteristics of fiber reinforcement [14]. To this purpose the same parameter has been herein tentatively adopted as previously employed for the mix-design and as an indicator of the fresh state performance: the average spacing d_{ss} of the solid particles (Table 2). Its definition (Eq. (2)) encompasses the geometrical dimensions and volume ratio of the fibers, their specific surface area, and their interaction with the aggregate grading.

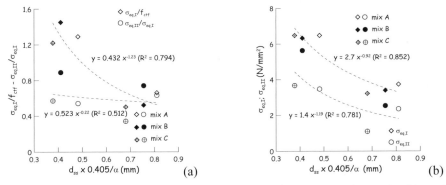

Figure 5: Toughness indicators (a); equivalent post-cracking residual strengths (b) vs. the average solid particle spacing d_{ss} [Eq. (2)] corrected by the normalized orientation factor

The role of the orientation factor has to be taken into account, due to its importance highlighted by experiments (Fig. 4). It is assumed that an orientation factor higher than the random isotropic one (0.405) corresponds to a tighter fiber spacing, which also means an improved efficacy of the fibers in guaranteeing stress transfer. For this reason an "orientation correction factor" equal to $0.405/\alpha$ has been applied to d_{ss}, (α values listed in Table 4). Fig. 5 highlights the effectiveness of this approach. The importance of the orientation factor is clear if the range of variability of d_{ss} computed for the three mixes (Table 2), for an isotropic reference situation, is compared with the one in Fig. 5. The effectiveness of the approach is proved also with reference to the results of splitting tension tests (Fig. 6).

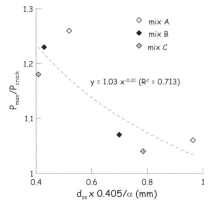

Figure 6: P_{max}/P_{crack} (splitting tests) vs. the average fiber spacing d_{ss} corrected by the normalized orientation factor

4. CONCLUSIONS AND FURTHER WORK

The results of an investigation aimed at assessing the correlations between the fresh state behavior, the fiber dispersion and orientation and the hardened state properties of self consolidating fiber reinforced concretes (SCSFRC) have been discussed in this study.

A mix-design model recently proposed for SCSFRC has been employed to analyze the performance in the fresh state, as measured through field tests. It is based on an average spacing of the solid particles, which accounts for the grading of aggregates and fibers; these are regarded as an equivalent aggregate with respect to the specific surface area. The average spacing of solid particles, d_{ss}, is an indicator of the degree of suspension of the solid particles into the fluid cement paste, characterized by fundamental rheological properties.

The effectiveness of the self consolidating concrete in driving the orientation of fibers along the casting direction and in guaranteeing a uniform dispersion of the fibers within the cast specimens, furthermore preventing their downward settlement, has been proved.

The performance of the composite in the hardened state, measured through 4 pb tests, has been shown to be strongly affected by the dispersion and orientation of fibers and have been effectively correlated to the same parameter, d_{ss}, employed for mix design and fresh state characterization. A correction factor has been suitably defined to include in this parameter the effect of the orientation of fibers, as influenced by the casting process, fresh state behavior of concrete and specimen geometry. The importance of this correction to assess a reliable correlation with the mechanical performance of the composite has been shown. This parameter, once corrected by the orientation factor term, can be hence regarded also as an indicator of the binding efficacy of aggregates and fibers by the hardened cement paste.

The multifold meaningfulness of the parameter d_{ss} makes the present approach attractive, aiming at a "design" of the material and of the casting process tailored to the dedicated application and to the anticipated structural performance. Further investigation to assess its reliability with reference to a wider range of cases is currently on going.

ACKNOWLEDGEMENTS

The authors thank Ms. Pamela Bonalumi and Mr. Alessio Caverzan for their help in performing tests and reducing experimental results.

REFERENCES

[1]   F. De Larrard, 'Concrete mixture proportioning. A scientific approach', E&FN Spoon, (1999).

[2]   S. Grunewald, Performance based design of self compacting steel fiber reinforced concrete", *PhD Thesis*, Delft University of Technology, (2004).

[3]   J.E. Wallevik, Relationships between Bingham parameters and slump, *Cement and Concrete Research*, 36 (2006) 1214-1221.

[4]   Ferrara, L. and Meda, A., 'Relationships between fibre distribution, workability and the mechanical properties of SFRC applied to precast roof elements', *Materials and Structures*, **39** (2006) 411-420.

[5]   Ozyurt, N., Woo, L.Y., Mason, T.O. and Shah, S.P., 'Monitoring fiber dispersion in fiber reinforced cementitious materials: comparison of AC-Impedance Spectroscopy and Image Analysis', *ACI Materials Journal,* **103** (5) (2006) 340-347.

[6]   Frachois, A., Taerwe, L. and Van Damme, S., 'A microwave probe for the non-destructive determination of the steel fiber content in concrete slabs', in Fiber Reinforced Concretes, Proceedings BEFIB 2004, M. di Prisco et al. eds., Varenna, Italy, September, 2004, 249-256.

[7]   Ferrara, L., Park, Y.D. and Shah, S.P., 'A method for mix-design of fiber reinforced self consolidating concrete', submittted for publication to *Cement and Concrete research*, Sept. 2006.

[8]   D'Aloia Schwartzentruber, L., Le Roy, R. and Cordin, J., 'Rheological behaviour of fresh cement pastes formulated from a Self Compacting Concrete', *Cement and Concrete Research,* **36** (7) (2006) 1203-1213.

[9]Roussel, N., and Le Roy, R., 'The Marsh cone: a test or a rheological apparatus?', *Cement and Concrete Research*, **35** (5) (2005) 823-830.

[10]Tregger, N., Ferrara, L. and Shah, S.P., 'Identification of rheological properties of self compacting concrete from cement paste rheology tests and numerical fluid dynamic modelling ', accepted for presentation to SCC2007, Ghent, Belgium, September 2007.

[11]Van Bui, K., Akkaya, Y. and Shah, S.P., 'Rheological model for self-consolidating concrete', *ACI Materials Journal*, **99** (6) (2002) 549-559.

[12]CNR DT-204: Guidelines for design and execution of SFRC structures (in Italian).

[13]Soroushian, P. and Lee, C.D., 'Distribution and orientation of fibers in steel fiber reinforced concrete' *ACI Materials Journal*, **87** (5) (1990) 433-439.

[14]Voigt, T., Van Bui, K. and Shah, S.P., 'Drying shrinkage of concrete reinforced with fibers and welded-wire fabric', *ACI Materials Journal*, **101** (3) (2004) 233-241.

MEASUREMENT AND MODELLING OF FIBRE DISTRIBUTION AND ORIENTATION IN UHPFRC

John Wuest, Emmanuel Denarié and Eugen Brühwiler

MCS, Ecole Polytechnique Fédérale de Lausanne, Switzerland

Abstract

Ultra High Performance Fibre Reinforced Concretes (UHPFRC) combine outstanding protective (extremely low permeability) and mechanical (high tensile strength and significant tensile strain hardening) properties. These materials can be used in composite UHPFRC-reinforced concrete members to provide long term durability and improved structural performance. However, their processing at fresh state and geometric boundary effects can induce significant anisotropic fibre distributions that must be considered when evaluating material characterisation test results or designing structural members to reliably benefit from their strain hardening properties.

The fibre distribution and the coefficient of orientation have been measured in UHPFRC tensile specimens cast in forms with different casting directions, and fibre length. A large-scale UHPFRC-reinforced concrete composite structural member has also been investigated to link tensile specimen test results and structural element performance.

Relationships have been found between the fibre distribution and orientation as a function of the form size vs. fibre length ratio, casting direction and the resulting mechanical properties. Furthermore, an original model for characterizing the fibre orientation from the determined number of fibres within three orthogonal cuts was developed, tested and successfully employed.

1.   INTRODUCTION

More and more durability and load carrying capacity problems emerge from the aging existing civil structures. In order to solve these problems, UHPFRC materials are being employed because of their easy on-site casting combined with their excellent strength and durability properties. UHPFRC combine a dense matrix with a high amount of steel fibres (2 to 9% in volume). These materials are characterized by a very low permeability and a significant strain hardening behaviour in tension.

Material characterization tests are conducted on relatively small specimens to determine the mechanical properties of UHPFRC cast on large-scale structural members. These specimens will have a different response depending on the casting direction, the form size, the mix workability and the fibre length. These parameters have an influence on the apparent material behaviour by extending the strain-hardening domain (if all fibres are orientated parallel to the principle stress direction) or eliminate a potential hardening (if all fibres are orientated perpendicular to the principle stress direction). Therefore material characterization test results should be interpreted as a function of the fibre distribution and orientation. Also the relevance of test results in view of structural application should be confirmed.

This article presents the fibre distribution and orientation measured in three directions on UHPFRC elements and identifies the influence of the fibre distribution and orientation on the UHPFRC hardening behaviour. Finally, a model for describing the fibre orientation is suggested, which describes the fibre orientation by two different angles.

2.   FIBRE ORIENTATION THEORY

2.1 Coefficient of orientation

Krenchel [1] suggested the coefficient of orientation for determining the fibre orientation:

$$C_{OR} = \frac{N_f \cdot \pi \cdot d_f^{\,2}}{V_f \cdot 4} \tag{1}$$

where N_f is the number of fibres per unit cross-area, d_f is the fibre diameter and V_f is the fibre volume. V_f can be determined as follows:

$$\rho_U V = \rho_m V_m + \rho_f V_f \;\Rightarrow\; V_f = \frac{\rho_U - \rho_m}{(\rho_f - \rho_m)} \tag{2}$$

where V is the total volume (equal to 1), V_m is the matrix volume, ρ_f is the fibre specific weight, ρ_m is the matrix, and ρ_U is the UHPFRC specific weight.

The C_{OR} value equals 1 if all the fibres are orientated in the same direction (1D); 0.637 if the fibres are orientated in 2D and 0.5 if the fibres are orientated in 3D.

2.2   Fibre orientation model

The orientation coefficient as defined by Eq. 1 depends on the fibre content (V_f) and distribution (N_f) which can vary significantly within a specimen. As a consequence, the orientation coefficient determined on the basis of three orthogonal cuts of a length significantly larger that the fibre length can lead to inconsistent results. The idea of the model is to "homogenize" the random fibre distribution and characterize it by means of "average" orientation angles combining the information from the three orthogonal cuts.

The following model is thus suggested for describing the fibre orientation within an element in a more global and consistent way. This model is based on three assumptions:

Assumption 1: All fibres within an element are equally spaced and their spacing is calculated as follows:

$$V_{tot} = ((n-1)\cdot s)^3 \text{ and } V_{tot} \cdot V_f = n^3 \cdot V_{1,f} \Rightarrow n = \sqrt[3]{\frac{V_{tot} \cdot V_f}{V_{1,f}}} \tag{3}$$

$$s = \frac{\sqrt[3]{V_{tot}}}{\sqrt[3]{\dfrac{4 \cdot V_{tot} \cdot V_f}{\pi \cdot d_f^2 \cdot L_f}} - 1} \tag{4}$$

where s is the fibre spacing, V_{tot} is the specimen volume (volume enclosed by all fibre centres uniformly distributed), n is the number of fibre centres in one direction, $V_{1,f}$ is the volume of a single fibre ($\pi d_f^2 \cdot L_f/4$) and L_f is the fibre length.

Assumption 2: All fibres have the same orientation defined by two angles α (orientation angle, around the z axis) and β (elevation angle, around the y axis) ranging from 0 to 90° (Fig. 1).

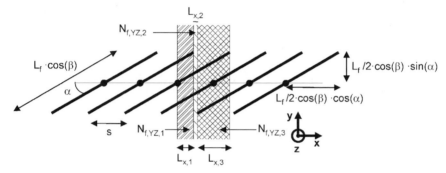

Figure 1: Description of the model for the x direction (here n_{tot}=3)

The weighted average of the number of fibres cut by a plane with respect to the projected length of half a fibre is calculated for the YZ plane using Eq. 5 (for the XZ and XY plane the equation is transformed accordingly).

$$N_{f,YZ} = \frac{2 \cdot \displaystyle\sum_{i=1}^{n_{tot}} N_{f,YZ,i} \cdot L_{x,i}}{L_f \cdot \cos(\alpha) \cdot \cos(\beta)} \cdot \frac{n^2}{A_u} \tag{5}$$

where $N_{f,YZ,i}$ and $L_{x,i}$ are respectively the number of fibres and the length from the different zones (Fig. 1), A_u is the element section and n_{tot} is the total number of zones considered.

Assumption 3: the number of fibres for a boundary area (area within $L_f/2$ from the boundary) is the average of the respective boundary surface number of fibres and the core number of fibres ([2] and [3]).

From the three orthogonal, experimentally determined, numbers of fibres ($N_{f,XY}$, $N_{f,YZ}$, $N_{f,XZ}$) a specific α and β combination is determined. The methodology is to first calculate the β angle from the $N_{f,XY}$. A α value, with the given β value, is then fitted to the $N_{f,YZ}$ and $N_{f,XZ}$ using the least squares method.

3.   MEASUREMENT OF FIBRE ORIENTATION

3.1   Specimens

Three tensile specimens of different UHPFRC and one slab element consisting of UHPFRC and reinforced concrete have been investigated. The three self-compacting UHPFRC mixes contain a high amount of cement (more than 1000 kg/m³), a relatively high quantity of macro fibres (V_f: 4-6%) and a low water/cement ratio (about 0.15). Table 1 gives the main characteristics of the investigated specimens. A higher aspect ratio was employed for TE-U-2, leading to a decrease in fibre volume to obtain sufficient workability.

Table 1: Characterization of the specimens

Specimen name	Mix	Macro fibres properties	Specimen type/casting direction	Number of analyzed surfaces
TE-U-1	1	V_f=6%; L_f/d_f=10/0.2	Dog bone horizontal	16
TE-N-1	1	V_f=6%; L_f/d_f=10/0.2	Notched Vertical	11
TE-U-2	2	V_f=4%; L_f/d_f=13/0.16	Dog bone horizontal	4
SE-S-3	3	V_f=6%; L_f/d_f=10/0.2	Slab element horizontal	20

The dog bone specimens have a total length of 70 cm, with a constant cross section of 5 by 10 cm² over a length of 30 cm. The notched element has a total length of 50 cm and a cross-section of 20 by 5 cm². A 2 cm deep notch was sawn on each side of the specimen. The slab element consists of a reinforced concrete slab of 200 by 200 cm² with a thickness of 20 cm. A rough interface surface was prepared by removing 0.25 to 0.5 cm of the cover surface by water jetting. A thin UHPFRC layer of 2.2 cm was then applied on top of the prepared surface.

All the analyzed elements were first cut in cubes of approximately 5 cm (Fig. 2) leading to the number of analyzed surfaces given in Table 1. On all tensile specimens, only one cut was done along the z direction for determining the number of fibres per unit cross-area in the XY plane (axis reference see Fig. 3). For the slab element, no measurements could be performed on the XY plane because of the small UHPFRC thickness (axis reference see Fig. 4).

3.2   Analysis of tensile specimens

a) Tensile behaviour

The three tensile specimens showed different responses. TE-U-2 showed an extended hardening domain compared to TE-U-1, while TE-N-1 exhibited only a softening behaviour (Fig. 2).

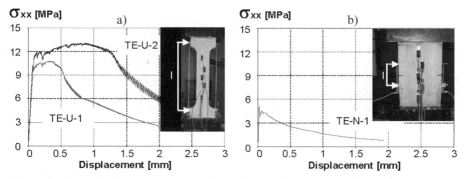

Figure 2: Stress-displacement relation for a) the two dog bone specimens (measurement length, l = 350 mm) b) the notched specimen (l = 150 mm).

b) Number of fibres and coefficient of orientation

The determination of the number of fibres was done by means of an image analysis software. The methodology for the image analysis process to count the fibres is addressed in [4] and [5].

The results of fibre counting in each plane (Table 2) show that TE-U-2 has the highest coefficient of orientation (0.66) in the principle stress direction, while it has the smallest fibre volume. Higher fibre length while maintaining the form size provides an increased coefficient of orientation in the principal stress direction. These parameters lead to a rather unidirectional flow of fibres during casting (restraining the fibres from being orientated randomly) and significantly reduced amount of fibres orientated in the other directions. Thus, the hardening domain is considerably extended.

Table 2: Results of fibre measurement in the three planes

Specimen	YZ			XZ			XY		
	N_f [fibres/mm^2]	V_f [%]	C_{or} [-]	N_f [fibres/mm^2]	V_f [%]	C_{or} [-]	N_f [fibres/mm^2]	V_f [%]	C_{or} [-]
TE-U-1	1.26 ±0.08	6.31 ±0.13	0.63 ±0.04	1.09 ±0.09	6.24 ±0.10	0.55 ±0.05	0.48	6.17	0.24
TE-N-1	0.70 ±0.15	5.88 ±0.11	0.37 ±0.08	1.37 ±0.11	5.82 ±0.14	0.74 ±0.05	1.16	5.79	0.63
TE-U-2	1.4 ±0.03	4.27	0.66 ±0.02	0.75	4.27	0.35	0.48	3.9	0.25
SE-S-3	1.11 ±0.22	6.00	0.58 ±0.11	1.29 ±0.19	6.00	0.67 ±0.10	No measurements		

Specimen TE-N-1 showed the smallest coefficient of orientation in the principle stress direction (0.37) because the fibres were mostly orientated perpendicular to the principle stress as a result of the casting direction and the gravity effect. Due to this forced orientation, TE-N-1 presented a higher N_f than all other tensile specimens in the XZ plane and XY plane. Moreover, due to the relatively small width of the form (5 cm) used for the vertical casting, the fibres were rather orientated following the y axis. If this element had been tested in the XZ or XY plane, it would have certainly shown a significant strain hardening behaviour. Moreover, the fibre orientation not only suppressed the hardening domain, but also severely reduced the first cracking resistance (first point where the curves deviate from the linearity (Fig. 2.)).

The standard deviation of $N_{f,YZ}$ along the specimen length for TE-U-1 (Fig. 3) and TE-U-2 is relatively small (<0.08 fibres/mm^2). This implies that the fibres are well distributed throughout the element and thus, no particularly unreinforced zones were detected. This is due to the uniaxial flow of the fibres created by the form during horizontal casting. In specimen TE-N-1, a higher standard deviation was determined which is principally due to the vertical casting process.

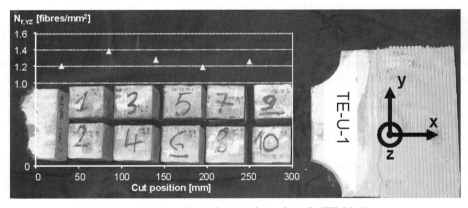

Figure 3: $N_{f,YZ}$ along the specimen length (TE-U-1).

c) Fibre orientation model

Table 3 presents the results using the fibre orientation model given in 2.2. The distance s between fibre centres is largest in TE-U-2 as it has the lowest fibre volume. The β angle in TE-U-1 and TE-U-2 is 16°, indicating that these fibres have a higher probability of being cut by a YZ or XZ plane than by a XY plane.

Table 3: Model representation of the three tensile test specimens

Specimen	s [mm]	α [°]	β [°]
TE-U-1	1.78	42	16
TE-U-2	1.90	26	16
TE-N-1	1.80	56	39

The α angle for TE-U-2 is relatively small compared to the TE-U-1 α angle. The two angles show that the fibres in TE-U-2 are almost orientated horizontally and parallel to the vertical boundaries. This confirms the conjecture stated previously that most of the fibres in this specimen are orientated in the x direction. Moreover, in TE-U-1, the orientation angle (42°) is very close to 45 ° corresponding to the same probability of being cut in the XZ and YZ direction. This means that the fibres in this element approach a uniform 2D distribution. The specimen TE-N-1 exhibited a β angle of 39°. This is higher than the 35.2° angle, which produces an equal probability for the fibre to be cut in a horizontal plane than in a vertical. Moreover, the 56° α angle shows that the fibres tend to be more oriented in the y than in the x direction. These high β and α angles confirm the conjecture stated in 3.2 b) that the YZ plane is almost devoid of fibres.

The potential fibre orientation given by the two averaged angles defined by this method was determined for the three tensile elements showing results which are in agreement with the results obtained from the fibre counting (error less than 7%).

3.3   Analysis of slab element

The results of fibre counting for the UHPFRC layer on the slab element are presented in Table 2 The first observation is that the N_f is higher in the XZ plane than in the YZ plane. This orientation is due to the levelling of the UHPFRC using a ruler to remove the extra UHPFRC. As a thin layer was cast (2.2 cm), this process may have orientated a significant amount of the fibres parallel to the levelling direction (y direction). Moreover, this orientation also corresponds to the casting direction (Fig. 4).

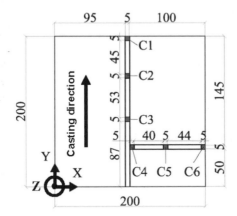

Figure 4: Location of the analyzed samples C1 to C6 from the slab (dimensions are in cm).

The obtained average N_f (for XZ and YZ) are very close to the tensile specimen TE-U-1, but the standard deviation is higher. The dog bone shaped form used for the tensile test specimen aligned the fibres with the casting flow and thus allowed a better distribution within the element. Since in the slab element, the boundaries have a small effect; fibres are less restricted to be orientated randomly. Moreover, within each series of tensile specimens a scatter has also been observed, not in the $N_{f,YZ}$ but in the tensile test behaviours. As the tensile specimen responses are dependent on the fibre orientation and distribution, the difference can thus be directly linked to the variation of $N_{f,YZ}$ in each specimens.

These results demonstrate that the prediction of the slab resistance by considering the experimental test results obtained from TE-U-2 would have been erroneous. In TE-U-2, the forms influenced the casting flow to orient the fibres parallel to the principle stress direction. In SE-S-3, the flow direction is controlled by the casting techniques and so, the fibres are less orientated. The slab resistance would have thus been considerably over estimated. These observations show that the size, casting process and testing procedure of the characterization of specimens, all influencing the fibre orientation, have to be defined for the structural element they represent.

4.   CONCLUSIONS

- An original model for the determination of fibre distribution and orientation of UHPFRC was presented and validated using measurements of three orthogonal cuts. This model defines an element's fibre orientation with an elevation and an orientation angle.
- Tensile test results should be accompanied by a fibre distribution and orientation analysis because fibre distribution and orientation highly influence the mechanical response of the UHPFRC element.
- The apparent hardening behaviour is increased in elements where the fibres are orientated in the principle stress direction compared to elements with a random fibre orientation.
- A larger scatter on the fibre distribution has been measured in the larger structural elements compared to the smaller tensile specimens.

ACKNOWLEDGEMENTS

The Swiss State Secretariat for Education and Research (SER) in the context of the European project Suinstainable and Advanced Materials for Roads Infrastructures (SAMARIS) have financially supported this research. The image analysis software has been developed by the Ecole d'Ingénieur de Genève (EIG).

REFERENCES

[1] Krenchel H., 'Fibre Reinforcement: Theoretical and practical investigations of the elasticity and strength of fibre-reinforced materials', Akademisk Forlag, (Copenhagen, 1964).
[2] Soroushian P., Lee C.D., 'Distribution and Orientation of Fibers in Steel Fiber Reinforced Concrete', ACI Mater. J. **87** (5) (1990) 433-438.
[3] Stroeven P. Effectiveness of steel wire reinforcement in a boundary layer of concrete. ACTA Stereol. **10** (1) (1991)113-22.
[4] Wuest J., Denarié E., Brühwiler E., 'Fibre distribution and orientation models for strain hardening UHPFRC elements', In preparation.
[5] Wuest J., Denarié E., Brühwiler E., Tamarit L., Kocher M., Galluci E., 'Image analysis method for the determination of fibre distribution and orientation in advanced cementitious materials', In preparation.

FIBER DISPERSION MONITORING USING AC-IMPEDANCE SPECTROSCOPY AND A CONVENTIONAL METHOD

Nilufer Ozyurt [(1)], Leta Y. Woo [(2)], Thomas O. Mason [(3)] and Surendra P. Shah [(4)]

(1) Bogazici University, Department of Civil Engineering, Istanbul, Turkey

(2) Lawrence Livermore National Laboratory, Livermore, CA, USA

(3) Northwestern University, Department of Materials Science and Engineering, Evanston, IL, USA

(4) Northwestern University, Center for Advanced Cement Based Materials, Evanston, IL, USA

Abstract

Fiber dispersion is an important and decisive parameter for composite material performance and should be well studied to describe material properties. Various methods are used for evaluating fiber dispersion characteristics in fiber-reinforced composites (FRCs). However, most of these methods are either destructive and/or time-consuming. New and non-destructive techniques are needed to effectively monitor distribution of fibers in composite materials. In the last decade, efforts have been made to use AC-Impedance Spectroscopy (AC-IS) to study fiber dispersion characteristics of FRCs. Previous work of the authors showed that AC-IS is sensitive to the presence of conductive fibers. This work has been undertaken to further study the findings of the previous study. A conventional method – Image Analysis – was employed to verify the results of AC-Impedance Spectroscopy. A comparison of the two methods was made. AC-IS was found to be an effective method to monitor fiber dispersion in FRCs.

1. INTRODUCTION

Image analysis has long been used for fiber dispersion monitoring in cement-based materials. It is a well-understood and trusted method if correctly applied. Nowadays it is possible to do higher precision measurements and faster data analysis owing to the use of high resolution scanning microscopes and powerful computer programs, respectively. Despite all of the advantages, image analysis may not be practical for some applications, especially if non-destructive and prompt results are needed.

Non-destructive sensing technology has also come a long way in the last decades. Extensive research has been conducted to develop practical methods to employ non-destructive techniques in a variety of applications? Furthermore, the use of non-destructive techniques to monitor cement-based materials is very common.

In this work a non-destructive electrical technique (alternating-current impedance spectroscopy) was used to study dispersion of fibers in steel fiber-reinforced cement-based materials. Information about the basic principles of the method and previous work can be found in [1-3]. In addition, image analysis was employed to measure fiber dispersion characteristics and the results obtained from image analysis and AC-IS were compared. Thus, it was possible to understand the ability of AC-IS to study fiber dispersion characteristics.

2. EXPERIMENTAL STUDY

Fiber-reinforced cement cubic specimens were cast for experimental study. The dimensions of the cubes were 89 mm x 89 mm x 89 mm. Two water-to-cement (w/c) ratios (0.30 and 0.35) and three fiber volume ratios (1%, 2%, 4%) were used. Short cut steel fibers with the length of 6 mm and diameter of 0.16 mm were provided by Bekaert. The mixing sequence was as follows. First, steel fibers were dry mixed with cement for 1 minute and then water was added. Then, the material was mixed for 1 minute at the lowest speed and 2 minutes at the highest speed. Specimens were stored under 100% relative humidity until the day of experiment.

2.1   Experimental Methods

2.1.1 AC-IS

AC-IS measurements were made 7 days after casting. For the experiments, artificial reservoirs were constructed on the top and bottom of the specimens. Electrodes were placed in the reservoirs and the reservoirs were filled with 1 M NaCl solution to provide good contact between the specimens and the electrodes. Measurements were made using a Solartron 1260 impedance gain/phase analyzer. The frequency range was 11 MHz to 100 MHz and voltage excitation was 1V. Matrix resistance (R_m) and composite (cement matrix + fibers) resistance (R) were obtained from the experiments and matrix normalized-conductivity (σ/σ_m) values were calculated (left hand side of Eq. 1). Further information about the experimental procedure could be found in [4].

2.1.2 Image analysis

Image analysis were conducted on the specimens following AC-IS measurements. For image analysis, the specimens were first cut into two parts either parallel or vertical to the casting direction. Specimen surfaces were then prepared to insure high quality images (good contrast of matrix and fibers were necessary) using a surface grinder and standard grit papers. Image capturing was done using an optical microscope (Wild M3Z stereo microscope with UV light source) and a high resolution digital camera.

3. RESULTS AND DISCUSSION

3.1 Fiber clumping

3.1.1 AC-IS

Fiber clumping was characterized using a pre-defined dispersion factor [5]. Equation 1 gives the matrix-normalized conductivity in the dilute limit for conductive particles/fibers. In Eq. 1, R_m, R, σ_m and σ stand for matrix resistance, composites resistance, matrix conductivity and composite conductivity, respectively. $[\sigma]_\infty$ and ϕ give intrinsic conductivity of fibers and fiber volume ratio, respectively.

$$\frac{R_m}{R} = \frac{\sigma}{\sigma_m} = 1 + [\sigma]_\Delta \phi, \qquad \Delta = \frac{\sigma_f}{\sigma_m} = \infty \text{ (for conductive fibers)} \tag{1}$$

Eq. 1 is used to define fiber clumping by means of a dispersion factor (Eq. 2). The dispersion factor compares the observed matrix-normalized conductivity of an actual FRC specimen to that of the theoretical value of a randomly dispersed FRC (given by Eq. 1).

$$Dispersion\ Factor\ (DF) = \left[\frac{\left(\frac{\sigma}{\sigma_m}\right)_{observed} - 1}{\left(\frac{\sigma}{\sigma_m}\right)_{theory} - 1}\right] = \frac{\phi'}{\phi} + \frac{\sum[\sigma]_{\Delta i}\phi_i}{[\sigma]_\Delta \phi} \tag{2}$$

3.1.2 Image analysis

A K-function of the point process statistics was used to evaluate fiber clumping using image analysis. The K-function gives the tendency of fibers to clump and repel each-other. Further information about point process statistics and K-function can be found in [6]. The estimator of the K-function is given as:

$$K = \frac{\text{Expected number of fibers within a distance r of x, given that x is a fiber location}}{\text{fiber intensity of the process}} \tag{3}$$

The observed value of the K-function was compared to the theoretical value to mathematically express how the fibers were dispersed in the specimens. Fig. 1 shows the K-functions for a specimen used in this study (1 vol. % of fibers and w/c=0.35) and for a spatially random dispersion. The K-function is equal to πr^2 for a spatially random dispersion. The upper curve, corresponding to the experimental K function, shows clumping. In Fig. 1, πr^2 corresponds to the K function of a random distribution, and C is the constant term of the curve for the experimental data.

$$Dispersion\ (IA) = \left(\frac{K_{theory}}{K_{observation}}\right) = \left(\frac{\pi r^2}{Cr^2}\right) \tag{4}$$

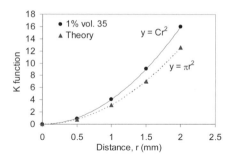

Figure 1: K-functions of a random dispersion (theoretically calculated) and an actual specimen (1 % vol.35)

Table 1 compares dispersion factors from the AC-IS and Image Analysis for the specimens. As is seen from the table, both methods give similar results.

Table 1: Dispersion factors from the AC-IS and Image Analysis

	Fiber volume, %	DF (AC-IS)	DF (Image A.)
w/c = 0.30	1	0.81 ± 0.17	0.83 ±
	2	0.88 ± 0.13	0.82 ±
	4	0.82 ± 0.11	0.83 ±
w/c = 0.35	1	0.83 ± 0.17	0.78 ±
	2	0.86 ± 0.13	0.77 ±
	4	0.83 ± 0.11	0.87 ±

3.2 Fiber orientation

3.2.1 AC-IS

For fiber orientation, 3-D measurements were carried out on the specimens and the results from the three directions were compared. To mathematically express the fiber orientation state of the specimens, an f-function was defined from Eq. 1 [7]. Previous work of the authors showed that AC-IS is sensitive to fiber directionality, meaning that the orientation of fibers affect conductivity of specimen [4]. If more of the conductive fibers are directed in the X direction than it is in the Z and Y directions, measured matrix-normalized conductivity in the X direction will be higher. Measurements using AC-IS were obtained in three directions and an effective f-function was calculated in the X, Y, and Z directions as shown below.

$$f_i = \left(\frac{R_m}{R}\right)_i - 1 = \left(\frac{\sigma_i}{\sigma_m}\right) - 1 = [\sigma]_{\infty,i}\,\phi \quad i = x, y, z \tag{5}$$

The effective f-function in each direction is then normalized using the total sum of the f-functions and the fractional effective f-functions are obtained.

$$\frac{f_i}{\sum\limits_{i=x,y,z} f_i} = \frac{[\sigma]_{\infty,i}}{[\sigma]_{\infty,x}\phi + [\sigma]_{\infty,y}\phi + [\sigma]_{\infty,z}\phi}; \quad i = x, y, z \tag{6}$$

3.2.2 Image Analysis

To describe the orientation of fibers using image analysis, a tensor description method was used. The orientation state of a single fiber can be defined using in-plane (ϕ) and out of plane angles (θ), as seen in Fig. 2. On the other hand, a more general description is needed to define the orientation state of fibers that are distributed in a volume (Eq. 7). Therefore, a tensor description method which is widely used in the fiber-reinforced polymer composite industry is employed. Detailed information about the method can be found in [8, 9].

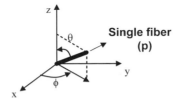

Figure 2: In-plane and out-of-plane angles of a single fiber

$$a_{ij} = \frac{\sum (p_i p_j)_n F_n}{\sum F_n} = \begin{pmatrix} a_{xx} & a_{xy} & a_{xz} \\ a_{yx} & a_{yy} & a_{yz} \\ a_{zx} & a_{zy} & a_{zz} \end{pmatrix} \quad i, j = x, y, z \tag{7}$$

In Eq. 7 a_{ij} stands for the components of the orientation tensor; p_x, p_y, and p_z and give the orientation state of a single fiber in reference directions and are calculated as follows (Eq. 8):

$$p_x = \sin\theta\cos\phi, \quad p_y = \sin\theta\sin\phi, \quad p_z = \cos\theta \tag{8}$$

In-plane (ϕ) and out-of-plane(θ) angles for every fiber were measured using an image analysis program. F in Eq. 7 gives the weighing function which is used to account for the effect of fiber orientation on the probability of a fiber being intercepted by the cross section under consideration (Eq.9). The probability of intercepting a fiber that is aligned vertical to the cutting plane is much higher compared to a fiber aligned parallel to the section.

$$F_n = \frac{1}{L}\frac{1}{\cos\theta_n} \text{ for } \theta < \theta_c, \quad F_n = \frac{L}{d} \quad \text{for} \quad \theta > \theta_c \text{ and } \theta_c = \arccos\left(\frac{d}{L}\right) \tag{9}$$

The main diagonal of the tensor in Eq. 7 is needed to obtain orientation states in the X, Y and Z directions. Therefore, only main diagonal components of the tensor are calculated for this study. Orientation density analyses were carried out on only one specimen due to time and labor intensity of the image processing. Fig. 3 shows the cross-section of the specimen (4 vol. % fiber content and w/c of 0.30) that was used to obtain orientation density. According to the results of the AC-IS measurement, the highest orientation was in the specimen with 4 vol. % fiber content and w/c of 0.30. Therefore, this specimen was used to study orientation density. The total number of fibers on the cross-section was approximately 6000. Considering the time and labor intensity, associated with the image processing, it was decided to choose a representative amount of subsections (20 subsections) and the orientation density analyses were carried out on only these subsections (Fig. 3).

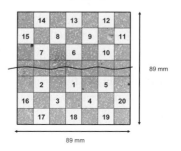

Figure 3. Schematic of the examined cross-section

Fig. 4 compares f-functions of AC-IS and fiber orientation densities of image analysis. Results of the two methods agreed well within the experimental uncertainty. Both methods showed low alignment in the Z direction. AC-IS showed similar alignment in the X and Y directions, while image analysis gave higher alignment in the X direction. Differences between the results were expected since the two methods are quite dissimilar in their measurement and analyzing techniques.

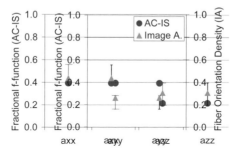

Figure 4. Fractional f-function (primary axis) and fiber orientation density (secondary axis) distributions

4. CONCLUSIONS

Two different methods (AC-IS and image analysis) were used to study fiber dispersion characteristics of FRCs. AC-IS was found to be sensitive to different dispersion phenomenon. Fiber clumping and fiber orientation in FRC specimens were measured using AC-IS and image analysis. The results of the two methods agreed well within experimental uncertainty, verifying the ability of AC-IS for non-destructive monitoring of fiber dispersion.

REFERENCES

[1] Ozyurt, N., 'Correlating, fiber dispersion, rheology, and mechanical performance for fiber-reinforced cement-based materials', PhD Thesis, Istanbul Technical University, 2006.

[2] Ozyurt, N., Mason, T.O., and Shah, S.P., 'Non-destructive monitoring of fiber orientation using AC-IS: An industrial scale application', *Cement and Concrete Research.* **36** (9) (2006) 1653-1660.

[3] Ozyurt, N., Mason, T.O., and Shah, S.P., 'Correlation of fiber dispersion, rheology, and mechanical performance of FRCs', *Cement and Concrete Composites.* **29** (2) (2007) 70-79.

[4] Ozyurt, N., Woo, Leta Y., Mu, B., Shah, S.P., Mason. T.O., 'Detection of fiber dispersion in fresh and hardened cement composites', in 'Advances in Concrete through Science and Engineering', An International Symposium during the RILEM Spring Meeting, Evanston, USA, 2003, on CD-ROM.

[5] Woo, L.Y., Wansom, S., Ozyurt, N., Mu, B., Shah, S.P., Mason. T.O., 'Characterizing fiber dispersion in cement composites using AC-Impedance Spectroscopy', *Cement and Concrete Composites.* **27** (6) (2005) 627-636

[6] Akkaya, Y., Picka, J., and Shah, S.P., 'Spatial distribution of aligned short fibers in cement composites', *Journal of Materials in Civil Engineering,* **12** (3) (2000) 272-279.

[7] Woo, L.Y., 'Characterizing fiber-reinforced composite structures using AC-Impedance Spectroscopy (AC-IS)', PhD Thesis, Northwestern University, 2005.

[8] Advani, S.G., and Tucker III, C.L., 'The use of tensors to describe and predict fiber orientation in short fiber composites', *Journal of Rheology,* **31** (8) (1987) 751-784.

[9] Mlekusch, B., 'Fibre orientation in short-fibre-reinforced thermoplastics II. Quantitative Measurements by Image Analysis', *Composites Science and Technology,* **59** (1999) 547-560.

SETTING AND HARDENING OF FRESH UHPFRCC MONITORED BY ULTRASOUND

Christian U. Grosse [(1)] **and Vazul Boros** [(2)]

(1) Department of Construction Materials, University of Stuttgart, Germany

(2) Department of Construction Materials and Engineering Geology, Budapest University of Technology and Economics, Hungary

Abstract
The behaviour of Ultra High Performance Fibre Reinforced Cementitious Composites (UHPFRCC) was monitored during setting and hardening by means of ultrasound. Advanced ultrasonic testing equipment can be used to study the effect of different UHPFRCC mixes or the influence of additives and fiber content. Different physical quantities are obtained during the stiffening process including velocity, energy and frequency development as well as the temperature evolution. A combined analysis of these quantities can help to control the quality of UHPFRCC mixes.

1.   INTRODUCTION

Non-destructive methods for testing fresh cementitious materials have been developed at the University of Stuttgart by the Department of Construction Materials [1; 2]. This method based on ultrasound techniques has been systematically improved during the last years [3; 4] and has already been used successfully for several applications [5; 6]. The technique allows for a continuous measurement during the setting and hardening of concrete.

On the basis of ultrasound techniques the properties of concrete and mortar mixtures can be measured – non-destructively, reproducible and largely objective. Of primary interest for quality control of fresh concrete is that the concrete parameters critically influencing the quality (e.g. the compressive strength) and workability (e.g. water-cement ratio, air-void contents), consistence, final strength, the effect of ad-mixtures and many more, have a significant effect on the ultrasonic signal parameters, such as wave velocity, amplitude and frequency content. In particular the setting process of fresh concrete and fresh mortar can be investigated in detail. Accordingly, these methods are directly connected with the elastic properties of the materials, rather than with the chemical properties (as with the hydration or maturity measurement methods). By this method, individual measured values like velocity, energy or frequency can be continuously recorded during concrete aging, and the concrete parameters derived from these values (e.g. onset of setting, final setting) extracted.

In this paper a mortar and two Ultra High Performance Fibre Reinforced Concrete mixtures where tested. Objective of the experiment was to investigate the materials behaviour in regard to setting and hardening with special focus on the influence of steel fibers.

2. MATERIALS TESTED

To investigate the applicability of the method for UHPFRCC first a reference mix of ordinary mortar was made as well as four different UHPFRCC mixtures. The UHPFRCC mixes followed mainly the results obtained at Kassel University [7]. The composition and the quantities had to be adjusted according to minor differences in the applied materials. The cement used was a CEM I 42,5 for the mortar and a CEM I 52,5 for the UHPFRCC mixtures. A superplasticizer on the basis of *polycarboxylic ether* was applied. The steel fibers were glued together and had a length of 30 mm with a diameter of 0.5 mm. The silica fume was added in a suspension with 50 % water content. All compositions are represented in Table 1.

Table 1: Composition of mortar and concrete mixtures (kg/m³)

Mixture	RS01	M1	M1F	M2Q	M2QF
Cement	380	900	900	900	900
Aggregate	1663	-	-	-	-
Silica sand	-	1016	1016	1016	1016
Fine silica	-	450	450	370	370
Steel fiber	-	-	192,5	-	192,5
Silica fume	-	-	-	200	200
Superplasticizer	-	28,2	28,2	28,2	28,2
Water	228	-	-	50	50

M1F and M2QF are two different UHPFRCC mixtures, one with silica fume and one without. The mixtures M1 and M2Q are similar but without steel fiber content. The mortar RS01 was made as a reference mix. From each UHPFRCC mix 2×3 prisms of the size 40 mm×40 mm×160 mm were made and tested after 7 and 28 days for compression strength. The prisms and the concrete in the FreshCon and Dewar container were compacted on a vibration table. The prisms were left in the formwork for 24 hours and cured in a water bath afterwards.

3. TEST SET-UP AND DATA ANALYSIS

3.1 Used hardware

At the Institute of Construction Materials (IWB), Universität Stuttgart, an apparatus was developed aimed at investigating the setting and hardening of cement-based materials in quality assurance. The method was eventually patented [8]. A detailed description of the individual developments can be found in publications by Grosse [3; 9]. In recent years, the technology has attained a good industrial standard. Proof of which, among others, is the fact that several research facilities and companies are by now successfully using the apparatus developed at the IWB. However, there are several other techniques similar than the described here. A good summary is the book edited by Reinhardt and Grosse [10].

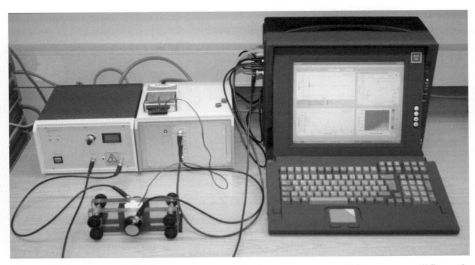

Figure 1: Overview of the FreshMor setup including a power-amplifier, pre-amplifiers, the container and a computer for data recording and analysis

The ultrasound device used for the investigations was the *FreshCon-2* system developed at the University of Stuttgart (Fig. 1). The container consists of two polymethacrylate (PMMA) walls which are tied together with four screws with spacers, with a U-shaped rubber foam element in between. This foam has high damping properties, suppressing waves from traveling through the mould and thus around the mortar. The volume of the mould is approximately 450 cm^3. With the aid of a piezoelectric transmitter, whose pulse energy is increased by a power amplifier, it is possible to produce signals that can be transmitted through fresh UHPFRCC. The reproducibility of the system is good and the sensors show a good linearity concerning the frequency response in the desired frequency range.

3.2   Data analysis methods
One of the most important parameters for assessing the hardened state and other material parameters is the ultrasonic velocity, which can be derived from the travel time of the wave following transmission through the material. For velocity v applies in general the well-known equation $v = s/t$ with travel time t and travel path s. When travel path s of the signal between transmitter and receiver (sensor) is known, the compressional wave velocity can be derived from the travel time of the signal. Measuring the transit times continuously and at fixed intervals, respectively, and derives from this the velocity of the waves, one will obtain characteristic – often s-shaped – curves that image the hardening and setting. Comparable curves and materials compositions can be obtained for all hardened materials (e.g. mortar or concrete) as well as e.g. all types of admixtures.

The software detects automatically the onset of the signal and calculates the according travel-time as well as velocity of the signal. The data can be displayed online graphically as shown in Fig. 2. The time interval between the measurements can be set from seconds to minutes or even hours and was set to 0.5 min during the first half hour, followed by 2 and 5 minutes intervals. All samples were examined for 24 hours in total.

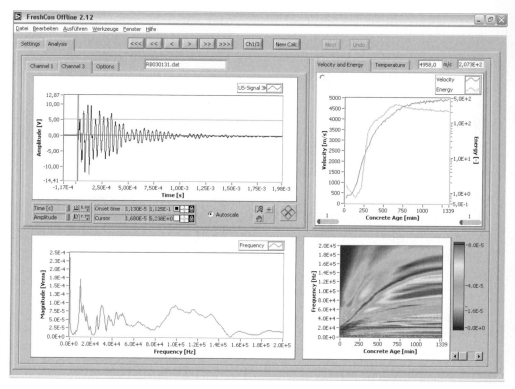

Figure 2: Snapshot of the online data evaluation software included in FreshCon-2 showing four different data analysis windows. Instead of the velocity and energy graph (upper right) the temperature evolution can be displayed

In order to broaden the possibilities of interpretation, additional parameters of the ultrasonic signals can be made use of. Further information can be derived from the change in signal amplitude (and energy, respectively) and frequency content in addition to the velocity. Investigating the signal energy development during the entire hardening process is helpful.

4.   RESULTS

4.1   Compressive strength

The compressive strength achieved (Tab. 2) is acceptable as the average strength reached by similar mixtures to M1F and M2QF at Kassel University was 128 N/mm² after 7 days and 153 N/mm² after 28 days under similar curing conditions [7]. As already described in several papers [11] a slight increase of compressive strength and a much better ductility, due to the addition of a significant amount of steel fibers, can be observed.

Table 2: Compressive strength and density of concrete specimen

Mix	7 days comp. strength [N/mm²] - average	28 days comp. strength [N/mm²] - average	Density of the prism [kg/m³] - average
M1	111.5	136.4	2315
M1F	125.7	147.1	2366
M2Q	111.4	123.0	2305
M2Q F	126.1	159.1	2414

4.2 Ultrasound and energy

A comparison of the ultrasound velocity and energy in the different mixtures can be seen in Fig. 3. It can be observed, that the UHPFRCC mixtures reach both a higher energy and higher velocity than the reference mortar mixture. Surprisingly even thought the concrete mixtures without steel fibers have a smaller compressive strength, higher ultrasound velocity is measured with these mixtures in the first 24 hours. The transmitted energy seems to reflect the higher strength of the steel fiber reinforced concrete. Both diagrams indicate that mixtures without steel fibers harden faster than the corresponding mix with fibers.

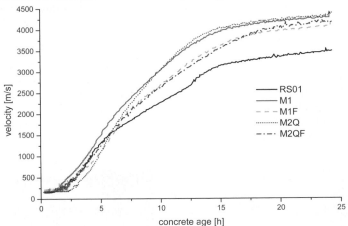

Figure 3: Changes of compressional wave velocity with concrete age for the mixes described in Table 1

The transmitted energy seems to reflect the higher strength of the steel fiber reinforced concrete. Both diagrams indicate that mixtures without steel fibers harden faster than the corresponding mix with fibers.

In addition to the elastic wave parameters obtained during the experiment the temperature was measured in three different ways including the ambient temperature, the temperature development in the FreshCon sample (measured using a thermocouple) as well as the temperature measured in a sample using a semi-adiabatic Dewar container. The results of these measurements for each different mix is giving information about the hydration process and described in the report by Boros [12].

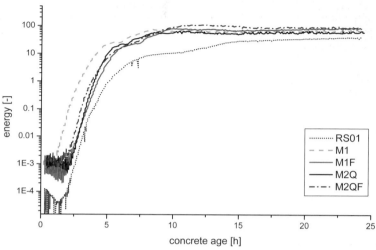

Figure 4: Changes of wave energy with concrete age for the mixes described in Table 1

4.3 Frequency

More details of the stiffening process can be obtained analyzing the signals in the frequency domain. Using Fast-Fourier-Transform (FFT) techniques these changes can be viewed in more detail [4]. Figure 5 shows the isoline representations of the frequency evolution for the mixtures M1 and M1F. The effect of the steel fibers causing a delay in the stiffening process can be observed again. Also the slight increase of strength is indicated by the more dominant contours of the plot for the mixture containing steel fibers. Similar observations can be made for the frequency plots of the mixtures M2Q and M2QF (Figure 6).

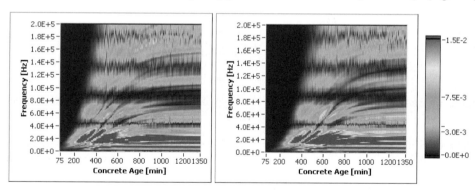

Figure 5: Frequency contour plot for mixtures M1 (left) and M1F (right)

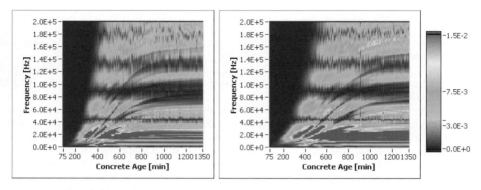

Figure 6: Frequency contour plot for mixtures M2Q (left) and M2QF (right)

All results regarding velocity, energy and frequency were made using the offline version of the FreshCon software. By picking the signal onset manually the error of the obtained data could be minimized. In each experiment the same computer, frequency generator, amplifier, ultrasound transmitter and FreshCon device was used in order to make the results comparable.

5.   CONCLUSIONS

Ultrasound transmission measurements can be used to observe the setting and hardening of Ultra High Performance Fiber Reinforced Cementitious Composites.

The investigation of several parameters such as ultrasound velocity and energy, frequency spectrum of the received signal and hydration temperature show, that the addition of steel fibers delays the hardening process.

Destructive tests carried out during the experiment and several papers show a higher compressive strength for steel fiber reinforced concrete. The results of the ultrasound energy correspond to this observation, but measurements show higher ultrasound velocity in the mixtures without fibers in the first 24 hours. It is the author's assumption that the inhomogenity of the material caused by the steel fibers is the reason for a lower velocity after the first day, whereas this has no effect on the transmitted energy. Further research is needed in this field, in particular to investigate the green concrete phase after 24 hours.

ACKNOWLEDGEMENTS

The described experiments were carried out at the Non-destructive Testing group of the University of Stuttgart and the authors are grateful for the support by Mr. G. Bahr, Mr. M. Schmidt, Dr.-Ing. M. Krüger. Additional scientific advice was given by Prof. Gy. Balázs from the Department of Construction Materials and Engineering Geology, Budapest University of Technology and Economics, Hungary, and Dr. E. Denarié from the Laboratoire de Maintenance, Construction et Sécurité des Ouvrages, EPFL, Lausanne, Switzerland.

REFERENCES

[1] Grosse, C.U. and Reinhardt, H. W., 'Continuous ultrasound measurements during setting and hardening of concrete'. Otto-Graf-Journal 5 (1994) 76–98.

[2] Grosse, C. U., 'Qualitätssicherung von Frischbeton mit Ultraschall' in Bauphysik Kalender, ISBN 3433017050 (Ernst & Sohn, Berlin, 2004) 397-403.

[3] Grosse, C. U., 'About the improvement of US measurement techniques for the quality control of fresh concrete' Otto Graf Journal **13** (2002) 93-110.

[4] Grosse, C. U. and Reinhardt, H. W., 'Ultrasound in through-transmission. Advanced testing of cement based materials during setting and hardening', in State-of-the-art Report No. 31, RILEM TC 185-ATC, (2006), 163-190.

[5] De Belie, N., et. al. 'Ultrasound monitoring of the influence of pozzolanic additions and accelerating admixtures on setting and hardening behavior of concrete and mortar', in Proc. 'Intern. Symp. Advanced testing of fresh cementitious materials', Stuttgart (2006), 55-64.

[6] Voigt, T., Grosse, C., Sun, Z., Shah, S.P., Reinhardt, H.W., 'Comparison of ultrasonic wave transmission and reflection measurements with P- and S-waves on early age mortar and concrete', J. of Mat. and Structure **38** (2005) 729-738.

[7] Fehling, E. et al., ,Entwicklung, Dauerhaftigkeit und Berechnung Ultrahochfester Betone (UHPC)', in ,Forschungsbericht DFG FE 497/1-1' (2005).

[8] Reinhardt, H.W., Grosse, C., Herb, A., Weiler, B., Schmidt, G., 'Method for examining a solidifying and/or hardening material using ultrasound, receptacle and ultrasound sensor for carrying out the method', patented under No. 09/857,536 at US Patent and Trademark Office, 2001.

[9] Grosse, C.U. and Reinhardt, H.W., 'New developments in quality control of concrete using ultrasound', in Proc. 'Intern. Symp. Non-Destructive Test. in Civ. Eng.' (NDTCE), vol. 85-CD, Berlin: DGZfP (2003).

[10] Reinhardt, H.W. and Grosse, C.U. (Eds.), 'Advanced testing of cement based materials during setting and hardening' in State-of-the-art report No. 31, RILEM TC 185-ATC, RILEM (2006).

[11] Balázs, L. Gy. & Polgár, L., 'Past, present and future of fiber reinforced concretes', in Proc. 'Intern. Symp. Fiber Reinforced Concrete, from research to practice', Budapest, 1999, 1-23.

[12] Boros, V., 'Ultrasound monitoring of the setting and hardening of Ultra High Performance Concrete'. Report, Budapest, Department of Construction Materials and Engineering Geology, Budapest University of Technology and Economics, October 2006.

High Performance Fiber Reinforced Cement Composites (HPFRCC5)
Mainz, Germany – July 10-13, 2007

PREPARATION AND APPLICATION OF SUPER-HIGH PUMPING STEEL FIBER REINFORCED CONCRETE

Sun Wei, Jiang Jinyang and Zhang Yunsheng

College of Materials Science and Engineering, Southeast University, P.R.China

Abstract

In this paper, a type of small-size fibers with dumbbells on two ends and notches in the middle are first designed to improve the workability of fresh steel fiber reinforced concrete (SFRC). By using the small-size fiber with specially designed appearance, the SFRC is successfully pumped to 306 meter high Sutong bridge tower once. The results demonstrate that the small-sized steel fiber not only can obviously restrain various shrinkages but also can greatly improve the axial tension strength, the toughness index and the bond strength between rebar and concrete, resulting in high resistance to non-loaded crack. The results also show the crack resistance of concrete beam is increased by approximately 40% due to an addition of small-sized steel fiber. Finally a full-scale model test is conducted to compare the cracking resistance between plain concrete and small-sized steel fiber reinforced concrete. It is found that the maximum crack width, cracking length and run-through crack number in the bridge anchorage zone made with SFRC are much less than those of plain concrete, which further indicates the small-sized steel fiber specially designed in this paper can effectively improve the structural crack resistance.

1. INTRODUCTION

It is well known that incorporation of steel fibers can meet the above-mentioned properties [1-3]. However, steel fiber addition greatly reduces the workability of fresh concrete, leading to the great difficulty in pumping process. At present, no published literature reports that SFRC can be continuously pumped over a height of 200 meters. In order to solve this problem, a new type of steel fiber with specially designed appearance and geometry are manufactured and used to prepare high flowable concrete with 300 meters of pumping height.

In this paper, a type of small-size fibers with 20 mm in length and 0.35 mm in diameter are first specially designed to improve the workability. In order to keep the fiber enhancement efficiencies, the appearance of fiber with dumbbells on two ends and notches in the middle is designed to increase the anchor-hold and friction between fibers and cement matrix. By using the small-size fiber with specially designed appearance and fly ash, the 306 meters high pumping test is also successfully performed in place. Finally, the shrinkage, cracking, axial tensile strength, toughness index and steel bar- SFRC matrix bonding strength were carried out in this study.

2. RAW MATERIALS AND EXPERIMENTAL PROGRAM

2.1   Raw materials

A Chinese standard Graded 42.5 ordinary Portland cement with the compressive strength of 47.6 MPa at age of 28 days is used, similar to ASTM C150 type II cement. Grade I fly ash, similar to Class F fly ash according to ASTM, are supplied by Nantong power plant, Jiangsu province, P.R.China. Rive sand with fineness modulus of 2.7 and continuous grade crushed basalt stone with maximum size of 16 mm are used as fine and coarse aggregate. A polycarboxylic-type superplasticizer with water reducing ratio of 25.8% is used, and the dosage is adjusted to keep the slump of fresh concrete mixture in the range of 200–220 mm. The special steel fibers with dumbbells on two sides and notches in the middle, have a length of 20 mm and an equivalent diameter of 0.35mm, the specific gravity and tensile strength of which are $7.8g \cdot cm^{-3}$ and $1.5kN \cdot mm^{-2}$, respectively. The commercial polypropylene fiber (PP fiber) with a rectangular cross-section and a length of 14 mm were also employed, the specific gravity, modulus of elasticity and tensile strength of which are $0.9g \cdot cm^{-3}$, $3.5kN \cdot mm^{-2}$ and 0.5-$0.65kN \cdot mm^{-2}$, respectively

2.2   Experimental program

A total of 6 bathes are made in this study. The details of experimental program are given in Table 1. Batch "SBH", "SBSF1", "SBSF2", "SBSF3" are used to compare the influence of fiber content (0, 0.6, 0.8, 1.0%). Batch "SBSF1" and Batch "SBSFIS" are used to investigate the fiber types (short fiber and long fiber). Batch "SBHSP" are specifically designed to investigate fiber hybrid addition approach (0.6% steel fiber and 0.1% PP fiber). The water/binder ratio is kept at 0.35 for all the batches. The corresponding physical and mechanical properties are also listed in Table 1.

Table 1: Mix proportions of sample / $kg.m^{-3}$

Batches	Cement	Fly ash	Sand	Gravel	Water	Fiber/kg	Superplas-ticizer
SBH	384	96	744	1070	160	0	3.82
SBSF1	384	96	778	990	161	Short fiber/46.8	4.22
SBSFI	384	96	778	990	161	Long fiber/46.8	4.22
SBSF2	388.8	97.2	806	946	163	Short fiber/62.4	4.37
SBSF3	393.5	98.4	833	903	165	Short fiber/78	4.92
SBHSP	391.2	97.8	778	990	164	Short fiber 46.8+PP 0.9	4.4

2.3   Pumping behavior

306 m high pumping test is conducted in Sutong bridge construction place in 2006. The SFRC made with the specially designed small-size steel fiber (fiber volume fraction = 0.8%) is successfully pumped up to 306 m high tower top once by using HBT90CH concrete pump. The oil pressure of the concrete pump is 26 MPa when performing the pump test, which is much lower than the maximum work pressure of 35 MPa. This indicates that it is feasible to continuously pump SRFC to an altitude of 306 meters or greater in as long as the steel fiber is properly designed. The detailed experimental parameters of SFRC in the process of pumping test are given in Table 2.

Table 2: Main parameters of SFRC in the process of pumping test

Time h	Slump out of machine mm	Spread out of machine mm	Slump out of tube (216 m) mm	Spread out of tube (216 m)	Oil pressure of the main system MPa	Pressure out of the machine MPa
0~0.5h	208	560	200	450	26	16.6

3. RESISTANCE TO SHRINKAGE

The shrinkage of high performance concrete has received great attention across the world. This paper conducted extensive studies on the various shrinkages such as plastic shrinkage and dry shrinkage of SFRC made with different fiber types and content.

3.1 Plastic shrinkage

Considering the SRFC made with the specially designed small-size fiber will be used in the anchorage zone in Sutong Bridge, the plastic shrinkage test in this paper is performed in the severest work condition that the steel anchorage box will be suffered from in service: 38^{L}, 40% relative humidity and average 10m/s wind speed. The mix proportions are shown in Table 1. The grade of cracking resistance was evaluated according to the evaluation method recommended in the Guide to Durability Design and Construction of Concrete Structure [4]. The experimental results are plotted in Fig. 1 and Fig. 2.

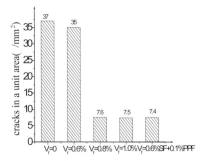

Figure 1: Effect of fiber content and type on the average cracking area

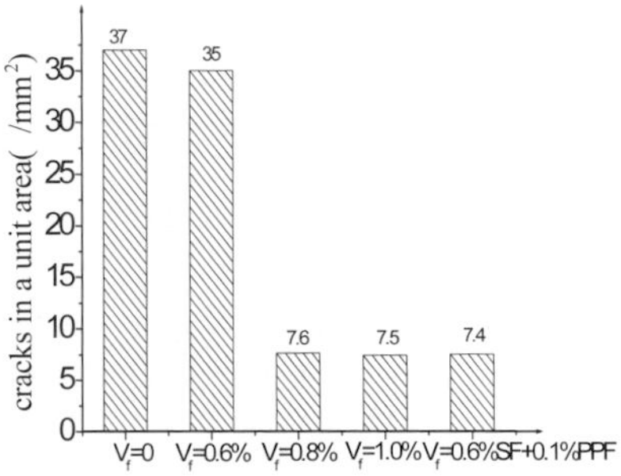

Figure 2: Effect of fiber content and type on the cracking number

The results shown in Fig 1 and 2 can demonstrate that:

It can be seen that when small-sized steel fiber is added into plain concrete, the cracking area and crack number per unit area will obviously reduced. And the more fiber content, the smaller cracking area and less crack number. It is due to cracking restraining effect of fiber that the cracking resistance capacity of SFRC above mentioned considerably improved. For example, the cracking resistance grade of plain concrete (SBH) is Grade V, while the SFRC made with 0.8% of steel fiber content (SBSF2 and SBSF3) is superior to the plain concrete. The corresponding cracking resistance is Grade I.

3.2   Drying shrinkage with restraint

The ring-type test is used to study the cracking due to dry. The diameter of the inner ring is 250 mm, the outer one is 300 mm, and the height is 150 mm. Because the space between the two rings is only 50 mm, the coarse aggregate were filtrated and the other components are left. The cracking behavior of the fiber reinforced cement mortar is shown in Fig. 3. It can be seen from Fig. 3 that for the plain cement mortar, the initial cracking occurs at an age of 9 days desiccation duration, and the maximum crack width reaches 0.58 mm after 50 days. Comparatively, when PP fiber is added, the initial cracking time is postponed to 15 days, and the maximum crack width is 0.3 mm after 50 days. When steel fiber is incorporated into plain cement mortar, the initial time is obviously postponed, even no crack is found in 50 days of testing duration in some cases. The maximum crack with is also greatly reduced at the end of test. For example, the initial cracking time is 28 days for these specimens with steel fibers of 0.6% volume fraction (SBSF1 and SBSFI). The maximum crack width is about 0.08 mm after 50 days. For the specimens made with 0.8% volume content of steel fiber (SBSF2 and SBSF3), no crack is observed in 50 days of testing duration. This indicates that the cracking caused by drying can be considerably reduced and prevented when fiber is added.

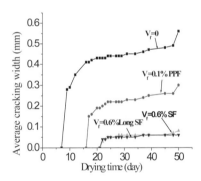 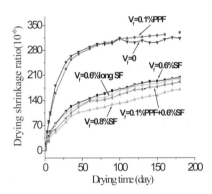

Figure 3: The effect of fiber type and content on average cracking width of cement mortars

Figure 4: The effect of fiber type and content on drying shrinkage rate of concrete

3.3 Drying shrinkage without restraint

According to Chinese standard GBJ82-85, the specimen for drying shrinkage test is 100 mm × 100 mm × 515 mm. The results of drying shrinkage in 180 days are shown in Fig. 4. It can seen that the drying shrinkage of plain concrete is much higher than that of steel fiber reinforced concrete. Compared with plain concrete specimen, the SFRC made with 0.8 volume fraction of fiber content has about 50% lower drying shrinkage. And the higher steel fiber content, the lower drying shrinkage.

Based on the above analysis of plastic shrinkage and drying shrinkage, it can be concluded that compared with the conventional long steel fibers, the specially designed small-sized fibers with dumbbell on two sides and notches in the middle section can also effectively prevent concrete from shrinking and cracking.

4. BASIC MECHANICAL BEHAVIOR

4.1 Bond strength between steel bar and steel fiber reinforced concrete

Bond strength test are carried out between steel bars and the concrete made with or without small-sized steel fiber according to Chinese standard for Hydraulic Concrete (DL/T 5150-2001). The experimental results are plotted in Fig. 5. It can be observed that the bond strength between steel bars and plain concrete is the smallest one. However, when small-sized steel fibers are added into plain concrete, the corresponding value is increased by about 40%. The high bond strength will guarantee that SFRC and steel anchor box can consistently work in service.

4.2 Tensile strength

The specimens for tensile test is 100 mm × 100 mm × 500 mm, and the clamp on the two ends are two rebars with a diameter of 200 mm. A length of 125 mm of the steel bars is embedded in the specimen. Four plain bars are welded on the 50 mm away from its end, which can reduce the stress concentration in the process of pulling [6]. The axial tensile strength of the concretes made with plain concrete and SFRC (0.8% volume fraction of steel fiber) are given in Fig. 6.

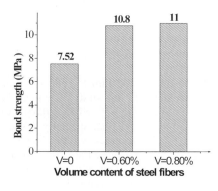
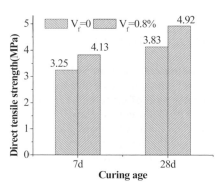

Figure 5: The effect of fiber content on bond strength between bar and concrete

Figure 6: The effect of fiber content on direct tensile strength

From the testing result, it can be concluded that the axial tensile strength of SFRC made with 0.8% volume fraction are increased about 30% compared with that of plain concrete. This will be especially benefit to improve cracking resistance.

4.3 Flexural behavior

Flexural test is performed according to ASTM C947. The flexural load-deflection curve and the initial cracking strength of the concrete made with or without steel fiber are tested and shown in Fig. 7 and Fig. 8. It can be seen from Fig. 7 and Fig. 8 that:

(1) Both the initital cracking strength and ultimate flexural strength can be increased with an increase in fiber content. For example, compared to the plain concrete, the initital cracking strength and ultimate flexural strength of the SFRC made with 0.8% volume fraction of small-sized steel fiber are increased by 15.6% and 31.4%, respectively.

(2) The flexural toughness of SFRC can aslo be increased when steel fiber is added. For SFRC made with 0.8% fiber content, the indices of flexural toughness I_5, I_{10} and I_{20} are increased 5.22, 8.7 and 12.39 times than plain concrete, respectively.

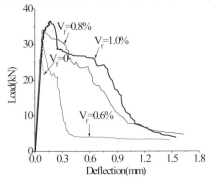

Figure 7: Contrast of load-deflection curve of SFRC with different volume fraction

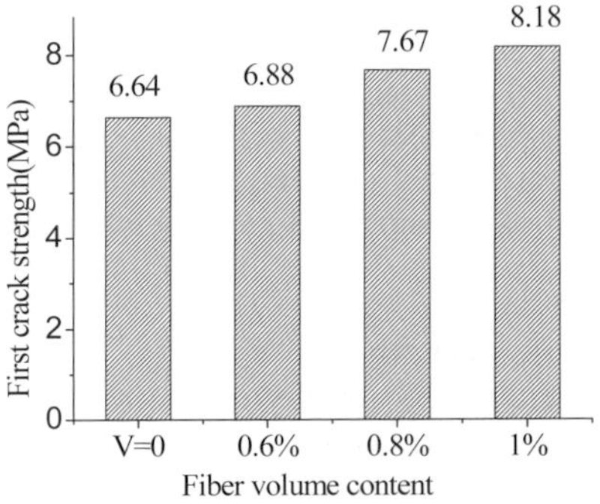

Figure 8: Comparison of first cracking strength of SFRC with different volume fraction

5. RESISTANCE TO STRUCTURAL CRACKS

5.1 Cracking resistance of SFRC beam

Flexural tests on six beams with the size of 150 mm × 200 mm × 1580 mm and the reinforcement ratio of 0.8% in the tensile zone are conducted in this study. The three beams are made with plain concrete and the other three ones are made with SFRC (0.8% volume fraction). The object is to investigate the effect of small-size steel fiber specially designed in this paper on the initial cracking load, the ultimate load, the crack width. The ultimate bending load is gradually reached. Both the Figs. 9 and 10 demonstrate the crack propagation of the concrete beam made with plain concrete and SFRC under different load levels, respectively. The development of cracks with increase in loads are given in Fig. 11. Based on the above experiment, the following conclusions can be drawn:

(1) The SFRC can remarkably improve the resistance to crack of concrete beam. When the volume fraction of steel fiber is 0.8%, the initial cracking load of SFRC beam is about 42.5kN, while the corresponding value is only 30kN for plain concrete beam. In other words, the initial cracking strength is increased by 40% when small-size steel fiber is incorporated.
(2) The SFRC can obviously reduce crack area and control crack width. The addition of steel fiber may transform the large cracks into many fine ones, leading to one multi-cracking mode. It should be noted that the small-sized steel fiber can reduce the maximum crack width. With the increase in load, the crack width of plain concrete beam rapidly increases, resulting in an instant failure, while a slow increase in crack width is clearly seen for the SFRC concrete beam.
(3) The ultimate load of the SFRC beam is 20% higher than that of the plain concrete beam. The addition of steel fiber also changes the failure of concrete beam from brittle mode to plastic one.

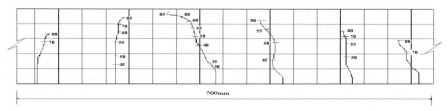

Figure 9: The crack propagation and shape of the middle of contrast concrete beam under the different load levels

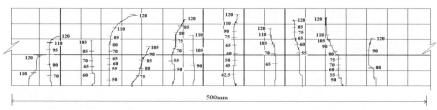

Figure 10: The crack propagation and shape of the middle of SRFC beam under the different load levels

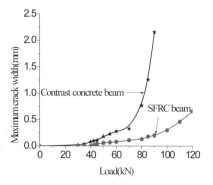

Figure 11: Comparison of the maximum crack width between SFRC beam and contrast concrete beam under the increasing load

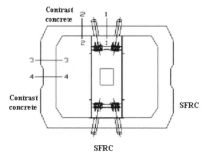

Figure 12: Testing design of full-scale model on anchorage zone

5.2   Cracking resistance of SFRC structure

In order to verify the resistance to structural crack of the SFRC above mentioned, a full-scale test that is used to simulate the anchorage zone of bridge tower that was carried out in this study, the half part of which was made with plain concrete and the other half was made with the specially designed small-sized steel fiber reinforced concrete, as shown in Fig. 12. The stress state on each section of the concrete tower is also shown in Fig. 12: Section 1-1 suffers from tension with small eccentricity; Section 2-2 bears pure bending load, both section 3-3 and section 4-4 bear tension with large eccentricity. In the case of normal service state, a single cable can bear 7500 kN load, which is labeled as P. When performing test, the loads are gradually increased from 0 to 1.7P by the counterforce device. Fig. 13 describes the development process of the maximum crack width of cable anchorage zone.

Fig. 14 shows the crack formation and propagation of the inner face of decorative notch groove, which are located at the longitudinal direction of bridge tower. Figs. 15 and 16 show the cracking shape of plain concrete and SFRC around the cable anchorage zone after holding the 1.7P load for 12 hours, respectively.

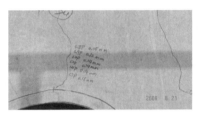

Figure 13: The maximum crack width of SFRC of cable anchorage zone under the increasing load

Figure 14: The crack formation and propagation of contrast concrete in the inner face of decorative notch groove under the increasing load

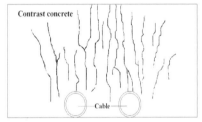

Figure 15: The cracking mode of contrasted concrete around cable anchorage zone under 1.7P loading

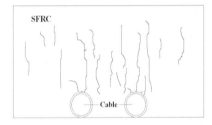

Figure 16: The cracking mode of SFRC around cable anchorage zone under 1.7P loading

According to the above testing results, the following conclusions can be reached:

(1) The SFRC exhibits excellent cracking resistance. When the cable's load reaches 0.6P, the plain concrete around cable zone begins to crack, while the initial cracking load is 0.8P for the SFRC. Compared to the plain concrete, the initial cracking strength of SFRC is increased by 33%. As for the decorative notch grooves on the sides of the anchorage zone, the similar phenomena is seen. Because two decorative notch grooves bear the tension with large eccentricity, two inner faces of the grooves are susceptible to crack. When the cable's load reaches 1.0P, the inner face of one notch groove made with plain concrete initiate cracking, while no crack can be found on the inner face of the other notch groove made with SFRC until the cable's load reaches 1.7P. It can be demonstrated that the SFRC posses excellent resistance to structural crack.

(2) The SFRC can greatly reduce the crack width of concrete structure around the cable anchorage zone. In the case of the regular service state, the maximum crack width is only 0.14 mm was for SFRC. When the cable's load continuously increases up to 1.7 P, the

maximum crack width is also very little, only 0.16 mm. Therefore, the SFRC can effectively inhibit the propagation of the crack around the cable anchorage zone.

(3) The SFRC can also prevent the formation and propagation of cracks. When the cable's load reaches 1.1P, the vertical cracks on the inner face of decorative notch groove made with plain concrete go through the tower wall from the bottom to the top. Correspondingly, the run-through crack can't be observed on the inner face of decorative notch groove made with SFRC when the cable's load reaches 1.7P. This demonstrates that SFRC possesses good resistance to initiation and propagation of structural cracks.

6. CONCLUSION

(1) By using the small-size fiber with specially designed appearance and fly ash, the SFRC can be pumped vertically to 306 m height. This will greatly promote SFRC to be applied in high-rise building construction.

(2) The plastic shrinkage and dry shrinkage of the concrete are greatly reduced due to the addition of the small-sized steel fibers. It is especially obvious when the volume fraction of steel fibers reaches 0.8%. The corresponding dry shrinkage can be reduced by 50%.

(3) The bond strength between steel bars and the concrete matrix made with small-sized steel fiber is increased by approximately 40% compared to that of plain concrete matrix. The axial tensile strength and flexural tougness are also improved greatly when small-sized steel fiber is added into the concrete matrix.

(4) The concrete structure made with small-sized steel fiber reinforced concrete possess good resistance to cracking. The numbers and width of cracks are very little at the normal service state. The initial cracking time is obviously postponed and the initial cracking strength is also improved.

REFERENCES

[1] Barragán, B.E., Gettu, R. Uniaxial tension test for steel fibre reinforced concrete-a parametric study. Cement and Concrete Composites 25 (2003), No. 7, 767-777.

[2] Lee, M.K., Barr, B.I.G. An overview of the fatigue behaviour of plain and fibre reinforced concrete. Cement & Concrete Composites 26 (2004), No. 4, 299-305.

[3] Song, P.S., Hwang, S. Mechanical properties of high-strength steel fiber-reinforced concrete. Construction and Building Materials 18 (2004), No. 9, 669-673.

[4] The project advisory group of durability of engineering structures and the safety, 'Design and construction of concrete structures durability Guide', 1st Edn, (Construction Industry Press, Beijing, 2004) 31-36 (In Chinese)

[5] Guofan, Z., Shouming, P. et al. Steel fiber reinforced concrete structure, 1st Edn. (Construction Industry Press, Beijing, 1999) 46-62 (In Chinese)

[6] Swaddiwudhipong, S., Lu, Hai-Rong, Wee, Tiong-Huan. Direct tension test and tensile strain capacity of concrete at early age, Cement and Concrete Research, 33 (2003), No. 12, 2077-2084.

SELF-CONSOLIDATING HIGH PERFORMANCE FIBER REINFORCED CONCRETE: SCHPFRC

Wen-Cheng Liao [1], Shih-Ho Chao [1], Sang-Yeol Park [2] and Antoine E. Naaman [1]

(1) University of Michigan, Ann Arbor, USA

(2) Cheju National University, Jeju-si, Korea

Abstract

Self-consolidating high performance fiber reinforced concrete (SCHPFRC) combines the self-consolidating property of self-consolidating concrete (SCC) with the strain-hardening and multiple cracking characteristics of high performance fiber reinforced cement composites (HPFRCC) [1, 2, 3]. SCHPFRC is a highly flowable, non-segregating concrete that can spread into place, fill the formwork, and encapsulate the reinforcing steel in typical concrete structures. It is being addressed as part of a project for the U.S. Network for Earthquake Engineering Simulation (NEES) with the objective to develop a SCHPFRC that can be easily manufactured and delivered by ready-mix trucks for use on the job site, with particular application in seismic resistant structures.

In this paper, the authors provide a brief summary of findings based on an extensive review of existing literature and numerous laboratory trials. Several SCHPFRC mixtures taken from previous studies were modified using the available local materials, leading to recommended mixtures with compressive strengths ranging from 35 to 65 MPa. These mixtures contain coarse aggregates having a 12 mm maximum size and 30 mm long steel fibers in volume fractions of 1.5% and 2%. The recommended SCHPFRC mixtures were achieved by adjusting the coarse to fine aggregate ratios, increasing paste volume, mixing in steps according to a pre-set procedure, and adding relevant admixtures. Spread diameter of the fresh SCHPFRC mixtures measured by using the standard slump flow test was approximately 600 mm. Results obtained from direct tensile tests showed that the strain-hardening response of the hardened composites were maintained up to large composite strains.

1. INTRODUCTION

Self-consolidating high performance fiber reinforced concrete (SCHPFRC) is the hybrid of self-consolidating concrete (SCC) and high performance fiber reinforced cement composites (HPFRCCs). It is a highly flowable, non-segregating concrete with a strain-hardening response under tension accompanied by multiple cracking. Six SCHPFRC mixtures with compressive strengths ranging from 35 to 65 MPa are recommended. These were first obtained from previous studies and modified using available local materials. Spread diameter of the fresh SCHPFRC mixtures measured by using the standard slump flow test was approximately 600 mm. Tensile response obtained from direct tensile tests showed that these composites exhibited significant strain-hardening behavior accompanied by multiple cracking. In addition, these mixtures were successfully used in large size applications; in some cases where heavier amount of reinforcing bars were present, minor vibration was needed.

2. PREVIOUS RESEARCH

Though adding fibers will extend the range of applications of SCC, a reduction in workability due to fiber addition may become a handicap in practice. Besides the fibers, there are also many parameters which affect the flowability of fresh SCC. Indeed, the type, diameter, aspect ratio, and volume fraction of fibers come in addition to the maximum aggregate size, coarse aggregate content, fine aggregate content to play an important role in flowability of SCC with fibers.

An earlier study by Swamy and Mangat [4] reported that the relative fiber-to-coarse aggregate volume and the fiber "balling up" phenomenon limit the maximum content of steel fibers. Edington et al [5] observed a relationship between the size of coarse aggregate and the fiber volume fraction. Narayanan and Kareem-Palanjian [6] found that the "optimum fiber content" (without balling) increased linearly with an increase in the percentage of sand to total aggregates. Johnston [7] remarked that the distribution of fibers and coarse aggregates was mainly determined by their relative sizes. While considering the effectiveness in the hardened state, Vandewalle [8] recommended choosing fibers longer than the maximum aggregate size. Grünewald [9] also suggested that the fiber length be 2 to 4 times that of the maximum coarse aggregate size, a recommendation similar to that generally suggested by ACI committee 544.

The addition of steel fibers into SCC mixtures has been studied by a number of researchers [10-13, 9, 14-21]. Moreover, numerous commercial laboratories have been involved in the development of SCC with fibers. Degussa Admixtures, Inc., (a division of Master Builders Technologies), which focuses on the development, manufacture and supply of chemicals and cementitious products for the construction industry, has been continuously improving the performance of SCC with fibers. Following are key findings based on their studies [15]:

1) The coarse-to-fine aggregate ratio in the mix needs to be reduced so that individual coarse aggregate particles are fully surrounded by a layer of mortar. Paste amount must be sufficient to fill the void between aggregates and fibers, and also cover around the aggregate particles and the fibers. Reduced coarse aggregate volume and higher paste volume are required for higher volume of fibers. Furthermore, it is recommended by [22] to reduce the volume of coarse aggregates at least 10 % compared with plain concrete to facilitate pumping.

2) Before addition of fibers, slump flow of SCC must be relatively high (as influenced by a lower coarse aggregate content, increased paste content, low water-to-powder ratio, increased superplasticizer rather than excess water, sometimes a viscosity modifying admixture). Johnston [22] indicated that initial slump of plain concrete should be 50 to 75 mm more than the desired final slump.

3) Everything else being equal, addition of fibers reduces slump flow of SCC; higher fiber volume and higher aspect ratio of fibers reduce slump flow of SCC as well, thereby leading to higher possibility of blocking.

3. EXPERIMENTAL PROGRAM

3.1 Materials

The cementitious materials used in this study are ASTM Type III Portland cement and a class C fly ash. The fine aggregate is #16 flint silica sand (ASTM 50-70). The coarse aggregate of 12 mm maximum size consists of solid crushed limestone or pea gravel from a local source with a density of 2.70 g/cm^3. Two polycarboxylate-based superplasticizers (SP1 and SP2) were used in all concrete mixtures. In addition to the superplasticizer, a viscosity modifying admixture (VMA) was used in some mixtures to enhance the viscosity and reduce fiber segregation in the presence of higher water to cementitious ratios. The physical and chemical properties of chemical admixtures are shown in Table 1. Two types of steel hooked fibers with circular cross section, one having high tensile strength (SF1) and the other one having regular tensile strength (SF2), were used. Table 2 gives the properties of fibers used.

Table 1: Physical and chemical properties of chemical admixtures used in this study

ID	Physical State	pH	Boiling Point (°C)	Freeze Point (°C)	Water Solubility	Specific Gravity	VOC* Concentration as applied (g/l)
SP 1	Liquid	5-7	100	N/A	Miscible	1.1	0
SP 2	Liquid	8.0	100	0	Completely soluble	1.002	0
VMA	Liquid	6.5	100	-6	Completely soluble	1.08	0

*VOC: Volatile Organic Compounds

Table 2: Properties of fibers used in this study

Fiber ID	Type	Diameter, (mm)	Length, (mm)	Density, (g/cc)	Tensile Strength, (MPa)	Elastic Modulus, (GPa)
SF 1	Hooked	0.38	30	7.85	2300	200
SF 2	Hooked	0.55	30	7.85	1100	200

3.2 Mix Proportions

Six different SCHPFRC mixtures were developed to cover a broad range of strength requirements. The mix proportions are summarized in Table 3. Their mechanical properties are described in Tables 4, 5, and 6. In this study, the amount of superplasticizer (SP) and the ratio of water-to-cementitious materials were selected as primary means to modify the compressive strengths. In addition, the fiber volume fraction for all mixtures was larger than or equal to 1.5%. Mixture 1 (Table 3) was the basis for numerous trial mixtures in extensive preliminary tests to estimate the feasibility of SCC with high volume fractions of fiber; the mixture was essentially taken from [15].

Table 3: Proportions by weight of cement for SCHPFRC mixtures used

Mix Proportion by weight of cement								
Series ID		Mix 1	Mix 2	Mix 3	Mix 4	Mix 5	Mix 6
Cement	C3*	1	1	1	1	1	1
Mineral Admixture	FA**	0.48	0.5	0.5	0.875	0.67	0.875
Fine Aggregates	Silica Sand (Flint)***	1.7	1.7	1.7	2.5	2.1	2.2
Coarse Aggregates	Crushed Limestone +	1.1	1	1	1.25		1.2
	Pea gravel ++					1.1	
Water	Water	0.45	0.6	0.6	0.84	0.67	0.8
Chemical Admixture	SP 1	0.027	0.015	0.01		0.013	
	SP 2 ×				0.0055		0.005
	VMA ×××		0.012	0.0095	0.065	0.013	0.038
Steel Fiber	SF 1		0.325	0.244	0.31	0.289	0.315
	SF 2	0.325					
Total Weight		5.082	5.152	5.0635	6.8455	5.871	6.433
V_f (%)		1.96	1.92	1.47	1.38	1.50	1.50

* ASTM Type III Portland cement; ** fly ash class C; *** ASTM 50-70; + max size about 12 mm; ++ max size about 8 mm; × these three chemical admixtures are typically added with the initial mix water and their concentration could be seen as 1.0; that is, it is not necessary to consider the amount of water in these chemical admixtures while calculating the total amount of water needed.

3.3 Mixing Procedure

Mixing procedure and mixing time are more critical in SCC as compared to conventional concrete mixtures. In addition, previous experimental studies suggest that each mixture proportion has its own optimum mix procedure, including the sequence by which different materials are placed in the mixer, the percentage of water demand added with time, the total time of mixing, and the total time of casting, etc. [23, 24, 19, 20, 9, 25]. Not only a minor change in proportioning, but a minor change in the mix procedure itself may change significantly the properties of freshly mixed concrete, such as its rheological behavior. The sequence of mixing is very important as well.

According to the previous research of various mixing procedures for SCC, the sequence of placing the various materials in the mixer plays an important role, especially when higher volume fraction of fibers are added. The advantages of two procedures found in prior studies have been incorporated in this study.

1) Pre-mixing water, SP, and VMA (if needed), then pouring the resulting fluid in several steps in order to develop a homogenous matrix without paste lumps before adding the coarse aggregates and fibers.

2) Reducing the coarse-to-fine aggregate ratio to provide a well-developed paste layer which can fully surround individual coarse aggregate. Paste amount must be sufficient not only to fill the void between aggregates and fibers, but also fully cover the aggregate particles and the fibers.

In this study the premixed liquid ((Water + SP + VMA (if needed)) was added in several steps as described below. This allowed supervision of the status of the mixtures in order to limit paste lumps. The following steps were used:

1) Dry-mix the cement, fly ash, and sand for 30 seconds.
2) Pour 1/2 of liquid (Water+SP+VMA) in the mixer. After mixing for about 1 minute, pour 1/4 of the remaining liquid (Water+SP+VMA).
3) After mixing for about 1 minute, pour 1/8 of liquid (Water+SP+VMA).
4) After mixing for about 1 minute, pour 1/16 of liquid (Water+SP+VMA).
5) After mixing for about 1 minute, pour all of the remaining liquid (Water+SP+VMA).
6) After mixing for about 1 minute, add all coarse aggregates in the mixer.
7) After mixing for about 2 minutes, slowly add all steel fibers in the mixer.
8) Continue mixing for about 3 minutes after all the fibers have been added. The mixture is then ready for pouring.

Note that if other types of SP and VMA are used, it is important to ascertain from the manufacturer's guidelines that they could be mixed together with the water in the same container, in order for the above procedure to succeed. It is also important to note that the quality of fresh SCHPFRC, such as flowability and segregation resistance, will be achieved only if the mix procedure is strictly followed.

3.4 Testing

The slump flow test (shown in Fig. 2(a); [26, 27, 19]), compression test [28], and direct tension test were carried out to estimate flowability, compressive strength, and tensile response, respectively.

The slump flow test was the easiest and most familiar way to evaluate the horizontal free flow (deformability) of SCC in the absence of obstructions. The test method is very similar to the conventional ASTM standard slump test of fresh concrete. However, instead of the loss in height, the diameter of the spread concrete is measured in two perpendicular directions and recorded as slump flow (Fig. 2(b)). In general, the average of diameters in two perpendicular directions should be larger than 600 mm for qualified SCC.

According to ASTM C39, the compressive strength of hardened concrete is determined from compression tests on standard cylindrical specimens. The cylinder specimens cast for this study had dimensions of 100 mm (diameter) × 200 mm (height). The cylinder specimens were submerged in water for curing after de-molding. During testing, 3 linear variable differential transformers (LVDTs) were used to measure the strains during compression tests.

The direct tension tests were needed to ascertain that the developed SCHPFRC composites give a strain-hardening response in tension after first cracking. Dog-bone shaped tensile specimens were prepared and tested for each SCHPFRC mixture. A typical specimen and the test setup are shown in Fig. 3. These specimens have a cross-sectional dimension of 25×50 mm. The applied load was monitored by the load cell of the testing machine and elongation was recorded by a pair of LVDTs attached to the specimen, with a gauge length of about 175 mm.

(a)   (b)

Figure 2: Slump flow test: (a) test setup; (b) Spreading diameter

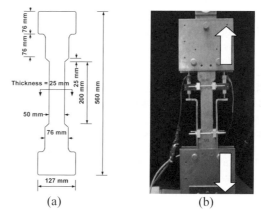

(a)   (b)

Figure 3: Photos illustrating the direct tensile test: (a) geometry of specimen; (b) test setup

4. EXPERIMENTAL RESULTS

4.1 Slump Flow Test

As described earlier, the final diameters of the concrete in two perpendicular directions were measured for each mix proportion, and are shown in Table 4.

Minor segregation was observed in Mix 1 which did not contain VMA. Because the mechanical performance of the hardened composite depends very much on fiber dispersion, it is better to trade off some loss in flowability for a reduced risk of segregation. Although the flowability of each SCHPFRC mixture was slightly lower than SCC without fibers, it can be considerably increased with a minimal external vibration.

4.2 Compressive Strength

The average compressive strengths of the mixtures with fibers tested in this study are shown in Table 4. Fig. 4(a) gives a comparison of the average compressive stress-strain curves for Mix 3, Mix 4, Mix 5 and Mix 6. As can be seen, SCHPFRCs behave as well-confined reinforced concrete in compression.

Table 4: Slump flow test results and average compressive strength (f_c) of SCHPFRCs

Series ID	Mix 1	Mix 2	Mix 3	Mix 4	Mix 5	Mix 6
Fiber Type (SF1: high strength, L/d=79; SF2: regular strength, L/d=50)	SF 2	SF 1	SF 1	SF 1	SF 1	SF 1
V_f (%)	1.96	1.92	1.47	1.38	1.50	1.50
Slump flow (mm)	565 578	518 525	603 601	582 568	613 602	579 552
(f_c) 14-day (MPa)	N/A	53.6	50.7	25	40.7	36.4
(f_c) 28-day (MPa)	65	67.9	65	36.4	43.6	39.3
(f_c) 90-day (MPa)	N/A	N/A	N/A	47.1	50	48.6

4.3 Tensile Response

As described earlier, the stress-strain curves were recorded from the dog-bone specimens tested. Typical curves are shown in Fig. 4(b). It can be observed that the tensile stress increases with an increase in strain after the first crack. Multiple cracks developed up to peak stress (post-cracking strength) at which crack localization occurred (Fig. 5). Thus these five mixtures all satisfy the requirement of strain-hardening behavior of HPFRCC. Beyond the peak stress, the tensile stress dropped gradually due to fiber pull out from the matrix. Some key results are summarized in Table 5. Tests for Mix 1 were not carried out.

Table 5: Average results of tensile tests for SCHPFRCs

Series ID	Mix 1	Mix 2	Mix 3	Mix 4	Mix 5	Mix 6
Average Post-Cracking Strength (MPa)	N/A	6.57	5.41	3.59	4.64	3.61
Average Strain at Peak Stress (%)	N/A	0.25	0.34	0.25	0.39	0.45
Stress at apparent strain = 0.5% (% of peak stress)	N/A	5.80 (88%)	4.85 (90%)	2.99 (83%)	3.86 (83%)	3.54 (98%)
Average Number of Cracks in the middle portion	N/A	5	9	6	9	6
Average Crack Spacing (mm)	N/A	29.7	18.0	25.7	18.0	25.6

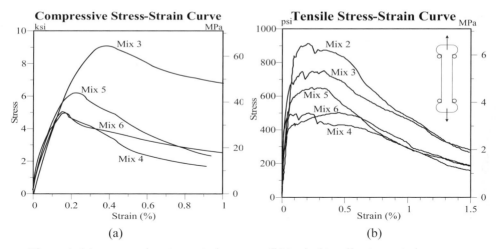

Figure 4: (a) compressive stress-strain curves; (b) typical tensile stress-strain curves

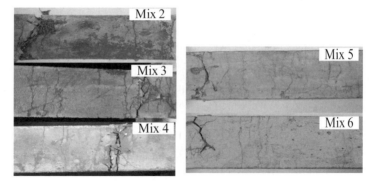

Figure 5: Multiple cracks observed in SCHPFRCs

5. CONCLUSIONS

Based on the experimental studies and analyses, the following conclusions can be drawn:

1. Flowability: only the slump flow test was used in this study to observe workability. Flow diameters about 600 mm were achieved in most cases. While the flowability of SCHPFRCs was not as high as for conventional SCC without fibers, it was deemed sufficient for practical implementation with slight vibration. In addition, larger scale specimens have been cast by using these mixtures and the flowability was quite satisfactory with no segregation observed (Fig. 6).

2. Segregation: segregation of fibers was greatly reduced by using viscosity modifying agent, VMA. The mixtures became viscous enough to bring fibers to the edge of the slump base plate during slump flow test.

3. Mixing Procedure: In order to achieve a good quality in fresh SCHPFRC mixtures, it is essential to strictly follow the recommended mixing procedure, in terms of time of mixing, addition of components, and sequence of material addition.
4. Mechanical Properties: Specimens made from the hardened composites were tested for compressive strength and tensile stress-strain response. The SCHPFRCs developed have compressive strengths ranging from about 35 to 65 MPa and a tensile strengths ranging from 3.5 to 6.5 MPa. They also showed strain-hardening response in tension, accompanied by multiple cracking. The peak strain capacity after first cracking in tension ranged from 0.25 % to 0.45 %.

(a)   (b)

Figure 6: Application of the developed SCHPFRC mixtures in larger scale specimens (a) SCHPFRC in the fresh state; (b) Pouring of coupling beam with minor vibration

ACKNOWLEDGEMENTS

The research described herein was sponsored by the National Science Foundation under Grant No. CMS 0530383 . The opinions expressed in this paper are those of the authors and do not necessarily reflect the views of the sponsor.

REFERENCES

[1] Naaman, A.E., "High Performance Fiber Reinforced Cement Composites," Proceedings of the IABSE Symposium on Concrete Structures for the Future, Paris, France, September 1987, pp. 371-376.
[2] Naaman, A. E., and Reinhardt, H. W., "Characterization of High Performance Fiber Reinforced Cement Composites—HPFRCC," High Performance Fiber Reinforced Cement Composites 2 (HPFRCC 2), Proceedings of the Second International RILEM Workshop, Naaman, A. E., and Reinhardt, H. W., eds., RILEM Publications, s.a.r.l., Cachan Cedex, France, 1996, pp. 1-24.
[3] Naaman, A. E., "Strain Hardening and Deflection Hardening Fiber Reinforced Cement Composites," HPFRCC 4 RILEM PRO 30, June 2003, pp. 95-113.
[4] Swamy, R.N. and Mangat, P.S., "Influence of fiber-aggregate interaction on some properties of steel fiber reinforced concrete," Materials and Structures, Volume 7, Number 5 / September 1974, pp. 307-314.
[5] Edgington, J.; Hannant, D. J.; Williams, R. I. T., "Steel fiber reinforced concrete," Fiber reinforced materials, The Construction Press, Lancaster, England, 1978, pp. 112-128.
[6] Narayanan, R., Kareem-Palanjian, A.S., "Factors influencing the workability of steel-fibre reinforced concrete," Concrete, Part 1: Vol.16, No. 10, 1982, pp.45-48, Part 2: Vol. 17, No. 2, 1982, pp. 43-44.

[7] Johnston, C.D., "Proportioning, mixing and placement of fibre-reinforced cements and concretes," Production Methods and Workability of Concrete, Edited by Bartos, Marrs and Cleland, E&FN Spon, London, 1996, pp. 155-179.

[8] Vandewalle, L., "Vezelversterkt Beton, Studiedag Speciale Betonsoorten en Toepassingen," Universiteit Leuven, Departement Burgerlijke Bouwkunde, 1993, pp. 77-98.

[9] Grünewald, Steffen, "Performance-based design of self-compacting fibre reinforced concrete," Ph.D. thesis, June 2006, p20-24.

[10] Groth, P. and Nemegeer, D., "The use of steel fibres in self-compacting concrete." In: Skarendahl A, Petersson O, editors. Proceedings of the first international RILEM symposium on self-compacting concrete. Stockholm, Sweden: 13-14 September 1999. pp. 497-507.

[11] Khayat, K. H. and Roussel, Y., "Testing and performance of fiber-reinforced, self-consolidating concrete." In: Skarendahl A, Petersson O, editors. Proceedings of the first international RILEM symposium on self-compacting concrete. Stockholm, Sweden: September 13-14, 1999. pp. 509-521.

[12] Massicotte, Bruno; Degrange, Gerard; Dzeletovic, Nikola, "Mix Design for SFRC Bridge Deck Construction," RILEM PRO15 Fibre-Reinforced Concretes BEFIB, 2000, pp. 119-128.

[13] Grünewald, Steffen and Walraven, Joost C., "Parameter-study on the influence of steel fibers and coarse aggregate content on the fresh properties of self-consolidating concrete," May 2001.

[14] Bui, V. K.; Geiker, M. R.; Shah, S. P., "Rheology of Fiber-Reinforced Cementitious Materials," RILEM PRO30 High Performance Fibre Reinforced Composites HPFRCC4, 2003, pp. 221-232.

[15] Bui, Van K. and Attiogbe, Emmmanuel., Degussa Admixtures, Inc., Seminar at UM on Oct. 27, 2005.

[16] Corinaldesi, V. and Moriconi, G., "Durable fiber reinforced self-compacting concrete," Cement and Concrete Research 34, 2004, pp. 249-254.

[17] Busterud, Lars; Johansen, Kåre and Døssland,Åse Lyslo, "Production of Fiber Reinforced SCC," SCC 2005, Session C-3: Fiber-Reinforced SCC, 2005.

[18] Dehn, Frank, Leipzig Germany, Private communication with Naaman, A.E., 2005.

[19] Sahmaran, Mustafa; Yurtseven, Alperen and Yaman, I. Ozgur, "Workability of hybrid fiber reinforced self-compacting concrete," Building and Environment 40, 2005, pp. 1672-1677.

[20] Sahmaran, Mustafa and Yaman, I. Ozgur, "Hybrid fiber reinforced self-compacting concrete with a high-volume coarse fly ash," Construction and Building Materials 21.1, Jan 2007, pp.150-156.

[21] Suter, R., and Butschi, P.Y., "Tunnel du Oenzberg / Voussoirs en Beton, avec ou sans fibres," in French, Mandat de Recherche No. P.0209, EIA-Fribourg, Switzerland, 2001.

[22] Johnston, C.D., "Fiber-Reinforced Cements and Concretes," Gordon and Breach Science Publishers, Amsterdam, 2001.

[23] Sedran, T., De Larrard, F., Hourst, F. y Contamines, C., "Mix design of self-compacting concrete," International RILEM Production Methods and Workability of Concrete, Edited by P.J.M. Bartos, D.L. Marrs y D.J. Cleand, Editorial: E & FN Spon, Londres, 1996, pp. 439-450.

[24] Brodowski, D., private communication with A.E. Naaman, 2005.

[25] Denarie, E., private communication with A.E. Naaman, 2006.

[26] EFNARC, "Specification and Guidelines for Self-Consolidating Concrete," February 2002.

[27] Nowak, Andrzej S.; Laumet, Pascal; Czarnecki, Artur A.; Kaszynska, Maria; Szerszen, Maria M. and Podhorecki, Piotr J., "US-Specific Self-Consolidating Concrete for Bridges," Final Report, July 2005.

[28] ASTM C39-96, "Standard Test Method for Compressive Strength of Cylindrical Concrete Specimens", West Conshohocken, PA., 1998.

PART FOUR

PERMEABILITY, DURABILITY AND TEMPERATURE EFFECTS

EFFECT OF CRACKING ON AIR-PERMEABILITY AND WATER AB-
SORPTION OF STRAIN HARDENING CEMENT-BASED COMPOSITES

Viktor Mechtcherine and Matthias Lieboldt

Institute for Building Materials, Technische Universitaet Dresden, Germany

Abstract

Strain-Hardening Cement-based Composites (SHCC) display a high strain capacity due to the gradual formation of a large number of fine, well-distributed cracks. The width of these cracks at strain levels, at least up to 1 %, is typically less than 0.1 mm. The influence of such cracking on transport properties of this new material, and subsequently on its durability, is still to be studied. The effect of cracking on air-permeability and water absorption of SHCC was investigated in the test series presented. Since testing of the material's transport properties was performed on unloaded specimens, special procedures were developed and applied in order to obtain characteristic crack widths that corresponded to the crack widths under loads at chosen strain levels. Both the air-permeability and water absorption clearly increased with increasing strain levels and related crack development. A strong correlation was found between the cumulative crack length at the specimen's surfaces and the transport properties under investigation. This paper includes a discussion on the testing procedures utilised and the results obtained, as well as considerations concerning further research in this area.

1.   INTRODUCTION

Most current applications of SHCC are non-structural. Fibre reinforcement is primarily used in controlling cracks due to shrinkage, as well as cracks induced by temperature change. However, considerable laboratory research has been performed in the last few years on the behaviour of structural members made of SHCC combined with conventional steel reinforcement.

In order to ensure the durability of the structure, first the durability of each of the applied materials should be assured. With regard to the durability of individual system components, and consequently, of the system as a whole, the following requirements could arise: (a) protection of steel reinforcement from corrosion; (b) durability of concrete (e.g., SHCC matrix); (c) fibre durability; and (d) absence of negative alterations to the bond (interface) properties between fibre and matrix. These complex durability issues can be influenced to a great extent by the transport properties of cementitious materials used as it was frequently shown for conventional reinforced concrete (requirements (a) and (b)); see e.g. [1], i.e. the transport behaviour of SHCC with regard to gases and fluids should be studied initially in order to provide basic information for subsequent investigations relative to given durability issues.

Apart from capillary porosity of the cement-based matrix and the bond interface between matrix and fibres, the transport properties of SHCC depend on the existing crack system. The design approach for elements made of SHCC implies that multiple cracking of this material may occur under operational conditions. Furthermore, it is reasonable to expect that elements made of SHCC, in general, may have a superior durability in comparison to conventional RC members [2] due to the presence of small crack widths (below 0.1 mm). Therefore, it appears necessary to explicitly consider the effect of cracking on the mass transport into and throughout SHCC.

First, two experimental procedures will be presented that were developed in order to obtain SHCC specimens with characteristic crack widths. Subsequently, the air-permeability and water absorption of SHCC will be investigated on both un-cracked and cracked material. The results obtained will be correlated to the strain levels applied during the preparation of the specimens, as well as to the cumulative crack lengths on each specimen's surface(s). Furthermore, the experimental results, the suitability of the test methods used, and the evaluation procedure will be discussed and conclusions regarding further purposeful examinations of the transport properties of SHCC will be developed.

2.   MATERIAL COMPOSITION AND GENERATION OF CRACKS

An SHCC with 2.25% by volume of PVA (Polyvinyl-Alcohol) fibres with a length of 12 mm was used for the experiments. This material was developed in previous investigations by the authors [3]. The composition of SHCC is given in Table 1. The details on the material design and the mechanical performance may be found in [3].

Table 1: Composition of SHCC used for the experiments

Cement [kg/m³]	Fly ash [kg/m³]	Quartzsand [kg/m³]	Water [kg/m³]	SP [kg/m³]	VA [kg/m³]	PVA fibers [kg/m³]
320	750	535	335	16.1	3.2	29.3

In monotonic tensile tests on dog-bone shaped prisms accompanying this research program, an average ultimate strain (strain capacity) of over 5 % was attained while the average values of the stress at first crack and tensile strength were 3.64 MPa and 4.29 MPa, respectively. The prisms had a cross-section of 60 mm by 100 mm; the gauge length was 250 mm; cf. Fig. 1. The loading was induced into the specimen via non-rotatable steel plates. The details concerning the production of the prisms and the test set-up are given in [3].

The same set-up and prism geometry were used for crack-generation test and subsequently for the production of the specimens for material transport property tests; cf. Fig. 1. Since the testing of the transport properties was performed on unloaded specimens, special procedures had been developed and applied in order to obtain characteristic crack widths that corresponded to the crack widths under loads at chosen strain levels.

The first procedure implied a deformation-controlled cyclic loading of the specimen in uniaxial tension until the strain remaining after unloading reached a desired value (e.g., 1%); cf. Fig. 2(a). In the second procedure, the tensile loading was first performed under deformation control until the strain value (e.g. 1%) chosen was attained in the loaded state. The load control was then applied to keep the attained stress constant in order to perform a kind of creep test; cf. Fig. 2(b). The loading continued until the strain increased by approximately 50% of the initial value; the specimens were then unloaded.

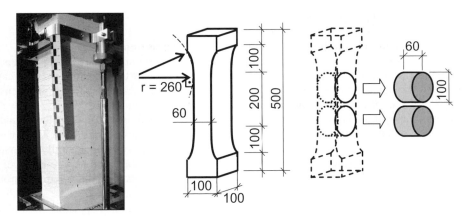

Figure 1: (a) Set-up of the loading in tension, (b) specimen geometry used for pre-damage of SHCC, and (c) location of specimens used for the testing of transport properties

These two methods delivered slightly different results with regard to the number of cracks and crack widths; however, in both cases, values were close to those of the crack characteristics observed under loads at corresponding strain levels.

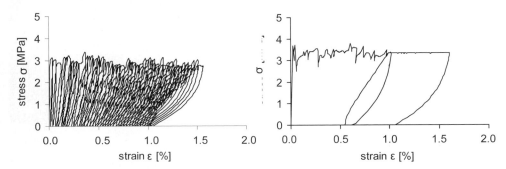

Figure 2: Representative stress-strain curves obtained from the tension tests used for pre-damage of SHCC for subsequent investigation of transport properties: (a) cyclic loading, (b) "creep" loading

The procedures described for the generation of cracks were performed at a concrete age of 28 days. The prisms were wrapped in foil and stored at room temperature prior to testing. Two cylinders, each with a diameter of 100 mm and a height of 60 mm, were extracted from each pre-damaged prisms by coring after crack generation was induced by tensile loading according to predefined strain levels; these strain levels ranged from 0% to 1%; cf. Fig. 1(c). A few cores were also taken from unloaded, undamaged prisms for reference.

3.   AIR-PERMEABILITY TESTS

3.1   Specimen preparation, test set-up and measuring technique

In total, 46 cored, cylindrical specimens (Ø 100 mm, h = 60 mm; cf. Fig. 1(c)) were tested. The cylinders were dried until mass stability was reached in order to remove water from capillaries and exclude the possible effect of varying moisture content of SHCC. The specimens, at an age of 45 to 50 days, were stored in standard climatic conditions (i.e., 20 °C / 65 % RH) for a minimum of 24 hours before testing. Additionally, the front surfaces of the cylinders were investigated and the crack pattern was recorded. These crack widths were, in all cases, smaller than 0.1 mm; the number of cracks differed significantly and, generally, increased with increasing strain levels. In order to quantify the degree of the specimen pre-damage, the cumulative crack length was measured for each individual cylinder, while only pass-through cracks (i.e., cracks going completely through the specimen) were considered.

Fig. 3 shows a schematic view of the test set-up used. A cylindrical specimen was placed in a metal test cell (Fig. 4) with an inflatable rubber cuff used to seal the lateral surfaces of the cylinder by means of the 500 kPa air pressure. Pressure levels ranging between 20 and 200 kPa were used for measuring air-permeability. Measurement began only after a constant pressure, stationary flow condition was attained (i.e., linear pressure distribution through the thickness of the cylinder). The flow rate was determined by using a gas meter to measure the runtime of a bubble in a measuring burette from one light reflection barrier to another.

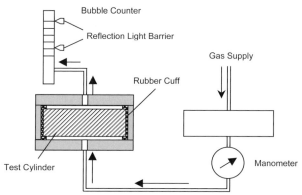
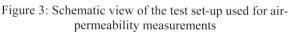

Figure 3: Schematic view of the test set-up used for air-permeability measurements

Figure 4: Test cell for the air-permeability testing

3.2   Test results

The calculation of the specific gas permeability was performed according to [4] using eq.1. This formula is analogue to the Hagen-Poiseuille's relationship.

$$k = \eta \frac{2 \cdot V \cdot p_0 \cdot h}{A \cdot t \cdot \left(p^2 - p_a^2\right)} \tag{1}$$

where: k is the permeability coefficient [m²]; η the dynamic viscosity of air [Ns/m²]; V the flow volume [m³]; p_0 the absolute pressure (atmospheric) during measurements [kPa]; h the thickness in [m]; A the surface area [m²]; t the flow time [s]; p the input absolute pressure [kPa] and p_a the outlet absolute pressure (atmospheric pressure) [kPa].

The calculations that use this formula are accurate for uncracked specimens only since this law implies a laminar flow in the pore system of the material tested. According to eq. 1 the gas permeability coefficient k for uncracked SHCC had an average value of $8.4 \cdot 10^{-16}$ m² which falls within the value range of conventional concrete [4] from 10^{-14} by 10^{-19} m².

The volume flow rate was considered instead of the permeability coefficient for the quantification of results on cracked specimens since an undefined flow modus exists within the crack pattern. A comparison of the individual results is meaningful, provided that the measurements are performed with constant pressure, temperature and same shaped specimens. All these requirements were met.

Preliminary tests with various pressure levels showed that a pressure difference of 50 kPa was suitable for the measurement of volume flow for the entire test spectrum, i.e., for all cracked specimens examined. The volume flow rate obtained for this pressure level is shown in Fig. 5 as a function of the cumulative crack length determined for each individual specimen. A pronounced linear correlation was derived between these two parameters in the strain range examined.

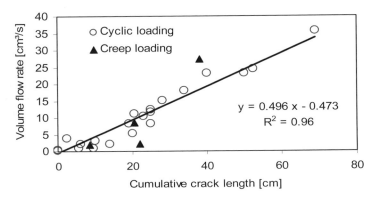

Figure 5: Effect of the cumulative crack length on the air volume flow rate (cylinders with Ø 100 mm and h = 60 mm; applied pressure 50 kPa; room temperature)

The correlation found between the volume flow rate and the remaining, induced non-elastic, average strain (the result of the tensile loading preceding air-permeability tests) was much less pronounced, although evident; cf. Fig. 6. In tests for smaller strain levels, the crack distribution (crack density) was quite uneven relative to the length of the dog-bone shaped prisms. As a result, for the same given average strain, various numbers of cracks were counted for individual cylindrical specimens taken from the cracked prisms at different sections. This explains a strong scattering of the results when the average strain is used as a measure of material damage instead of the cumulative crack length. Nevertheless, a linear correlation can be established between the volume flow rate and the values of the non-elastic strain. Based on such regression functions, for instance, it can be stated that the volume flow increased from 0.35 cm³/s, as measured on the uncracked cylinders, to approximately

30 cm³/s for specimens with induced non-elastic strain of 1 %, i.e., by a factor 86 under the given test conditions.

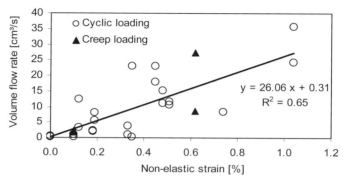

Figure 6: Effect of the non-elastic strain on air volume flow rate (cylinders with Ø 100 mm and h = 60 mm; applied pressure 50 kPa; room temperature)

4. WATER ABSORPTION TESTS

4.1 Preparation of the specimens and test procedure
The cylinders, already pre-conditioned as described in Section 3.1, were used for measuring the area-related capillary water absorption W_{ak} after air-permeability tests were completed. The lateral surfaces of the cylinders were coated with a waterproof sealant before immersing one of each specimen's front faces 5 mm deep into a water bath for at least 72 h for this purpose. These tests were performed under standard climatic conditions (20 °C / 65 % RH). The amount of water absorbed was determined at given time intervals from these data, and the area-related capillary water absorption were calculated according to the procedure described in [4, 5].

4.2 Test results
The water absorption coefficient w_{24}, which corresponds to the average area-related capillary water absorption per time unit during the first 24 hours after immersing the specimen in water, was calculated for a straightforward but robust evaluation of the tests results. The choice of this parameter, instead of the "usual" water absorption coefficient w, resulted from the fact that a linear relationship cannot always be found between water absorption and the square root of time, which may primarily be traced back to the swelling of specimens.

The average value measured for the water absorption coefficient w_{24} was 260 g/(m²·h$^{0.5}$) for uncracked specimens. The cumulative crack length on the front face, in contact with water, was used as a suitable scale basis in order to evaluate the results of the tests on cracked SHCC. A linear relationship was observed between the water absorption and the cumulative crack length (Fig. 7).

Only a weak correlation was found between the capillary water absorption and the non-elastic strain induced prior to transport measurement similarly to the results obtained from the air-permeability tests. Once again, this can be traced to a less-than-distinctive relationship between the cumulative crack length of individual cylinders tested, the decisive parameter for transport properties of SHCC, and the average strain level attained for the entire dog-bone prisms. Fig. 7 shows exemplary strain bands corresponding to given water absorption coeffi-cients w_{24}.

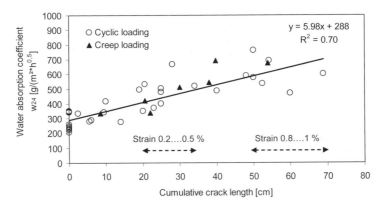

Figure 7: Effect of the cumulative crack length on the water absorption coefficient w_{24} as measured for cylindrical specimens with a diameter of 100 mm and a height of 60 mm

From analysis of the data, the water absorption coefficient w_{24} doubles, for example, at a strain level of 0.5 % ($w_{24} = 525$ g/ (m²·h$^{0.5}$)) compared to the w_{24} value obtained for the un-cracked material. According to [6], a material with a water absorption coefficient of 500 to 2000 g/(m²·h$^{0.5}$) can be referred to as "water retardant". In the case of SHCC investigated, this corresponds to the performance of the cracked specimens from prisms with a non-elastic strain of approximately 0.5 % to 1 %. According to this classification, SHCC investigated displayed a "water repellent" property (i.e., water absorption coefficient less than 500 g/ (m²·h$^{0.5}$)), when pre-loaded up to a stain level below 0.5 %.

5.   DISCUSSION AND OUTLOOK

The results obtained from the air-permeability tests and water absorption tests clearly show the effect of cracks in SHCC on the transport properties of this material, while the condition of the crack system is the decisive parameter. A "close-to-reality" quantification of the crack sys-tem condition is a challenging task which not only implies a very accurate recording and evaluation of the geometry of the surface cracks (crack widths and lengths), but also the conti-nuity of cracks throughout a specimen. In the present study, the cumulative length of pass-through cracks was used as a rough approximation to describe the cracks on a basis of a visual inspection of both front sides of the cylinders tested. An attempt to "look inside the specimen" using computer tomography has thus far only enabled to trace wide cracks. The relatively large size of the specimens limited the resolution of these measurements so that no detailed image of the entire crack system was obtained. In the on-going work of the authors, the performance of photogrammetry procedures has been tested which should enable recording and automatic evaluation of local displacements including accurate monitoring of cracking during tension tests preceding the testing of transport properties. This procedure should deliver both the information on the distribution of local strains throughout the specimen length and a quantitative description of all surface cracks. Furthermore, specimens will be impregnated after the transport testing using fluorescent epoxy resin and subsequently cut into slices and studied using equipment for image analyses for the investigation of the internal crack system.

The results obtained from the air-permeability testing are valid for the material investigated for applied pre-treatment and would differ with changing moisture content. This effect should be investigated in the future work. Since, the volume flow rate must be used as a transport measure for cracked SHCC instead of the permeation coefficient, a comparison to the performance of other materials can be only made if the same testing condition are used (specimen geometry, air pressure, etc.). Therefore, a standardised procedure should be adopted by the SHCC community.

Certainly, also time-dependent micro-structural changes due to continuing hydration, pozzolanic reactions, and carbonization should be considered explicitly in the future work, for all types of transport mechanisms. For this, the transport processes in uncracked material must be studied, as well. In particular, the effect of the bond interface between fibre and cement-based matrix on the transport of fluid and gases must be evaluated using morphological investigations.

Finally, it should be underlined that the investigation of transport properties is only the first step toward the estimation of durability of the material, itself, and structures built from it. Great efforts are needed in order to be able to define threshold values which would ensure an unerring durability design of structures made of SHCC. For this, a great deal of conceptual work must be performed along with extensive durability experiments (e.g., carbonation, frost, etc.).

6.   SUMMARY

Procedures for testing of transport behaviour of cracked SHCC was developed and tested. The air-permeability and capillary water absorption increased linearly with increasing non-elastic strain levels imposed on the specimens or the cumulative crack length. The air-permeability coefficient obtained for the uncracked SHCC was in the range for conventional concretes.

The capillary water absorption at strain levels of up to 1% was comparable to the corresponding behaviour of uncracked ordinary concrete. SHCC was classified as water repellent for strains imposed below 0.5%.

Much work must still be done in order to describe the transport of fluids and gases through crack systems in SHCC. Further research on the durability performance of SHCC is needed, as well, and an effort must be made to establish a quantitative link between the transport properties of SHCC and the durability of structures made of this new material.

REFERENCES

[1] Hilsdorf, H. K., Schönlin, K., Tauscher, F.: Durability of concrete. Beton-Verlag GmbH, Düsseldorf, 1997 (in German).

[2] Li, V. C., Stang, H.: Elevating FRC material ductility to infrastructure durability. Proceedings of BEFIB, pp. 171-186, 2004.

[3] Mechtcherine, V., Schulze, J.: Ultra-ductile concrete – material design concept and testing. CPI Concrete Plant International, No. 5, pp. 88-98, 2005.

[4] Bunke, N.: Testing of concrete – Recommendations and references as a complement to DIN 1048. DAfStb, Vol. 422, Beuth Verlag GmbH, Berlin, 1991 (in German).

[5] DIN 52617: Determination of the water absorption coefficient of building materials, 1987-05.

[6] Hohmann, R., Setzer, J.: Formula and tables for conctruction physics. Werner-Verlag GmbH, Düsseldorf, 1995 (in German).

EFFECT OF CRACKING AND HEALING ON DURABILITY OF ENGINEERED CEMENTITIOUS COMPOSITES UNDER MARINE ENVIRONMENT

Mo Li, Mustafa Sahmaran, and Victor C. Li

Department of Civil and Environmental Engineering, University of Michigan, USA

ABSTRACT

Engineered Cementitious Composites (ECC) offer significant potential for durable civil infrastructures under marine environment, due to its high tensile strain capacity of more than 3%, and controlled micro-crack width of less than 60 μm. An experimental study was designed to investigate the durability of ECC material with regard to cracking and healing under combined mechanical loading and environmental loading conditions. ECC coupon specimens were firstly preloaded under uniaxial tension to different strain levels, and then exposed to a chloride environment for 1, 2 and 3 months and subsequently reloaded up to failure. The reloaded specimens retained multiple micro-cracking behavior and tensile strain capacity of more than 3%, although the average crack width increases from 40 μm to 100 μm and the tensile strength was reduced by 10%. The test results indicated strong evidence of self-healing of the micro-cracked ECC material, which can still carry considerable tensile stress and strain. The phenomenon of self-healing effectively closes the microcracks. These results confirmed that ECC, both uncracked and micro-cracked, remain durable despite exposure to a severe marine environment.

1. INTRODUCTION

Cracking is usually a result of various physical and chemical interactions between concrete and its environment, and it may occur at different stages throughout the life of a structure. The durability of concrete structures is commonly affected by the presence of cracks. Cracks can reduce the strength and stiffness of the concrete structure and accelerate the ingress of aggressive ions, leading to other types of concrete deterioration and resulting in further cracking and disintegration [1]. Concrete shrinkage, thermal deformations, chemical reactions, poor construction practices and mechanical loads are some of the causes of cracks in concrete [2]. A summary of maximum allowable crack widths in various codes and specifications by technical committees for design of reinforced concrete structures in marine exposure is shown in Figure 1. As seen from Figure 1, the most stringent requirements are specified by JSCE and ACI 224.

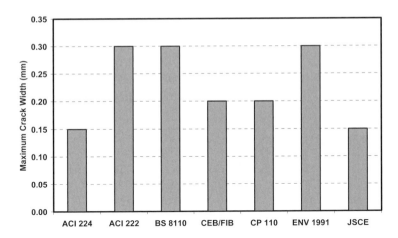

Figure 1: Comparison of allowable crack widths: Marine exposure [2-8]

Self healing is generally attributed to the hydration of previously unhydrated cementitious material, calcite formation, expansion of the concrete in the crack flanks, crystallization, closing of cracks by solid matter in the water and closing of the cracks by spalling of loose concrete particles resulting from cracking [9]. Self healing of cracks should also be taken into account when specifying tolerable crack widths. Evardsen [10], and Reinhardt and Jooss [11] proposed that cracks of less than 0.1 mm can easily be closed by self healing process.

Despite extensive research, reliable crack width control using steel reinforcements in concrete structures remains difficult to be realized in practice. Recently, a new high performance cementitious composite has been developed by Li and co-workers [12] called Engineered Cementitious Composites (ECC). ECC is a high performance fiber reinforced cementitious composite with substantial benefit in both high ductility and improved durability due to tight crack width. By employing micromechanics-based material design, maximum ductility in excess of 3% under uniaxial tensile loading can be attained, and ECC changes the cracking behavior from a single crack with large crack width to multiple microcracks. Even at large imposed deformation, crack widths of ECC remain nearly constant, less than 70 µm, while the number of cracks increases. Figure 2 shows a typical uniaxial tensile stress-strain curve of an ECC containing 2% PVA fiber. The characteristic strain-hardening after first cracking is accompanied by multiple micro-cracking. The crack width development during inelastic straining is also shown in Figure 2. Even at ultimate load, the crack width remains on the order of 50 µm to 70 µm. Under marine environment, ECC's tight crack width can greatly reduce the chloride penetration rate, and its tensile ductility helps prevent spalling resulting from the expansion of the corroding reinforcement.

Little research has been conducted on the long term durability of ECC in the cracked and uncracked state, and self healing of fine cracks under marine environment. In this study, an experimental program was designed to investigate the durability of ECC material under combined mechanical loading and environmental loading conditions. ECC coupon specimens were preloaded under uniaxial tension to the strain of 0.5%, 1.0% and 1.5%, to simulate different strain levels applied to an in-service structure. The pre-applied strain can be a combination of strain due to vehicle load, prestressing load, shrinkage, thermal load, etc. Later on, the specimens were exposed to a chloride environment with the chloride concentration of 3% for 1, 2 and 3 months and subsequently reloaded up to failure. The effect of autogenous healing was assessed by measuring the retained stiffness, ultimate tensile strength and tensile strain capacity of ECC.

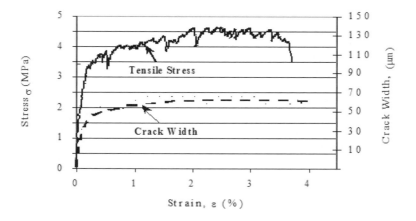

Figure 2: Uniaxial tensile stress-strain curve and crack development of ECC

2. EXPERIMENTAL PROGRAM

2.1 Mixture Proportions

The mix proportions for ECC are summarized in Table 1. The materials used were ordinary Portland cement, silica sand passing 200 μm sieve with average grain size 110 μm, Class-F fly ash, high range water reducer (HRWR), poly-vinyl-alcohol (PVA) fiber and water. A special poly-vinyl-alcohol (PVA) fiber designed particularly for ECC applications is used at 2% (by volume) in this ECC mixture. This fiber has a length of 8 mm, a diameter of 39 μm, and a nominal tensile strength of 1620 MPa. The density of the PVA fiber is 1300 kg/m³.

ECC mixture was prepared in a standard mortar mixer. The mixing sequence is as follows: the cement, fly ash, sand and water were first mixed, and then the HRWR was slowly added while mixing continued, and finally the fiber was incorporated. From ECC mixture, 152.4 × 76.2 × 12.7 mm³ coupon specimens were prepared for the direct uniaxial tensile test. The fresh ECC was then covered with plastic sheets and demoulded after 24 h. The specimens were cured in plastic bag at 95 ± 5% RH, 23 ± 2 °C for 6 days. The specimens were then left to cure in laboratory air, under uncontrolled conditions of humidity and temperature until the age of 28 days for testing. The direct tensile cracks were introduced in the coupon specimens as described in the next section. After pre-cracking, these specimens were stored in sodium chloride solution. For control study, some specimens without precracking were cured in laboratory air and then exposed to sodium chloride solution.

Table 1. Mixture properties of ECC by weight

	ECC (M45)
FA/C	1.2
W/CM*	0.27
Water (W), kg/m^3	331
Cement (C), kg/m^3	570
Fly ash (FA), kg/m^3	684
Sand (S), kg/m^3	455
Fiber (PVA), kg/m^3	26
High range water reducer (HRWR), kg/m^3	5.1

* CM: Cementitious materials (PC+FA)

2.2 Pre-Cracking and Uniaxial Tensile Testing

After 28 days of curing, the coupon specimens were pre-loaded to 0.5, 1.0 and 1.5% direct tensile strain to achieve various amounts of microcracking before exposure to sodium chloride solution. Before testing, aluminum plates were glued to both ends of the coupon specimen to facilitate gripping. Tests were conducted on an MTS machine with 25 kN capacity under displacement control at a rate of 0.005 mm/s. Typical stress-strain curves of the preloaded specimens are shown in Figure 3.

The pre-cracked ECC specimens were then continuously immersed in a 3% NaCl solution at room temperature, together with some uncracked specimens without preloading, for 30, 60 and 90 days. Subsequently direct tensile measurements on these specimens were conducted and stress-strain curves were recorded. In the case of uncracked specimens, average strain capacity and ultimate strength of ECC are an average of four specimens. In the case of pre-cracked specimens, average strain capacity and ultimate strength of ECC are calculated from a minimum of four and maximum of six specimens. The sodium chloride solution was replaced with a fresh solution every month.

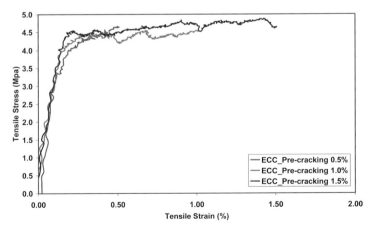

Figure 3: Typical pre-cracking tensile stress-strain curves of ECC

3. EXPERIMENTAL RESULTS AND DISCUSSION

Table 2 summarized the tensile strain capacity, tensile strength, and crack width of ECC with various preloaded strain value, and NaCl exposure conditions. Typical tensile stress-strain curves obtained for specimens before and after exposure to NaCl solution are shown in Figure 4. For the uncracked specimens, exposure to NaCl appears to reduce the cracking strength and ultimate strength by about 10%. However, the tensile strain capacity does not appear to be affected. For the pre-cracked specimens, exposure to NaCl appears to be similarly affected, such that the influence of pre-cracking even up to 1.5% does not exacerbate the deterioration.

Table 2. Tensile Properties of ECC under different NaCl exposure conditions

Curing Condition	Pre-loaded Strain (%)	Tensile Strain Capacity (%)	Ultimate tensile strength (MPa)	Average crack width (μm)
28 days air + 30 days air or NaCl	0.0 (Air curing)	2.86 ± 0.58	4.81 ± 0.64	~ 45
	0.0 (3% NaCl)	2.79 ± 0.54	4.34 ± 0.62	~ 100
	0.5 (3% NaCl)	3.85 ± 0.61	4.59 ± 0.29	~ 100
	1.0 (3% NaCl)	2.66 ± 0.66	3.85 ± 0.09	~ 100
	1.5 (3% NaCl)	2.48 ± 0.94	3.87 ± 0.73	~ 100
28 days air + 60 days air or NaCl	0.0 (Air curing)	2.51±0.19	4.75 ± 0.32	~ 35
	0.0 (3% NaCl)	2.37±0.50	4.25 ± 0.47	~ 100
	0.5 (3% NaCl)	3.16±0.26	4.05 ± 0.47	~ 100
	1.0 (3% NaCl)	3.28± 0.42	4.18 ± 0.22	~ 100
	1.5 (3% NaCl)	2.97± 0.69	4.07 ± 0.47	~ 80
28 days air + 90 days air or NaCl	0.0 (Air curing)	2.51±0.19	4.75 ± 0.32	~ 35
	0.0 (3% NaCl)	2.37±0.50	4.25 ± 0.47	~ 100
	0.5 (3% NaCl)	3.16±0.26	4.05 ± 0.47	~ 100
	1.0 (3% NaCl)	3.28± 0.42	4.18 ± 0.22	~ 100
	1.5 (3% NaCl)	2.97± 0.69	4.07 ± 0.47	~ 80

Figure 4 shows also the tensile properties of ECC specimens that had been pre-cracked to 0.5, 1.0% and 1.5% strain levels, then unloaded, and reloaded 1 day after pre-cracked. Thus these specimens had no time to undergo any crack healing which is found in specimens exposed to NaCl solution. As expected, there is a remarkable difference in initial stiffness between virgin specimen and pre-cracked specimen under direct tension. This is due to re-opening of cracks within pre-cracked specimens during reloading [13]. The opening of these cracks offers very little resistance to load, as the crack simply opens to its previous crack width before fiber bridging is re-engaged. Once fiber bridging is re-engaged, however, the load capacity resumes, and further tensile straining of the intact material can take place.

By comparing the initial material stiffness of reloaded ECC specimens exposed to NaCl solution in Figure 4, it can be observed that a significant recovery of mechanical stiffness has been achieved. This suggests that between the time of inducing pre-cracking and the time of testing, after exposure to NaCl solution, healing of the micro-cracks has occurred in the ECC specimens. This can be attributed primarily to the high cementitious material content and relatively low water to binder ratio within the ECC mixture. As a result of the formation of micro-cracks due to mechanical loading, unhydrated cementitious particles are easily exposed to the sodium chloride solution during the immersion period, which leads to development of further hydration processes. Finally micro-cracks under conditions of a damp environment were closed by newly formed products. These investigations indicated that the formation of re-hydration products in micro-cracks is possible. In ECC, the re-healing process is especially aided by the innately tight crack width.

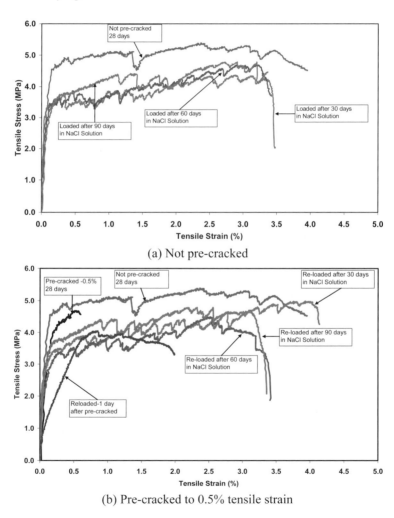

(a) Not pre-cracked

(b) Pre-cracked to 0.5% tensile strain

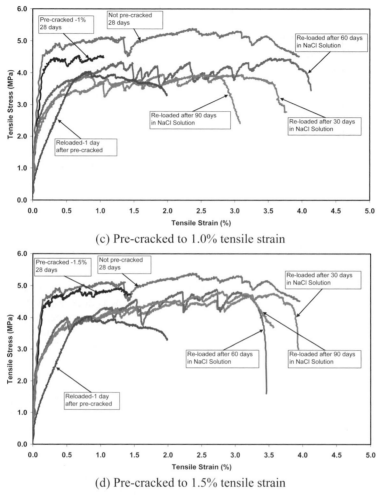

(c) Pre-cracked to 1.0% tensile strain

(d) Pre-cracked to 1.5% tensile strain

Figure 4: Tensile stress-tensile strain curves of ECC specimens before and after exposed to 3% NaCl solution

The average ultimate tensile strength values are shown in Figure 5. Compared to control specimens cured in laboratory air, the test results indicate that the specimens (pre-cracked and uncracked) stored in sodium chloride solution show a 10% reduction in ultimate tensile strength for all exposure ages; this may be attributed to the effects of leaching of calcium hydroxide from the specimens. Water not saturated with calcium hydroxide (high-calcium hydrated lime) may affect test results due to leaching of lime from the test specimens [14]. However, more experimental studies on a micro-mechanical scale are necessary to understand the reasons of the reduction in the ultimate tensile strength and increased crack width.

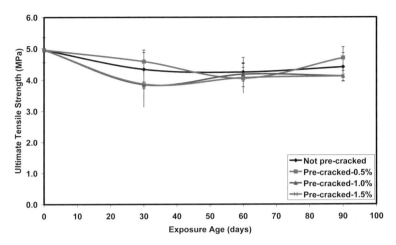

Figure 5: Influence of sodium chloride solution and mechanical loading on ECC ultimate tensile strength

Figure 6 shows the average of tensile strain capacity of ECC specimens stored in NaCl solution. The tensile strain capacity reported for these specimens does not include the residual strain from the pre-cracking load. By neglecting this residual strain, the large variability in material relaxation during unloading is avoided, and a conservative estimation for ultimate strain capacity of the material is presented. The tensile strain capacity of uncracked and pre-cracked ECC specimens exposed to NaCl solution averaged between 2.4% and 3.8%. This value is higher than or similar to that of air cured specimens (averaging 2.5% to 2.8%).

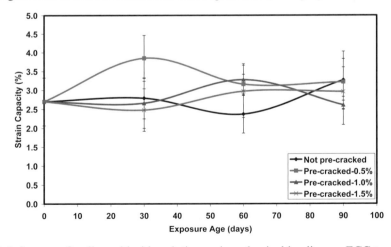

Figure 6: Influence of sodium chloride solution and mechanical loading on ECC tensile strain capacity

In the case of pre-cracked specimens exposed to NaCl solution, a distinct white deposit was visible, which formed a continuous dense layer over the crack surface (Figure 7). The deposits were most probably caused by efflorescence due to the leaching of calcium hydroxide into cracks [15]. It has also been suggested that in marine environment this effect may arrest chloride transportation by healing of cracks. From the present study, healing of micro-cracks of ECC under NaCl solution is evident from the mechanical properties discussed before. The mechanical properties indicate that micro-cracks of ECC exposed to NaCl solution healed almost completely. This can be attributed primarily to the high cementitious material content and relatively low water to binder ratio within the ECC mixture. The continued hydration of unhydrated cementitious material cause the self-healing of the crack and then may also reduce the ingress of aggressive ions.

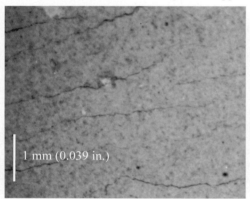
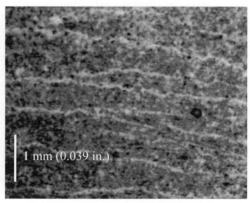

(a) ECC cracks before NaCl exposure   (b) ECC cracks after NaCl exposure

Figure 7: Self healing products in ECC microcracks before and after salt ponding test

4. CONCLUSION

Specimens pre-loaded up to 1.5% strain capacity showed almost complete recovery of stiffness when re-loaded in direct tensile tests even after periods of only one month in NaCl solution exposure. Preloaded ECC specimens with microcracks at 45 μm crack width induced by mechanical loading and then exposed to sodium chloride solution almost fully recovered their tensile strain. However, both pre-cracked and uncracked ECC specimens exposed to NaCl solution lost more than 10% of their ultimate tensile strength due to the leaching of calcium hydroxide under sodium chloride solution for all exposure ages. Furthermore, the crack width increased to around 100 μm compared with 45 μm in air curing condition. This phenomenon suggests possible change in the fiber/matrix interface bond properties. Microcracks of ECC specimen that were subjected to sodium chloride solution appear completely sealed as a result of self-healing. Hence, it is expected that transport properties recover to their original values before microcracking occurs.

The results presented in this study provide a preliminary database for the durability of cracked and uncracked ECC under combined mechanical loading and marine environmental loading conditions. For a complete understanding of durability of ECC in marine environment, it will be necessary to conduct further research on a micro-mechanical scale to investigate changes of ECC matrix toughness and fiber/matrix interface properties.

REFERENCES

[1]   Mehta, P. K., and Gerwick, B. C., "Cracking-Corrosion Interaction in Concrete Exposed to Marine Environment," *Concrete International,* V. 4, No. 10, Oct. 1982, pp. 45-51.

[2]   ACI Committee 224R-2001, Control of Cracking in Concrete Structures, ACI Manual of Concrete Practice, Part 3, American Concrete Institute, Farmington Hills, Michigan, 2001.

[3]   British Standards Institution. ENV 1991-1-1, BSI, London (1992).

[4]   British Standards Institution. BS 8110: Pt.1, BSI, London (1997).

[5]   CEB-FIP Model Code 1990, CEB Information Report No. 213/214, Comite Euro-International DuBeton, Lausanne, May 1993.

[6]   Code of Practice for the Structural Use of Concrete - Part 1. Design, Materials and Workmanship, British Standards Institution Publication CP 110, London, England, November 1972 (Amended May 1977).

[7]   Standard Specification for Design and Construction of Concrete Structures - 1986, Part 1 (Design), Japan Society of Civil Engineers, SP-1, Tokyo, Japan, 1986.

[8]   ACI Committee 222, "Corrosion of Metals in Concrete," ACI 222R-89, American Concrete Institute, Detroit, Michigan.

[9]   Ramm, W., and Biscoping, M., "Autogenous healing and reinforcement corrosion of water-penetrated separation cracks in reinforced concrete." Nuclear Engineering and Design 179, 191-200, 1998.

[10]   Evardsen, C. "Water Permeability and Autogenous Healing of Cracks in Concrete" ACI Materials Journal. Vol. 96 No. 4. 1999. pp. 448-454.

[11]   Reinhardt, H.W., Jooss, M. "Permeability and self-healing of cracked concrete as a function of temperature and crack width" Cement and Concrete Research. Vol. 33 (2003), pp 981-985.

[12]   Li, V.C., "High Performance Fiber Reinforced Cementitious Composites as Durable Material for Concrete Structure Repair," Int'l J. for Restoration of Buildings and Monuments, Vol. 10, No 2, 163–180 (2004).

[13]   Y. Yang, M.D. Lepech, V.C. Li, Self-healing of ECC under cyclic wetting and drying, Proceedings of Int'l workshop on durability of reinforced concrete under combined mechanical and climatic loads, Qingdao, China, 2005, pp. 231-242.

[14]   ASTM C 511, Standard Specification for Moist Cabinets, Moist Rooms, and Water Storage Tanks Used in the Testing of Hydraulic Cements and Concretes, *American Society for Testing and Materials*, West Conshohocken, PA, Vol. 04, No. 02, (2002).

[15]   Mindess, S. and F. Young. 1981. *Concrete*, Prentice Hall Inc., Englewood Cliffs, New Jersey.

USE OF HYBRID HPFRC MEMBERS TO SATISFY PERFORMANCE CRITERIA FOR UNLINED CONCRETE PRIMARY LNG TANKS

Neven Krstulovic-Opara

ExxonMobil Development Company, Houston, USA

Abstract

Significant interest has been generated in recent years in the development, design and construction of liquefied gas containment tanks, such as Liquefied Natural Gas (LNG) tanks. Consequently, a large number of LNG tanks are planned for construction in the near future. Concrete is particularly well suited for construction of such tanks. This paper presents a method of using stay-in-place HPFRC formwork in construction of unlined primary concrete tanks. Use of HPFRCs controls tank cracking and thus enables unlined primary concrete tanks to meet performance requirements prescribed by the code. Design charts for flexural design of such composite members are provided.

Keywords: All Concrete LNG tank, SIMCON, tension, hybrid section, design charts.

1. INTRODUCTION

In recent years the US is simultaneously experiencing an increase in energy demand, a dwindling supply of domestic natural gas (NG) and rising cost of NG. Therefore, the U.S. is once again looking into importing large quantities of NG to supplement domestic resources.

Liquefying gases by cooling to cryogenic temperatures (e.g., - 160°C, i.e. -260°F) is a widely used method for significantly reducing their volume (e.g., 600 times) and thus making their transportation over long distances economically attractive. In the US, increasing demand for NG leads to importing liquefied natural gas (LNG) in large quantities over long distances from countries such as North Africa and the Middle East. This increased demand for LNG has led to a significant increase in the number of new import and storage facilities. As a result a large number of LNG tanks are planned for construction in the near future.

Concrete material is particularly well suited for the storage of cryogenic liquids since most of its properties and behavior improve substantially as temperature is lowered into the cryogenic range (e.g., see [1-8]). However, no standard or code is currently available in the world for the design of concrete LNG tanks. For this reason ACI has tasked ACI Committee 376 to develop the first US standard titled *"Design and Construction of Concrete Structures for the Containment of Refrigerated Liquefied Gases"* [9].

In developing the standard, the committee has encountered issues related to performance of the "primary" concrete tanks, i.e., the tank directly containing LNG liquid. Preliminary investigations indicate that performance criteria for liquid tightness and product containment might be hard to meet if unlined primary concrete tanks are used. More specifically, cracking condition during service and extreme events might not be possible to satisfy if tensile capacity of concrete has been previously exhausted. A solution to this problem is in the use of High Performance Fiber Reinforced Concretes (HPFRCs), which is the focus of this paper. HPFRCs have both (a) high tensile capacity even at strain levels significantly beyond yielding of steel reinforcement, as well as (b) excellent crack control, and can thus enable the unlined primary concrete tanks to meet cracking requirements prescribed by the code.

2.   BACKGROUND

2.1   LNG Tank Types
Various types of Refrigerated Liquid Gas (RLG) concrete tanks have been used in the past. In general, there are two main categories: single-containment and double containment tanks. The single-containment tank systems consist of only one tank. An additional concrete bund wall is used to contain the product in an event of the tank failure. For double-containment tank systems, the secondary tank wall contains the product if the primary tank fails. Tank types can be further subdivided into following categories, as shown in Figures 1 and 2:
1) single-containment steel or concrete tank systems with concrete bund walls (dikes),
2) double-containment tank systems with the primary container made of steel and the secondary container made of concrete,
3) double-containment tank systems with both walls made of concrete,
4) full-containment tank systems with the primary container made of steel and the secondary container made of concrete, as shown in Figure 1 a,
5) full-containment tank systems with both the primary and the secondary container made of concrete, as shown in Figure 1 b, and
6) membrane tanks with concrete primary container walls [1].

The key difference among these tank types is how the pressurized product vapor is contained. LNG storage requires a pressurized gas vapor boundary that can be either the primary or the secondary container. For the tank types 1 to 3 pressurized gas is contained by the primary container, while the secondary container is at atmospheric pressure. In the case of tank types 4 to 6, pressurized gas is contained by the secondary container. This paper deals with the tank type 5, i.e., ACLNG tanks made with the unlined primary container.

In all of the above cases, concrete can be exposed to cryogenic liquids. Two types of exposure are possible: temporary and long term. Concrete in the primary container is exposed to cryogenic temperatures for most of its design life. Concrete in the secondary container can only be exposed to cryogenic temperatures if the primary container ruptures.

2.2   Tank Loading Phases
During life of the tank, the tank experiences following loading phases:
1. Construction phase – this phase includes two stages. The first stage includes loads tank experiences prior to wall prestressing. The second stage includes prestressing loads and other construction loads. Most significant loads during the first stage are (a) loads due to concrete shrinkage, thermal and/or moisture effects, and (b) loads due to the settlement of the primary tank [10 – 12]. It is important to note that the wall acts as a reinforced concrete member during this phase, i.e., prestressing has no effect on preventing cracking.

2. Commissioning phase - Thermal loading during the cool down is the most significant loading during this phase. While the cooling rate is controlled to minimize cracking, economic reasons put a limit on the minimum cool down rate.

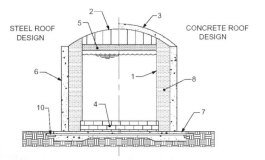

1) Primary container (steel)
2) Steel roof
3) Concrete roof
4) Bottom insulation
5) Ceiling insulation
6) Secondary container and vapor barrier (prestressed concrete)
7) Foundation slab
8) Pearlite insulation
10) Foundation heating system

Figure 1: Example of Refrigerated Liquefied Gas full-containment tank with only the secondary containment wall made of concrete (Adopted from EN 1473).

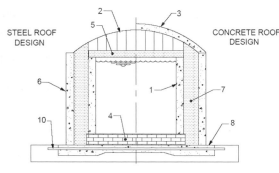

1) Primary container (prestressed concrete)
2) Steel roof
3) Concrete roof
4) Bottom insulation
5) Ceiling insulation
6) Secondary container and vapor barrier (prestressed concrete)
7) Foundation slab
8) Pearlite insulation
10) Foundation heating system

Figure 2: Example of Refrigerated Liquefied Gas full-containment tank with both the primary and secondary containment wall made of concrete (Adopted from EN 1473).

3. Operation under normal loading conditions – the most significant loading to the primary tank wall during this phase is the product loading.
4. Operation under abnormal loading conditions – the most significant loading of the primary tank during this phase is the product loading and earthquake. Two levels of earthquake are usually considered: Operating Basis Earthquake (OBE) and Safe Shutdown Earthquake (SSE). OBE is an earthquake after which the facility must continue to operate. SSE is a significantly higher level of earthquake after which the facility will be closed and repaired. However, the facility must be able to be safely shut down.

2.2 Performance Criteria

Current code requirements specify that under the product load, as well as under the product load plus OBE, the primary tank must remain liquid tight. Under the product load plus SSE the primary tank must retain its containment capability.

For an unlined tank, liquid tightness and containment capabilities are specified in terms of section cracking, such that:

a) Liquid tightness under product load conditions is achieved by assuring that: (i) the net resultant force in a section is compression, and (ii) a compressive zone of either 50 % of the section thickness or 0.2 m, whichever is greater, is maintained.

b) Liquid tightness under product loads plus OBE is achieved by assuring that the compressive zone is at least the maximum of either 50 % of the section thickness or 0.2 m.

c) Containment capability under operation loads plus SSE is achieved by assuring that the compressive zone is at least the maximum of either 25 % of the section thickness or 0.1 m.

Furthermore, for the product and product plus OBE loading conditions, tensile capacity of concrete can not be used in the analysis. For the product plus SSE loading condition, tensile capacity of concrete can only be used if the load history justifies it.

2.3 Issues Associated with Unlined Primary Concrete Tanks

An in-depth finite element analysis of ACLNG tanks with unlined primary tank was performed to better understand cracking and its effect on wall behavior [13]. The effect of shrinkage and thermal strains [10] on concrete capacity was introduced by specifying that concrete has no tensile capacity.

Analysis demonstrated that significant through-cracking developed in the lower 1/5 of the wall height prior to prestressing. Further through-cracking developed during the cooldown in the same region, as well as at the top 1/8 of the wall height. Additional interior surface cracking, with crack depths ranging between 15% to 25% of the section thickness, developed along the entire wall height in the cool down phase.

Related preliminary design-investigation of large tanks indicated that in the case of such loss of concrete tensile capacity, it might not be possible to economically meet code performance criteria. This problem might be eliminated by using FRCs, as explained next.

3. POTENTIAL FOR USE OF FRCS IN ACLNG TANKS

Contrary to conventional concrete, FRCs and HPFRCs exhibit significantly improved behavior under serviceability, ultimate and post-ultimate limit states. HPFRCs in particular exhibit high tensile strengths at strains that are significantly higher than yield strain of steel, as shown in Figure 3 a. Therefore, contrary to current code requirements, when HPFRCs are used in tank walls, tensile capacity of concrete should be accounted for in calculating the size of the uncracked zone under product, product plus OBE and product plus SSE conditions. Furthermore, since fibers are added during construction, they are efficient in eliminating or at least significantly decreasing detrimental effects of thermal and shrinkage strains on exhausting tensile capacity of concrete prior to wall prestressing. FRCs have also been shown to exhibit excellent behavior at cryogenic temperatures [14, 15]. This all makes them ideal for improving performance of unlined primary LNG tank walls.

3.1 Construction Issues

Two options exist for adding fibers: (a) placing fibers throughout the section during casting, and (b) applying a layer of higher fiber volume fraction HPFRCs at wall faces experiencing the highest stress demand, as shown in Figure 3b.

LNG tank walls are made using either slip forming or jump-forming techniques. Neither are well suited for casting-in-place section made entirely of FRC. The other option is to use precast FRC of HPFRC panels that act as stay-in-place formwork, while the rest of the section is made using conventional concrete, as shown in Figure 3 b.

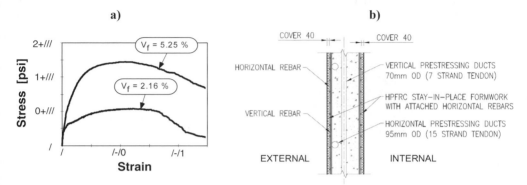

Figure 3: (a) Stress-Strain behavior of SIMCON in tension [17]. (b) An example of stay-in-place SIMCON formwork for LNG tank construction [16].

3.2   Background on SIMCON

One of the HPFRCs that is well suited for stay-in-place formwork application shown in Figure 3, is Slurry Infiltrated Mat Concrete (SIMCON). SIMCON is made by infiltrating pre-placed continuous fiber-mats, shown in Figure 4 a, with very flowable high-strength slurry [16 - 18]. Due to its fiber-mat configuration SIMCON is well suited for casting thin elements such as stay-in-place formwork shown in Figure 4 b. The result is a markedly improved crack control, load capacity, ductility and overall seismic / blast / impact performance [20 – 30].

4.   DESIGN CHARTS

The main challenge for implementing proposed FRC stay-in-place formwork into LNG tank design is lack of design tools that can be both referenced by the ACI 376 standard [9], and easily used by the practicing engineers. The existing commercially available computer programs do not allow easy implementation of stress-strain curves for HPFRC materials. Furthermore, available approaches for analysis of hybrid HPFRC sections usually require use of non-linear section-analysis programs that have to be developed by the end user [20]. Therefore, the goal of this paper was to simplify the design of hybrid HPFRC-RC wall sections by developing design charts similar to those presented in BS 8110-3.

4.2   Material Properties

SIMCON material properties used in this paper are as defined in [17 - 19]. 5.25% fiber volume fraction SIMCON layer was used throughout the analysis. Examples of SIMCON tensile behavior are shown in Figure 3 b.

Compressive 28 day cylinder strength was 40 MPa (5.8 ksi). Compressive stress-strain concrete curves were as defined in BS 8110. Tensile behavior was as defined in [32].

A bi-linear stress-strain curve was used for steel reinforcement. Yield steel strengths were 400 MPa and 500 MPa (58 and 73 ksi), which are usual steel strengths used in LNG tanks.

a)

b)

Figure 4: (a) Continuous fiber-mats used in manufacturing of SIMCON. (b) The 2.5 cm (1 in.) thick 1.52 m (5 ft) long, 40.6 cm (16 in.) high and 25.4 cm (10 in.) wide SIMCON stay-in-place formwork. Shear studs bolted directly into the formwork sides are visible [26, 28].

4.3   Section Analysis

Analysis of the composite section was performed using an internal Arup section analysis program [31]. Section thicknesses between 0.5 m to 1 m were considered. This is the usual range of primary tank wall thicknesses for 160,000 m^3 LNG tanks and larger tanks.

4 cm (1.6 in) thick SIMCON layer was used throughout the analysis. Reinforcement quantities varied between 0.5% and 4%. The ratio of 0.5% is the minimum ratio required by the standard [9]. The total reinforcement was distributed symmetrically on both wall faces.

It should be noted that if analysis is conducted for load phases when the primary tank is exposed to cryogenic temperatures, adequate cryogenic reinforcement should be used.

4.3.1   Selected Strain Limits

Tensile behavior of HPFRCs is characterized by a multiple-cracking mechanism, i.e., development of a series of very fine and disconnected cracks. These cracks develop up to the point of the maximum tensile strength of HPFRCs. At the maximum tensile strength one critical crack opens up and all further deformation is concentrated in the opening of this single crack. Prior to the opening of the critical crack, all other cracks are very fine and disconnected [18]. This was clearly visible in the case of SIMCON retrofitted reinforced concrete beams [20]. Even after beams were loaded up to the ultimate load level and except for the single critical crack, all other maximum crack sizes at the end of testing were less or equal to 0.09 mm (0.0039 in.). These crack sizes are well within the crack size limits of 0.198 mm (0.0078 in.) required by ACI standards for the reinforced concrete elements exposed to severe environments. Furthermore, it should be kept in mind that crack width limits defined by ACI were developed for continuous cracks, characteristic of conventional reinforced concrete. SIMCON cracks are discontinuous and, therefore, their level of impermeability is even higher than that of the same width reinforced concrete cracks allowed by the code.

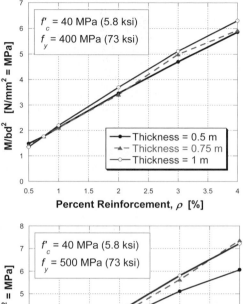

Figure 5: Design charts for wall sections for 400 MPa reinforcement. 5.25% fiber volume fraction and 4 cm (1.6 in) thick SIMCON stay-in-place formwork was used in the analysis.

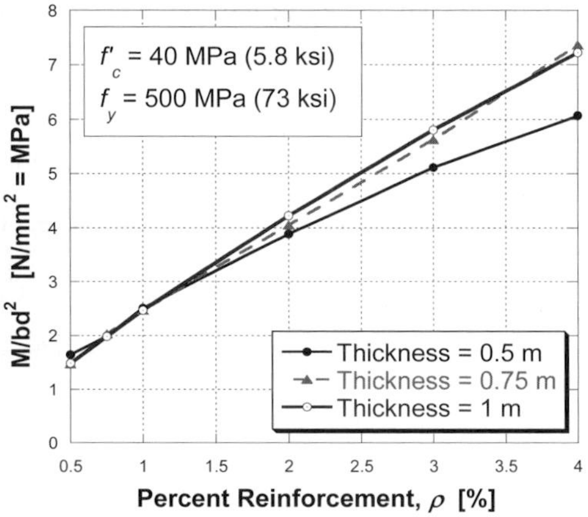

Figure 6: Design charts for wall sections with 500 MPa reinforcement. 5.25% fiber volume fraction and 4 cm (1.6 in) thick SIMCON stay-in-place formwork was used in the analysis.

The maximum tensile stress and strain values for 5.25% fiber volume fraction SIMCON are in the range of 16 MPa (2.3 ksi) and 1.1 %, respectively. A limiting tensile strain, corresponding to 75% of the tensile strength, was selected based on known tensile behavior of SIMCON. In the case of 5.25% fiber volume fraction this corresponded to a strain of 0.25%.

Two strain limits were satisfied in developing the design charts (a) limiting SIMCON tensile strain of 0.25%, measured at exterior wall surface, and (b) limiting steel yield strain measured at the level of reinforcement.

5. RESULTS

Developed design charts are shown in Figures 5 and 6. In line with BS 8110-3 limiting flexural loads are presented in terms of M/bd^2 ratio, where M is the limiting moment, b is the section length of 1 m, and d is the depth of tension reinforcement. No strength reduction factors, material factors or load factors were used (i.e., all factors equal 1.0).

6.   DISCUSSION AND CONCLUSIONS

- Presented results (e.g., Figure 3 a) demonstrate that contrary to current code requirements, when HPFRCs are used tensile capacity of concrete should be accounted for when calculating the size of the uncracked zone. This is valid for all loading conditions including product, product plus OBE and product plus SSE cases.
- The maximum tensile strain in the SIMOCN layer should be limited to that corresponding to 75% of the ultimate tensile strength. In this range SIMCON stress-strain behavior is predominantly elastic and majority of the existing multiple-cracks are so small that they are not visible to the naked eye (e.g., see [18]). In the case of 5.25 % fiber volume fraction SIMCON, this limiting strain is in the range of 0.25%.
- Presented design charts were developed assuming that prestressing has not yet been applied. After wall prestressing, the effect of the prestressing load and additional straining of tendons should be accounted for. Since in this load range section response still remains elastic, these effects can be accounted for using the principle of superposition.
- Presented approach should be investigated in a greater detail by extending the non-linear finite element analysis to include full load and deformation history of the tank construction (e.g., include effects of shrinkage and thermal strains prior to prestressing).

REFERENCES

[1]   Fédération Internationale de la Précontrainte (FIP), "Cryogenic Behaviour of Materials for Prestressed Concrete", *State of the Art Report*, May 1982.

[2]   Van der Veen, C., *Properties of Concrete at Very Low Temperatures*, Delft University of Technology, Netherlands, Report 25-87-2, 1987.

[3]   Monfore, G.E., and Lentz, A.E., "Physical Properties of Concrete at Very Low Temperatures", *Journal of the PCA*, Research and Development Laboratories, 1962, pp. 33-39.

[4]   Reinhardt, H. W., "Mechanische en fysische eigenschappen van beton tussen -190°C en +400°C", *Cement*, Vol. 31, No. 1, 1979, pp. 7-13.

[5]   Stockhausen, N.; *Die dilatation hochporker Festkorper bei Wasseraufnahme und Eisbildung*, Ph.D. Thesis, Technical University of Munich, 1981.

[6]   Wiedemann, G.; *Zum einfluss tiefer Temperaturen auf Festigkeit und Verformung von Beton*, Ph.D. Thesis, Technical University of Braunschweig, 1982.

[7]   Berner, D.E., *Behavior of Prestressed Concrete Subjected to Low Temperatures arid Cyclic Leading*, PhD Dissertation, University of California, Berkeley, 1984.

[8]   Bamforth, P.B., *The Structural Permeability of Concrete at Cryogenic Temperatures*, PhD Thesis, The University of Aston at Birmingham, UK, 1987.

[9]   ACI Committee 376, *Design and Construction of Concrete Structures for the Containment of Refrigerated Liquefied Gases (RLG) (ACI 376-XX) and Commentary (ACI 376R-XX)*, ACI Standard, In progress, American Concrete Institute, 2007.

[10]   van Breugel, K., and van der Veen, C., "Prediction of Temperature Induced Crack Patterns in Cylindrical Concrete Structures", *Long-Term Serviceability of Concrete Structures*, ACI-SP 117, American Concrete Institute, October 1, 1989, pp. 27 – 44.

[11]   Hamada, S., Oshiro, T., and Hino, S., "Vertical Cracking of Concrete Tank Walls", ACI *Concrete International*, American Concrete Institute, October 1987, pp. 50 – 55.

[12]   Anson, M., and Rowlinson, P.M., "Early-age Strain and Temperature Measurements in Concrete Tan Walls", *Magazine of Concrete Research*, Vol. 40, No. 145, December 1988, pp 216 – 226.

[13]   Gration, D., "Inner Tank Design Report", Report No. 97055-RP1-SG-001, *BP ACLNG Peer Review,* Arup Energy for BP America Inc., January 2007.

[14] Rostasy, F.S., and Sprenger, H., "Strength and Deformation of Steel Fiber Reinforced Concrete at Very Low Temperature", *The international Journal of cement Composites and Lightweight Concrete*, Vol. 6, No. 1, February 1984, pp. 47 – 51.

[15] Kormeling, H. A., *Strain rate and Temperature Behavior of Steel Fibre Concrete in Tension*, Delft University Press, 1986.

[16] Moncarz, P., and Krstulovic-Opara, N., "Tougher Concrete Structures to Service and Protect Oil and Gas Operations", Proceedings of the *ATCE 2005*, Society of Petroleum Engineers International Symposium, Dallas, October 9 – 12, 2005, Paper No. SPE-97258-MS.

[17] Krstulovic-Opara, N., Malak, S., "Tensile Behavior of Slurry Infiltrated Mat Concrete (SIMCON)", ACI *Materials J,*, January – Feb., 1997, pp. 39 - 46.

[18] Krstulovic-Opara, N., Malak, S., "Micromechanical Tensile Behavior of Slurry Infiltrated Fiber Mat Concrete (SIMCON)", ACI *Materials J,*, Sept, - Oct, 1997, Vol. 94, No. 5, pp. 373 - 384.

[19] Krstulovic-Opara, N., Al-Shannag, M. J., "Compressive Behavior of Slurry Infiltrated Mat Concrete (SIMCON)", ACI *Ma. J.*, May – Ju. 1999, pp. 367-377.

[20] Krstulovic-Opara, N., Dogan, E., Uang, C. -M, Haghayeghi, A., "Flexural Behavior of Composite R.C. - SIMCON Beams", ACI *Structural Journal*, Sept.-Oct. 1997, pp. 502 - 512.

[21] Krstulovic-Opara, N., Al-Shannag, M. J., "SIMCON - Based Shear Retrofit of Reinforced Concrete Members", ACI *Struct. J.*, Jan. – Feb. 1999, pp. 105 - 114.

[22] Dogan, E., *Retrofit of Non-Ductile Reinforced Concrete Frames Using H.-P. Fiber Reinforced. Composites*, Ph.D. Thesis, North Carolina State University, 1998.

[23] Dogan, E., Hill, H., Krstulovic-Opara, N., "Suggested Design Guidel. for Seismic Retrofit With SIMCON & SIFCON", *HPFRC in Infrastr. Repair and Retr.*, ACI SP-185, 1999, pp. 207-248.

[24] Krstulovic-Opara, N., LaFave, J., Dogan, E., Uang, C. - M., "Seismic Retrofit With Discont. SIMCON Jackets", *HPFRC in Infrastr. Repair and Retrofit*, ACI SP-185, 1999, pp. 141-185.

[25] Dogan, E. and Krstulovic-Opara, N., "Seismic Retrofit With Continuous SIMCON Jackets," *ACI Structural J.*, Nov.-Dec. 2003, pp. 713 - 722.

[26] Ply, C, *High-Performance Composite Column Members Made With Advanced Cementitious Composites*, MS Thesis, North Carolina State University, 1999.

[27] Brezac, B., *Seismic Behavior of Hybrid SIMCON Jacket. – High Strength Lightweight Aggregate FRC Filled Steel Tubes*, MS Th., 2002.

[28] Krstulovic – Opara, N., and Kilar, V., "Development and Seismic Behavior of H.-P. Composite Frames", *Concrete: Material Science to Applications*, ACI SP-206, 2002, pp. 453 – 471.

[29] N. Krstulovic-Opara, M. Adan, and V. Kilar, "High-Performance Composite Frames for Increased Resistance to Seismic or Blast Loadings", Proceedings of the 4th International Conference on *Analytical Models and New Concepts in Concrete & Masonry Structures*, AMCM-2002, Krakow, Poland, June 5-7, 2002, pp. 93-100.

[30] P. Moncarz and N. Krstulovic-Opara, "Tougher Concrete Structures to Service and Protect Oil and Gas Operations", *Proceedings of ATCE 2005*, Society of Petroleum Engineers International Symposium, Dallas, October 9 – 12, 2005.

[31] Oasys Ltd, *AdSec*, Version 8.0, Arup, London, 2007.

[32] Scott, R. H., "Technical Note 372 - The Short Term Moment Curvature Relationship for RC Beams", *Proc. of the Institution of Civil Eng.*, Vol. 75, Part 2, Dec. 1983, pp. 725 – 734.

INVESTIGATION OF THE DURABILITY OF TEXTILE REINFORCED CONCRETE – TEST EQUIPMENT AND MODELLING THE LONG-TERM BEHAVIOUR

Till Büttner, Jeanette Orlowsky and Michael Raupach

Institute of Building Materials, RWTH Aachen University

Abstract

Textile reinforced concrete (TRC) is one promising possibility to produce thin-walled high load bearing structural elements. Besides the maximum load bearing capacity, the durability under various conditions is one major issue for future applications. This paper deals with the technical requirements needed to investigate aspects of the durability of TRC. The investigations include short- and long-term loading tests, which were carried out under different climates. The test rig used to investigate the long-term performance of TRC-specimen will also be presented. The results show a reduction of the strength loss of the AR-Glass due to the alkalinity of the concrete, when polymers are used for impregnating the reinforcement.

1. INTRODUCTION

Concrete reinforced with fibres offers several advantages as a building material. Fibre reinforced concrete (FRC) is used since over 30 years. Some typical fields of application are claddings, filigree construction elements and industrial floors. Textile reinforced concrete (TRC) represents an interesting new construction material, offering several additional advantages compared to steel or fibre reinforced concrete. These advantages dominate in those fields of applications where thin-walled, structural elements with a high load-carrying capacity are required.

Mainly alkali resistant (AR-) glass rovings, carbon rovings and aramid rovings consisting of several filaments are used to produce textiles as reinforcement materials. Table 1 gives an overview over the mainly used reinforcement materials for the current research. One possibility to improve the load bearing capacity of the reinforcement is to use an impregnation. In the current research two different epoxy resins were used – the epoxy resin called EPL is based on an epichlorhydrine with an amine hardener, the other one (called PRE) is a prepreg epoxy resin. The detailed mechanical and chemical properties of these epoxy resins can be found in [1]. One major difference is the glass transition temperature (T_G), which is an indicator for the behavior of the resin at increased temperatures. The T_G of the epoxy resin is below 50 °C, the T_G of the Prepreg Resin is above 50 °C. The concrete mixture used for the investigations was developed at the Institute for Building Materials Research, Aachen University, ibac, as a fine-grain concrete (also called: micro-concrete). The composition and the mechanical properties are described in [2]. The pH value of this mixture is 13.5.

Even if the reinforcement is called alkali resistant glass, there is a strength loss due the alkalinity of the concrete [3]. So the aim of this work is to present the tools required to investigate the durability of textile reinforced concrete. As materials different types of reinforcement are used, the mechanical properties are shown in Table 1.

Table 1: Characteristics of the reinforcement including standard deviation [4], [3]

	Unit	Filament	Roving				Textile
Name	-	VET-**F**-ARG-2400-1-03	VET-**RO**-ARG-2400-1-03	Roving – EPL Impregnated	Roving – PRE Epoxy		MAG-07-03
Density	g/cm³	2.68	--	--	--		--
Titer	tex	1.55	2400	2400	2400		--
Tensile strength	N/mm²	1691 ± 275	695 ± 67	1885	1800		968 ± 105 *
E-Modulus		53340	53000	63200	56200		51330 *

*: in 0° direction (direction of the applied load)

2. TEST METHODS TO INVESTIGATE THE DURABILITY

In order to investigate the durability of textile reinforced concrete four different test setups have been used. In the following the test setups will be presented and the relevance of the results discussed.

2.1 Single Filament Test

To investigate the chemical attack on AR-glass in alkaline solutions, tensile tests on single filaments have been performed (see Fig. 1). Before testing, the filaments were stored in an alkaline solution in order accelerate the aging of the specimen. The configuration of this alkaline solution was chosen according to the previous mentioned micro-concrete [1].

Fig. 1 shows the tensile test specimen. Each single filament was glued between two U-shaped papers before testing. In order to test these specimens a special testing machine was developed at ibac. The tensile load is applied on the filament with a rate of 0.546 mm/min. A load cell measures the applied load and two LVDTs are used to determine the displacement.

The preparation of the test specimens requires a high degree of accuracy and caution because the tested filaments have a diameter of only about 27 µm. The filament diameter has a standard deviation of 1 µm, which results in a rather high scatter of the filament tensile strength. Nevertheless it is possible to calculate the area of the effective filament cross section (since filament diameters are measured using a microscope and camera). This is a decisive advantage compared to tensile tests on rovings (multifilament yarns), since not all filaments in a roving contribute equally in taking the load, making interpretation of results very complex.

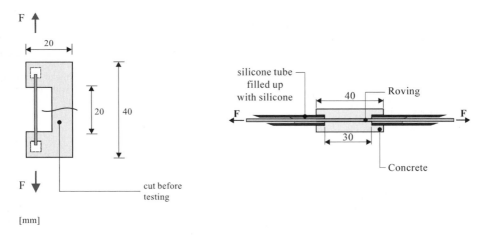

[mm]

Figure 1: Testing of a filament specimen   Figure 2: Testing of a SIC specimen

2.2   SIC-Test (Strand in Cement)

The change of tensile strength of a roving embedded in concrete after climatic stress (for example hot water) can be measured with the SIC-Test [5]. For the SIC-Test a roving is concentrically cast into fine-grained concrete. The test specimens are 40 mm long, 10 mm high and 10 mm wide and stored after a hardening period of 28 days at 23 °C and 95 % relative humidity several times in water at different temperatures. Silicone tubes are used to protect the roving outside the concrete from the water ingress (Fig. 2). Filling the silicone tubes with silicone avoids the concrete from entering the tubes. Furthermore this measure allows the precise definition of the embedded length of the roving in the specimen.

A tensile force can be applied to the roving ends outside the concrete for measuring the loss in tensile strength of the embedded rovings after climatic stress. The SIC-Tests are carried out at a displacement rate of 1 mm/min.

2.3   TSP-Test (Dog Bone Shaped Specimen)

The TSP-Test (dog boned specimen specimens in tensile test) allows conclusions concerning the changes in the stress-elongation behaviour, the cracking image and the maximum roving tensile strength after climatic stress. This test allows an assessment of the long-term behaviour of textile reinforced concrete. The geometry of the TSP specimens can be seen in Fig. 3. In order to achieve a roving failure the amount of reinforcement depends on the used rovings – e.g. using 2400 tex roving 8 rovings are required. During testing the change of length is measured on two sides over 250 mm using electrical gauges. The rovings, which are sticking out of the sample body, are glued with epoxy resin at the ends of the specimen. So the individual filaments are fixed at each end of the sample. During the loading process, filaments are unable to slip towards the centre of the sample from the sample edges. Therefore the rovings can reach their maximum tensile strength. The tensile load is applied via rounded off steel elements, as shown in Fig. 3. The TSP-Tests are carried out at a displacement rate of 0.5 mm/min.

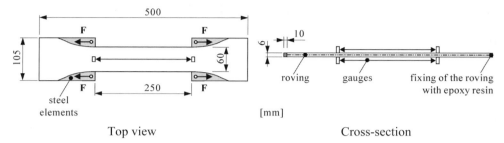

Top view   Cross-section

Figure 3: Testing of a TSP specimen – Left: Top view of the specimen; right: Cross-section

2.4   Setup and Test procedure to measure the fatigue strength

The influence of a permanent static load is investigated on TSP-specimens, which are presented in the previous section. The test setup for constant load tests was developed at the ibac and is shown in Fig. 4. The axial load is applied in the waist shaped area of the test specimens and assured by a weight at a crank of a lever. The force is measured by a load cell and the elongation is measured with two LVDTs. The storage conditions can be varied by applying a tank to the test setup. This tank allows a variation of the storage humidity up to under water storage at different temperatures.

In order to control the force application of the constant load test the force-elongation diagram was measured and compared to a diagram recorded with a displacement controlled test. This test has been performed on a displacement-controlled testing machine with a displacement rate of 0.5 mm/min. Fig. 5 shows the comparison of two exemplary curves. In addition one possible load level, e.g. 80 % of the fracture load, is shown.

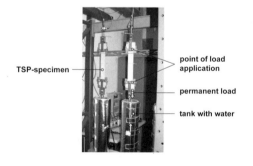
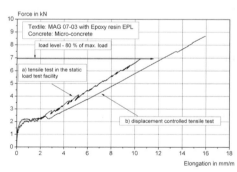

Figure 4a: Setup of the test facility to measure the behaviour of textile reinforced concrete under permanent static load

Figure 4b: Comparison of the force-elongation curves a) displacement controlled and b) load controlled in the constant load test facility

3. DURABILITY MODEL FOR AR-GLASS REINFORCEMENT IN TRC

In order to allow a prediction of the AR-Glass strength loss over time, a durability model has been developed [3]. The schematic design of the durability model is given in Fig. 5.

Splitting the life time of a TRC element in small time slices the degree of strength loss can be calculated for each time slice t_i. As input parameters for the calculation of the strength loss in a time slice the following parameter are required: temperature T and humidity h_R at the reinforcement level in the concrete for the time slice, as well as the degree of strength loss up to this time Δf_i (t_{i-1}) (see Eq. 1). First it has to be checked if the water content at the reinforcement h_R is above the critical water humidity h_{lim}. If this is not the case, the degree of strength loss sums up to zero in this time slice, if the humidity is above the critical humidity, the next step has to follow. As soon as the static load σ exceeds a critical load σ_{lim}, the specimen fails [6]. If the static load is lower than the critical load, the carbonation depth X_c will be important: if the concrete around the reinforcement is carbonated ($X_c \geq c$), the strength loss is negligible, if this is not the case, the corrosion model [7] has to be used to calculate the strength loss during this time slice. The accumulated loss in strength of all time slices results in the strength loss at the end of the proposed life time of the TRC component. As shown the existing model can take various material parameters into account and predict the durability of this combination.

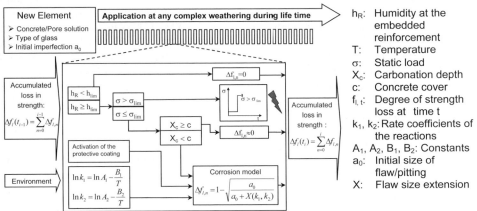

Figure 5: Schematic design of the durability model

In order to calculate the long term behavior of TRC the humidity of the concrete as a function of the weathering time has to be known. So in a second step the model will be expanded in order to have the possibility to calculate the influence of the outside humidity on the water content at the reinforcement inside the concrete. Then it will be possible to include any climatic data and predict the durability of TRC. The results of this research will be presented in further publications.

4. SELECTED RESULTS OF THE DURABILITY INVESTIGATIONS ON VAROIUS REINFORCEMENT MATERIALS

In the following, the results of various tests will be presented according to the previous section. The results show the difference between impregnated and non-impregnated rovings and textiles. The degree of strength loss Δf_l can be calculated using Eq. 1:

$$\Delta f_{l,t} = 1 - \frac{f_t}{f_{t=0}} \qquad (1)$$

where $\Delta f_{l,t}$ degree of strength loss at time t
            f_t tensile strength of the specimen at time t

In order to get an idea about the influence of the alkalinity of the concrete matrix, single filament tensile tests were performed at first. Fig. 6 left shows the degree of strength loss of AR-glass filaments with and without impregnation with epoxy resin prior to their storage in alkaline solution at 50 °C. The pH value of the solution is equal to 13.5 and matches so the pore solution of the used concrete. The film thickness of the epoxy-layer on a single filament is below 1 µm. The tensile tests were performed with 10 single filaments after 7, 14 and 28 days of storage in alkaline solution at 50 °C. As shown in Fig. 6 left the impregnation shows no influence on the degree of strength loss of the AR-glass reinforcement. After a period of 7 days, the degree of strength loss is approx. 40 %. This value increases within the next 14 days up to 60 %. These results have to be seen under consideration of the following two aspects: the impregnation with epoxy resin on a single filament has a very low thickness and the attack area of the alkaline solution is equal to the whole filament area. Rovings which are used as reinforcement in concrete show a greater impregnation layer thickness and a much smaller attack area, because the alkaline solution only accesses the roving in the pores of the concrete. The increased thickness is due to the impregnation process, because single filaments are very sensitive to mechanical treatments. So the results have to be interpreted very carefully.

This influence of the attack area can also be seen in Fig. 6 right which displays the results of the TSP tests (dog-boned shaped specimen) stored in water. One test series for each point of time contains three single specimens.

The impregnated textiles reveal a significant lower degree of strength loss than the non-impregnated textiles. This reduction in the degree of strength loss is probably a result of the noticeable lower attack area of the alkaline solution in the pore system and the increased thickness of the epoxy resin compared to the filament tests. The influence of the thickness of the epoxy resin will be investigated in further test series. Also the influence of different types of epoxy resins, such as the prepreg epoxy resin, and modifications of the resins are an element of the current research and will be presented later on.

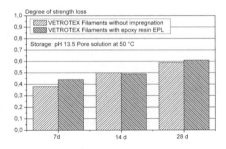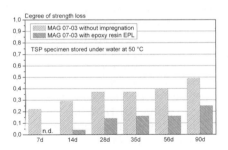

Figure 6 left: Degree of strength loss of filaments after storage in alkaline solution at 50 °C ;
right: Degree of strength loss of TSP specimens after storage in accelerated ageing
(50 °C/water); both with and without epoxy resin EPL – n.d. – not determined

Besides the influence of the alkalinity, also the influence of a constant load has to be investigated, in order to evaluate the durability of TRC. In the following the maximum times to failure of different specimens – using three different types of reinforcement : non-impregnated textiles (MAG-07-03) ; impregnated textiles (MAG 07-03) using both types of exopy resin – are given.

Table 2: Times to failure of TSP Specimen under constant load

Reinforcement	Storage RH/T	Percentage of fracture load	Time to failure
-	°C / %	%	h
VET-RO-ARG-2400-1-03	23/50	80	18000
	23/50	90	1440
	23/100 (Water)	80	0.01-0.08
MAG 07-03 with epoxy-resin	23/50	60	> 170[1]
	23/95		> 1770[1]
	23/100 (Water)		> 160[1]
MAG 07-03 with Prepreg Epoxy	50/50	60	> 300
	50/95		
	50/100 (Water)		

1) Storage temperature was increased after the indicated time – failure at approx. 40 °C

The results shown in Table 2 indicate clearly that the impregnation of the textiles increases the times to failure significantly, if the specimens are stored under water. The rapid failure of non-impregnated textiles under constant load and storage under water is probably mainly caused by a reduction of the friction between the filaments [3]. This thesis is backed by the fact, that every specimen with a non-impregnated reinforcement fails directly after water is applied. This failure mechanism is supposed to be avoided by the impregnation of the textiles, because, as shown in previous tests the cross-section of a roving is totally filled with epoxy resin [1]. However, the positive effect of an impregnation can be destroyed by the usage of an epoxy resin, which is not able to keep a stable impregnation at higher temperatures. The glass transition temperature (T_G) is one indicator for the stability of a polymer at higher temperatures, but it is not necessarily equal to the temperature at which the maximum strength of a polymer decreases. This value can be detected by using a thermo-mechanical analysis. As mentioned before the T_G of the epoxy resin is below 50 °C, which explains the failure of the specimens at temperatures around 40 °C. Using a more temperature stable epoxy resin, such as the prepreg resin, an increased temperature did not lead to a failure of the specimens.

As described in chapter 3, a model is available to predict the durability of textile reinforced concrete. The loss of strength is modeled as a function of the climatic parameters such as temperature and relative humidity. In order to calibrate the model the specimens have to be stored at different climatic conditions in the laboratory – also known as accelerated aging. Then the results are verified with specimens stored outside. Fig. 7 shows the results of the accelerated aging on the left side and then, on the right side, the calculated curves for a time of 50 yrs. One very important fact is that the curves are calibrated for the climate in Aachen and not valid for other climates. Because the calibration for the epoxy-impregnated textiles is not finished yet, the loss of strength after 50 yrs. can not be predicted yet. But, because of the significantly lower loss of strength after the accelerated ageing, it can be assumed that the loss of strength after 50 yrs. for impregnated textiles is considerably lower than for non-impregnated textiles.

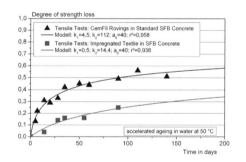 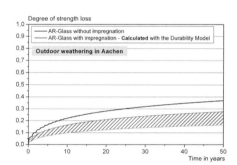

Figure 7: Degree of strength loss of impregnated and non-impregnated reinforcement as a function of time – Calculations done with [3]

5. CONCLUSION AND OUTLOOK

In this paper different test setups to investigate the strength loss of AR-glass used as reinforcement in TRC were presented. The test setups can cover all variations of the material TRC from the smallest element – single filament – up to a compound specimen. Also selected results which lead to an also presented durability model were shown. The following conclusions can be drawn out of this research:

- The durability of impregnated AR-glass textiles embedded in the micro-concrete is improved compared to the non-impregnated AR-glass textiles. This improvement seems to be a function of the thickness of the impregnation layer and the contact area between the alkaline (pore) solution and the reinforcement.
- The load bearing capacity under constant load is also improved by the usage of polymermodified rovings. However the tests also show that the change of mechanical properties caused by the temperature can not be neglected.
- Current research deals with the evaluation of the remaining load bearing capacity of TRC specimens, which were stored under a constant load for a certain time. The results will be presented later and show the magnitude of the applied load level on the strength loss of the AR-glass reinforcement.
- Also in current research, the influence of the polymer formulation and the type of applying the coating are analysed.

ACKNOWLEDGEMENTS

The investigations at the ibac, RWTH Aachen University, are part of the Collaborative Research Center 532 "Textile reinforced concrete – Basics for the development of a new technology" and sponsored by the Deutsche Forschungsgemeinschaft (DFG). The support is gratefully acknowledged.

REFERENCES

[1] Raupach, M., Orlowsky, J., Büttner, T., Dilthey, U., Schleser, M.: Epoxy-Impregnated Textiles in Concrete - Load Bearing Capacity and Durability. Bagneux: RILEM, 2006. - In: Textile Reinforced Concrete. Proceedings of the 1st International RILEM Symposium, Aachen, 6./7. September 2006, (Hegger, J. ; Brameshuber, W. ; Will, N. (Eds.)), S. 77-88

[2] Brameshuber, W.; Brockmann, T.; Hegger J.; Molter, M.: Untersuchungen zum textilbewehrten Beton. Beton 52 (2002) Nr.9, S. 424-429

[3] Orlowsky, J.: Zur Dauerhaftigkeit von AR-Glasbewehrung in Textilbeton. Berlin: Beuth. - In: Schriftenreihe des Deutschen Ausschusses für Stahlbeton (2005), Nr. 558

[4] Banholzer, B.: Bond Behaviour of a Multi-Filament Yarn Embedded in a Cementitious Matrix. In: Schriftenreihe Aachener Beiträge zur Bauforschung, Institut für Bauforschung der RWTH Aachen (2004), Nr. 12

[5] GRCA Method of test for strength retention of glassfibre in cements and mortars. Gerrards Cross 1984

[6] Orlowsky J, Antons U, Raupach M (2003) Behaviour of Glass-Filament-Yarns in Concrete as a Function of Time and Environmental Conditions. Cambridge: Woodhead Publishing Limited. Proceedings of the 7th International Symposium on Brittle Matrix Composites, Warsaw, 13-15 October 2003, (Brandt, A.M. ; Li, V.C.; Marshall, I.H. (Ed.)), S.233-241

[7] Orlowsky, J., Raupach, M.: Modelling the Loss in Strength of AR-Glass Fibres in Textile-Reinforced Concrete. In: Materials and Structures (RILEM) 39 (2006), Nr. 6, S. 635-643

QUANTIFICATION OF GLASSFIBRE - CEMENT INTERFACIAL PROPERTIES BY SEM-BASED PUSH-OUT TEST

Michal A. Glinicki and Andrzej M. Brandt

Institute of Fundamental Technological Research, Polish Academy of Sciences, Warsaw, Poland

Abstract

The toughness of cement composites reinforced with glassfibres (GFRC) is known to degrade in the long term in spite of high alkali resistance of fibres. The stability of fibre-matrix interface is a key factor for high performance composites. For the interfacial characterization of glassfibre and cement composites SEM-based push-out tests were performed. The materials studied included strands of zirconia glass filaments of diameters ranging from 13 to 15 µm and cementitious matrices modified with mineral additives. The push-out tests were performed on thin slices of about 450-600 µm, cut out of the specimens perpendicularly to the direction of the glass filaments. During testing a continuous recording of load and displacement of a fibre was performed at a constant push velocity of about 0.2 µm/s. Test results revealed significant differences due to introduced matrix modifications as well as to ageing of the specimens. Both stress-based approach and energy-based approach was applied for characterization the interfacial properties.

1. INTRODUCTION

The toughness of cement composites reinforced with glass fibres (GFRC) is known to degrade in the long term in spite of high alkali resistance of fibres. Application of pozzolanic additives to GFRC is found to improve the long-term performance, particularly in wet and warm environment [1-3]. The stability of fibre-matrix interface can be considered as a key factor for providing a high performance characteristic since the overall performance of fibre reinforced composite materials is controlled to a great extent by the properties of the interfaces. In brittle matrix composites the interface debonding shear strength and frictional shear stress are the key parameters governing their fracture behaviour. The strength of the bonding between fibre and matrix plays a major role in the ability of the composite to bridge or deflect cracks along the interface. In order for such toughening mechanisms to occur, however, the fibre-matrix interface must have an optimal bonding strength.

Several tests have been and are being developed with the objective of measuring the interfacial properties in fibre-reinforced composites [4]. The pull-out of a single glass filament is difficult because fibres mostly rupture rather than are pulled out from hardened cement matrix. Moreover, in the pull-out technique it is nearly impossible to determine the influence of other fibres in the bundle on the single fibre-matrix bond. The push-out (called also push-in) technique test involves axial loading of a single fibre using a punch until it completely debonds and slides out of the specimen. The push-out test is based on an indentation technique, which was originally developed for testing ceramic matrix composites [5]. The schematic representation of the push-out technique is shown in Fig. 1. An effective use of such a test was reported for various matrix composites, [6], [7], The basic analysis of push-out data involves a determination of the bond strength and the sliding stress. The interfacial shear strength (bond strength) is defined by the stress corresponding to fibre debonding from the matrix. The sliding stress is measured as the fibre moves out of the matrix. In a simple formulation the bond strength or the sliding stress is defined as follows:

τ - is the bond strength or the sliding stress; $\tau = P/ (\pi D t)$
P – is the axial load at the point of interest (debonding, sliding)
D – is the fibre diameter
t - is the specimen thickness

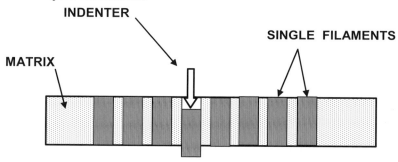

Figure 1: Schematic representation of the push-out technique

A typical load-displacement (or stress-time) curve is shown in Fig. 2, where characteristic values of the shear bond stress τ are indicated: τ_0 represents the initial debonding stress, the partial debonding stress τ_p , the maximum debonding stress τ_m and the complete debonding stress or frictional stress τ_{fr} .

More detailed analysis of push-out data is possible considering the fibre expansion due to the effect of Poisson coefficient, contact length changes during progressive sliding of fibre out of the matrix or even residual stresses and thermal effects. An extensive review of analytical studies of the fibre push-out test was proposed by Zhou et. al. [8] without considering any particular materials for fibres and matrix. There were used basically two different theoretical models for this problem, applied for both pull-out and push-out situations. One is based on a criterion of shear bond stress, according to which debonding appears when the interfacial stress exceeds the shear bond strength. The second one is derived from fracture mechanics concept of a crack that propagates along the fibre, according to the input of energy from external loading. Basic difference between pull-out and push-out techniques is in the influence of Poisson coefficient of the fibre whose influence of the stress distribution around the fibre has opposite sign.

Some push-out test data for glassfibres in cement matrix were reported in [9] and [10]. This paper presents the investigation included in a larger research program on toughness mechanisms and the durability of GFRC composites, reported in [11]. The objective was to provide the quantitative data on interfacial properties for design of glassfibre cement composites.

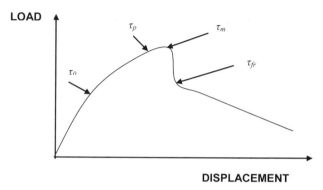

Figure 2: Load-displacement curve from the push-out test

2. EXPERIMENTAL

2.1. Materials and specimens

Strands of high zirconia glassfibres were applied. The diameter of a single glass filament was about 13-15 µm. The following materials were used for manufacturing the cementitious matrix: pure Portland cement, highly reactive metakaolin, superplasticizer and tap water. The investigated matrix modifications were achieved by substituting highly reactive metakaolin for an equal mass of cement in the mix. Such substitutions ranging up to 40% of cement were studied. The mix proportions for the series of specimens are indicated in Table 1.

Table 1: Cement paste mix proportions

Material	Content [g]			
	Reference CP	MK_20	MK_30	MK_40
Cement CEM I 42.5 NA	1000	800	697	600
High reactivity metakaolin	-	200	303	400
Superplasticizer	5	15	24	25
Water	403	421	430	439

Cement paste mix was prepared using a standard cement mixer. The specimens were manufactured in the special moulds 200 x 50 x 15 mm with precision grooves to guide unidirectionally strands of AR glass fibres. After positioning the fibre strands the mould was gently filled with fluid matrix material. The specimens were cured for 7 days in water and later in a dry laboratory conditions until the age of 28 days. Later the specimens were stored in accelerated ageing conditions and tested after ageing. The accelerated ageing procedure was a warm water immersion at 50°C during 84 days. Using an acceleration factor based on Arrhenius law one can estimate this ageing period as approximately equivalent to 30 years of natural exposure in Central-European climate.

2.2. Test method

Push-out tests were performed on thin slices about 440-600 μm, cut out of the specimens perpendicularly to the direction of glass filaments. Precision cutting was performed using a diamond wire saw and using Struer's polishing machine to obtain the required thickness of the slice.

The push-out apparatus used was a Touchstone Research Laboratory device, placed in a vacuum chamber of SEM microscope Carl Zeiss 962. The push-out tests were performed at the EMPA laboratory in Thun, Switzerland. Specimens were mounted on a grooved stub that was then placed on the SEM stage. The displacement rate was about 0.2 μm/s, the maximum load applied was 70 N. A very thin (6.2 μm in diameter) diamond conical tip was used and any damages and splitting of the tested filaments have been avoided.

Single glass fibres in selected locations within the strand were loaded and pushed-out from the matrix. The selection of glassfibres was made in purpose to distinguish properties of the 'inner' fibres, surrounded by other fibres and interstitial material, and the 'outer' fibres, located at the boundary of the strand. The load data was digitally recorded with precision up to 1 mN and the push-out process was observed in situ, at high magnification, during load application.

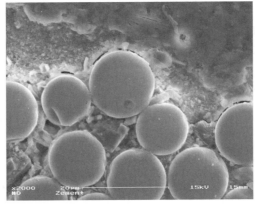

Figure 3: Single filaments surrounded by interstitial material

3. TEST RESULTS

An enlarged fragment of the glassfibre strand in cementitious matrix shown in Fig. 3 illustrates the distinction of the 'inner' fibres and 'outer' fibres at the boundary of the strand.

Some representative push-out curves for 'inner' and 'outer' fibres in the matrix with 30% of metakaolin are shown in Fig. 4 as obtained for unaged specimens. On the basis of obtained load-displacement curves a quantitative difference in push-out performance of single fibres could be provided. Debonding stresses and frictional stresses were higher for fibres located at the boundary of the strand than for inner fibres. The recorded values of shear stress and the displacement at the ultimate and the friction stress during sliding are given in Table 2 for the aged specimens.

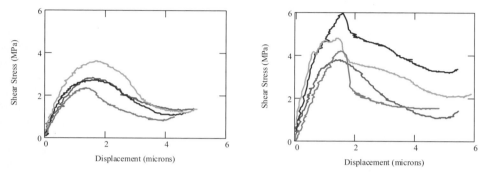

Figure 4: Examples of push-out curves for 'inner' fibres (left) and 'outer' fibres (right) in the matrix with 30% of metakaolin (unaged specimens)

Table 2: Push-out data for aged specimens (average and standard deviation for 4 to 8 fibres)

Matrix	Filament location	Bond strength τ_m		Ultimate displacement u_m		Friction stress τ_{fr}	
		[MPa]		[µm]		[MPa]	
specimen thickness 600 µm							
CP	Outer filaments	7.53	±0.87	6.36	±0.41	4.11	±0.82
MK_20		7.35	±0.83	7.93	±1.38	5.17	±1.09
MK_30		5.70	±0.72	5.17	±1.25	2.95	±0.55
MK_40		4.94	±0.72	3.45	±0.51	2.48	±0.43
CP	Inner filaments	7.47	±1.40	6.21	±1.26	3.66	±0.71
MK_20		6.17	±0.73	5.92	±0.65	3.30	±0.82
MK_30		5.28	±1.25	5.32	±0.82	2.67	±0.49
MK_40		4.11	±0.88	3.47	±0.68	2.28	±0.34
specimen thickness. 440 µm							
CP	Outer filaments	6.23	±1.13	2.45	±0.36	3.06	±0.30
MK_30		5.22	±0.95	2.72	±0.76	1.88	±0.44
CP	Inner filaments	5.51	±0.67	2.53	±0.60	2.05	±0.28
MK_30		4.09	±1.01	2.50	±0.51	1.49	±0.32

The bond strength decreased from 7.5 MPa down to appr. 4 MPa with increasing content of metakaolin and systematically higher values were obtained for the outer fibres than for the inner ones. Simple linear relationships are proposed:

$\tau_m = 7.89\ (1-0.85\ m_{me})$, r^2=0.82 - for outer fibres

$\tau_m = 7.61\ (1-1.08\ m_{me})$, r^2=0.98 - for inner fibres

where m_{me} is the fraction of cement mass replaced by high reactivity metakaolin.

The influence of metakaolin content on the recorded frictional stress can be approximated by the following simple formula:

τ_{fr} = 4.23 (1-0.95 m_{me}) - both for the inner and the outer fibres.

The differences due to fibre location within the strand disappear for the reference matrix, i.e. for pure portland cement paste. So the ageing process affects equally these fibres in the reference matrix while for the increasing content of metakaolin these differences are increased.

Recorded high bond stresses were correlated with high axial stresses in single filaments 0.7-1.3 GPa and such data should be considered in relation to the long term tensile strength of glass filaments. West and Majumdar [12] have found that the tensile strength of zirconia glass fibres removed from cementitious matrix after a prolonged wet storage was about 1.1 GPa. As shown in Fig. 5 using this value as the approximation of the long term tensile strength of glass filaments the three modes of fibre failure, reported in [12], can be distinguished. So called telescopic fracture is seen when the filaments at the strand boundary break and the inner filaments pull-out.

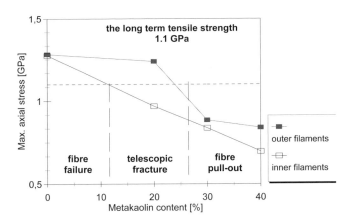

Figure 5: The influence of metakaolin content on the recorded axial stress in glass filaments (aged specimens)

Further interpretation of test data was done using the model proposed by Marshall and Oliver [5]. Assuming a linear distribution of axial stresses in the fibre and a constant friction stress after debonding the energy balance for an increase of debonding crack gives the following formula for the displacement of the loaded fibre end u:

$$u = \frac{F^2}{4\pi r_f^3 \tau E_f} - \frac{2\Gamma_i}{\tau}$$

where F – the axial load, r_f – the fibre radius, E_f – the Young's modulus of fibre, 2 Γ_i – the fracture surface energy in mode II fracture, τ - the fibre-matrix friction stress. The parameters

Γ_i and τ are considered as characteristic for the fibre-matrix interface. Since the formula above yields a linear relationship between F square and u, using the recorded load-displacement data it is possible to estimate the values of Γ_i and τ for each tested fibre. The values of Γ_i and τ extracted from such a linear approximation are presented in Table 3 for aged specimens (average values and standard deviation values for 4 to 8 fibres). A decrease of Γ_i and τ with increasing content of metakaolin is evident:

$\Gamma_i = 2.42\ (1\text{-}1.46\ m_{me})$, $r^2 = 0.97$ - for the outer fibres
$\Gamma_i = 2.48\ (1\text{-}1.80\ m_{me})$, $r^2 = 0.99$ - for the inner fibres
$\tau = 6.52\ (1\text{-}0.76\ m_{me})$, $r^2 = 0.97$ - for the outer fibres
$\tau = 7.26\ (1\text{-}1.24\ m_{me})$, $r^2 = 0.97$ - for the inner fibres

The differences in the performance of the inner fibres and the outer fibres is also evident as far as Γ_i is concerned, due to the data scatter such a difference is not certain for τ.

Table 3: The parameters Γ_i and τ of Marshall-Oliver model for aged specimens

Metakaolin content [%]	Γ_i [N/m]		τ [MPa]	
	outer fibres	inner fibres	outer fibres	inner fibres
0	2.34 ±0.20	2.44 ±0.52	6.6 ±1.6	7.5 ±0.8
20	1.87 ±0.06	1.72 ±0.29	5.5 ±0.9	5.0 ±1.3
30	1.33 ±0.33	1.06 ±0.17	4.8 ±0.5	4.6 ±1.2
40	0.94 ±0.28	0.69 ±0.06	4.7 ±1.1	3.8 ±0.8

Comparing two sets of data for different filament location the significant differences can be noted due to position of a tested fibre within the bundle. The interface between the matrix and the fibres at the edge of the bundle was characterized by higher shear strength and higher fracture energy. Between the inner filaments some empty spaces can be seen that resulted in lower shear stresses during push-out. Such a complex performance of fibres in a bundle could be a result of a process of filling-up of interfilamentary spaces that could be associated with migration of pore-water solutions into bundle and crystallization from solutions.

4. CONCLUSIONS

The following conclusions could be drawn on the basis of presented results.
- For the matrices modified with metakaolin increase of the maximum bond stresses τ_m were observed after accelerated ageing, namely 57-143% for outer filaments and 39-127% for inner filaments.
- The increase for the frictional stress τ_{fr} was also observed, but reduced to 44-97% and 25-62%, for outer and inner filaments, respectively.
- For increasing content of metakaolin a proportional decrease of the maximum bond stress τ_m and the frictional stress τ_{fr} after ageing was observed.
- Marshall-Oliver model provided a very good description of push-out data.

- Identification of bond properties of glassfibres to modified matrices by push-out test may be applied in design.

ACKNOWLEDGMENT

The cooperation of Dr. J. Janczak-Rusch from Empa, Switzerland, is gratefully acknowledged.

REFERENCES

[1] Majumdar, A.J., Laws, V., *Glass Fibre Reinforced Cement*, Oxford BSP professional Books, London, 1991

[2] Marikunte, S., Aldea, C., Shah, S.P., Matrix modification to improve the durability of glass fiber reinforced cement composites, in: *'Brittle Matrix Composites 5'*, A.M.Brandt, V.C.Li and I.H.Marshall eds., Woodhead Publ. - Bigraf, Cambridge and Warsaw, 1997, 90-102

[3] Rajczyk, K., Giergiczny, E., Glinicki, M.A., The influence of pozzolanic materials on the durability of glass fibre reinforced cement composites, *in: 'Brittle Matrix Composites 5'*, A.M.Brandt, V.C.Li and I.H.Marshall eds., Woodhead Publ. - Bigraf, Cambridge and Warsaw, 1997, 103-112

[4] Bartos, P., Review paper: Bond in fibre-reinforced cements and concretes. *Int.J. of Cement Comp.& Lightweight Concrete*, vol.3, no 3, 1981, 159-177

[5] Marshall D.B., Oliver, W.C., Measurement of interfacial mechanical properties in fiber-reinforced ceramic composites, *Jour. of American Ceramic Soc.*, vol. 70, no 8, 1987, 542-572

[6] Janczak, J., Stackpole, R., Bürki, G., Rohr, L., The use of push-out technique for determination of interfacial properties of metal-matrix composites, *17th Int. SAMPE Europe Conf. of the Society for the Advancement of Materials and Process Engineering*, Basel, 1996, 7p.

[7] Kalton A. F. , Howard S. J. , Janczak-Rusch J., Clyne T. W. , Measurement of interfacial fracture energy by single fibre push-out testing and its application to the titanium-silicon carbide system, *Acta Materialia*, vol. 46, no 9, 1998, 3175-3189

[8] Zhou, L.M., Mai, Y.W., Ye, L., Analyses of fibre push-out test based on the fracture mechanics approach. *Composites Engineering*, vol.5, no 10-11, 1995, 1199-1219

[9] Zhu, W., Bartos, P.J.M., Assessment of interfacial microstructure and bond properties in aged GRC using a novel microindentation method, *Cement and Concrete Research.*, vol.27, no 11, 1997, 1701-1711

[10] Glinicki M.A., Effects of diatomite on toughness of premix glass fibre reinforced cement composites, in: *Proc. 11th International Congress of GRCA*, Cambridge, April 14-16, 1998, paper 4, 10p.

[11] Brandt, A. M., Glinicki, M. A., Effects of pozzolanic additives on long-term flexural toughness of HPGFRC, in: *Int. Workshop on High Performance Fiber Reinforced Cement Composites HPFRCC-4*, A.E.Naaman and H.W.Reinhardt eds, Ann Arbor, Michigan 2003, 399-408

[12] West, J.M., Majumdar, A.J., Strength of glass fibres in cement environments, *J. Materials Science Letters*, 1, 1982, 214-216

NUMERICAL INVESTIGATION OF FIRE TESTS ON TEXTILE-REINFORCED CONCRETE ELEMENTS

Hans W. Reinhardt, Joško Ožbolt, Markus Krüger and Goran Periškić

Department of Construction Materials, University of Stuttgart, Germany

Abstract

Four fire tests have been performed on textile-reinforced concrete (TRC) sections (I-sections). The textiles were AR glass and carbon. These experiments showed that the load bearing behaviour of textile-reinforced structural components in fire greatly depends on the textile used, their bond to the concrete, and the behaviour of the concrete under high temperatures. Based on the test results numerical investigations were made using a transient three-dimensional FE-model. The present paper describes the numerical analysis.

1. INTRODUCTION

When textile reinforced concrete elements are used in fire relevant structures such as buildings they have to have a certain fire endurance which depends on the function of the rooms. The requirements include for example a sufficient load bearing capacity and a limit of maximum deformation as well as temperature differencies between the cold and the warm side to ensure a room enclosing function in the event of fire. Since the behaviour of textile reinforced concrete elements in fire is very rarely investigated tests have been carried out at the University of Stuttgart on four types of textile reinforced concrete elements. The results of the tests are described in [1]. Additionally, a numerical study has been performed in order to simulate the fire behaviour of these elements. The analysis is subject of this contribution.

In the present paper a transient thermal three-dimensional (3D) FE Analysis of a carbon reinforced concrete beam has been performed using a 3D model that is based on the thermo-mechanical coupling between mechanical properties of concrete and temperature. The microplane model [2] is used as a constitutive law for concrete whose model parameters are made temperature dependent. The finite element analysis is performed in two steps. In the first step the temperature distribution is calculated for given temperature boundary conditions (air temperature and/or concrete surface temperature). In the second step the required load history is applied where the influence of temperature on the mechanical properties of concrete is considered.

2. TRANSIENT THERMAL ANALYSIS

As the first step of coupling the mechanical properties of concrete with the temperature, for a given thermal boundary condition at time t, the temperature distribution over a solid structure of volume Ω has to be calculated. In each point of continuum, which is defined by the Cartesian coordinates (x,y,z), the conservation of energy has to be fulfilled. This can be expressed by the following equation:

$$\lambda \Delta T(x,y,z,t) + W(x,y,z,t,T) - c\rho \frac{\partial T}{\partial t}(x,y,z,t) = 0 \tag{1}$$

where T = temperature, λ = conductivity, c = heat capacity, ρ = mass density, W = internal source of heating and Δ = Laplace-Operator. The surface boundary condition that has to be satisfied reads:

$$\lambda \frac{\partial T}{\partial \mathbf{n}} = \alpha(T_M - T) \tag{2}$$

with $\mathbf{n}$ = normal to the boundary surface Γ, α = transfer or radiation coefficient and T_M = temperature of the media in which surface Γ of the solid Ω is exposed to (for instance temperature of air). To solve the problem by the finite element method the above differential equations (1) and (2) have to be written in the weak (integral) form [3].

3. DECOMPOSITION OF STRAIN

3.1   Strain tensor

In the present model the total strain tensor ε_{ij} (indicial notation) for stressed concrete exposed to high temperature can be decomposed as [4, 5, 6]:

$$\varepsilon_{ij} = \varepsilon_{ij}^m(T,\sigma_{kl}) + \varepsilon_{ij}^{ft}(T) + \varepsilon_{ij}^{tm}(T,\sigma_{kl}) + \varepsilon_{ij}^c(T,\sigma_{kl}) \tag{3}$$

where ε_{ij}^m = mechanical strain tensor, ε_{ij}^{ft} = free thermal train tensor, ε_{ij}^{tm} = thermo-mechanical strain tensor and ε_{ij}^c are strains that are due to the temperature dependent creep of concrete.

In general, the mechanical strain component can be decomposed into an elastic, plastic and damage part. In the present model these strain components are obtained from the constitutive law. The free thermal strain is stress independent and it is experimentally obtained by measurements on the load-free specimen. In such experiments it is not possible to isolate shrinkage of concrete, therefore, the temperature dependent shrinkage is contained in the free thermal strain. The thermo-mechanical strain is stress and temperature dependent. It appears only during the first heating and not during the subsequent cooling and heating cycles [4]. This strain is irrecoverable and leads in concrete structures to severe tensile stresses during cooling. The temperature dependent creep strain is of the same nature as the thermo-mechanical strain except that it is partly recoverable. In the experiment, it is not possible to isolate it. For low temperature rates, what is the normal case in the experiments, this strain component compared to the thermo-mechanical strain is small. Therefore, the temperature dependent creep strain is neglected in the present model.

3.2 Mechanical strain

The mechanical strain components are obtained from the constitutive law of concrete. In the proposed model the microplane model is used for the temperature independent (isothermal) constitutive law [2]. In the microplane model the material is characterized by a relation between the stress and strain components on planes of various orientations. The basic concept behind the microplane model was advanced by G.I. Taylor [7] and developed in detail for plasticity by Batdorf and Budianski [8] under the name "slip theory of plasticity". The microplane model used in the present paper was recently proposed by Ožbolt et al. [2]. The temperature dependency of the microplane model is adopted such that the macroscopic properties of concrete (Young's modulus, compressive and tensile strength and fracture energy) are made temperature dependent, according to the available experimental data [5, 9, 10].

3.3 Free thermal strain

The experimental evidence [5] indicates that the free thermal strains in concrete specimens mainly depend on the type and amount of the aggregate. Although the experiments indicate that the free thermal strain depends on the rate of the temperature, in the present model is assumed that this strain depends only on the temperature. Moreover, it is assumed that in the case of a stress free specimen, the thermal strains in all three mutually perpendicular directions are the same (isotropic thermal strains). The temperature dependency of the free thermal strain, as adopted in the present model, reads:

$$\dot{\varepsilon}_{ij}^{ft} = \alpha \dot{T} \delta_{ij}$$

$$\begin{aligned} &for\ \ 0 \le \theta \le 6 \quad \alpha = \frac{6.0\ 10^{-5}}{7.0-\theta} \\ &for\ \ \theta > 6 \qquad \alpha = 0 \qquad \text{with } \theta = \left(T - T_0\right)/100°C \end{aligned} \tag{4}$$

3.4 Stress induced thermal strain – creep

When a concrete specimen is first loaded and than exposed to high temperature, the resulting thermal strain is different from the case when the specimen is not loaded [6, 11, 12]. The difference can be obtained if the free thermal strain is subtracted from the resulting thermal strain; the so called stress induced thermal strain. The stress induced thermal strain consists of two parts – irrecoverable part and partly recoverable part (temperature dependent creep). Since the partly recoverable part has only a theoretical meaning and is much smaller than the irrecoverable part, it is neglected in the present model, i.e. the total stress dependent thermal strain is assumed to be irrecoverable. The bi-parabolic thermo-mechanical strain model is used [13], which reads:

$$\dot{\varepsilon}^{tm}(T,\sigma) = \frac{\sigma}{f_c^{T_0}} \beta \dot{T}$$

$$\beta = 0.01 \cdot \begin{cases} 2 \cdot A \cdot \theta + B & for \quad 0 \le \theta \le \theta^* = 4.5 \\ 2 \cdot C \cdot (\theta - \theta^*) + 2 \cdot A \cdot \theta^* + B & for \quad \theta > \theta^* \end{cases} \tag{5}$$

where θ^* is a dimensionless transition temperature between the two expressions (470°C). The above two expressions are introduced to account for abrupt change in behaviour detected in the experiments. *A*, *B* and *C* are experimentally obtained constants that are in the present model set as: $A = 0.0005$, $B = 0.00125$ and $C = 0.0085$.

4. NUMERICAL SIMULATION - MODEL DESCRIPTION

The performance of the carbon textile reinforced concrete beam (MAG-5-03) was numerically investigated. The goal of the numerical analysis was to investigate whether the numerical analysis is able to realistically predict experimental results. In the analysis the same geometry as in experiment was used (see Fig. 1). In order to save computational time, only one quarter of the geometry was modelled, i.e. the double symmetry was utilized (see Fig. 2). Discretization of concrete was performed by eight-node elements. Carbon reinforcement was modelled using one-dimensional bar elements. Perfect bond between concrete and textile reinforcement was assumed. The material properties used in the numerical analysis are summarised in Table 1. Note that Young's modulus and tensile strength of the textile are obtained from test results of a textile roving.

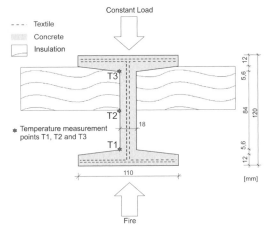

Figure 1: The experimental setup in cross-section; one side of the specimen is exposed to fire

Table 1: Material properties

	Concrete	Carbon reinforcement
Young's modulus E [MPa]	35000	180000
Poisson's ratio ν	0.18	0.4
Tensile strength f_t [MPa]	3.5	1100
Uniaxial compressive strength f_c [MPa]	45	-
Fracture energy G_F [N/mm]	0.12	-

a)   b)

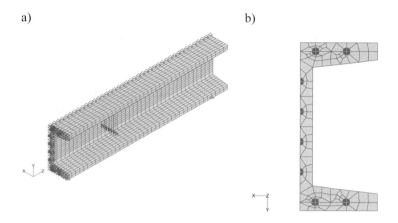

Figure 2: 3D FE discretization: a) Model of simulated beam and b) Position of
Carbon rovings

5.   RESULTS OF THE NUMERICAL ANALYSIS

5.1   Static analysis of carbon reinforced concrete beam

A simple static analysis of the carbon reinforced concrete beam without influence of fire
was first carried out. The goal was to investigate whether the numerical model is able to predict the beam response under isothermal conditions realistically. The test setup is shown in
Fig. 3. The specimen was subjected to four-point bending that was applied by displacement
control. Fig. 3 shows the load-deflection curves obtained in the analysis and measured in the
experiment. It can be seen that both, predicted ultimate load and stiffness of the response,
agree very well with the experimental results.

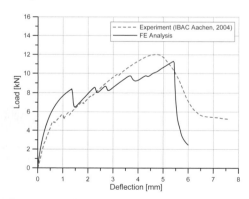

Figure 3: Load-deflection curves obtained by the 3D FE analysis and measured in the experiment (isothermal conditions)

Fig. 4 shows a typical crack pattern (maximal principal strains) of the examined concrete beam. Cracks in the tensile flange and the bottom chord can be observed. The failure of the beam follows after the tensile strength of the carbon reinforcement has been reached.

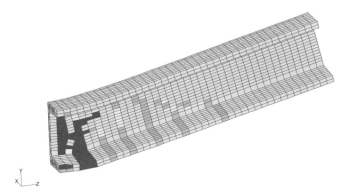

Figure 4: Typical crack pattern obtained by the static isothermal 3D FE analysis

5.2   Thermal analysis of carbon reinforced concrete beam

As already mentioned, the transient thermal analysis consists of two steps: In the first step temperature distribution is calculated and then in second step this distribution is used as a thermal loading of the beam. As in the test, the lower side of the flange has been heated with the heated area matching to the one being exposed to fire in the fire room. The heating was simulated such that the air below the heated concrete area was heated for 90 minutes according to the ISO-834 standard curve with a transfer coefficient α=8.0 W/(m^{2}K). Thermal properties of concrete have been taken as follows: conductivity λ=2.9 W/(mK), heat capacity c=900 J/(kgK) and density ρ=2300 kg/m^3. Thermal properties of carbon reinforcement have not been taken into account by the calculation of temperature distribution. The starting temperature of 20°C was assumed. Model setup for the calculation of temperature as well as temperature distribution after 90 minutes of heating is shown in Fig. 5.

a)   b)

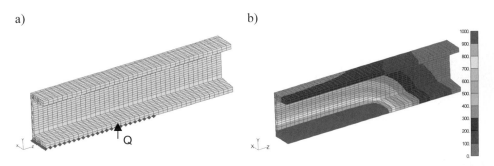

Figure 5: a) Model setup for calculation of temperature and b) temperature distribution after 90 min. of heating

In the analysis the specimen was first subjected to static loading in four-point bending and then exposed to heating. The static load corresponds to the 1/3 of the ultimate bearing capacity at isothermal loading conditions. Results of the thermal transient numerical analysis are shown in Fig 6. The total deflection of the beam is shown as a function of time. It can be observed that the maximal deflection as well as the maximal bending moment disagree with the experimental results, however, the numerical results are qualitatively in good agreement with the experimental results. Namely, at the beginning of heating the deflection of the beam increases as a result of bending, but as the temperature in the flange and the bottom chord increases the carbon reinforcement start to contract, because of the negative temperature coefficient of extension $\alpha_T = -0.4\times10^{-6}$ K^{-1}, and causes compressive stresses in the flange and the chord. This causes the decrease of the beam deflection. With further heating the stress in the carbon rovings increases until it reaches the tensile strength, which causes failure of the beam.

The reason for the difference between the experimental and numerical results is probably due to the complexity of the problem that is in the numerical simulation greatly simplified. For instance, the moisture transport during heating and change of thermal properties of concrete due to the increase of temperature were not taken into account in the simulation. Moreover, pore pressure due to the heating of concrete and the interaction between thermal and mechanical properties are not considered in the model. Obviously, to predict more accurate response of the beam the above influencing factors should be taken into account.

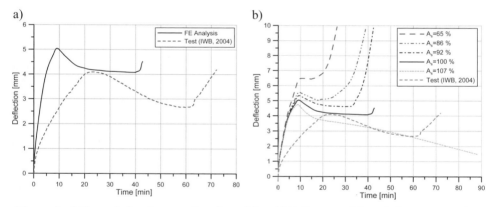

Figure 6: a) Beam deflection as a function of time b) Influence of the reinforcement ratio on the deflection-time dependency

To investigate the influence of the carbon rovings on the deflection of the carbon reinforced beam, numerical analysis was performed for beams with different reinforcement ratios. The results of the analysis are shown in Fig. 6b. It can be seen that for higher amount of reinforcement the tensile stress in the reinforcement does not reach the tensile strength, deflection decreases for almost the whole 90 minutes of heating and the specimen does not fail. On the other hand, when the reinforcement area decreases the maximal deflection increases and the tensile strength of the carbon rowing is reached earlier.

Fig. 7 shows a typical crack pattern at failure load compared to a picture of a specimen after fire test. It can be seen that the crack indicating the failure of the specimen appears in both cases almost at the same place.

a)

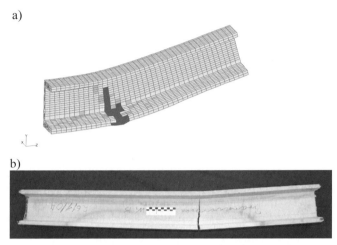

b)

Figure 7: a) Typical crack pattern from a thermal FE analysis and b) specimen after fire test

In Fig. 8a the temperatures in the measurement point T1 (see Fig. 1) from the numerical analysis have been compared to the equivalent temperatures from the experiment. It can be observed, that the temperature in the numerical analysis increases much faster than in the experiment. As already mentioned before, the reason for this difference is probably due to the fact that the moisture transport was not taken into account in the calculation of the temperature distribution. Therefore, to get more realistic temperature distribution over the concrete beam, a modified air temperature curve was used. The modification was performed such that the temperature difference between numerical and test data in the measurement point T1 has been subtracted from the original input air temperature (ISO-834). This changed air temperature has then been used as input data in calculation of the temperature distribution. The results of the new analysis are shown in Fig. 8a. Again, a certain difference can be observed in the first 20 minutes, but afterwards the numerical and experimental results agree well.

The new temperature data have then been used to perform additional static analysis, with the material properties the same as in the experiment. The results are shown in Fig 8b. It can be seen that, in comparison with the original numerical analysis, the deflection process as well as the development of the tensile force in the rovings is considerably slower. The time point of the maximal deflection agrees well with the experiment (ca. 25 minutes). Also, the time point where the ultimate strength of the rovings is reached shows relatively good agreement with experimental data. The failure was equivalent to the one observed in the experiment.

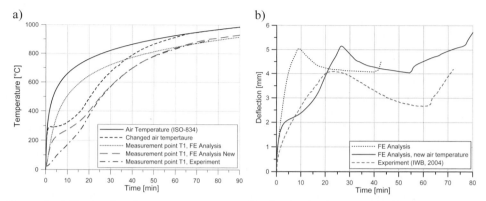

Figure 8: a) Comparison between temperature distribution in the FE analysis and experiment and b) results of the failure analysis with the use of the modified distribution of the air temperature curve

6. ASSESSMENT OF THE NUMERICAL INVESTIGATIONS

In the present paper the behaviour of the carbon reinforced concrete beam under fire loading has been numerically investigated using a transient three-dimensional thermo-mechanical model for concrete. The calculation consists of two steps. In the first step for a given heating a temperature distribution over a concrete member is calculated. In the second step this distribution of temperature is applied as a thermal load with taking into account the influence of the temperature on the concrete mechanical properties. To investigate whether the 3D FE code is able to realistically predict failure of carbon reinforced beam at isothermal conditions, the beam was first loaded in four point bending up to failure. The results of the analysis show good agreement with the experimental results. Subsequently, 3D FE thermal and thermo-mechanical analyses of the beam were performed. The results of both analyses were compared with the test results. Principally, the agreement between numerical and experimental results is good. However, it is obvious that the relatively simple thermo-mechanical model for concrete need to be improved, i.e. the interaction between the hydro-thermo-mechanical properties should be taken into account in order to predict the structural response under fire loading more realistically. The parametric study in which the influence of the reinforcement on the behaviour of beam was studied show that with increase of the reinforcement ratio the failure of the beam can be avoided for the whole period of 90 minutes of heating. Finally, it can be concluded that the presented, relatively simple, model is a powerful numerical tool which can be used to clarify the behaviour of a number of structures and structural details exposed to fire.

7. OUTLOOK

The numerical investigations have shown that the fire behaviour of textile reinforced concrete elements could be modelled. However, the material behaviour at very high temperatures is of high complexity and knowledge is still limited.

In summary, in particular three aspects would have to be investigated more closely in future: The behaviour of fine concrete in high temperatures, the strength and the thermal expansion behaviour, and the development of the bond of textile reinforcement in high temperatures.

REFERENCES

[1]   Krüger, M., Reinhardt, H.W., Raupach, M., Orlowsky, J.: Textilbewehrter Beton unter Brandbeanspruchung. Betonwerk + Fertigteil-Technik 71 (2005), Nr. 10, S. 38-48

[2]   Ožbolt, J., Li, Y.-J. and Kožar, I.: Microplane model for concrete with relaxed kinematic constraint, International Journal of Solids and Structures, Vol. 38, No. 16, 2001, 2683-2711.

[3]   Ožbolt, J., Kožar, I., Eligehausen, R. and Periškić, G.: Three-dimensional FE Analysis of headed stud anchors exposed to fire, Computers & Concrete, Vol. 2, No. 4, 2005, 249-266.

[4]   Khoury, G.A., Grainger, B.N. and Sullivan, P.J.E.: Transient thermal strain of concrete: literature review, conditions within specimens and behaviour of individual constituents, Magazine of concrete research, Vol. 37, No. 132, 1985a, 131-144.

[5]   Schneider, U.: Properties of Materials at High Temperatures, Concrete, 2nd. Edition, Kassel, RILEM Technical Comitee 44-PHT, Technical University of Kassel, 1986.

[6]   Thelandersson, S.: Modeling of combined thermal and mechanical action in concrete, Journal of Engineered Mechanics, Vol. 113, No. 6, 1987, 893-906.

[7]   Taylor, G.I.: Plastic strain in metals, Journal of the Institute of Metals, Vol. 62, 1938, 307-324.

[8]   Batdorf, S.B. and Budianski, B.: A mathematical theory of plasticity based on the concept of slip, Technical Note No. 1871, Washington D.C., National Advisory Committee for Aeronautics, 1949.

[9]   Zhang, B. and Bićanić, N.: "Residual Fracture Toughness of Normal- and High-Strength Gravel Concrete after Heating to 600°C", ACI Materials Journal, Vol. 99, No 3, 2002, 217-226.

[10] Thelandersson, S.: On the multiaxial behaviour of concrete exposed to high temperature, Nuclear Engineering and Design, Vol. 75, No. 2, 1982, 271-282.

[11] Bažant, Z.P. and Chern, J.C.: Stress-induced thermal and shrinkage strains in concrete, Journal of Engineering Mechanics, Vol. 113, No. 10, 1987, 1493-1511.

[12] Khoury, G.A., Grainger, B.N. and Sullivan, P.J.E.: Strain of concrete during first heating to 600°C under load, Magazine of concrete research, Vol. 37, No. 133, 1985b, 195-215.

[13] Nielsen, C.V., Pearce, C.J. and Bićanić, N.: Improved phenomenological modeling of transient thermal strains for concrete at high temperatures, Computers & Concrete, Vol. 1, No. 2, 2004, 189-209.

FIRE RESISTANCE TESTS OF TEXTILE REINFORCED CONCRETE UNDER STATIC LOADING – RESULTS AND FUTURE DEVELOPMENTS

Till Büttner, Jeanette Orlowsky and Michael Raupach

Institute of Building Materials, RWTH Aachen University

Abstract
One major application field of textile reinforced concrete as an innovative building material are load bearing structural elements in various types of buildings. Due to this, the fire resistance is a very crucial point, which has to be taken into account while investigating such a new building material. Within the Collaborative Research Center SFB 532 and in cooperation with the University of Stuttgart several fire resistance tests under static loads were already carried out. The tests were performed on I-shaped concrete beams reinforced with alkali-resistance (AR-) glass and carbon textiles. The results reveal that the carbon textile reinforced specimen can bear a standardized fire load up to 95 minutes. However, the tests also show that the fire resistance of TRC with AR-Glass reinforcement needs to be improved for certain applications. So in this paper ways to improve the fire resistance of TRC-specimen reinforced with AR-Glass and the aim of future research will be presented.

1. INTRODUCTION

The advantages of the new construction material textile reinforced concrete (TRC) dominate in fields of applications where thin-walled structural elements with a high load bearing capacity are required. As reinforcement mainly alkali resistant (AR-) glass rovings, carbon rovings and aramid rovings are used. The collaborate research center "SFB 532" at Aachen University deals with the scientific questions which have to be solved in order to develop this new technology. One important aspect for structural elements, besides the load bearing capacity and the durability, is the fire resistance. It is one key element for ruling out the application areas of a construction material and regulated in the German DIN 4102 containing on one hand the requirements for all types of building materials and on the other hand the requirements for testing building materials. Large scale fire tests were carried out at the University of Stuttgart [1], which are described in this paper.

2. FIRE RESISTANCE REQUIREMENTS IN GERMANY

In Germany two major standard series deal with fire resistance. The first part is the DIN 4102:1998, in which the requirements for testing the fire resistance and the classification of the results in so called fire resistance classes are defined. The second part is represented by the county building regulations which deal with the usage of the fire resistance classes. These county regulations are based on a prototype regulation ("Musterbauordnung") and also there are additional regulations for special buildings like theatres, which are not part of this current reflection.

The declaration of a fire resistance class contains two informations – the maximum time which the construction material is able to bear a fire load according to the standardized temperature curve, in intervals of 30 min. from 30 up to 180 minutes, and a classification whether the material is fire-proof (A), flammable (B) or predominantly fire-proof (AB). In order to achieve one fire resistance class not only the time until failure of a series of at least two specimens has to be greater than the desired class but also certain requirements on the deflection speed and the temperature difference over the cross section have to be met

The utilization of those fire resistance classes in Germany has to be carried out according to the county building regulations ("Landesbauordnung"). In these regulations the requirements for construction details are listed. In the following table 1 and table 2 an extract of the county building regulation of North Rhine-Westphalia ("BauO NRW") is given. In this regulation "buildings of small height" are defined as buildings in which no living space is above 7 m over ground (see §2 BauO NRW).

Table 1: Extract of §29 of the county building regulations of North-Rhine Westphalia (BauO NRW) – Walls and columns

Column	Structural element	Free-standing residential house with one apartment	Residential house of small height, with no more than 2 appartments	Building of small height	Other buildings
1a	load-bearing walls and columns	no requirements	F30	F30	F90-AB
1b	as 1a in basements	no requirements	F30-AB	F90-AB	F90-AB
1c	as 1a in top floors with possible accommodation above	no requirements	F30	F30	F90
1d	as 1a in top floors with **no** possible accommodation above	no requirements			
2	non load-bearing outdoor walls	no requirements			A or F30

Table 2: Extract of §34 of the county building regulations of North-Rhine Westphalia (BauO NRW) – ceilings

Column	Structural element	Free-standing residential house with one apartment	Residential house of small height, with no more than 2 apartments	Building of small height	Other buildings
1	ceiling	no requirements	F30	F30	F90-AB
2	ceilings over basements	no requirements	F30	F90-AB	F90-AB
3	as 1a in top floors with possible accommodation above	no requirements	F30	F30	F90
4	as 1a in top floors with **no** possible accommodation above	no requirements	no requirements, but construction details according to §30 have to be met		

3. FIRE RESISTANCE TEST

3.1 Materials

The materials have been selected within the Collaborative Research Center "SFB 532" at Aachen University. The concrete is a so called micro-concrete, which was developed at the Institute for Building Materials Research, Aachen University. In order to achieve a good compound, a high floating ability and low diameters of aggregate are required. As consequence the micro-concrete has a maximum grain size of 0.6 mm. The composition and the mechanical properties are given in Table 3 and in [2].

Table 3: Composition of the fine-grained concrete

Binder system	Type of cement	Cement content	Additives				Binder content	w/b-ratio	Porosity
			Fly ash	Silica fume	Water reducer	Stabilizer			
			kg/m³			-	kg/m³	-	% by Vol.
OPC	CEM I 52.5	490	175	35	1 [1]	-	700	0.4	15 [2]

[1]: Mass percentage in relation to cement content
[2]: Storage of the specimen: 90 d under water

As reinforcement two-dimensional AR-glass and Carbon Textiles have been used, which are produced at the Institute of Textile Technology, RWTH-Aachen University. The characteristics of the reinforcement are summarized in table 4 [2] and the paper "Investigation of the durability of TRC – Test methods and modeling the long-term behaviour" of this conference.

Table 4: Characteristics of the reinforcement

		MAG 07-03	MAG 07-03 impregnated	MAG 04-03
Basic roving		VET-RO-ARG 2400-1-03	VET-RO-ARG 2400-1-03 impregnated with epoxy resin (EPL)	TEN-RO-CAR-1600-2-02
Material		AR-Glass	AR-Glass	Carbon
Titer per Roving	tex	2400	2400	1600
Mesh size	mm	8	8	8
Tensile strength [N/mm²] *	N/mm²	970	-	1100

*: in 0° direction (direction of the applied load)

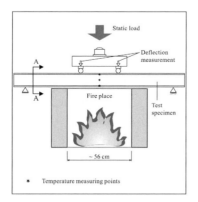 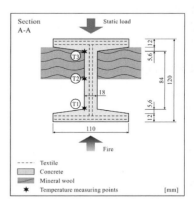

Figure 1: Test setup of the fire resistance tests

3.2 Test Setup

In this paper two series of fire resistance tests are presented. The test parameters of the two series are given in table 5. Fig. 1 gives an overview over the test setup. As test specimen a concrete I-beam with a four point loading was used. The top chord of the I-beam was covered by a mineral wool in order to achieve a one dimensional heat flow within the specimen. The external static load was applied before starting the fire exposure of the specimen; the fire load was applied according to the standardized temperature curve (called "ETK") according to the DIN 4102 given in Fig. 2. The curve reflects the temperature of a natural fire after the "Flash-Over", the point after which the fire is fully developed. The temperature after 30 min. is above 800 °C; 30 minutes later it is above 900 °C and after 120 minutes of testing the temperature is greater than 1000 °C. The fire tests are performed until the specimens fail.

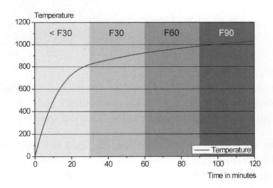

Figure 2: Standardized temperature curve according to DIN 4102 and fire resistance classes under the assumption that all other requirements, e.g. displacement speed, are met

Table 5: Test parameters of the performed fire resistance tests according to DIN 4102

Specimen	Reinforcement material	Static load as percentage of fracture load	Age of the specimens
-	-	%	d
1-AR-1	AR-Glass Textile (MAG 07-03)	33	> 90
1-C-1	Carbon Textile (MAG 04-03)		
1-C-2			
2-AR-1	AR-Glass Textile (MAG 07-03)	50	
2-AREP-1	AR-Glass Textile (MAG 07-03) impregnated with epoxy resin (EPL)		
2-C-1	Carbon Textile (MAG 04-03)		

4. TEST RESULTS

4.1 First test series

The first test series contains three specimens with AR-Glass and Carbon reinforcement. The static load was chosen to be one third of the fracture load of the specimens. The results can be seen in Fig. 3.

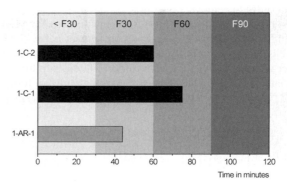

Figure 3: Times up to failure of the specimens 1-C-1; 1-C-2; 1-AR-1 at 1/3 of the fracture
load and indication of possible fire resistance classes under the assumption
that all other requirements, e.g. displacement speed, are met

It can be seen that all specimens can bear the fire load between 45 and 75 minutes of
testing. The carbon fibre reinforced specimen last longer than the AR-glass fibre reinforced
specimen. It also has to be noted, that the concrete of the specimen 1-C-2 was deteriorated on
the bottom side after approx. 15 min. of testing. The test was then continued for another 45
minutes. The carbon did not show any failure due to the fire test. In Fig. 5 the specimen can
be seen after the testing.

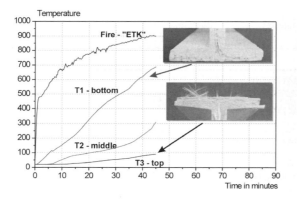

Figure 4a: Temperature curve of specimen 1-AR-1 and
pictures of the AR-glass reinforcement after fire exposure

Figure 4b: Carbon fibre
reinforcement after fire
exposure

Figure 5: Deteriorated bottom of the specimen 1-C-2

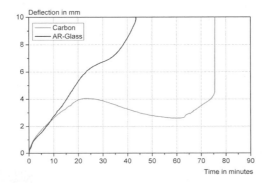

Figure 6: Deflection curves of the specimen 1-AR-1 and 1-C-1

Pictures 4a and 4b show the difference of the two reinforcement materials in the area where the failure of the specimen occurred. The carbon fibers do not deteriorate due to the fire like the AR-glass fibers, which have been deteriorated completly in the bottom of the specimen. The temperature measurements show that the temperature at the bottom of the specimen 1-AR-1 at failure of the specimen is approx. 680 °C. Because there are no temperature-strength curves for AR-Glass available at the time, the curves for E-Glass have to be used to get an indication what the remaining strength of AR-Glass might be at such a temperature. For E-Glass with a softening temperature of 750 °C, the remaining strength at 680 °C is only 7 – 10 % of the strength at room temperature. The AR-Glass used in the presented tests has a softening temperature of 860 °C, so it is likely that the remaining strength here at temperatures between 600 and 700 °C is also very low [3].

Besides the times to failure the deflection speed is one other important aspect of fire resistance testing. For all three specimens, the requirements of the deflection speed according to DIN 4102:1988 were fulfilled. Comparing the time-deflection curves of the specimen 1-C-1 and 1-AR-1 it is obvious that the deflection of the specimen 1-AR-1 shows a constant increase over time. The deflection of the specimen 1-C-1 decreases after approx. 25 minutes of testing. This is probably due to the fact, that carbon has a negative temperature elongation modulus and so the carbon reinforcement compresses itself and leads to a decrease of the deflection.

4.2 Second test series

The second test series contains also three specimens with partly a different reinforcement and a static loading of one half of the fracture load. As reinforcement also Carbon and AR-glass textiles were used. One of the specimens (2-AREP-1) was produced by using an epoxy impregnated textile as reinforcement (see also table 2). The impregnation leads to a higher strength of the textile and the compound material [3]. Because of the low temperature stability of the epoxy impregnation was not supposed to increase the fire resistance, but the impacts of such an impregnation of the behavior under a fire load were supposed to be of interest. The results of the second series can be found in Fig. 7.

At first sight the results reveal the same trend as the results of the first test series. The carbon fiber reinforced concrete specimen fails a considerable time after the two AR-glass fiber reinforced beams. The failure of the specimen (2-C-1) even occurs later than the failure of the two specimens (1-C-1;2) of the first series, unnoted of the higher load.

The AR-glass reinforced specimens of the second test series show a different result in comparison to the first test series. Both specimen fail after 15 minutes of testing and cannot even fulfill the minimum requirement of 30 minutes withstanding the fire, which has been fulfilled by the first test series. The influence of the epoxy impregnation on the fire resistance is not positive or negative – the specimen 2-AREP-1 lasts also only 15 minutes.

The previously described failure pattern of the reinforcement (see Figs. 4a and 4b) could also be noticed here. Also the deflection speed and the decrease of the deflection caused by the negative temperature elongation modulus of carbon can be observed here.

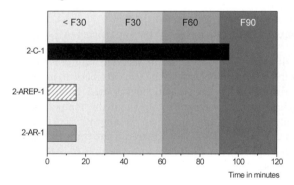

Figure 7: Times to failure of the specimens 2-C-1; 2-AREP-1; 2-AR-1 at 1/2 of the fracture load and indication of possible fire resistance classes under the assumption that all other requirements, e.g. displacement speed, are met

5. DISCUSSION OF THE RESULTS

Taking all six specimens into account a clear trend regarding the fire resistance of TRC specimen can be noted under the premises that the test setup is only valid for research purposes and can only be carefully transferred to real structural elements. Regarding the micro-concrete only in one case a concrete failure occurred. All the other tests did not reveal any concrete failure.

The other aspect of this composite material is the reinforcement. Regarding the carbon fiber reinforcement it is obvious that this material can withstand at least 60 minutes of fire according to the German standardized temperature curve. Even an increase of the load during the fire testing could not decrease the time to failure.

The results of the AR-glass reinforced specimen reveal certain problems. It is obvious that all specimens reinforced with AR-Glass fail within a relatively short time. This is due to the fact that the temperatures in the specimens rise very quickly and glass looses its strength rapidly with an increased temperature. The tensile strength of E-Glass (there are not yet data available for AR-Glass, but E-Glass may be used as comparison), at 500 °C is only 50 % of the original value. This temperature is reached after approx. 5 minutes of testing. So, because the low concrete cover – in the presented tests, the concrete cover was approx. 5 mm – is not able to distribute the heat, possibilities have to be found to increase the fire resistance of TRC using AR-glass fibers. Current research leads to the following options:

- increasing the concrete cover
- combining carbon and AR-Glass fibers
- using fire protective intumescent coatings
- changing the micro-concrete

The first two options may not be helpful, because an increase of the concrete cover would lead to thicker construction elements and so be contrary to the idea of TRC, which is predestinated to produce thin and lightweight elements. Preliminary computer simulations show that a decrease of 100 °C can be reached by increasing the concrete cover by approx. 15 mm. The combination of different reinforcement materials is certainly an option which maintains the idea of TRC, but the costs of Carbon compared to AR-Glass have to be considered. The combination of both materials might only be a realistic solution, if small amounts of carbon fibers lead to a significant increase of the fire resistance.

Because steel elements show also a loss of strength under the influence of temperature, the use of fire protective coatings seems to be the most promising option at this time. An already planned third test series will contain specimen with such a fire resistance coatings. Also a different micro-concrete will be part of this third test series.

6. CONCLUSION AND OUTLOOK

In this paper two series of fire resistant tests were presented. Both series were performed at the University of Stuttgart according to the DIN 4102:1998 and contain different reinforcement materials and two different load levels. The results lead to the following conclusions:

- TRC components reinforced with Carbon textiles were able bear the fire up to 95 minutes of testing. The negative temperature elongation modulus leads to a negative deflection during the testing. In the presented tests, this negative deflection does not lead to any negative effect. Future research has to show whether this is independent from the test setup or not.
- AR-Glass reinforced specimen show under 50 % of the fracture and fire loading a very low load bearing ability, which leads to a rapid failure of the specimen. Regarding the

temperature distribution of the concrete beam, the failure is due to the decreased material strength under the influence of temperature.

Future research has to be carried out regarding two major aspects. On the one hand, the high temperature behavior of the used materials separated from each other has to be investigated. The already conducted scientific research mainly focuses on temperatures up to approx. 300 °C, but for building purposes temperatures up to 1000 °C are relevant. On the other hand, possible ways to increase the fire resistance of AR-Glass fiber reinforced specimen have to be investigated.

ACKNOWLEDGEMENTS

The investigations at the ibac, RWTH Aachen University, are part of the Collaborative Research Center 532 "Textile reinforced concrete – Basics for the development of a new technology" and sponsored by the Deutsche Forschungsgemeinschaft (DFG). The support is gratefully acknowledged.

REFERENCES

[1] Krüger, M. ; Reinhardt, H.W. ; Raupach, M. ; Orlowsky, J.: Textilbewehrter Beton unter Brandbeanspruchung : Untersuchungen zum Tragverhalten im Brandfall. In: Betonwerk und Fertigteil-Technik 71 (2005), Nr. 10, S. 38-48

[2] Brameshuber, W.; Brockmann, T.; Hegger J.; Molter, M.: Untersuchungen zum textilbewehrten Beton. Beton 52 (2002) Nr.9, S. 424-429

[3] Raupach, M. ; Orlowsky, J. ; Büttner, T. ; Dilthey, U. ; Schleser, M.: Epoxy-Impregnated Textiles in Concrete - Load Bearing Capacity and Durability. Bagneux : RILEM, 2006. - In: Textile Reinforced Concrete. Proceedings of the 1st International RILEM Symposium, Aachen, 6./7. September 2006, (Hegger, J. ; Brameshuber, W. ; Will, N. (Eds.)), S. 77-88

[4] Kleineberg, M.; Herbeck, L.; Brosinger, A.; CFPR APU INTAKE DUCT for MEGALINER, SAMPE Europe Conference and Exhibition, 2004

FIBER-REINFORCED CEMENT COMPOSITES UNDER ELEVATED TEMPERATURES

Kiang Hwee Tan and Yu Qian Zhou

Department of Civil Engineering, National University of Singapore, Singapore

Abstract

In this study, the performance of fiber reinforced cement mortar under elevated temperatures was investigated. Ninety prism specimens comprising one control group, three groups strengthened with discrete steel fibers and two groups strengthened with polypropylene fibers, were fabricated. The specimens were subjected to elevated temperatures of up to 1010°C in a furnace before they were tested to failure under four-point bending. According to the test results, the ultimate strength of the specimens generally decreased with an increase in the maximum imposed temperature. Steel fiber reinforced cement mortar performed better than polypropylene fiber reinforced cement mortar in terms of peak strength and post-peak behavior, when subjected to the same elevated temperature.

1.   INTRODUCTION

Short discrete fibers are traditionally used as a secondary reinforcement in concrete or mortar. They are known to inhibit crack initiation and propagation, and enhance the toughness and ductility of cement composites. Their application has thus gained popularity in structures such as pavements, runways for airports and slab-type sleepers for high-speed trains. Recent applications include the use of fiber-reinforced cement composites (FRCC) in blast or impact-resisting structures.

Extreme events such as blasts or explosions are often accompanied by fire. It is therefore pertinent to investigate the performance of FRCC under elevated temperatures, for which little work has been reported. Such information would also be useful for the application of FRCC as fire insulation for externally bonded fiber reinforced polymer (FRP) systems that have become popularly used in the strengthening and rehabilitation of reinforced concrete structures [1]. Without fire insulation, FRP systems would lose their structural integrity and polymer resins would ignite or burn when the temperatures rise beyond their glass transition temperatures which are in the order of 150°C.

With the above objective in mind, a study was carried out to investigate the performance of fiber reinforced cement mortar under elevated temperatures of up to 1010°C. Small mortar prism specimens were fabricated with short steel or polypropylene fibers as reinforcement. After being placed in a furnace up to the target temperature followed by natural cooling, the prisms were subjected to four point bending tests. The load-deflection characteristics including the ultimate loads and post-cracking behavior are discussed with respect to the maximum imposed temperature, fiber type and fiber content.

2.   TEST PROGRAM

2.1   Test specimens and Temperature-Time Curve

A total of ninety prism specimens were fabricated. Each specimen measured 50 mm by 25 mm in cross-section and 200 mm in length. As shown in Table 1, the specimens were divided into six groups, A to F. Group A specimens constituted the control group, made with cement mortar only. Groups B, C and D consisted of steel fiber-reinforced cement mortar specimens with the steel fiber content at 0.5%, 1.0% and 1.5% by volume, respectively. Groups E and F specimens were made with polypropylene fiber-reinforced cement mortar with volume fractions of 0.25% and 0.5% respectively.

Each group comprised fifteen specimens. Among these, three specimens were tested under bending without subjecting to heating, that is, they were tested at the ambient temperature of 30°C. For the remaining specimens, three specimens each were subjected to elevated temperatures of 500, 600, 800 and 1010°C. The specimens were designated by the symbol "Xy" where X refers to the group and y indicates the target elevated temperature in 100 degrees, with A representing the ambient temperature.

The specimens were heated in an electrical furnace. Although the heating process was intended to follow the standard time-temperature curve given by ASTM E-119 [2], the initial heating rate could not be as fast as the standard curve as shown in Fig. 1, because the heat was produced by means of electrical wire spirals instead of gas burners. However, the actual temperature-time curve approached the standard curve after about one hour, and was adopted in this study.

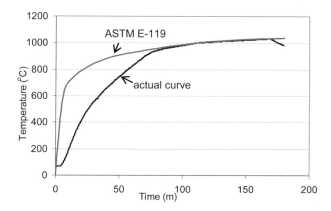

Figure 1: Temperature-time curve

Table 1: Specimen details

Group	Specimen	Fiber Type	V_f (%)	Target T (°C)	Actual T (°C)	Age (days)
A	AA	-	0	30	30	49
	A5	-	0	500	438	49
	A6*	-	0	600	596	56
	A8	-	0	800	765	57
	A10	-	0	1010	1083	52
B	BA	steel fiber	0.5	30	30	49
	B5	steel fiber	0.5	500	438	45
	B6*	steel fiber	0.5	600	596	54
	B8	steel fiber	0.5	800	765	55
	B10	steel fiber	0.5	1010	1083	50
C	CA	steel fiber	1	30	30	48
	C5	steel fiber	1	500	522	69
	C6	steel fiber	1	600	624	47
	C8	steel fiber	1	800	788	75
	C10	steel fiber	1	1010	1007	56
D	DA	steel fiber	1.5	30	30	46
	D5	steel fiber	1.5	500	532	70
	D6	steel fiber	1.5	600	624	44
	D8	steel fiber	1.5	800	788	72
	D10	steel fiber	1.5	1010	1007	58
E	EA	PP fiber	0.25	30	30	58
	E5	PP fiber	0.25	500	507	77
	E6	PP fiber	0.25	600	600	78
	E8	PP fiber	0.25	800	834	80
	E10	PP fiber	0.25	1010	1005	73
F	FA	PP fiber	0.5	30	30	57
	F5	PP fiber	0.5	500	507	76
	F6	PP fiber	0.5	600	600	78
	F8	PP fiber	0.5	800	834	79
	F10	PP fiber	0.5	1010	1005	72

Note: * Specimens were accidentally subjected to prolonged heating at the target temperature.

2.2 Materials

The prism specimens were fabricated using the same mix proportion of normal Portland cement, sand and water in the ratio of 1:2:0.4 by weight. The steel fibers were of the hooked-end type, with a length of 35 mm and a diameter of 0.75 mm. The polypropylene fibers were of the filament type with a length of 10 mm and a diameter of 9.6 μm.

2.3   Instrumentation and test procedure

Each time, six prism specimens from two different groups were placed in the general purpose chamber furnace. The specimens were then heated to the target temperature following the temperature-time curve shown in Fig. 1.

After the target temperature was reached, the heating process was stopped and the specimens were allowed to cool down in the chamber overnight to the ambient temperature of about 30°C. By accident, Group A6 and B6 specimens were however subjected to prolonged heating for about an hour after the target temperature of 600°C was reached; the results of these specimens would be viewed with this in mind.

The prisms were then subjected to four-point bending tests over a span of 180 mm in an Instron machine with a 50-ton capacity. The load was applied at third-points at a rate of 0.05 mm/min. A linear variable deformation transducer was placed at the mid-span of the prism to measure the displacement. In addition, a strain gauge was attached on the top face of the prism at the mid-span, while an omega strain gauge was installed at the same location on the bottom face to measure the strains.

The bending test was stopped when there was an obvious drop in the load-carrying capacity or when sufficient deflection has been recorded.

3.   TEST RESULTS AND DISCUSSION

3.1   Effect of elevated temperatures

Fig. 2 shows the typical load-deflection characteristics of each group of prism specimens.

For Group A, E and F specimens, that is unreinforced mortar and PP fiber-reinforced mortar specimens, the load-deflection curve is characterized by a linear relation up to the peak (ultimate) load when flexural cracks first appeared, followed by a drop in load-carrying capacity to almost zero, except for reinforced specimens (EA and FA) that were not subjected to elevated temperatures.

The drop in load-carrying capacity from the peak value was very sharp where the elevated temperature was less than about 600°C, and more gradual otherwise. There was also a significant drop in the peak load (that is, by more than 50%) when the elevated temperature went beyond 600°C.

For Group B, C and D specimens that were reinforced with steel fibers, the load-deflection curves also exhibited a linear relation up to the first crack load, followed by a sharp but limited drop in load-carrying capacity and strain hardening thereafter for specimens not subjected to heating. For specimens subjected to heating, fine cracks were observed in the specimens prior to bending tests. This resulted in the load-deflection curve having a gradually decreasing slope (corresponding to a reduction in flexural stiffness) with an increase in applied load.

After the maximum (ultimate) load was reached, the load-carrying capacity began to drop gradually to a residual value which was maintained with increasing deflection. For each of these groups, the ultimate load again dropped significantly when the elevated temperature went beyond 600°C.

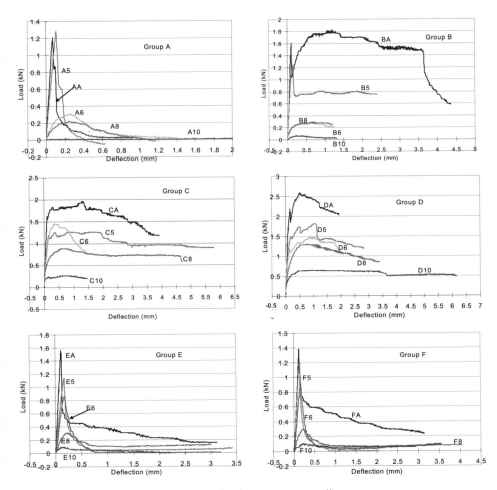

Figure 2: Load-deflection curves according to group

3.2 Effect of fiber inclusion

Fig. 3 shows typical load-deflection curves of the prism specimens subjected to the same target temperature, ranging from ambient temperature of about 30°C to 1010°C.

For specimens not subjected to heating and tested at ambient temperature, the inclusion of PP fibers led to an increase in the ultimate load and the presence of a residual load carrying capacity after the peak load, which however did not differ very much for the fiber content investigated. The inclusion of steel fibers, on the other hand, led to deflection hardening with the effect increasing with the fiber content.

When subjected to elevated temperatures, specimens reinforced with PP fibers (Group E and F) did not show any difference with the unreinforced (Group A) specimens. This was because the PP fibers would have been disintegrated by the heat and therefore lost their effectiveness.

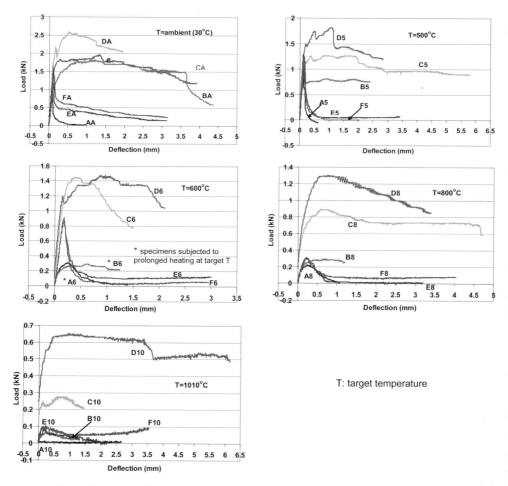

Figure 3: Load-deflection curves according to maximum imposed temperature

For Group B to D specimens that were subjected to heating, the inclusion of steel fibers resulted in a higher ultimate load and more ductile behavior, especially with a higher fiber content and lower elevated temperatures. With the elevated temperatures going above 600°C, the fibers were not effective for the case where the fibre content was 0.5%. It appeared that a fiber content of 1.5% would be necessary to ensure an ultimate strength after heating to 800°C that would be comparable to that of an unreinforced, unheated specimen (that is, comparing D8 and AA), with improved post-peak behavior.

4. CONCLUSIONS

From the study carried out, the following conclusions are deduced:
- Regardless of the fiber type and content, the ultimate strength of fiber-reinforced cement mortar decreased with an increase in the maximum imposed temperature.
- Polypropylene fibers were not effective in enhancing the strength or improving the post-cracking characteristics of cement mortar.
- Steel fibers were effective in enhancing the ultimate strength and improving the ductility of cement mortar under elevated temperatures.
- A steel fiber of 1.5% by volume would be necessary to ensure an ultimate strength after heating to 800°C that is comparable to that of unreinforced, unheated cement mortar while improving the post-peak behavior.

ACKNOWLEDGEMENTS

The tests were carried out with the assistance of Ms Mun Yee Grace Wong, for which the authors are grateful. The steel fibers used in the investigation were provided by Arcelor Group. The polypropylene fibers were provided by Brasilit Com. E Ind. Ltda. The authors thank the companies for generously donating the materials. The opinions expressed in this paper are solely those of the authors and do not reflect the views of the sponsors.

REFERENCES

[1] American Concrete Institute, ACI 440.2R-02, "Guide for the Design and Construction of Externally Bonded FRP Systems for Strengthening Concrete Structures", Farmington Hills, Michigan, United States, 2002.
[2] ASTM International, ASTM E 119-00a, "Standard Test Methods for Fire Tests of Building Construction and Materials", West Conshohocken, United States, 2000, 21.

High Performance Fiber Reinforced Cement Composites (HPFRCC5)
Mainz, Germany – July 10-13, 2007

USING X-RAY TOMOGRAPHY TO IMAGE CRACKS IN CEMENT PASTE

François Paradis [1] **and Jason Weiss** [2]

(1) Laval University, Canada

(2) Purdue University, USA

Abstract
The durability of a concrete structure is related to its ability to impede, or greatly reduce, the rate of fluid transport. A great deal of research has been performed to assess the durability of concrete structures. However, the majority of previous research has focused on undamaged concrete, and comparatively little work has been performed to quantitatively describe how these transport properties change in the presence of damage or sustained loading, which frequently occur in the field. Describing the effects of cracking can be complicated as the morphology of the cracks is difficult to fully characterize. This paper describes an investigation to determine crack size and crack morphology using three-dimensional x-ray tomography. Fiber reinforcement has the potential to substantially change the nature of the cracks that form. As a result, fiber reinforcement can alter the rate of fluid transport and thereby substantially improve durability if the fiber reinforcement changes the morphology of the cracks.

1. INTRODUCTION

The deterioration of the concrete infrastructure is a major problem around the world. Many researchers have conducted tests to determine the transport properties of concrete to describe the movement of fluid through the concrete. This information has led to a better understanding of the mechanisms that control the degradation processes of concrete and has even resulted in the development of service life models [1-7]. However, the majority of this research has focused on undamaged concrete, and little work has been performed to quantitatively describe how these properties change due to the presence of damage (i.e., cracking) in concrete.

X-ray tomography techniques have been previously used to study cracking in building materials. Landis et al. [8-10] have used x-ray tomography to locate and image cracks caused by compressive loading in specimen with a 4 mm diameter and a 4 mm height. Similar studies were performed by Lawler et al. [11] on specimens under compressive load. In each of these studies, x-ray absorption was used to detect a difference in material density due to the presence of a void or crack. Other researchers have used the x-ray absorption approach to study the change in material density that occurs as a result of water movements in paste [12-13]. This approach was used to assess moisture movement in cracked concrete using point by point measurement [14]. The point by point measurements were extremely time consuming.

This paper describes the development of an x-ray tomography system to image cracks in paste. The ultimate goal is to be able to use this system to measure cracking and the effects of cracking in larger scale concrete elements. The objective of this paper is to describe some of the initial calibration of this system and describe the technique and apparatus used to obtain a three dimensional image of cracking in a specimen.

2.   GENERAL EQUIPMENT DESCRIPTION

The equipment used for testing is a GNI x-ray absorption system which is located at Purdue University. This system consists of an x-ray source placed at a specific distance from a detector in an environmentally controlled chamber (see Fig. 1). The apparatus has the ability to measure the x-ray with two devices; a CCD camera (i.e., which will be used in this paper) or a single point detector. The CCD camera records the total intensity of x-rays at each pixel with a surface of 252 x 256 pixels. The detector measures the photon count at a single point over 256 channels (i.e., as a function of KeV) providing a measure of the energy spectrum. The x-ray source beam has a diameter of approximately 3 mm and can be moved using a programmable x-y positioning table with a ± 0.001 mm precision. The Focus to Detector Distance (FDD, i.e., the distance between the source and the detector), can be adjusted from 10 mm to 500 mm. For this study, the FDD was fixed at 500 mm. The specimens analysed in this study are mounted on a linear stage, which allows the user to control the crack opening to a precision of 0.02 mm. The linear stage is fixed on a turntable (see Fig. 1) that enables tomography of the specimen to be performed, (i.e., take measurement by rotating the specimen up to 360 degrees for reconstruction of the specimen in 3D). The sample can be placed anywhere between the beam source and the detector to have a precise Focus to Object Distance (FOD). The FOD influences the specimen exposure area, and then, the precision of the measurement as described in section 3.

3.   RESOLUTION AS A FUNCTION OF FOD

Resolution of the measurement is an important issue. Some researchers have demonstrated that crack width, as low as 50 μm can have an influence on the penetration of aggressive agents [15-16]. Tests have been performed with the x-ray equipment to assess the relationship between the location of a sample and the physical size represented by each pixel. The resolution improves as the sample gets closer to the source (i.e., smaller FOD). For instance, with this apparatus, a FOD of 25 mm gives a resolution for each pixel about 6 x 6 μm and the total exposure area is about 1.6 mm x 1.6 mm. As the FOD increases, the exposure area reaches a size of 18 mm x 18 mm at a FOD of 300 mm. Fig. 2 relates the size measured by each pixel of the camera to the FOD.

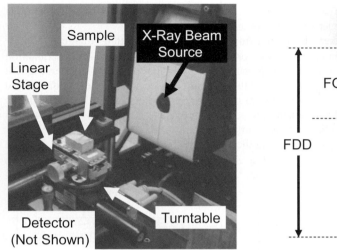
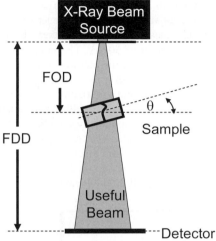

Figure 1: Equipment Layout: a) a Photo of the Specimen in the X-ray Chamber and b) a Schematic Illustration of the Geometry of the Problem

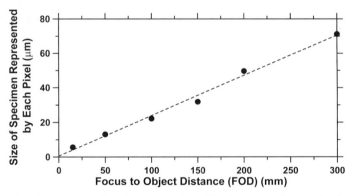

Figure 2: Size of Specimen Represented by One Pixel versus Distance to the Detector

4.   CRACKS IN TWO DIMENSIONS

X-ray measurements were performed on cracked paste samples. The tests were done using two specimens prepared with different crack morphologies. The crack face in the first sample is a flat plane while the crack face in the second sample is a rougher, more tortuous surface. The morphology of the second specimen was manufactured using the number 9 surface from ICRI [17]. The paste samples were cast in a two-part procedure. The first part of this procedure consisted of casting the paste against a surface mold (i.e., flat plane or ICRI rough surface). In the second part of this procedure the surface mold was removed and the second part of the sample was cast. The final size of the specimen was 40 mm long, 22 mm wide, and 15 mm high. After curing, the specimens were split and the crack width was fixed at 0.1 mm apart with the linear stage as shown on Fig. 1. The linear stage was also used to simulate cracks of varying width, however they will not described in this paper.

The measurements were taken at 200 mm from the x-ray source with a voltage of 65 keV and a current of 50 µA. The integration time for each image was 1000 ms. After acquisition by CCD camera, the pictures were examined using an intensity per pixel as shown in Fig. 3a. It can be seen that the crack (as shown by the dark pixels) occurs in the middle of the specimen (around a horizontal distance of 6.25 mm) however these images also show erratic points or "bad pixels" with unexplained spikes. To improve the analysis, a filter has been developed and applied systematically to each image to remove pixels that are not stable (i.e., "bad pixels"). The filter consists in removing the "bad pixel" and replacing the pixel with the average value of the 8 surrounding pixels. Fig. 3b presents the same image shown in Fig. 3a after the filter was applied. It can be seen that the majority of the high intensity pixels now correspond only to the location of the crack.

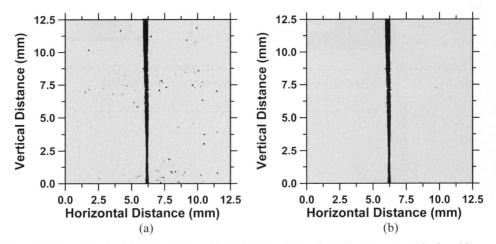

Figure 3: Plane Crack a) Without Filter, b) With Filter (Note the Black Denotes Pixels with a High Intensity, while the Grey Denotes Pixels with a Low Intensity)

Cracks can be analyzed in two dimensions if the crack is aligned with axis of the x-ray beam shown in Fig. 1b. However, the two dimensional picture can make it difficult to evaluate the crack width if the x-ray beam is not perfectly aligned with the main crack axis or if the crack is tortuous. Fig. 4 presents the normalized intensity of the x-ray reaching the detector as function of the horizontal distance along the specimen for both the plane and the rough crack. Fig. 4 represents the mean of 10 rows of pixels taken at the middle of the picture (i.e., a 0.5 mm band centered at a height of 6.25 mm in the vertical direction in Fig. 3). The plane crack graph with the 0.1 mm crack aligned with the x-ray beam (i.e., zero degree) shows an intensity is much higher and narrower than other orientations. If the sample is rotated the high intensity region widens and however the maximum intensity decreases.

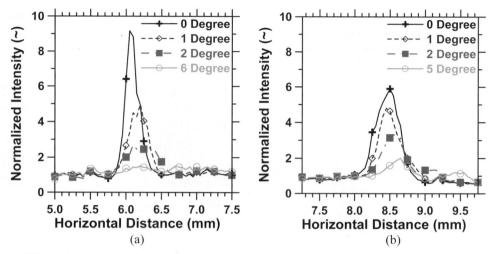

Figure 4: Intensity of 10 Rows of Pixels for Various Orientations with the Crack, a) Plane Crack b) Rough Crack (Each Pixel is Approximately 50 Microns Apart)

It should be noted that if the specimen is not perfectly aligned (i.e., even for a rotation as low as one degree) the x-rays cannot pass directly through the crack. The recorded signal is then lower and has a wider spread as shown in Fig. 4b. This observation is similar with the rough crack. However, for the rougher crack, the width of the crack is very difficult to determine. In fact, as the crack is not plane, the x-ray is unable to pass through the crack without touching the face of the crack. This results in a wider and lower signal. Direct evaluation of the crack width is difficult to determine from a single measurement with any precision. A three dimensional reconstruction is needed for this analysis.

5. CRACKS IN THREE DIMENSIONS

In order to be able to visualize cracking in three dimensions, x-ray tomography was performed. Tomography was performed by taking a series of images at different angles and using these images to reconstruct a three dimensional image. Tomography was performed on a round mortar sample that was prepared exactly in the same way as describe previously. A photo of the rough surface is presented in Fig. 5. The crack was opened to a width of 0.5 mm for the reconstruction shown below. The tomography was performed by taking a series of 360 images each at increment of 0.5 degrees from the previous image. A three dimensional reconstruction was then performed using the COBRA software, which takes all projections, analyzes the results, and merges them together to produce slices of the sample. Fig. 6 presents slices from the three dimensional reconstruction for the sample with a rough surface. Data obtained from the slices in Fig. 6 can be used to determine the width of the crack. Calculations on the reconstruct crack using images with intensities that are over 60,000 KeV*µA (similar to the intensity without a sample between the source and the detector) (i.e,, black spaces) suggest its width to be approximately 9 to 10 pixels wide which corresponds to a width of 0.45 mm to 0.50 mm which is very comparable to the dimensions of the specimen. Fig. 6b also shows an artefact which appears in some slices due to the inability to filter out all 'bad pixels' in the current process. Continued research is being performed to improve the three dimensional reconstruction.

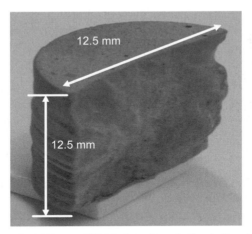

Figure 5: A Photo of Half of the Rough Crack Specimen

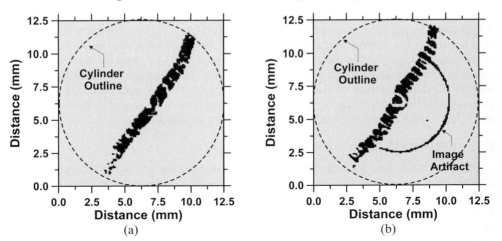

(a)   (b)

Figure 6: a) Image Reconstruction of Slices from a) the Middle and b) the Bottom of the Paste Sample Shown in Fig. 5

6.   SUMMARY

In summary, this paper presented results from a series of experiments that have been performed using a newly developed x-ray imaging system to examine cracking in paste specimens. The paper presents results that indicate the relationship between the location of the sample and the area measured by each pixel. An example was used to demonstrate the need for image cleaning to remove 'bad pixels'. Analysis was performed to assess cracking using a single measurement with the x-ray beam parallel to the length of the crack. It was shown that rougher cracks and cracks with the beam not aligned directly along the beam demonstrate a wide rise in x ray intensity while more aligned, smoother cracks demonstrate a higher intensity signal. Finally, tomography was used to reconstruct the images in three dimensions to observe cracks. This technique is promising for assessing cracks in three dimensions, however further work is needed to refine the image reconstruction process.

ACKNOWLEDGEMENTS

The authors gratefully acknowledge support received from the National Science Foundation (NSF) under Grant No. 0134272: a CAREER AWARD granted to the second author. Any opinions, findings, and conclusions or recommendations expressed in this material are those of the authors and do not necessarily reflect the views of the National Science Foundation. In addition the authors acknowledge support from the center for Advanced Cement Based Materials Center and the Centre de Recherche en Infrastructure sur le Béton (CRIB). This work was conducted in the Materials Sensing and Simulation Laboratory using the x-ray tomography equipment which was made possible through a grant to the second author for the development of a Materials and Moisture Characterization Laboratory.

REFERENCES

[1] Boddy, A., Bentz, E.C., Thomas, M.D.A. and Hooton, R.D., 'On overview and sensivitivity study of multimechanistic chloride transport model', *Cem. Concr. Res.* **29**(6) (1999) 827-827.

[2] Liang, M.T., Wang, K.L. and Liang, C.H., 'Service Life prediction of reinforced concrete structures', *Cem. Concr. Res.* **29**(9) (1999) 1411-1418.

[3] Matin-Pérez, B., Zibara, H., Hooton, R.D., Thomas, M.D.A., 'A study of the effect of chloride binding on service life predictions', *Cem. Concr. Res.* **30**(8) (2000) 1215-1223.

[4] Kirkpatrick, T.J., Weyers, R.E., Anderson-Cook, C.M., Sprinkel, M.M., 'Probabilistic model for the chloride-induced corrosion service life of bridge decks', *Cem. Concr. Res.* **32**(12) (2002) 1943-1960.

[5] Thomas, M.D.A. and Bentz, 'Life-365 Computer program for predicting the service life and life-cycle costs of reinforced concrete exposed to chlorides', American Concrete Institute Committee 365 (2000).

[6] Truc, O., Olivier J.P. and Nilsson L.O., 'Numerical simulation of multi-species transport through saturated concrete during a migration test – MsDiff code', *Cem. Concr. Res.* **30**(10) (2000) 1581-1592.

[7] Maltais, Y., Samson, E., Marchand, J., 'Predicting the durability of Portland cement systems in aggressive environments – laboratory validation", *Cement and Concrete Research*, 34 (2004) 1579-1589

[8] Landis, E.N., Zhang, T., Nagy, E.N., Nagy, G., and Franklin, W.R., "Cracking, damage and fracture in four dimensions", *Materials and Structures*, 40(4) (2007) 357-364

[9] Landis, E.N., Nagy, E.N., Keane D.T., and Nagy, G., Technique to Measure 3D Work-of-Fracture of concrete in Compression, *J. of Eng. Mechanics*, June (1999) 599-605

[10] Landis E.N., "Damage variables based on three-Dimensional Measurement of Crack geometry", *Strength, Fracture and Complexity 3* (2005) 163-173

[11] Lawler, J. S., Keane, D.T., and Shah S.P., Measuring three-dimensional damage in concrete under compression, *ACI Mat. J.*, 98(6) (2001) 465-475

[12] Bentz, D.P., Hansen, K.K., "Preliminary observations of water movement in cement pastes during curing using X-ray absorption", *Cem. Concr. Res.*, 30(7) (2000) 1157-1168.

[13] Bentz, D.P., Quenard, D.A., Kunzel, H.M., Baruchel, J., Peyrin, F., Martys, N.S., Garboczi, E.J., "Microstructure and transport properties of porous building materials. II: Three-dimensional X-ray tomographic studies", *Materials and Structures*, 33(227) (2000) 147-153

[14] Weiss J., Geiker, M.R., Hansen, K.K., "Using X-Ray Absorption to Detect Fluid Ingress in Cracked Concrete", submitted to Journal of Testing and Evaluation

[15] Ismail, M., Toumi, A., François, R., and Gagné, R., "Effect of crack opening on the local diffusion of chloride in inert materials", *Cement and Concrete Research*, 34(4) (2004) 711-716.

[16] Rodriguez, O.G., and Hooton, R.D., "Influence of cracks on chloride ingress into concrete", *ACI Materials Journal*, 100(2) (2003) 120-126

[17] ICRI, "Selecting and Specifying Concrete Surface Preparation for Sealers, Coatings, and Polymer Overlays", Guideline No.03732, Technical Guidelines, 1997

PART FIVE

RETROFIT AND STRENGTHENING

STRENGTHENING OF R/C BEAMS WITH HIGH PERFORMANCE FIBER REINFORCED CEMENTITIOUS COMPOSITES

Giovanni Martinola [(1)], **Alberto Meda** [(2)], **Giovanni A. Plizzari** [(3)] **and Zila Rinaldi** [(4)]

(1) Concretum Construction Science AG, Switzerland

(2) Dept. of Engineering Design and Technologies, University of Bergamo, Italy

(3) Dept. DICATA, University of Brescia, Italy

(4) Dept. of Civil Engineering, University of Roma "Tor Vergata", Italy

Abstract
The possibility of using a thin layer of concrete with tensile hardening behavior (High Performance Fiber Reinforced Cementitious Composites, HPFRCC) for strengthening R/C beams is investigated herein. In order to verify the effectiveness of the proposed solution, full scale tests have been performed on 4.55 m long beams. The obtained results show the effectiveness of the proposed technique both at ultimate and serviceability limit states. The experimental results have been modeled by means of numerical FE analysis with a commercial program (DIANA) and of an analytical approach. The comparison of the results allowed several considerations on the effect of a HPFRCC layers on existing R/C beams.

1.   INTRODUCTION

In the last few years the use of concrete reinforced with fibers has been continuously increased due to the enhanced properties in cracking stage [1, 2]. As a result, Fiber Reinforced Concrete (FRC) is nowadays extensively used in applications where the fiber reinforcement is not essential for the structure safe (e.g. industrial pavements or shotcrete in tunnels). Besides these applications, there are structures where the fiber reinforcement is used as totally substitute of the traditional reinforcement [3, 4]. In particular, several studies demonstrated that fiber can be used in replace of transverse reinforcement [5, 6]. In all these applications a low volume fraction of fibers (lower than 0.6%-0.8%) is usually adopted and FRC exhibits a post peak softening behavior in tension.

Recently, FRC materials having a hardening behavior in tension, usually named High Performance Fiber Reinforced Cementitious Composite (HPFRCC), are available for practical uses [7-10] and allow proposing interesting applications. As a matter of fact, the hardening behavior allows to avoid brittle collapse and, consequently, the traditional reinforcement (rebars or welded mesh) can be removed [11, 12]. These new materials can be used for designing structures with new geometries and shapes that are no longer bounded to the reinforcement placement limitations. Unfortunately, the cost of these materials is not comparable with the traditional reinforced concrete and this is still a limit for common applications. Nevertheless, it can be of interest the use of HPRCC for strengthening and repair existing concrete beams with several advantages in comparing with traditional solutions such as the "beton plaque" or the R/C jacketing [13] and new solutions such as the application of FRP (fiber reinforced polymer) [14]. The strengthening technique proposed herein is based on the application of a HPRCC jacket on existing beams. The effectiveness of this application is shown with experimental flexural tests on full scale beams (4.55 m long and 0.50 m depth) reinforced with a 40 mm thick jacket.

The experiments were modeled by means of FE analyses where the HPFRCC constitutive law was determined by performing inverse analyses from uniaxial tensile and bending tests. An analytical approach was also used in order to propose a simplified method for the design the HPRCC jacket strengthening of existing beams.

2.   EXPERIMENTAL TESTS

The effectiveness of the proposed HPFRCC jacketing technique has been investigated by performing full-scale experimental tests on three 4.55 mm long beams having a depth of 500 mm and a with of 300 mm (Fig. 1). One of the beams was cast without any reinforcement while in the other two beams were reinforced with two bottom longitudinal rebars (Ø 16 mm) and two top longitudinal rebars (Ø 12 mm).All the rebars ends were welded to steel plates in order to guarantee a good anchorage and to avoid any slip. Two legged stirrups having a diameter of 8 mm were placed at a distance of 150 mm at the beams ends in order to avoid shear failure. The beams were cast with a C20/25 concrete. Such low resistance, with the low reinforcement percentage (0.3%), was chosen in order to simulate the real case of a weak beam and to highlight the strengthening effectiveness.

One of the reinforced beams was used as the reference specimen while a 40 mm thick layer of HPFRCC was applied on the other beams, as shown in Fig. 2. The strengthening material is a FRC with 2.5% (by volume) of straight microsteel fibers having a length of 12 mm and a diameter of 0.18 mm.

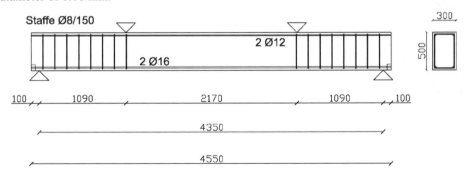

Figure 1: Geometry of the specimens.

Direct tensile test on dog-bone specimens and bending tests on small beams were performed in order to characterize the material. The results of the tests together with the specimen geometries are reported in Fig. 3.

The compressive strength, as measured on 100 mm side cubes, was 176.8 MPa.

Figure 2: Strengthening scheme.

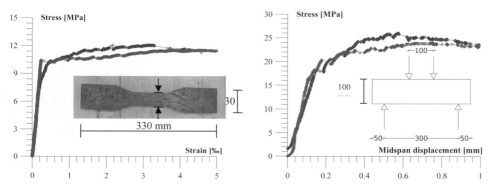

Figure 3: HPFRCC characterization: a) direct tensile test on dog-bone specimen (thickness equal to 13mm); b) flexural test (100x100 mm cross-section).

The HPFRCC jacket was applied on the full scale beams after a sandblasting that produced a mean depth of roughness of 1-2 mm, considered enough to avoid the use of primer products. Preliminary tests have been performed on small beams to verify the effectiveness of the adhesion [15]. The HPFRCC material was prepared in concrete mixers (with vertical axis) and placed without any vibration. A plastic layer was placed on the surface in order to limit the evaporation during curing in laboratory. Further information on the technology adopted for the HPFRCC jacket application and on the testing procedures can be found in [15].

The comparison of the experimental results of the three beams is shown in Fig. 4. For the sake of brevity, in the following the discussion will be focalized on two R/C beams with and without strengthening jacket. It can be noticed as the HPFRCC layer allows to increase the bearing capacity of the beam (2.15 times), even if the post peak behavior becomes softening. In any case, at the end of the softening branch the load stabilizes with a plastic branch, with a value higher than that obtained in the unstrengthened R/C beam.

The proposed technique allows a remarkable stiffness increase of the beam, with a behavior similar to the uncracked stage in the un-reinforced beam (Fig. 4). Indeed the HPFRCC jacket limits the development of macrocracking with evident advantages in terms of stiffness. If a total service load of 80 kN is considered, the use of the HPFRCC jacket leads to a decrease of the midspan displacement from 6 mm to 0.5 mm (12 times less; Fig. 4). This effect is comparable to that obtained with an external pretension action, where the cracking is avoided with a complete reacting section. From the technological point of view, the use of an HPFRCC jacket can be easily proposed as an alternative to external prestressing cables.

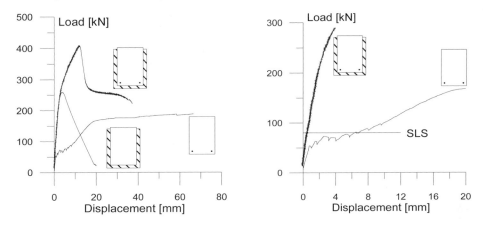

Figure 4: Comparison between the experimental results

3. NUMERICAL AND ANALYTICAL MODELS

The experimental behavior of the reinforced beams has been further simulated with numerical and analytical models, with the aim of completely clarify and deepen the mechanisms governing the flexural response of the analyzed reinforced beams. The main parameters affecting the local and global behavior are highlighted in order to optimize the proposed strengthening technique.

3.1 Numerical analyses un-reinforced beam

The numerical analyses have been performed with the FEM program Diana 9 [16]. Preliminary studies on the un-reinforced schemes have been performed, in order to test the program and to characterize the concrete and steel properties. In particular, the concrete in compression has been simulated with the Thorenfeld curve [17], whose parameters have been assigned on the basis of the outcome of compression tests performed on cubic specimens. In particular an average stress of about 27 MPa was experimentally obtained. The cylindrical stress (22 MPa), the Young's modulus (28 GPa) and the tensile peak stress (2.36 MPa) have been evaluated according to the Eurocode 2 rules starting from the cubic strength. Tensile behavior of concrete is simulated with a "multi-linear total strain rotating crack model" that defines the pre-peak behavior as a stress-strain relationship, and the post-peak response in terms of stress-crack opening.

The steel behavior is characterized by an elastic-plastic relationship, whose parameters, (yielding stress ≈ 560 MPa, ultimate stress ≈ 678 MPa, ultimate strain ≈ 10%), have been experimentally determined from the steel rebars used in the experiments.

Fig. 5 shows the mesh and the numerical results obtained with the FE analyses.

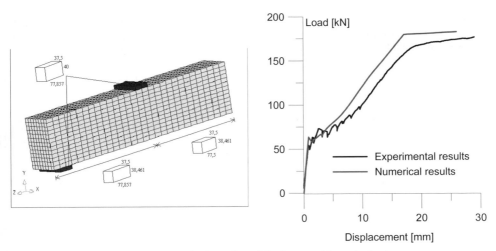

Figure 5: Numerical results of the beam without jacketing.

It can be noted that the elastic stiffness of the un-reinforced beam is perfectly caught by the model. The small differences in the second stage are probably related to the formation of splitting cracks (along the rebars), observed during the test; these cracks were not reproducible in the numerical analyses because of the assumed hypotheses of perfect bond between the concrete and the steel rebar. The analysis of the crack pattern at collapse further confirms the effectiveness of the numerical model. As in the experimental results, the cracks appear close to the tensile steel rebars, with multiple cracks in the shear span and an opened inclined crack close to the point load.

3.2   Numerical analyses of the reinforced beam

The numerical model for the analysis of the reinforced beam requires particular care for the definition of the constitutive parameters characterizing the tensile behavior of the HPFRCC. At this aim, the behavior of the beam specimens subjected to four point bending test, described in Fig. 3b, has been simulated to properly calibrate the constitutive relationship of the material, with particular reference to its post-cracking tensile strength.

The tensile behavior of HPFRCC (Fig. 3a) has been represented by a multi-linear total strain rotating crack model [16]. As already mentioned, this model allows the adoption of a stress-strain relationship before cracking, and of a stress-crack opening law after cracking (Fig. 6). In particular the parameters defining the softening branch have been calibrated on the basis of the experimental results obtained from the small beam specimens.

The behavior in compression is again simulated with Thorenfeld curve [17], characterized by a maximum stress equal to 177 MPa and the Young's modulus equal to 44000 MPa.

Due to the symmetry of the scheme, only half of the beam is considered (Fig. 7). Iso-parametric brick elements with 20 joints are adopted and the mesh is about 250x200x200 mm. The obtained results, compared with the experimental ones, are depicted in Fig. 7 showing a very satisfactory agreement.

Once defined the FRC constitutive relationships, the full scale beam was numerically simulated. Fig. 8 shows the beam mesh (made of iso-parametric brick elements with 20 joints): perfect bond has been assumed at the interfaces between steel rebar and concrete and concrete and HPFRCC. The latter assumption is based on the preliminary experimental results obtained from small beams [15].

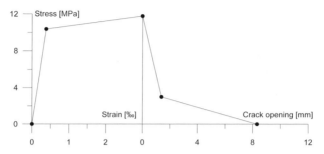

Figure 6: Modeling law of the HPFRCC material.

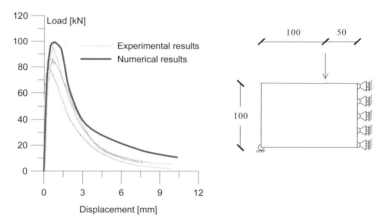

Figure 7: Numerical vs. experimental results for the four point beam (100x100x400 mm).

The numerical load displacement curve is compared with the experimental one in Fig. 8 where a significant difference in the second and third stages can be observed. This phenomenon could be related to a kind of "notch-effect" due to the onset and development of the macro-cracks in the ordinary concrete that can induce a premature localization in the HPFRCC material. As a matter of fact, even if the fiber reinforcement delays the macro-cracks formation and propagation, the contact with a more brittle material where the strains tend to concentrate easily, anticipates this macro-crack onset. On the basis of this assumption, the behavior of the fiber reinforcement in tension has been modified, shifting the softening branch in order to reduce the hardening phase, as shown in Fig. 9. The adoption of the new constitutive relationship provides the global response of the beam depicted in Fig. 10, with experimental and numerical response in good agreement. In particular, the model catches well the main phases characterizing the structural response, i.e. the elastic stage, the second stage whose stiffness is governed by the multiple cracking in the fibre reinforcement, the softening branch, whose slope is due to the macro-crack localization and the residual strength. Also the numerical final crack pattern is similar to the experimental one.

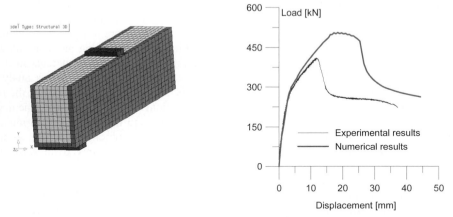

Figure 8: Numerical results of the beam with HPFRC jacket.

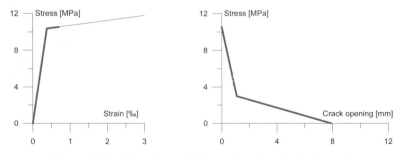

Figure 9: Modeling low with the reduced hardening branch.

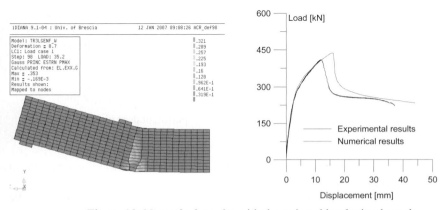

Figure 10: Numerical results with the reduced hardening branch.

3.3   Analytical model

The influence of the reinforcement layer on the beam response has been finally studied with an analytical model developed for the evaluation of the non-linear behavior of reinforced concrete elements [18], and extended to the case of external strengthening [19]. The main aim of the model is the definition of the bending moment-mean curvature of a reference element, whose length is equal to the crack spacing, subjected to constant bending moment and axial force. The hypothesis of perfect bond between the different materials (concrete, steel and FRC) is removed in all the sections except the cracked one. In order to obtain analytical formulations, the bond-slip relationship is assumed to be rigid-plastic and a decay of the bond strength is introduced. The concrete and the steel constitutive laws are in agreement with those adopted in the numerical analyses. It is worth mentioning that the model formulation does not require the definition of the limit bond strength, nor the crack spacing, as these parameters represent the outcome of the procedure. The problem is solved for subsequent steps, from the cracking stage up to failure, in strain control, by using equilibrium and compatibility equations in the sections and along the concrete-steel and concrete-PFR interfaces. The obtained moment-(mean) curvature relationship can be adopted for the analysis of simple structures; in particular, it allows the evaluation of displacements and rotations, through simple integrations along the element length. The description of the whole procedure is beyond the scope of the paper and can be found elsewhere [18].

The analytical model is then used for the simulation of the beams under study, by assuming the same constitutive relationships of the numerical model previously described. As for the numerical simulations, in order to obtain a good agreement between analytical and experimental results, it is necessary to modify the softening branch of HPFRCC. The obtain force-displacement bending moment- mean curvature relationship for the un-reinforced and reinforced beams are plotted and compared with the experimental response in Fig. 11.

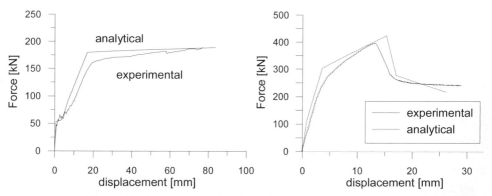

Figure 11: Comparison of analytical and experimental results.

4.   CONCLUDING REMARKS

The research present herein represents a valuable application of HPFRCC and the cost of the solution is comparable with other strengthening features.

On the basis of the experimental and numerical results the following conclusion can be drawn:

- the strengthening with a HPFRCC jacket has provided an increase of the bearing capacity of R/C beams and a remarkably increase of its stiffness (12 times);
- the application of the HPFRCC jacket is relatively simple as well as the preparation of the original R/C beam;
- the numerical analyses evidence the development of a premature localization in the HPFRCC due to the original concrete cracking that can be taken into account by a reduction in the hardening branch;
- the numerical analyses properly simulate the behavior of R/C beams strengthened with HPFRCC;
- good results can also be obtained with a analytical procedure that allows to predict the behavior with an easy procedure.

The main advantages of the proposed solution are: (a) the possibility of easily repair and strengthening R/C beams, (b) the application of an HPFRCC jacket can increase remarkably the durability, (c) the technique is suitable for the reparation of structures damaged to fire exposure.

ACKNOWLEDGEMENTS

The presented research has been founded by the Tecnochem Italiana S.p.a. The Authors thank Mr. Dario Rosignoli for his trust in the proposed application. The Authors are finally grateful to Dr. Fausto Minelli and Dr Luca Cominoli for their support during the experimental tests as well as to Cristina Zanotti and Nicola Rossini for the work carried out during their graduation thesis.

REFERENCES

[1] Rossi, P. and Chanvillard, G., '5th RILEM Symposium on Fibre Reinforced Concretes (BEFIB 2000)', (RILEM Publications, Cachan France, 2000).

[2] di Prisco, M., Plizzari, G. A., Felicetti, R., '6th RILEM Symposium on Fibre Reinforced Concretes (BEFIB 2004)', (RILEM Publications, Bagneux France, 2004).

[3] Falkner, H., Henke, V., Hinke, U., 'Stahlfaserbeton für tiefe Baugruben im Grundwasser', *Bauingenieur*, **72** (1997).

[4] ACI 544.4R, 'Design consideration for steel fiber reinforced concrete (Reported by ACI Committee 544)', *ACI Structural Journal* **85** (5) (1988).

[5] Meda, A., Minelli, F., Plizzari, G. A., Riva, P., 'Shear behavior of steel fiber reinforced concrete beams', *Materials and Structures*. **38** (277) (2005).

[6] Minelli, F., Cominoli, L., Meda, A., Plizzari, G. A., Riva, P., 'Full-scale tests on HPSFR prestressed roof elements subjected to longitudinal flexure', RILEM – PRO 49 *International Rilem Workshop on High performance fiber reinforced cementitious composites (HPFRCC) in structural applications*, (Rilem Publications S.A.R.L, 2006).

[7] Li, V.C., 'From Micromechanics to Structural Engineering - the design of cementitious composites for civil engineering applications', *JSCE Journal of Structural Mechanics and Earthquakes Engineering*, **10** (2) (1993).

[8] Rossi, P., 'High Performance multimodal fiber reinforced fibre reinforced cement composite (HPMFRCC): the LPC experience', *ACI Materials Journal*, **94** (6) (1997).

[9] RILEM – PRO 49, 'International Rilem Workshop on High performance fiber reinforced cementitious composites (HPFRCC) in structural applications', (Rilem Publications, Bagneux France, 2006).

[10] van Mier, J. G. M., 'Cementitious composites with high tensile strength and ductility through hybrid fibres', *6th RILEM Symposium on Fibre-Reinforced Concretes*, (RILEM Publications, Bagneaux France, 2004).

[11] Vicenzino, E., Culhman, G., Perry, V. H., Zakariasen, D., Chow, T. S., 2005. 'The first use of UHPFRC in thin precast roof shell for LRT Canadian station', *PCI Journal*. September-October (2005).

[12] Shimoyama, Y., Uzawa, M., 'Taiheiyo Cement Kenkyu Hokoku', *Journal of the Taiheiyo Cement Corporation*, Japan, **142** (2002).

[13] Bulletin d'Information 162, 'Assessment of concrete structures and design procedures for upgrading (redesign)', (CEB, Lausanne, 1983).

[14] Fib bulletin 14, Fib bulletin 14. 2001. 'Externally bonded FRP reinforcement for RC structures', (Fib, Lausanne, 2001).

[15] Martinola, G., Meda, A., Plizzari, G.A., Rinaldi, Z. 'An application of high performance fiber reinforced cementitious composites for R/C beams strengthening', 6th Int. Conference on Fracture Mechanics of Concrete and Concrete Structures, *Framcos VI*, Catania, 17-22 June 2007.

[16] Diana v. 9.1. 'Material Library', TNO DIANA BV, Delft (The Netherlands, 2005).

[17] Thorenfeldt, E., Tomaszewicz, A., and Jensen, J.J. 'Mechanical properties of high-strength concrete and applications in design'. In Proc. Symp. Utilization of High-Strength Concrete (Stavanger, Norway, 1987).

[18] Rinaldi, Z. An analytical model for the evaluation of the local ductility of R/C members. Studies and Researches-Politecnico di Milano, ed. by A. Migliacci, P.G. Gambarova and F. Mola, publ. by Starrylink (Brescia, Italy), V.26, pp.75-102.(2006)

[19] Rinaldi Z., Grimaldi A., Olivito R. Behaviour of r.c. beams reinforced with FRC material: analytical-experimental evaluation"; *6th RILEM Symposium on Fibre-Reinforced Concretes*, (RILEM Publications, Bagneux France, 2004). 20-22 September, Varenna.

DURABILITY OF HES-ECC REPAIR UNDER MECHANICAL AND ENVIRONMENTAL LOADING CONDITIONS

Mo Li and Victor C. Li

The Advanced Civil Engineering Materials Research Laboratory (ACE-MRL), Department of Civil and Environmental Engineering, University of Michigan, USA

Abstract
   The lack of durability in concrete repairs induces premature repair deterioration and endless "repair of repairs". This paper suggests High Early Strength Engineered Cementitious Composites (HES-ECC) as a material solution to repair failures under both mechanical and environmental loading conditions. HES-ECC is a new class of HPFRCC, which has been micromechanically designed for concrete structure repair applications with high early strength, high ductility and toughness indicated by multiple micro-cracking behavior under uniaxial tension. Experimental study shows that when subject to monotonic flexural loading, the HES-ECC layered repair system showed 100% increased load carrying capacity, and 10 times the deformation capacity of HES-Concrete layered repair system. When under the same level of fatigue flexural loading, HES-ECC layered repair system exhibited significantly longer service life. In addition, the high ductility of HES-ECC could relieve shrinkage induced stresses in the HES-ECC repair layer and at the HES-ECC/concrete interface, thereby suppressing large surface cracks and interface delamination. The concept of translating ECC repair material ductility to the whole repair system durability can be widely applied to many concrete structures repair applications for developing cost-effective and durable concrete repairs.

1. INTRODUCTION

   The purpose of this research is to overcome the lack of durability in concrete repair, through innovations of cement based repair materials with ultra ductility in tension. It has been reported [1] that about 50% of repairs fail in the field. Concrete repairs are often perceived to lack both early age performance and long-term durability. While knowledge of the causes of failure and the recognition of the need for material compatibility has been increasing in recent years, a robust and cost-effective solution appears lacking. In this research, focus is placed on the source of the problem: a lack of tensile ductility in current repair mortars so that surface cracks, spalling and delamination are common failure phenomena.

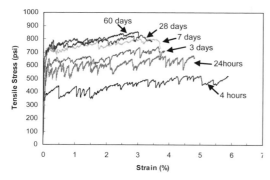

Figure 1: Tensile stress-strain curve of
HES-ECC

The approach of this research is to utilize High Early Strength Engineered Cementitious Composites (HES-ECC) as a repair material to improve durability of repaired concrete structures. HES-ECC has been developed under the guidance of micromechanical models for concrete structures repair applications. HES-ECC can achieve high early age compressive strength of around 20 MPa at 4 h, 35 MPa at 6 h, 40 MPa at 24 h, and high late age compressive strength of around 50 MPa at 7 d, 55 MPa psi at 28 d, and 57 MPa at 60 d. It also has high tensile strain capacity of more than 3% and toughness indicated by multiple micro-cracking behavior under uniaxial tensile loading. Its tensile stress-strain curves at different ages are shown in Fig. 1.

2. HES-ECC REPAIR UNDER MECHANICAL LOADING

Mechanical loading can cause repair cracking and interface delamination between the repair layer and the concrete substrate. When cracks exist in the concrete substrate, mechanical loading such as traffic loading will induce the maximum bending stress in the repair layer near to the cracks. This is because there is no load transfer through the existing cracks. Interface delamination can also happen around existing cracks due to the lack of the deformation compatibility between the two layers. Therefore, the whole delaminated section in the repair layer is subject to the maximum bending stress. Cracking happens in the repair layer when the maximum stress exceeds the repair material's tensile strength. This phenomina is normally refered to "reflective cracking". The detailed discussion on stress distribution and failure mechanism in a repair system under mechanical loading can be found in Zhang and Li (2002) [2]. In this research, experimental study was made on the performance of a layered repair system under monotonic and fatigue flexural loading. The repair cracking, interface delamination, load carrying capacity and deformation carrying capacity of the repair system was investigated. Influence of concrete substrate surface preparation on the repair system's overall performance was also evaluated and reported here.

2.1 Experimental Program

A layered repair system was investigated for resistance to spalling and delamination under mechanical loading, such as that induced by wheel loading. This system contains a layer of repair material cast on a substrate layer of old concrete with initial crack and little extent of interfacial delamination. The layered system was initially used by Lim and Li (1997) [3] and Kamada and Li (2000) [4] to simulate the reflective cracking in overlaid pavement. As shown in Fig. 2, a vertical crack in the old concrete substrate was initially introduced to simulate already existed cracking in concrete structure. A horizontal interfacial crack between the repair layer and the substrate layer was also produced before testing to simulate an initial debonding zone above the crack location in the old concrete. The specimen was subjected to four-point bending load with load-deflection curve monitored during testing. The deflection of the specimen at the center was measured by two linear variable differential transducers (LVDTs), which were mounted on both sides at the center of the layered beam.

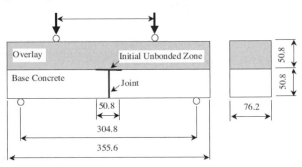

Figure 2: Dimensions of layered repair system under mechanical loading in mm

Both the monotonic and cyclic loading tests were conducted on a 250kN load capacity, MTS-810 testing machine equipped for closed-loop testing. The monotonic flexural test was carried out with deformation controlled by the displacement of the actuator. The displacement was increased at a constant rate of 0.1mm/min similar to ASTM C1018 "Standard Test Method for Flexural Toughness and First-Crack Strength of Fiber-Reinforced Concrete". The fatigue flexural test was conducted with load controlled using a sinusoidal waveform with a frequency of 2 Hz. It started with a ramp to the maximum load Pmax at a rate of 0.1 kN/s followed by a sine waveform fatigue loading. The maximum load (Pmax) is 0.9, 0.8 and 0.7 of the average load-carrying capacity of the layered repair system, which was obtained from the monotonic flexural test results. The ratio R between the minimum and maximum load levels was constant at $R = P_{min}/P_{max} = 0.1$. 3 specimens will be tested for each category.

Two different repair materials, HES-ECC and HES-Concrete, were investigated in this study. HES-Concrete was employed as control. The mixing proportion and properties of the repair materials are listed in Table 1 and Table 2.

Concrete beams with dimensions of 355.6 mm × 76.2 mm × 50.8 mm were first cast, and demolded after 24 hours. After demolding, the beams were cured in water at 22-26°C for 28 days. Then each beam was cut using a diamond saw into four concrete blocks with size of 177.8 mm ×76.2 cm × 50.8 cm. The blocks were then stored in the laboratory condition for another week and then smooth plastic tape was used to form vertical cracking and interfacial debonding before the repair layer was cast. The vertical cracking was in the middle of the concrete substrate, and the interfacial debonding length was 50.8 cm. Each repair layer, made of either HES-ECC or HES-concrete, was cast on the top of two concrete blocks which formed the concrete substrate. The layered specimens were then demolded at 6 hours, air cured, and tested at the age of 28 days.

The cotact surface was roughened in the fresh state using a chisel to remove slurry cement from external surfaces of coarse aggregates. Before placing the repair layers, the substrate surfaces were recleaned with a brush and high-pressure air to ensure a clean bonding surface, and then they were dampened to achieve better bonding with the repair layers. After that, 50.8-cm-thick repair layers made of each of the two repair materials were cast on the top of the concrete substrates.

Table 1: Repair materials composition

Material	C [a]	W	S	CA	SP	AC	V_f
HES-Concrete	1.0	0.4	1.3	1.3	0.005	0.04	--
HES-SFRC	1.0	0.4	1.3	1.3	0.005	0.04	0.01 [c]
HES-ECC (Mix 7)	1.0	0.33	1.0	0.064 [b]	0.0075	0.04	0.02 [d]

[a] Portland type III cement, [b] Polystyrene beads as coarse aggregates for HES-ECC,
[c] Steel hooked fiber, [d] PVA fiber

Table 2: Repair materials mechanical properties

Material	ε_u %	f_c' (MPa) [a]	E (GPa) [a]	Tensile Behavior
HES-Concrete	0.01	49.9±1.6 (7d) 54.2±2.4 (28d)	26.2±1.4 (7d) 27.8±1.5 (28d)	brittle
HES-SFRC	0.01	51.4±2.4 (7d) 56.9±2.0 (28d)	25.7±2.0 (7d) 27.9±1.3 (28d)	quasi-brittle
HES-ECC	2.5~5	47.5± 1.9 (7d) 55.6±2.2 (28d)	20.6±0.7 (7d) 23.2±1.0 (28d)	ductile

[a] Mean ± standard deviation

2.2 Experimental Results

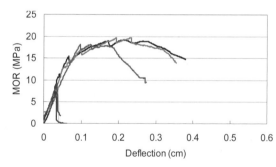

Figure 3: Flexural behavior of HES-ECC and
HES-Concrete layered repair system under
monotonic loading

The flexural behavior of HES-ECC repair system compared with HES-Concrete repair system under monotonic loading is shown in Fig. 3. The modulus of rupture (MOR) of the specimens were determined by

$$MOR = \frac{M}{bh^2/6}$$

where M is the bending moment at the center of the specimen, b is the width of the repair layer, and h is the thickness of the repair layer. It can be seen that HES-ECC layered repair system exhibited very ductile failure mode. This was in contrast with the sudden brittle failure mode of the HES-Concrete layered repair system. The flexural load carrying capacity of the HES-ECC repair system was significantly higher than HES-Concrete repair system. The MOR of the HES-ECC repair system was more than 100% higher than the HES-Concrete repair system. Furthermore, the deformation capacity of HES-ECC repaired system, represented by the specimen's center deflection at peak load, was 5 to 10 times higher than that of HES-Concrete repaired system. The greatly increased MOR and deformation capacity were contributed by the strain hardening behavior and high ductility of HES-ECC, which is in contrast with the tension softening behavior and brittle nature of HES-Concrete.

Figure 4: Cracking and interface delamination of different layered repair systems

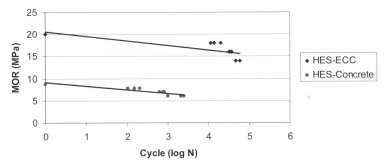

Figure 5: Fatigue life of different layered repair systems

The cracking pattern of the different layered repair systems can be seen in Fig. 4. The HES-Concrete / Concrete layered repair system had a sudden failure with one single crack formed in the repair layer. In contrast, the HES-ECC / Concrete layered repair system exhibited multiple micro-cracking behavior, with very tight crack width below 50μm. The significant difference of between the HES-ECC and HES-Concrete layered repair systems came from the kink-crack trapping mechanism: In the case of HES-Concrete repair, the initial interfacial crack always kinked into the repair layer and formed spalling. However for HES-ECC, the initial interfacial crack firstly kinked into the repair layer, and then trapped inside the HES-ECC because of the high toughness of the material. As the flexural load increased, the interfacial crack grew a little, and the kink-crack mechanism repeated till the final failure when the HES-ECC layer had its flexural strength exhausted. This kink-crack mechanism of HES-ECC repair helped to suppress repair spalling.

The fatigue flexural performance of different layered repair systems is shown in Fig. 5 in terms of MOR versus fatigue life (S-N). It is obvious that when the traffic loading is at the same level, the fatigue life of HES-ECC repair system is significantly longer than that of the HES-Concrete repair system.

3. HES-ECC REPAIR UNDER ENVIRONTAL LOADING

3.1 Background

In concrete repair applications, "new" repair materials are often bonded with "old" concrete substrates which have undergone shrinkage. After placement, the repair material will immediately begin shrinkage. However, the shrinkage deformation of the repair material is restrained by the concrete substrate, so that tensile stress will be developed in the repair layer, and both tensile stress and shear stress will be developed along the interface between the repair and the concrete substrate. The combination of these stresses is the reason to cause repair cracking and interface delamination.

Li (2004) [5] illustrated the effect of inelastic strain capacity of cementitious material on the deformation behavior of a 2-D slab geometry restrained at its ends. For brittle or quasi-brittle repair material with tension softening behavior, the cracking potential under restrained shrinkage is defined as:

$$p = (\varepsilon_{sh} - (\varepsilon_e + \varepsilon_{cp}))$$

where ε_{sh} is material shrinkage strain, ε_e is material elastic tensile strain capacity, and ε_{cp} is material tensile creep strain. If $p \geq 0$, one single crack forms in the repair material, with crack width proportional to the cracking potential p and increasing with the brittleness of the material.

In the case of a repair layer, the boundary conditions are different from what described above, because restraints are applied at the base of the slab rather than at its ends. This type of restraints will lead to a number of distributed cracks along the repair layer. In the case of plain concrete, these traction-free cracks will again open with crack widths proportional to p, resulting in relaxation of most of the tensile stress built up, and little or no shear stress at the layer/substrate interface. As a result, delamination at the interface is expected to be small.

For common tension-softening Fiber Reinforced Concrete (FRC) materials, shrinkage induced stresses are expected to induce surface cracking similar to normal concrete. However, since the cracks are bridged by fibers, the crack widths may be expected to be smaller, so that some tensile stress can still be maintained in the layer. As a result, the interface shear stress is not relieved, so that delamination may be more prominent compared with normal concrete.

In order to suppress both surface cracking of the repair layer and interface delamination, the repair material will need to exhibit "plastic straining" in order to relieve the tensile stress built up by restrained shrinkage. Once plastic straining occurs, the interfacial shear stress will also be relaxed, and interface delamination may be minimized. Plasticity in the form of microcrack damage has been demonstrated in HES-ECC, as this material exhibit an ultimate strength higher than the first cracking strength, accompanied by a large strain capacity ε_i at ultimate strength. For HES-ECC, the cracking potential [5] is modified as

$$p = (\varepsilon_{sh} - (\varepsilon_e + \varepsilon_i + \varepsilon_{cp}))$$

The cracking potential p for concrete, SFRC, and ECC can be estimated, as shown in Table 3. The p-values for the three materials confirm that concrete and SFRC are subjected to tensile fracturing when undergoing restrained drying shrinkage, while ECC will experience microcrack damage in the inelastic straining range.

Table 3: Concrete, SFRC and ECC cracking potential estimation

Properties	Concrete	SFRC	ECC
ε_{sh} (%)	0.07	0.053	0.177
ε_e (%)	0.01	0.01	0.015
ε_i (%)	0	0	2.5 ~ 5
ε_{cp} (%)	0.02 ~ 0.06	0.02 ~ 0.06	0.07
$p = \varepsilon_{sh} - (\varepsilon_e + \varepsilon_i + \varepsilon_{cp})$ (%)	0 ~ 0.04	(-0.017) ~ 0.023	(-4.908) ~ (-2.408)

3.2 Experimental Program

Three different repair materials — HES-Concrete, HES-Steel Fiber Reinforced Concrete (HES-SFRC) with tension softening stress-strain curve and HES-ECC were investigated. HES-Concrete and HES-SFRC were employed as controls since they have been used in repair applications. The mixing proportion and properties of the repair materials are listed in Table 1 and Table 2.

Layered repair systems were experimentally investigated with each of the three repair materials – HES-Concrete, HES-SFRC and HES-ECC. Concrete substrates were cast initially with dimensions of 1560mm×100mm×100mm, as shown in Fig. 6. The concrete substrates were moisture cured until age of 28 days, and then left to dry in ambient condition for an additional 60 days before the repair layers were placed. The additional 60 days were for the purpose of allowing any potential shrinkage in the substrates to occur before bonding the repairs. The contact surfaces of the substrates were prepared the same way as the layered specimen under mechanical loading described in section 2.2.

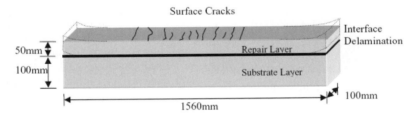

Figure 6: Layered repair system configuration and potential failure modes

After a clean bonding surface with appropriate moisture level was achieved, a 50-mm-thick repair layer made of each of the three repair materials was cast on the top of the concrete substrate. The repair layers were moisture cured for 24 hours and then demolded. After demolding, the layered specimens were moved into a room with ambient conditions of 20-30℃, and 25-55% RH.

3.3 Experimental Results

The surface cracking pattern of HES-Concrete, HES-SFRC and HES-ECC repairs are shown in Fig. 7. Table 4 summarizes crack number and crack width of the three repaired systems respectively at the age of 60 days. Three specimens were tested for each repair material. It can be seen that when HES-Concrete was used as the repair material, 3-4 cracks localized at age of 60 days. The maximum crack width of the three specimens was 520μm.

When HES-SFRC was used as the repair material, 1-4 localized cracks formed, and the maximum crack width of the three specimens was 130µm. The smaller crack width of HES-SFRC repair can be contributed by the steel fiber's bridging effect. It should be noted that because of a positive shrinkage cracking potential, the restrained shrinkage induced crack width for HES-Concrete or HES-SFRC repair is a structural property, which is dependent on structural dimensions.

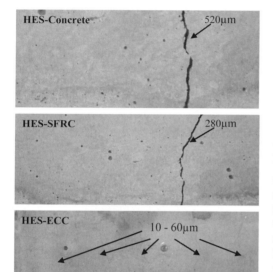

Figure 7: Repair surface cracking

In contrast, when HES-ECC was used as the repair material, 83-113 micro-cracks were formed with the maximum crack width of 60µm, which was much smaller than that of HES-Concrete or HES-SFRC repair. The average crack width of HES-ECC repair was around 30µm. No localized fracture was observed. Since shrinkage strain of HES-ECC was less than 0.3 % (Table 3), it was much below HES-ECC's tensile strain capacity of 2.5-5 %. Therefore, the restrained shrinkage cracking of HES-ECC was occurring in its strain-hardening stage, during which the material formed multiple microcracks with steady crack width. This indicates that the restrained shrinkage crack width of HES-ECC repair is a material property, which is independent of structural dimensions. Even for larger scale repair applications with different types of restrained conditions, HES-ECC repair is still expected to exhibit tight crack width below 60µm.

Table 4: Interface delamination and surface cracking of different layered repair systems

Repair Material	Specimen Number	Cracking	
		Number	Width (µm)
HES-Concrete	(1)	3	169 ; 370 ; 520
	(2)	4	190 ; 340 ; 360 ; 490
	(3)	4	70 ; 380 ;420 ; 450
HES-SFRC	(1)	2	110 ; 120
	(2)	4	50 ; 90 ; 120 ; 130
	(3)	1	280
HES-ECC	(1)	83	10 - 50
	(2)	109	10 - 60
	(3)	113	10- 50

At the age of 60 days, both the HES-ECC and the HES-Concrete repaired systems exhibited relatively low delamination heights at the specimen ends, which were 80μm for the former and 90μm for the latter at the maximum. The maximum delamination length was 80mm for the HES-ECC repair and 170mm for the HES-Concrete repair at the maximum. The HES-SFRC repaired system had much larger delamination height than the HES-ECC or HES-Concrete repaired system at the age of 60 days, which is 290μm. Its delamination length was also larger, around 340mm. Fig. 8 shows the interface delamination profiles of the three layer repair systems at different ages, which are vertical displacement/delamination of the repair layers at different locations along the repair/substrate interface. These profiles are approximately symmetric about the mid-point of the specimen, as would be expected.

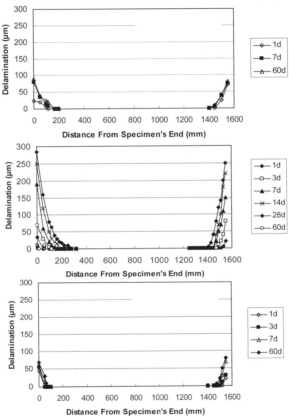

Figure 8: Interface delamination profile of HES-Concrete, HES-ECC and HES-SFRC repaired systems

4. CONCLUSIONS

This study evaluated performance of HES-ECC layered repair system under both mechanical and environmental loading conditions. When subject to monotonic loading, the

HES-ECC layered repair system exhibited 100% increased load carrying capacity, and 10 times the deformation capacity of HES-Concrete layered repair system. Instead of forming one single crack in the HES-Concrete repair layer, the initial interfacial crack would kink into the HES-ECC repair layer, and then trapped there. Upon additional loading, delamination resumes at the interface. The unique kink-trap-cracking behavior repeated itself with increasing flexural loading till the flexural strength of HES-ECC was exhausted. In this way, repair spalling was successfully suppressed by using HES-ECC.

When under the same level of fatigue loading, HES-ECC layered repair system showed significantly longer service life than HES-Concrete layered repair system. The interface properties did not exhibited effect on the cycles experienced before failure. Like the monotonic flexural test, the deformation capacity of the HES-ECC layered repair system was much larger than the HES-Concrete layered repair system. And the maximum deflection before failure was bigger when the interface is smooth. There was no evident difference on the specimen's cracking pattern under the monotonic and the fatigue loading conditions.

When subject to restrained drying shrinkage, the high ductility of the HES-ECC repair layer could accommodate the shrinkage deformation by forming multiple micro-cracks with tight crack width. By this means, tensile and shear stresses at the interface was released, so that both repair cracking and interface delamination could be suppressed. For the traditional HES-Concrete repair, several localized cracks normally formed in the repair layer with large crack width. For the HES-SFRC repair, still several localized cracks formed, but the cracks were bridged by steel fibers. Since the cracks could not open freely to accommodate the repair layer's shrinkage deformation, the interface delamination was much larger than HES-Concrete and HES-ECC repairs.

The above experimental results suggest that HES-ECC can be a very durable repair material with prolonged service life, no matter under environmental loading or mechanical loading. The common failure modes such as large surface cracking, spalling and interface delamination can be successfully suppressed by the uniquely large tensile strain capacity of HES-ECC material.

REFERENCES

[1] Vaysburd, A. M., Brown, C. D., Bissonnette, B, and Emmons, P. H., ""Realcrete" versus "Labcrete"", Concrete International, Vol. 26 No.2, pp 90-94 , 2004

[2] Zhang J., Li, V.C., "Monotonic and Fatigue Performance in Bending of Fiber Reinforced Engineered Cementitious Composite in Overlay System ," J. of Cement and Concrete Research, Vol. 32, No.3, pp. 415-423, 2002

[3] Lim, Y.M. and V.C. Li, "Durable Repair of Aged Infrastructures Using Trapping Mechanism of Engineered Cementitious Composites," J. Cement and Concrete Composites, Vol. 19, No. 4, pp. 373-385, 1997.

[4] Kamada, T. and V.C. Li, "The Effects of Surface Preparation on the Fracture Behavior of ECC/Concrete Repair System," J. of Cement and Concrete Composites, Vol. 22, No. 6, pp.423-431, 2000.

[5] Li, V. C., "High Performance Fiber Reinforced Cementitious Composites as Durable Material for Concrete Structure Repair," Int. J. for Restoration of Buildings and Monuments, Vol. 10, No 2, pp 163–180, 2004

RC BEAMS RETROFITTED WITH CARDIFRC -- BEHAVIOUR AFTER THERMAL CYCLING

Farhat A. Farhat [(1)] and Bhushan Karihaloo [(2)]

(1) Higher Institute of Technical Science, Hoon, Libya

(2) School of Engineering, Cardiff University, Cardiff, UK

Abstract

A new retrofitting technique using CARDIFRC, a material compatible with concrete, has recently been developed at Cardiff University. It overcomes some of the problems associated with the current techniques based on externally bonded steel plates and FRP which are due to the mismatch of their tensile strength, stiffness and coefficient of linear thermal expansion with that of concrete structure being retrofitted. It has now been tested under thermal cycling. Each thermal cycle tried to mimic a 24-hour temperature variation in hot dry climate when exposed concrete surfaces are known to reach very high temperatures. It consisted of a temperature rise period from room temperature to 90°C, followed by a dwell period of 8 hours at this elevated temperature and a slow cooling period back to room temperature. The test and analytical results show that thermal exposure does not cause any degradation to the retrofitted beam strength, or to the bond between concrete and CARDIFRC. It is therefore a very promising material for repair and retrofit in high temperature environments

1. INTRODUCTION

Concrete structures can deteriorate and therefore need repair after long periods in service. Also, to accommodate for a load carrying capacity higher than the original design value, members may need to be strengthened through retrofitting. A common repair and strengthening technique for concrete beams is by bonding a steel plate to the tension side of the beam. However, several problems have been encountered with this technique, including the occurrence of undesirable shear failures, difficulty in handling heavy steel plates, corrosion of steel that can cause deterioration of the bond at a glued steel-concrete interface, and the need of butt joint systems as a result of limited workable lengths [1, 2].

Recently, attention has been directed towards the use of FRP plates, which offer higher strength/weight and improved durability over their steel counterparts [3, 4]. Retrofitting using FRP is also vulnerable to undesirable brittle failures due to a large mismatch in the tensile strength and stiffness with that of concrete. Another problem, which has also been observed with this technique, is the effect of long exposure to temperature variations [5-7].

A new retrofitting technique using CARDIFRC, a material compatible with concrete, has recently been developed at Cardiff University. It overcomes some of the problems associated with the current techniques based on externally bonded steel plates and FRP which are due to the mismatch of their tensile strength, stiffness and coefficient of linear thermal expansion with that of concrete structure being retrofitted [8]

It has now been tested under thermal cycling. Each thermal cycle tried to mimic a 24-hour temperature variation in hot dry climate when exposed concrete surfaces are known to reach very high temperatures. It consisted of a temperature rise period from room temperature to $90^{0}C$, followed by a dwell period of 8 hours at this elevated temperature and a slow cooling period back to room temperature. The test and analytical results show that thermal exposure does not cause any degradation to the retrofitted beam strength, or to the bond between concrete and CARDIFRC. It is therefore a very promising material for repair and retrofit in high temperature environments

2. RETROFITTING RC BEAMS

To make this paper as self-contained as possible, we begin with details of the retrofitting procedure. CARDIFRC denotes a whole class of HPFRCC mixes. The mix proportions of a typical CARDIFRC mix, designated Mix I are given in Table 1 and its typical mechanical properties shown in Table 2. We will now describe briefly the performance of CARDIFRC as a material for retrofitting damaged concrete flexural members at elevated temperatures. The moment resistance and the load-deflection behaviour of the retrofitted beams have been predicted by two approaches developed by Alaee and Karihaloo [9, 10]. The results of these approaches have been compared with test data and very good agreement found. However, due to lack of space the analytical approaches will not be described in this paper. It will be shown that thermal cycling of flexural members retrofitted with CARDIFRC has no effect either on the bond between concrete and CARDIFRC or on their performance.

3. CARDIFRC

CARDIFRC is a new class of high-performance fibre-reinforced cementitious composite (HPFRCC) characterised by high compressive strength (in excess of 200 MPa), tensile/flexural strength (up to 30 MPa) and high-energy absorption capacity (up to 20,000 J/m^2). This has been made possible by the use of large amounts (up to 8 % by volume) of brass-coated short steel fibres (6-13 mm long, 0.16 mm diameter) in a cementitious matrix densified by the use of silica fume. The matrix contains only very fine graded quartz sand, instead of ordinary river sand and coarse aggregates. By optimising the grading of fine quartz sands, the water demand was considerably reduced without affecting the workability of the mix. This was achieved using novel mixing procedures. Computer Tomography imaging and sectioning of specimens have confirmed that these procedures ensure remarkably homogeneous mix with a uniform distribution of fibres [11]. The mix proportions of a mix of the CARDIFRC class are given in Table 1.

Table 1: Mix proportions for CARDIFRC

Constituents (Kg)	Mix I
Cement	855
Quartz sand:	
9-300µm	470
250-600µm	470
Microsilica	214
Water	188
Superplasticizer	28
Fibres: -6 mm	390
-13 mm	78
Water/cement ratio	0.22
Water/binder ratio	0.18

Table 2: Typical material properties of CARDIFRC Mix I

Material properties	Mix I
Indirect tensile strength (MPa)	27
Fracture energy (J/m^2)	17000
Compressive strength (MPa)	200
Modulus of elasticity (GPa)	48

4. TEST BEAMS

Forty-eight under-reinforced RC beams were prepared. Of these, 32 were retrofitted with CARDIFRC and 16 left as control. The beams were fabricated in 12 batches, with each batch consisting of 4 beams. Along with each batch of beams, three cylinders (100 mm in diameter x 200 mm high) and three cubes (100 mm) were also cast. The beams were allowed to cure in a water bath for 28 days. The cement: fine aggregate: coarse aggregate proportions in the concrete mix were 1:1.8:2.8 by weight and the water/cement ratio was 0.50. Ordinary Portland cement was used and the maximum size of aggregate was 10 mm.

Two types of reinforced concrete beam have been investigated in this study: beams without shear reinforcement, which were designed to fail in flexure or in shear, and beams with sufficient shear reinforcement. The former, reinforced with a single 12 mm rebar, were 1200 mm long, 100 mm wide and 150 mm deep. The remaining beams were provided with shear stirrups in their shear spans. According to the British Standard BS8110 the beams were overdesigned for shear to prevent brittle failure due to the increased shear load on the strengthened beam so the flexural behaviour could be observed throughout the loading up to failure. Shear reinforcement consisted of 6 mm deformed bars placed at 65 mm spacing.

Two different configurations of retrofitting were investigated; one strip bonded on the tension face (Fig. 1a) and three strips (one bonded on the tension face and the others on the vertical sides (Fig. 1b)).

All beams were simply supported on a clear span of 1100 mm and were tested under four-point loading. The loading points were 400 mm apart. The beams were incrementally loaded to failure.

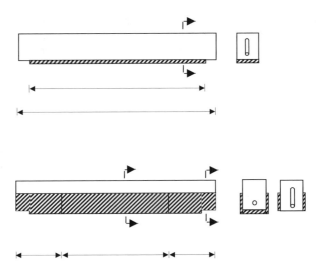

Figure 1: Configurations of retrofitting. Beams retrofitted with: (a) one strip on the tension face, and (b) one strip on the tension and two continuous strips on sides, fully covering supports and tension strip sides.

5. CARDIFRC STRIPS

The retrofit material, CARDIFRC was cast as flat strips in 1030 mm long and 100 mm wide steel moulds with a well oiled base and raised border whose height is 16 mm. The moulds were filled on a non-magnetic vibrating table at a frequency of 50 Hz and smoothed over with a float. To ensure a uniform thickness (within 1 mm) a glass panel was located on top of the raised border. The strips were left to cure in the moulds for 24 hours at 20 C before de-moulding. The retrofit strips were then hot-cured at 90° C for a further 7 days. In order to avoid large thermal gradients a gradual increase in temperature from ambient temperature to 90° C and vice versa was found necessary. The strips were left in the tank for a total period of 9 days. On the first day the temperature of the water was increased gradually from 20° C to 90° C and on the ninth day it was decreased from 90° to 20° C.

Mechanical degradation (pre-cracking) of test beams

Strengthening activities are often to be carried out on existing concrete structures that are normally cracked under the service load. To simulate a RC element more realistically, the test beams were pre-cracked at 75 percent of the ultimate strength of the control beams to induce flexural cracking.

6. RETROFITTING PROCEDURE

Having been loaded to 75 percent of the failure load at which flexural cracks became visible, the beams were unloaded and retrofitted using CARDIFRC strips and epoxy-based adhesive (Sikadur 31). In order to improve the bond between the repair material and the original concrete, the contact surfaces of concrete were carefully cleaned. Before bonding the CARDIFRC strip to the concrete, the surface of the specimens was roughened by creating a grid of grooves to improve mechanical interlocking. An angular grinder was used to create the grooves approximately 3 mm deep at a spacing of 50 mm on the contacting surfaces of the original concrete. The rough, irregular, and often deep surface topography creates a structural morphology that allows the adhesive to penetrate into the irregularities, forming a strong interfacial layer.

The CARDIFRC strips were bonded to the prepared surfaces of the concrete with the thixotropic epoxy adhesive, Sikadur 31. The two parts of the adhesive were thoroughly mixed and applied with a serrated trowel to a uniform thickness of 3 mm. The repair material was placed on the adhesive and evenly pressed. The adhesive was allowed to cure for 24 hours.

7. THERMAL CYCLING

The test programme comprised of 12 control, 24 retrofitted reinforced concrete beams, six 100 mm cubes for compressive strength and six 100x200 mm cylinders for in-direct tensile strength. The specimens were placed in an electrical furnace and heated to a maximum temperature of 90° C from a room temperature of about 25° C. They were heated in the furnace from room temperature to the maximum temperature in about 20 minutes. The aim was to keep the average heating rate at about 3 degrees per minute, to avoid the risk of the beams being thermally shocked during heating. The maximum temperature was then maintained for another eight hours before the beams were cooled down to the room temperature in a further 16 hours. The above 24-hour heating, hold and cooling period constitutes one thermal cycle. The specimens were exposed to 30 or 90 thermal cycles. After the requisite number of thermal cycles, the beams were tested at room temperature in four-point bending.

8. TEST RESULTS

Table 3 shows the effect of thermal cycling on the mechanical properties of CARDIFRC. As can be seen, the mechanical properties of CARDIFRC seem to be unaffected by thermal cycling, thanks to the presence of fibres. The fibres have been shown to reduce concrete damage by hot and cold cycles in the temperature range from 25 to 150^0C.

Table 3: Mechanical properties of CARDIFRC after thermal cycling

Material properties	Thermal cycles		
	0	30	90
Indirect tensile strength (MPa)	27	31	31
Compressive strength (MPa)	200	224	225
Modulus of rupture (MPa)	33	33	34
Modulus of Elasticity (GPa)	48	49	49

The compressive and splitting strengths of ordinary concrete used in test beams after 0, 30 and 90 thermal cycling are shown in Tables 4. The results reveal a relative increase in the compressive and tensile strengths at the elevated temperature of 90°C, irrespective of the number of thermal cycles.

Table 4: Compressive and splitting strengths of ordinary concrete used in test beams

Thermal cycles	Average Compressive strength (MPa)	COV (%)	Average Splitting strength (MPa)	COV (%)
0	56.10	1.8	4.46	2.3
30	66.73	1.7	5.10	7.0
90	60.67	2.5	4.84	2.7

The results of 16 control and 32 retrofitted beams exposed to 0, 30 and 90 thermal cycles are summarized in Table 5. The failure mode and ultimate strength of each beam are noted. In the following sections, the test results will be discussed in detail.

8.1 Beams without shear reinforcement

Of the eight beams retrofitted only on the tension face and subjected to 0, 30 and 90 thermal cycles, three beams failed in shear, four in flexure and one beam failed due to interfacial failure (debonding) at the strip-adhesive interface situated at the end of the retrofit strip. Visual investigation revealed that this debonding occurred due to poor bonding. The shear failure happened in a brittle manner. The flexural failure observed was characterised by a single flexural crack occurring in the loading span extending upwards to the concrete top fibre and downwards through the retrofit strip. All beams exhibit greater load carrying capacity and stiffness than the control beams. Of the eight beams retrofitted on the tension face and the sides and subjected to 0, 30 and 90 thermal cycles, two beams failed suddenly in shear. One failed because the flexural strength at the mid-span of the beam exceeded the shear strength of the beam near the supports. To prevent such shear failure, a system of repair with three continuous strips and four short strips was adopted. The other beam failed due to weak bonding of the side short strip at the support. The behaviour of the remaining six beams was as expected; in the first stage of loading the beams exhibited a linear elastic behaviour. Then the load-deflection response deviated gradually from the initial straight line. The first crack appeared in the middle third of the tension strip, propagated in the side strips and opened up gradually until the load reached the maximum and the load-deflection curve started to descend gently. All the six beams exhibited a plastic behaviour with the yielding of steel. As can be seen from Table 5 the average failure load increased from 40.20 kN to 75 kN for beams kept at room temperature, from 46.85 kN to 88.92 kN for beams exposed to 30 thermal cycles and from 41.62 kN to 86.94 kN for beams exposed to 90 thermal cycles. Therefore, it can be concluded that the load carrying capacity of retrofitted beams exposed to 30 thermal cycles increased by 18.40 percent over the room temperature value, but after 90 thermal cycles the average load carrying capacity increased by only 15.76 percent.

Table 5: Four-point test results of control and retrofitted beams after different thermal cycles

Configurations	TC	Beams without shear reinforcement				Beams with shear reinforcement				
		Sp. No	Max Load (kN)	Avg (kN)	Failure mode	Sp. No	Max Load (kN)	Avg (kN)	Failure mode	Model prediction kN
Control	0	CF-1	40.20	39.92	S-F	CS-1	45.10	45.64	F	42.86
		CF-2	39.64		S-F	CS-2	46.18		F	
	30	CF-3	47.39		S-F	CS-3	47.78		F	
		CF-4	47.24	46.85	F	CS-4	48.80	47.65	F	43.43
		CF-5	45.92		S-F	CS-5	46.59		F	
	90	CF-6	41.4		S	CS-6	47.77		F	
		CF-7	41.35	41.62	S	CS-7	47.79	47.37	F	42.97
		CF-8	42.10		S-F	CS-8	47.55		F	
Retrofitted	0	RF-1	47.39	49.49	F	RS-1	49.80	51.50	F	54.29
		RF-2	51.6		S	RS-2	53.20		F	
	30	RF-3	65.67		S	RS-3	57.57		F	
		RF-4	58.27	62.88	F	RS-4	55.24	57.73	F	55.14
		RF-5	64.7		D	RS-5	60.40		F	
	90	RF-6	55.00		F	RS-6	53.38		F	
		RF-7	59.30	56.37	F	RS-7	48.82	52.06	F	54.86
		RF-8	54.80		S	RS-8	53.97		F	
	0	RF-9	76.00	75.10	F	RS-9	74.00	76.00	F	74.57
		RF-10	74.20		S	RS-10	78.19		F	
	30	RF-11	93.14		F	RS-11	92.68		F	
		RF-12	87.40	88.92	F	RS-12	89.30	90.18	F	76.00
		RF-13	86.23		F	RS-13	88.55		F	
	90	RF-14	88.87		D	RS-14	79.48		F	
		RF-15	87.78	86.94	F	RS-15	87.60	85.22	F	75.90
		RF-16	84.32		F	RS-16	88.60		S	

TC: Thermal cycles, S: Shear Failure, F: Flexural failure, S-F: Shear and flexural failure, D: Debonding

8.2 Beams with sufficient shear reinforcement

The test results show that the response of the control beams has very little scatter, especially before the attainment of the maximum load. It appears that thermal cycling has very little effect on the load carrying capacity of control beams reinforced in flexure and shear. After 90 thermal cycles the shear reinforcement seems to counteract the reduction expected due to the reduction in compressive strength (Table 4).

As expected, all beams retrofitted with one strip failed in pure flexure. The flexural failures observed were generally characterized by a single flexural crack occurring in the middle third of the beam extending upwards to the concrete top fibre between the load points and downwards through the retrofit material (Fig. 2a). All beams failed at loads higher than the average failure load of control beams. Moreover, both the deflection behaviour and failure modes were similar for all exposure conditions.

(a)   (b)

Figure 2: Flexural cracking in a beam retrofitted with: (a) one strip on the tension face and (b) one strip on the tension face, two continuous strips and four short strips on the sides.

Of the eight beams retrofitted with three continuous and four short strips only one beam failed in shear. This failure occurred through the joint connecting the long and short strip. Due to the bridging action of the tension strip, the crack was arrested in the CARDIFRC tension strip. This type of failure can be classified as a ductile shear failure. All the remaining beams failed in pure flexure. The first crack appeared in the middle third of the tension strip. As the load was increased, this crack propagated vertically in the side strips and the mouth of the initial crack in the tension strip opened gradually. As the load was increased further the propagation of the cracks on both sides of the beam towards the compression top fibre became visible. After the peak load, the load-deflection curves descended gently. Finally, the beam exhibited plastic behaviour with the yielding of steel. The results of the fracture-mechanics based analytical model [10] are compared with the test results in Fig. 3. For the analytical modelling the compressive and tensile (including tension softening) constitutive equations of CARDIFRC [12, 13] were used together with those of concrete and of reinforcing steel.

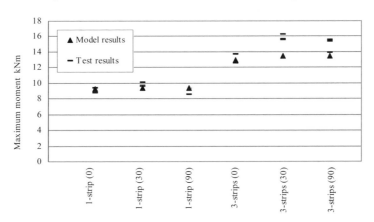

Figure 3: Comparison of moment resistance of beams with predictions of model

9. CONCLUSION

The test and analytical results confirmed that thermal exposure does not cause any degradation to the retrofitted beam strength, or to the bond between concrete and CARDIFRC. CARDIFRC is therefore a very promising material for repair and retrofit in high temperature environments.

REFERENCES

[1] Jones R., Swamy RN and Charif A. Plate separation and anchorage of reinforced concrete beams strengthened by epoxy-bonded steel plates. *Structural Engineer (London)*, 1988; 66(5), 85-94.

[2] Ziraba Y, Baluch MB, Basenbul IA, Sharif AM and Azad AK, Al-Sulaimani GJ. Guidelines towards the design of reinforced concrete beams with external plates. *ACI Structural Journal*, 1994; 91(6), 639-646.

[3] Meier U, Deuring M, Meier H and Schwegler G. Strengthening of structures with CFRP Laminates: Research and Application in Switzerland. *Advanced composite materials in bridges and structures*, Canadian Society for Civil Engineering, 1992; 243-251.

[4] Meier U. Post strengthening by continues fibre laminates in Europe, Non-metallic (FRP) reinforcement for concrete structures, *Japan Concrete Institute*, 1997; 1, 41-56.

[5] Sen R, Mullins G, Shahawy M and Spain J. Durability of CFRP/epoxy/Concrete bond. Composites in the transportation industry, *Proceedings of the ACUN-2 International Composite Conference*, University of South Wales, Australia, 2000.

[6] Zhen M and Chung DDL. Effects of temperature and stress on the interface between concrete and its fibre-matrix composite retrofit, studies by electrical resistance measurement. *Cement and Concrete Research*, 2000; 30, 799-802.

[7] Toutanji HA and Gomez W. Durability characteristics of concrete externally bonded with FRP composite sheets. *Cement and Concrete Composites*, 1997; 19, 351-358.

[8] Karihaloo BL, Alaee FJ and Benson SDP. A new technique for retrofitting damaged concrete structures. *Proc. of the Institution of Civil Engineers, Building & Structures*, 2002; 152(4), 309-318.

[9] Alaee FJ and Karihaloo BL. Retrofitting of reinforced concrete beams with CARDIFRC®. *ASCE Journal of Composites for Construction*, 2003; 7(3), 174-186.

[10] Alaee FJ and Karihaloo BL. A fracture model for flexural failure of beams retrofitted with CARDIFRC®. *ASCE Journal of Engineering Mechanics*, 2003; 129(9), 1028-1038.

[11] Benson S, Nicolaides D and Karihaloo B L. CARDIFRC – Development and mechanical properties, Part II: Fibre distribution. *Magazine of Concrete Research*, 2005; 57(7), 421-432

[12] Benson S and Karihaloo B L., CARDIFRC – Development and mechanical properties. Part III: Uniaxial tensile response and other mechanical properties. *Magazine of Concrete Research*, 2005; 57(8), 433-443

[13] Benson S and Karihaloo, B L., CARDIFRC – Manufacture and constitutive behaviour, Proc HPFRCC4 RILEM PRO 30, Rilem Publications s.a.r.l, Bagneux, France, 2003, 65-79

OUT-OF-PLANE BEHAVIOR OF MASONRY WALLS STRENGTHENED WITH FIBER-REINFORCED MATERIALS: A COMPARATIVE STUDY

Kiang Hwee Tan [(1)], Samsu Sukaimi Hendra [(1)] and Shen Ping Chen [(2)]

(1) Department of Civil Engineering, National University of Singapore, Singapore

(2) College of Civil Engineering, Hubei University of Technology, Hubei, China

Abstract

The out-of-plane behavior of masonry walls strengthened with an overlay using various fiber-reinforced materials was investigated. A total of 14 wall specimens including an unstrengthened wall, were tested. The strengthening materials were: (a) ferrocement and steel fiber-reinforced ferrocement; (b) steel fiber-reinforced mortar; and (c) hybrid fiber-reinforced mortar. The overlay was applied on the tension face of the walls. All walls were subjected to a uniform patch load applied using an airbag at their center. Test results indicated a substantial increase in ultimate load-carrying capacity and ductility of the walls due to the overlay. In general, a higher percentage of fine wire mesh in the ferrocement overlay gives a higher strength with a correspondingly lower ductility. Adding steel fibers in the ferrocement overlay resulted in higher initial stiffness but lower ductility. For higher total volume fraction of reinforcement, fine wiremesh is preferable over steel fibers. Using mortar overlay reinforced with discrete fibers alone gives smaller increase in both strength and ductility of the walls. The use of continuous steel bars with a combination of both steel and polypropylene fibers in the strengthening overlay gives the most desirable performance in terms of initial stiffness, ultimate strength, ductility and energy absorption capacity.

1. INTRODUCTION

Unreinforced masonry walls, which form the envelope of a building, generally constitute the most vulnerable element in a structure in terms of resistance to out-of-plane forces that may result from seismic or blast events. As the failure of such walls is sudden and severe, which results in debris flying through the cavity of the failed wall and causing injuries to inhabitants, it is necessary to enhance the performance of masonry walls in terms of stiffness, ultimate strength, ductility or energy absorption capacity. This may be facilitated by using an externally bonded cementitious overlay which could be reinforced by continuous (skeletal steel and wire mesh) or discrete (steel and polypropylene fibers) reinforcement.

While structural members strengthened with ferrocement laminates had been shown to exhibit significant increase in shear strength, flexural capacity and ductility [1-4], the use of steel fiber-reinforced mortar has not been well established as a repair material due to its relatively low tensile strength. On the other hand, it has been reported that combining different kinds, types, and sizes of fibers, such as in the case of polypropylene (PP) and steel fibers can improve the mechanical properties of the composites [5, 6]. In this investigation, three groups of materials were examined for use in overlays for the strengthening of masonry walls. They are: (a) ferrocement (denoted by prefix F) and steel fiber-reinforced ferrocement (FS); (b) steel fiber-reinforced mortar (S); and (c) hybrid fiber-reinforced mortar (H).

Masonry wall specimens strengthened with these materials were simply supported on four edges and subjected to a center patch load using an airbag. The load-deflection characteristics of the strengthened walls were compared in terms of stiffness, strength, ductility and energy absorption capacity. The effectiveness of the overlay was also compared to the use of fiber-reinforced polymer (FRP) systems on similar walls, tested earlier by the first author [7].

2. TEST PROGRAM

2.1 Test walls

Fourteen wall specimens, each measuring 1 m by 1 m in elevation and 115 mm in thickness, were constructed. The specimens consisted of one unstrengthened and 13 strengthened walls, as shown in Table 1. All the strengthened walls were reinforced with a 30-mm thick overlay on the tension face.

Table 1: Details of wall specimens

| Series | Specimen Designation | Volume Fraction of Reinforcement* (%) | | | | | $f_{cu}^{\#}$ (MPa) | Remarks** |
		$V_{f,\text{ss}}$	$V_{f,\text{wm}}$	$V_{f,\text{sf}}$	$V_{f,\text{pf}}$	V_f		
	REF	-	-	-	-	-	n.a.	n.a.
I	F11	1.31	0.65	-	-	1.96	52.9	C:S:W= 1:2:0.5
	F12	1.31	1.30	-	-	2.61	52.9	
	FS10	1.31	-	0.5	-	1.81	53.8	
	FS11	1.31	0.65	0.5	-	2.46	53.8	
II	S1	-	-	1.0	-	1.0	58.9	C:S:W= 1:2:0.4
	S2	-	-	1.5	-	1.5	55.6	
	S3	-	-	2.0	-	2.0	56.7	
	S4	-	-	2.5	-	2.5	57.6	
III	H00-22	-	-	1.0	0.5	1.5	69.7	C:S:W= 1:2:0.4 1.5% super-plasticizer 7.5% SF
	H10-20	1.31	-	1.0	-	2.31	63.6	
	H10-13	1.31	-	0.5	0.75	2.56	65.0	
	H10-22	1.31	-	1.0	0.5	2.81	69.7	
	H10-23	1.31	-	1.0	0.75	3.06	69.5	

* $V_{f,\text{ss}}$= volume fraction of skeletal steel; $V_{f,\text{wm}}$= volume fraction of fine mesh; $V_{f,\text{sf}}$= volume fraction of steel fibers; $V_{f,\text{pf}}$= volume fraction of polypropylene fibers; V_f= total volume fraction of reinforcement
** C= cement; S= sand; W= water; SF= silica fume; $\#f_{cu}$= mortar compressive strength

The walls are divided into three series. Series I consisted of five wall specimens, two of which were strengthened with a ferrocement overlay (F11 and F12), another two with a steel fiber-reinforced ferrocement overlay (FS10 and FS11), and the remaining unstrengthened wall serving as a reference (REF) specimen. Besides a layer of skeletal steel with a volume fraction of 1.31 percent, the ferrocement overlay was reinforced with a fine wiremesh having a volume fraction of 0.65 or 1.30 percent and steel fibers of 0.5 percent.

In Series II, a steel fiber-reinforced mortar overlay with fiber volume fraction ranging from 1 to 2.5 percent in steps of 0.5 percent was used to strengthen four walls (S1 to S4). Series III comprised five walls strengthened with an overlay that was reinforced with different combination of skeletal steel bars, short steel fibers and polypropylene (PP) fibers. The walls were designated H00-sp or H10-sp for walls without and with skeletal steel bars respectively, with "s" denoting the volume fraction of steel fibers (in "0.5s" percent) and "p" the volume fraction of polypropylene fibers (in "0.25p" percent).

The strengthened wall specimens had a total volume fraction of reinforcement ranging from 1.5 percent (in S1 and H00-22) to 3.06 percent (in H10-23).

2.2 Materials
All walls were fabricated with solid clay bricks having a dimension of $72 \times 95 \times 215$ mm. The bricks were laid in running bond with a mortar joint of about 10 mm in thickness for which the mix proportion was 1:3 by volume of cement to sand. The cement used in all mortar mixes was ASTM Type I normal Portland cement. The sand used was natural river sand with a specific gravity of 2.65. For hybrid-fiber reinforced mortar mixes, silica fume and superplasticizer were added to improve workability.

Two types of steel meshes were used to reinforce the overlay: skeletal steel consisting of 6-mm diameter bars welded in orthogonal directions with 150-mm square openings, and galvanized wire mesh with 1.25-mm wire diameter and 12.5-mm square openings. The yield strength of the skeletal steel and the wire mesh were 650 MPa and 369 MPa, respectively.

As for the discrete reinforcement, the steel fibers were of the hooked-end type, with a length of 35 mm and a diameter of 0.75 mm, while the PP fibers were of a monofilament type, with a length of 10 mm and a diameter of 12 μm.

2.3 Test procedure
Each wall was laid horizontally with the strengthened face downwards, and simply supported along all four edges on round steel bar supports with the corners free to lift and free to rotate about the support lines (see Fig. 1). The effective span was 900 mm in each direction.

The walls were subjected to a uniform load applied using an airbag over a square loading area of approximately 750 mm by 750 mm at the center of the specimen. To measure the wall deflection, a linear variable displacement transducer (LVDT) was placed at the bottom of the wall at its center. The applied load and deflection of the wall were monitored throughout the test until failure.

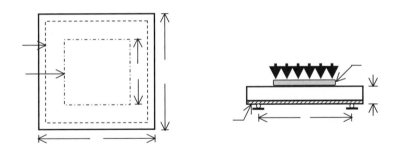

Figure 1: Test set-up

3.   TEST RESULTS AND DISCUSSION

3.1   Load-deflection characteristics

Fig. 2 shows the load-deflection curves of the walls in each series. The test results of similar walls strengthened with FRP systems[7] are also shown for the purpose of comparison.

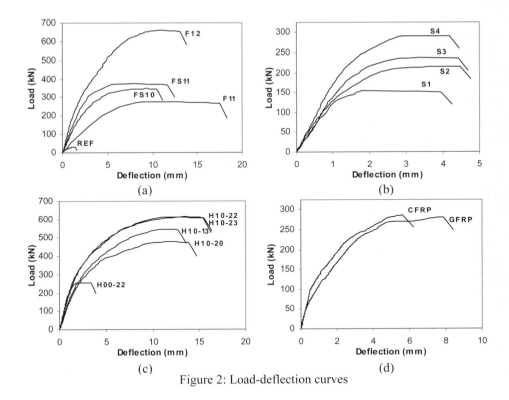

Figure 2: Load-deflection curves

Series I: Walls strengthened with ferrocement and fiber-reinforced ferrocement. - The load-deflection curves shown in Fig. 2(a) illustrate the effects of various volume fractions of reinforcement and the addition of steel fibers. The test results showed that:

1. Compared to the reference (unstrengthened) wall, the stiffness, load carrying capacity and the ductility (defined by the extent of the plateau of the curve) of the strengthened walls were greatly enhanced.
2. A higher volume fraction of reinforcement in the form of fine wiremesh led to a higher load-carrying capacity and a correspondingly lower ductility, as indicated by walls F1 and F12, although in the former wall, early debonding of the ferrocement laminate from the wall was observed.
3. Compared with F11, the addition of steel fibers in FS11 resulted in higher initial stiffness but lower ductility of the wall.
4. For approximately the same total volume of reinforcement, wall F12 (V_f = 2.61%) performed better than specimen FS11 (V_f = 2.46%) in terms of initial stiffness, ultimate strength and ductility; whereas F11 (V_f = 1.96%) performed better than specimen FS10 (V_f = 1.81%) only in terms of ductility, partly because of the unexpected debonding of overlay in F11. For higher total volume fraction of reinforcement, it appears that fine wiremesh is preferable over steel fibers due to the mixing problem associated with steel fibers.

Series II: Walls strengthened with steel fiber-reinforced mortar. - Unlike composites with continuous steel reinforcement that failed mainly due to yielding, steel fiber-reinforced mortar failed due to the pull-out of fibers from the matrix. The walls failed in a ductile manner. From Fig. 2(b), it can be seen that:

1. The load-carrying capacity of the walls increased with an increase in volume fraction of steel fibers. The capacity of wall S4 (V_f = 2.5%) was moderately lower than that of FS11 (V_f = 2.46%).
2. The maximum deflections were independent from of the volume fraction of fibers and ranged from 4 to 4.5 mm. These were much lesser than the values observed in walls with ferrocement overlays.

Series III: Walls strengthened with hybrid fiber-reinforced mortar. - Fig. 2(c) shows that:

1. All walls except H00-22 exhibited higher initial stiffness, ultimate strength, maximum deflection and ductility than walls strengthened with ferrocement or steel fiber-reinforced mortar overlays.
2. Wall H00-22 that was strengthened with an overlay having discrete steel and polypropylene fibers only exhibited lesser load-carrying and deformation capacities.
3. A higher volume fraction of discrete fibers led to higher load-carrying and deformation capacities; however, an increase in volume fraction of polypropylene fibers above 0.5% appears to have no beneficial effect, as indicated by H10-22 and H10-23.

Fig. 2(d) shows the test results of similar wall specimens[7] strengthened with carbon and glass fiber-reinforced polymer (FRP) systems, and subjected to the same loading as those in the current study. The FRP laminates were placed in one ply in each orthogonal direction. The FRP-strengthened walls had ultimate strength equal to those of walls strengthened with steel fiber-reinforced mortar overlay, but with maximum deflections between those of walls strengthened with steel fiber-reinforced mortar overlay and ferrocement overlays. Thus, the use of skeletal steel with discrete fibers in overlays is a viable and more economical way to strengthen masonry walls against lateral loads.

3.2 Energy absorption capacity

Instead of strength and ductility, the energy absorption capacity, defined as the area under the load-deflection curve, is used herein to compare quantitatively the performance of the strengthened walls against lateral loads. The energy absorption capacities obtained are shown in Table 2, while Figs. 3 and 4 illustrate the relation between the energy absorption capacity of the wall and its reinforcement ratio and the tensile capacity of the overlay, respectively.

The reinforcement ratio is defined as the area of reinforcement divided by the cross-section area (that is, width times overall thickness) of the strengthened wall. For discrete fibers, the area of reinforcement is taken as half the volume fraction times the overlay thickness. The tensile capacity is taken as the area of reinforcement multiplied by the tensile strength for continuous reinforcement. In the case of discrete fibres, tests were carried out to establish the tensile capacity using fiber-reinforced mortar specimens.

Table 2: Energy absorption capacities

Specimen Designation	Reinft. Ratio (%)	Tensile capacity (kN/m)	Ultimate Capacity (kN)	Ultimate Deflection (mm)	Failure Modes*	Energy Absorption Capacity (kNmm)
F11	0.20	164.3	277.4	17.52	FT	3982
F12	0.27	200.5	660.9	13.05	FT	6628
FS10	0.19	153.6	348.1	11.69	FT	2907
FS11	0.25	189.8	372.2	10.54	FT	3777
S1	0.10	50.7	154.3	3.95	FT	505
S2	0.16	76.2	214.6	4.47	FT	753
S3	0.21	101.7	237.1	4.42	FT	819
S4	0.26	127.2	290.9	4.18	FT	931
H00-22	0.16	93.0	256.1	3.39	FT	699
H10-20	0.24	181.8	479.3	13.87	FT	5745
H10-13	0.26	179.0	546.4	12.73	FT	4992
H10-22	0.29	221.1	614.3	15.53	FT	7825
H10-23	0.32	223.2	610.6	15.39	FT	7904
CFRP	0.15	577.5	285.5	5.60	FC	1155
GFRP	0.61	1507.5	280.2	7.86	FC	1666

Note: * FT= flexural tension (by rupture/pullout of steel reinforcement); FC= flexural compression.

As shown in Figs. 3 and 4, the energy absorption capacity of the strengthened walls increased with its reinforcement ratio or the tensile capacity of the overlay. The increase is most significant with overlays containing both continuous and discrete reinforcements. Ferrocement overlays are slightly less efficient although the trend is in line with hybrid fiber-reinforced overlays, especially when viewed with respect to the tensile capacity of the overlays. Wall FS11 did not perform as well due to premature debonding as mentioned earlier.

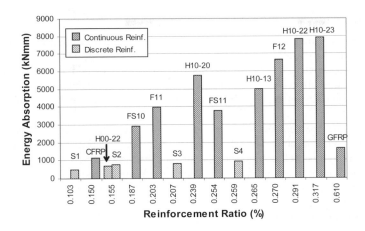

Figure 3: Relationship between energy absorption and reinforcement ratio

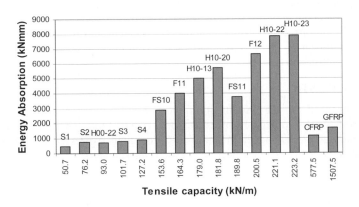

Figure 4: Relationship between energy absorption capacity and tensile capacity of overlay

Steel fiber-reinforced mortar overlays are not as efficient due to the low tensile capacity. As for FRP systems, carbon FRP lamintates gave comparable or slightly better performance as steel fiber-reinforced overlays when viewed with respect to reinforcement ratio. However, from the viewpoint of tensile capacity, both glass and carbon FRP laminates did not result in higher energy absorption capacity of the wall, than ferrocement or hybrid fiber-reinforced overlays. This is attributed to the thinness of FRP laminates which adds little to the rigidity and shear resistance of the wall. Unlike walls using reinforced mortar overlays, which were able to sustain the load until the reinforcement failed in rupture or pullout, walls strengthened with FRP systems lost their resistance soon after the masonry wall cracked under the load.

4.   CONCLUSIONS

This investigation reported in this paper involved an experimental evaluation of the out-of-plane behavior of masonry walls strengthened with externally bonded overlays comprising various fibre-reinforced materials. The following conclusions may be deduced from the study:

1.   Strengthening of unreinforced masonry walls using reinforced cement composite overlays contributes substantially to the flexural performance of the walls in terms of stiffness, strength and ductility.
2.   In general, a higher percentage of fine wire mesh in the ferrocement overlay gives a higher strength with a correspondingly lower ductility. Adding steel fibers in the ferrocement overlay resulted in higher initial stiffness but lower ductility. For higher total volume fraction of reinforcement, fine wiremesh is preferred over steel fibers.
3.   Using mortar overlay reinforced with discrete fibers alone gives smaller increase in both strength and ductility of the walls.
4.   The use of continuous steel bars with a combination of both steel and polypropylene fibers in the strengthening overlay gives the most desirable performance in terms of initial stiffness, ultimate strength, ductility and energy absorption capacity.
5.   In general, the energy absorption capacity of the strengthened walls increased with the reinforcement ratio and the tensile capacity of the overlays.
6.   Compared to fiber-reinforced polymer systems, ferrocement and hybrid fiber-reinforced mortar overlays appear to be a viable and more economical method in strengthening masonry walls against lateral loads.

ACKNOWLEDGEMENTS

The steel fibers used in the investigation were provided by Arcelor Group. The polypropylene fibers were provided by Brasilit Com. E Ind. Ltda. The authors thank the companies for generously donating the materials. The opinions expressed in this paper are solely those of the authors and do not reflect the views of the sponsors.

REFERENCES

[1] Iorns, M., 'Laminated ferrocement for better repair', *Concrete International: Design and Construction* **9** (9) (1987) 34-38.
[2] Paramasivam, P., Lim, C.T.E., and Ong, K.C.G., 'Strengthening of RC beams with ferrocement laminates', *Cement and Concrete Composites* **20** (1) (1998) 53-65.
[3] Kazemi, M.T., Morshed, R., 'Seismic shear strengthening of reinforced concrete column with ferrocement jacket', *Cement and Concrete Composites* **27** (7) (2005) 834-842.
[4] Al-Kubaisy, M.A., Jumaat, M.Z., 'Flexural behaviour of reinforced concrete slabs with ferrocement tension cover zone', *Construction and Building Materials* **14** (5) (2000) 245-252.
[5] Bentur, A., Mindess, S., 'Fibre reinforced cementitious composites', (Elsevier Applied Science, London, 1990).
[6] Qian, C., Stroeven, P., 'Fracture properties of concrete reinforced with steel-polypropylene hybrid fibres', *Cement and Concrete Composites* **22** (5) (2000) 343-351.
[7] Tan, K.H., Patoary, M.K.H., 'Strengthening of masonry walls against out-of-plane loads using fiber-reinforced polymer reinforcement', *Journal of Composite for Construction* **8** (1) (2004) 79-87.

MITIGATION OF DAMAGE DUE TO CRACK OF RC ELEMENTS UTILIZING HIGH PERFORMANCE FIBER REINFORCED CEMENTITIOUS COMPOSITES

Hiroshi Fukuyama [1], Masato Iso [2], Atsuhisa Ogawa [3] and Haruhiko Suwada [1]

(1) Building Research Institute, Tsukuba, Japan

(2) Fukui University, Fukui, Japan

(3) Kuraray, Okayama, Japan

Abstract

Two damage mitigation techniques by using HPFRCC are introduced in this paper. The one is HPFRCC thin-board used as form. The damage properties of beams were tested in the cases with and without HPFRCC board. Because of the multiple cracking properties of HPFRCC board, no visible crack were observed before failure in shear. The shear crack width as well as flexural crack width can be successfully reduced.

The other technique is HPFRCC shear wall precast panel. The HPFRCC wall panel was casted at the precast plant by using the same mixer and methods as those in the case of production of RC precast wall panel. The nonstructural wall with openings made by HPFRCC showed little damage by 1/100 rad. in deflection angle. In the contrast, the RC non-structural wall with the same configuration showed the severe damage with many large shear cracks. Since the strength of HPFRCC wall was not decrease by the 1/100 rad. the contribution of it to the seismic performance of the structure can be taken in the account as a structural elements.

1. INTRODUCTION

High Performance Fiber Reinforced Cementitious Composite (HPFRCC) has unique characteristics including strain-hardening and multiple cracking. This paper proposes a new idea to prevent and control the cracking damage (the damage caused by major cracks which may impair the building function) by using HPFRCC. The outline of the structural experiments which were carried out for investigation is also introduced.

2. NEED FOR DAMAGE MITIGATION

When the 1995 Hyogo-ken Nanbu Earthquake (Kobe Earthquake) occurred, most of the Reinforced Concrete (RC) buildings designed according to the current seismic code didn't collapse and protected many human lives. It was meeting with the code requirement as minimum requirement. However, unfortunately, not a little RC buildings were eventually reconstructed because there were critical damages observed including a lot of excessive cracks, the yielding and buckling of reinforcement, and the concrete compression failure and as a result, the cost of the restoration estimated to overrun the reconstruction cost (see examples in Photo 1). In the 1978 Miyagi-ken Oki Earthquake and the 2005 Fukuoka-ken Seiho Oki Earthquake (see Photo 2), since nonstructural walls of condominiums were damaged so heavily a substantial decrease in the required function for safety and serviceability of buildings were found. From those experiences, it is cleared that the damage mitigation technology including damage control and prevention is needed as well as the security of human lives on the huge earthquake.

(a) View of the building. The structural system of its long direction is RC frame	(b) Damage of columns	(c) Damage of beam-column joints

Photo 1: A building, not collapsed but severely damaged due to the 1995 Kobe Earthquake, which was designed according to the Japanese current seismic code

Photo 2: Damage of nonstructural wall and door of a residential building caused by the 2005 Fukuoka-ken Seiho-oki Earthquake

From the environmental view, it is natural that the demand for long life structures is growing year by year. Unlike the above examples, long life structures should survive an earthquake, and as such, they should adapt the technology of damage control. On top of that, a great number of building stocks in Japan were constructed during the high-speed-growth period after World War II. Today and in the very near future, most of them are facing the problems of renovation or reconstruction. By the time of the renovation, the technology development of damage control should be complemented.

Central Disaster Prevention Council of the Japanese Cabinet Office issued "the Business Continuing Guideline; First Edition" in 2005. The guideline requires every company to establish its own Business Continuity Plan (BCP). According to the guideline, a BCP should emphasize on the quick recovery of building functions and business operations in order to minimize the effect of malfunctions because of the natural disaster including earthquakes. Among a variety of countermeasures, to maintain the building function from the view of structural engineering, the damage prevention and control of structural frame and nonstructural members should be given the first priority.

3. MITIGATION OF DAMAGE DUE TO CRACK

Based on the historical background, following two technologies to mitigate the damage due to cracks are proposed in this paper. Effect of multiple cracking by HPFRCC can be expected in both technologies.
1) Using high performance fiber reinforced cement board (HPFRCC thin cement board) for the surface of columns, beams, and walls, as formwork panels
2) Producing Precast (PCa) nonstructural walls using HPFRCC and constructing them in the same way as the conventional PCa-RC nonstructural walls.

The structural experiments to examine the feasibility of these ideas are outlined in the following chapters.

4. DAMAGE REDUCTION OF RC BEAMS USING HPFRCC CEMENT BOARDS AS FORMWORK PANELS

In this study, the ready-made PVA-HPFRCC cement board is used as a formwork panel from the view point of aiming "the reduction of tropical timber plywood" as well as the main purpose of "the damage control". Accordingly, it aims to develop the cracking resistant new RC members which can secure the same level of workability as the conventional RC members. It also places an emphasis on the possibility if it can control the width of shear crack.

4.1   Experimental outline

The list of test specimens is shown in Table 1 and the configuration of test specimens including the bar arrangements are shown in Fig. 1. The HPFRCC cement board with 8 mm thick was used as a formwork panel. It was formed by many layers of thin sheets from a slurry of PVA fiber, pulp, cement and water. It was placed in order the fiber direction to keep in an axial member. All the specimens shared the following common factors: cross section b x D was 175mm x 270 mm, shear span ration a/D was 1.5, and shear reinforcements were D6-@180; deformed bar with 6-mm in diameter placed in 180 mm interval. High strength reinforcements; SHD685 (685 N/mm^2 in nominal yield strength) were used as a longitudinal bar so as that the shear failure preceded. The design strength of concrete was 18 N/mm^2. Variable of the test is the surface configuration, smooth or rough, of formwork panels which could influences on the crack characteristics. The No. 3 specimen had an artificially rough-cast surface on a formwork panel. The No. 2 specimen had a smooth-cast surface on it. The No. 1 specimen was a standard RC specimen without using a formwork panel as a control specimen.

Table 1: Test specimens

Nunber of beam specimen	Variables
No. 1	without HPFRCC formwork panel (Control RC beam)
No. 2	with HPFRCC formwork panel having smooth cast surface in both sides
No. 3	with HPFRCC formwork panel having artificial rough cast surface in one side, and smooth cast surface in another side

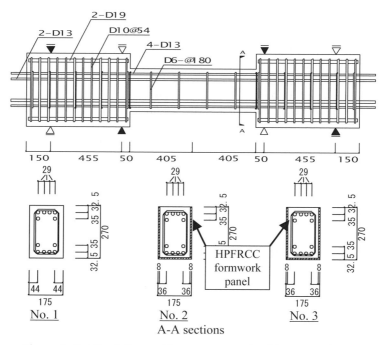

Figure 1: Configulation and bar arrangements of beam specimens

Test results of Reinforced concrete materials and formwork panels are shown in Table 2 and 3, respectively. In Fig. 2 is shown a tension stress (σ)-strain (ε) relationship of a formwork panel which has a rough-cast surface on one side. In this case, the loading direction is parallel to the fiber direction. The uniaxial tensile properties of this formwork panel was determined as multiple cracking properties while the strain hardening characteristics was observed with 2 percent of strain capacity after cracking occurs. Crackings were invisible until at the last loading when a width of one cracking was observed.

Specimens were loaded by Ohno method to represent an antisymmetrical moment condition. The reversed cyclic loading was performed under the control by deformation angle, 1/200, 1/100, 1/50 and 1/33rad, respectively.

Table 2: Material properties of steel reinforcements and concrete

Type of reinforcements (diameter and class)	Yield strength (N/mm^2)	Tensile strength (N/mm^2)	Young's modulus (kN/mm^2)
Longitudinal reinforcement (D13, SHD 685)	742	936	215
Shear reinforcement (D6, SD295A)	426	559	185
Type of concrete	Tensile strength (N/mm^2)	Compressive Strength (N/mm^2)	Young's modulus (kN/mm^2)
Normal concrete (Fc 18)	2.33	30.7	23.7

Table 3: Material properties of PVA-HPFRCC formwork panels

Surface condition	Loading direction	Tensile strength (N/mm^2)	Bending strength (N/mm^2)	Young's modulus (kN/mm^2)
smooth cast surface in both sides	Parallel to the fiber direction	14.5	38.6	13.5
	Perpendicular to the fiber direction	7.62	20.0	12.9
artificial rough cast surface in one side, and smooth cast surface in another side	Parallel to the fiber direction	20.2	45.7	16.2
	Perpendicular to the fiber direction	9.5	25.9	13.8

Pieces for tensile test : 30 x 8 x 300 (mm), Pieces for bending test : 100 x 8 x 400 (mm)

4.2   Test results

1) Failure properties

The photos of crack properties when the deformation angle was +1/100 rad. are shown in Photo 3. In any event, RC specimen (No. 1) had more number of cracks than No. 2 or No. 3 which used formwork panels. In particular, the No. 3 specimen with an artificially rough-cast surface on a formwork panel had remarkably smaller cracks than other two specimens. Until the maximum capacity due to shear failure, however, No. 2 and No. 3 showed the same level of crack properties. Therefore, no distinguished differences between No. 2 and No. 3 can be observed when these beams are not failed in shear as usual case in design. All the three specimens showed the typical mechanism of shear tensile failure; the shear reinforcing bars' yielding led the shear capacity. After the shear capacity, the separation of the underside-board on No. 2 specimen was aobserved at -1/100 rad., and that of the left-side-board on No. 3 specimen was observed at +1/50 rad. The widening of the separation became more obvious with increasing deformation. The multiple cracking of No. 3 specimen at 1/100 rad. is shown in Photo 4. This is a close up picture taken by CCD camera system. The good characteristics of the multiple cracking can be observed by the photo in which the width of cracks is less than 0.1 mm and the spacing of them is less than 1mm. The visible cracks are only marked as shown in Photo 3.

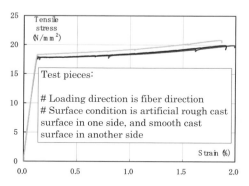

Figure 2: Tensile stress – strain relationships of the formwork panel

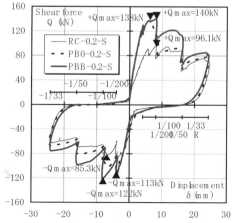

Figure 3: Shear force - displacement relationship

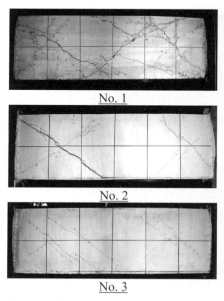

No. 1

No. 2

No. 3

Photo 3: Crack properties at +1/100 rad.

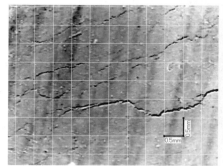

Photo 4: Multiple cracking of No. 3 at 1/100 rad.

2) Shear capacity and deformation properties

The shear force (Q)-relative displacement (δ) relationship is shown in Fig. 3. Secured by the formwork boards, the stiffness and the shear capacity of No. 2 and No. 3 specimens after the shear cracking are higher than those of No. 1 specimen. No. 2 specimen with smooth-cast surface of formwork panel and No. 3 specimen with rough-cast surface showed almost same stiffness and shear capacity after the shear cracking. The difference of the cast surface did not influence on the failure properties nor ultimate capacity.

By using formwork panel, the shear strengthening effect can be expected as well as the crack damage prevention because the shear capacity of No. 2 and No. 3 specimens were much higher than that of No. 1 specimen.

- Wall length x height : 1760 x 1100 mm
- Wall thickness : 40mm
- Wall reinforcements : D4@200
- Column section : 240 x 240 mm

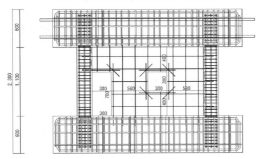

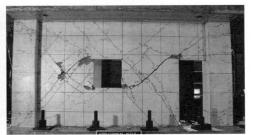

Figure 4: Configuration and bar arrangements wall specimens

Figure 5: Lateral force-displacement of relationships

(a) HPFRCC wall

(b) RC non-structural wall [1]

Photo 5: Comparison of damage at 1/200 rad. in drift angle

5. REDUCTION OF DAMAGE DUE TO CRACK OF NONSTRUCTURAL WALLS UTILIZING HPFRCC

In the past earthquakes, the performance of the structural members was adversely affected by nonstructural walls or the nonstructural walls were heavily damaged. Therefore, nowadays, it is recommended to use slits for isolation between structural and nonstructural members. However, having complete slits could cause problems concerning waterproofing, sound isolation, and airtightness. In particular, for waterproofing there is a defect liability system for 10 years, therefore, using slits has not been always acceptable. Still now, unfortunately, the damage and the destruction of nonstructural members are widely observed when a huge earthquake occurs.

Based on the facts, this study is aiming to newly develop the high performance wall members. Those new members should be able to mitigate the damage of nonstructural walls without structural slits and to work as shear walls with large openings.

5.1 Experimental outline

The configuration of test specimens and the bar arrangements are shown in Fig. 4. This specimen employs the same configuration and the bar arrangement as the RC cast-in-situ nonstructural wall introduced in reference [1]. The difference is that the specimen in this study is using HPFRCC instead of wall panel concrete. Wall panels were produced in the precast concrete works for practical application. Used HPFRCC is hybrid HPFRCC of which volume fraction is 0.75 % of polyethylene fiber (6 mm length, 12 μm diameter) and 0.75 % of steel code (32 mm length, 405 μm diameter). A forced mixing type biaxial mixer of 1 m^3 capacity which is usually used in the precast concrete plants, was used for mixing the HPFRCC. The reversed cyclic lateral force was applied to the center of the upper beam with constant axial load; axial force ratio 0.1, applied on each columns. For the details of an experiment, see reference [1].

5.2 Test results

Load-deformation curves are shown in Fig. 5. The envelope of RC nonstructural wall in reference [1] is also shown in the figure. HPFRCC wall didn't show any strength reduction until deformation angle (1/100 rad), while RC nonstructural wall showed remarkable strength reduction at 1/400 rad. The ultimate strength of HPFRCC wall was higher than that of RC nonstructural wall on the negative side of the curve and lower on the positive side. The main factor for the lower ultimate strength on the positive side is presumably the slippage on the surface because shear cotters were equipped on the left and right sides, but not on the top or bottom sides of HPFRCC wall. It followed the usual specification of precast walls.

Crack patterns of HPFRCC walls and RC nonstructural walls at -1/200 rad. are shown in Photo 5, respectively. On HPFRCC walls, only fine cracks can be observed. The damage mitigation effects are noticeable. The maximum width of cracks is about 12 mm on the RC nonstructural wall and about 0.3 mm on the HPFRCC wall.

It is also significant that the ultimate strength (about 700kN) of HPFRCC nonstructural wall with openings (wall thickness;40 mm) approximates closely to the ultimate strength (about 800 kN) of RC seismic wall without opening (wall thichness;60 mm) [2].

6. CONCLUSION

The followings were confirmed:
1) By using HPFRCC cement board as a formwork panel for RC members, cracking damage can be drastically mitigated and stiffness and shear capacity can be improved.
2) By using HPFRCC wall instead of conventional RC nonstructural wall, cracking damage can be drastically mitigated and the structural performance can be substantially improved.
Further research and investigation will be continued for quantitative evaluation.

REFERENCES

[1] K. Shirai, T. Watanabe, T. Mukai, H. Suwada, H. Fukuyama, S. Nomura: Experimental study on seismic retrofit with PCa-walls using UFC, Proc. of AIJ annual meeting, Structure IV, pp.535-538, 2005-9 *(in Japanese)*

[2] H. Fukuyama, H. Suwada, T. Mukai, T. Watanabe and, S. Nomura: Structural Test on High Performance Seismic Resistance Elements with High Strength, Stiffness, Ductility, Proc. of AIJ annual meeting, Structure IV, pp.487-490, 2005-9 *(in Japanese)*

LAP SPLICE PERFORMANCE OF REINFORCING BAR IN HIGH PERFORMANCE SYNTHETIC FIBER REINFORCED CEMENTITIOUS COMPOSITES UNDER REPEATED LOADINGS

Esther Jeon, Sun-Woo Kim, Young-Oh Lee, Jang-Bae Byun and Hyun-Do Yun

Dept. of Architectural Engineering, Chungnam National University, Republic of Korea

Abstract

The primary objective of this research is to investigate the lap splice performance and bond stress of deformed reinforcing bars embedded in high-performance fiber-reinforced cementitious composites (HPFRCC). In this paper, the effects of reinforcing fibers on the lap splice strength of reinforcing bars in tension were experimentally investigated. A total of 6 specimens were made and tested in axial tension. The variables in this study covered matrix ductility [reinforcing fibers: polypropylene (PP) and polyethylene (PE) fiber] and lap splice length (90 and 120% of development/splice length in ACI 318-05 lap splice provisions). Three strain gages located on the surface of reinforcing bar were placed to monitor the strain of the reinforcement during the deformation process. The scope of the investigations on the splice strength of reinforcing bars in tension in absence of transverse reinforcement in comparison with plain unconfined concrete. The current experimental results demonstrated clearly that the addition of synthetic fibers in cement matrixes increases significantly the lap splice performance of reinforcing bars in tension. Lap splice strength by adding PE fiber in 1.5 percent by volume increased 30.11 ~ 88.63 percent more than that of normal concrete. Also, the presence of fibers increased the number of cracks formed around the spliced bars, delayed the growth of the splitting cracks, and consequently, improved the ductility of bond failure.

1.   INTRODUCTION

In Korea, precast concrete frame construction has been used extensively for industrial and commercial facilities due to its potential benefits in term of construction speed, high quality control, and saving in costs. However, it is required to develop a adequate connection between the precast members because recently, seismic design code in Korea is more intensified in consideration of increasing the seismic hazards in the Korean Peninsula. Such a precast member connection must meet the demands of strength and damage tolerance such as ductility and energy dissipation capacity. It is well known that the seismic performance of precast component connections is dependent on the amount/details of joint reinforcements and CIP(Cast-in-place) joint materials [1]. In essence, an increased amount and complicated details of connection reinforcement result in the increase in construction time and cost.

In the past decade, efforts [2, 3] to improve quasi-brittle characteristic of fiber-reinforced concrete (FRC) have led to innovative materials i.e. HPFRCC which uniquely exhibit multiple, fine cracks and ductile strain-hardening behavior resembling ductile metal upon loading in tension. Advances in HPFRCC have been so rapid that the application of several HPFRCC materials to seismic-resistant structures has been discussed [4].

This research aimed at developing a strong and damage-tolerant connections between precast components is a preceding study. This paper provides the basic characteristics of the two types of HPFRCC with polypropylene (PP) and polyethylene(PE) fiber in terms of uniaxial tensile tests. Also, the effects of HPFRCC's tensile characteristics on the the lap splice performance and crack procedure are experimentally investigated.

2. CHARACTERISTICS OF HPFRCC

2.1 Materials and mix proportions

The synthetic fibers used in this study were PP and PE. As shown in Table 1, the PP fiber had a diameter of 0.04 mm, a length of 15 mm and a tensile strength of 600 MPa. Also, the PE fibers 15 mm in length and tensile strength of 2,500 MPa were used. Silica sand with a specific gravity of 2.61 and grain sizes ranging from 105 to 120 μm was used. Superplasticizers were used to control the workability of high strength cement composite(50 MPa).

The mix proportions of PP2.0, PE1.5 and normal concrete(Concrete) are shown in Table 2. Test specimens were named according to the types of reinforcing fibers (PP2.0 for PP-HPFRCC, PE1.5 for PE-HPFRCC) and fiber volume fraction. In PP2.0 and PE1.5, the content of fiber was 2.0, 1.5% by volume fraction respectively. The cement composites was made using ASTM Type III cement, commercial silica sand and aggregate, at w/c ratio of 0.37 for concrete and 0.45 for PP2.0 and PE1.5.

Table 1: Proportions of fibres

Fiber type	Specific gravity (kg/m³)	Length (mm)	Diameter (μm)	Aspect ratio (l/d_f)	Tensile strength (MPa)	Young's modulus (GPa)
PP	0.91	15	40	375	600	5
PE(DYN-A)	0.97	15	12	1,250	2,500	75

Table 2: Mixture proportions of composites

Specimen notation	W/C	V_f (%)	Unit weight(kg/m³)			
			Cement	Sand	Aggregate	Water
Concrete	0.37	-	459.0	759.0	570.0	170.0
PP2.0	0.45	2.0	1036.0	414.4	-	466.2
PE1.5	0.45	1.5	1041.5	416.6	-	468.7

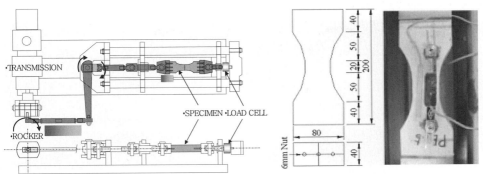

Figure 1: Set-up of uniaxial tensile test   Figure 2: Shape of tensile specimen

2.2   Testing procedure

Uniaxial tensile tests were performed using the dogbone-shaped specimens to examine the effect of reinforcing fiber types on the tensile response and fracture process of HPFRCC. Figs. 1 and 2 show the test set-up and specimen configuration, respectively. The cross-section of tensile specimen is 80 x 40 mm. This specimen is directly subjected to tensile load with pin-fixed boundary condition as shown in Fig. 1. The displacement of this central region was measured by means of PI gauge, and the tensile strain was calculated by dividing this measured displacement by the reference length of 100 mm.

2.3   Tensile response and crack patterns

Tensile stress-strain curves for PP2.0 and PE1.5 are shown in Fig. 3. PE1.5 composites reinforced with high elastic modulus PE fibres show more tensile stiffness than PP2.0 composite with low elastic modulus PP fibres. PE1.5 composites clearly indicated the pseudo strain hardening characteristics and multiple cracks while PP2.0 composites exhibit just ductile strain hardening characteristics. After initial crack in the PP2.0, the tensile stress decreased abruptly due to low elastic modulus, strength, and bond stress of PP fiber. PE 1.5 composites exhibited stable strain hardening without sudden decrease of tensile stress. PP2.0 and PE1.5 HPFRCC properties obtained from direct tension test are first cracking strengths of 2.08 MPa at 0.17% strain and 2.03 MPa at 0.05% strain, respectively and ultimate tensile strengths of 4.20 MPa at 2.26% strain and 5.58 MPa at 2.27 % strain, respectively.

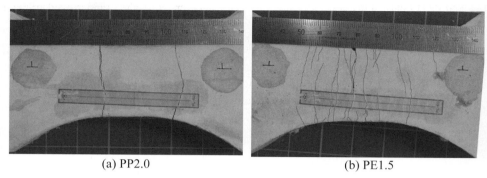

(a) PP2.0   (b) PE1.5

Figure 3: Typical tensile response of HPFRCC

3.   PERFORMANCE OF LAP SPLICES IN HPFRCC

3.1   Specimen configuration

A summary of the test specimens is provided in Table 3. The dimensions and reinforcing bar arrangements of the specimens are shown in Fig. 4. Parameters cover lap splice length and matrix type. Lap splice specimen had 120 x 100 mm of cross section and 600 (730) mm of length. The spliced length of the bars was 400 (530) mm [90(120) percent of lap splice length(l_d) calculated by ACI 318-05 lap splice provisions]. A 19 mm diameter deformed bars were spliced centrally.

3.2   Test rig and procedure

As shown in Fig. 4, two linear variable differential transducers (LVDTs) were installed to measure the displacement of the specimen of lap splice region. Three wire strain gauges were attached to estimate the strain distribution of reinforcing bar according to splice length. Loading is carried out with repeated manner. The tests were carried out using a displacement control (500 to 4,000 strain in term of strain of reinforcing bar embedded in HPFRCC). All specimens were loaded vertically in a 1,000 kN capacity servo-hydraulic Universal Testing Machine and gripped at the protruding ends of the steel reinforcement so that the tensile load was transferred from the reinforcing bar to lap splice at the center of specimen.

3.3   Failure patterns

A typical crack pattern of the lap splice has been shown in Fig. 5. During the early stage of load application, tensile cracks initiated at the lap splice edge of reinforcing bars. As the load increased, tensile cracks formed randomly along the entire length of the lap splice region. These cracks progressed to the center of specimen. For Concrete specimen, there is no distributed cracking that occurs before localization. Only four cracks formed in the specimen before one of the cracks began to localize. The use of PE fiber, compared with PP, greatly improved the fracture process by allowing for the formation of multiple microcracks before the macrocrack began to localize. The addition of the microfibers reduced the widening of coalesced cracks and induced the formation of multiple cracks before the peak load. The formation of multiple cracking increased the deformation capacity of the material and the corresponding delay in the development of a critical macrocrack resulted in increased strength.

Table 3: Mixture proportions of composites

Specimen notation	Bar size number	Splice length (mm, %)	V_f (%)
Concrete-19-90	19	400(90)	-
Concrete-19-120	19	530(120)	-
PP2.0-19-90	19	400(90)	2.0
PP2.0-19-120	19	530(120)	2.0
PE1.5-19-90	19	400(90)	1.5
PE1.5-19-120	19	530(120)	1.5

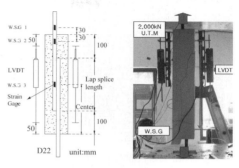

(a)Details of specimen　　(b) Set-up

Figure 4: Test set-up

3.4　Tensile load-displacement responses

Fig. 6 shows the tensile load versus displacement response for six specimens under repeated loading. As shown in the figure, the tensile load-displacement curves before ultimate load is typical of concrete members loaded in tensile, with no significance difference in the strength of the load-displacement response between the PP2.0 and Concrete specimen.

However, following the ultimate load of Concrete specimen, there is a very sudden decrease in the tensile load versus displacement due to a large energy release at crack location. The PP2.0 failed rather gradually. The load resistance decreased slightly after reaching ultimate and continued to drop gradually with increasing displacement.

Lap splice strength of PE1.5 specimen reinforced with high modulus PE fibers increased by up to 25.86~51.61 percent more than that of PP fiber up to 2.0 percent by volume. Lap splice strength of PE1.5 specimen with 90 and 120% of standard lap splice length by ACI code was reached the ultimate strength (168.56kN) of reinforcing bars. Thus, although lap splice length is 90% of American Concrete Institute (ACI) code requirements for reinforcing bars in concrete, PE1.5 specimen represents sufficient lap splice performance.

The presence of fibers increased the number of cracks formed around the spliced bars, delayed the growth of the splitting cracks, and consequently, improved the ductility of bond failure.

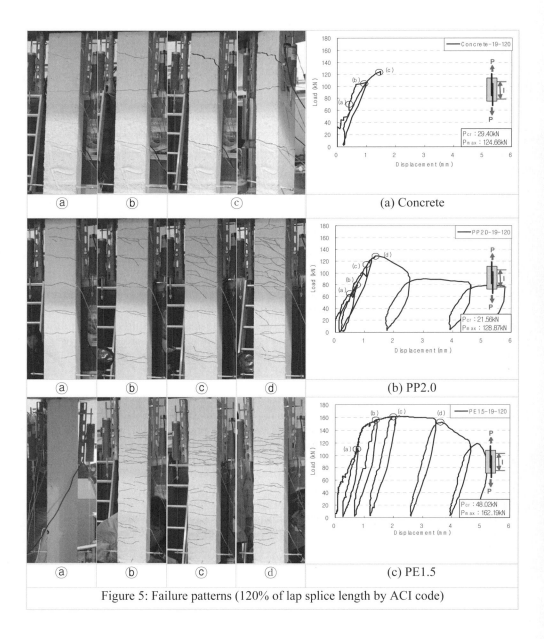

Figure 5: Failure patterns (120% of lap splice length by ACI code)

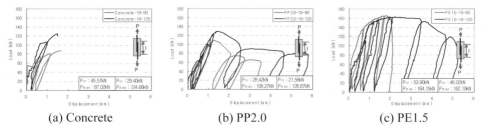

(a) Concrete   (b) PP2.0   (c) PE1.5

Figure 6: Load-displacement relationship

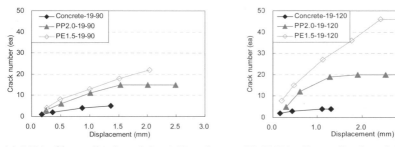

(a) 90% of lap splice length by ACI code   (b) 120% of lap splice length by ACI code

Figure 7: Crack number-displacement relationship

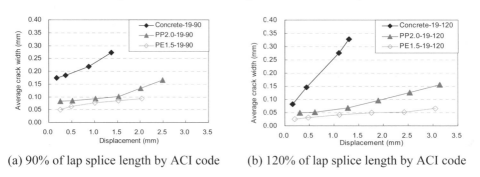

(a) 90% of lap splice length by ACI code   (b) 120% of lap splice length by ACI code

Figure 8: Average crack width-displacement relationship

3.5 Crack spacing and width

Crack number-displacement and average crack width-displacement relationship of specimens are shown in Fig. 7 and 8. The average crack width was calculated by dividing this measured crack number by displacement (by LVDTs). In the PP and PE specimens, the cracks which formed in the splice region were small in width but large in number, whereas, they were larger in width but fewer in number in the Concrete specimens. The ability of fiber reinforced composites to develop large number of small width cracks prior to failure is the main reason behind their ductile behaviour in the post-splitting range. Fiber reinforcement controlled cracking even in the post-yielding range. It prevented excessive opening of the developed cracks at failure and, in effect, maintained the integrity of the specimens.

4. CONCLUSIONS

– The presence of synthetic fibers considerably increases the development/splice strength of reinforcing bars in tension. Lap splice strength of HPFRCC increased 30.11 ~ 88.63 percent more than that of normal concrete.
– Adding PE fiber in up to 1.5 percent by volume fraction increased the splice strength of reinforcing bars by up to 25.86 ~ 51.61 percent in comparison with PP fiber in up to 2.0 percent. Tensile strength and lap splice performance depends on fiber tensile stress and elastic modulus more than fiber volume fraction.
– After cracking and significant deformations, the normal concrete suffered macro cracks and lost a significant amount of its lap splice. But HPFRCC matrix stiffens the tension member at uncracked sections and also strengthens it at cracked sections. Hence, the composite tensile response is significantly improved in terms of load carrying capacity as well as ductility.

ACKNOWLEDGEMENTS

This research was supported by the Brain Korea 21 and Korea Science and Engineering Foundation Grant (R01-2005-000-10546-0) funded by the Korea Government.

REFERENCES

[1] Soubra, K.S., Wight, J.K. and Naaman, A.E. "Cyclic Response of Fibrous Cast-in-Place Connections in Precast Beam-Column Subassemblages, ACI Structural Journal, 90 (1993), No. 3, pp. 316-323
[2] JCI: Proceedings of the JCI international Workshop on DFRCC, (2002), p. 298
[3] Reinhardt, H.W. and Naaman, A.E. "High Performance Fiber Reinforced Cement Composites: HPFRCC(1-4)," Proceedings of the 1st-4th international RILEM Workshop, 1991, 1995, 1999, 2003.
[4] Parra-Montesinos, G.J. "High-Performance Fiber-Reinforced Cement Composites : An Alternative for Seismic Design of Structures," ACI Structural Journal, 102 (2005), No. 5, pp. 668-675

PART SIX

IMPACT, BLAST
AND SEISMIC LOADING

ARAMID FIBER MESH-REINFORCED THIN SHEET RESPONSE TO IMPACT LOADS

Kyu Hyuk Kyung and Christian Meyer

Columbia University, New York, USA

Abstract

The response of structures to impact loads has gained considerable interest during the last few years. Whereas the design and construction of new structures to resist such loads poses not so much technical as economical challenges, this is even more true in the case of hardening and strengthening of existing structures. Thin sheets, consisting of a fine-grained cement matrix reinforced with a suitable fiber mesh made of high-performance materials such as aramid, are now being studied for their suitability in such situations. A considerable body of knowledge can be found in the body-armor literature. It is the objective of a study currently in its initial phase to combine this knowledge with the state of the art of penetration dynamics in order to determine the feasibility and effectiveness of such strengthening technology. A brief overview of the state of the art of both of these technologies is given, together with a preliminary feasibility assessment.

1. INTRODUCTION

Although aramid fibers are widely known to be the material of choice for composites used in the body armor industry [1], research on aramid fiber-reinforced composites for civil engineering applications has been rather limited. A study of thin-sheet cement composites reinforced with aramid fiber mesh at Columbia University [2, 3] has shown that such composites have a potential for various practical applications. A follow-up preliminary study has been performed to review the suitability of aramid fiber mesh as reinforcement of thin cementitious sheets subjected to impact loads [4]. Since thin concrete sheets reinforced with aramid fabrics, such as Kevlar and Twaron, have an enormous capacity of absorbing and dissipating energy, such structural components have the potential of greatly enhancing the resistance of structures to impact loads. The primary objective of the proposed research will be to study analytically and experimentally the mechanisms by which composites that consist of inherently brittle materials are capable of dissipating large amounts of energy. Especially, the strain rate effect on fine grained concrete and aramid fiber mesh will be investigated thoroughly. Based on the outcome of this research, the feasibility of using such thin sheets in civil engineering applications will be explored. Of particular interest will be the hardening or strengthening of existing structures.

2. FUNDAMENTAL RESPONSE MECHANISMS

The strain rate effect of materials is one of the major factors determining impact resistance. Its inclusion in numerical simulations requires a much larger computational effort, especially if complex nonlinear material models are involved. The concrete and steel in reinforced concrete structures subjected to such loads experience strain rates of the order of $10s^{-1}$ to $1000s^{-1}$. At these high strain rates the apparent strength of the materials can increase by more than 50 percent for the reinforcing steel, by more than 100 percent for concrete in compression, and by more than 600 percent for concrete in tension [5]. Such strain rate induced strength increases are typically expressed in terms of a Dynamic Increase Factor defined as the ratio of the dynamic response to the quasi-static response. It is well established that fiber-reinforced concrete exhibits considerably improved impact resistance compared with plain concrete. The flexural strength of steel fiber-reinforced mortar appears to be slightly more strain rate sensitive than plain mortar, which is likely to be due to the multiple cracking of the matrix [6]. The energy absorbed by steel fiber-reinforced concrete under impact loads can be about 20 to 100 times that absorbed by plain concrete. For example, it has been shown that the flexural energy absorption of fiber-reinforced concrete (FRC) beam specimens increases significantly with the strain rate – see Fig. 1, which also depicts the load-deflection curves for two extreme strain rates.

The dynamic mechanical properties of Twaron fabrics were examined by high-speed tensile tests on specimens using a split Hopkinson bar [7]. The stress-strain curves of Fig. 2 are representative of both the static and dynamic behavior of Twaron fibers. The strain rates of $495s^{-1}$ and $238s^{-1}$ are clearly dynamic, while the strain rates of $1s^{-1}$, $0.1s^{-1}$ and $0.01s^{-1}$ represent basically static loadings. The energy absorption capacity of a material, defined by the area under the stress-strain curve, is affected both by the failure strain and the maximum stress. This area is significantly smaller for the high strain rate ($\dot{\varepsilon}=495s^{-1}$) than that for a low strain rate ($\dot{\varepsilon}=238\ s^{-1}$), Fig. 2. If the fibers are to sustain load, they first need to be straightened and realigned due to the initial crimping. The straightening process stiffens the material and contributes to the nonlinear response. Unlike at low strain rates, there is insufficient time at high strain rates for this effect to take place. In addition, at low strain rates, intermolecular slippage in the polymer chains becomes significant. Therefore, the phenomenon involves plastic flow and deformation, which dissipates additional energy.

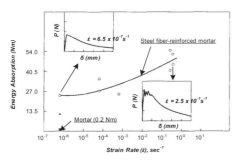

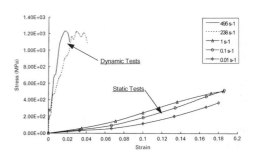

Figure 1: Strain Rate Effect on a FRC Beam [6]   Figure 2: Strain Rate Effect on Twaron Fibers [7]

Another parameter that determines structural response to impact loads is the kinetic energy density delivered by the projectile, which is defined as the kinetic energy of the projectile divided by its cross-sectional area. In the subhydrodynamic regime of penetration in which the kinetic energy density is low, conventional material parameters determine the penetration mechanism. However, the kinetic energy density is much higher for longer, thinner, heavier, and faster projectiles. In this case the strengths of the materials are negligible and the impact needs to be characterized as a fluid-structure interaction, governed by the laws of fluid dynamics. This is known as the hydrodynamic regime. Although fluid flow governs the interaction in the transition between two zones, with density being the dominant physical parameter, material strength still proves to be a significant factor [8].

3. ANALYTICAL / NUMERICAL APPROACH

This study will have analytical, numerical and experimental components to develop a new technology to harden or strengthen existing structures by improving our understanding of structural response mechanisms to impact loads. Once these mechanisms are understood sufficiently well, analytical models can be developed to allow the numerical simulation of material response. Such numerical simulations will be useful when identifying potential strategies to support the experimental effort.

3.1 Analytical approach

The structural response analysis to impact loads requires realistic analytical models. Several analytical and empirical models have been proposed in the body armor literature to consider the nonlinear characteristics of ballistic performance and the strain rate effect on various composite materials [9]. These are generally algebraic relations and ordinary differential equations. Most analytical penetration models are based on localized interaction models (LIM). The combined effect on the interaction between the medium and a moving projectile can be expressed as the superposition of all local interactions. It is determined both by the local geometric and kinematic parameters of the surface element and by the global parameters that take into account the integral characteristics of the medium. The typical mathematical form of LIM is expressed in Eqs. 1 and 2, Fig. 3 [9].

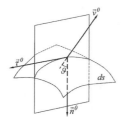
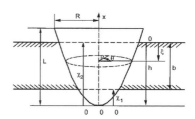

Figure 3: Definition of LIM [9]   Figure 4: Coordinates and Notations [9]

$$\begin{cases} d\vec{F} = [\Omega_n\,(\vec{a};u,v)\,\vec{n}^0 + \Omega_\tau\,(\vec{a};u,v)\,\vec{\tau}^0]\,ds & if \quad 0 < u < 1 \\ d\vec{F} = \Omega_n\,(\vec{a};1,v)\,\vec{n}^0\,ds & if \quad u = 1 \\ d\vec{F} = 0 & if \quad u \le 0 \end{cases} \tag{1}$$

$$\vec{\tau}^0 = -(\vec{v}^0 + u \cdot \vec{n}^0)/\sqrt{1-u^2} \quad \& \quad u = -\vec{v}^0 \cdot \vec{n}^0 = \cos\theta \tag{2}$$

where $d\vec{F}$ is the force acting on the surface element ds of the projectile. $\vec{n}^0$ is the inner normal unit vector and $\vec{\tau}^0$ is the inner tangent unit vector. $\vec{v}^0$ is a unit vector of the projectile velocity $\vec{v}$. θ is the angle between $\vec{n}^0$ and $-\vec{v}^0$. Ω_n and Ω_τ are the functions which determine the projectile-medium interaction. In general, it is assumed that $\Omega_\tau = 0$ or $\Omega_\tau = k\Omega_n$, where k is the coefficient of friction between the impactor and the shield. $\vec{a}$ is a vector with components which characterize the properties of the host medium.

The analytical model for a shield with a finite thickness (SFT) is shown in Fig. 4 [9]. The projectile is represented in the cylindrical coordinates x, ρ, θ, and the shape of the projectile is determined by the equation of $\rho = \Phi(x, \theta)$, where, Φ is a function which determines the shape of the impactor, b is the thickness of the shield, L is the impactor's nose length, and h is the penetration depth. In both a shield with finite thickness (SFT) and a semi-infinite shield (SIS), the total force $\vec{F}$ is determined by integrating the local force over the impactor-shield contact surface. The drag force is expressed as $D = \vec{F} \cdot (-\vec{v}^0)$, which is a function of $\vec{a}, h$, and v. The equation of motion of an impactor with mass m can be represented by Eq. 3.

$$mv\frac{dv}{dh} + D(\vec{a};h,v) = 0 \tag{3}$$

In a SFT, the ballistic limit velocity v_{bl} is defined as the initial velocity of the impactor required to emerge from the shield with zero velocity. In a SIS, the depth of penetration h is usually considered as a characteristic parameter. These two primary penetration factors are obtained by solving a first-order ordinary differential equation, Eq. 3.

For nonhomogeneous or layered shields with different material properties such as reinforced concrete panels strengthened by thin cementitious composites, $\vec{a}$ can be expressed as a function of the depth of the shield, ξ. The LIM is very useful to investigate impact dynamics problems because it can consider the interaction between various shapes of the projectile and the medium as well as simulate the motion of an impactor in a shield.

3.2 Numerical approach

The failure process on the macroscopic scale is comprised of several local damage and failure mechanisms at the lower scales. The fundamental mechanisms at the micro-scale are the rupture of single filaments and their debonding from the matrix. These changes in the material micro-structure propagate to the meso-scale in the form of yarn damage and yarn debonding, as well as crack initiation. These effects explain the macroscopically observable effects like delamination of the textile layer. It is assumed that the cementitious matrix is homogeneous, which means that no distinction is made between the cement paste and sand aggregate.

In general, the complex damage and failure processes call for micromechanical models, which may require a great amount of computational effort. In order to avoid this problem, textile reinforced concrete (TRC) components can be modeled on the macroscopic scale and simplified as two-dimensional elements since they are generally used for thin-walled structural elements or for hardening / strengthening of existing planar structures. Therefore, layered shell and layered folded plate elements can be employed in the modeling on the macroscopic scale [10]. The Microplane-Damage-Model, e.g., is available for the layered shell model [11]. The effect of textile reinforcement has been included at the material point level in the form of a direction-specific damage law and tension-stiffening effect associated with differently oriented microplanes. An alternative model to represent a specific multi-layer continuum by introducing an extended layered model is the Multi-Reference-Plane Model [12], which includes regular concrete layers, steel reinforcement layers, strengthening layers with textile reinforcement, and interface layers.

4. TRC-STRENGTHENED COMPOSITES

Strengthening methods using aramid fiber mesh-reinforced thin cementitious sheets have the potential to be superior over other strengthening technologies because of their mechanical properties and relative ease of application. It is one of the objectives of the proposed research to verify such intuitive conjecture. TRC exhibits a high degree of heterogeneity for the matrix and the reinforcement. As a result, the damage localization processes of TRC are comprised of interactions between elementary failure mechanisms within the matrix, the reinforcement, and those along their interfaces controlled by bond behavior. Due to these damage interactions, existing models for concrete and composites are not directly applicable to TRC. When TRC-strengthened thin composites are subjected to impact loads, a projectile will be blunted by the strike plate comprised of aramid fiber mesh-reinforced thin sheets, and the load induced by the projectile is distributed over a larger area. Subsequently, the backing material deforms to absorb the projectile's remaining kinetic energy by delaying the initiation of tensile failure of the TRC and backing materials.

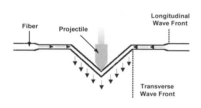

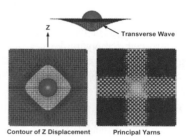

Figure 5: Transv. Impact on a Single Fiber [13]   Figure 6: Transv. Impact on a Single Ply [13]

To understand the mechanism of energy dissipation in such composite systems, consider a simple case of transverse impact on a single fiber, Fig. 5 [13]. There are two waves propagating from the point of ballistic impact, a longitudinal and a transverse wave. The longitudinal tensile wave travels along the fiber axis. As it propagates away from the point of impact, the material behind the wave front flows toward the impact point, which is deflecting in the direction of motion of the moving projectile. This transverse movement of the fiber initiates the transverse wave. This observation can be expanded to the transverse impact on a single ply of fabric mesh, Fig. 6. When a projectile strikes the fabric, it causes a transverse deflection of the yarns that are in direct contact with the projectile, defined as principal yarns. The impact also generates longitudinal strain waves, which move along the axes of the yarns. Subsequently, the orthogonal yarns, which intersect the principal yarns, are pulled out of the original fabric plane by the principal yarns. These orthogonal yarns undergo large deformations and develop their own strain waves. Most of the kinetic energy of the projectile is transferred to the principal yarns as strain and kinetic energy, whereas the contribution of the orthogonal yarns to energy absorption is relatively small [13]. In this study, both reinforced concrete (RC) panels and other composites strengthened on one or both sides with aramid fiber mesh-reinforced thin sheets will be analyzed as shown in Fig. 7 and the effects of the strengthening measures will be evaluated.

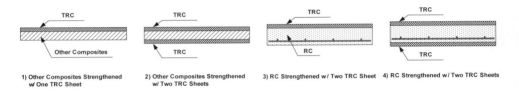

1) Other Composites Strengthened w/ One TRC Sheet   2) Other Composites Strengthened w/ Two TRC Sheets   3) RC Strengthened w/ Two TRC Sheet   4) RC Strengthened w/ Two TRC Sheets

Figure 7: TRC-Strengthened RC and Other Composites

5. CONCLUSIONS

The body-armor products and impact-resistant thin cementitious composites are similar in that inherently brittle component materials are combined to form composites that are capable of dissipating large amounts of energy. The main difference between these two types of applications appears to be the material selected for the outer face such as strike plates. Only a minimum of ductility is required for both the strike face materials in body-armor composites and the cement-based thin sheet panels. Therefore, any nonlinear behavior displayed by a fiber reinforced composite derives from the irreversible slippage of individual fibers within a roving as well as large-deformation effects. It will be the challenge for the development of impact-resisting panels to fully exploit such mechanisms.

REFERENCES

[1]   Phoenix, S. L. and Porwal, P. K., 2003, "A New Membrane Model for the Ballistic Impact Response and V50 Performance of Multi-Ply Fibrous Systems", *International Journal of Solids and Structures*, Vol. 40, pp. 6723 – 6765

[2]   Vilkner, G., 2003, *Glass Concrete Thin Sheets Reinforced with Prestressed Aramid Fabrics*, Ph.D. Dissertation, Columbia University, New York, NY

[3]   Meyer, C. and Vilkner, G., 2003, "Glass Concrete Thin Sheets Prestressed with Aramid Fiber Mesh", Pro. Of the Fourth Int. RILEM Workshop on High Performance Fiber Reinforced Cement Composites (HPFRCC4), A. E. Naaman and H. W. Reinhardt Eds., pp. 325-336.

[4]   Kyung, K. H. and Meyer, C., 2006, "Aramid Fiber Mesh as Reinforcement of Concrete Panels under High Strain Rates", Proceedings of the 1st International RILEM Conference, Aachen, Germany, pp. 351-358.

[5]   Malvar, L. J. and Ross, C. A., 1998, "Review of Strain Rate Effects for Concrete in Tension", *ACI Materials Journal*, Vol. 95, No. 6, pp. 735-739.

[6]   Suaris, W. and Shah, S. P., 1982, "Strain-Rate Effects in Fiber-Reinforced Concrete Subjected to Impact and Impulsive Loading", *Composites*, April, pp. 153-159.

[7]   Shim, V. P. W., Lim, C. T. and Foo, K. J., 2001, "Dynamic Mechanical Properties of Fabric Armour", *International Journal of Impact Engineering*, Vol. 25, pp. 1-15.

[8]   Smith, P. D. and Hetherington, J. G., 1994, *Blast and Ballistic Loading of Structures*, Butterworth Heinemann.

[9]   Ben-Dor, G. et al., 2005, "Ballistic Impact: Recent Advances in Analytical Modeling of Plate Penetration Dynamics – A Review", *Applied Mechanics Review*, Vol. 58, pp. 355 – 371.

[10] Brameshuber, W., Ed., 2006, "Textile Reinforced Concrete", *State-of-the-art Report of RILEM Technical Committee TC 201-TRC 'Textile Reinforced Concrete'*, RILEM Publications S.A.R.I., Report 36, Bagneux, France

[11] Jirazek, M., Bažant, Z., 2002, *Inelastic Analysis of Structures*, John Wiley & Sons.

[12] Steinigen, F., Möller, B., Graf, W., Hoffmann, A., 2003, "RC structures with textile reinforcement and strengthening", Computational Modeling of Concrete Structures, Proceedings of the Euro-Conference St. Johann im Pongau, pp759-768.

[13] Cheeseman, B. A. and Bogetti, T. A., 2003, "Ballistic Impact into Fabric and Compliant Composite Laminates", *Composites Structures*, Vol. 61, pp. 161 – 173.

TEXTILES AS REINFORCEMENTS FOR CEMENT COMPOSITES UNDER IMPACT LOADING

Alva Peled

Structural Engineering Department, Ben Gurion University, Israel

Abstract

Cementitious materials can be subjected to dynamic loading for variety of reasons. Due to the inherent brittleness and low tensile strength of most cement-based elements, such impact loadings can cause severe damage, resulting in extensive cracking. To date dynamic properties of cement composites have been studied mainly for short fibers composites. The research to date clearly demonstrates a significant improvement in the energy absorption capacity of fabric reinforced cement composites under static loading as compared to plain concrete materials and other fiber cement composites. The aim of this work was to study the dynamic behavior of textile-cement based composites. A pendulum impact set up was used to study the impact behavior of the cement composites. Composites with different fabrics were examined made from AR glass with two different mesh sizes, polyethylene and carbon. Also, specimens made from short AR glass fibers were studied for comparison. The benefit of using fabrics as reinforcements for cement-based elements exposed to dynamic loading was clearly demonstrated in this study. Composites reinforced with fabrics were shown significantly grater impact behavior compared to those reinforced with short fibers. The best impact strength was obtained of composite reinforced with carbon fabric.

1. INTRODUCTION

Modern textile technology offers a wide variety of fabrics with great flexibility in fabric design and control of yarn geometry and orientation. This flexibility allows engineering of composite performance for various cement products. Several researchers reported that fabrics could significantly improve the mechanical behavior of cement matrices [1-3]. In addition to the improved strength, these fabric-reinforced composites exhibited strain-hardening behavior even when the reinforcing yarns had low modulus of elasticity. This was explained by enhancement in bonding due to mechanical anchoring provided by the non-linear geometry of the individual yarns within the fabric, induced by the fabric structure.

Cementitious materials can be subjected to dynamic loading for variety of reasons including: fast moving traffic, wind gusts, blast explosions, missiles, earthquakes, projectiles, and machine vibration. Due to the inherent brittleness and low tensile strength of most cement-based elements, such impact loadings can cause severe damage, resulting in extensive cracking. Any attempt at improving the energy absorption capacity of these elements by enhancing their post-fracture stress transfer capability will therefore be an effective way of improving its resistance to impact loads. Fiber reinforcement is one of the most effective means of enhancing the impact and blast resistance, in both strength and energy. To date dynamic properties of cement composites have been studied mainly for short fibers composites [4-6]. This improvement is dependent on the type and geometry of the fiber. Fabric-cement composites have clearly demonstrated a significant improvement in the energy absorption capacity under static loading as compared to plain concrete materials and other fiber cement composites [1-3, 7]. It is speculated that they can potentially exhibit high resistance under impact loads as well [8].

The aim of this work was to study the dynamic behavior of textile-cement based composites. Composites with different fabric structures and materials were examined, made from AR glass, carbon and polypropylene. Also composites with short AR glass fibers were examined for comparison. A pendulum impact set up was used to study the impact behavior of the cement composites reinforced with the different textiles. The time, impact loads and accelerations were recorded for the different tested composites. The crack pattern of the different composites was also studied.

2.   EXPERIMENTAL PROGRAM

2.1   Fabrics and composites preparation

Three types of fabrics were used in this study: bonded, warp knitted weft insertion, and short weft knitted. The weft insertion knitted fabric was composed of multifilament carbon. Two bonded fabrics were studied having different densities, both made from multifilament AR glass yarns. The short weft knitted fabric was made from monofilament polyethylene (PE) yarns. Table 1 presents the geometry and properties of the and fabrics and yarns made up the fabrics.

Table 1: Fabrics and yarns geometry and properties

Fabric type	Fabric geometry	Fabric density (opening) (mm^2)	Yarn nature	Modulus of elasticity (yarns) (GPa)	Tensile strength (yarns) MPa
AR Glass – Dense – Open	Bonded	0.30 0.60	Bundle	72	1360
Carbon	Weft insertion knitted	1.60	Bundle	240	2200
PE	Short weft knitted	0.19	Monofilament	1.76	260

Composite specimens were prepared by lay-up of fabrics in a cement matrix. The matrix used was made of cement paste (only water and cement) with water/cement ratio of 0.4, by weight.

Several types of laminate fabric composites were prepared all with dimensions of 400 x 400 mm and thickness of 20 mm (in a plate shape):

(i) Six layers of fabrics were placed in the cement matrix with 2 mm cement paste in between each two layers. The layers of the fabrics were located at the bottom of the specimen up to about 10 mm of its thickness. Another 10 mm of plain cement paste was placed on top of these layers up to specimen thickness of 20 mm. In this way the fabrics layers were located at the tensile zone of the tested composite during impact loading. Specimens made from PE fabric and AR glass fabrics with dense and open structures were prepared.

(ii) Two layers of fabrics were located at the bottom of the specimen similar to the specimens described above. Carbon fabric and dense glass fabric were used to prepare these composites.

(iii) Twenty layers of fabric were located in the matrix through the entire specimen thickness (20 mm). This composite was prepared with PE fabric only.

The first two sets of specimens were prepared by hand lay up of the fabrics in the matrix (casting). The third set, with the 20 layers of fabrics, was prepared by the pultrusion process [3, 7]. Also specimens with similar dimensions made from short AR glass fibers were prepared for comparison. The short glass fibers were added during mixing. The number of layers for each fabric type and the reinforcing yarns by volume for each composite set are provided in Table 2. Note that the volume fractions were calculated based on the bundle diameter and assume no penetration of the cement matrix between the filaments of the bundles.

The cement composite plates were cured in 100% relative humidity for 7 days and then at room environment until testing in impact, 28 days after casting. Before testing, each composite plate was cut to three slices providing specimens with a length of 400 mm, width of 120 mm, and thickness of 20 mm.

Table 2: Impact properties of the composites

Type of reinforcement	Layers number	V_f %	Impact strength (bending) MPa	Efficiency factor	Deflection, (Max.) mm	End of testing
Short AR Glass fibers	-----	5.0	15.8	0.23	-----	Failed
Open AR Glass fabric	6	1.8	25.2	1.03	13.6	Cracking
Dense AR Glass fabric	6	2.7	29.8	0.81	----	Failed
	2	0.9	11.5	0.94	----	Failed
Carbon fabric	2	3.2	38.2	0.54	14.5	Cracking
Polyethylene fabric (PE)	6	1.7	10.4	2.35	4.3	Cracking
	20	5.9	13.0	0.85	25.4	Cracking

2.2 Impact tests

A pendulum impact set up was used to study the impact behavior (three point bending) of the cement composites reinforced with the different textiles (Fig. 1). This impact test facility was based on a pendulum that hanged on a steel frame at a height of 7m, using 4 cables to ensure horizontal motion with a total weight of 150 kg. The impactor was installed on the head of the pendulum, and a 50kN load cell was placed between them. The pendulum can provide a load profile with a rise time of minimum 0.1 msec, duration up to 100 msec, and a pressure of 10 MPa. The maximum velocity reached by the pendulum when it hits the specimen is 10 m/s. Two accelerometers were used: one was placed on the hammer and the second on the specimen (opposite to the impactor) having a range up to 5000 g. The outputs from the measuring devices were collected using a data acquisition system (IOTECH model WaveBook/516), which had 8 channels, 16 bit, at a rate of 1 MHz. Different dropping heights of the impactor were examined: 5, 10, 15 and 25 mm.

The impact (three point bending) stresses were calculate and plotted vs. time. Typical stresses vs. time curves were chosen to compare between the different tested systems. Also the maximum stresses as well as the strength efficiency factor were calculated for each composite. The efficiency factors were calculated by dividing the composite strength with the volume content of reinforcement and fabric tensile strength, in order to compare the different composites on a similar basis.

Figure 1: Impact test set up

3.   RESULTS

3.1   Pendulum dropping height

Fig. 2a presents the impact loads of composites reinforced with 20 layers of PE fabrics (pultruded) for several dropping heights. Increasing the dropping height of the pendulum greater impact loads were recorded, as expected. No complete failure was observed with these specimens even with dropping height of 25 mm. Dense crack pattern, of multiple cracking behavior, was observed with these PE composites (Fig. 2b).

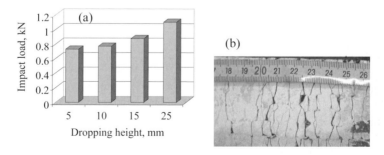

Figure 2: PE composites: (a) impact load for several dropping heights (b) crack pattern

The stress vs. time behavior of the PE composite is presented in Fig. 3a (for dropping height of 25 mm). Stiff behavior of up to about stress of 5 MPa and maximum stress of about 13 MPa are observed. Maximum deflection of 25 mm was obtained with this composite, calculated based on the acceleration data of the accelerometer located on the specimen at its tension zone (opposite to the pendulum). The large deflection of the specimen is also clear in Fig. 3b, taken after ending the impact test. These results indicate the ability of the composite with the PE fabric to sustain impact loading without failure (for dropping high of 25 mm), and the high energy absorption capacity of this component.

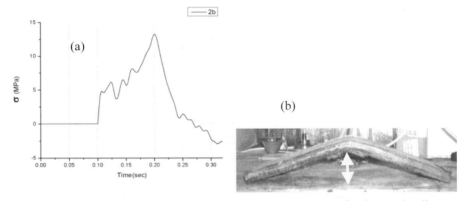

Figure 3: (a) Impact behavior of PE composite, (b) the specimen after impact loading

Dropping height of 25 mm was used in this work to test the different composites with the different fabric types, fabric densities and number of fabric layers as well as the system with the short glass fibers. The average impact results of the different composites are presented in Table 2.

3.2   Effect of fabric geometry

Fig. 4a shows the stress vs. time behavior of two composites reinforced with AR glass fabrics (6 layers of fabrics with different densities) and a composite reinforced with short AR glass fibers (randomly dispersed). The benefit of using fabrics as reinforcement for cement composite exposed to impact loading compared to composite reinforced with short fibers is obvious in this figure, as both composites with the fabrics exhibit improved impact resistance. Impact strength of ~30 MPa is observed for the dense glass fabric composite, as compared to much lower impact strength of ~16 MPa for the short glass fibers composite (Table 2). This gives improvement of about twofold by the fabric structure. Note that the volume content of the reinforced fabric is lower than that of the short fibers. The differences between the behavior of the fabric and short fibers composites are also clear when comparing their acceleration behavior (Fig. 4b). Moreover, the composite with the short fibers was shown complete failure, in a catastrophic mode of failure. On the contrary, no complete failure but rather multiple crack behavior was observed for the composite reinforced with the open net fabric structure, similar to Fig. 2b.

In addition, Fig. 4a indicates that the glass fabric composite with the dense structure exhibits greater impact resistance than that of the glass fabric with the open structure. This might be due to the relatively high volume content of the dense fabric in the composite (Table 2). In order to compare the two glass fabric systems on similar basis, efficiency factors were calculated which taking in consideration the differences in volume content of the reinforcement at each system. Greater efficiency factor of 1.05 was calculated for the composite with the open mesh glass structure whereas efficiency factor of 0.81 was calculated for the denser fabric structure system. Moreover, the composite with the open fabric structure was exhibited multiple crack behavior with no complete failure at the end of the impact testing. However the composite with the dense fabric structure was completely failed during testing. The open fabric structure may allow better mechanical anchoring with the cement matrix, due to improved cement penetrability in between the openings of the fabric. This can lead to better utilization of this fabric under impact loading and improved energy absorption.

The above results indicate that fabric structures can be very attractive as reinforcements for cement components when they exposed to dynamic (impact) loading.

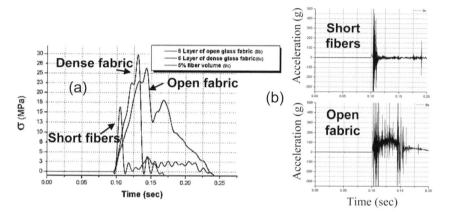

Figure 4: AR glass composites: (a) impact behavior of fabrics and short fibers composites, (b) acceleration vs. time of open fabric and short fibers composites

3.3 Effect of fabric type and number of layers

Comparison of the composites with the different fabrics is presented in Table 2 along with their efficiency factors. The carbon fabric composite exhibits the best impact strength following by the AR glass fabrics with the 6 layers. The lowest impact strength is recorded for the PE fabric composites. Similar deflection at the end of testing of about 14 mm is obtained for the composites with the carbon and the open glass fabrics. These two composites were exhibited multiple cracking with no complete failure during testing. The PE composite was not reached complete failure either and also exhibited multiple cracking at the end of testing with deflection of about 4 mm (with 6 layers of fabric). The volume content of reinforcement of the carbon fabric composite is relatively high, 3.2%, as compared to the open glass and PE composites with volume fractions of 1.8% and 1.7%, respectively. The high volume fraction of the carbon fabric can result some of the improved impact performance of the composite in addition to its high properties (Table 1). When comparing the efficiency factors of these composites the trends are quite different. The calculated efficiency factor of the PE fabric composite (with 6 fabric layers) is as high as 2.35 and only 0.54 for the carbon fabric composite. The efficiency factor of the open glass composite is 1.03, i.e., higher than that of the carbon composite but lower than the PE composite. However, increasing the content of the PE fabrics up to 6% by volume (20 layers), the benefit of using this type of fabric is reduced, exhibiting efficiency factor of only 0.85. In this case the fabric layers are located not only at the tension zone but also at the compression zone of the composite during impact loading. This might cause the reduced reinforcing efficiency of the PE fabric in the composite. This low modulus PE fabric composite with high content of reinforcement exhibits quite high deflection of above 25 mm.

Fig. 5 presents the surface area where the pendulum was hit the composite, of carbon (2 fabric layers) and PE (6 fabric layers) systems. Severe damage is observed of the carbon composite, as big part of the hardened cement paste is crashed and failed at this area (Fig. 5b). Similar damaged surface was observed with the AR open glass fabric composite (6 fabric layers). On the other hand, no such damage is observed for the PE fabric composite, the surface is smooth and undamaged (Fig. 5a). The maximum deflection of the PE specimen is about 4 mm, and no full recovery of this deflection is observed at the end of testing (Fig. 5a), i.e., the composite is not fully returned to its original location. The open glass and carbon composites are highly bent during the impact tests (deflection of about 14 mm was recorded), however after testing, the specimen is returned to its original location and no remaining of the specimen curvature is observed (Fig. 5b). This forward and backward displacement of the carbon and glass specimen including the high impact forces apply on the weak zone of the specimen (where no fabrics are located) can result the damaging of the surface at the pendulum zone of these composites.

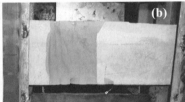

Figure 5: Specimens after impact loading: (a) PE fabric, (b) carbon fabric

The number of fabric layers also influences the impact resistance of the composite. Increasing the number of fabric layers results in better resistance to impact (Table 2). Maximum stress of 29.8 is calculated for the composite with the 6 layers of fabrics as compared to only 11.5 MPa tensile strength of the composite with the 2 fabric layers. When comparing the efficiency factors of these systems, with 6 and 2 fabric layers, no significant difference is observed. Note that these two composites were failed completely during testing.

4.   SUMMARY AND CONCLUSIONS

– Based on this study it can be concluded that fabric structures can be very attractive reinforcements for cement-based elements exposed to dynamic (impact) loading. Composites reinforced with fabrics were exhibited significantly grater impact behavior compared to those reinforced with short fibers (glass). Improvement of about twofold was observed with the fabric-cement composite. The impact behavior of fabric-cement composites should further be explored.

–   Carbon fabric was provided the greatest impact strength of the composite following by the AR glass fabric with relatively open structure. The PE fabric composite was exhibited the lowest impact resistance. However the greatest reinforcement efficiency was found with the PE fabric when 6 layers of fabrics were located at the tension zone of the composite during the impact tests.

–   Composite reinforced with relatively open fabric structure was shown improved impact behavior as compared to composite reinforced with denser fabric structure, observed in this work with bonded glass fabrics. This might be due to improved mechanical anchoring of the open fabric with the cement matrix by better matrix penetrability in between fabric openings.

ACKNOWLEDGEMENTS

The author would like to acknowledge Polysack Ltd. Israel, the Textile Institute at Aachen University (ITA), and SAINT-GOBAIN for their cooperation and for the effort they made to provide the fabrics and fibers used in this study. The author would like to acknowledge the Protective Technologies Research and Development Center at the Department of Mechanical Engineering in Ben Gurion University for the help with the impact tests. Talia Levi and Oded Talfus are gratefully acknowledged for their help with the experimental program.

REFERENCES

[1] Peled, A., Bentur, A., 'Geometrical characteristics and efficiency of textile fabrics for reinforcing composites', Cement and Concrete Research, **30** (2000) 781-790.

[2] Peled, A., Bentur, A., Yankelevsky, D., 'Flexural performance of cementitious composites reinforced by woven fabrics', Materials in Civil Engineering (ASCE), **11** (4), (1999) 325-330

[3] Peled, A., Mobasher, B., 'Pultruded fabric-cement composites', ACI Materials J., **102** (1) (2005) 15-23

[4] Banthia, N., 'Crack growth resistance of hybrid fiber reinforced cement composites', Cement and Concrete Composites, **25** (1) (2003) 3-9.

[5] Gupta, P., Banthia, N., 'Fiber reinforced wet-mix shotcrete under impact', J. of Materials in Civil Engineering (ASCE) (February 2000) 81-90

[6] Suaris, W., Shah, S. P., 'Properties of Concrete Subjected to Impact', J. of Structural Engineering, **109** (7) (1983) 1727-1741

[7] Peled, A., Mobasher, B., Sueki, S., 'Technology methods in textile cement-based composites', In 'Concrete Science and Engineering, A Tribute to Arnon Bentur', March, Chicago, 2004, (RILEM 2004) 187-202

[8] Butnariu, E., Peled, A., and Mobasher, B., 'Impact Behavior of Fabric-Cement Based Composites,' in 'Brittle Matrix Composites (BMC8)' Proceedings of the 8th International Symposium, Warsaw, October, 2006, 293-302.

STATIC AND IMPACT BEHAVIOR OF FABRIC REINFORCED CEMENT COMPOSITES IN FLEXURE

Mustafa Gencoglu [(1)] **and Barzin Mobasher** [(2)]

(1) Istanbul Technical University, Faculty of Civil Engineering, Istanbul, Turkey

(2) Arizona State University, Dept. of Civil and Environmental Engineering, Tempe, USA

Abstract

Fabric-cement composites developed using the pultrusion production process have demonstrated impressive tensile and flexural properties. AR Glass and PE fabric reinforced composites exhibit strain-hardening behavior in addition to tensile strength in the range of 20 to 25 MPa and strain capacity of the order of 2 to 5%. Impact properties were investigated under three point bending conditions using an instrumented drop weight system. Test parameters include the fabric type, specimen orientation, and drop height of hammer. Preliminary results indicate that for the same drop height, the vertical type (beam) specimens are stiffer; however, they have a lower ultimate deflection and higher load carrying capacity than the horizontal (plate type) specimens. By increasing the impact energy beyond 5 Joules, the impact strength of the horizontal specimens made with glass fabrics sharply decreased, while there was no incremental change in the impact strength of the vertical specimens. Results are compared with the static flexural tests conducted under closed loop deflection controlled tests.

1. INTRODUCTION

Concrete structural elements such as piles, hydraulic structures, airport pavements, military structures, and industrial floor overlays may be subjected to severe impact loads [1]. High stress rates occur during such dynamic loads as a large amount of energy is transmitted to the structure in a short duration. Structural elements subjected to dynamic forces should have enough strength, toughness, and ductility to maintain integrity without collapse. Fibers are added into concrete to improve the ductility, tension, impact and flexural strength of concrete. Lok and Zhao [2], showed that the post-peak ductility of SFRC is lost at strain rates exceeding 50 s^{-1} because fragments can no longer bond onto the steel fibers. Bindiganavile et al. [3, 4, 5], showed that compact reinforced composites under impact was capable of dissipating much higher energy compared with conventional fiber reinforced concrete with polymeric or steel fiber. Manolis et al. [6] showed that fibrillated polypropylene fibers significantly improve the impact resistance of concrete slabs without affecting the natural frequency while the static compression and flexural strength decrease with increasing fiber content. Tang and Saadatmanesh [7] showed that composite laminates significantly increased the capacity of concrete beams to resist impact loading, reduced the maximum deflection, and increased the shear strength of the beam by preventing widening of cracks. In this study, the static and impact behavior of PE and AR Glass fabric reinforced cement composites was investigated.

2. EXPERIMENTAL PROGRAM

2.1 Material properties and mix design

The mix design for cement paste of fabric reinforced cement-based composites was 42% cement, 5% silica fume, 0.1% superplasticizer and 50% water by volume as the water/cement ratio by weight was 0.4. The AR Glass and PE fabric used for this study are shown in Figs. 1a and b respectively. The AR glass fibers were with tensile strength of 1270 to 2450 MPa, elasticity modulus of 78,000 MPa and filament diameter of 13.5 microns. The PE fibers were with tensile strength of 260 MPa, 1760 MPa modulus of elasticity and 0.25 mm diameter. The pultrusion process was used to produce the fabric-cement based composite specimens [8]. Each composite was made with 6 layers of fabrics, resulting in reinforcement content of about 4.0% and 8.0% by volume of AR glass fibers and PE fibers, respectively.

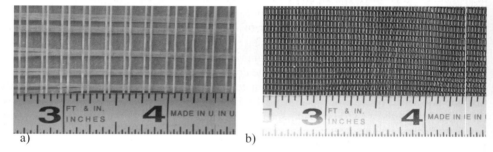

a)   b)

Figure 1: a) AR Glass Fabric, b) Polyethylene Fabric

2.2 Pultrusion Process

In the pultrusion process, the fabrics were immersed in a slurry infiltration chamber, and then pulled through a set of rollers to squeeze the paste in the openings of the fabric, and remove excessive paste. The pultrusion process is shown in Fig. 2. Composite laminates were formed on a rotating mandrel. The panels produced by using PE and AR Glass fabric were cut to dimensions of 50 mm x 150 mm, and eighteen specimens consisting of six layers of fabric were obtained for each fabric type. The thickness of the PE panels was between 10 mm and 12 mm. The AR Glass-Cement Paste panels were thinner than the panels with PE fabric at around 7 to 9 mm. This was attributed to the larger opening of the AR Glass mesh than the PE mesh resulting in a better compaction.

2.3 Experimental test set up and instrumentation

An impact test set up based on a free-fall drop of an instrumented hammer on a three point bending specimen was developed. The schematic of the system is presented in Fig. 3. The drop heights range from 1 to 160 cm, and can be controlled by means of an electronic hoist and release mechanism. After impact, an anti-rebound system consisting of a pneumatic brake system triggered by a contact type switch is used to stop the hammer after the duration of impact is completed. A device based on a lever arm mechanism was used to measure the specimen defection directly under the loading point. The experimental set-up included: two load cells rated at 90 kN capacity at the hammer and the support each; a linear variable displacement transducer with a range of $\pm$ 3.17 mm; and two accelerometers with ranges of $\pm$ 10 g and $\pm$ 100 g attached to the hammer and specimen respectively.

| Figure 2: Pultrusion process | Figure 3: Schematics of the impact test set up. |

The hammer weight includes the free weight, frictionless bearing assembly, load cell, connection plate, and the threaded rods weighing at 137 N (30.79 lbs). The data acquisition system used LABVIEW VI's and recorded signals from load cell, accelerometers and the LVDT at a sampling rate up to 100 kHz. The test lasted approximately 0.2 second. Matlab programs were developed for data processing to compute the frequency content, filter, smooth, plot, and calculate the parameters such as initial stiffness, toughness etc.

Figs. 4a and b represent a time-history of load, deflection and acceleration response of a Polyethylene (PE) and AR Glass reinforced fabric composites subjected to low impact velocity. Note that both the acceleration and deceleration response of the hammer and the specimen are recorded. The acceleration signals indicate that the specimen may accelerate after the initial contact to as high as 50 g, and the load experienced by the sample could reach as high as 2700 N. The phase lag in the deflection signal is due to the loading of the specimen. The maximum deflection is achieved as the load drops significantly; the specimen decelerates and comes to rest after the impact event. The load and strain signals stabilize after the impact event; however permanent deflection and post failure oscillations exist in the specimen after the impact event. The event duration is longer for the PE composites in comparison to the AR-Glass composites which may be attributed to the distributed cracking which gives rise to oscillations recorded in the accelerometer signals. The superior energy absorption of fabric composite can be observed, especially if these data are compared to the plain concrete specimens.

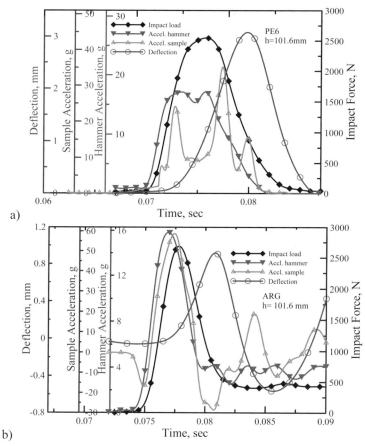

Figure 4: Time history of load, deflection, and acceleration of a fabric reinforced composite subjected to low impact velocity. a) Polyethylene fabric, b) Alkali Resistant Glass Fabric.

3. DISCUSSION OF THE TEST RESULTS

The FRCC specimens were tested in both vertical and horizontal positions with respect to the directions of applied impact load. The composites in the vertical orientation (beam type) were parallel to the direction of load, while in the horizontal specimens the fabrics were perpendicular to the direction of load application (plate type). The horizontal composites with AR Glass Fabric (6 layers) were tested for only the drop height of 50.8 mm since these test specimens failed at higher drop height levels due to shear delamination of the layers. The span of composite beams was 127 mm for three point flexural impact tests.

3.1   Effect of Drop Height

The hammer drop height was used as a variable ranging from 50.8 to 203.2 mm representing input energy from 5 to 20 Joules. At the same drop heights, the impact loads resisted by the composites held in a vertical manner for both AR Glass and PE fabrics were almost equal to each other. It was observed that the impact force and stress carried by vertical composite specimens produced using AR Glass and PE fabrics increased as the drop height increased until the drop height of 101.6 mm (see Fig. 5).

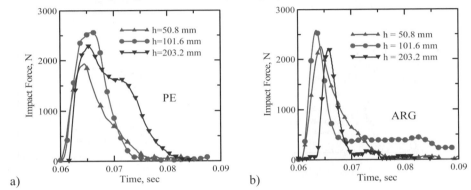

a)   b)

Figure 5: Time–impact force variation for vertical Fabric-Cement Paste Composites according to different drop heights

The maximum impact load and stress at the height of 203.2 mm was less than the respective values at 101.6 mm. The impact loads sustained by the horizontal composites with PE fabrics subjected to a drop height of 101.6 mm were almost equal to the impact loads at the drop height of 203.2 mm (see Fig. 6), the impact stress of the horizontal composites with PE for the drop height of 101.6 mm was 10 % higher than ones at the drop height of 203.2 mm due to the differences of sectional size between two specimens. According to these results, a drop height of 101.6 mm, corresponding to impact energy of 14.02 Joules, can be identified as the height corresponding to maximum impact load carrying capacity. The stress vs. deflection variations are shown for vertical specimens in Fig. 6a and b respectively. These figures indicate that fabric-cement paste composites for each fabric type have the highest stress at the hammer drop height of 101.6 mm.

3.2   Effect of Fabric Type

Figs. 5 and 6 indicate that the composites with AR Glass fabric are stronger but are more brittle than composites with PE fabric at each drop height level. This is shown by the PE fabric composites which exhibit more load carrying capacity at large deflections than the AR Glass fabric specimens. The ductility effect is more pronounced after the peak stress when data at the same drop heights are compared. The processing may also contribute to the differences in the results. Due to the size of the opening in the PE fabric, even with the use of pultrusion process, the cement paste may not sufficiently penetrate in between the yarns as well as AR Glass Fabric. This is because the sizes of openings in the PE fabric are too small to allow full penetration. Therefore, composites with AR Glass fabric are thinner than composites with PE. Although the impact load carrying capacity of PE composites is almost equal to those with AR Glass for same drop height, the impact flexural stress of composites with AR Glass is higher due to the thickness differences between the two systems. It was observed that AR Glass fabrics maintained the bond far better than the PE composites which exhibited signs of delamination after the impact load. It may be concluded that composites with AR Glass fabric have stronger interlaminar bonding than PE fabrics.

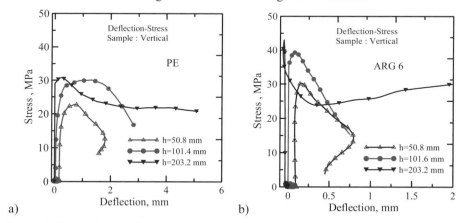

a)   b)

Figure 6: Time – impact force variation for horizontal Fabric-Cement Paste Composites according to different drop heights

3.3 Monotonic flexural tests for three point bending

Static flexural tests were conducted using a displacement controlled test procedure on a closed loop controlled MTS Hydraulic Systems with capacity of 90 kN. The deflections at the mid-span were measured using a linear variable displacement transducer with a range of ± 2.54 mm using a deflection rate of 5 mm per minute. Composite specimens of 10 mm × 50 mm × 150 mm in size were tested in horizontal and vertical direction under three point bending. Stress vs. deflection responses, as shown in Fig. 7a, indicate that AR Glass fabric specimens have as much as twice the strength under impact conditions as compared with statically loaded specimens.

3.4 Energy Absorption

The energy absorbed by composite specimens subjected to impact loads was calculated as area under impact load-deflection curve. The input potential energy was determined as a function of the hammer height and weight, assuming that no frictional losses took place during the free fall. The ratio of the absorbed energy to the input potential energy was determined for each drop height according to the fabric types and specimen orientation. The variations of this ratio and absorbed energy as a function of drop height are shown in Fig. 7b for vertical specimens of PE and AR Glass. Although the composites with AR Glass fabric carried higher impact loads than composites with PE fabric, Fig. 7b also illustrates that the absorbed energy amounts of the composites with PE fabric are higher than the composites produced using AR Glass fabric. This result indicates that the composites made of PE fabric with cement paste are more ductile than the composites with AR Glass fabric.

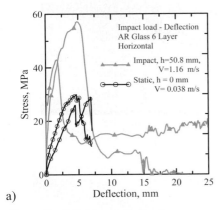

a)

Figure 7: a) Stress vs. Deflection response of composites under static three point bend flexural test compared with impact conditions

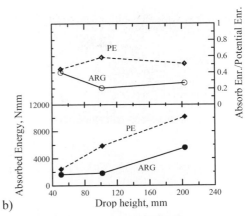

b)

Figure 7: b) Effect of drop height on the absorbed energy and ratio of absorbed energy to the input potential energy for vertical composites specimens

3.5   Orientations of specimens

A typical pattern of distributed cracks under the impact condition of the fabric composite is shown in Fig. 8. Both the vertically held, and also horizontally held specimens for the AR Glass are shown in Fig. 8a, and 8c respectively. Corresponding figures for the PE facrics are shown in Figs. 8b, and 8d. Significant microcracking in the form of radial fan cracking is observed in the flexural vertical specimens. The compression failure at the point of impact also causes degradation, however, the main parameter observed in the distributed cracking in the tensile zone. Distributed cracking is also observed in the horizontally held specimens. Fig. 8d indicates that the horizontal composites with PE fabrics have better crack distribution capability than AR glass specimens.

4. CONCLUSIONS

The impact and static flexural behaviors of the cement based composites made of PE and AR Glass fabrics were studied. The direction of fabric in the composite affects the load carrying capacity, and deflections. Stresses as high as 30 for the PE and 60 for the Alkali resistant glass are observed when subjected to a range of input impact ebnergy in the range of 5 to 15 Joules. The amount of energy absorbed is approximately bewteen 20% to 50% of the applied input potential energy.

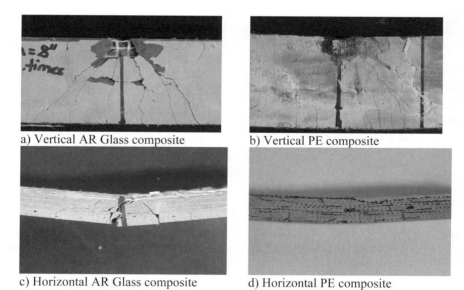

a) Vertical AR Glass composite   b) Vertical PE composite

c) Horizontal AR Glass composite   d) Horizontal PE composite

Figure 8: The views of damages on the cement based composites after impact load for the drop height of 203.2 mm (8")

REFERENCES

[1] Wang Nianzhi, Sidney Mindess and Keith Ko, (1996). "Fiber Reinforced Concrete Beams Under Impact Loading", *Cement and Concrete Composites*, V.26, 3, 363-376.
[2] Lok T. S., and Zhao P. J. (2004). "Impact Response of Steel Fiber-Reinforced Concrete Using a Split Hopkinson Pressure Bar.", ASCE *J. of Materials in Civil Engineering*, 16(1), 54–59.
[3] Bindiganavile, V., Banthia, N and Aarup, B., (2002). "Impact response of ultra-high strength fiber reinforced cement composite", *ACI Materials Journal,* 99(6), 543-548.
[4] Bindiganavile, V. and Banthia, N., (2001). "Polymer and Steel Fiber-Reinforced Cementitious Composites under Impact Loading, Part 1: Bond-Slip Response", *ACI Materials Journal*, 98(1), 10-16.
[5] Bindiganavile, V. and Banthia, N., (2001). "Polymer and Steel Fiber-Reinforced Cementitious Composites under Impact Loading, Part 2: Flexural Toughness", *ACI Materials Journal*, 98(1), 17-24.
[6] Manolis G. D., Gareis P. J., Tsono A. D., and Neal J. A.,(1997). "Dynamic Properties of Poly-propylene Fiber-Reinforced Concrete Slabs.", *Cement and Concrete Composites,* 19, 341-349.
[7] Tang T. T., and Saadatmanesh H. P. E., (2003). "Behavior of Concrete Beams Strengthened with Fiber-Reinforced Polymer Laminates under Impact Loading", *Journal of Composites for Construction,* 7(3), 209–218.
[8] Peled, A. and Mobasher, B., (2005), "Pultruded Fabric-Cement Composites," ACI Materials Journal, Vol. 102 , No. 1, pp. 15-23.

DYNAMIC MECHANICAL BEHAVIOUR OF ULTRA-HIGH PERFORMANCE CEMENTITIOUS COMPOSITES UNDER REPEATED IMPACT

Sun Wei, Lai Jianzhong, Rong Zhidan, Zhang Yunsheng and Zhang Yamei

College of Materials Science and Engineering, Southeast University, Nanjing, China

Abstract

Ecological ultra-high performance cementitious composites(UHPCC) were prepared by substitution of ultra-fine industrial waste powder for 60% cement by weight. Repeated compressive impact were on UHPCC in four kinds of impact modes with split Hopkinson pressure bar (SHPB). Standard strength of repeated impact is defined to compare the ability of resistance against repeated impact among different materials. Results show that the peak stress and elastic modulus decrease and the strain rate and peak strain increase gradually with the increase of impact times. The rate of the reduction of standard strength decreases under repeated impact by fiber reinforcement. The rate of damage is slowed down and the ability of repeated impact resistance of UHPCC is improved with the increase of fiber volume fraction.

1. INTRODUCTION

Ultra-high performance cementitious composites(UHPCC) is a new type of building material with very high strength and durability [1-5]. In this paper, Ecological ultra-high performance cementitious composites was prepared by substitution of ultra-fine industrial waste powder for 60% cement by weight. The ground fine quartz sand with maximal diameter of 600 μm was totally replaced by natural fine aggregates with maximal diameter of 2.5 mm. The advantages of granular packing and component complementing are achieved by the means of trinary composition of ultra-fine industrial waste powder.

Materials and structures in use usually suffered more than one time impact. Split Hopkinson pressure bar (SHPB) is effective to obtain the dynamic stress-strain behaviour [6-10]. The dynamic mechanical behaviour of UHPCC was researched under repeated impact in different impact modes by the means of SHPB. The paper also discovered the effects of material composition, impact times and load modes on the behaviour of UHPCC under repeated impact.

2. MATERIALS PREPARATION AND STATIC MECHANICAL PROPERTIES

Four cementitious materials were used in the preparation of UHPCC including portland cement, silica fume, ultra-fine fly ash and ultra-fine Slag. The strength grade of cement is P •II 52.5 according to the relevant Chinese standard. The maximum particle size of natural sand is

2.5 mm with a fineness modulus of 2.6. The superplasticizer was produced by Grace Company in Shanghai China with a water-reducing ratio more than 40%. The equivalent diameter, length and tensile strength of the fine steel fiber are 0.2 mm, 13 mm and 1800 MPa respectively.

Three types of UHPCC matrix were prepared which were $UHPCCV_0$, $UHPCCV_3$ and $UHPCCV_4$. The mix proportion is listed in Table 1. 60% of cement was replaced by ultra-fine industrial waste powder. Ground fine quartz sand was totally replaced by natural fine aggregates. The water-binder and sand-binder ratio were 0.15 and 1.2 respectively. The volume fraction of steel fiber was 0% to 4%. The static compressive results are shown in table 2. Results show that the static strength, elastic modulus and toughness are improved with the increase of fiber volume fraction.

Table 1: Mix proportion of UHPCC(%)

Materials	Cement	Silica fume	fly ash	Slag	Fiber volume fraction
$UHPCCV_0$					0
$UHPCCV_3$	40	10	25	25	3
$UHPCCV_4$					4

Notes: water/ binder=0.15; sand/ binder=1.2; Superplasticizer/ binder=0.02

Table 2: Uniaxial compressive results

Material	Uniaxial compressive strength (MPa)	Peak strain ($\times 10^{-3}$)	Elastic modulus (GPa)	Toughness index		
				η_{c5}	η_{c10}	η_{c30}
$UHPCCV_0$	143	2.817	54.7	2.43	2.43	2.43
$UHPCCV_3$	186	3.857	57.3	3.59	5.08	5.57
$UHPCCV_4$	204	4.165	57.9	4.57	6.32	7.39

3. EXPERIMENTAL METHOD OF REPEATED IMPACT

The cylinder dimension for SHPB test was 70 mm in diameter and 35 mm in length. A typical SHPB set-up is outlined in Fig. 1. It is composed of elastic input and output bar with a short specimen placed between them. The impact of the projectile at the free end of the input bar develops a compressive longitudinal incident wave $\varepsilon_I(t)$. Once this wave reaches the bar specimen interface, a part of it $\varepsilon_R(t)$, is reflected, whereas another part goes through the specimen and transmits to the output bar $\varepsilon_T(t)$. Those three basic waves are recorded by the gauges pasted on the input and output bars. According to the wave propagation theory, the average stress, strain and strain rate of specimens can be calculated by the following equation:

$$\sigma = E\varepsilon_R(t)\frac{A}{A_0}, \quad \dot{\varepsilon} = -\frac{2c_0}{l_0}[\varepsilon_T(t) - \varepsilon_I(t)], \quad \varepsilon = \int_0^t \dot{\varepsilon}(\tau)d\tau, \tag{1}$$

Where, E is Young's modulus. A and A_0 are the cross section area of the bar and the specimen respectively. l_0 and c_0 are the length of the specimen and the elastic wave speed respectively.

Figure 1: SHPB test set-up

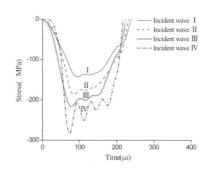

Figure 2: Incident waves on repeated impact

Repeated impacts on UHPCC by four kinds of loading modes of different incidents wave(Fig. 2) are as follows:

Mode A：the first impact is from incident wave Ⅰ, others are from incident wave Ⅱ;
Mode B：the first impact is from incident wave Ⅱ, others are from incident wave Ⅱ;
Mode C：the first impact is from incident waveⅢ, others are from incident wave Ⅱ;
Mode D：the first impact is from incident waveⅣ, others are from incident wave Ⅱ.

4. RESULTS AND ANALYSIS

4.1 Stress waves under repeated impact

Fig. 3 shows the stress waves transmitted through the same material under repeated impact in different loading modes. The incident and transmitter waves under first impact strengthened with the speed of first impact and the damage of specimens increased at the same time. The same speed of the second and the third impact produced the similar incident waves on the second and the third impact but the transmitted wave weakened with the increase of material damage. The more the first impact damage the faster the weakening rate of the transmitter wave and the reflective wave strengthened.

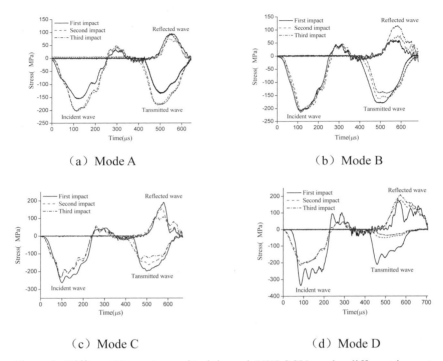

（a）Mode A　　　　　　　　　　　　　　（b）Mode B

（c）Mode C　　　　　　　　　　　　　　（d）Mode D

Figure 3: Different Waves transmitted through UHPCCV$_4$ under different impact

4.2 Dynamic mechanical properties of UHPCC on repeated impacts

4.2.1　The effect of impact times on the dynamic mechanical properties of UHPCC

Fig. 4 and Table 3 show the strain-stress curves and the test results under repeated impact in mode A. The weak resistance of UHPCC matrix against repeated impacts results in complete crack of the matrix specimen after the second impact so it cannot tolerate any impact any more. The resistance of UHPCC against repeated impact was strengthened massively by fiber reinforcement. With the speed of projectile at second impact higher than that of the first impact in mode A, the peak stress of the specimen is greater than that of the first impact but decreases gradually after each impact because of increasing damage of the material. The decreasing rate of peak stress is reduced by increasing fiber volume fraction. Especially UHPCCV$_4$ with the fiber volume fraction of 4%, the peak stress of it remained almost the same at the second and third impact and above 100 MPa at the forth and fifth impact, which shows its excellence in resistance against repeated impact. Fig. 5 shows that the weak damage of the specimen and the stress-strain curve bends back under the first impact, and that the slope of the rising stress-strain curve decreases and like what metal does, a yielding stage will appear after peak stress with the increasing time of impact. Stress-strain curves show that the peak stress decreased largely with the increase of impact times when the specimen strain is over 0.01 and the strain rate is over 60/s. The strain of UHPCCV$_4$ is below

0.01 and its strain rate is below 50/s after successively five times of impact, and the decline of its peak stress is no more than 15%. Table 1 shows that the strain rate and peak strain increase while the peak stress and elastic modulus decrease gradually with the increasing of impact times, which illustrates the accumulation of material damage under repeated impact.

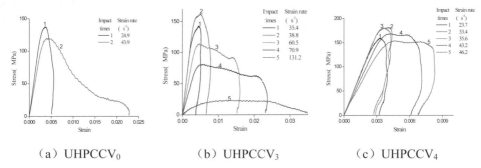

（a）UHPCCV$_0$　　　　　（b）UHPCCV$_3$　　　　　（c）UHPCCV$_4$

Figure 4: Stress-strain curves of UHPCC at different impact times in mode A

Table 3: Experimental results of UHPCC at different impact times in mode A

Materials	Impact times	Stain rate (s^{-1})	Elastic modulus （GPa）	Peak strain （$\times 10^{-6}$）	Peak stress （MPa）
UHPCCV$_0$	1	24.9	50.1	3588	138
	2	43.9	39.2	4051	120
UHPCCV$_3$	1	35.4	48.7	4518	143
	2	38.8	49.2	4956	162
	3	60.5	31.2	5629	114
	4	70.9	20.5	6087	81
	5	131.2	4.6	12197	24
UHPCCV$_4$	1	23.7	55.3	3270	160
	2	33.4	56.7	4094	182
	3	35.6	56.1	3629	181
	4	43.2	46.7	4272	169
	5	46.2	40.9	4579	154

4.2.2　The effect of impact mode on the mechanical properties of UHPCC

Fig. 5 and Table 4 show the different strain-stress curves and the test results of repeated impact in different mode. Results show that the strain rate, elastic modulus , peak stress and peak strain increasing gradually under the first impact in the order from mode A to mode D in that the amplitude of incident wave increases gradually with the changing of impact modes while the material damage accumulates. With the same amplitude of incident wave of the second impact but different material damage for each mode, the stress-strain curves on second impact change in the pattern contrary to that of the first impact, namely, the elastic modulus and peak stress on second impact decreases from mode A to mode D. In the same mode the elastic modulus and peak stress

decrease while the strain rate and peak strain increase with the increase of impact times. In mode
B and mode C, the reduction of elastic modulus and peak stress decreases with the increase of
fiber volume fraction. In mode D the strain rates of different materials were all over 90/s and the
strain was over 0.02 on the first impact while the elastic modulus and peak stress decreased
significantly to a similar degree on the second and third impact, which can be concluded that
when the damage at the high strain rate under the first impact over a certain degree leads to the
similar effects of the second and third impact or the effects of different material composition on
the ability of resistance against repeated impacts remain insignificantly.

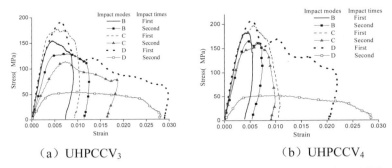

（a）UHPCCV$_3$　　　　　　　　　　　　　（b）UHPCCV$_4$

Figure 5: Effect of impact modes on the stress-strain curves of UHPCC

Table 4: Experimental results of UHPCC in different impact modes

Materials	Impact mode	Impact times	Stain rate (s^{-1})	Elastic modulus （GPa）	Peak strain （$\times 10^{-6}$）	Peak stress （MPa）
UPC1V$_3$	B	1	38.8	49.6	4421	155
		2	59.9	33.1	7607	130
		3	87.6	16.0	9057	78
	C	1	66.8	53.7	5575	178
		2	82.1	27.2	7304	115
		3	88.4	13.7	5764	56
	D	1	99.2	57.4	6308	192
		2	98.9	16.2	9969	55
		3	131.8	8.5	8854	34
UPC1V$_4$	B	1	35.5	57.3	4418	183
		2	39.9	43.7	4769	165
		3	66.2	36.4	8708	144
	C	1	67.1	57.2	5570	199
		2	69.8	47.5	6337	164
		3	57.3	36.8	4798	134
	D	1	90.3	65.1	5399	207
		2	102.9	15.0	9650	52
		3	139.5	9.4	10991	38

4.2.3   The standard strength of UHPCC on repeated impacts
The standard strength of materials is defined as:

$$I_n = \frac{F_n}{F_0} \tag{2}$$

Where, I_n is the standard strength of the specimen after n times impacts, F0 and Fn are the peak load of the specimen on the first and nth impact respectively.

Fig. 6 shows the changing process of the standard strength of UHPCC under repeated impact in different impact modes. The matrix of UHPCC usually cracked completely on the first impact, but only in mode A can it be impacted for the second time where the second standard strength I2 decreased to 86% while the I2 of UHPCC with fiber reinforcement increased by more than 10% compared with that of I1 and then I_n decreased with the increase of impact times. The reduction of I_n falls more slowly with the increase of the fiber volume fraction. The standard strength of UHPCCV4 reduced only by 10% after 5 times of impact which justifies its excellence in repeated impact resistance. As the material damage caused by the first impact increased from mode A to mode D, the reduction rate of standard strength increased gradually. The reduction rate of standard strength of UHPCCV4 is smaller than that of UHPCCV3. In mode B, the reduction of I2 of UHPCCV3 and I3 of UHPCCV4 is no more than 20% compared with I1 which shows high ability of repeated impact resistance of fiber reinforced UHPCC. In mode C, I2 of UHPCCV3 and UHPCCV4 is about 48% and 68% respectively which shows the remaining ability of resistance against the repeated impact.

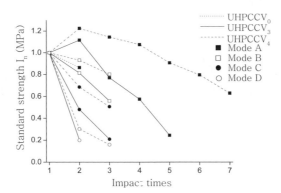

Figure 6: Effect of steel fiber fraction on the standard strength of UHPCC

In mode D, I2 of UHPCC reduced to 20%~30% and I3 to 15%. Thus it can be seen that the more the fiber volume fraction increases, the greater the ability of resistance against repeated impact UHPCC displays. The damage caused by the first impact has significant effect on the ability of resistance against repeated impact. Materials with lower damage have higher ability of resistance against repeated impact.

4.3 The fracture pattern of UHPCC on repeated impact
Fig. 7 to Fig. 9 show the fracture pattern of UHPCC on repeated impact. The matrix of

UHPCC cracked severely after the first two times of impact and with the increasing of first impact load the damage degree increased with pieces dropping from the edge to total cracking into small parts. The fiber reinforcement improved greatly UHPCC's ability of resistance against repeated impact. In mode A, UPC1V$_3$ and UPC1V$_4$ suffered significant damage on 5 and 10 times of impact respectively. Under repeated impacts, slight crack appeared on the side of fiber reinforced specimens before the crack extended to the center of the specimens at a low speed with the help of the fiber reinforcement. The specimens still appeared intact although cracks across the middle of them appeared after several times of impacts. Materials damage on the second and third impact deteriorates with the increase of damage on the first impact. In mode D, obvious cracks appeared on the side of specimens UPC1V$_3$ and UPC1V$_4$ on the second impact and crack existed in the middle of specimens on the third impact. The damage of UPC1V$_4$ is less severe than that of UPC1V$_3$ after the same times of impact.

First impact   Second impact   First impact   First impact
（a）Mode A   （b）Mode B   （c）Mode D

Figure 7: Fracture pattern of UHPCCV$_0$ under repeated impact

First impact   First impact   First impact   Second impact   Third impact
（a）Mode A   （b）Mode B   （c）Mode D

Figure 8: Fracture pattern of UHPCCV$_3$ under repeated impact

First impact   First impact   First impact   Second impact   Third impact
（a）Mode A   （b）Mode B   （c）Mode D

Figure 9: Fracture pattern of UHPCCV$_4$ under repeated impact

5. CONCLUSION

(1) Ecological ultra-high performance cementitious composites with 200 MPa compressive strength was prepared by substitution of ultra-fine industrial waste powder for 60% cement by weight and replacing ground fine quartz sand totally with natural fine aggregates whose maximal diameter is 2.5 mm.

(2) The dynamic behaviour of UHPCC with three different steel fiber volume fractions under repeated impacts by four kinds of load modes was researched using SHPB. The ability of repeated impacts resistance of UHPCC is improved with the increase of fiber volume fraction.

(3) The damage development is controlled by fiber reinforcement under repeated impact. Only by the composition of high strength fine fibers the ability of UHPCC can be fully displayed.

ACKNOWLEDGEMENT

The authors are thankful to the support of the National Natural Science Foundation of China with project No. 59938170.

REFERENCES

[1] Man-Chung Tang. High Performance Concrete-Past, Present and Future. In: M. Schmidt, E. Fehling, C. Geisenhanslüke (Eds.). Proceedings of the International Symposium on Ultra High Performance Concrete. Kassel, Germany. September 13-15, 2004. 3-9.

[2] Resplendino, Jacques. First recommendation for Ultra-High Performance Concrete and example of application. In: M. Schmidt, E. Fehling, C. Geisenhanslüke (Eds.). Proceedings of the International Symposium on Ultra High Performance Concrete. Kassel, Germany. September 13-15, 2004. 79-90

[3] Reda, M.M., Shrive, N.G., Gillott, J.E. Microstructural investigation of innovative UHPC. Cement and Concrete Research 29 (1999), 323-329

[4] Bonneau, Oliver, Poulin, Claude, Dugat, Jerome. Reactive powder concrete: from theory to practice.Concrete International 18 (1996), No. 4, 47-49

[5] Richard, P, Cheyrezy, M. Composition of reactive powder concrete.Cement and Concrete Research 25 (1995), No. 7, 1501-1511

[6] Han Zhao. A study on testing techniques for concrete-like materials under compressive impact loading. Cement and Concrete Composites 20 (1998), 293-299

[7] Han Zhao, Gerard, Gary. On the use SHPB techniques to determine the dynamic behavior of materials in the range of small strains. Journal of International Solids Structures 33 (1996), No. 23, 3363-3375

[8] Ross, C A, Tedesco, J W, Kuennen, S.T. Effects of strain rate on concrete strength. ACI Materials Journal 92 (1995) ,No. 1, 37-47.

[9] Lok, T.S., ASCE, M., Li, X. B. et al. Testing and Response of Large Diameter Brittle Materials Subjected to High Strain Rate. Journal of materials in civil engineering 14 (2002), No. 3, 262-269

[10] Grote, D.L., Park, S.W., Zhou, M. Dynamic behavior of concrete at high strain rates and pressures: I. experimental characterization. International Journal of Impact Engineering 25 (2001), 869-886

HIGH-PERFORMANCE FIBER REINFORCED CONCRETE FOR EARTHQUAKE-RESISTANT DESIGN OF COUPLED WALL SYSTEMS

James K. Wight, Gustavo J. Parra-Montesinos and Rémy D. Lequesne

University of Michigan, Ann Arbor, USA

Abstract

This study integrates research in the fields of high performance fiber reinforced concrete, reinforced concrete structures, and large-scale experimentation to develop new coupled wall systems that are easier to construct and offer improved earthquake performance. It was conceived from the idea that the next generation of reinforced concrete (RC) structures should utilize ductile cementitious materials in critical regions, rather than extensive reinforcement detailing to provide shear resistance, concrete confinement and thus, an increase in deformation capacity of structural members and systems. In other words, the approach is to use a "better material" rather than "more material".

The structural application reported in this paper is for the use of HPFRC in coupling beams of reinforced concrete structural wall systems. Coupled structural walls are a popular lateral load resisting system for medium-rise structures in zones of moderate to high seismicity. During a large earthquake it is anticipated that the coupling beams will undergo significant inelastic deformations and it is important for these beams to have a high energy dissipation capability and good stiffness retention. Steel reinforcement detailing required in reinforced concrete coupling beams to resist earthquake-induced forces and deformations is labor intensive and costly, which often leads practicing engineers to discard the use of such coupling beams in medium- and high-rise construction.

The seismic behavior of precast, lightly reinforced HPFRC coupling beams is discussed based on results from large-scale tests under displacement reversals. HPFRC is used: 1) as a replacement for steel confinement reinforcement, 2) to provide additional shear resistance, and 3) to increase coupling beam damage tolerance.

1. INTRODUCTION

Coupled concrete structural wall systems are often an efficient lateral bracing system for both medium-rise steel frame and concrete structures. These wall systems can develop significant lateral strength with good stiffness retention through large displacement reversals. The efficiency of the system is improved through proper coupling of two or more consecutive structural walls through the use of short coupling beams. The demand for flexural rigidity of the individual walls can be reduced by taking advantage of the axial stiffness of the structural walls through the coupling action provided by the short coupling beam elements.

These coupling beams must ideally retain a significant shear force capacity through large displacement reversals, while suffering a modest degradation of stiffness for the satisfactory performance of this structural system during a seismic event. For span-to-depth ratios of less than two, it has been shown [1] that special diagonal reinforcement detailing is required to eliminate the development of brittle diagonal tension or sliding shear failures and provide adequate ductility and stiffness retention to achieve the design goals of the system. However, the detailing required to provide stable behavior of the bi-diagonally reinforced coupling beam is difficult to construct, and often fails to sustain the integrity of the full concrete element through large displacement reversals. Other alternatives have been proposed and investigated [2], including steel and hybrid steel-concrete beams. Despite simplified detailing and improved hysteretic behavior, providing proper anchorage of the steel element without disrupting reinforcement in the structural wall is a significant challenge.

HPFRCs provide significantly improved ductility over more traditional cement based materials, and are therefore ideal for consideration as an improvement to the seismic design of coupling beams. The improved tensile properties of HPFRCs have been shown [3] to not only enhance bond with the reinforcement, but also to provide adequate confinement of the diagonal reinforcement to eliminate the need for steel confinement of each group of diagonal bars. This not only simplifies detailing, but also gives the engineer the freedom to select as few as one diagonal bar in each direction.

Furthermore, HPFRCs offer the potential, through their enhanced tensile strength at high strains (beyond 5% in some cases) [4], to support a significant portion of the applied shear stress after cracking, thereby reducing the need for diagonal reinforcement while improving the ductility of the entire element. Essentially, coupling beam behavior would no longer be reduced to relying solely on the two sets of diagonal bars to sustain the applied shear at large drifts. Rather, the HPFRC would ideally maintain its integrity through large displacement reversals, and thus, continue to share the diagonal tension with the diagonal reinforcement.

2. RESEARCH SIGNIFICANCE

It has been shown previously [3] in tests of short coupling beams with a span-to-depth ratio of 1.0 that incorporating HPFRCC can: 1) eliminate the need for steel confinement of the diagonals, 2) delay the development of crack localization by dispersing damage over multiple finer cracks, and 3) provide improved shear capacity, drift capacity, and stiffness retention over conventional bi-diagonally reinforced coupling beams, thereby significantly improving energy dissipation. It is the goal of this current research to investigate the effects of incorporating HPFRC in the design of coupling beams with longer aspect ratios ($1/d = 1.75$), where flexural deformations play a larger role, interacting with shear to contribute to the drift of the element. To further simplify the construction process and reduce costs, this research will continue to investigate the possibility of precasting the coupling beam, as in previous research by Canbolat et al. [3], but with a focus on evaluating possible embedment strategies that provide sufficient development of the precast section into the structural wall without interfering with wall reinforcement.

3. MATERIALS

The tests performed by Canbolat et al. [3], and discussed below, allow a comparison of the behavior of a conventionally reinforced concrete coupling beam to one incorporating an HPFRCC composite. The concrete in Specimen 1 was conventional, with a 28-day compressive strength of 43.0 MPa (6.2 ksi). Specimen 4 consisted of a mortar mixture reinforced with a 1.5% volume fraction of twisted steel (Torex) fibers. The 28-day compressive strength was 59.6 MPa (8.6 ksi); the peak tensile strength was 5.9 MPa (860 psi).

Recent work at the University of Michigan [5] has developed a highly flowable HPFRC mix which reinforces a concrete matrix with a 1.5% volume fraction of high strength hooked steel fibers. This mixture was selected for use in the current series of tests. For Specimen CB-1, discussed below in Section 5, the 28-day compressive strength was 37.2 MPa (5.4 ksi). All tensile tests showed strain-hardening behavior with an average peak tensile strength of 2.4 MPa (350 psi) occurring at about 0.2% strain. Five beam tests were also conducted according to ASTM C 1609 [6], which consistently showed deflection-hardening. The mean maximum equivalent bending stress was 45% higher than the mean bending stress at first cracking. Minimal vibration was necessary for placement despite narrow openings between steel reinforcement and forms.

4. PREVIOUS RESEARCH

Because conventional detailing of short coupling beams with an effective span-to-depth ratio less than two has been shown by Paulay [7], and others since, to exhibit unacceptably brittle behavior due to either diagonal tension failure or sliding shear failure at the ends of the beam, several solutions have been investigated by researchers to improve the hysteretic behavior of these elements.

In 1996, Tassios et al. [8] presented the results from a series of tests which systematically compared the most commonly proposed reinforcement schemes applied to beams with l/d ratios of 1.0 and 1.66. The results presented clearly illustrate several key points, summarized as follows:
- while dowel bars in the end regions of the beam may help prevent sliding shear failure, stiffness degradation and severe pinching in the hysteresis response are not improved,
- although a rhombic layout of diagonal reinforcement requires less complicated detailing than bi-diagonally reinforced coupling beams, and exhibits less stiffness degradation than conventionally reinforced coupling beams, severe pinching of the hysteresis loops is still present,
- bi-diagonal reinforcement does appear to provide the most stable behavior and highest energy dissipation, but providing sufficient confinement to ensure stability of the diagonal bars is "indispensable", and presents significant field placement difficulties.

With these difficulties in mind, researchers have explored other options, as discussed by Harries, Gong, and Shahrooz [2], including steel and hybrid coupling beam designs. These alternatives respond very favorably in shear, showing stable behavior with wide hysteresis loops. However, the steel element requires a long embedment into the structural wall to ensure full development of its capacity, which inevitably interferes with critical transverse reinforcement providing confinement to the boundary region of the structural walls.

4.1 HPFRCC Coupling Beam Tests

To address these issues, Canbolat et al. [3] proposed using HPFRCC to both simplify the design of reinforced concrete coupling beams by providing sufficient confinement to the diagonal reinforcement, as well as improving the cyclic behavior in terms of energy dissipation, stiffness retention, and damage mitigation. Reproduced in Fig. 1 are the reinforcement details for the series of tests which were included in the study.

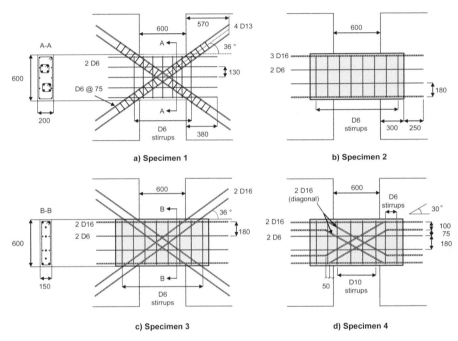

Figure 1: Reinforcement details for specimens included in Canbolat [9], dimensions in mm

Specimen 1 is conventional concrete, reinforced with bi-diagonal steel, and cast monolithically with the structural walls, as is done in practice today. Specimen 2 explores eliminating the bi-diagonal reinforcement entirely and relying on the HPFRCC for ductility, while Specimen 3 considers removing only the confining reinforcement around the diagonal steel. Specimens 2 and 3 also explored the possibility of precasting the coupling beam to further simplify jobsite construction and to reduce material costs by incorporating fiber reinforcement only in the most critical regions. Finally, Specimen 4 ties these efforts together into a precast, bi-diagonally reinforced, HPFRCC section with bent diagonals to ease placement of the precast section on the jobsite.

Of most interest to the current discussion is a comparison of the hysteretic behavior of Specimens 1 and 4, as presented in Fig. 2. While the cross-sectional area and orientation of diagonal reinforcement are nearly equal, the shear stress capacity and drift capacity are both markedly improved in the HPFRCC member. This shows clearly that stability of the diagonal reinforcement can be adequately maintained by the surrounding HPFRCC matrix. Further, it is evidence that the enhanced properties of HPFRCC contribute appreciably to increasing the shear strength of the member up to drifts nearing 6%, even in heavily shear dominated members. It should also be noted that the stiffness degrades more gradually in the HPFRCC member, which is evidence that the HPFRCC suffers less localization of damage than the reinforced concrete member at comparable drifts.

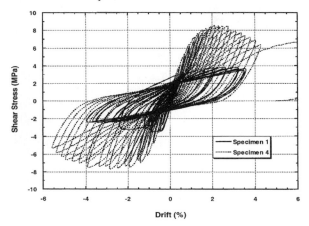

Figure 2: Shear stress vs. drift response comparison of Specimen 1 (reinforced concrete) and Specimen 4 (HPFRCC) from Canbolat [9]

5. CURRENT PROJECT

5.1 Embedment

The idea that HPFRC may be advantageously utilized in critical regions to improve the ductility of structural elements and alleviate congestion is a major thrust behind much of the current research project. The cost, however, of incorporating fiber reinforcement throughout a structure is prohibitive. The solution proposed previously [3], to precast the HPFRC section and embed it into the reinforced concrete structural walls, has proven promising and has the added benefit of providing a more controlled environment for manufacturing and ensuring quality of construction for coupling beams. However, similar to the steel and hybrid coupling beams discussed earlier, interference with critical transverse reinforcement in the boundary region of the wall is still an issue.

The current research project is proposing to precast the HPFRC section, but to terminate the HPFRC portion only 25 mm (1 inch) into the wall, relying extensively on steel reinforcement to transfer shear and moment between the coupling beam and the structural wall. The 25 mm (1 inch) of embedment allows the precast coupling beams to be placed on the adjacent walls, and provides some resistance to sliding shear through bearing on the cover and interlocking created by the presence of shear keys, as shown in Fig. 3. However, force transferred through bearing on the cover and shear keys is not a reliable mechanism, so the end regions are designed to conservatively transfer the full shear force through dowel action and shear friction, due to clamping action, provided by the steel protruding from the end of the precast section.

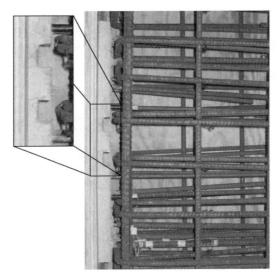

Figure 3: Embedment of precast section into structural wall with shear key detail

Similarly, the full moment capacity of the coupling beam (making sure to consider the flexural-tension contribution of the HPFRC) must be transferred into the structural wall. This is done by providing some minimal additional steel reinforcement at the interface between the HPFRC coupling beam and the wall concrete. Fig. 4a shows that two U-shaped steel bars are specified at each interface, which extend 150 mm (6 inches) into the coupling beam before being bent for anchorage. This results in a situation where the ratio of moment capacity to moment demand at the termination of the U-shaped steel in the coupling beam is similar to the equivalent ratio at the cold joint, thereby avoiding a localization of rotation at the interface.

One coupling beam test has been completed and it appears that this proposed solution effectively transfers the shear and moment capacity of the coupling beam into the structural wall and avoids any localization of failure in the boundary region.

5.2 Interaction of HPFRC and reinforcement

The hysteretic shear vs. drift response of the first HPFRC coupling beam test in the current study is shown in Fig. 4b. Although the behavior degrades around 2.5% drift, it is a direct result of a detailing issue, as described below, which is being addressed in future tests. Fig. 4a shows that the diagonal reinforcement is bent before entering the wall. This is done to ease placement of the precast section and to increase the shear contribution of the diagonal bars by increasing the angle of elevation relative to the horizontal. This results in a force component that will tend to burst through the top and bottom of the coupling beam if not sufficiently restrained by stirrups. Adequate restraint of this force component was not provided in the first test, but is being evaluated in future tests. However, it is worth noting that the behavior up to 2.5% drift showed no evidence of instability of the diagonal bars, which supports the assertion that HPFRC can be relied on to provide adequate confinement of the bi-diagonal reinforcement.

Another interesting observation from the testing of the first specimen relates to the improved bond developed between the HPFRC and the steel reinforcement, compared to conventional reinforced concrete. Due to the double curvature condition imposed on coupling beams, a single longitudinal steel bar, placed along either the top or bottom of the beam, should ideally have one half experience tension and the other half experience compression. Due to a severe degradation of bond, coupled with elongation of the beam due to damage, conventional concrete coupling beams often show evidence that longitudinal bars are under tension for the entire length of the beam [1]. The initial HPFRC coupling beam test performed for this study showed that at large drifts, a longitudinal bar may show compressive strains at one end of the beam, while yielding in tension at the other end. Thus, the HPFRC matrix is capable of retaining its integrity through large displacement reversals.

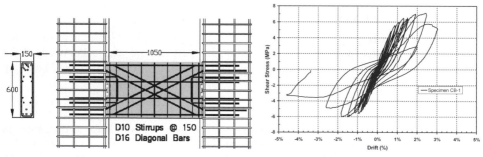

Figure 4a: Specimen CB-1 reinforcement detail   Figure 4b: Specimen CB-1 shear stress vs. drift response

6. CONCLUSIONS

The tests of HPFRC coupling beams described herein show evidence that the enhanced material properties of HPFRC can both simplify and enhance the design of short coupling beams by having an appreciable impact on preventing brittle failure mechanisms from developing. The following observations are indicative of the potential which HPFRC coupling beams may offer:

– HPFRC can be relied on to provide adequate confinement for the bi-diagonal reinforcement of coupling beams, which significantly simplifies detailing and construction of coupling beams.

– HPFRC will disperse damage to a structural element over more numerous, finer cracks than conventional concrete, thus delaying the localization of damage and the subsequent development of an undesirable failure mechanism. The structural implications of this are evidenced by the more gradual degradation of stiffness through multiple displacement reversals. This has important implications for a coupled wall system, where dissipating energy and maintaining a consistent degree of coupling are critical for adequate behavior of the structure during a seismic event.

– It appears to be possible to adequately develop both moment and shear capacities of the coupling beam without interfering with structural wall reinforcement. This makes precast

HPFRC more attractive than steel for coupling beams, from a construction viewpoint, while improving quality control of concrete coupling beam construction.
- Short coupling beams that incorporate HPFRC show a higher shear stress capacity than traditional bi-diagonally reinforced coupling beams, as well as an improved drift capacity. This results in more stable hysteretic behavior and greater energy dissipation.

7. CONTINUING RESEARCH

The current research includes an effort to study the effects of incorporating HPFRC in the design of longer span coupling beams ($l/d = 1.75$). Further, through a hybrid, pseudo-dynamic, full-scale test, the implications of incorporating precast HPFRC coupling beams on the seismic response of the overall system will be investigated.

ACKNOWLEDGEMENTS

The current research project is funded by NSF grant #CMS 0530383, and is a part of the national NEES research program. The efforts of Dr. Canbolat are also acknowledged for working at length with the two first authors to complete the series of short HPFRCC coupling beam tests discussed herein.

REFERENCES

[1] Paulay, T. and Binney, J.R., 'Diagonally Reinforced Coupling Beams of Shear Walls', *Shear in Reinforced Concrete,* ACI Publication SP-42 by ACI-ASCE Shear Committee, **2** (1974) 579-598.

[2] Harries, K., Gong, B., and Shahrooz, B., 'Behavior and Design of Reinforced Concrete, Steel, and Steel-Concrete Coupling Beams', *Earthquake Spectra* **16** (4) (2000) 775-799.

[3] Canbolat, B.A., Parra-Montesinos, G., and Wight, J., 'Experimental Study on Seismic Behavior of High-Performance Fiber-Reinforced Cement Composite Coupling Beams', *ACI Structural Journal* **102** (1) (2005) 159-166.

[4] Li, V.C., Wang, S., and Wu, C., 'Tensile Strain Hardening Behavior of PVA-ECC', *ACI Materials Journal* **98** (6) (2001) 64-97.

[5] Liao, W.C., Chao, S.H., Park, S.Y., and Naaman, A.E., 'Self-Consolidating High Performance Fiber Reinforced Concrete (SCHPFRC) – Preliminary Investigation' Technical Report, University of Michigan, Ann Arbor, Report No. UMCEE 06-02 (2006).

[6] ASTM C1609/C1609M–06, *Standard Test Method for Flexural Performance of Fiber-Reinforced Concrete (Using Beam With Third-Point Loading)*, ASTM International.

[7] Paulay, T., 'Coupling Beams of Reinforced Concrete Walls', *Journal of the Structural Division, ASCE* **97** (ST3) (1971) 843-862.

[8] Tassios, T., Moretti, M., and Bezas, A., 'On the Behavior and Ductility of Reinforced Concrete Coupling Beams of Shear Walls', *ACI Structural Journal* **93** (6) (1996) 711-720.

[9] Canbolat, B.A., 'Seismic Behavior of High-Performance Fiber Reinforced Cementitious Composite Coupling Beams', Ph.D. Dissertation, University of Michigan, Ann Arbor, Report No. UMCEE 04-11 (2004).

PUNCHING SHEAR RESISTANCE AND DEFORMATION CAPACITY OF FIBER REINFORCED CONCRETE SLAB-COLUMN CONNECTIONS SUBJECTED TO MONOTONIC AND REVERSED CYCLIC DISPLACEMENTS

Min-Yuan Cheng[1] and Gustavo J. Parra-Montesinos[2]

(1) Graduate Student Research Assistant, Department of Civil and Environmental Engineering, University of Michigan, USA

(2) Associate Professor, Department of Civil and Environmental Engineering, University of Michigan, USA

Abstract

The use of fiber reinforced concrete (FRC) as a means to increase punching shear resistance in slab-column connections subjected to either gravity-type loading or combined gravity and earthquake-induced loads was experimentally investigated. The testing program was two-fold. First, ten slab-column connections were tested monotonically to failure to evaluate the ability of various steel fiber reinforced concretes to increase punching shear resistance under gravity-type loading. These tests also allowed the selection of the best materials for use in the second testing phase, which consisted of the testing of two slab-column subassemblies subjected to gravity punching shear stresses of $0.17\text{-}0.2\sqrt{f_c'}$ (MPa) combined with lateral displacement reversals. Two types of hooked steel (Dramix) fibers and one type of twisted (Helix) fiber were evaluated. The hooked steel fibers had an aspect ratio of 55 and 80, and were made of regular strength wire ($f_u = 1100$ MPa) and high-strength wire ($f_u = 2300$ MPa), respectively. The twisted steel fibers had an aspect ratio of 60 and were made of high-strength wire. Strain-hardening or high-performance tensile behavior was observed in the FRC with high-strength hooked fibers.

Test results showed that FRCs reinforced with a 1.5% volume fraction of hooked steel fibers (either regular or high strength) offered the best results in terms of punching shear strength and ductility under monotonic loading and thus, they were selected for further investigation under displacement reversals. The two FRC slab-column connections subjected to combined gravity and lateral loading showed excellent behavior with drift capacity of at least 4%. The connection that featured a 1.5% volume fraction of high-strength hooked fibers (high-performance FRC material) could not be failed and showed only minor damage at 5% drift.

1.   INTRODUCTION

Slab-column framed systems, where slabs are supported directly by columns, have long been a popular structural system, particularly when large open spaces and reductions in story heights are required for space usage and economy. While the elimination of beams from the floor system facilitates formwork and allows a reduction in story height, it leads to a substantial reduction in lateral stiffness and the potential for punching shear failures in the connections between the slab and the columns. In order to provide adequate lateral stiffness and strength, slab-column frames are often combined with either structural walls or moment-resisting frames. On the other hand, the potential for punching shear failure in slab-column connections is generally addressed by thickening the slab (e.g. drop panels) or by providing steel shear reinforcement (e.g. shear stud reinforcement) in the connection region (Fig. 1).

Figure 1: Stud reinforcement in slab-column connection (courtesy of Jack P. Moehle)

In slab-column construction in regions with earthquake hazard, connections are even more susceptible to punching shear failures because of the potential for inelastic rotations and additional punching shear stresses induced during an earthquake. Test and analysis results [1,2] have shown that connection unbalanced moments and deformations induced by lateral frame displacements could trigger punching shear failures. Further, good correlation was found between the level of punching shear stress induced by gravity loads and frame drift capacity; the larger the gravity shear stress, the lower the drift capacity. This interaction is recognized in the ACI Building Code [3], where a drift limit above which shear reinforcement is required in slab-column connections is specified as follows,

$$Drift\ Limit = 0.035 - 0.05\,(\frac{V_u}{\phi V_c}) \geq 0.005 \tag{1}$$

where V_u is the factored shear force in the slab-column connection, ϕ is the strength reduction factor (0.75), and V_c is the punching shear strength of the connection (without shear reinforcement), generally equal to $1/3 \sqrt{f_c'}\ b_o d$, where f_c' is the specified concrete compressive strength (MPa), b_o is the critical perimeter, and d is the slab effective depth. The ratio V_u/V_c is typically referred to as the gravity shear ratio. Based on Equation (1) and neglecting the ϕ factor, a gravity shear ratio of 0.5 (shear stress of $1/6\sqrt{f_c'}$, MPa) would require the use of punching shear reinforcement whenever the design drift ratio exceeds 1%.

In this investigation, the use of fiber reinforced concrete (FRC) in cases where shear reinforcement is required per Equation (1) was evaluated. The tensile ductility and post-cracking strength exhibited by some FRCs, particularly those with strain-hardening behavior or high-performance fiber reinforced concretes (HPFRCs), are believed to have the potential to increase punching shear strength not only under gravity loading, as demonstrated in previous research [for example 4,5], but also under displacement reversals induced by earthquakes.

2. EXPERIMENTAL INVESTIGATION

The experimental program can be divided into two phases. The first phase was aimed at evaluating the punching shear resistance of FRC slab-column connections under monotonic loading. The second phase focused on the evaluation of punching shear strength and deformation capacity of FRC slab-column connections subjected to reversed cyclic loading.

2.1 Tests of slab-column connections under monotonic loading

A total of five pairs of specimens were tested in this phase. Two specimens were tested for each material investigated, one with a tension reinforcement ratio of 0.67% in each principal direction and the other with a 1% longitudinal reinforcement ratio. Each slab specimen was 1.5 m square and 15 cm thick, simply supported along its periphery. Load was applied through a column stub, 15 cm square and located at the center of the slab. Fig. 2 shows a photo of the test setup, while Table 1 lists the main features of the test specimens.

Figure 2: Test setup for slab-column specimens subjected to monotonic loading

As shown in Table 1, the first pair of specimens was constructed with regular concrete and the results used for comparison purposes. Three pairs of specimens featured FRC containing hooked steel (Dramix) fibers in either 1% or 1.5% volume fraction, while the last pair of specimens was constructed with an FRC containing a 1.5% volume fraction of twisted steel (Helix) fibers. Fiber properties are also listed in Table 1. All FRCs with hooked steel fibers contained course aggregate with a 10 mm maximum aggregate size, while only fine aggregate was used in the mixture containing twisted steel fibers.

Table 1: Summary of features and test results for slab-column connection specimens subjected to monotonic loading

Spec	ρ (%)	Fiber Type (V_f)	l_f/d_f	f_u (MPa)	f'_c (MPa)	f_y (MPa)	Peak Load (kN)	$v_u/\sqrt{f_c'}$ (MPa)
S1	1	-	-	-	47.7	471	433	0.44
S2	0.67	-	-	-	47.7	471	379	0.39
S3	1	SH (1%)	55	1100	25.4	445	386	0.54
S4	0.67	SH (1%)	55	1100	25.4	445	390	0.55
S5	1	SH (1.5%)	55	1100	31.0	449	522	0.66
S6	0.67	SH (1.5%)	55	1100	31.0	449	472	0.60
S7	1	HSH (1.5%)	80	2300	46.1	449	531	0.55
S8	0.67	HSH (1.5%)	80	2300	59.1	449	503	0.46
S9	1	ST (1.5%)	60	2400	59.3	471	530	0.49
S10	0.67	ST (1.5%)	60	2400	58.3	471	444	0.41

ρ: longitudinal reinforcement ratio in each direction; SH: steel hooked fiber; HSH: high-strength steel hooked fiber; ST: steel twisted fiber; V_f: fiber volume fraction; l_f: fiber length; d_f: fiber diameter; f_u: fiber tensile strength; f'_c: concrete (or mortar) compressive strength; f_y: yield strength of slab steel bars; v_u: peak punching shear stress calculated according to ACI 318 [3].

The test slabs with a 1% reinforcement ratio typically exhibited limited or no yielding prior to punching shear failure. On the other hand, the slab specimens with a 0.67% reinforcement ratio showed various degrees of flexural yielding prior to failing in punching shear. Both regular concrete specimens, Specimens S1 and S2, failed suddenly by punching shear at a shear stress of 0.44 and 0.39 $\sqrt{f_c'}$, respectively, which is 33% and 18% higher than the ACI Code limit of 0.33 $\sqrt{f_c'}$. These two specimens exhibited a rather limited rotation capacity, particularly the specimen with a 1% reinforcement ratio, which failed almost immediately after reinforcement yielding initiated.

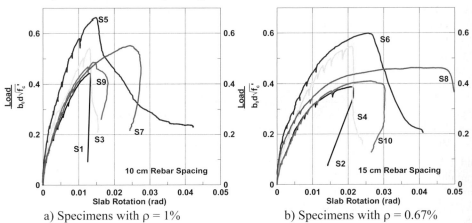

a) Specimens with $\rho = 1\%$ b) Specimens with $\rho = 0.67\%$

Figure 3: Normalized shear stress versus rotation response for slab specimens subjected to monotonic loading

Fig. 3 shows the shear stress versus rotation response for all test slabs. Rotation represents the average rotation measured over 30 cm from each column stub face. As can be seen, all FRC specimens exhibited larger ductility and/or punching shear strength compared to the regular concrete slabs. Among the specimens with a 1% reinforcement ratio, Specimens S5 and S7 with 1.5% volume fraction of hooked steel fibers showed the best behavior in terms of shear strength and ductility, respectively (Fig. 3a). Specimen S5 exhibited a nearly linear response up to a peak shear stress of $2/3\sqrt{f_c'}$, at which point a sudden punching shear failure occurred. Some yielding in the slab reinforcing bars was observed through strain gauge readings prior to failure, with peak tensile strains ranging between 0.003 and 0.008. Specimen S7 with high strength hooked steel fibers, on the other hand, exhibited appreciable flexural yielding prior to punching shear failure, which occurred at a shear stress of $0.55\sqrt{f_c'}$. Tensile strains at failure exceeded 1.5% in several slab bars of Specimen S7. Specimen S9, with twisted steel (Helix) fibers, behaved comparably to Specimen S5 in terms of displacement capacity, but sustained a 26% lower normalized shear stress ($0.49\sqrt{f_c'}$).

Extensive flexural yielding prior to punching shear failure was observed in some of the specimens with a 0.67% reinforcement ratio, particularly in the specimens with a 1.5% volume fraction of steel fibers (hooked or twisted). Overall, the behavior of Specimen S8, with high strength hooked steel fibers, could be argued to be the best. This specimen sustained a peak shear stress of $0.46\sqrt{f_c'}$, governed by the flexural capacity of the slab, and a rotation capacity of nearly 0.05 rad. Specimens S6 and S10 showed similar rotation capacity (0.025-0.03 rad), but Specimen S6 sustained a nearly 50% higher shear stress. Because the strength of Specimens S6 and S8 was basically controlled by the flexural capacity of the slabs, the maximum force applied to these two specimens was nearly the same (6% difference). The differences in normalized peak shear stress demand seen in Fig. 3b and Table 1 were thus caused by differences in the concrete compressive strength.

2.2 Tests of slab-column subassemblies under displacement reversals

Two approximately half-scale slab-column connection subassemblies, Specimens SC1 and SC2, were tested under combined gravity load and lateral displacement reversals. The objective of these tests was to evaluate the effectiveness of using FRC in the slab-column connection region to increase connection ductility and frame drift capacity under earthquake-induced displacements. Overall specimen dimensions and test setup are shown in Figs. 4 and 6a. As shown in the figure, slab vertical movement at its corners was restrained through four "rigid" links. In addition, vertical deflections along the slab perimeter were minimized by providing steel channels "sandwiching" the slab.

Based on the results from the slab punching shear tests under monotonic loading, two FRCs were selected for further investigation: 1) FRC with 1.5% volume fraction of high-strength hooked steel fibers ($l_f = 30$ mm; $l_f/d_f = 80$; $f_u = 2300$ MPa), and 2) FRC with 1.5% volume fraction of regular strength hooked steel fibers ($l_f = 30$ mm; $l_f/d_f = 55$; $f_u = 1100$ MPa). The FRC with high-strength hooked fibers falls under the category of strain-hardening, HPFRC, while the FRC material with regular strength hooked steel fibers represents a strain-softening FRC.

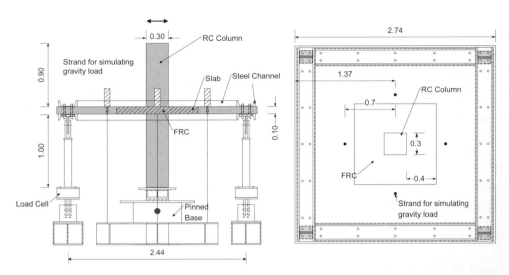

Figure 4: Slab-column subassembly specimens (dimensions in meters)

In the two slab-column connection subassemblies, FRC was used only in the slab region extending up to approximately four times the slab thickness from each column face (Fig. 4). Casting of FRC in the connection region was performed first, immediately followed by casting of regular concrete in the remaining portions of the slab.

Simulated gravity load on the slab was achieved through four hydraulic jacks pulling down on the slab, as shown in Fig. 4. The initial gravity shear ratio applied to the test specimens was ½ ($v_g = 0.17\sqrt{f_c'}$), which was monitored through a load cell at the column base. Pressure on the jacks was adjusted throughout the test in order to maintain a nearly constant gravity shear ratio.

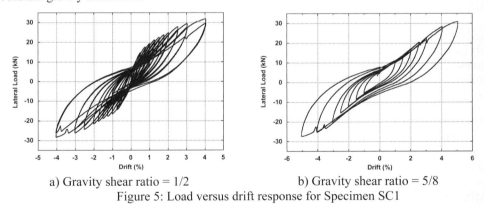

a) Gravity shear ratio = 1/2   b) Gravity shear ratio = 5/8
Figure 5: Load versus drift response for Specimen SC1

Fig. 5a shows the lateral load versus drift (lateral displacement ÷ column height) response for Specimen SC1. As can be seen, this specimen sustained several displacement cycles of increasing magnitude up to a drift of 4% without a significant loss of lateral stiffness and maintaining its ability to sustain gravity loads. At this stage, no appreciable damage was observed in the connection region (Fig. 6). Given the large magnitude of the applied drift, it was decided to increase the gravity shear ratio to 5/8 ($v_g = 0.21 \sqrt{f_c'}$) and start a new series of lateral displacement cycles. The lateral load versus drift hysteresis loops for this new test are shown in Fig. 5b. Lateral displacements up to 5% drift were applied, but only minor connection damage was observed. The specimen was once more unloaded and subjected to increasing simulated gravity loads (without lateral displacements) to evaluate the residual punching shear strength of the slab. Because of limitations in the jacking system, the peak punching shear stress applied corresponded to $v_g = 0.33 \sqrt{f_c'}$. No major signs of distress in the connection were observed.

a) Side view of Specimen SC1   b) Connection region
Figure 6: Specimen SC1 at 4% drift (gravity shear ratio = ½)

Because of the large punching shear resistance and drift capacity observed in Specimen SC1, regular strength hooked steel fibers, as opposed to high-strength fibers, were used in the connection region of Specimen SC2. As in Specimen SC1, the initial gravity shear stress in the connection corresponded to a gravity shear ratio of ½. Similarly to Specimen SC1, no major damage was observed in this specimen when subjected to drift cycles of up to 4% drift. Under an increased gravity shear ratio of 5/8, Specimen SC2 sustained drift cycles of up to 5% drift, the displacement at which a punching shear failure became evident.

3.   CONCLUSIONS
From the test results and discussion presented, the following conclusions can be drawn,

-    The use of fiber reinforced concrete with deformed steel fibers in volume fractions between 1% and 1.5% led to an appreciable increase in deformation capacity and/or punching shear strength in slabs subjected to monotonic punching shear loading. Among the various FRC materials evaluated, a concrete mixture with 10 mm maximum aggregate size and a 1.5% volume fraction of hooked steel fibers ($l_f = 30$ mm; $l_f/d_f = 80$; $f_u = 2300$ MPa) led to the best behavior in terms of punching shear strength and ductility.

- The use of steel fiber reinforced concrete with a 1.5% volume fraction of hooked steel fibers, whether made of regular strength or high strength wire, led to outstanding drift capacity in the two slab-column subassemblies tested under displacement reversals. Both test specimens sustained drift demands of up to 4% combined with gravity shear stresses as large as $0.21\sqrt{f_c'}$ (MPa). Specimen SC1, with high-strength hooked fibers, did not exhibit any appreciable damage in the slab-column connection at the end of the test, while Specimen SC2, with regular strength hooked fibers, failed by punching shear during the cycles to 5% drift under a gravity shear stress of $0.21\sqrt{f_c'}$ (MPa).

4.   ACKNOWLEDGEMENTS

This research is sponsored by the National Science Foundation, as part of the Network for Earthquake Engineering Simulation (NEES) Program, under Grant No. CMS 0421180. It is part of a broader research project led by the senior writer, Professor Jerome P. Lynch from the University of Michigan, and Professor Carol K. Shield from the University of Minnesota. The opinions expressed in this paper are those of the writers and do not necessarily express the views of the sponsor.

REFERENCES

[1]   Pan, A.D. and Moehle, J.P., 'An experimental study of slab-column connections', *ACI Struct. J.*, **89** (6) (1992) 626-638.

[2]   Hueste, M.B.D. and Wight, J.K., 'Evaluation of a four-story reinforced concrete building damaged during the Northridge Earthquake', *Earthquake Spectra*, **13** (3) (1997) 387-414.

[3]   ACI Committee 318, 'Building code and commentary', Report ACI 318-05/318R-06 (American Concrete Institute, Farmington Hills, 2005).

[4]   Alexander, S.D.B. and Simmonds, S.H., 'Punching shear tests of concrete slab-column joints containing fiber reinforcement', *ACI Struct. J.*, **89** (4) (1992) 425-432.

[5]   Harajli, M.H., Maalouf, D. and Khatib, H., 'Effect of fibers on the punching shear strength of slab-column connections', *Cement and Concrete Composites*, Elsevier Science Limited, **17** (2) (1995) 161-170.

STUDY ON SEISMIC RETROFIT USING ULTRA HIGH STRENGTH FIBER REINFORCED CONCRETE

Kazuyoshi Shirai [1], **Makoto Katagiri** [1], **Hiroshi Fukuyama** [2], **Haruhiko Suwada** [2], **Tomohisa Mukai** [2], **Takeshi Watanabe** [3] and **Hideyuki Kinugasa** [3]

(1) Taiheiyo Cement Corporation, Japan

(2) Building Research Institute, Japan

(3) Tokyo University of Science, Japan

Abstract

A seismic retrofit of an RC building frame was developed using shear wall, medium wall and sidewall consisting of ultra high strength fiber reinforced concrete (UFC) panels. To investigate the effect, static loading tests were conducted. UFC sidewalls and medium walls strengthened the existing columns and walls appropriately. The performance of the sidewall varied, depending on how UFC panels and the column were jointed. UFC medium wall fractured at the joint between the panel and RC frame, and the panel was scarcely damaged. UFC shear wall and that with lattice openings both fractured with the shear capacity. The maximum force of the wall without openings was 1.5 times the RC shear wall, which was twice the thickness. Even the wall with lattice openings showed 85% of the RC shear wall in maximum force. From the above results, the capability of thin, lightweight seismic retrofit using UFC was demonstrated.

1. INTRODUCTION

From a social viewpoint, old middle to high-rise concrete residential buildings must be renovated, not rebuilt, using the existing frame to make flexible space for the enlargement of rooms or the remodeling of facilities. In such renovations, seismic retrofit technology should satisfy the following requirements: (a) building weight should increase at minimum; (b) seismic members should not block windows or openings to disturb day lighting or changing in the room layout; (c) appearance of members should be appropriate for concrete structures.

To meet these requirements, we are developing a seismic retrofitting method using ultra high strength fiber reinforced concrete (UFC) panels that can minimize the number, dimensions, and weight of seismic members. This paper describes the results of a series of loading tests that were conducted on frames retrofitted with UFC panels, along with an examination of the joint method between the panel and the existing concrete frame.

2. SEISMIC PANELS USING ULTRA HIGH STRENGTH FIBER REINFORCED CONCRETE

2.1 Ultra high strength fiber reinforced concrete (UFC)

UFC consists of a matrix with an optimum proportional mix of Portland cement, siliceous powder, and quartz sand with steel fibers added 2% by volume, which is based on the reactive powder concrete by Richard and Cheyrezy [1]. The matrix of UFC is supplied as premix powder blended in a premix plant. UFC is produced by mixing the powder, water, and superplasticizer, followed by adding steel fibers. UFC also has high fluidity with its zero-hit flow of 250 to 270 mm.

UFC members after casting are cured primarily for about 24 hours at ambient temperature, followed by heat treatment at 90°C for 48 hours. With these processes, the compressive strength reaches to 200 N/mm^2. The characteristic values for the mechanical properties of UFC made of the standard mix of materials are prescribed in the recommendations (draft) established by the Japan Society of Civil Engineers [2]. According to the recommendations, characteristic values are 180 N/mm^2 for compression, 8 N/mm^2 for first cracking strength, and 8.8 N/mm^2 for tensile strength.

2.2 Seismic retrofit using UFC

The advantages of seismic retrofitting using UFC can be listed as follows:
- High strength of the material leads to a thin, light structure.
- Steel fibers provide tensile reinforcement. Stirrups could be omitted in some cases.
- When used with reinforcing bars, UFC bonds with the bars well, so anchoring length can be shortened. Concrete cover can also be thinner.
- Design flexibility and accordance with concrete structure are obtained.

To develop a seismic retrofit using UFC, the following problems are listed.
- Development of an easy and assured method to joint the panels and existing frames.
- Establishment of a design and evaluation method for UFC panels and buildings retrofitted with UFC.

There can be a variety of retrofitting methods using UFC. Here, the most basic and simple one is cited. Fig. 1 shows the method in which a UFC panel is attached to a non-structural wall located on the boundary between dwellings and a common space. For such non-structural walls, UFC panels provide sufficient strength and ductility. Likewise, some methods can be listed such that UFC panels cover columns lacking ductility, attached to columns as sidewalls, or placed between windows as medium walls.

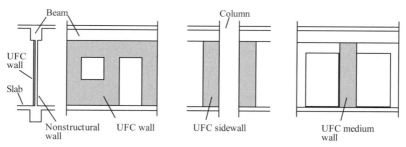

Figure 1: Seismic retrofit using UFC panels

3.   SHEAR TEST FOR THE JOINT

3.1   Test outline
In order to evaluate the strength of the joint between the UFC panel and the existing frame, shear tests using joint model specimen which represents the force transfer mechanism between UFC panel and existing concrete frame were conducted. Test parameters were the joint method, grouted material, diameter of anchors, etc. The length of the anchors had been determined with previous tensile tests.

The testing method is shown in Fig. 2. For the joint method, the following three methods were tested: through anchor method, lap anchor method, and indirect joint method. The tests were conducted on the condition in which lateral slip was free by putting PTFE sheets beneath the specimens in order to eliminate compressive stress in the bonded area and obtain the minimum value for shear strength. In comparison, a few specimens using the indirect method were tested with steel bars to induce compressive stress into the bonded area.

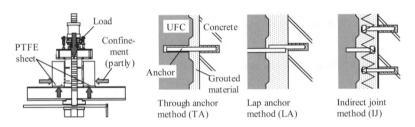

Figure 2: Shear test diagram

3.2   Test results
The expected failure mode of the specimens was, the yielding of the anchor bars, the fracture of the shear cotter and the bond failure that the bond between the grouted material and the concrete was gradually lost. Fig. 3 shows the shear force vs. slip curves when changing the jointing method or grouted material (no-shrink mortar or UFC). The through anchor method showed an expected failure mode, whereas the lap anchor method ended in low maximum load due to the lack of developing length of the bar. By replacing the grouted material with UFC, the maximum load was improved up to that of the through anchor method.

The indirect joint method without confinement collapsed under one-half the load of the other two methods due to the lack of transfer of flexural tension at the lower side of the specimen. By confining the specimen, maximum load increased up to more than twice that without confinement.

Fig. 4 shows the comparison of the measured maximum load and Q_a calculated with equation (1) prescribed in the design guidelines for seismic retrofit of RC buildings [3].

$$Q_a = n \times \min\left[0.7\,_m\sigma_y \cdot _s a_e, 0.4\sqrt{E_c\sigma_B} \cdot _s a_e\right] \tag{1}$$

where Q_a: shear capacity (N), n: number of anchors, $_m\sigma_y$: yield point of anchor (N/mm^2), $_s a_e$: cross section of anchor (mm^2), E_c: Young's modulus of concrete (N/mm^2), σ_B: concrete strength (N/mm^2)

Note that the shear capacity of the joint methods can be evaluated with existing equations except for several problematic cases.

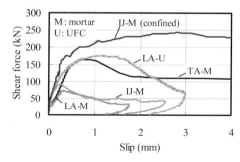

Figure 3: Shear force vs. slip   Figure 4: Measured and calculated Q_a

4.   CYCLIC LATERAL LOADING TEST

4.1   Specimens

In order to understand the performance of seismic retrofits using UFC panels, static loading tests were conducted on frames installed with UFC shear walls, columns installed with UFC sidewalls, and a wall installed with a UFC medium wall.

Fig. 5 and Table 1 show the dimensions and reinforcing bar arrangement of the test specimens. All specimens were 1/2.5 scaled models. Details of the specimens are as follows:

Table 1: Test specimens

| Name | Member | Compressive strength (N/mm²) | | | Anchor | | Column |
		UFC	Grouted material	Concrete	Shape/ Method	σ_y (N/mm²)	$p_w\sigma_y$ (N/mm²)
No. 1	Column	-	-	38	-	-	0.28
No. 2, No. 3	Column + Sidewall	229	73	38	D10/IJ	375	0.28
No. 4	Wall + Medium wall	229	73	38	D10/IJ	375	-
No. 5	Frame + Shear wall	229	92	42	D10/IJ	375	0.28
No. 6		212	194	28	D6/LA	340	0.45
No. 7		-	-	28	-	-	1.79

σ_y: yield point, p_w: lateral reinforcement ratio

No. 1 is a column where the ratio of shear capacity to flexural capacity is 0.55. No. 2 and No. 3 are the same as column No. 1 but retrofitted with UFC sidewalls. UFC panels and the

stab are jointed with the indirect joint method. In addition, in No. 3, UFC panels and the
column are also jointed.

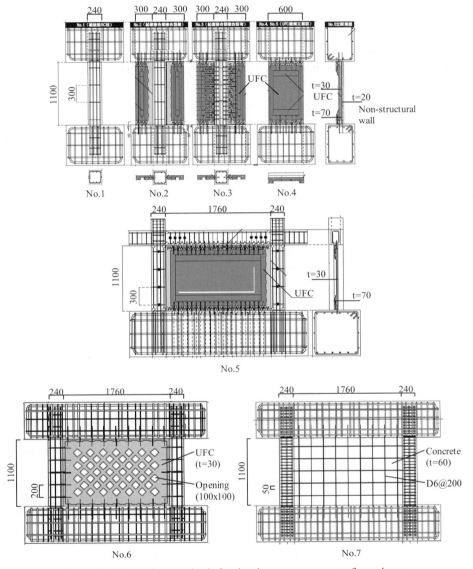

Figure 5: Dimensions and reinforcing bar arrangement of specimens

No. 4 is a non-structural wall retrofitted with a UFC medium wall. The top and bottom
ends of the UFC panel are jointed to concrete stabs with the indirect joint method. The gap
between the UFC panel and the non-structural wall are grouted with mortar.

No. 5 is a concrete frame retrofitted with a UFC shear wall. The top and bottom ends of the panel are jointed to a beam with the indirect joint method. In No. 6, the UFC shear wall inside the frame has lattice openings that can be used to maintain visibility. No. 7 is a conventional concrete shear wall cast together with the frame.

To joint the panel of No. 1 to No. 5, the indirect method joint was used in consideration of the simplicity of the work. In No. 6, the lap anchor method with UFC grout was used. The through anchor method was not used because of the difficulty in the accuracy of the work. In addition, although No. 5, No. 6, and No. 7 used slightly different shapes and reinforcement in the existing frame, the influence was considered rather small.

4.2   Loading method

Specimens were subjected to cyclic lateral loading. Fig. 6 shows the apparatus used for loading. The axial load was 10-% of the product of concrete strength and the cross section of a column for No. 1 to No. 4, being that of two columns for No. 5 to No. 7. The story drift index was given by dividing lateral displacement by the height of the columns/walls for No. 1 to No. 4 and by the distance from the wall bottom to the height of loading for No. 5 to No. 7.

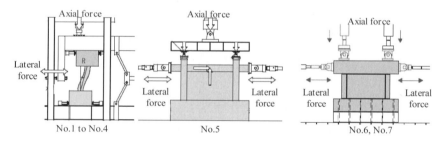

Figure 6: Loading method

5.   RESULTS OF LOADING TESTS

5.1   Columns and UFC sidewalls

Fig. 7 shows the relationships between shear force Q and story drift index R for No. 1 to No. 4. Failure patterns are also shown in the figure.

In No. 1, a lateral reinforcement at the column top yielded, cover concrete crushed and shear failure took place with diagonal large crack.

In No. 2, failure took place with flexural cracks stretching to shear cracks in the column. Finally the outer end of the horizontal joint area crushed and fell, with lateral load decreasing. Since the bond between the column and grouted mortar at the vertical joint was lost early, there were a small number of cracks on the UFC sidewalls.

In No. 3, many cracks were observed on the vertical joint area, whereas the column and UFC panels behaved uniformly because they were combined. The jointed column and UFC panels were subjected to diagonal force, and finally, the outer end of the horizontal joint area crushed with shear failure taking place on the column.

5.2   Medium walls

In No. 4, from the early cycle, the joint area fractured and the UFC panel rotated. Then, a part of the anchor bars yielded, whereas the lateral force decreased with the cone fracture of joint area expanding. Since the fracture was concentrated in the joint area, almost no cracks were observed on the panel.

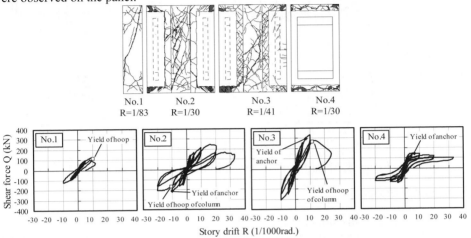

Figure 7: Shear force vs. story drift index for No. 1 to No. 4

5.3   Shear walls

In No. 5, the first crack in the mortar of the horizontal joint area was followed by fine shear cracks on the UFC panel. As the loading progressed, cracks increased and then became localized. Finally, the wall fractured with the shear crack penetrating the joint area and the beam.

In No. 6, first, fine cracks perpendicular to each bar of the lattice were observed on several bars. The number of cracks increased and then the lattice suddenly fractured at several bars in a chain reaction.

In No. 7, shear cracks were first observed at the center of the wall and then stretched to the column bottom. As the loading progressed, concrete crushed at the angle of the wall and shear cracks in the column expanded.

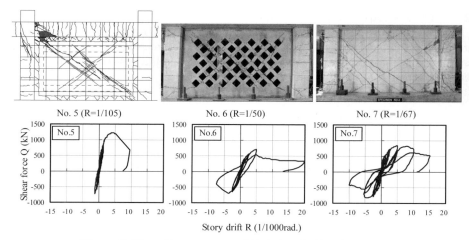

Figure 8: Shear force vs. story drift index for No. 5 to No. 7

6.   DISCUSSIONS

6.1   Effect of sidewalls and medium walls

To see Fig. 7, note that the strength and stiffness of the column increased by retrofitting with UFC panels. Anchoring the vertical joint between the column and the panel made them much stronger, but made their failure more brittle.

No. 4 has bearing forces of 140 kN, almost equal to one column. Although most of the anchors yielded, lateral load decreased as the cone fracture expanded in the tension area and the mortar crushed in the compression area. Grouted material should be improved for such members.

6.2   Effect of shear walls

To see Fig. 8, note that the strength and stiffness of the frame retrofitted with a UFC panel increased remarkably. The strength was 1.5 times greater than that of a conventional concrete shear wall, even though the UFC panel was half the thickness of the concrete shear wall and had no reinforcement. In addition, the UFC panel with lattice openings bore the force up to 85-% of that of the concrete shear wall, which demonstrates the capability of the new type of lightweight seismic retrofitting.

7.   CONCLUSIONS

In order to understand the seismic performance of retrofitting with UFC, a series of tests was conducted for sidewalls, a medium wall, and shear walls made of UFC panels. The results are summarized as follows:

- By combining the anchor and grouted material appropriately, joint methods with sufficient strength were obtained.
- UFC sidewalls and UFC medium walls are able to strengthen existing columns and walls appropriately. The performance of the sidewall varied, depending on whether the column and the panel were jointed.

- – UFC shear walls showed excellent reinforcing performance in strength that was 1.5 times greater than that of a conventional concrete shear wall twice as thick.

This method of using UFC represents the capability of the new type of lightweight seismic retrofitting. Practical use will be desired after the design equations are determined.

REFERENCES

[1] Richard, P. and Cheyrezy, M., 'Reactive Powder Concretes with high ductility and 200-800 MPa compressive strength', ACI, SP144-24 (1994) 507-518.
[2] 'Recommendations for design and construction of ultra high strength fiber reinforced concrete structures (draft)', Japan Society of Civil Engineers (2006).
[3] 'Seismic evaluation and retrofit', Japan Building Disaster Prevention Association (2001).

DAMAGE TOLERANCE OF STEEL PLATE REINFORCED HPFRCC COUPLING BEAMS

Wan-Shin Park, Hyund-Do Yun, Sun-Woo Kim, Esther Jeon and Won-Suk Lee

Dept. of Architectural Engineering, Chungnam National University, Daejeon, Republic of Korea

Abstract

The objective of this study is to evaluate the seismic performance of the steel plate - reinforced high performance fiber reinforced cementitious composites (HPFRCC) coupling beams under cyclic loading and to investigate the influence of cementitious composite properties, particularly strain hardening and multiple cracking, on the damage tolerance of coupling beams when subjected to large displacement reversals. The evaluation and quantification of damage tolerance was conducted through the use of seismic damage indices. The combination of a ductile cementitious matrix and steel plate for shear reinforcement is found to result in improved energy dissipation capacity and inelastic deformability of shear dominant coupling beam. Test results showed that the steel plate reinforced coupling beam constructed with HPFRCC exhibited excellent strength, deformation capacity, and damage tolerance capacity, in comparison with steel plate reinforced coupling beam constructed with a conventional concrete.

1.   INTRODUCTION

In high multistory reinforced concrete buildings, coupled shear walls can provide an efficient structural system to resist shear force due to wind and seismic loads. Seismic resistance of medium-rise reinforced concrete buildings typically relies on structural walls due to their good lateral strength and stiffness properties. Architectural considerations usually result in window and door openings in structural walls, which divide a single wall into more slender walls connected by short and deep beams, referred to as coupling beams. The use of coupling beams leads to a more efficient and economical structural system than individual walls because properly designed coupled wall systems possess significantly higher strength, stiffness, and energy dissipation capacity [1-3].

However, it is confirmed that RC coupling beams with conventional or diagonal reinforcement in shear wall system have insufficient strength, ductility, damage tolerance capacity, and have a number of problems about damage tolerance and construction. As an alternative, a new type of coupling beam with HPFRCC has recently been developed [4, 5].

In this study, the seismic behavior and damage tolerance of steel plate reinforced coupling beams with HPFRCC subjected to high shear are investigated and compared to steel plate reinforced coupling beams with a conventional concrete.

2. EXPERIMENTAL PROGRAM

2.1 Specimen configuration and construction

For this experimental program, two coupling beam specimens were tested under displacement reversals to evaluate the feasibility of using HPFRCC materials in coupling beam with steel plate. The two specimens were of identical dimensions and reinforcement details as shown in Fig. 1, and span-to-depth ratio of the coupling beam was selected as 1.0. The first specimen (PCB-PC) consisted of a reinforced concrete coupling beam. The second specimen (PCB-PH) was constructed with a HPFRCC material containing 0.75% five twisted steel fibers (steel cord, SC) and 0.75% ultra-high molecular weight polyethylene (PE).

2.2 Test set-up and procedure

The specimens were horizontally cast, then rotated and placed into the test setup with one of the walls fixed to the reaction floor as shown in Fig. 2. In this horizontal position, displacement cycles were applied to the coupling beam specimen through a hydraulic actuator with its line of action passing through the upper of wall. To simulate the demands during an earthquake, the planned lateral displacement history started from a coupling beam drift of 0.1% and went 4.0%, with three cycles performed at each new drift level.

2.3 Mechanical properties of material

The HPFRCC is composed of a Portland cement-based mortar (water-cement ratio of 45%, sand-cement ratio of 45%) that is reinforced with both 15 mm long, 0.012 mm diameter PE fibers and 32 mm long, 0.405 mm SC in diameter with respective volume fractions of 0.75% and 0.75%.

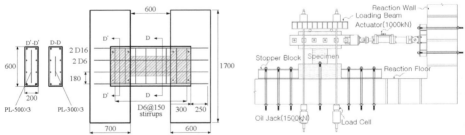

Figure 1: Specimen configuration (Unit: mm)   Figure 2: Test setup

Fig. 3 shows the stress-strain relationship curves of HPFRCC. The HPFRCC and concrete have similar ranges of tensile and compressive strength (3.25 to 3.56 MPa and 44 to 48 MPa, respectively). The cyclic compression behavior of HPFRCC was similar to the monotonic compressive result in both the compressive strength and the strain level at the onset of softening. The tensile strain capacity is similar to the uniaxial tension test results for two schemes, as shown in Fig. 3. Cyclic loading does not limit the tensile strain capacity of the hybrid fiber-reinforced cementitious composite used in this study. The horizontal reinforcing bars at the top and bottom were 16 mm deformed bars. The yield and ultimate strengths for these bars were 470 and 562 MPa, while the yield and ultimate strength of 152 and 201 MPa were obtained for steel plate encased in coupling beam, respectively.

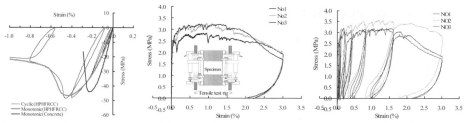

(a) Compression response   (b) Monotonic tensile response   (c) Repeated tensile response
Figure 3: Stress-strain relationship curve of HPFRCC

3. TEST RESULTS

3.1 Cracking pattern and hysteretic response

Fig. 4 shows the comparison of the shear cracking pattern and hysteretic responses for two coupling beams during the cyclic loading, and crack width of each specimen was also compared as shown in Fig. 6. In specimen PCB-PC, initial flexural cracks were first observed at the lower of coupling beam when the rotational angle was about 0.1%. At a rotational angle of about 0.2%, inclined crack was propagated from lower to middle face of coupling beam. As the rotational angle was increased, a number of cracks were generated around the inclined crack and crushing started below the compression face. At a rotational angle of about 1.4%, clear shear crack occurred in the full face of coupling beam. At a rotational angle of about 1.6%, specimen represents the peak strength of 551.01 kN in the positive direction and shows ductility ratio of 1.27 until a rotational angle of about 2.04%, 80% of peak strength. After this rotational angle, new crack did not occur but only width of previous shear cracks was intended to increase continuously. At rotational angle larger than 2%, spalling of concrete had occurred and coupling beam failed finally.

In specimen PCB-PH , micro-cracks first observed at the lower of coupling beam during the cycles to the rotational angle of about 0.3%. At the rotational angle of about 0.6%, the initial crack was propagated at the lower of coupling beam, and inclined shape of crack occurred middle level of coupling beam in the negative loading direction. At the 0.8% rotational angle, micro inclined crack at the upper face of coupling beam, a larger number of hairline cracks are observed at the lower face of coupling beam. At the rotational angle of about 1.0%, compression layer at the lower face of coupling beam was crushed, and inclined crack was generated and propagated at the rotational angle of about 1.2%.

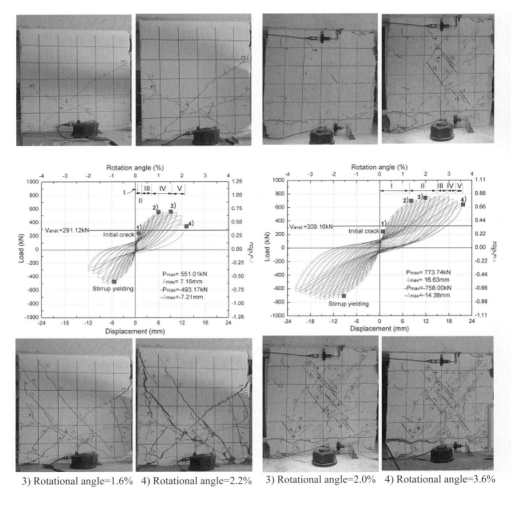

3) Rotational angle=1.6%   4) Rotational angle=2.2%   3) Rotational angle=2.0%   4) Rotational angle=3.6%

(a) Specimen PCB-PC   (b) Specimen PCB-PH

Figure 4: Cracking pattern and hysteretic response

As the rotational angle was increased, it is not observed that crack width of the previous level did not grow rapidly but only multiple cracks were tended to grow around of the previous cracks. At the rotational angle of about 2.8%, specimen PCB-PH represents the peak strength of 773.04 kN in the positive direction and shows ductility ratio of 1.29 until the rotational angle of about 3.58% corresponding to 80% of the peak strength. Strength and ductility of specimen PCB-PH was more increased 40.42% and 1.97% than specimen PCB-PC, respectively. It may result in the ductility improvement effect due to the bridging of reinforcing fiber. After this rotational angle, clear shear crack was not observed until the rotational angle of about 3.4%, and coupling beam failed at this level. At the end of the test, the coupling beam failed with gradual increasing of the previous crack width (Fig. 4(b)).

3.2   Seismic performance indices

The dissipated energy was defined as the area enclosed within the load-displacement hysteretic loop for that cycle. In order to determine the effect of matrix ductility on the energy dissipation capacity of the coupling beams, different method (Work index, damage index) was used and compared. Work index, I_w, is proposed by Gosain et al. [6] to estimate energy dissipate capacity and inelastic deformation capacity of structural member, and I_w can be obtained from Eq. 1

$$I_w = \sum \frac{F_i \delta_i}{F_{max} \delta_y} \qquad (1)$$

Where, F_i and d_i are peak strength and displacement at ith cycle, and F_{max} and d_y are maximum strength and yielding displacement.

Damage index, D_{ew}, is proposed by Ehsani and Wright [7] in terms of dissipated energy and elastic energy at each cycle. D_{ew} can be obtained from Eq. 2

$$D_{ew} = \frac{1}{F_{max} \delta_y} \sum E_i \left(\frac{K_i}{K_y} \right) \left(\frac{\delta_i}{\delta_y} \right)^2 \qquad (2)$$

Where, K_i and K_y are stiffness at i th cycle and yielding stiffness, E_i is dissipated energy at ith cycle. Fig. 5 shows the value of the cumulative dissipated energy calculated by work index and damage index at each cyclic loading level. All specimens represent similar value of I_w and D_{ew} until 20th cycles of the rotational angle of about 1.6% corresponding the peak strength of specimen PCB-PC. However, at the 22nd cycle corresponding to the rotational angle of about 2.2%, I_w and D_{ew} of specimen PCB-PH were about 342.48% and 90.40% greater than specimen PCB-PC, respectively. After this cycle, D_{ew}, was increased rapidly as damages advanced. It was confirmed that proposed index, I_w and D_{ew}, are adequate for estimation on the physical damage of structure member. In addition, it is clarified that D_{ew} could represent damage progress of HPFRCC coupling beams more than I_w.

3.3   Crack width

JBDPA [8] proposed a scale in which five levels of damage were defined in terms of visible damage characteristics (especially crack width), as listed in Table 1.

Fig. 6 shows the maximum crack width at the peak strength of each cycle on the line drawn perpendicular to the cracks on surface, facilitated by optical microscopy. As can be seen in the figure, while crack widths in PCB-DH at the rotational angle of about 1.4% were 0.1 mm (very slight damage), maximum crack width in PCB-DC at same rotational angle with specimen PCB-PH, were 1.8 mm which corresponds to the damage class III (moderate damage). Also, at the rotational angle of about 1.6% which corresponds maximum strength of specimen PCB-PC, while maximum shear crack width of specimen PCB-PC was 2.0mm, a large number of hairline cracks which has 0.4 mm of maximum crack width were measured in the specimen PCB-PH .

3.4   Damage tolerance evaluation

In the Seismic Evaluation Standard[8], the seismic capacity reduction factor, η, aims to give a consistent numerical indication of the damage level across a wide range of structures and loading types. The factor, η, is defined by the following Eq. 3

$$\eta = E_r / E_t \tag{3}$$

Where E_d and E_r are the dissipated energy and residual absorbable energy, respectively, and E_t is the entire absorbable engrgy which is defined as the sum of E_d and E_r.

Fig. 7 shows the relationships between η and maximum crack widths. In this study, the effect of the matrix ductility on the damage tolerance of coupling beams was evaluated by the seismic capacity reduction factor η. The comparison of PCB-PC and PCB-PH indicates a sudden drop in reinforced concrete after 2.0 mm of crack width (Damage class III) due to lower damage tolerance, that is, lower strain energy at a given displacement relative to HPFRCC coupling beam.

Table 1: Damage class for RC structural member [8]

Damage Class	Observed Damage on Structural Members
I	Some cracks are found. Crack width is smaller than 0.2mm.
II	Crack of 0.2-1 mm with are found.
III	Heavy cracks of 1-2 mm wide are found. Some spalling of concrete is observed.
IV	Many heavy cracks are found. Crack width is larger than 2mm. Reinforcing bars are exposed due to spalling of the covering concrete.
V	Buckling of reinforcement, crushing of concrete and vertical deformation of columns and/or shear walls are found. Side-sway, subsidence of upper floors, and/or fracture of reinforcing bars are observed in some cases.

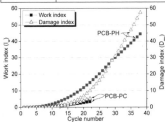

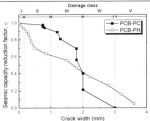

Figure 5: Comparison of   Figure 6: Crack width variation   Figure 7: Seismic capacity
damage indices for specimens   of specimens   reduction factor

4.   CONCLUSION

The following conclusions were derived from the experimental results of steel plate-reinforced composite coupling beams with high performance hybrid fiber-reinforced cement composite subjected to high shear in a coupled shear wall system.

- Specimen PCB-PC shows ductility ratio of 1.27 until the rotational angle of about 2.04% corresponding to 80% of the peak strength. The ductility of specimen PCB-PH was 1.97% larger than specimen PCB-PC. It may result in the ductility improvement effect due to the bridging action of reinforcing fiber.
- While maximum shear crack width of specimen PCB-PC at the rotational angle of about 1.6% which corresponds maximum strength, was 2.0 mm, a large number of hairline cracks which has maximum crack width of 0.4 mm were measured in the specimen PCB-PH .
- At the 22nd cycle corresponding to the rotational angle of about 2.2%, I_w and D_{ew} of specimen PCB-PH were about 342.48% and 90.40% greater than specimen PCB-PC, respectively. After this cycle, I_w and D_{ew} of specimen PCB-PH were also increased continuosly as damages advanced. It was confirmed that damage tolerance capacity of HPFRCC coupling beam has been improved due to bridging action between reinforcing fibers and cement matrix.
- The comparison of specimens PCB-PC and PCB-PH indicates a sudden drop in reinforced concrete after 2.0 mm of crack width (Damage class III) due to lower damage tolerance, that is, lower strain energy at a given displacement relative to HPFRCC coupling beam.

ACKNOWLEDGEMENTS

This work was supported by Korea Research Foundation Grant funded by the Korean Government (MOEHRD) (KRF-2006-353-D00039).

REFERENCES

[1] Harries, K.A., 'Seismic Design and Retrofit of Coupled Walls Using Structural Steel', *Ph. D thesis*, McGill University, Montreal, Canada, (1995).
[2] Park, W.S. and Yun, H.D., 'Seismic behaviour of steel coupling beams linking reinforced concrete shear walls', *J. Eng. Struct.* **27** (7) (2005) 1024–1039.
[3] Gong, B. and Shahrooz, B.M., 'Concrete-steel composite coupling beams', *J. Struct. Div.* **127** (6) (2001) 625–631.
[4] Yun, H.D., Kim, S.W., Jeon, E. and Park, W.S., 'Effect of matrix ductility on damage tolerance of diagonally reinforced coupling beams', *Key Engineering Material.* **324-325** (2006) 723-726.
[5] B. A. Canbolat, G. J. Parra-Montensinos, and J. K. Wight, 'Experimental Study on Seismic Behavior of High-Performance Fiber-Reinforced Cement Composite Coupling Beams', *ACI Structural Journal*, **102** (1) (2005) 159-166.
[6] Gosain, N.K., Brown, R.H. and Jirsa, J.O., 'Shear requirements for load reversals on RC. members', *J. Struct. Eng., ASCE.* **103** (7) (1977) 1461-1476.
[7] Ehsani, M.R. and Wright, J.K., 'Confinement steel requirements for connections in ductile frames', *Journal of Structural Engineering.* **116** (3) (1990) 751-767.
[8] The Japan Building Disaster Prevention Association (JBDPA). (1991)

Author Index

The numbers refer to the opening page of the relevant papers.

Subject Index

The numbers refer to the opening page of the relevant papers.

High Performance Fiber Reinforced Cement Composites (HPFRCC5)
Mainz, Germany – July 10-13, 2007

Directeur de publication : Michel BRUSIN

Dépôt légal : 3ème trimestre 2007

Imprimé en FRANCE

Printed in France

Imprimerie Compédit Beauregard S.A.

61600 La Ferté-Macé FRANCE

ISBN : 978-2-35158-046-2

RILEM Proceedings PRO 53